CHURCHILL AND FISHER

Churchill and Fisher

Titans at the Admiralty

Barry Gough

Seaforth
PUBLISHING

Dedicated to the memory of Sir Martin Gilbert

Copyright © Barry Gough 2017

First published in Great Britain in 2017 by
Seaforth Publishing,
A division of Pen & Sword Books Ltd,47 Church Street,
Barnsley S70 2AS

www.seaforthpublishing.com

British Library Cataloguing in Publication Data
A catalogue record for this book is available from the British Library

ISBN 978 1 5267 0356 9 (HARDBACK)
ISBN 978 1 5267 0357 6 (KINDLE)
ISBN 978 1 5267 0358 3 (EPUB)

Typeset and designed by MATS Typesetters, Leigh on Sea, Essex
Printed and bound in Great Britain by CPI Group (UK) Ltd, Croydon, CR0 4YY

*Memories of old days crowd upon me, and I have thought much of you
these last few hours. It all seems so far away and yet so near.
Where should we all be to-day, were it not for your foresight, your bold
determination? ... Really, the prophets were not in it with you.
And what a story the whole thing would make ...*
Viscount Esher to Lord Fisher, 1918

*Still the most volcanic and furious spirit of his generation ... the most
distinguished British Naval Officer since Nelson*, said Churchill of Fisher.
And on Admirals Fisher and Wilson: *It was to these two great old men and
weather-beaten sea-dogs, who for more than half a century had braved the
battle and the breeze, and were Captains afloat when I was in my cradle, that
the professional conduct of the naval war was now to be confided.*
Winston S Churchill, *The World Crisis* (1923)

*So far as the Navy is concerned, the tendency of these 'Thinking
Establishments' on shore is to convert splendid Sea officers
into very indifferent clerks.*
Admiral of the Fleet Lord Fisher

Two very strong and clever men, one [Fisher] *old, wily, and of vast
experience, one* [Churchill] *young, self-assertive with great self-satisfaction
but unstable. They cannot work together; they cannot both run the show.*
Rear-Admiral Sir David Beatty, December 1914

Contents

List of Illustrations

ATLANTIC
OCEAN

Shetland Islands

NORWAY

Oslo

N

SWEDEN

Orkney Islands

Pentland Firth *Scapa Flow*

Wick

The Minch

Invergordon *Cromarty Firth*

SCOTLAND

Rosyth *Firth of Forth*

Edinburgh

Lindesnes *Skagerrak*

*North
Sea*

DENMARK *Kattegat*

*Baltic
Sea*

*Kaiser
Wilhelm
Canal*

Kiel

Newcastle

IRELAND

*Irish
Sea*

Hull

*Dogger
Bank*

Heligoland

Borkum *Islands*

Frisian Islands

Emden Wilhelmshaven

Hamburg

Bremen

WALES

ENGLAND

Harwich

HOLLAND

GERMANY

London

Zeebrugge

Chatham Dover

Antwerp

Portsmouth Calais Ostend

BELGIUM

English Channel

Paris

FRANCE

ATLANTIC
OCEAN

0   200 miles

0   200 km

Basel

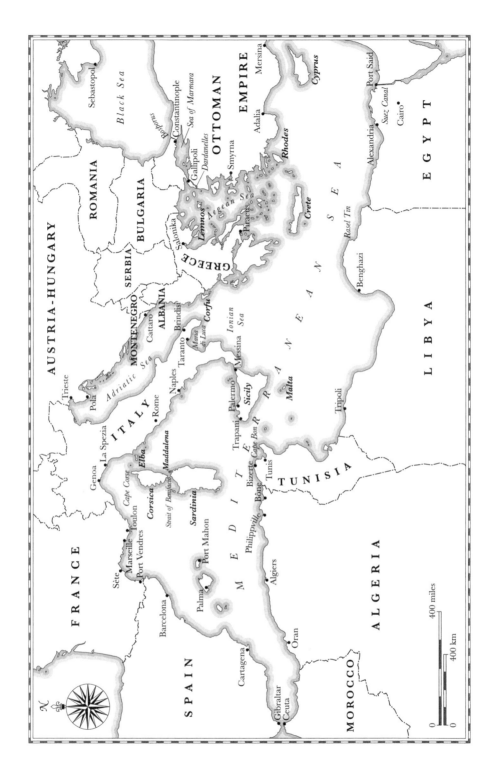

FRANCE

SPAIN

MOROCCO

ALGERIA

TUNISIA

LIBYA

EGYPT

ITALY

AUSTRIA-HUNGARY

ROMANIA

SERBIA

BULGARIA

MONTENEGRO

ALBANIA

GREECE

OTTOMAN EMPIRE

Black Sea

Sea of Marmara

Bosporus

Aegean Sea

Dardanelles

Ionian Sea

Adriatic Sea

MEDITERRANEAN SEA

Sebastopol

Constantinople

Gallipoli

Smyrna

Salonika

Lemnos

Thaso

Mersina

Cyprus

Adalia

Rhodes

Crete

Alexandria

Port Said

Suez Canal

Cairo

Benghazi

Ras el Tin

Tripoli

Malta

Sicily

Palermo

Messina

Trapani

Maria di Leuca

Taranto

Brindisi

Corfu

Cattaro

Pola

Trieste

Naples

Rome

Genoa

La Spezia

Cape Corse

Corsica

Elba

Maddalena

Strait of Bonifacio

Sardinia

Bizerte

Cape Bon R.

Bône

Philippville

Tunis

Palma

Port Mahon

Barcelona

Cartagena

Oran

Algiers

Gibraltar

Ceuta

Sète

Marseille

Toulon

Port Vendres

0   400 miles

0   400 km

xii

Preface

The interlocking lives of Winston Spencer Churchill and John 'Jacky' Arbuthnot Fisher command centre stage in any compelling study of the First World War, especially from the point of view of Britain and the British Empire. The remarkable, though sometimes problematic, and, in the end, tragic partnership of these two personages has rightly gained legendary proportions. However, partisan and therefore unreliable attempts at explanation have been made, often inspired by prejudice rising to invective against Churchill or Fisher. Biographers invariably defend their subjects, and it is their right and duty to do so. In writing this new look into the ever-changing and tortuous relationship between the civilian head of the Royal Navy and its professional head, I have been guided by the goal of providing a perspective unencumbered by any ill-founded preference to tell Winston's or Jacky's story.

The study of history leads necessarily to the examination of the personality and character of those who made history. Although other forces, not least fate and what is called synchronicity, shape any unfolding drama, it is individuals who make their entrances on the stage of history, play their parts, triumph or fail, falter or rise to glory, then exit offstage, where they face re-evaluation by the historians and critics. This book examines, among other things, leadership under crisis. How health, physical and mental, affected the actions of the principals is a subject of newer interest. As with many other notable men in history, unhappy childhoods, challenging early years, or sometimes both, evoked a fixed sense of purpose and tenacity that brought them to greatness and to courageous action. Arthur Marder, the distinguished American naval historian and author of the magisterial *From the Dreadnought to Scapa Flow*, found fascinating 'the war behind the war'. What follows here owes much to his disclosures. All the same, it goes deeper into the various personal relationships in the British leadership, political and naval, that directed (and misdirected) the course of the naval war – a great unravelling tragedy made acceptable to the British public only by the coming Armistice and the end of armed conflict.

The years 1901 to 1918 were vivid and eventful, made remarkably so by the transformation the Royal Navy underwent in types of ships and, in consequence, tactical methods. In 1901 the Fleet consisted of coal-burning battleships and cruisers, and some destroyers. The submarine was in its infancy and largely untried. The efficiency of main armaments was tested at just over a mile. Torpedoes ran for about 800yds. By 1914 the Fleet consisted of fast, big-gun battleships and battlecruisers with main armaments capable of engaging the enemy at an unheard-of 20,000yds. Over one hundred destroyers could launch torpedoes with ranges of 8,000yds. The submarine had become a potent main unit, capable of deployment against naval and merchant vessels in an oceanic environment in which it could disappear. At the same time, naval officers and designers were turning their minds to a ship that could carry aircraft to accompany and defend the Fleet or engage in reconnaissance or offensive operations.

It was a war of technological surprises, of innovations that changed the nature of war: Zeppelins, aircraft (fighter, bomber, reconnaissance), and tanks all played new and unexpected roles. Wireless, cable, and codes made for new forms of communication not fully understood as to operations (and attendant complications). Naval intelligence assumed a vital role. This was a dynamic period, calling for officers and men willing to adapt to changing circumstances caused by the technological shifts and inventions of the age. The means of hunting German submarines (U-boats) electronically was urgently sought and came into existence only near the war's end.

In August 1914 Fisher and other admirals began the war confident that predominance in numbers of dreadnoughts – battleships and battlecruisers – would ensure command of the sea. This confidence was rudely shaken by the U-boat menace, which brought the population of the British Isles nearly to the point of starvation. With reluctance, the Admiralty adopted the convoy, the saving grace. And in the end, and not too soon, the British blockade brought Germany to its knees. This, too, was a triumph of supreme power at sea – the silent and often unglamorous as well as endless demonstration of 'the price of admiralty'.

Neither Churchill nor Fisher wanted to fight a continental war. Long before 1914 they had made this abundantly clear, in their separate ways. Like many leading men of their time, they were amphibian in their thinking. The maritime strategist Sir Julian Corbett, who wrote, and lectured to naval officers, on this theme, was their partial guide. Churchill and Fisher hated to be chained to the requirements of British and Empire land forces on the Western Front. Mobility of force was prized, and their wish was to carry the war to enemy frontiers on the margins of great theatres. All the same, they lacked experience in the waging of amphibious operations. Inter-Service co-operation was despised by Fisher. He opposed being shackled to the War Office in any way and preferred to think of the Army as a projectile to be fired by the Navy. Such naval staff planning as existed was seldom followed. Both Churchill and Fisher favoured some sort of Baltic project, sending British maritime power to Germany's doorstep, but in the distant theatre of the Dardanelles in the eastern Mediterranean, where their greatest opportunity to mount a new front presented itself, they could never reach agreement on how to prosecute that campaign. When the chance came in early 1915, they faltered. 'By ships alone' proved an unrealistic and badly thought-out war plan. The Dardanelles, as Fisher predicted, became their grave.

This book is therefore about Churchill's and Fisher's war – how each fought it, how they waged it together, and how they fought against each other, face to face or behind the scenes. The pages of history reveal other such dramatic struggles in high military command – the relationship of General Patton and General Bradley of the US Army comes to mind. The result was that both Churchill and Fisher were constantly shifting their positions so as to stay influential in the high councils of state. They were also making odd departures from the scene, many unauthorised by convention or responsibilities of office. Examples abound. At one time, Churchill departed the Admiralty to defend Antwerp against German assault, unsuccessfully; on another occasion, Fisher irresponsibly, but perhaps justifiably, walked from the highest post at the Admiralty, leaving it unguarded. Churchill, uncertain of the future, left London to command a battalion in France. They sought allies where and when they could find them, and they were individually blind to the colossal collapse that would come upon British arms in the horrors of that desperate year of 1915. The next year, 1916, brought no solace, only the unsatisfactory Battle of Jutland and the rising U-boat menace. From then until the war's conclusion, they eagerly sought a return to places of influence. Being on the sidelines was anathema to them both. By this time their respective political credit had run out, and only Churchill was brought back into the administration with executive powers – as Minister of Munitions – through the influence of his old ally, now prime minister, David Lloyd George. There he did great work contributing to victory. Fisher, by contrast, never fully enjoyed government's confidence and, sadly, continued to be unquenchable in his pronouncements. He was generally ostracised from councils of influence. As for Churchill, he changed parties yet again, returned to the Conservatives, and eventually, after some years in the wilderness, was again First Lord of the Admiralty at the outset of the Second World War. The First World War held many lessons for him, and he was quick to learn from them. Fisher was too obstinate to learn lessons. He passed from this earth an embittered man, one mindful of how the great conflict had changed all civilisations and brought forth a darker present. At the end, he went quietly into the night.

In the struggle to control the past and refurbish his reputation, time favoured Churchill over Fisher. Prominent historian that he was, Churchill could make vigorous assessments of those to whom he had been harnessed during his time at the Admiralty in the war, notably Fisher. (This he did in the first two volumes of *The World Crisis*: 'Winston has written a book about himself,' chuckled the former prime minister Arthur Balfour, 'and has called it the World Crisis.') Naval writers closely scrutinised those volumes at the time of publication. As a prominent journalist after the war, Churchill was able to challenge Admiral Reginald H Bacon, authorised biographer of Fisher, who defended his man against Churchill. Longevity has its benefits – Churchill invariably had the last word and, therefore, the advantage. He was not only one of the principal actors in the long saga but also came, in time, to be in command of history. Those who die last and are good writers always have the advantage in any battle against rivals.

Worth keeping in mind, as historian Paul Addison reminds us in the *Oxford Dictionary of National Biography*, is that Churchill was 'a restless, intuitive force who re-invented himself at frequent intervals and hardly knew where imagination and opportunity would carry him next.' Any attempt to show Churchill on a linear path is complicated by the perennial shifts of fate. Fisher, by contrast, shows a narrower trajectory and, to a certain degree, a more centred one, and it must always be remembered that he was a generation older than Churchill. He was the guardian of the Navy at all costs. He was a materialist, a weapons man, and a shipbuilder. Churchill, politician and statesman, was invariably protecting his career and his future.

Other persons important in the historical record enter our story. That powerful force in political and military affairs, Arthur Balfour, haunts the fringes. The Earl of Selborne, First Lord of the Admiralty, was the key politician making Fisher's reforms possible. Churchill's preferment of Admiral Sir David Beatty makes the great sailor a central figure here. Fisher's preferment of Admiral Sir John Jellicoe runs on a parallel course. Jellicoe and Beatty form the main naval figures of the age, and their personalities and characteristics, their different actions in the great but inconclusive action at the Battle of Jutland, weave through the latter half of this book, partisan figures to the last. Even the interment of Earl Beatty beside Viscount Jellicoe in the crypt of St Paul's became a subject of controversy, as the Dowager Countess Jellicoe sought to protect her husband's reputation against someone she thought a pretender to greatness. Montagues and Capulets abound: Jutland will be a battle without end.

Admiral Prince Louis of Battenberg, one of the Navy's finest officers, fell victim to the rising Germanophobia of late 1914, though he was hardly the forceful head of the naval staff that was required to be placed on the block in the heat of battle. As we will see, Fisher was brought in by Churchill to replace Battenberg.

Fisher's intractable quarrel with the publicly popular Admiral Lord Charles Beresford was a smouldering volcano that threatened to erupt at any moment during the last years of Fisher's first tenure as First Sea Lord. Fortunately, in this heated circumstance, Fisher was curtailed by that man of backstairs influence Lord Esher, prominent in these pages, and by H H Asquith, the prime minister. Beresford had also quarrelled with Admiral Sir Percy Scott, another figure of note. Brilliant at gunnery inventions, 'Aim Straight' Scott was one of the key figures of Fisher's technological revolution. Beresford, believing him a spy for the First Sea Lord, took the opportunity to humiliate Scott, who did not help the cause by signalling to one of his cruisers that paintwork seemed more in demand than gunnery. Beresford could stand on ceremony and, like Fisher, commanded obedience and punctuality. Reginald Bacon, from the same epoch, backed Fisher and came to his unquestioned support as biographer.

Fisher could be, and was often, a harsh judge of fellow officers and of politicians, and he had a long memory in these things that tended toward the unforgiving. He had what might be described as Sicilian tendencies. Churchill was the opposite, and although he could hire and fire at will, as many a general could attest, he did not bear grudges. It was his wife, Clementine, who had the long memory in these matters. She was one of the 'women behind the fleet', ever so important in British naval affairs.

Jacky Fisher may have been a great man – one of the greatest Englishmen of his age – but for many he left a trail of sorrow and uncertainty. That the Navy did so brilliantly in the Second World War is a tribute to certain lessons learned in the First. The ending of partisan leadership at the Board of Admiralty formed the essential preliminary to waging a successful war at sea – and a second defeat of Germany within two and a half decades. Those are stories for other times and other places. Here it serves us well to remember that the Fisher era of the Royal Navy was much like the man himself – volatile, exciting, uncertain, partisan, and full of crises. This then is an inquiry into the psychology of military competence and the role of personality and character in the making of history.

***

Of late, a lurid and irresponsible tendency to embrace the counterfactual has solidified professional careers and even made historians into soothsayers. Years ago I was taught to beware of the bogus. Yes, it would be grand had Britain not entered the war in 1914. Like most of the British Cabinet of the age, including Churchill, the nation wanted peace. But it was a matter of honour and obligation that Britain entered the war against Germany and the Central Powers. It did so in accord with understandings with allies, and in conformity to the integrity of international law as to national independence of nations and governments that would fall under the control of an alien power, specifically Belgium in regards to Imperial Germany's aggression. A sense of honour and duty also brought the British Empire's peoples and nations into the same fight. The bugles of England were bleating powerfully from the home islands. They were heard around the world. From our comfortable seats a century later it's easy to postulate, as some have done, that Britain should not have entered the war, and that Churchill was a warmonger. But such proponents do a disservice to history and do a violence to the historical record.

Such arguments are also strange apologies for the German position, which was not defensive but was, in fact, aggressive and in defiance of international law and order. Bernard Shaw once said that the English could quickly take a moral position on just about any subject. I do not question that, and I rather applaud it as part of living in a democratic society. I do object, however, to misleading arguments by historians who use the commercial media to advance counterfactual and inaccurate positions that do not stand the test of historical scholarship. As voyeurs of the past, these pretenders have abdicated all responsibility as judge and jury of the historical record. To be specific: any viewpoint that would charge Winston Churchill with leading Britain into war in 1914 would do well to look at the life and record of Sir Edward Grey, the Foreign Secretary. It was his arguments that sealed 'the continental commitment'. And as Arthur Marder, the famed American historian, wrote so wonderfully, naval rivalry did not cause the war, but it ensured that when war did break out, Britain would be on the side of Germany's enemies. The German high command understood this, and one need only read the words of Friedrich von Holstein, head of the political section of the German Foreign Office, to the effect that the German fleet increased the number of Germany's enemies but would never be strong enough to vanquish them. Germany could not hope, then or later, for an equal fight at sea. This is a factor in the unfolding great tragedy.

All students of this subject, and particularly of naval aspects of the First World War, are beholden to Professor Marder, editor of selections of Jacky Fisher's letters in three volumes and author of *From the Dreadnought to Scapa Flow* in five volumes, all about what Marder called 'the Fisher era', 1904–1919. Fisher's remarkable books *Memories* and *Records* are not autobiography in the complete sense; they are fragments thrown together. They represent, adroitly, the fragmented progress that was his life. Many biographies of Fisher guide our path, among them most notably that by Ruddock Mackay and the generalist Richard Hough, though the shorter work of Richard Ollard suggests the nuances of the relationship that the First Sea Lord had with the First Lord of the Admiralty. Geoffrey Penn and Richard Freeman's books have lain open Beresford's vendetta against Fisher, though others have thought it a quarrel or a feud. I am beholden to Professor Paul Halpern for the supreme quality of his documents editions and for his sober and wide-ranging appraisals of naval affairs of the age. Even in death, and within living memory of his time at the Admiralty, Jacky was the source of controversy among leading naval authorities, as the pages of the *Naval Review* attest. My bibliography gives the essential items by A H Pollen, A C Dewar, Lord Sydenham, and others.

For Churchill, we have his official life, commenced by son Randolph Churchill and completed by Sir Martin Gilbert. This last historian, the greatest chronicler of Churchill, was also a compiler of companion volumes of documents. Churchill is the subject of numerous biographies and countless other studies of almost Napoleonic proportions. In my estimation, Robert Rhodes James's examination of the years of Churchill's floundering, 1900 to 1939, greatly helps us understand the nature of his character and the difficulties of the circumstances he faced in the years covered in this book. Equal in rank, though of a different order, is the first and prodigious volume of William Manchester's biography, *Last Lion*. Rhodes James and Manchester present nuanced treatments and third dimensions of character not found in the official biography (or, it might be added, in many another biography). Trumbull Higgins's sadly neglected study of Churchill and the Dardanelles also provides insights not found elsewhere. Tim Travers's *Gallipoli 1915* gives new evidence, laudably refuses to pin the blame on individuals, and provides important Ottoman and German material.

As to the politics of the era, Max Aitken, Lord Beaverbrook, gives a behind-the-scenes account of how Fisher was the doyen of the Unionists and courted them – to Churchill's cost. Among the studies of Churchill and the Royal Navy of this time, those by Vice-Admiral Sir Peter Gretton, Captain Stephen Roskill, and Professor Christopher M Bell demonstrate Churchill's desire to dominate the scene and control the Fleet. Bell's *Churchill and the Dardanelles* covers new ground, notably the Dardanelles Commission. The periodic tension between Churchill and Fisher reflected the politics of Admiralty affairs and difficulties any First Lord probably faced with his professional naval advisers to develop policy and concurrently administer a far-flung navy. Personalities rather than process usually drove the development of policy. In this regard, Nicholas Rodger's and C I Hamilton's books on the Admiralty are our guides. As to other works, Robert Massie's pairing *Dreadnought* and *Castles of Steel* retains popular attraction as well as authenticity, though not deeply rooted in documentary research. Throughout I have been guided by Paul Halpern's rich survey *A Naval History of World War I* and the supreme oversight of Basil Liddell Hart. Details of all these works, and others, are to be found in the Bibliography.

Students of this subject are eager to learn how Churchill's experience in the First World War influenced his actions upon return to the Admiralty in 1939 and after, until the end of the Second World War. In my epilogue I have specifically dealt with this matter. It may be wondered if past practice finds new methods on account of experience – and the trials of war.

In the past few decades many new revelations have come to light through the re-evaluation of technical, financial, and strategic issues of this era. The noteworthy and specialised contributions of, particularly, Jon Tetsuro Sumida and Nicholas Lambert are significant, although this so-called new history has not replaced the mainline narratives that form our appreciation of the naval issues of the age. Their focus is on the Fisher era and the Fisher naval revolution, and unlike Manchester, who wrote about the Krupps, has not yet entered the commercial and industrial military complex. Rather than replacing the great canon of history written by Marder and those of his times, their work in the pre-war period supplements and enriches the earlier narratives. Matthew Seligmann's innovative work on armed defensive cruisers shows that the protection of seaborne trade was the essential thing against rival German cruiser capabilities. The curious and unexpected unravelling of the naval war in all its dimensions after August 1914 places all predetermined or imagined scenarios in situations of uncertainty. As the war unfolded, so too did strategy, tactics, materials, and priorities. Those who have written so much about the lead-up to 1914 and the Fisher revolution that formed part of it need to know that the end result cannot be reduced arbitrarily to the effectiveness of director firing, the explosion of shells on contact, or the disposition and composition of fleets. The personal and moral factors, the traditions and the will to fight, so often ignored by contemporary historians, are essential features in victory or defeat.

My theme, different from recent historical preoccupations, plays on aspects of character and personality. Reverting to the original documents helps put these matters in better perspective. The war was waged in the minds of men, perhaps more important in the long run than that waged by those who fought the campaigns at sea, on land, and in the air – which does not diminish war at the sharp end, or the sacrifices. This analysis is principally based on extensive evaluation of the manuscript papers of both Fisher and Churchill, now held in the Churchill Archives Centre, Churchill College, Cambridge. The rich Churchill Papers and the Fisher Papers are as comprehensive as one is likely to find when undertaking research in the contemporary history of the early twentieth century. It has taken me two years as resident Archives Fellow at Churchill College, plus numerous additional visits, some of months' duration, to complete the enjoyable labour, the results of which are demonstrated in this book. While the interaction of Churchill and Fisher has been the subject of other authors, including Richard Ollard, Arthur Marder, Ruddock Mackay, and Geoffrey Penn, to name the most prominent, and I have benefited from their findings and explanations, none of them enjoyed the advantage that was accorded to me. The Churchill Archives Centre made the full range of Churchill Papers available to me shortly after its accession. Similarly, the complete run of the Fisher Papers, gathered over many years at the same repository, was likewise available in full. Previous scholars had been hampered by inability to access the full files, but the secrets they hold can now be disclosed. This book represents the first full use of these marvellous collections.

Supplementing the Churchill and Fisher manuscripts are others in the Churchill Archives Centre, notably those of Reginald Brett (2nd Viscount Esher); Shane Leslie, Beatty's intended biographer; and Captain Stephen Roskill, the famed naval historian. In the National Maritime Museum, the papers of Earl Beatty, which supplement those in the British Library; the papers of Earl Jellicoe and Arthur Balfour in the British Library; and other collections have been partially used. At The National Archives, Kew, the Admiralty Papers provide the official record of the Lords of the Admiralty in addition to the operational and intelligence papers of the Royal Navy during the period. Selections of Fisher, Jellicoe, Keyes, and Beatty manuscripts have been printed in edited form by the distinguished and reliable Navy Records Society (see the Bibliography). They are used here, as are the excerpted documents and the printed correspondence of Churchill published in the authorised biography, begun by Randolph Churchill and completed by Sir Martin Gilbert. A selection of correspondence to and from Fisher, as prepared by Arthur Marder in three volumes, has also been used extensively. Lord Selborne's key relevant papers about Fisher's rise are in print. The papers of the Dardanelles Commission, and allied correspondence, provide further insights into the workings of this pair.

A work such as this owes much to the previous labours and insights of a host of researchers and writers, and in the Acknowledgements I indicate those who have given assistance. I thank many professional associates and friends who have read sections of this work or otherwise given advice. I alone am responsible for the interpretations and use of documentation, and any errors of fact are mine alone.

Barry Gough
June 2017

A Note on the Board of Admiralty

From medieval times, specifically 1391, the office of the Lord High Admiral denoted administrative and operational control of the Royal Navy. Officers executing that office when it was put into commission (that is, when it was not held by a single person) were known as Lords Commissioners of the Admiralty, and their committee was the Board of Admiralty. This system continued until 1964, when the Admiralty was absorbed, with the Army and the Royal Air Force, into the Ministry of Defence.

Over centuries the Admiralty grew into one of the great state offices of the Crown, unique in its capacities due to its direct connection to the monarch of the day, with an independent attitude to match its historical functions as chief defender of trade, protector of seaborne commerce, and regulator of jurisdiction in maritime affairs upon which the power and the profit of Great Britain and the British Empire depended. Its influence was global.

The Board of Admiralty consisted of the civilian First Lord of the Admiralty, a Cabinet minister and member of the House of Lords or House of Commons. There was, too, a Civil Lord, a Parliamentary and Financial Secretary, a Permanent Secretary, and four professional sea or naval lords. The old title of 'sea lords' dated from 1613. However, the term was altered to 'naval lords' early in the nineteenth century, reverting to the old term when Admiral Sir John Fisher became First Sea Lord in 1904.

The First Lord of the Admiralty had the duty of general direction and supervision, and was responsible for presenting the annual naval estimates to Parliament. The First Sea Lord, paramount officer on the board, was responsible for advice on naval policy, disposition of the Fleet, and its fighting strength and efficiency. He was also Chief of Naval Staff. He was expected to provide advice to his political chief, the First Lord of the Admiralty, on all naval matters. The Second Sea Lord's responsibilities concerned personnel, including manning and mobilisation. The Third Sea Lord, or Controller, had charge of the materiel of the Fleet, while the Fourth Sea Lord managed the supplies and transport. (The position of Fifth Sea Lord, responsible for naval aviation, was instituted in 1917.) The Civil Lord looked after buildings and works. The Parliamentary and Financial Secretary was responsible for the department's finances. The Permanent Secretary of the Admiralty, the 'nerve centre' of the Board, looked after correspondence and office administration.

As will be shown in the following pages, the men who formulated naval policy were the First Lord of the Admiralty and the First Sea Lord. In 1869 the

First Lord was made responsible to the sovereign and to Parliament for all Admiralty business. Accordingly, members of the Board were advisers of and subordinate to the First Lord. Should their advice not be accepted, they had no remedy except protest or resignation. Just before Fisher became First Sea Lord, a special Order in Council reduced the authority of the junior naval lords and transferred strategy and operations to the First Sea Lord. The Director of Naval Intelligence, whose department, founded in 1886, was a fact-gathering office, advised on the state of foreign navies and potential rivals at sea.

The Admiralty was brought into the Imperial Defence Commitee early in the twentieth century, though reluctantly, and in 1904 the Committee of Imperial Defence (CID) was established as an advisory or consultative body on defence matters. The Admiralty and the War Office (which administered the Army) met on common ground at the CID, though seldom with unanimity of opinion or purpose. The CID had a Permanent Secretary, advisory to the Cabinet, which directed the affairs of state. From this committee came significant developments relating to strategy, and in the three years leading to war in 1914, the CID exercised considerable influence in defence matters without encroaching on the prerogatives of the Admiralty or the War Office.

Introduction: The Daemonic Duo

Throughout English history, control of those vital 'narrow seas' that separate the British Isles from the European continent formed a central tenet of British national statecraft and policy. From King Alfred's reign down to and after the era that is the focus of this book, sea power – that is, the instrumental means of naval protection and coercion – has been an essential feature guarding the profit and power of the British state, on which the well-being of the island nation is assured. With control over the seaboards of other naval powers of Europe, Great Britain ensured the security of the home islands and, at the same time, that of her widespread colonial possessions.

The American historian Alfred Thayer Mahan made this approach clear in 1890 with publication of *The Influence of Sea Power upon History*. British admirals knew it to be true all along. By contrast, and at the same time as Mahan's pronouncements, British politicians did not always fully grasp the essential requirement: that the Royal Navy had to be maintained in such prominence that it always enjoyed a margin of superiority in size and number of manned ships so that it could deal effectively with any challenge to its command of the sea. That meant superiority against any contender who wished to grasp the trident of Neptune held by Britannia, but also against any combination of rivals who might form a hostile alliance to seize the trident. By the late nineteenth century, this Two-Power Standard was the agreed-upon measure, with the Navy being theoretically capable of dealing with a combination of two rivals, say France and Russia. In anxious days ahead, however, this formula had to be surrendered in favour of a policy of alliances.

In asserting this policy of Great Britain as 'mistress of the seas', politicians and statesmen in Westminster and Whitehall forged Britannia's sceptre and kept it in their firm grasp. Whereas the nation, and the well-informed person in the street, might understand the dependence of the kingdom on sea power, it was the rulers who made the policies that were fundamental to progressive naval development. These were the 'sea kings' dating from the time of King Alfred.

Navies are artificial creations of state. They do not spring up naturally from the seafaring tendencies of coastal societies. Admirals with their fleets are weapons wielded in the hands of statesmen.

These were time-honoured appreciations. More than two centuries before the epoch covered in this book, and in consequence of that great test of strength, the near-fatal wars against the Dutch in the seventeenth century, the Admiralty took speedy measures to bolster Britain's capabilities at sea, not least so as to prevent an invasion from the Continent. When Napoleon Bonaparte rose to prominence and threatened invasion in purpose-built landing craft assembled at Boulogne in 1803, it was British sea power that stood in the way. That great sea king Earl St Vincent was able to assure the nation that the French would not come by sea. Nelson's resounding victory at Trafalgar secured a ten-year interval, and blockade and campaigns on the Continent, plus a grand European alliance including Britain, were factors that brought Napoleon's defeat at Waterloo and his surrender. His quest to become master of the Mediterranean Sea, with an empire stretching from Egypt to India, had been shattered by the efforts of British ships and sailors. Trafalgar and Waterloo gave Britain an undisputed global advantage. The benefits were manifest. In the subsequent hundred years Britain not only ruled the waves but also established a dominant world order known as Pax Britannica, a unique interval in modern history in which, by British men-of-war on distant station or in reserve, the outward ramparts of empire were secured, slavery was abolished and the slave trade ended, and large-scale piracy was eradicated. British statesmen and politicians of all stripes and persuasions knew the benefits of British strength at sea. It was on seaborne trade that the wealth of the nation principally depended, and in this scenario profit and power had jointly to be considered.[1] *The Times* put this well on 3 February 1902:

> England is mistress of the seas, not by virtue of any arrogant or aggressive pretensions, but by virtue of her history, of her geographical situation, and of her economic antecedents and conditions, and of her Imperial position and expansion. These conditions have given the dominion of the seas to her, not by any prescriptive right, but by a normal and almost natural process of evolution; and, so long as they subsist and she is true to herself, they will retain it for her.

Here was a most optimistic view on a rapidly changing scene.

As the twentieth century dawned, politicians and statesmen often expressed radically different views on how large the British navy should be in time of peace. Invariably, threats by foreign rivals riveted their attention. As a rule, the Conservatives, or Unionists, strongly argued the need for a powerful navy. Their defence policy during their years in power, from 1895 under, in turn, prime ministers Salisbury and Balfour, right down to their electoral defeat in 1905, called for vigorous measures in the design and building of new ships; the fortification of dockyards and bases around the world, such as Bermuda, Gibraltar, Simonstown, Esquimalt, and Singapore; and the general readiness for war. By contrast, the Liberals, or Radicals, as they were then occasionally called, opposed massive military expenditures. Inheriting anti-militaristic views expressed during the time of William Ewart Gladstone (he resigned the premiership in 1894 on account of what he thought were unconscionably high naval estimates), the Liberals had a pronounced agenda of social reforms befitting a modern industrial state. Here was a 'guns or butter' scenario.

The 'naval question' was a preoccupation at a time of many other pressing concerns: Home Rule for Ireland, votes for women and the suffragette movement, unemployment, wages and wage controls, industrial action including coal strikes, public house licensing, and reform of the House of Lords preoccupied most politicians. Pushed to the background was naval preparedness. And thus it was that as the world lurched almost unknowingly toward war in 1914, the Conservatives were most attuned to the naval and military requirements of the modern state, and the Liberals were much less aware of the threat posed to the power, prestige, and profit of the British state and empire by Imperial Germany. With the Liberals holding a commanding majority in the Commons, and the Conservatives controlling the House of Lords, what might be called 'the politics of naval supremacy' was widely discussed. It was hotly contested in and out of Parliament, in the press, and in the drawing rooms and clubs of the nation. The politicians were mindful of the dangers then approaching, and some books of the age, notably Erskine Childers's *Riddle of the Sands* (1903), attracted much attention and put up warning signs.

Through the ten years leading to the outbreak of war, governments and Parliament were determined to prevent the conflict. At the same time – as Winston Churchill, an observer of and participant in events, wrote later in *The World Crisis* – 'the sinister hypothesis was continually present in their thoughts, and was repeatedly brought to the attention of the ministers by disquieting incidents and tendencies.' He continues:

During the whole of those ten years this duality and discordance were the keynote of British politics; and those whose duty it was to watch over the safety of the country lived simultaneously in two different worlds of thought. There was the actual visible world with its peaceful activities and cosmopolitan aims; and there was the hypothetical world, a world 'beneath the threshold,' as it were, a world at one moment utterly fantastic, at the next seeming about to leap into reality – a world of monstrous shadows moving in convulsive combinations through vistas of fathomless catastrophe.[2]

As the months and years rolled relentlessly toward August 1914, the strength and the readiness of the Royal Navy became more and more the essential subject of consideration. The reasons were clear. The security of seaborne trade, and the future of the British Empire, rested on His Majesty's ships at sea, on their bases and material resources at home, and on the officers and men who served these men-of-war. The responsibility was as vast as the future was in doubt. Armageddon was fast approaching. For on German shores and in German dockyards was arising the supreme rival, the navy of the Kaiser and of Admiral von Tirpitz, and all indications were that it was rising with malicious intent.

It was at this critical point in the affairs of Britain and the British Empire that two unlikely and certainly remarkable persons directed the preparation, readiness, and deployment of the largest military instrument then known to mankind, the Royal Navy.[3] At this decisive moment, these two sea lords dominated the affairs of the Admiralty, that all-powerful and ancient ministry of government responsible for the Fleet and its manning, and, indeed, all things connected to the Navy. One was First Lord of the Admiralty, the Rt Hon Winston Leonard Spencer Churchill, MP, PC; the other, First Sea Lord, Admiral Sir John Fisher (Baron Fisher of Kilverstone after 1910).

On the shoulders of this duo – and of those who worked immediately with and under them – fell the heavy obligation of maintaining Britain's naval primacy; safeguarding the seaborne commerce upon which the lifeblood of the island kingdom and its many outlying dominions, colonies, bases, and ramparts depended; and keeping the seas free for all who should pass on their lawful occasions. The immediate task at hand was to defeat Imperial Germany and its allies, foes with which they were engaged in mortal combat. Seldom if ever in the course of history were the burdens so heavy, the challenges so mighty, and the stakes so high.

'The history of the War,' the biographer of Arthur Balfour, sometime prime minister and First Lord of the Admiralty, astutely observed, 'is very largely a history of personal combinations.' 'No more instructive illustration of this is to be found than at the Board of Admiralty.'[4] The historian is struck, invariably, by the role played by personality in the course of history. Had it been the statesman Balfour instead of Churchill dealing with Fisher at the Admiralty during the Dardanelles crisis, what sort of quieter, more accommodating effects might have resulted instead of the grinding difficulties that were continually asserting themselves? Or, to pose another possibility, had Churchill's opposite not been Fisher but, say, Admiral Sir Henry Jackson – with his technical mastery of communications, especially wireless, and who served at the Admiralty as First Sea Lord with Balfour – how would Churchill have contended with such a person, who was so much less volatile and far more malleable than Jacky

Fisher? We are naturally left wondering about the tantalising might-have-beens, but the reality was the daemonic duo of Churchill and Fisher, a powerful combination with tragic consequences for waging a successful war at sea.

Many additional difficulties, some of a systemic nature, stood in the way of British successes. At the War Office, the amalgamation of ministerial and professional functions under Lord Kitchener had brought that august figure unimagined powers of centralisation, and from these came unfortunate struggles with the Admiralty in early 1915. As a result, every aspect of staff work was in disarray. Arthur Balfour, reviewing this state of affairs in the lead-up to the Dardanelles disaster, described the position of the government in terms of personalities: 'the principal actors at home were a soldier without strategic genius, who controlled the military machine, a sailor equally without strategic genius, who ought to have controlled, but did not, the naval machine, and a brilliant amateur who attempted, but failed, to dominate both.'[5] This is a fair assessment by an onlooker to events unfolding. The Kitchener–Fisher–Churchill combination spelled disaster, and each of these men was to pay heavily for his inability to work with the others, though in their individual capabilities they might have been great leaders. Altogether they stand at the centre of the unfolding tragedy.

These problems of command and control, and of government departments working with one another, stemmed from the old and palmy days of the late nineteenth century, when the Admiralty had few reasons to talk to the War Office, except to discuss fortifications of naval bases or gunnery questions. The performance of the British Army in the South African, or Boer, War called for radical measures of reform, particularly in army administration. That became the preoccupation of Arthur Balfour's Conservative administration and was continued by Lord Haldane at the War Office under the Liberals. Fisher did not seek accommodation with the War Office; for good or ill, he fought for the Admiralty's primacy.

Another great challenge presented itself in those complicated and restless days. The reassuring era of the Pax Britannica was quickly drawing to a close. On every sea and ocean annexe, new contenders were appearing to challenge Britain's naval supremacy, pegging out spheres of empire on distant shores and islands. Fisher, a little boastfully (as was his wont), always contended that the Admiralty ranged far ahead of the Foreign Office in realising the dangers presented by rival nations. Fisher's bravado in these matters rested on the fact that the Admiralty had its own means of gathering data – all sorts of details on foreign ships launched or building, dockyards constructed or expanded, canals and waterways widened or otherwise improved, appointments made, and ships deployed. On 14 September 1902 Vice-Admiral Sir Reginald Custance, the Director of Naval Intelligence and a man of suspicious outlook, drew the

Admiralty's attention to the danger posed by the upstart German fleet in the North Sea. Around that time, key personnel in the Foreign Office came to the same conclusion as Custance, for alarming information from Berlin and elsewhere had suggested that the Kaiser's navy was the rival coming forward to challenge the Royal Navy and the Pax Britannica. This newly formed instrument of sea power was the creation of that remarkable professional sailor and administrator Grand Admiral Alfred von Tirpitz. Successive German naval bills after 1900 indicated to the Foreign Office, the Admiralty, the War Office, the Cabinet, and its recently created Committee on Imperial Defence (designed specifically to assess Britain's readiness for war) that Germany intended to become a potent sea power, with a fleet big enough to back up any German moves to expand colonial interests, trade, and naval bases globally – in the Caribbean, on the coast of Africa, and in East Asia. To the First Lord of the Admiralty fell the heavy burden of bringing forward in Parliament the customary annual naval estimates. And as the nation and empire drew unavoidably closer to war, so, too, did that burden increase.

In the naval affairs of that age, the dominant, virulent, volcanic, and uncompromising personality of John Arbuthnot Fisher towered above all others. Besides being domineering, he was warm, sociable, and outgoing. As a naval commander, admiral, and sea lord, he had shaken his fist in the face of everyone of importance and influence. He had made many enemies (and he feared no one who stood in his way). He was of indomitable courage. If in charge of a gunnery establishment, a torpedo school, or a dockyard, he had always thrown himself into his work. He was a professional technocrat.

The times favoured the man, and Fisher's genius had been given the fullest scope. One writer likened Fisher to that previous giant of naval administration, the Earl of St Vincent:

> Both were ruthless, relentless, and remorseless in quelling opposition; both were ardent reformers; both became much-hated men during the process of reform. And while St Vincent made the fleet that won Trafalgar, Fisher was largely responsible for the Navy that fought in the Great War. The work of both had an outstanding and lasting effect upon the Great Service to which they belonged, while their respective careers afford interesting sidelights upon the history of the Navy at two periods a century apart.[6]

Many who observed Fisher thought him mad, and said so to his face. The eminent psychologist Norman Dixon, authority on military incompetence, wrote, in praise of Fisher: 'As might be expected of a man with an ego of positively tank-like proportion, Fisher suffered little repression of sex or aggression ... A great womanizer, and loved by women in return, his warmth and humanity extended far beyond the confines of sex and marriage.' The comfort of the officers and men under his command was of abiding concern to him. He was particularly kind to younger officers and midshipmen. 'Autocratic but non-authoritarian' is Professor Dixon's classification of his managerial style. 'All in all, Fisher, like Nelson, was well equipped to use his intelligence and drive in the pursuit of naval efficiency. He was apparently quite unhampered by those feelings of infantile inferiority that have crippled other military and naval leaders. It was not without insight that he wrote: "I attribute my present vitality to the imbibing of my mother's milk beyond the legal period of nine months."'[7]

Winston Spencer Churchill, similarly, was an agent of change, a provocateur, with large scope for individual action and initiative. This he shared with his professional counterpart. As another commented: 'Fisher's relationship with Churchill is the key to Churchill's relation to the navy. Both, essentially, were, for all their dazzling gifts of communication and their power to entrance, men who were a cause unto themselves, to use the old medieval definition of freedom. Both were irreverent, witty, Radical.'[8] Like Fisher, Churchill was a foe to complacency. He was ruthless, volcanic, and pugilistic, defiant of opposition. For seven months formally, and for many more informally both before and after the great crisis of the Dardanelles, Fisher and Churchill worked closely together. Sir Alfred Ewing, the brains behind the formation of Room 40 for naval intelligence, a witness to their combination at the Admiralty, thought these two were 'well mated in force, courage, and vision.'[9]

Fisher and Churchill exhibited the same dynamic energy. They showed insight and they showed genius, thus displaying the rare instincts of Nelson in combination. They were forward thinking, progressive, and activist. They were risk-takers. They were prepared to leave certain aspects of war-making to chance. They possessed anticipation, a rare capacity to foresee what might happen and thus make preparations. Moreover, they shared the unusual capacity to force their firmly held ideas ruthlessly on their respective colleagues. In naval matters, Fisher was the professional and Churchill the gifted amateur. Both had read about strategy and tactics (Churchill officially at Sandhurst; Fisher as part of the day-to-day efforts in senior command), and both had read history. Churchill took the study of history seriously; Fisher looked for the changes of history, the departure from the norms: 'History is the record of exploded ideas!' was his constant cry as a technical revolutionary, a materialist. Neither had great gifts in strategic thinking; then again, they lived in an age that had hardly seen great wars at sea, except for the Russo-Japanese War, which led them to believe that another Trafalgar would occur along the line of Tsushima, the Trafalgar of the East, when the Imperial Japanese navy annihilated the Imperial Russian Baltic squadron. Churchill and Fisher were ready for war. They were courageous, and they were influential in the particular way that they made the Admiralty into a powerful machine of war-making.

Brought together by strange circumstances, they forged a remarkable alliance, one tested to the full by the unravelling of events, which they also sought to control. They could see or imagine the far horizons.

They were, it now seems, locked in a strange and fatal destiny. Their contemporary, the politician and journalist Max Aitken, Lord Beaverbrook, writing of those same days, of which he was a close observer, said that these two men were chained together, so if one went overboard, the other did too.[10] This was so obviously the case. For when Fisher resigned his post in May 1915 and walked from his office irresponsibly, Churchill was left virtually high and dry – his political fortunes in shambles. A dark cloud hung over his head for many a year after the Dardanelles disaster, the set-piece tragedy of this book. Many a critic thought him untrustworthy, and he had several long years in the political wilderness. Intriguingly, when he became First Lord of the Admiralty once more in 1939, and then prime minister in 1940, he retained the position of Minister of Defence, a post that gave him powers of surveillance and authority over the full gamut of military and security affairs, besides abundant diplomatic initiatives of an Allied nature. He had learned his lesson from the Dardanelles campaign. Moreover, he took pains to make sure that the service heads were not only subservient to their political chiefs but also acted according to the protocols and regulations of a modern democratic state at war. He had things written down, not left to chance or oral recollection. In other words, Churchill learned from the lessons of history. In addition, by writing his own histories of these wars, he made certain that his interpretations and judgements would be recorded persuasively. Like Herodotus, and others of the ancient world, he recorded and recounted the particulars of his own campaign. Such is his profound literary legacy.

In Jacky Fisher's time, and predating Churchill's arrival, the Admiralty stood as an exalted and particularly proud and independent department of state, unique in its time and circumstances. The Admiralty was at the pinnacle of the military-industrial complex of the United Kingdom, and the Navy was the largest expenditure of the state. The whole Admiralty establishment shook and trembled during Fisher's tenure. Churchill raised its profile, too, after he became First Lord in 1911. He was in the most important position for the defence of British trade and imperial interests in the lead-up to the war, and under his leadership many super-dreadnoughts were authorised for construction. However, the fortunes of war did not sustain the public's support for the Admiralty, or for Churchill or Fisher. The Admiralty fell from grace in consequence of the tragedy that worked itself out in the war. As was the case for the dreadnoughts, the Admiralty's power and influence passed to new engines of war in sub-surface and aerial warfare. But many who served in the Navy during the First World War were present again in the Second, and perhaps a little surprisingly they found themselves dealing with a domineering Churchill, an agent of aggressiveness and uniquely inspired strategic planning whom they found, as Fisher had done in 1915, strategically unsound and personally distasteful.

Such was the odd combination. The angular and dynamic personalities of these two characters were bound to rub against one another. But the fact is, as their correspondence discloses, their partnership lasted a good long time, often informally and behind the scenes. It went through various phases. It was forged in peace. It faced numerous difficulties during urgent measures. It was nurtured during successful warfare. And it fell apart during a military expedition the likes of which the world had not seen to that date, a hastily arranged affair fought at a time when British naval superiority was being tested on the high seas – that is, in the North Sea, and then in the U-boat war against Allied shipping. Even in defeat they shared their perspectives on the direction of the war. Fisher and Churchill did not fight the war they wanted to: they never fought a war for the shallow waters of the Baltic, one they thought would turn the tide of events in the continental war. Instead, their dreams of bold action against Germany and in support of Russia, which would have relieved the pressure on the Western Front and perhaps ended the war early, died a long and miserable death.

In the circumstances, Fisher and Churchill found themselves obliged to fight the unexpected campaign in the Dardanelles and Gallipoli. In this they paid the great penalty for inadequate planning, poor relations with the Army and with their French ally, lack of surprise, and insufficient reconnaissance to determine what the enemy had in mind with regards to the mine, the submarine, and the torpedo in the narrow waters leading from the eastern Mediterranean to the Sea of Marmara. In all, it was a tragic scenario, and much ink has been spilt on it. But the episode masks some larger questions about the naval affairs of the United Kingdom and the British Empire.

The revolution in naval warfare was swift and unrelenting. Fisher and his rebels stood at the vortex. If technological innovations were changing the material features of war at sea, tactical matters and ship management were often far astern. Fisher and many of his fellow officers, especially those in high command, had been trained in the old sailing navy. They could remember how Their Lordships had reluctantly adopted innovations in steam propulsion and gunnery. They could also remember what naval warfare was like before the age of the mine and the torpedo and, certainly, the submarine. Their grandfathers, too, had fought in the age of fighting sail, when the battle was determined by the natural movements of ships and by formations that were predicated on winds and tides. Now, and suddenly, the machine age had come to naval warfare, bringing with it all sorts of new dimensions and abundant difficulties. Resistance to change was natural in a service dedicated to traditions. 'It was a world in which war with a capital "W" was hardly ever thought of,' recalled one admiral, and another officer said: 'Although it cannot be denied that we bred great seamen in those days when books were seldom opened and the university of the seaman was the sea, yet, owing to world changes and the ever onward trend of science, modifications became necessary. So, with the progress of time, the old wooden ships disappeared, nor could they be the home of those who were to be the naval officers of the future.'[11]

Great changes were likewise afoot in the Royal Navy concerning the education of cadets, the future officers. The Blue Book for the information of those parents thinking of the Royal Navy as a career for their young and tender sons advised that certain characteristics were likely to help one become a good officer and a man of action: resourcefulness, resolution, decisiveness and readiness to act on decisions, and, above all, willingness to learn the secret of command, which was through the discipline of obedience. The New Scheme, the so-called Selborne Scheme (after the reform-minded Earl of Selborne, First Lord of the Admiralty from 1900 to 1905), in which Fisher played a decisive part, necessitated rapid changes through the various naval training establishments and dockyard schools at Devonport and Portsmouth. Naval colleges were opened at Osborne House in the Isle of Wight and at Dartmouth in Devon, and for the first time cadets spent hours in workshops and laboratories learning about marine engineering, the design of ships, and the intricacies of how a modern warship worked. Engineering had gone to sea, and it was to have a profound influence ashore. Naval diehards naturally fought against such changes.

Selborne sent Fisher to become Commander-in-Chief, Portsmouth, where, in charge of naval activities ashore, including dockyard work, he could supervise the implementation of the scheme. Many were happy to see him out of the Admiralty for a time, tired as they were of his incessant reforming tendencies and his determined views. When he was at Portsmouth, his energetic and all-consuming actions pressed forward the naval revolution. Fisher may not have fully understood the scientific and technical aspects of this material shift – he had no university education and no service background in the engineering branch – but he kept himself well informed on developments in naval weaponry, particularly guns and torpedoes. His interest in ship speed and mobility set him apart from almost every other officer who rose to the dizzying heights in the Board of Admiralty. This is a recurrent theme in these pages, and the changes that Fisher proposed often set off alarm bells. One senior officer who viewed Fisher with suspicion, Rear-Admiral Sir Reginald Custance, wrote to his friend Vice-Admiral Sir Cyprian Bridge, Commander-in-Chief on the China station, 'Fisher arrives next week. Heaven knows what he may not attempt to run. Any wild cat scheme finds a supporter in him.'[12]

It bears remembering that this was an age, too, of unbridled public expectations in the Navy's success in any prospective war. Decades of British children had been raised to believe in Britannia's invincibility. Nelson was the naval ideal. Teachers, politicians, and writers, parsons, fathers, and uncles, and many others besides had told them so. It was a national love affair, with the Navy as Britain's prize asset, its sure shield of defence. As one admiral who witnessed the transition from the Old to the New Navy put it, 'Doings of the Old Navy, of hand-to-hand and ship-to-ship fighting, with its spectacular incidents and records of heroism, had from youth up stirred the blood and the emotions of the nation, and therefore bitter disappointment was felt at the undramatic and prosaic *dénouement* of the only modern fleet action that was fought.'[13] He was referring to the Battle of Jutland, 31 May to 1 June 1916, the largest naval battle of the war, in which the Royal Navy fell well short of the total victory expected by the public. Disappearing, too, at this time, was much that was picturesque in the manners and customs at sea, but the tradition of the Service continued. And it was in this tradition that the Royal Navy held its trump card in the contest against the strong hand of its newest, strongest and most dangerous rival.[14]

In any possible engagement with that new naval power, Germany, the greatness and invincibility of the British Fleet was expected to be demonstrated. The public, press, and Parliament expected no less, especially as the stakes were high at this critical period of modern times. When war came, the Fleet was prepared. It may seem brutally frank in its clinical assessment, but the following evaluation from the distinguished engineer officer Vice-Admiral Sir Louis Le Bailly, who entered the Royal Navy in 1929, rings down through the years and is a testament to Fisher's greatness as well as a comment on those hazardous times in which desperately needed reforms were brought about:

If Admiral Sir John Fisher and his fellow rebels had not been born the Royal Navy would have remained the rather primitive organisation they inherited. In that case the newly built German fleet might have well annihilated the more numerous British fleet, and an invasion or a total blockade and ultimate starvation would have occurred. As things turned out, a much improved, but very far from perfect British fleet was at its northern watchtower in Scapa Flow when war was declared in August 1914.[15]

In this Churchill played a key part: that the Fleet had been placed at its war station owed much to Churchill's foresight, direction, and even political deviousness in those terrible days.

In many dark years that lay ahead, what I call the Britannic tragedy came to be, and it came in unwanted and unexpected fashion. The run-up to the catastrophe of the 1914 war had its own senseless logic. And when the crisis came, few in high places of office or command were prepared. Nor, once it had begun, did they have a clue as to how it might end. The return to peace was everyone's wish, but an increasingly vain hope.

Of Churchill's and Fisher's roles in this grander, extenuated tragedy, together and separately, no critic could slight their zeal or doubt their patriotism. In large measure the opened floodgates of history engulfed them in that storm-laden period. They did their best as the German juggernaut set to sea – in cruiser formations, then in the High Seas Fleet, and ultimately in the deadly U-boat arm. In the face of early defeats or inconsequential results for British arms, Churchill and Fisher believed that war could be brought to an early end if only the supreme command were placed in their hands. They never lost faith in their own abilities and remained steadfast in the face of the formidable challenges that confronted them. They were well acquainted with what might be called 'the supreme command' of their day – and all its frailties. At one time Fisher made a multi-point demand, listing what he would need to win the war. At another he told Churchill he was the best man to become generalissimo. It took another great war to put in place the joint political-military structures at the top of both the national and allied realms that would bring victory, this time against stronger but equally ruthless powers.

Early warnings of a change in international politics came with the new century. The great Queen-Empress Victoria passed from the scene on 22 January 1901. So long had she held exalted office that popular fantasy might be excused for thinking her immortal. She had become an institution, an emblem of the Empire's unity, its permanence. After her accession she had restored the prestige of the position, and her clear intellect, firm will, and high integrity gave persons in office at home and abroad reassurance that the popularity of the monarchy was due to the personality of the Queen herself.

Into the sorrowful scene on the occasion of her funeral marched a jingoist and a bully in the form of Kaiser Wilhelm II. Throughout the doleful proceedings, King Edward VII, aged fifty-nine, had his nephew the German Emperor at his side. Never were there two such opposites, for whereas the Kaiser was consciously seeking publicity, the King was unable to avoid it. The Kaiser preferred pomp and circumstance to informal gatherings. 'He was forever playing Providence,' commented an astute Viennese reporter, who had observed them both over many years. Edward VII was a past master of tact, knowledge of men, and worldly wisdom, said the same observer, and lived for the moment, disliking rhetoric or bluff, 'the most natural of all princes'.[16] On the surface all seemed to give fair indication of good allies at this time of bereavement and mourning. However, as the day wore on, the Kaiser, breaching the protocol that such an occasion required, conversed with Lord Lansdowne, the Foreign Secretary, as well as with the King, on political and diplomatic matters. When Lansdowne, by way of reply, raised for the first time the old question of the balance of power among the European nations, which lay in England's hand, the Kaiser bluntly stated, as reported by the secretary of the German embassy in London, 'that the balance of power now rested with the 22 German army corps, that England was no longer in a position to isolate herself as in former years from the rest of Europe, but must move together with the continent.'[17] The events of that afternoon were as if the Kaiser had brought a loaded pistol into the room.[18]

The Kaiser lunched at Marlborough House with King Edward the next day, in the presence of forty persons. The King's official biographer recounts that at the close of the meal the King proposed a toast to his nephew's health. The German Emperor replied with expressions of thanks at the magnificent reception, but then continued in words bound to alarm the leading figures in London and Berlin: 'We ought to form an Anglo-Saxon alliance, you to keep the seas while we would be responsible for the land; with such an alliance, not a mouse could stir in Europe without our permission, and the nations would, in time, come to see the necessity of reducing their armaments.' The Kaiser's notion that the two great nations should 'stand together to help in keeping the peace of the world' failed to be properly reported in the Berlin press. He took this as a slight and made a point of blaming the King and the English press. On his return to Berlin, his friendliness to England rapidly flagged.[19]

The Queen's death and Edward VII's succession brought other responses. Russia's Tsar expressed earnest hope that their two countries might become even closer than in the past. 'May the new century bring England and Russia together for our mutual interests and for the general peace of the world.' The president of the French Republic sent expressions of sorrow and regret, and when a British emissary arrived in Paris, he was told by the president, 'I and my ministers would consider it a crime if any one, I care not who, were to make mischief between France and England.'[20] As for the King, he began an active round of visits and gestures that brought about a closer association with France and then Russia, though no specific treaties of alliance were signed. These were understandings based on cordial greetings and similar positions.

A few years earlier, in 1895, Winston Churchill, then a young officer, had the pleasure of lunching with Sir William Harcourt, one of the powerful political figures of the time. During the conversation, in which Churchill admits he took none too modest a share, he asked the great man, 'What will happen then?' 'My dear Winston,' replied the old Victorian statesman with abundant calm, 'the experiences of a long life have convinced me that nothing ever happens.' Churchill took note of what the great man said, and in later years liked to bring to mind just how the force of events had dramatically altered Harcourt's assessment of the state of affairs. In the opening pages of his history and memoir of the war, Churchill reflected that since the very moment of his discussion with Harcourt, things had never ceased happening. Indeed, the world of British politics was enveloped in a flood of events.

> The growth of the great antagonisms abroad was accompanied by the progressive aggravation of party strife at home. The scale on which events have shaped themselves, has dwarfed the episodes of the Victorian Era. Its small wars between great nations, its earnest disputes about superficial issues, the high, keen intellectualism of its personages, the sober, frugal, narrow limitations of their action, belong to a vanished period. The smooth river with its eddies and ripples along which we then sailed, seems inconceivably remote from the cataract down which we have been hurled and the rapids in whose turbulence we are now struggling.[21]

One crisis, or anxious moment, followed another in swift order: first came the Jameson Raid in 1896, heralding the South African war. This ill-starred event brought Germany closer to challenging Britain's imperial agenda in Africa and elsewhere. Then, in 1902 Lord Salisbury, the Conservative prime minister for most of the previous seventeen years, resigned, replaced by Arthur Balfour, who inherited a weak government with a dismal future. Education and tariff reforms further weakened the Conservative position. The Russo-Japanese war brought disquiet. Closer relations with France and formation of the Committee of Imperial Defence ('the instrument of our preparedness', as Churchill rightly judges it) could not halt the government's demise. In November 1905 Balfour tendered his resignation, and Sir Henry Campbell-Bannerman formed a Liberal government. Then in rapid succession came the revolution in British foreign policy, the end of 'splendid isolation', the rise of the Kaiser's navy and its worrying consequences, the Moroccan crisis of 1906, the Agadir crisis of 1911, the reform of the British Army, and the attempted reform of the Admiralty so that it would have a naval staff. Two general elections of 1910 were followed by a crisis about the constitutional (some thought obstructionist) powers of the House of Lords. The Irish struggle entered the verge of civil war. Then there were all those episodes, major and minor, in the Balkans, many quite beyond Britain's control or influence, that brought the world to war in late July and early August 1914. This period Churchill rightly called 'Milestones to Armageddon'.

Many books have been written on these themes, but none of them portrays the Royal Navy as unprepared for war. The credit for that state of affairs goes to Fisher as to Churchill. The Senior Service may have been inexperienced in recent naval combat. It may have been unprepared to deal with a hostile submarine force. It may have been a moth-ridden organisation. It had many lessons to learn. It had not neglected its traditions, but it had neglected the administrative genius that it had held during the wars against France and Napoleon. It did not know how to co-operate with the Army, and it was inadequate in its efforts to prepare for amphibious operations. The rush of events that Churchill describes came upon Whitehall and Parliament with such a flourish that though the ships might well have been sent to sea or taking up their station, they did not know what next to expect, or where and when the German navy would strike. Naval intelligence soon gave the British an advantage. Many sorties taken by British submarines and destroyer flotillas brought success. On the other hand, many disasters overtook British warships and their complements in the first year of the war. The advantage lay with the offensive – and the German command. The next year opened with better prospects but soon brought despair with the failures of the Dardanelles and Gallipoli. The broad, sunlit horizons had narrowed quickly.

From Churchill's viewpoint, and that of Fisher, too, these were momentous days. In 1923 Churchill, putting the best face on it, recalls in *The World Crisis*:

> From October 25, 1911, to May 28, 1915, I was, in the words of the Royal Letters Patent and Orders in Council, 'responsible to Crown and Parliament for all the business of the Admiralty.' This period comprised the final stage in the preparation against a war with Germany; the mobilisation and concentration of the Fleet before the outbreak; the organisation of the Blockade; the gathering in 1914 of the Imperial forces from all over the world; the clearance from the oceans of all the German cruisers and commerce destroyers; the reinforcement of the Fleet by new construction in 1914 and 1915; the frustration and defeat of the first German submarine attack upon merchant shipping in 1915; and the initiation of the enterprise against the Dardanelles. It was marked before the war by a complete revision of British naval war plans; by the building of a fast division of battleships armed with 15-inch guns and driven by oil fuel; by the proposals, rejected by Germany, for a naval holiday; and by the largest supplies till then ever voted by Parliament for the British Fleet. It was distinguished during the war for the victories of the Heligoland Bight, of the Falkland Islands and the Dogger Bank; and for the attempt to succour Antwerp. It was memorable for the disaster to the three cruisers off the Dutch Coast; the loss of Admiral Cradock's squadron at Coronel; and the failure of the Navy to force the Dardanelles.[22]

During these hurried days, with all their rocky, violent eruptions and uncertain results, Churchill and Fisher, separately and together, faced an alarming set of circumstances offering no possible solution. Europe and the world found itself convulsed in the great catastrophe. In such a scenario, heads rolled, and they rolled easily. In due course, empires fell and their monarchs, too. New nations were brought into existence. The most powerful of states, Imperial Germany, was humbled at the peace table after being defeated on land and on sea. But in those days when Churchill and Fisher prepared for the war and then fought through as long as they could – or as long as their colleagues allowed them to do so – they were, in effect, clutching at straws. Every expectation of an easy and early victory vanished. They did not realise the scale of the war that they were fighting, and they were caught up in the maelstrom. No matter how much they had prepared for Armageddon, and anticipated its arrival, they were unable to shape its destiny or direct its course. Thus they shared the agony of each and every defeat to British arms, and they particularly grew weary and increasingly anxious when their bold voices and stout hearts were no longer welcome at the conference tables. They were pushed aside by the events of the war, sidelined partly because of their own inventiveness and power of intellect and argument, and mainly because the support that had sustained them in earlier times had melted from under their feet. Less masters of their own misfortune, they were victims of changing circumstances, circumstances far beyond their control. Long before the outset of the catastrophe that was the war, they had prepared for the day they hoped would not present itself.

PART ONE

The Naval Revolutionary

1

Fisher Ashore and Afloat

Part Machiavelli, part child

In many ways, John Arbuthnot Fisher appeared as the most unlikely of British admirals, for he bore a strangely Asiatic appearance. His face captured the imagination of many.[1] He delighted in rumours that he was Malay, the son of a Cingalese princess, and from this he would say with a quick and gleaming grin so characteristic of him, 'Hence my oriental cunning and duplicity.'[2] Some even were so bold as to call him, rather affectionately, 'the yellow peril'. Lovingly, Churchill referred to him, in correspondence with his wife, Clementine, as 'the old Malay'. He had extraordinary light eyes that gave a prominent and snake-like look. His hair was grey-white, made notable by a wiry tuft that fell across his forehead. His broad forehead, his mouth with a grim sardonic line, and his intensely pugnacious face all suggested the East. He was of medium height and stocky build. His conversation, always animated, was punctuated by laughter and would invariably end in a big smile. His voice was unexpectedly high-pitched. He was talkative. He was vitality personified. Many found him loveable. Others were not so inclined. At the height of his influence, that singular face, both inscrutable and mobile, gave no hint of human emotion. 'The full eye with its curiously small pupil, the wide, full-lipped mouth drooping mercilessly at the corners, the jaw jutting out a good-humoured challenge to the world, all proclaim a man who neither gives nor asks quarter. He laughs, he cracks jokes, he talks with voluminous geniality; but behind all these breezy externals of the seaman are his three "R's" of war – Ruthless, Relentless, Remorseless – and his three "H's" of battle – Hit first, Hit hard, Keep on Hitting.'[3] At any opportunity he loved to derive a dramatic effect.

His personal private secretary, Esther Meynell, thought his rapid way of talking to be really a sort of smokescreen, under which a great deal of work got done. And while others were laughing at some drollery or vehemence he was, in fact, pursuing some matter unknown to them. Thus her evaluation that he was 'a mixture of Machiavelli and a child which must have been extraordinarily baffling to politicians and men of the world.'[4] Another who knew him well, the newspaperman Harold Begbie, thought Fisher's single-minded purpose of the security of Britain something quite childlike. 'No man I have met ever gave me so authentic a feeling of originality as this dare-devil of genius, this pirate of private life, who more than any other Englishman saved British democracy from a Prussian domination.' Here was a man of exceptional force, said the same authority, 'a man posessed of a daemon of inspiration.' 'He sought the safety, honour, and glory of Great Britain.' In the eyes of his enemies, when this overmastering purpose was set aside, he was seen as 'a monster, a scoundrel, and an imbecile'.[5] In all, Jacky Fisher was a strange mixture, a genetic and social rarity, a modernist, even a revolutionary. No wonder he called his enemies in the Service 'fossils', and politicians who would not do his bidding 'a flabby lot'.

His letters were a delight, penned in large script with green or red ink, most bearing delightful salutations, and all closing with some variant of 'Yours till Hell freezes', his favourite, or 'Yours till the Angels smile upon us'. His biblical knowledge would challenge that of any clergyman, and he would in private correspondence quote and cite from the Old Testament freely and with telling effect. He regarded the British as one of the Ten Lost Tribes of Israel. He attended Westminister Abbey two, three, or even four times a day, and the Dean of Westminster warned him that he would suffer from spiritual indigestion. He liked to think that if his life ended successfully he would find himself memorialised among the great in the Abbey, but if not then he certainly deserved to be cast into the sea. On one occasion, Fisher took the Dean to Portsmouth to see the revolutionary *Dreadnought*; the clergyman had never seen a battleship before. Fisher liked to recount gleefully the grateful Dean's letter: 'The *Dreadnought*'s all right; she is exactly the same length as Westminster Abbey!'[6] If listening to sermons was one of Fisher's weaknesses, the other was dancing, and many are the stories of the turns on the ship's deck he would take with female visitors or with fellow sailors, while ashore at some gala occasion he would dance the night away with one chosen female partner. Here was a most unusual fellow, a delightful oddity, but a man sworn to secure England's future unlike any other except the monarch of the day.

He seemed to be the personification of youth. He said in an unpublished recollection of his life that he was 'first born on January 25th, 1841, and reborn many times since into curiously new worlds.' He first saw light east of Suez, born in Rambodde, Ceylon, son of a Colonial Service army officer (captain in the 78th Highlanders and aide-de-camp to the Governor of Ceylon, Lord Robert Wilmot-Horton).[7] His mother, the beautiful Sophia Lambe, daughter of a New Bond Street wine merchant, was on her brother's coffee plantation in Ceylon when she met and married the tall Captain Fisher. Captain and Mrs

Fisher had seven children, four of whom lived. During Fisher's early years, his father faced serious financial difficulties. Young Jack, age six, was sent to school in England; he never again saw his father. Although not quite a waif and a stray, he was taken under the wing of Lord and Lady Wilmot-Horton, who lived at Catton Hall in Derbyshire and became his nominal guardians. There were many children in this family, and Jack vied for attention. In country shooting pursuits, Jack was given advice that he never forgot: 'Don't hesitate. Shoot quickly.'

Jack's pathway to the Navy was cleared by these guardians. Admiral Sir William Parker, Commander-in-Chief, Plymouth, lived near the Wilmot-Hortons and had at his disposal two nominations for cadetships. When his friend and neighbour Lady Wilmot-Horton asked if young Jack might be presented for the entrance examination, Parker obliged. Jack's younger brother Frederic William joined the Navy as well and became a full admiral in his own right. Their father placed strong emphasis on deportment and honourable behaviour as central to their career prospects. This was key to their rise, since the Navy, while class-ridden, still offered a favourable opportunity and an honourable profession for those of limited means.[8] Many another flag officer found his way into the upper echelons of the Service on account of landed wealth, ecclesiastical connection, or other station (for example, Fisher's rival and nemesis Lord Charles Beresford, the second son of the Marquess of Waterford and an MP, whom we will meet in detail later), but Fisher had to rise to the top on his merits as a seaman and leader of naval men – and on his persuasive powers, which were exceptional. He could not play to aristocratic privilege. Fisher was a meritocrat, and he owed his own rise to become one of the greatest Englishmen (or world-renowned admirals) to his application and determination. He undoubtedly had genius but he was largely self-created. Therein lies his magic.

Fisher entered the Navy on 12 July 1854. He was then thirteen years of age. In later years he loved to remember that he was nominated to the Navy by the last of Nelson's captains, Admiral Parker. Fisher had a small collection of Nelson memorabilia, pictures and relics, and he thought the world of Emma, Lady Hamilton, for she had helped Nelson. He liked to think of his progress from the nursery to Admiral of the Fleet as a Nelsonic progress. Fifty years later, on his selection as First Sea Lord, he arranged to enter the Admiralty on the ninety-ninth anniversary of Trafalgar. In fact, he mistook the date by one day, an indication that he sometimes faltered when it came to historical details. But no matter to him: he was conscious of the legacy of British command of the seas, and that was the essential fact. Nothing else mattered to him. He was the Navy personified. He took on its aura as its guardian angel, and he fought for it as its vigorous and muscled King Neptune: he was Britannia's servant. Therein lay his charm, and everyone who met him realised this in him, whether early in his life or in his last days.

Like many bound eventually for the quarterdeck and command, Fisher entered the Navy as a Volunteer First Class. 'I wrote out the Lord's Prayer, and the doctor made me jump over a chair naked, and I was given a glass of Sherry on being in the Navy.' He also had to be able to compute by the rule of three (eg 'If a yard of cloth costs 1s. 4d., how much will three yards cost?'). Jacky then bought his uniform and reported on board *Victory*. 'They were holystoning the decks, and the white-haired First Lieutenant, with his trousers turned up above his knees and no shoes or stockings, roared at me like the Bull of Basham and afterwards gave me an orange when he met me outside his cabin in the cockpit.' Young Jack, he said of himself, was then 'penniless, friendless and forlorn'. He was duly assigned to the old ship *Calcutta* and sailed to the Baltic in the closing stages of the war against Russia. Then it was on to the Black Sea to bring back troops from the Crimea and, as a fully-fledged midshipman, to China in the steam corvette *Highflyer*. He first saw action at the Battle of Fatshan (Foshan) Creek in 1857, and after other actions in rivers and against Chinese forts at Peiho, where he demonstrated bravery and leadership, he was promoted acting lieutenant.

Fisher returned from China to Britain in *Furious* in August 1861. He qualified in navigation and then was appointed to HMS *Excellent* at Portsmouth. This was his first spell of duty at this formidable and experimental gunnery establishment. He became, in March 1863, gunnery lieutenant of *Warrior*, the Navy's first ironclad warship – the Royal Navy's answer to French innovations in the same sort of warship. He returned to *Excellent* in 1864 and pursued the use of electricity in the evolution of mines. This led naturally to later interest in locomotive – that is, self-propelled – torpedoes. Guns and armament held great fascination for him, and speed of ships. Torpedoes were the new weapon, with the submarine still largely an experimental weapons platform. Fisher lived a life at the edge of the technological revolution in naval warfare.

While many 'middies' who aspired to be admirals spent time snipe hunting, fly-fishing, placing bets at the racecourse, or riding to hounds, Fisher did none of these. He had little time, and, more to the point, little money, for these sorts of extracurricular activities. He eschewed sports such as cricket and polo, partly because he could not afford them but more likely because he did not fit the social mould of the upper classes, a breed unto themselves in their self-consciousness and desire to perpetuate their own kind. He was an outsider. Nor did he exhibit such patience as was required to play up and play the game. He was married quite young as a junior lieutenant and could not afford to spend money foolishly. His abiding concern for economy transferred to his career in the Service. He remained conscious of the need to save money where possible, and not simply throw more and more money at the Navy.[9] He saw himself as the personal agent of economy, and while many senior officers were demanding more naval assets, Fisher would be examining ways to achieve greater efficiency and reduce waste. Reforming zeal coursed through his veins. That, too, made him an unlikely admiral. At the same time it made him many friends among the politicians. He had a fascination for women, and his boyish innocence and heart-warming persona made him an attractive figure. He gained the affection and support of many women of influence right up to his death,[10] and his experience illustrates the fact that many wives and sweethearts of naval officers 'wore more gold braid' than their male mates or lovers. In Fisher's life we have two interesting examples – his wife, Katharine Delves Broughton (later Lady Fisher), and his lover and confidante, Nina, Duchess of Hamilton.

On 4 April 1866 Fisher, aged twenty-five, married into the gentry when he took as his wife Frances Katharine Josepha Delves Broughton, daughter of the Reverend Thomas Delves Broughton and Frances Corcran. There were many Army and Navy connections on her side of the family. She was to bear him three daughters, Beatrix, Dorothy, and Pamela, and a son, Cecil, later Cecil Vavasseur Fisher, 2nd Baron Fisher (1868–1955), and when he was elevated to the peerage in 1910, she took the title Baroness Fisher. Steadiness was her great attribute, and thank goodness she had it, for it was essential to the task of marriage to the volcanic admiral, with independence of mind a good accompaniment. It was a happy marriage. She seems not to have concerned herself with his wild schemes and notable social flirtations. From her perspective, we might imagine, detachment from public affairs and naval matters was a unique benefit. That having been said, she is one of the most important figures who could be included in the yet-to-be-written book 'the women behind the fleet'. She was never in the public eye, and she liked it that way. So did he. In time, Jacky's friendship with Nina, Duchess of Hamilton, wife of an invalided naval officer, though never the subject of gossip or disdain, became central to his emotional well-being. In the duchess he found his greatest female friend and undivided supporter. She enters our story at a later stage.

Three years after his marriage, Fisher was promoted to commander at the early age of twenty-eight. He was appointed executive officer of the screw ship *Donegal* on the China station. When he went out there again, all eyes were on him, for he was responsible for the ship's complement, its organisation, routine, discipline, leave, efficiency, and happiness. A strict disciplinarian, he was also meticulous in dealing with the ship's company.

The China seas, with all their cross-currents of international rivalry, opium traffic, piracy, quarrels ashore, besieged colonial authority at Hong Kong, and enforcement of the British imperium of the Treaty Ports, were no new thing to Fisher. Ten years previously, in action against the Taku forts, Midshipman Fisher had been closely attached as aide-de-camp to Admiral Sir James Hope, Commander-in-Chief of the East Indies and China station, who flew his flag in

Chesapeake. Fisher saw much action in small boats and developed a strong sense of self-confidence. He became the life and soul of the wardroom, well respected for his attention to duty and his punctiliousness. When he came home from China, he had an enlarged view of British responsibilities and the complications inherent in warships wearing the White Ensign in such intricate littorals and estuaries.

Fisher shared a then common view of what is called nowadays by British historians 'the fear of falling' – that is, worry about losing a place of absolute prominence in the world. He may have had a somewhat eschatological view of naval affairs that was tied to a social Darwinist fear of Britain's eclipse as a Great Power. Naval battles, to his way of thinking, were not minor collisions at sea but held the potential for annihilation.[11] 'Naval Supremacy once destroyed is destroyed forever,' he wrote. 'Carthage, Spain, Holland, the great commercial nations of the past, had the sea wrested from them, and then they fell.'[12] (Without really understanding history, he liked to exploit it whenever possible for his own use.) Perhaps he saw Britain as some kind of new Israel and himself as an Old Testament prophet. 'With the great harbour of Scapa Flow in the North and the narrow straits of Dover in the South,' he once proclaimed, 'there is no doubt, sir, that we are God's chosen people.'[13]

Fisher had all the makings of a popular hero, and he came undoubtedly close to being so, had not certain self-destructive characteristics acted against universal and unbridled acclaim. On the one hand, he could be extraordinarily charming and invariably popular with the lower deck, while on the other he was often a terror to the self-perpetuating establishment types. He charmed both Queen Victoria and King Edward VII (no mean feat in either case). He was on intimate terms with many others who might be called the great and the good of the realm. He was well known at court and was generally treated with respect, though often with caution. He was known abroad. Kaiser Wilhelm II knew him by reputation. Tsar Nicholas II knew him similarly and met him at Reval in 1907. In the United States, his contemporary, Admiral William Sampson, knew him closely from the days of the Spanish-American War. In fact, in those days Fisher was known in every admiralty of the world. He was watched carefully by the Foreign Office, which thought him dangerous. But Fisher thought the Navy more alive to the world's shifts and crises than the ambassadors and clerks at the Foreign Office. He once said, 'The absolute fact is that the Admiralty always knows better than the Foreign Office.'[14]

As his career progressed, Fisher retained his buoyant self-confidence. However, as he climbed the ladder of promotion, his ego grew faster than his intellect. As one writer has noted, 'There is no evidence to suggest that he had grown intellectually since he was a commander, or that he had any idea of his own limitations. What had undoubtedly grown, and small wonder considering his success, was his "ego".'[15]

From the outset of his time in the Navy, Fisher expressed interest in technical improvements, especially those that had changed or would change naval warfare in the future. He was a materialist, of that there can be no doubt. However, and fatally, he did not always possess the necessary technical know-how. The technological developments of the era, and the rapid strides taken in naval architecture and engineering, lay with the professionals of that age – the naval architects, the steam engineers, the armaments manufacturers, and those who made explosives. That did not stop Fisher from advocating new weapons of war. Just the opposite. Fisher was an expert in gunnery, not an uncommon thing for a naval officer. This competence led him naturally to explore what could be done with a newfangled contraption called the torpedo. In fact, as early as 1869 he had advocated study of its use.[16] What he then had in mind was not a locomotive, or self-propelled, torpedo but a towed one.

When appointed to the gunnery establishment at Portsmouth, HMS *Excellent*, Captain Fisher was told to start a new section, all to do with the torpedo. A passionate believer in this new dangerous weapon, and a powerful instructor, he took advantage of the opportunity and began to exert his reformist zeal regarding weaponry. He rightly saw in the torpedo a weapon that would revolutionise naval warfare. 'His passionate belief in the importance of his work was infectious,' writes one admiral-historian. 'Elderly post captains, sent on a course to fill in time, found themselves, in Jacky Fisher's classes, pulling an oar in a boat, laying out mines and hauling on sliming moorings with youthful enthusiasm.' 'If you are a gunnery man, [he told them,] you must believe and teach that the world must be saved by gunnery. If you are a torpedoman you must lecture and teach the same thing about torpedoes. But be in earnest, terribly in earnest. The man who doubts, or who is half-hearted, never does anything for himself or his country.'[17]

Later he had charge of HMS *Vernon*, the new torpedo establishment for experimental work. In that capacity he was sent to Fiume, Austria, to witness trials of Robert Whitehead's torpedo (which was ultimately adopted by the Royal Navy). It was a slow-moving contrivance and carried only a small explosive charge. Nonetheless, Fisher championed it. In 1876 he prophesied, with unerring insight, 'The issue of the next naval war will chiefly depend upon the use that is made of the torpedo, not only in naval warfare, but for the purposes of blockade.'[18] When he went to sea in the armoured cruiser *Northampton*, he made sure torpedo practice received repeated attention. He saw much sea time in the late 1870s, necessary for promotion to flag rank. Details of his various assignments need not delay us here, and it is only necessary to say that in all his posts he learned much and caught the attention of many, including Vice-Admiral Geoffrey T Phipps Hornby on the Mediterranean station.

He was a product of the Old Navy, but something stirred in him in the way of innovation. He was restless. He delighted in making people think about naval changes. He could point in his own career to innovations, even in the form of naval combat and amphibious operations. He saw inefficiencies at work. He saw military, that is to say Army, ineffectiveness also.

He was equally capable of sensational self-advertisement so as to make his points. The statesmen and journalists of the age invariably took him at his word, so powerful was he in his declarations. He sped the evolution of the telegraph, the submarine cable, and the wireless. These early technical reforms may have given him a wider scope and responsibility than was possible as a fleet gunnery or navigation specialist. Put differently, he was a generalist but one with far-seeing horizons. He was an unlikely admiral in more ways than just his odd appearance. He did not have all-important social and political connections. Such posts as he got, however, gave him the opportunity to shine on his own merit. He never missed a chance to use these positions or to exploit his friends. He adored the attention of the press, and he savoured the notoriety of the moment. On the other hand, his metier, he confessed, was behind the scenes or underground. You could follow his progress, he liked to say, as you followed the passage of a mole that throws up dirt mounds in its wake: 'Trace me by upheavals!'[19]

In 1881 Fisher was appointed to command the new battleship *Inflexible*, part of the Mediterranean Fleet. One of the events of his naval career that always caught the imagination of the press took place at Alexandria, Egypt, in July 1882 – the first occasion since the Crimean War that British battleships were in action. Bombarding from the sea, British warships had engaged and totally destroyed the Egyptian army mutineers ashore. Four of the forts were blown up, the Khedive's palace set ablaze, and the lighthouse damaged. Ashore, civil unrest reigned in the streets. Fisher was given command of the landing party after the bombardment. He took with him, as his Naval Provost Marshal, Lord Charles Beresford, already mentioned as the near contemporary of Fisher who was to play a notorious role in Fisher's life. In the subsequent land operations, a naval armoured railway train, a complete novelty in military practice, was employed. It was Fisher who contrived the whole – the locomotive fortress consisted of six trucks protected with iron shields, the engine being in the centre. A Nordenfeldt rapid-fire gun looked over the bows of the leading truck, and three Gatlings similarly over the stern of the hindmost. Two field guns were also carried.[20] As much as the armoured train captured the public imagination, it was the woeful inefficiency of the British naval gunnery that alarmed Jack Fisher. From anchor, the eight warships had scored only ten hits from three thousand rounds fired at the Egyptian fortress guns. After the bombardment, he commanded the naval brigade that took possession of the city and held it for weeks in precarious circumstances. The Khedive returned in triumph to his capital, British influence in Egypt restored. The Admiralty expressed satisfaction at the service of Captains Fisher and Beresford.

As a result of his actions during and after the bombardment, Fisher became a public figure. He was created a Companion of the Bath for services at Alexandria and was disappointed that Beresford received no honour of distinction.[21] He also contracted severe dysentery, compounded by malaria, suffering great weight loss and needing almost four years to recover fully. He could not leave his ship at his own expense, and feared loss of pay. In the end, the First Lord of the Admiralty, Lord Northbrook, brought him back to England, saying: 'We can get many *Inflexible*s, but only one Jack Fisher.' From the lower deck came this respectful and affectionate letter: 'May you receive your share of rewards and laurels and your Ship's company will then feel as proud and prouder than if it was bestowed on themselves.' After convalescence, Fisher stayed at Osborne House, Isle of Wight, a guest of Queen Victoria, the first of several visits.[22] He was uncharacteristically listless, but gradually his health improved, partly in consequence of his 'taking the waters' in various places in Bohemia and in Switzerland. Later, he suffered from pleurisy, a dangerous state of affairs in which the lining of the lungs become infected. This also required rest and repair. Despite these illnesses, Fisher always gave the impression of good health and a good constitution.

In April 1883 Fisher was appointed to command the gunnery establishment *Excellent*. He was thirty-three and young for this top post in ship armaments and gunnery drill. To this point, he had spent a disproportionate amount of his career as Controller, responsible for procurement and materiel, as well as at the weapons training establishments *Excellent* and *Vernon*. He did not have a reputation as a fighting admiral in the Service: there were plenty of other officers who were more qualified in that line. Instead, Fisher, owing to his organisational genius, energy, and commitment to detail, became a ships' contractor and a weapons enthusiast. He liked the building of ships (of all classes and sizes) and getting the work done on time. A warship is a weapons-carrying platform, and Fisher saw the warship as a high point of mankind's material achievements. It was in these capacities that Fisher became familiar with the leading gunnery manufacturers of Britain, led by Sir William Armstrong, a pioneer in hydraulic engineering and electical applications. The story of the modern gun lies elsewhere in technical studies, but here we note that by 1880 it had become a revolutionary breech-loading mechanical giant of steel, built up in construction, rifled, and firing elongated, cylindrical and explosive shells over vast distances. Every part of this gun was controlled by machinery, and such prodigious weapons operated with an accuracy and power of hitherto unimaginable proportions. Fisher saw this revolution through, and it made possible, in due course, the revolutionary dreadnought. (Later, as the submarine came into prominence, Fisher lauded its abilities and warned of its dangers – notably, making capital ships obsolete – another story for another time, but important here to show that Fisher was at the lead edge of technological change, even if he did not have the technical or engineering competence.)

In the early 1880s Britain's naval primacy began to be subverted by French naval expansion and by neglect or indifference at home from Gladstone's Liberal government, which was interested mainly in economy and the Irish question. Lords of the Admiralty became flustered, unable to get the prime minister's attention on this matter. Gladstone himself refused to consider those 'portentous weapons' (the big guns aboard great warships), dismissing them as beyond common comprehension. Neglect of the Fleet continued; building plans were set aside. The French continued to expand their navy.

Unknown to the general public and to the admirals of the day, two persons staged a revolution, and Fisher fed them the critical information. The first figure was Hugh Oakeley Arnold-Forster, a barrister and political secretary, who watched the decaying Navy with dismay. Determined to take the matter into his own hands, he went to see a journalist, William Thomas Stead, son of a Congregationalist minister, who published the *Pall Mall Gazette*. It was Stead who had sent General 'Chinese' Gordon to Khartoum, for he had embarrassed Gladstone into reluctant action. Stead liked to set the alarm bells ringing. Arnold-Forster revealed to Stead sheaves of statistical details, ship plans, French naval estimates, Admiralty delay in decision-making, and much else. Stead needed professional naval confirmation. A clandestine scheme was hatched. Fisher was brought on board.

In The Goat, a public house just off New Bond Street in Mayfair, a stocky captain climbed the stairs to the upper room for regular meetings with the inquisitive Stead. These clandestine meetings went on late at night, and in other locales, too. Week in and week out, the journalist scribbled down facts and opinions. He took note of the dire warnings, then put pen to paper. 'What Is the Truth about the Navy' was the series of articles Stead published, the first appearing 15 September 1884. Free trade, said Stead, needed a strong and protective navy, and Britain needed to have 'an undisputed and indispensible ascendancy on every sea'. He gingerly cleared the prime minister, Gladstone, of any neglect, and reverted to the great man's Midlothian declaration of maintaining supremacy at seas. That having been said, he then went into a line-by-line indictment – old ships, foreign intrigues and shipbuilding mismanagement, inadequate coal supplies, insufficient coaling stations, poorly defended harbours, vulnerable merchant shipping, and much else.

Stead and Fisher conducted a newspaper campaign to reorganise and strengthen the Navy. 'The minds of these two men flashed at each other across Europe,' wrote Viscount Esher (of whom more below), 'the outcome being a new naval policy for England – a policy that stood the test of the South African War, guaranteed to our country the neutrality of Germany, France, and Russia in those difficult years, and paved the way for that still greater Navy to which we owe in large measure the victory of 1918.'[23] Of Stead's enthusiasm for the Navy, Fisher said, 'It never cooled: he was saturated with the great patriotic belief that the British Empire floated on the British Navy, and that it floated on nothing else. When I was First Sea Lord he had one of his famous interviews with a great foreign personage who said to him: "Don't be frightened." Stead answered: "Oh no, for every ship you build we'll build two."'[24] He was not far off the mark.

The power of sensational revelations in the press had noted effect. In June 1885 Gladstone's Liberals lost to Lord Salisbury's Conservatives, who gave the Navy a new budget, and Europe a new arms race, fuelled by Fisher and the press. The Naval Defence Act of 1889 demonstrated the government's will that the Navy should truly be pre-eminent: seventy new ships were to be built, and at all times the Navy would be at least equal to the combined strength of the next two largest navies. One admiral recalled, 'There is no doubt that had we gone to war with France in those days we might well have been swept off the face of the globe ... The Naval Defence Act ... saved the country.'[25] When, a year later, US authority Alfred Thayer Mahan published *The Influence of Sea Power on History*, which stressed the importance of a strong British navy as a determinant in modern naval history dating from the wars against the Dutch through to his own times, Parliament began to give more attention to 'blue water' concerns. These were, essentially, the protection of seaborne commerce, the 'fleet in being' (a strategy in which a nation's fleet is a threat without leaving port or engaging in battle, by forcing the opposition to expend resources preparing for potential battle or protecting its shipping or other assets against possible attack by the enemy fleet), and the primacy of the great fleet that, in time of war, would provide the sure shield of Britain and the Empire. Steed's journalism and Mahan's histories presaged that a greater naval rivalry would lie ahead, but still the government was reluctant to build ships when none seemed to be needed.[26]

Meanwhile, Fisher stuck to his regular tasks. But after his success with Stead, he never forgot the benefits of the press to his schemes, or the value of press leaks. He had no scruples about such conduct. From that point on he cultivated the national press and the navalist writers assiduously, including James R Thursfield, naval correspondent of *The Times*, and Arnold White, the liveliest of journalists, who was on the executive council of the Navy League, a charitable organisation that supported the Royal Navy. In his hands they became powerful influencers of public opinion and Parliament. White described Fisher's instructions 'burn and destroy' on a letter to actually mean 'publish as widely as possible, but don't give me away'.[27]

Fisher was an enthusiast for efficiency, and though he took no master's degree in business administration, he learned the principles of management by observation. For instance, he could see that the gunnery production at Woolwich Arsenal was slow and bogged down. At Elswick, Newcastle, by contrast, Sir William Armstrong was making great strides in production efficiencies. Fisher recommended to the Admiralty that it start to shift its contracts to the private sector, because it could build ships and armaments better and cheaper than government yards.

All the same, the Navy was making great ships and Fisher was the major provider. An early, great opportunity in this line came in 1891, when Rear-Admiral Fisher (as he was then) became Admiral-Superintendent of Portsmouth Dockyard. He was good at co-ordinating ship construction with the supply of guns and other armaments, and he built the new *Royal Sovereign* in record time. It was generally said that the British Fleet was 'the fleet that Jack built'. All the great changes in ship technology came during his watch: the adoption of water-tube boilers, the introduction of the steam turbine, and the use of fuel oil, whether for raising steam in boilers or for the direct production of power in internal combustion engines. All were tied up with that never-ending struggle for more power with less weight of machinery and fuel. And all were associated with the name of Fisher. He was the driving force and had the full support of the Engineer-in-Chief of the Fleet, Vice-Admiral Sir A J Dunston; his assistant, Vice-Admiral Sir Henry J Oram; and Engineer Vice-Admiral G G Goodwin, names now virtually lost to history. More often than not it was the engine rooms and the engine-room staff in British warships that did excellent duty in battles at sea. Jellicoe and Beatty, when in charge of fleets, acclaimed the engineers and the stokers. Churchill praised the engine rooms: 'Here is a squadron of the Fleet which does not lie in harbour but is far away from its dockyard; and which during six months of war has been constantly at sea. All of a sudden the greatest trial is demanded of their engines, and they all excel all the previous peacetime records. Can you conceive a more remarkable proof of the excellence of British machinery, of the glorious industry of the engine-room branch?'[28]

These engineering developments still lay in the future when Fisher was made Knight Commander of the Bath in 1894 and promoted vice-admiral in 1896. In 1897 he took up the command of the North America and West Indies station. It was indeed time to go to sea again, for he had been in shore assignments for fifteen years and needed a fleet command for further rise in the Service. Fisher was even permitted to take as his flagship the newly commissioned *Renown* – a pretty compliment from Lord Goschen, the First Lord. Fisher was aware that the appointment would arouse some jealousy within the Royal Navy.[29] *Renown* was one of three shallow-draught battleships constructed for operations on distant seas and littorals. Never a great success, these ships were nonetheless the newest of innovations.

On the North America and West Indies station, hardly a backwater in the days of United States naval expansion, Fisher's key task was watching events unfolding in Cuba during the Spanish-American War. There were contentious French fishing issues to be dealt with at St Pierre and Miquelon, near Newfoundland, a potentially explosive issue during the Fashoda incident of September 1898, as was the tetchy quarrel between Britain and France over colonial claims in Africa. Should war with France take place, the story goes, Fisher planned to rescue, in the middle of the night, the falsely accused French army officer Alfred Dreyfus, a Jew, then imprisoned on Devil's Island, and return him to Europe. This bold, if irrational, stroke was designed to add to the burdens of the French government. From Admiralty files we now know that Fisher did indeed make plans for the mobilisation of troops, transport, and escort vessels, including five cruisers, five smaller vessels, and the troopship *Malabar* at Bermuda, ready to sail with twenty-four hours' notice, and to carry 1,000 troops, field guns, horses, ammunition, and provisions. No military objective is specified for this secret expedition.[30] And in the event of war, when no French battleship could contest British naval power in those seas, Fisher planned to cut the submarine cable to France, steam *Renown* to Gibraltar, and join the Atlantic Fleet. It was a madcap scheme and would likely have been done on Fisher's own hook, independent of Admiralty instructions, but in time it grew to be part of the Fisher legend.

From these days we can see early signs of Fisher's insistence on professional accountability as a factor in tactics. He disliked the signals system of the late nineteenth century (1871), which he saw, unerringly, as useless in close action because it fettered the responsibilities of individual captains. With proper training and doctrine, individual captains could be trusted to take initiative on their own without relying on signals from the flagship.[31] However, technological advances in communications were working in the opposite direction. The Spanish-American War was a telegraph and submarine cable war. These technologies gave the victor immense advantage in deploying squadrons and individual ships. Centralisation of command reduced the very individual initiative in decision-making that Fisher proclaimed. On the North America and West Indies station Fisher saw this at first hand. The control and use of communications was an essential feature of ruling the waves. Better than most admirals of his era he grasped the concept of centralised command and control.

Fisher's notable achievement on the North America and West Indies station was to effect a closer relationship with the United States Navy. Among all the powers, Britain had remained strictly neutral in the Spanish-American War, and the United States had recognised that fact with grateful appreciation. On Admiralty instructions, Fisher had invited his opposite, Admiral William Sampson, to an official banquet in Bermuda on 4 July 1899. Before the assembled officers of both navies, Fisher had proclaimed the American naval greatness and toasted his opposite. It was on this occasion that Sampson, never garrulous, issued the memorable reply: 'It was a fine old hen that hatched the American Eagle.' From this event and these circumstances can be dated closer relations in Anglo-American naval affairs, and already Fisher was proclaiming Admiral Mahan's wisdom on the influence of sea power on history, first published in 1890.[32]

Fisher was keen on closer relations with the Russians, too, and it was the invitation from the Tsar's government for the great powers to meet at The Hague to discuss military and naval limitations that brought Fisher onto the international stage as a diplomat and a crusader for the benefits of a strong British navy. In 1899 the Cabinet, on Lord Salisbury's advice, selected Fisher as its naval delegate to the conference in The Hague, called to decide on rules for war. Fisher cut a large figure there. He charmed the other delegates but rejected as preposterous the idea of moderating war.[33] He was all for peace, and said so. For him, by definition, war was brutal and deadly. It therefore stood to reason, his thinking ran, that the power most ruthless and determined would win out in the end, regardless of any rules. The sooner this could be done the better. He was also dismissive of the rights of neutrals in wartime. He put it this way:

> Suppose that war breaks out, and I am expecting to fight a new Trafalgar on the morrow. Some neutral colliers try to steam past us into the enemy's waters. If the enemy gets their coal into his bunkers, it may make all the difference in the coming fight. You tell me I must not seize the colliers. I tell you that nothing that you, or any power on earth, can say will stop me from sending them to the bottom, if I can in no other way keep their coal out of the enemy's hands; for to-morrow I am to fight the battle which will save or wreck the Empire. If I win it, I shall be far too big a man to be affected about protests about the neutral colliers; if I lose it, I shall go down with my ship into the deep and then protests will affect me still less.[34]

In all conference proceedings and diplomatic arrangements, Fisher proved the perfect British naval delegate. He exuded charm and goodwill. He was generous in friendship and fellowship. He was quick to draw the line. He was forthright and brutally frank. In discussions, he opposed any restriction on or abolition of materials of war that would weaken Britain at sea or otherwise proscribe its greatness, yet he steered into channels for future discussion those contentious issues that could not be immediately wrestled to the ground.

On the other hand, in private channels he repeatedly made it clear that Britain ruled the waves and did so for the betterment of mankind. 'The supremacy of the British Navy is the best security for the peace of the world,' he proclaimed. According to the German naval delegate, Captain S Siegel, Fisher said that he had been chosen as delegate to the conference because his views on sea warfare were known: he acknowledged but a single axiom, which was Might is Right. The same German officer, obviously envious of the British and presaging the new German Naval Law of 1900, gave the following summary of Fisher's views:

1. England holds more than ever the fixed conviction that her position in the world, her power and her prosperity depend on the fleet, and that everything must be done to make the fleet as strong as national policy requires.
2. Currently the fleet has attained a strength that is equal to all demands. It suffices on its own to crush a combination of all other states ... The fleet is perfectly capable of protecting all British trade.
3. England is firmly resolved to employ with all cunning and ruthlessness, in case of need, the instrument of war which she possesses in her fleet according to the principle: Might is Right.[35]

Fisher's apparent ruthlessness now became the subject of discussion in the admiralties and chancelleries of Europe. The Germans refused to talk of excessive armaments or restictions on the same. There was reason for this.

A year before the conference, in 1898, the Reichstag passed the first of several Naval Laws, which called for a naval establishment to protect Germany's sea trade and colonies. It envisioned a fleet of sufficient strength that even the adversary with the greatest sea power would see that a war against the German navy would involve hazards that could actually endanger its position in the world. This was the 'risk theory', and in consequence the battle fleet had to be as strong as that of the greatest naval power as soon as possible. The greatest continental military power was now to present a seaborne challenge to the British, their seaborne commerce, and the British Empire overseas. As the young Imperial German navy entered upon its first great building programme, most British statesmen thought little of it. Churchill, for one, did not think that Germany had much salt-water experience, which was true. However, he was one of the first to realise that these Naval Laws called for the maintenance of the fleet at a certain size – in other words, with replacement capacities built in. In the press the Germanic surge at sea was hardly noticed (at least as a threat) during these years of quietude, and it was in Africa, where the Germans wanted and won territorial gains and concessions, that the attention of the Foreign Office was heightened.

By the late 1890s, all this changed, especially after June 1897, when Rear-Admiral Alfred von Tirpitz arrived in Berlin as State Secretary of the Imperial Naval Office. He was to dominate Germany's naval high command for the next two decades.[36] Tirpitz posesssed the same drive and determination as Fisher, and like his British opposite was a torpedo man. He had expertise in fleet tactics and administration – and a well-earned reputation for intrigue, operating from a fog to conceal his next move and then moving into the sunlight to reveal the next urgent plans. He studied the precepts of Alfred Thayer Mahan, absorbed the deterministic views of the historian von Treitschke, and was a great admirer of British naval traditions and achievements. (He even sent his daughters to Cheltenham Ladies' College, one of the best of the girls' boarding schools.) He exploited the German press and had his own propaganda office, a ministry of information. Churchill eyed Tirpitz warily. He did not like what he saw, calling him a 'sincere, wrongheaded, purblind old Prussian', a comment not far off the mark.[37] Tirpitz entered the highest echelons of naval command just at the time that German industrial capacity and shipbuilding prowess had become global and even dominant. His father had a profound dislike for Britain and what he saw as its selfishness. This fuelled the son's offensive spirit. He wanted heavily armoured ships capable of throttling French naval actions in the English Channel in wartime, thus taking the fight to the British in turn. His naval planning was designed to link up with the German army's emerging Schlieffen Plan, which would take the coasts of Holland and Belgium. He saw the merits of Zeebrugge and Ostend, with their interlocking shipping canals, for U-boat operations. With these ports in German possession, the navy would have places from which to project power against England.

The Grossadmiral (for so he soon became), ambitious to give Germany world-class maritime and naval status, found an active supporter in Wilhelm II. The Kaiser had spent many summers at Osborne, the residence of his grandmother, Queen Victoria, and knew by sight the capital ships from the great Portsmouth base. He was a keen yachtsman – his *Meteor II* had won the Queen's Cup at Cowes (though he took exception to the handicapping that the Prince of Wales, the Commodore of the Royal Yacht Squadron, had approved) – and a 'blue water' man, who became an admiral of the British Fleet, the rank conferred on him by Victoria. He had always been fascinated by sea power. He read Mahan's *The Influence of Sea Power on History* (1890) and accepted its premises without question. He ordered a copy of the German translation for every wardroom in his warships. In 1897 he declared roundly, 'The trident is in German hands ... our future lies on the water.'[38] That same year, Tirpitz found himself closeted with the Kaiser and the sympathetic new secretary of state for foreign affairs, Bernhard von Bülow, making naval plans; from out of this there emerged a basic strategy that called for the completion by 1905 of eleven battleships, five large cruisers, and seventeen smaller ones. Against the size of the Royal Navy this could be counted as small potatoes. But Tirpitz never rested. The new Naval Law of 1900, put together at the time of The Hague conference, followed, and its deliberate choice of a battleship navy of considerable size was something to contend with in the future. It also saddled Germany with the *Weltpolitik* then adopted.

What inkling Fisher had of this it is impossible to say. But he was fast learning about new thoughts and directions being taken by Tirpitz. As the years passed, Germany announced extensions to the original plans. The Kaiser made wild proposals for an Anglo-German agreement on colonial differences, followed by furious outbursts against England for not agreeing to his wishes. The Foreign Office watched the Kaiser with dismay as he insulted Lord Salisbury's government and even warned that misunderstandings and recrimination between the two nations might lead to bloodshed. The Kaiser paid a state visit to England in November 1899, but by then the South African War had broken out, and the Kaiser intimated that Britain should accept its reverses in South Africa. If diplomacy could not bring peace, he said, 'It would certainly be better to bring matters to a settlement. Even the best football club, if it is beaten notwithstanding the most gallant defence, accepts finally its defeat with equanimity. Last year in the great cricket match of England *v.* Australia, the former took the victory of the latter quietly, with chivalrous acknowledgement of her opponent.'[39] With just cause and uncanny insight, Sir Edward Grey at the Foreign Office wrote, 'The German Emperor is ageing me; he is like a battleship with steam up and screws going, but with no rudder, and he will run into something one day and cause a catastrophe.'[40]

'Look out, here comes Jack'

The Hague discussions had interrupted Fisher's assignments at sea. Now sixty-three, he seemed anxious that his advancing age would preclude his being appointed First Sea Lord. But others were watching his progress with approval. At The Hague he had demonstrated that he was one of the few among the delegates who had any practical knowledge of modern warfare at sea. He spoke his mind and was frequently able to make clear statements that corrected the altruistic enthusiasm that was displayed. And it was at The Hague that he began to realise the North Sea would become the new campaign ground for naval mastery.

In 1899, following the conference and according to the Admiralty's plan, Fisher took up command of the Mediterranean Fleet, based on Malta. He continued to fly his flag in *Renown*. This was the most influential and

19

challenging British naval command afloat. An admiral-historian wrote of him, 'As a young lieutenant he had been recognized as an officer of rare accomplishments and in every subsequent rank he had left his mark on the service.'[41] The Mediterranean was a perch from which to survey the future. Fisher saw it as one he could use to get the attention of the statesmen and politicians at home. Here his vision and energy had ample scope. He was revolutionary in technique: he encouraged younger officers to think for themselves. He lectured to his officers on naval gunnery and strategy, expounding on themes that later appeared in his new scheme for the future organisation and administration of the Admiralty. William Fisher, later Admiral Sir William W Fisher, noted that the Commander-in-Chief used hardly a single note and talked for two hours, 'simply magnificent. Very interesting and humorous too. His smile is irresistible.'[42] Jacky Fisher had an eagle eye for those efficient and enterprising young officers who could enter the golden age of advancement, where so many opportunities now presented themselves. He was also immensely popular with the lower deck, whose interests he championed after centuries of neglect.

Fisher cut a dramatic figure as a commander-in-chief. You could not mistake him in a crowd. 'I still have a vivid recollection of the awe which the "great Jack" inspired whilst on board,' a young lieutenant recounted, 'not that he did any of us any harm, but he had such a terrific face and jaw, rather like a tiger, and he prowled around with the steady rhythmical tread of a panther. The quarterdeck shook, and all hands shook with it. The word was quickly passed from mouth to mouth when he came on deck, "Look out, here comes Jack." Everyone then stood terribly to attention, while the great one passed on and away.' Immaculately dressed, Fisher took on himself 'the licence of the Great'. 'He loved dash and making a fine effect.' He watched his Fleet with closest care, and hardly a day passed when he did not send for 'the brains' of the Fleet to help him make some machine against *der Tag*. He was plumbing the depths of competent naval thinking on various problems and possibilities: torpedoes, gunnery, and the great future ship, *Dreadnought*. Devoted to his country and to the Service, he welcomed ideas presented by others, and he welcomed the chance to try out his ideas on younger officers who served under him. He took a keen interest in fellow officers. But he would not accept inefficiency, and he played personal favourites on grounds of efficiency. He wanted everything done at full speed. 'There were no half-measures with Jacky,' wrote another lieutenant, 'it was first in everything or – look out!' 'He always had at heart the comfort of the officers and men under his command, and there were few among those who served under him who had not some good reason to be grateful to him.'[43]

At year's end, Fisher received as his new second in command in the Mediterranean the recently promoted Rear-Admiral Lord Charles Beresford.

This Irish aristocrat and noted foxhunter, and a sometime Member of Parliament as a Unionist, had a modicum of experience afloat. It has been suggested that politicians eager to be rid of him in Parliament engineered his appointment to the Mediterranean.[44] Whatever the case, at the beginning, Fisher and Beresford got on well together. Fisher wrote to his wife: 'Beresford did uncommonly well and he is much pleased at my praising him, which he thoroughly deserved.'[45] However, Beresford was as headstrong as he was proud, and a breach between the two, which ultimately led to Beresford's vendetta against his superior officer, may have begun as early as 1900, when Beresford's ship *Ramillies* was clumsily handled in the tight entrance to harbour in Malta. The ship lay almost athwart the entrance until a corrective manoeuvre could be completed, delaying the entrance of a second division into harbour. Fisher publicly reprimanded Beresford, signalling to him, 'Your flagship is to proceed to sea and come in again in a seamanlike manner.' In spite of this incident, the two remained on fairly good terms until 1906, as we will see in the next chapter.

By the 1890s, the Mediterranean was the cockpit of empires, the oceanic space of instabilities and rivalries. Britain had kept a naval armament in the Mediterranean, with bases at Gibraltar, Malta, and Alexandria, throughout the nineteenth century so as to control communications and deter the French from any claim that the Mediterranean was their sea. The Suez Canal, opened in 1867 and acquired by British majority share in 1875, needed guarding. Keeping the Ottoman Empire strong, and discouraging Russian aspirations of gaining the Bosporus, was part of the foreign policy developed by Lord Palmerston and others. This required a great number of battleships and cruisers, plus smaller vessels on station. British naval strategy had always favoured blockading the enemy coast and carrying the war to the enemy in his waters. This forward strategy in favour at the Admiralty relied on watchfulness and strangulation of trade, and the annals of national naval history are replete with just such a demonstration of naval power. In 1893, however, the British began to worry when they learned that the French were getting 24 knots out of their torpedo boats. After the Fashoda incident in what is now South Sudan, which nearly led to war between France and Britain in 1898, the French were determined to rebuild their navy along lines that would give them a technological advantage against the British. Rather than seeking to engage the British Fleet proper, the French settled on the *guerre de course* (war of the chase) strategy, hunting the enemy's merchant ships and keeping their main fleets in masterful inactivity – a fleet in being. In consequence of this revolution in naval thinking, they abandoned the battleship and the battle fleet as the main instruments of naval power projection, concentrating instead on cruisers of all types. The principal weapon was to be the torpedo, delivered by torpedo boats against blockading British cruisers.

In London, the Director of Naval Intelligence put the Russian naval disposition and assets in the same category as the French,[46] and the British concluded that they would hardly be able to sustain a blockade of the sort that would defeat the enemy. Naval regeneration was obviously needed to secure Britannia's pre-eminence. In the interim, the tasks of the British Fleet in a future war were designed to protect seaborne commerce coming to and from the United Kingdom (under the principle of freedom of the seas), and all shipping under the Union Jack. Cruisers were in short supply. In consequence, the policy response was to arm British merchant cruisers.

The emergence of the torpedo and the torpedo boat also obliged the British to think differently about countermeasures. Thus was born the 'catcher', or as the shipbuilder Alfred Yarrow suggested to Fisher, the 'destroyer', called in early days the 'torpedo-boat destroyer'.[47] Designed to be faster than enemy torpedo boats, by 1914 a turbine-powered destroyer could do 30 knots and in many instances higher, which gave it the advantage. During Fisher's time in the Mediterranean, the destroyer was regarded as the means of blockading an enemy port, such as Toulon, and it was deemed necessary that destroyers and torpedo-gunboats would work in the formation of a 'flotilla' against French naval units (mainly torpedo boats, arranged against such an attack). The French fleet, meantime, was to be engaged far from Toulon's support. Spain and Italy were to be watched. The Dardanelles was to be closely observed, and the Suez Canal and Alexandria guarded by one coastal-defence ship each. Their Lordships' instructions to Fisher bore the Nelsonian touch:

> Make such dispositions of your ships on the general lines indicated in this letter as will best enable you to take, sink, burn, and otherwise destroy any ships or vessels belonging to the enemy, observing that until the strength of the enemy's navy has been broken, attacks on fortified positions will not be admissible.[48]

Fisher undoubtedly had a role in the shaping of these orders, or at least in giving advice on the fundamentals they contained.

However, from the outset of Fisher's appointment to the Mediterranean command, he turned to the game of attempting to outdo the Foreign Office in its appreciation of the possible enemy or combinations of belligerents to appeal to his bosses at the Admiralty for more material resources for his fleet. He was rarely satisfied with what Their Lordships could spare from already-taxed resources, for the needs were unending and global. No sooner was he on station, his base at Valletta, Malta, than he put up a warning to London of a likely French and Russian combination, a potent mix that was bound to involve the Ottomans and the Greeks. This came on top of a growing pile of intelligence reports and recommendations from commanders-in-chief dating back to

Admiral Tryon in 1891. The most recent were from Rear-Admiral Gerard Noel, Beresford's predecessor as second in command and the great expert on Fleet manoeuvres of his time. In the event of war, Noel had called for the Mediterranean Fleet to join with that of the Channel Command, based at Gibraltar. The object was to guard against the French at Toulon, freeing a detachment based on Malta to attend to Egypt's defence and check Russian aggrandisements and pretensions. Noel's position and reputation gave authenticity to Fisher's views.[49]

Still, in Whitehall, Fisher's strong perspectives and insistent claims did not quite ring true. Admiral Lord Walter Kerr, the epitome of tradition and sage counsel, was the first to complain about Fisher's exaggerations. He minuted, in reference to Jacky: 'The C. in C. has a habit, noticeable in some of his communications, of indulging in strong phrases to emphasize his arguments such as "disastrous consequences", "imperative necessity", "immediate large increase", "I earnestly press", etc.' Kerr thought these were the outcome of impulse rather than calm, deliberate judgement, and hence ought not to be taken seriously. Constantly 'crying wolf' would not do. Kerr thought Fisher's demands unreasonable, for if such forces were sent to the Mediterranean, England's Channel ports would be deprived of the means to defend against torpedo-boat flotillas based on the northern ports of France. Kerr's response bordered on anger: 'Their Lordships have a right to expect something better than a demand for impossibilities from an officer holding the position of the C. in C. in the Mediterranean [the most senior command afloat]. They might fairly expect to receive from him a well matured scheme as to how to use to the best advantage the destroyers at his disposal.' Kerr went on to counter the exaggerations and misunderstandings of a committee Fisher had convened on the subject of dealing with French torpedo boats and ports.[50] Kerr knew his man: he thought Fisher misguided and prone to exaggeration – implying instability and even unsuitability for command. He rightly recognised the Commander-in-Chief's manipulative ways.

Fisher, however, never shied away from the strategic realities and complexities of the Mediterranean command. No one in Whitehall doubted the complications of that command in those days. Britain had boosted Gibraltar's defences and upped its protection of Egypt at the Alexandria base. But Britain's relations with the Ottoman Empire bordered on the fragile and were daily in danger of collapsing in the face of German intrigues at Constantinople. Russia stood waiting to control the Dardanelles. Spain, Italy, and Greece held independent positions, with the latter realising that its future depended on England countering Russia in the Mediterranean. Fisher's in-letters to the Secretary of the Admiralty may read like a screed of paranoia, but these years were in fact the last of Pax Britannica – before the whole edifice of solitary power and splendid isolation collapsed. The lamps at the Foreign Office burned long and late as the secretaries and analysts took measures to shore up what no end of battleships and destroyers could do.

Early in 1901 Selborne, as First Lord of the Admiralty, decided to go out to the Mediterranean to see for himself the state of affairs that Fisher was describing with alarming effect. When Selborne told his father-in-law, Lord Salisbury (then in his final term as prime minister), that he was going to investigate Fisher's demands, the venerable statesman replied in lugubrious fashion that although Admiral Fisher was subject to those hallucinations of which all admirals were victims, he had hoped that by now Fisher would be over that sort of thing. In any event, Selborne, with Cabinet knowledge, sailed in the *Majestic*-class battleship *Caesar*. With him were the First Sea Lord, Admiral Lord Walter Kerr, and his head of 'the naval department of transports', actually the Director of Naval Intelligence, Vice-Admiral Sir Reginald Custance. In Malta, in mid-April 1901, Selborne was able to gain an appreciation of Fisher and the Mediterranean situation that no amount of correspondence could reveal.

Although young – only forty-three – William Waldegrave Palmer, 2nd Earl of Selborne, cut a powerful figure. He was as obstinate as he was progressive. He played a big part in Unionist politics and was reputed to be trustworthy and fair-minded, someone who, to use his own phrase, would be a safe companion on a tiger hunt. Besides being son-in-law of the prime minister, he was a cousin of Arthur Balfour, the rising Unionist who was soon to become premier. Selborne told his colleagues that the British margin over its naval rivals, French and Russian, was thin and, moreover, the Navy was not in a state of fighting readiness. He possessed outstanding analytical skills, and he had in H O Arnold-Forster, the naval evangelist, a competent if high-strung parliamentary secretary, with a seat in the House of Commons. In many respects, Selborne was the necessary naval revolutionary – the enabler – clearing the way for Jacky. Upon taking office, he asked Fisher to write to him from time to time on naval matters. For his part, Fisher, not losing the opportunity, courted him closely. Fisher placed readiness for war above all other considerations. Selborne wanted economies and modernisation.

Selborne disliked the tendency of Fisher and Beresford to exaggerate. The personal visit was called for because, as Selborne knew, if the problems of the day had to be sorted out by letter it would take until the 'crack of doom'. To Lord Curzon he confided that 'it is very aggravating to have to argue with men who calmly ignore this [the Royal Navy's worldwide responsibilities], and who also exaggerate so systematically as Fisher and Beresford do, and who apparently do not mind in the least being found out. The kind of balance sheet they draw up as between us and the French and Russians is one, in which we have no assets and the other party no liabilities, which is absurd.'[51]

24

Once arrived at Malta, Selborne, Kerr, and Custance listened to Fisher's analysis of the Mediterranean situation in disbelief. 'Do you consider Lord Salisbury a d– fool?' Selborne asked Fisher in reference to the former Foreign Secretary's understanding of events and circumstances. 'No,' replied Fisher with classic cheek, 'but all the same, this is the state of affairs in the Mediterranean.'[52] The view was different in Malta than from Whitehall, and Fisher had the ability to expose and exploit it. All the same it is probably true, as Selborne concluded, that Fisher's concentration on the Mediterranean led him to ignore British responsibilities on other seas and oceans.

Thus began the process by which Selborne conceived of bringing Fisher to the Admiralty as the great reformer,[53] though that was more than a year away. For the moment, Selborne took an interest in Fisher's considerations about the Mediterranean as the prime place of British naval interest and activity. At the same time, the sudden and dramatic emergence of Germany as a naval power and chief rival to the British Empire alerted him to the necessity of giving sufficient credence to the geopolitical shift. In November 1901 he drew the Cabinet's attention to German naval policy and to the Kaiser, who seemed 'determined that the power of Germany shall be used all the world over to push German commerce, possessions and interest.' From that point on, and enriched by Arnold-Forster's strident tone, Selborne pushed a naval policy to deal with a 'conviction that the great new German navy is being carefully built up from the point of view of a war with us.'[54] It is certain that Selborne was far in advance of Fisher in understanding the German menace, though this is not to say that Fisher was unaware of the challenge from Berlin. At The Hague, Fisher had met German admirals who brazenly informed him that the British Fleet was useless and vulnerable. The Germans in wartime, they boasted, would sink the whole lot with their torpedo boats and destroyers. Fisher was not shaken. To a committee of the Mediterranean Fleet preparing the details for the Fleet manoeuvres, Fisher recounted the episode. 'Now,' he told them, 'I have come out here and will prove that this is all nonsense.' He had as yet no plan, at least not one he was prepared to disclose. He asked the officers for suggestions – he was always glad to do so – and in this case the matter concerned torpedo-boat manoeuvres.

On the committee sat Captain Reginald Bacon, later Fisher's devoted biographer. Bacon, noted for improvements he made to the range of the torpedo, had studied these matters closely. He sketched out a plan for Malta using the antiquated craft then available and sent them to Fisher. The next morning, Bacon was astonished to receive a long signal eulogising him and his views. Along with this came an order to attend on Fisher at Admiralty House at noon. Bacon did so. 'After this he kept me constantly at work – both on Fleet and torpedo-boat manoeuvres on preparations for war,' recalled Bacon. 'Every officer with ideas was consulted and their view assimilated, till Sir John became the embodiment of the advanced ideas of all classes of officers of the Fleet.'[55]

All the same, Fisher continued to harp on the French menace at sea. He constantly complained that the force at his disposal was inadequate, and he told the Board of Admiralty he needed more destroyers. The sixteen he had on station in 1900 were not enough; he demanded sixty-two. 'His reiterated demands became tedious,' minuted Admiral Lord Walter Kerr. Fisher saw destroyers as accompaniments to the Fleet at sea – in other words, fleet escorts; by contrast, Kerr continued to see them as originally intended – that is, ships to operate from bases against enemy torpedo boats. Kerr maintained that Fisher wanted to employ destroyers where light cruisers and gunboats were called for, but Fisher had it right: 'To steam a Fleet at night without a fringe of destroyers is like marching an army into an enemy's country without advance guard, flanking parties and scouts!' Fisher guarded his naval assets, championing the concept of the fleet in being. British naval strategy and tactical thinking were shifting in his hands, and Kerr's notion (also held by others) of taking out the enemy's torpedo boats at source was giving way to a more defensive attitude – the protection of the Fleet at sea. This was to have profound implications in 1915 and 1916. The British built destroyers mightily in the years running up to the outbreak of the war. Their need for stouter hulls and more heavily gunned destroyers led to development of the River class and later the early Tribal class, more powerful destroyers with extended cruising capabilities. The 35-knot *Scout* class (with four 4in quick-firing guns) were designated flotilla leaders. By 1914 the Navy had nine flotilla-leader destroyers and 237 of the smaller torpedo-boat destroyers.[56]

Fisher found frustrating the numerous distractions of naval administration that took the C-in-C, Mediterranean, away from his most important duty: carrying out active fleet operations to make the Fleet efficient for war. He needed more cruisers and destoyers so that he could carry out those exercises that would make the Fleet ready for instant war. He did not want to see a naval scenario that mirrored what had happened during the Boer War, when the army was unprepared. As Fisher said, he had a noose around his neck. He cited what had happened to Admiral Byng at Minorca in the Seven Years War. Byng was court-martialled and executed because he was unable to defend a British garrison from a French fleet. The stakes were high, and the naval capabilities of the British needed to be of sufficient size to deal with the most likely enemy – the French – and defend and protect those communications and outposts of a great oceanic and global empire. Against this line of reasoning, politicians – 'the frocks' – were hard pressed to say no to Jack's importunities. Parliament, however, had to pass the annual naval estimates, and the costs of running this great naval instrument of state never seemed to diminish. But, as will be seen, Fisher knew where to effect economies, and that pleased his supporters and his rivals.

In his abiding attempt to gain more resources for the Mediterranean Fleet, Fisher stopped at nothing. He was the master of intrigue and of manipulation. In later years such actions would be regarded as breaches of trust, but Fisher always seemed to defy the conventions of his times – and, more, to get away with it. Not content just to appeal to the Admiralty, he wrote directly to his favourite journalists as well as to a former Liberal prime minister, Lord Rosebery, then in opposition to the Conservative government of Lord Salisbury.[57] To James R Thursfield, naval correspondent of *The Times*, Fisher complained of the weakness of the Mediterranean Fleet as well as the dilatory leadership of the Admiralty.[58] And to the lively and effective journalist Arnold White he sent thanks for exerting pressure on the Admiralty, with the result that, as described, Selborne as well as Kerr and Custance sailed to Malta in order to discuss Fisher's strategic and naval problems face to face.[59]

So much depended on the successful movement of the Fleet against its opponent in combat. Thus Fisher emphasised fleet exercises while C-in-C, Mediterranean. These exercises were to test battleships, battlecruisers, and destroyers in operations, and to test 'wireless scouting in searching for and keeping touch with an enemy'. He wanted aggressive, not passive, tactics. 'The whole and sole object of strategy,' he said, 'is to bring a superior force to bear on an inferior force.' Tactics were thus to be designed to bring superior gunfire to bear on the enemy and annihilate them.[60] As he informed Selborne, '*I maintain it to be a cardinal principle (that should never be departed from) that the Mediterranean Fleet should be kept constituted for instant war*' (italics in original).[61] In other words, the secret was to 'cross the T' but not so close as to allow the enemy to bring his torpedoes to bear.[62]

His command in the Mediterranean gave Fisher the chance to advance his long-held belief that the key to naval warfare was not just gunnery, but long-range gunnery.[63] Secondary armament was becoming increasingly incapable of penetrating the secondary armour in foreign ships, in his view, and he stated, 'One big shell in an open battery would be fearfully destructive and demoralizing.'[64] This dependency on the big gun as the primary, or even sole, armament had tactical weaknesses not foreseen by Fisher. He was a big-gun man, and he championed the cause.

Fisher's crowded time as Commander-in-Chief, Mediterranean, came to a close on 2 June 1902. The three years had been momentous ones, most notably in British imperial affairs and particularly in fighting the Boers in the South African War and dealing with the Boxer Rebellion in China. Fisher had not lost the opportunity to get the Fleet into fighting trim to take on all comers as required. Beresford, in a professional mood not yet hampered by his distrust of Fisher and his own vaunted ego, nicely summarised Fisher's Mediterranean years:

> While Vice-Admiral Sir John Fisher was Commander-in-Chief of the Mediterranean Fleet, he greatly improved its fighting efficiency. As a result of his representations, the stocks of coal at Malta and Gibraltar were increased, the torpedo flotillas were strengthened, and the new breakwaters at Malta were begun. Some of Sir John Fisher's reforms were confidential; but among his achievements which became common knowledge, the following are notable: From a 12-knot Fleet with breakdowns, he made a 15-knot Fleet without breakdowns; introduced long range target practice, and instituted the Challenge Cup for heavy gun shooting; instituted various war practices for officers and men; invited, with excellent results, officers to formulate their opinions upon cruising and battle formation; drew up complete instructions for torpedo flotillas; exercised cruisers in towing destroyers and battleships in towing one another, thereby proving the utility of the device for saving coal in an emergency; and generally carried into execution Fleet exercises based, not on tradition, but on the probabilities of war.[65]

Fisher came home from the Mediterranean a full admiral. Many honours had come his way, notably the Knight Commander of the Bath and the Order of Osmanieth from the Sultan of Turkey. He stood near the apex of power. He was ambitious for more and needed a new vent for his enthusiasms and his professional zeal. Gunnery exercises on the bright blue Mediterranean Sea had proved the value of the great gun firing at long ranges. From a powerfully armoured, fast-moving warship these great guns constituted the new arbiter of power. He had brought his fleet to a state of efficiency heretofore only imagined. His knowledge of technical matters, if not clouded by the specifics, gave him an advantage over many senior naval officers. Seniority and experience had hardened his views. His star was in the ascendant. In naval matters he was remarkably iconoclastic, which set him apart from all other admirals. He could not be out-argued in naval matters. His sense of humour was compelling to many who encountered him and added to his charm. His social reforming instincts, mirroring some national preoccupations, placed him in an unusual category, and he was interested in the welfare of the lower deck, as was Churchill. He was a meritocrat. He hated the old-guard favouritisms (though all the same, promoting by devious means his own favourites). Partly by covert methods he had gained the attention of the press, and he was known to all the navalists of the age. He was on the edge of great things, though even greater challenges lay ahead and in these were sown the seeds of the growing suspicion that would split the Navy between his followers, 'the Fishpond', and his mortal enemies. The war that he had forecast, the Armageddon, lay nearly a dozen years away. He made furious preparations for it but in the end, like all the main participants and observers, could do nothing to stop the approaching catastrophe. The rapid expansion of the Fleet, already in place when he arrived back in London, favoured his schemes. Gearing up for war readiness made the issue of an adequate supply of well-trained and well-educated naval officers one commanding attention and need. Only Fisher could have imagined the social changes required, the opposition from 'the old fossils', and the political complications (never fully overcome) that lay ahead.

The Selborne Scheme: attempting a great revolution

'The fact is that we are going to make a great revolution,' H O Arnold-Forster, MP, the forceful and flamboyant Parliamentary Secretary to the Admiralty, said in November 1902, '... a revolution which will leave its mark on the Naval service for many a year to come.'[66] The government of the day, under Prime Minister Arthur Balfour, favoured the time-honoured maintenance of British naval supremacy as a means of securing the profit and the power upon which British trade and foreign influence rested. This Conservative administration was alive to the changing international shifts and far outdistanced its Liberal opposition in the concept of 'look to your moat'. The South African War had revealed Germany's intention of challenging British pre-eminence at sea, and British statesmen were alive to the possibility of similar unwelcome interventions in the future. Balfour initiated the reorganisation of the Army and constituted the Committee of Imperial Defence. The Conservatives, with vigour, also set about restoring the strength of the Navy by revolutionary measures.

The Earl of Selborne, whom we have already briefly met, was First Lord of the Admiralty in Balfour's government. A member of the aristocracy, he came in the guise of a social revolutionary. He was attuned to the perils of the age, and an expert in South African colonial administration at a time when the national mood was caught up in Kipling's 'Recessional'. Selborne had been appalled by British military disasters in South Africa, and he took the humiliation that came with the self-exalted state of British affairs as an opportunity for a beneficent improvement, a merciful discipline. He thought being First Lord of the Admiralty the most delectable role after that of prime minister. In late 1901 Selborne began to consider who might be the successor to Admiral Sir Archibald Douglas as Second Sea Lord, the office that administered personnel. Selborne saw in Fisher the characteristics needed. For the present, however, Selborne was alone in his views. Senior admirals stood on guard against change, and most were suspicious of Jacky Fisher. They saw him as a wild card – a man not to be trusted.

Selborne consulted his professional colleague Lord Walter Kerr, the First Sea Lord, about whom he should appoint Second Sea Lord. In a letter to Kerr, he put forward Fisher's name as his first choice. He made it clear that he viewed Fisher as being especially capable of addressing personnel or the 'manning question', the most difficult and, indeed, the main challenge then faced. The rapid enlargement of the Fleet meant a similar expansion in the need for all sorts of men who would comprise 'the lower deck', including warrant officers, petty officers, leading seamen, able seamen, gunnery and torpedo specialists, paymasters, assistants, stokers, oilers, boatswains, and others. Moreover, more officers of all ranks were needed – navigators, gunnery specialists, torpedo experts, submariners and aviators, engineers, and those destined for the bridge – for the increasingly large battleships, battlecruisers, light cruisers, and others that were being launched. More young lieutenants were needed for the growing number of destroyers being built and commissioned.

However, one of the most intractable problems in the Navy was the great divide between those who walked the quarterdeck, who were invariably specialists in navigation, gunnery, and torpedoes, and those of the lower deck, who were increasingly men with technical knowledge and proficiency. In the age of Nelson, less distinction existed between those who navigated the ships and those who literally knew the ropes, were proficient seamen and served the guns; the coming of steam propulsion created the naval engineer. Engineer officers became responsible for the propulsive machinery of the ship and nothing else, while the other officers were responsible for fighting the enemy. The divide, which included social implications as well as the effects of their different roles, was created by the different and separate ways the two groups were trained.[67] By the end of the nineteenth century, the *Britannia* system of training had evolved for the executive class: after going to preparatory or cramming schools, these boys entered the Navy as cadets at the age of fourteen to fifteen and a half and began three terms aboard the wooden ships *Britannia* and *Hindustan*, permanently moored in the river at Dartmouth, and one term aboard the training cruiser *Isis*. After fifteen months' training, they then passed into the Fleet as midshipmen and eventually became officers. The engineers invariably entered the Navy as enlistments and rose up through the ranks over many years, proud of their social station but anxious to improve it – not as social revolutionaries but as those proud of their work and in need of recognition by others, including the state, of their importance. This separation meant a social stigma became attached to those who worked the engines.[68] As well, there tended to be a distinct class difference between the executive officers and the engineers, with the engineers having a comparative lack of education and a lesser family background. These differences went hand in hand with a difference in status when aboard ship, especially as the engineer could never command a vessel.[69]

In the final decades of the nineteenth century, widespread recognition existed in naval circles that reforms to the system were necessary.[70] The education received by cadets aboard *Britannia* was condemned, and some questioned the second stage of their instruction aboard a seagoing ship. As well, for years the engineers, supported by the technical press, had carried on a powerful agitation against their inferior status; there was a call for equal treatment of engineers and executive officers, and even for similar uniforms.[71] Thursfield at *The Times*, a confidant of Fisher, gave prominent support for reforms in education and training in the Navy.[72] One early advocate of reform was Colonel Sir John Colomb, Royal Marines, a prominent writer on defence issues, who had supported the principle of common entry for many years. Rear-Admiral C C Penrose Fitzgerald likewise argued that a 'complete revolution' was required, and that the executive officers required more technical training.[73] By contrast, in 1901 *Monthly Review* editor Henry Newbolt and contributors Commander Carlyon Bellairs and Admiral E R Fremantle kept to the old line of maintaining the separation of executive and engineer officers during their training.[74] Sweeping away established methods was by no means easy, and battle lines were being drawn.

Selborne was aware of the agitation regarding the position of engineers in the Royal Navy, and the need for reform. Increasing agitation also came from the trade unions (and supporters in the press) that wanted engineers and those who worked in engine rooms, the artificers, to be given better recognition for their technical capacities. In a letter to the First Sea Lord, he noted that he foresaw 'much future difficulty and trouble in connection with the engineer officers of the Navy'. On a recent visit to the Royal Naval Engineering College, Keyham, the training establishment for engineer officers (founded 1880), he had learned that the number of candidates presenting themselves for vacancies was steadily diminishing. This he attributed to the 'agitation on the position of engineer officers now proceeding in Parliament and the Press.'[75] Indeed, he noted:

> The numbers of engineer officers are and will be constantly increasing. The public imagination is already greatly impressed with the importance and value of their services. They are supported and will be more and more so, by what I may describe as a Trades Union of immense influence and power, the Civil Engineers of the United Kingdom.

Selborne thought it a 'very bad thing for the Navy that so large a body of its officers should be growing up in a different atmosphere of tradition and aspiration to that of the executive officers.' In his mind, there could be only one possible remedy: rather than a 'sudden' fusion of the two branches, 'in the future all officers whether engineer or executive should enter the Navy at the same age and under the same conditions, should up to a certain point be trained in the same way, and that then a sufficient number of them should specialize in engineering in exactly the same way neither more nor less, as specialization now exists among the executive officers of the Navy in gunnery or torpedo work.'[76]

Selborne reasoned that Fisher's genius for organisation was exactly what was required to grapple with the vexed matter.[77] Walter Kerr was unconvinced. The First Sea Lord credited Fisher with 'all his abilities and powers of organisation', but also made abundantly clear to his political boss that Fisher not only had many faults but that other prospective admirals who might be made Second Sea Lord were equally capable of undertaking the vast organisational work that was required to deal with the manning question.

Unlike Selborne, Kerr had no stomach for significant change in the relationship between engineer and executive officers. He feared too sudden change in a Service essentially traditional and conservative in nature, and he imagined that Fisher could be expected to initiate new systems. Kerr argued that the technical training essential to the engineers could not possibly be worked into the education of those who were to become executive officers. He believed that the line of education would have to split from the point at which the cadets left the *Britannia*, and that the age of twenty was too late to begin to specialise in engineering.[78] Unhappy with his political master, Kerr repeated his belief that there was no fundamental deficiency in the means by which new officers were trained in the Royal Navy.

The First Sea Lord raised another point: he was keen to caution the First Lord that from Fisher's new position as Second Sea Lord he would be next in line by seniority and position to become First Sea Lord. As he put it bluntly, 'I should advise you to think a great deal before you placed Fisher in this position – he certainly does not possess the confidence of the Service and his appointment as Senior Naval Lord would be universally condemned.' These were early warning signs. Kerr reiterated that Fisher 'always asks for more and unreasonably more.'[79] Moreover, he contended, not without reason, that when Fisher was C-in-C, Mediterranean, he was guilty of feeding information to 'Navy Leaguers and kindred spirits', thus bringing the public into discussion of delicate matters, and breaching security.[80] So the issue really came down to whether Selborne and the Cabinet were prepared to let Fisher become First Sea Lord when the time came.

'His loyalty has not always been unimpeachable,' Selborne agreed in a letter to Kerr, 'his judgment is sometimes hasty and even flighty; he is supposed to think too much of No. 1; the arts of advertisement are not quite unknown to him.' And again: 'you said he was impressionable, greatly affected by his environment, easily influenced in certain directions for good or evil.' Selborne agreed with Kerr on this, and he deduced 'that at the Admiralty between you and me he would run straight. His particular sphere of work would not easily lend itself to disloyalty.'[81]

In a sudden and swift gesture Selborne brushed aside Kerr's resistance. Against the advice of the senior naval authority on the Board of Admiralty, the politician offered Fisher the post of Second Sea Lord on 19 February 1902,[82] bringing him to the Admiralty with all his difficulties and all his methods, all his friends and all his enemies. He would tackle the manning question, but in doing so would be kept under close surveillance.

Helping to manage Fisher was Reginald Brett, 2nd Viscount Esher, a man who can only be described as 'the fixer'. A courtier of the old school, close confidant of the King, just as he had been an adviser to Queen Victoria, Esher worked the inner circles of state, giving advice where required, guiding ministers of state, as well as high-placed sailors and soldiers who did the work of power and progress. He had Liberal party connections, was at one time a Member of Parliament, and had often been asked to become permanent undersecretary at the War Office, but he preferred the workings of Windsor Castle and Buckingham Palace, where he was on royal retainer, arranging royal coronations and funerals, running the royal archives, and advising the King. He aimed to be non-partisan, and he was convinced that he could manipulate events more effectively from backstage. On these grounds he declined many attractive offices, ministerial and diplomatic. Along the way he acquired honours and many friendships. Lord Esher worked the back rooms of power as a courtier and an adviser to the Committee of Imperial Defence, which he had a hand in establishing in 1902, as a progressive force. He therefore, and delightfully, moved back and forth as required – at the War Office one day, the Admiralty the next, 10 Downing Street one day, Windsor to see the King the next – never on a regular cycle but always well arranged so as to give appropriate advice or send messages against taking unwanted actions.

Some thought Esher an insidious intriguer, and one naval officer with exceptional opportunities to observe the conduct of high policy thought there was a myserious power at work in the government machine. He speculated that it might be vaguely referred to as the Treasury, though less benignly designated the Judaeo-Masonic combination.[83] In any event, Esher sat at the heart of policy-making.

Esher became Fisher's adviser. In return, Fisher responded to Esher's guidance and friendship. Esher aided and abetted the naval revolution, but at the centre of it, as Arnold-Forster and those in the Cabinet knew, lay their messenger, their agent: Jacky Fisher. He was essential to the revitalisation of the Navy at the critical hour, but it was the political heads of that age who needed him, more than even they were prepared to admit, or than historians have since acknowledged. He was their instrument: he never disappointed, though more often than not they disappointed him and earned his opinion that politicians were 'a flabby lot'.

Fisher's success in gaining Selborne's confidence lay in his ability to use to his advantage the advice of what Fisher called 'the seven brains', seven serving officers – all of them up-and-coming figures in the service or engineering: Captain Henry Jackson, FRS, later Admiral of the Fleet and First Sea Lord; Captain John Jellicoe, later Admiral of the Fleet, Commander-in-Chief of the Grand Fleet, and First Sea Lord; Captain Reginald H Bacon (biographer of Fisher and of Jellicoe); Captain Charles Madden, Jellicoe's Chief of Staff, later Admiral of the Fleet and First Sea Lord; Commander Wilfred Henderson; William H Gard, Chief Constructor at Portsmouth Dockyard, who became Assistant Director of Naval Construction and later Deputy Director; and Alexander Gracie of Fairfield Shipbuilding and Engineering. One might call this a cabal, and so it looked to suspicious outsiders. In the Navy, well-ordered authority was customary, everyone answerable to someone senior, but Fisher was injecting a new system that would serve as a sounding board for his own ideas. Fisher disclosed the names of the brains to Selborne and explained to his political superior that he had been trying out various ideas on these men for some considerable time. He told Selborne this so that the First Lord would not think the reforming agenda was coming merely from Jack, and would know that the ideas had been tested by some of the best brains in the Navy. For some years Fisher had had his own private printing press, a thing unheard of in the Service. His extraordinary charm enabled him to get recipients of the sheets that came off the press to admit to sworn secrecy. 'Burn this!' was the mantra. It was high risk – and dangerous for Fisher.

Jacky arrived at the Admiralty as Second Sea Lord on 10 June 1902, a momentous occasion in the history of the Navy. Dervish-like, he set to work on proposals, as he described to his son some months later: 'At 10 minutes to 12 I said "how d'ye do" to Lord Selborne. At 5 minutes to 12 he gave me practically *carte blanche*, and at 12 I was read in at the Board, and five minutes after, I commenced operations in my room at the Admiralty in sending the first pages to the printer of the preamble of the new schemes of training, entry, etc.'[84]

He set to work with prodigious results. That year, wrote his private secretary Sir Charles Walker, 'witnessed an activity at the Admiralty which had never before occurred in time of peace. Reform after reform ... was brought about by Sir John Fisher with bewildering rapidity.'[85] Within six days the new Second Sea Lord had drafted and sent to Selborne three papers that dealt with proposed reforms. Of these three papers, only the third dealt with an issue that fell under the purview of the Second Sea Lord. The first two addressed the necessity of a naval staff and the redistribution of the fleets; the third was on the engineer question, the issue he was brought in to address by Selborne. In this paper, Fisher put his case as follows:

The deck officers have no longer what really was an all-absorbing task in becoming proficient in handling a ship under sail ...

These qualities, no longer required on deck, are acquired now and required now (but both in a lesser degree) amongst the engines and boilers and it would be good for our officers as a body to get much more than the present scanty attendance of the midshipmen when the ship is under steam and their entire absence when the maximum propelling power is being exerted which is the most impressive time for instruction.

This alteration in training so essential for the efficiency of the Navy can be readily brought about by following precisely the same method as was employed to make the navigation of his Majesty's ships more efficient, a plan attended by the most signal success as the Hydrographer will testify, for never has the British Navy been better navigated than in the present time. The method then pursued to attain the present excellent results was gradually to stop the entry of the old navigating class and increase that of naval cadets and for officers who so elected (and in view of the advantages and extra pay there has been no lack of candidates) to take up navigating duties as sub-lieutenants, as lieutenants, and as commanders, following on to the Captains' List and the Flag List in the usual course. Such a plan is suggested with a feeling of absolute confidence in its ultimate success in regard to the engineering duties of the Navy.

This course is not proposed on account of the present engineer agitation, it is proposed solely in the interests of the Service ... The general good and efficiency of the Navy renders it imperative that the entry of engineer students as at present arranged should be gradually stopped and the entry of naval cadets gradually increased in the like proportion and that instruction from the moment of entry into the college at Dartmouth should in a large measure, *at least half the time*, be devoted to engineering. That like gunnery, torpedo, and navigating officers as at present, there shall be engineer officers, sub-lieutenants, lieutenants, and commanders and going on perhaps to the Captains' List and Flag List but the pay in view of greater responsibilities (the extra pay that is) should be such as would perhaps induce officers to prefer remaining in the engineering class.

The present college at Keyham would serve the same purpose as the *Excellent* and *Vernon* for qualifying and re-qualifying engineer officers. The artificer engineers would require to be largely increased which would be most popular and conducive to efficiency.[86]

This paper contained two main proposals: common entry, which as has been seen was previously advocated by Selborne; and the idea that these engineer officers could progress onto the Captains' List and Flag List, and hence be eligible to command ships (which became known as 'interchangeability'), an idea that had not been previously advanced by Selborne.[87]

On the same day that Fisher sent his three papers to the Admiralty, Selborne issued a confidential memorandum entitled 'Position of Naval Engineers'. He reiterated his belief in the strength of the agitation for change, especially from the engineering institutions and their potential allies, the chambers of commerce. He argued that it would be preferable if the Navy instituted changes on its own rather than have them imposed by a Royal Commission or a Committee of the House of Commons. He listed what he believed the engineer officers desired: (a) for the Chief Engineer to have similar power over the stokers as the Senior Officer of Marines had over his men; (b) to be included in the Military branch; (c) to exchange the present engineer ranks with normal rank names followed by 'E'; and (d) to have the same uniform as the executive branch. Selborne said that these changes would not nearly be sufficient, though, as they would only satisfy those engineers currently in the Navy. Those arguing for reform outside the Navy would not be satisfied, and what satisfaction might result for the naval engineers would likely be short-lived once they realised that the changes had not fundamentally altered the situation. He believed that the source of the problem was the difference in social origin, entry, and training of the two branches of officers, and the only solution that would go to the root of the problem would be common entry. Selborne concluded the memorandum by listing some of the problems facing any such efforts at reform, adding that it might not be possible to surmount all of them. He also stated that the new Second Sea Lord should commence a complete examination into the subject.[88]

Kerr, though cautious, caved in and indicated that he was 'generally in agreement' with the contents of Selborne's memorandum. He also expressed his belief that the majority of the agitation originated from outside the Service, and that while internally the relations between the engineers and the executive officers were 'very satisfactory', pressure from Parliament could force their hands. That having been said, he did not think that the Navy could ever make a good job of interchangeable officers. Kerr knew the Navy better than the reforming Selborne; he correctly concluded that the social side of the issue would present the greatest difficulty.[89]

This first instalment of the proposed reforms, entitled 'A Brief Summary of Reasons and Proposals for altering the present System of Entry and Training of Officers and Men of the Navy', was returned from the printing press on 2 July 1902. Selborne attached a cover letter to the memorandum, stating that copies were to be distributed only to members of the Admiralty Board, were to be treated as '*very confidential*', and would serve as a basis 'for discussion' after the summer holidays. Fisher included in the memorandum a critical letter, dated 26 May, from Rear-Admiral HSH Prince Louis of Battenberg, then Director of

Naval Intelligence, showing that his views of those who opposed the changes had maybe not yet hardened to the degree they would in the near future.[90]

Fisher brought in Sir Alfred Ewing, then professor of mechanical engineering at Cambridge, to fill the new post styled Director of Naval Education. Many an officer must have scratched his head in disbelief, for it was well understood that 'Training' was the thing, and 'Education' quite a secondary proposition. But change was in the wind, and social revolution, too. The intent was to bring Ewing's wide range of engineering knowledge to bear on the new education scheme for naval officers. Ewing did what he could, and brought to the post an enormous reputation at home and aboard. For twelve years he laboured to bring success to Fisher's design. Then the war came and brought everything in that line to a standstill.

On 14 November 1902 Fisher confided to his son that 'I've gotten through the biggest part of the big scheme I have been working on since June 10th last, and Lord Selborne seems very pleased; but I think the rest of my colleagues look on me as a sort of combined Robespierre and Gambetta!'[91] Elsewhere he wrote of 'the old Mandarins who are coming out'. Young officers were in favour; the old fogies were the pessimists. To journalist Arnold White he wrote:

> The Naval Rip Van Winkles (N.B.: *that phrase is copyright!*) have dubbed it 'a d—d revolutionary scheme!' So it is! And perhaps they are going to vilify me and identify it as my work alone, so as to discredit it! It would be disastrous to the prestige of the scheme if it were in any way otherwise than what it is, which is *the unanimous decision of the whole Board of Admiralty*, and therefore I send this line of caution, in case your kindly feelings might entice you to mention my name in association with the scheme, as then the enemy would blaspheme at once![92]

Arriving in many a home as an unwelcome yuletide present was the final proposal, published in the press on Christmas Day 1902, entitled 'Memorandum Dealing with the Entry, Training, and Employment of Officers and Men of the Royal Navy and of the Royal Marines'.[93] (It came also to be known as the Selborne Scheme, the New Scheme, and the New Admiralty Scheme). The historical introduction summarised how technology had affected the Navy. Now a new look was called for: in short, a naval officer 'must be a seaman, a gunner, a soldier, an engineer, and a man of science as well'. Stating that the 'highest type of Naval Officer was that wherein great professional knowledge is added to force of character', the memorandum went on to say that:

> the Executive, the Engineer, and the Marine Officers are all necessary for the efficiency of the Fleet; they all have to serve side by side throughout their career; their unity of sentiment is essential to the welfare of the Navy; yet they

all enter the Service under different regulations, and they have nothing in common in their early training. The result is that the Executive Officer, unless he is a gunnery or torpedo specialist, has been taught but a limited amount of engineering, although the ship in which he serves is one huge box of engines; that the Engineering Officer has never had any training in executive duties; that from lack of early sea training the Marine Officer is compelled, sorely against his will, to remain comparatively idle on board ship.

Henceforth all future officers – executive, engineer or Royal Marine – would enter under the same conditions as cadets, age twelve to thirteen, and they would be trained to the same system until they had passed to the rank of sub-lieutenant between the age of nineteen and twenty. This meant a coalescing of the branches of the Service. The result intended:

is, to a certain point, community of knowledge and lifelong community of sentiment. The only machinery which can produce this result is early companionship and community of instruction. These opportunities will be secured by a policy of:

One System of Supply
One System of Entry
One System of Training.

When the Selborne Scheme was released to the public, clamour arose as to whether or not senior engineer officers could move into executive positions and command ships. The implication of the above was that the division between the three branches at the age of twenty would be final, a position that was confirmed elsewhere in the memorandum. This raised the question of how recruits for the engineering specialisation would be obtained. As far as possible, each officer would be allowed to choose which branch he would join, subject to the proviso that all branches were satisfactorily filled. Preference (other things being equal) would be given to those boys whose parents or guardians declared for them that they would be ready to enter any of the three branches of the Service. The social revolution also confirmed that the rate of promotion would be the same for engineers and executive officers, and that the ranks of engineer officers would correspond to executive officers, with the addition of '(E)'. Also, the engineer officers would receive additional pay, and 'every endeavour will be made to provide those who enter the Engineer branch with opportunities equal to those of the Executive branch including the same opportunity of rising to Flag Rank.'[94]

The final sentence implied that interchangeability might be available to some engineer officers. Fisher himself had hoped to retain interchangeability for all officers, but he recognised that such a proposal was not contained in the memorandum. In the margins of a copy of the memorandum in 1906 he wrote: 'It was the intention and was the only sound basis to have complete interchangeability, but in deference to a strongly expressed desire not to fetter unduly future Boards, the separation into three branches was reluctantly acquiesced in.'[95]

The reason given for including the Royal Marines in the new scheme was that, under existing arrangements, Marines received no naval training. While on board ship they had only about six to twelve hours of duty each week; they were not trained to be of any use for the rest of the time. By including them in the new scheme, it was hoped that they would be more useful aboard ship and would become more a part of the ship's company.[96] It was a vain hope, for Marine officers did not feel that the common training would provide their new recruits with adequate instruction in the specialised tasks of Marines as 'soldiers of the sea'. Thus in 1906 the Marines were excluded from the Selborne Scheme, and Marine officers subsequently entered the Service separately.[97]

The Selborne Scheme faced stiff opposition, and almost every aspect of it attracted fire. Retired Admiral of the Fleet Sir Frederick Richards, for one, declared that the new scheme was a 'hazardous experiment' and demanded an inquiry into its scope and effect.[98] Others who attacked the reforms were Vice-Admiral Sir Lewis Beaumont, Admiral Gerald Noel, and former First Lord Goschen.[99] Fisher sensed that 'two pre-historic admirals', Admiral Penrose Fitzgerald and Sir Vesey Hamilton, led the opposition.[100] In a letter to the *Daily Graphic* on 10 March 1906, Admiral Fitzgerald wrote of 'the curious composite officer now being manufactured at Osborne and Dartmouth to perform alternately the duties of a seaman, a marine, and an engineer.'[101] The 'old fossils' did not fully carry the day. Among more thoughtful critics, such as Sir George Clarke (first Secretary of the Committee of Imperial Defence, the CID), Admiral W H Henderson, and Sir Rowland Blennerhasset, the Selborne Scheme was opposed mainly for one or more of the following reasons: (1) the concentration on engineering would threaten to displace the study of tactics and strategy; (2) any one of the three branches required complete attention in order for an officer to achieve proficiency; and (3) the duties of the executive officer and the engineer officer were completely different, and the increasingly complicated engines and boilers required the undivided attention and further specialisation of the engineer officer class.[102]

Foremost among the Selborne Scheme's critics were the existing engineer officers. Although some realised that the scheme would benefit the Navy, and hence did not stand in the way of its implementation,[103] others saw that they would have the burden of training the new engineer officers, while they would not benefit themselves from the changes that the newer officers would benefit from. As well, the perception arose that, under the new scheme, no more attention would be paid to engineering than to, say, gunnery. More importantly, the scheme appeared to do nothing about the existing order of things in the Navy, as the existing engineer officers would still be without military status, while their subordinates were to be executive officers. An attempt was made to rectify this on 28 March 1903 when military titles were granted to the engineers via an Order in Council. They would now be known as Engineer Rear-Admirals instead of Chief Inspectors of Machinery, Engineer Captains instead of Inspectors of Machinery, etc. However, a distinction was still made between these new ranks and the new-style Lieutenants (E).

Among Fisher's hearty champions of change at this stage was his later arch-opponent Lord Charles Beresford, who wrote:

> The strongest opponent of the scheme will acknowledge that it is a brilliant and statesmanlike effort to grapple with a problem upon the sound settlement of which depends the future efficiency of the British Navy ... The executive officer of to-day should possess an intimate knowledge of all that relates to his profession. Up to now he has been fairly educated in the different branches. The most important, however – in that we depend entirely upon it – that relating to steam and machinery, has been sadly neglected ... the engineer officer has never received that recognition to which the importance of his duties and responsibilities so justly entitled him ... The abolition of distinction regarding entry has settled this point once and for ever, and it is satisfactory to find that constituted authority has taken the matter in hand before it became a political or party question ...
>
> The memo referring to the marines will be, I believe, received with the greatest satisfaction by the splendid corps as a whole as by the Service as a whole ...
>
> I consider the return to the early age of entry of infinite value.[104]

In support of his position, Fisher often referred to a long letter written to him by Beresford, dated 14 April 1903. In it, Beresford stated, 'I regret the opposition in this country to the present scheme', and 'I am certain that such opposition is unfounded and unsound, and if still in the House of Commons I could have knocked the bottom out of it.'[105] Fisher frequently quoted from this letter in his subsequent conflict with Beresford.

Fisher was open to all sorts of prospects for improving the education and training of officers and men. To that date, no navigational school had been formed, and the young Herbert Richmond, one of the brightest 'sparks' in the Navy, was arguing for just such an institution. Employing his friend Henry Oliver, then a commander, Richmond advanced the cause with Jacky Fisher. Almost immediately a powerful committee was struck, in which Richmond and Oliver were both made members under Fisher's chairmanship. Richmond noted admiringly in his diary: 'It really is wonderful to have a man at the Head of Affairs who can take up a matter as Fisher has, who is so absolutely approachable and ready to listen to suggestions and act on them.' Richmond was not alone in his admiration of Jacky. In later years, Oliver wrote wistfully of Fisher that 'in the everlasting war against Downing Street ... old Jack could handle Civil Servants and Cabinet Ministers and get things done whatever his faults may have been.'[106]

As the dust settled in the first half of 1903, Fisher presided over an education committee that was tasked with, among other items, the development of Osborne House as a naval college. Osborne had formerly been a residence of Queen Victoria, but the new King decided that he would not have any use for it, and donated the main building as a military hospital. The stables were converted to a naval college.[107] As Dartmouth would not be ready to accept cadets until 1905, Osborne had to be made ready to accept cadets as of September 1903 in order to educate the first and second years of the new-style entrants.[108] Lord Esher, on a royal visit to Osborne in February 1906, wrote: 'We went to the college this afternoon. Four hundred boys looking splendid. The gym is much improved. There is a portrait of Nelson hung in the gallery – with a motto under it in enormous letters: "There is nothing the Navy cannot do" ... The place is good and a God-send ... as you can imagine.'[109] Fisher contended that Osborne would become the best and most popular public school in the kingdom, but again he exaggerated.

In 1905, as the last of the old-entry cadets entered Keyham, the Royal Naval Engineering College, the Cawdor Memorandum (named for Lord Cawdor, Selborne's replacement as First Lord of the Admiralty) was published. In addition to dealing with a number of topics ranging from *Dreadnought* to fleet distribution, it also announced that in future there would only be one class of officers, regardless of the type of work they performed, and henceforth all would be executive officers.[110]

The stigma of engineer officers persisted. In 1905 Rosslyn Wemyss, Captain of Royal Naval College, Osborne, noted 'a tendency on the part of the parents of some cadets at Osborne to hope at least that their sons might never become Lieutenants (E), with no chance of commanding ships or fleets, and I have a suspicion that, for this reason, they have in some cases even discouraged their sons in their engineering studies.'[111]

'Nothing can stop this scheme,' Fisher declared in March 1906. 'Prejudice cannot stop it. Parliament cannot stop it. Satan cannot stop it. Not even the Treasury can stop it. They might as well try to stop an avalanche.' Fisher received indirect support from an American naval officer who, after a visit of a United States fleet to British waters, reported that Royal Navy officers believed the Selborne Scheme to have been an improvement.[112] He also received support from Admiral Sir Reginald Custance, Admiral Sir John Hopkins, and the Chief Inspector of Machinery, Sir Henry Benbow.[113] Even so, in 1911, nearly a year after he retired as First Sea Lord, Fisher remained concerned about the reforms, as he told naval writer John Leyland. There was a conspiracy afoot by Beresford's supporters to hamper the scheme, and this conspiracy was receiving a somewhat sympathetic ear in high places. As well, he argued that those cadets who chose engineering received ridicule and abuse from others. He stated that if he was still in charge, three or four commanders of battleships would be sent ashore on half-pay, and a dozen midshipmen sent home to their parents for another line of work, adding, 'I always think it was so nice of Lord St Vincent that he headed-up a man in a cask and threw him overboard, not that he had committed any overt act of mutiny, but *'he looked sulky'* as St Vincent passed him! *It wants a bit of St. Vincent now!'*[114]

In August 1912, under the initiative of Churchill, now First Lord of the Admiralty, the age of entry into Osborne was raised to thirteen and a half so as to correspond with the age at which boys finished their preparatory school work. As well, shore courses were reintroduced prior to the examination for the rank of lieutenant.[115] A supplementary scheme of entry was started to cope with the threatened shortage of officers, which was the result of the rapid expansion of building programmes after 1909, as well as the growth of the submarine service, the fleet air services, and the dominion navies. Under the existing scheme, it took nine years to produce a lieutenant. Under the supplementary scheme, a number of boys between seventeen and a half and eighteen and a half years of age, who were finished products of the public school system, were admitted as cadets. These cadets received eighteen months of intensive training and then were sent to the Fleet as midshipmen, meaning that an officer was turned out in a little less than half the time of the existing scheme.[116]

In 1910, when the last class of students who had entered into Keyham College under the old scheme had passed through, the college was closed.[117] Later, in April 1914, the Keyham Naval Engineering College was reopened for the first of those common-entry cadets who had chosen engineering as their specialisation. They took a specialist course in engineering as part of their training to become Lieutenants (E). It was also announced that in deciding on officers to command submarines, preference would be given to officers who had specialised in engineering.[118]

In summary, Fisher had attempted the unimaginable, but with political leadership making it possible. On the eve of the press's publication of the Selborne scheme, 24 December 1902, H O Arnold-Forster, Parliamentary Secretary to the Admiralty, had written to his sister on the matter of who deserved credit for the reforms:

It is well that credit should be given where credit is due. It is really due to three men. Principally to Sir John Fisher, whose originality, perseverance, and energy have made the thing possible. Next to Sir John credit is due to the First Lord [Selborne], on whom, after all, all the responsibility rests, and on whom the chief blame will fall if the scheme fails; and thirdly, and in a high degree, credit is due to Lord Walter Kerr, a splendid, thoroughgoing, old-school sailor of the best kind, who has justly earned the perfect confidence of the officers ... A smaller man would have simply set his face against the whole thing, and either have made it impossible or have sulked. Lord Walter, on the contrary, having once made up his mind to accept the new principles, has been most loyal, and has done everything in his power to make it a success. The mere fact of his acquiescence is worth an immense amount.[119]

Eventually the scheme failed. The difference between quarterdeck and engine room increased with demand for specialisation and technical knowledge. As of 1902, however, Fisher stood against the diehards.

Reconstructing the War Office: the Esher Committee and Portsmouth

In September 1903 Fisher was sent to Portsmouth as Commander-in-Chief to make sure that the 'Osborne scheme' for entry and training of officers should not suffer any interference from a less co-operative C-in-C. Probably he requested this appointment, as a relief from the pressures of Whitehall and the Admiralty. It was, in any case, an important command, for it signified how the future officers of the Senior Service would be trained and educated. By his presence, Fisher could ward off the old guard, who were habituated to traditional ways of cadet entry and officer training. At Portsmouth, Fisher's essential job was as guardian, or defender, of policies already adopted by politcal masters. All eyes were upon him.

Fisher liked to entertain, and the history-laden facilities at HM Naval Dockyard Portsmouth favoured his intentions. He flew his flag in the famed *Victory*, Nelson's flagship at Trafalgar, and the ship Fisher had first been assigned to. King Edward VII was entertained at Portsmouth on occasion. He deplored the submarine shown to him by Jacky, fearing he could never get out of it. (Portly fellow that he was, he had reason for concern.) On another occasion, Rudyard Kipling, bard of empire, accepted Fisher's invitation 'to go down in a submarine'. Kipling had the same rooms ashore that had been reserved for the monarch, and he liked that. As to Fisher's motives for bringing the bard down from his residence, Bateman's, Kipling could see through it all: 'Jacky has taken an ungodly shine to me for ulterior purposes I imagine but he's a good man.'[120]

These were expansive and restorative days for Fisher in Portsmouth, near the great ships, the gunnery and torpedo establishments, and the comings and goings of the Fleet – and with the breath of fresh sea air in his nostrils. Truth to tell, Fisher's presence at the Admiralty as Second Sea Lord had hardly been conducive to harmony. No one likes a revolutionary in their midst unless they are on side with the intentions of the leader. Thus, when he departed for Portsmouth, sighs of relief went up in certain offices. The Director of Naval Ordnance, Angus MacLeod, told a friend that he too was glad to be out of the Admiralty 'with all its scheming'. But many of Fisher's associates remained in place, and Fisher's force continued to radiate through the corridors. The First Sea Lord, Lord Walter Kerr, now muted in influence by the power of Lord Selborne, the First Lord, seemed helpless, as if he was marking time. So even in his absence from London, Fisher was practically running the Admiralty through the Director of Naval Intelligence (Battenberg) and Captain Hugh Tyrwhitt, who served as Private Secretary to Lord Selborne.

From time to time Fisher was back in London. In his lifetime, though an agreeable and vocal personality, Fisher gave only four public speeches. He preferred to make his pronouncements through the press, using his carefully cultivated editors and his naval writer associates to articulate his points of view. On 2 May 1903, however, he had occasion to give a reply to a toast 'to Imperial Forces' at the Royal Academy Banquet, London. Present were the Prince of Wales (the future George V) and St John Brodrick, Secretary of State for War. Fisher stated: 'On the British Navy rests the British Empire. Nothing else is any use without it, not even the Army. We are different from Continental Nations. No soldier of ours can go anywhere unless a sailor carries him there on his back. I am not disparaging the Army. I am looking forward to their coming to sea with us as they did in the old days ... I think I may say that we now have a Board of Admiralty that is united, progressive, and determined, and you may sleep quietly in your beds.'[121] These words were stirring enough, and they are memorable in another sense, for laughter had followed the cheers, when, in emphasising his point with a wave of the arm, he swept a glass of port into the immaculate front of Broderick, who was sitting next to him.

At the time, War Office reform was on the lips of the politicians, not least because of the Army's poor performance during the South African War. But how was reform to be effected against such a well-entrenched institution of the British state, one with its own strong and independent sense of itself? The Conservatives decided that it was time for review and reform, and while Fisher was at Portsmouth, Balfour appointed him to the War Office Reconstruction Committee. This placed Fisher in almost daily connection again with Reginald Brett, 2nd Viscount Esher, who chaired the committee (which soon came to be known as the Esher Committee) and who had an abiding interest in military reorganisation. Esher was a man-about-government, as it were, and he had much to do with choosing who should sit on the committee that would carry out the necessary changes in the War Office. At one time Esher suggested that just he and Fisher should be allowed to do the work, but Balfour vetoed this suggestion. One suspects it was on grounds of his mistrust of Fisher.[122]

Fisher and Esher had known one another for a decade, and on first meeting had taken to one another. They had much in common in ways of work and in reforming ambitions. And they had the same sort of mind, recalled one who knew them both well: 'Both had the early Italian type of mind. Both preferred to come in at the back door instead of the front,' remarked Sir Frederick Ponsonby, who mused at how well they got on with one another. 'There was something tortuous about both of them, but while Fisher loved a fight and was prepared to stand or fall by his measures, Esher was very susceptible to public opinion and shrank from any responsibility. I always think that Esher's strong point was that he never minded who got credit for any measure he devised so long as it was adopted by the authorities.'[123]

Fisher had come under pressure from the Admiralty, in particular from Prince Louis of Battenberg, not to serve on the committee. He brushed this aside. At the same time, Fisher, always wiggling for elbow room, had serious objections to serving with General Brackenbury,[124] so another general, Grenfell, in England commanding the 4th Army Corps, was suggested. When he proved unsuitable, Sir George Clarke, at that point in distant Australia as Governor of Victoria, was appointed. As Clarke was 12,000 miles away, Esher noted that he and Fisher would begin the work and Clarke would have to catch up when he returned to England.[125] Fisher and Esher became even faster friends, partners in their good and compelling work of reform. They played on one another's sympathies. Clarke, when he joined them, was the odd man out. A rough fellow who had the capacity to fall out with everyone sooner or later, Clarke was also one of the sharpest minds of the day on defence matters, and he later played a powerful role in imperial defence review. He shared Esher's and Fisher's views of implementing the 'blue water' school, cutting back Army waste, and reorganising the War Office along the lines of Army–Navy co-operation. However, he thought Fisher's scrapping of gunboats and closures of squadrons and bases had gone too far; he thought *Dreadnought* was a disaster of policy; and he accused Fisher of running a one-man show. He was, too, a strong critic of how Churchill liked to write, and rewrite, history. But these matters lay in the future. For the present the committee got down to the hard, even thankless, task of reforming the War Office. Fisher's sweeping reforms at the Admiralty had been undertaken with comparative ease. Within the Army, however, resistance to change was strong. In letters to Esher, Fisher advocated a full 'root and branch' reform of the War Office, noting that 'the British public loves a root and branch reform. One remnant left of the old gang or the organisations and you taint the whole new scheme!'[126] Fisher could not bring about these reforms by himself, and he never contended that he could do so. With Esher in support, a revolution in Army affairs could be effected.

Fisher's main contribution to the Esher Committee was his consistent advocacy of navalisation, and his insistence that the problem was not with home defence, as the Navy could handle that, but with foreign defence. He argued that the regular Army was a 'projectile to be fired by the Navy'.[127] But many did not share Fisher's view that the Army ought to be kept small, a sort of corporal's guard looking after the affairs of the home island. What would happen, Ponsonby asked Fisher on one occasion, if the enemy made a successful landing on British shores and held the nation hostage? Here was 'the invasion bogey' raised yet again. Fisher's answer always lay in 'blue water' policy: the Navy would provide the security of the kingdom, free from invasion.

The credit for most of the great changes effected by the committee belonged to Esher, who contributed to the development of the CID, and to Lieutenant-Colonel G F Ellison, secretary to the committee, who dealt with the Army's staff organisation. Clarke concentrated on financial aspects. Among the consequences of the Esher Committee was the abolition of the post of Commander-in-Chief, the creation of the posts of Chief of the General Staff and Director of Military Operations, and the creation of a General Staff. It is interesting to note that while Fisher advocated a General Staff for the War Office, he did not implement the same for the Admiralty.[128] Fisher also emphasised that the formation of the Army Council did not mean a lessening of the parliamentary responsibility of the Secretary of State for War, as he remained in the exact same position as the First Lord of the Admiralty.[129] And so the reform of the War Office was completed. Afterwards, Major-General Douglas Haig wrote to Esher that he never thought such a reorganisation could take place without a prior military disaster.[130]

In January 1904 Fisher sent Esher four names as recommendations for the posts on the new Army Council. He did so with customary bravado, even threatening resignation from the committee over the possibility that 'old grey hairs' in the Army were going to continue in authority. In his view, 'new measures require new men'. In particular, Fisher objected to the sharp-tongued General Sir William Nicholson ('Old Nick', Fisher called him), a person 'so hateful to the Admiralty and such a thorough cad' that Admirals Kerr and Battenberg had declined to work further with him. Finally: 'Over every fellow's door at the War Office under the new regime has got to be written in large letters: "No looking back. Remember Lot's wife."'[131] On the 22nd, Fisher sent a telegram to Esher that Arnold-Forster had written to say that the four names had been 'cordially accepted', and he would settle them the next day at Windsor with the King. Fisher wrote in florid fashion: 'I heartily congratulate you as a skilful pilot on our prosperous passage between the Scylla of sentiment and the Charybdis of pessimists.'[132]

On 11 January 1904 the first part of the Esher Report was published, with a recommendation to strengthen the existing CID. The second part detailed the establishment of a General Staff, and the third stressed the duties of both agencies to anticipate contingencies that could arise in the field of military policy.[133] The most important consequence of the acceptance of the Esher report was the formalisation of the CID. It was a consultative body only, but with Balfour as its guiding genius started work on matters that the heads of the Army and the Navy concerned themselves with: fortifications abroad, coaling stations, submarine cables, and colonial and imperial defence. This was defence by committee, a necessary preliminary to greater co-operation in the urgent times of peace leading to war in 1914. One close observer of events, Lieutenant-Colonel Charles à Court Repington, military correspondent of *The Times*, recalled that real reform at the War Office had been needed and that the reforms undertaken after the Esher Committee stood Britain in good stead and had actually been along German lines with respect to the General Staff: 'The Esher Committee made an end of the Commander-in-Chief and the old dominance of the Adjutant-General. They framed Army Council on Admiralty lines, going beyond the Board of Admiralty model, and clothing the Admiralty skeleton with flesh and blood. The change was made with scant courtesy and consideration.'[134] Jacky Fisher's hand in these matters was clearly visible. 'Look out, here comes Jack' was now the new watchword in Whitehall.

From 19–22 February 1904, Edward VII paid a visit to Admiralty House, Portsmouth, where he was the guest of the admiral. It was a long visit, and during it Fisher got to know the King well. More and more King Edward relied on Fisher in naval matters; moreover, he enjoyed the fun and frolic Fisher often brought to otherwise stiff occasions. Fisher's biographer, Captain Bacon, recounted that on one occasion 'the King suddenly called to Fisher across the table: "Admiral, Lady – says that you sailors have a wife in every port." Without an instant's pause, Fisher rapped out: "Wouldn't you have liked to have been a sailor, sir?" For just a moment a severe look came over the King's face, and then he burst out into a genuine hearty laugh.'[135] Fisher noted in *Records* that he had 'never more enjoyed such a visit', even if it meant that he was no longer master in his own house. Lord Knollys, Edward VII's private secretary, subsequently wrote to Fisher about the royal visit:

I am desired by the King to write and thank you again for your hospitality. His Majesty also desires me to express his great appreciation of all the arrangements, which were excellent, and they reflect the greatest credit both on you and on those who worked under your orders.

I am very glad the visit was such a great success and went off so well. The King was evidently extremely pleased with and interested in everything.[136]

Thus commenced Fisher's long correspondence with Knollys and the King. Edward VII called Fisher's letters 'effusions!'[137] Perhaps Fisher bored the King with his stream of ideas about the betterment of the Navy. His Majesty may have suffered from fatigue. Fisher once commented to Esher that although the King was attentive and appeared to be supportive of the cause of reform, 'He can't grasp details', and it was difficult to make a lasting impression.[138] But the friendship was enduring, and reassuring to Fisher.

The King did not share Fisher's enthusiasms but he raised no opposition. In circumstances of growing social intimacy, and in later years between spells as First Sea Lord, Fisher spent summers at Karlsbad 'drinking the waters'. In these regular excursions to Bohemia he was often in the presence of Edward VII. The King would come over to Karlsbad, a sort of anteroom to the royal apartments at Marienbad, to visit friends and associates. Fisher was then seeing a great deal of the Grand Duchess Olga Alexandrovna, the Tsar's sister. The King had arranged this attachment. Fisher, a great dancer, taught her to waltz at the Savoy Hotel. Despite, or perhaps because of his strange facial appearance, women found him irresistible. According to the correspondent of a prominent Vienna newspaper, Dr Sigmund Munz, whose reporter's beat concentrated heavily on the goings on in Karlsbad and Marienbad, Fisher also instructed the Russian minister, Count Isvolsky, in Germanophobia. Isvolsky is the man credited with forging the Russian alliance with Britain. However, he was not to be taken in by Fisher. There, too, Fisher got to know the Russian ambassador in London, Count Benckendorff. The statesman Clemenceau of France would join them from time to time. It is tempting to think that the Great War was instigated in these places of 'taking the waters', but this is not so. As the Viennese correspondent suggests, there was but one member of the group who would have preferred to strike immediately rather than await the course of events, and that was Fisher, 'physically and morally of the rough-hewn type, his irrepressible vigour and vitality shining from a clean-shaven Malay face which, to his amusement, had given rise to the legend that his mother was a Cingalese Princess. I had many talks with him and should have been inclined to class him as a genuine wit had it not been for a certain occasional uncouthness unusual in distinguished Englishmen.'[139]

Fisher liked to preach the preventive war. His statements, amounting to harangues, exhibited Old Testament fervour. Some thought he had a touch of Machiavelli in his nature, and one of his aphorisms was '"Tact" is insulting a man without his knowing it.' The observant Munz records that Fisher once told him that he had wanted to become a missionary but decided it would be better to be First Sea Lord. Fisher liked Nelsonic tendencies – resourcefulness, self-reliance, the taking of initiative, and the fearlessness of responsibility. Many statements indicated his belligerent disposition, none better than his venomous phrase 'to Copenhagen the German fleet à la Nelson'.[140] 'Think in oceans – shoot at sight' was a familiar, striking utterance, vintage Fisher.

To this point in Fisher's career, all pointed to his own high intellectual attainments and his devotion to his profession. In advance of most of his fellow officers approaching flag rank, he seemed devoted to technical advancements, though not a technocrat himself. He moved at the edges of the naval revolution in gunnery, armour, and propulsion, and his knowledge of guns, explosives, mines, and torpedoes had won him recognition, if not acclaim. He was developing a knowledge of underwater warfare, something rather rare in a service largely devoted to surface warfare. He was intellectually above average, with a strong sense of inquiry, particularly if he could get the assistance of others who knew more than he did in technical matters. He took an interest in 'the private sector', those industrialists and engineers developing fast engines, big guns, and strong hulls. He exhibited a strong drive coupled with powers of persuasion, unique in his profession. That, alone, set him apart from his contemporaries, and it made him attractive to his superiors. He cultivated and entertained those who mattered, whether they were in the Navy or in politics or in the press. He was devoted to his own advancement, as, we note, was Churchill. Fisher was determined to make the most of himself, and it may be suggested that this was owing to his insecurities exhibited as a youngster and the heady competition that he faced when he made his entry into the Navy. His preoccupation with religious matters was an additional factor, though of indirect value but nonetheless important in his growing self-assuredness with the right of conviction at his side. In a sense this was a messianic disposition, and in an age of high evangelism and Christian dispositions, he was not then regarded as the unusual fellow in this line that he is in our own times. He courted royalty and did so successfully, and it was the events at Alexandria that brought him into prominence. His contemporaries in the Service were bound to watch him with some admiration but with growing concern at his self-assertive ways. There was little room in the Navy for a man 'on the make'. He was to prove them wrong, but with unavoidable consequences for his actions.

2

Fisher's Reforms

Fisher arrives at the Admiralty

When Fisher went to Portsmouth as Commander-in-Chief in 1902, he knew he would return to the Admiralty as First Sea Lord. Prime Minister Balfour and First Lord of the Admiralty Selborne had said so. As of early 1904, the name of Sir John Fisher was on everyone's lips as likely to succeed Admiral Lord Walter Kerr as First Sea Lord. To date all his postings favoured the grand prize, and with it the greatest of professional obligations that could face a British sailor in administration. He had commanded the North America and West Indies station; was conversant with the United States Navy; had been in charge of the top command, the Mediterranean; had been British naval delegate to The Hague conference; been Second Sea Lord; and had served the bulk of his career in administration and policy-making. His knowledge of gunnery, mines, torpedoes, propulsion systems, and shipbuilding marked him out as a leader in these fields. He had not confined himself to professional matters only; in fact, he was a wild publicist of his views and concepts – and was an ardent expansionist in the material lines of naval power and influence. He was seen as the prospective great provider of the materiel of the Navy. Through these posts, he was already well placed to gain extraordinary contacts with leading statesmen, the press, and, perhaps most importantly, the King. He had never lost an opportunity to champion the fact that the security of the British Empire rested with the Royal Navy. This was an undeniable fact. At the turn of the century the monarch still had a great deal to say about military and naval appointments. As Esher wrote, Fisher could count on the support of the King regardless of the pending elections of 1905: 'Remember, not more than a dozen people in England count for anything (a large estimate) and you happen to be one of them.'[1] Apart from Lord Charles Beresford, he was the best-known naval personality in the land.

Esher had wanted Fisher to write an early document setting out his intended great and sweeping naval reforms. Fisher had other ideas. As he told his courtier-confidant on 28 July 1904:

Selborne has been trying to draw me but I have steadfastly declined to say a word or write a line before I am installed on Trafalgar Day! *One exception*! I drew up a scheme for the re-organization of the Admiralty. He has swallowed it whole & got the vote in Council for it! *The new scheme gives me nothing to do*! It also resuscitates the old titles of *Sea Lords* dating from A.D. 1613 but which some silly ass 100 years ago altered to *Naval Lords*. *Don't say a word of all this*! As Evan Macgregor [Secretary of the Admiralty] says Selborne is most anxious it should appear as *his own scheme*!'[2]

Fisher likened Selborne to alternating electrical current – 'of cordiality and jealousy' – and on Selborne's visit to Portsmouth claimed, 'I shook my fist in his face for 2¼ hours without a check!'[3]

Much of this was pure Fisher bravado, for without Selborne's guidance and backing, Fisher would have failed to undertake the big and fundamental reforms that are generally credited to him. Professional heads of the Navy, and all Lords of the Admiralty, as much as they might like to think of themselves as independent of the state, in all real measures depended on political support, principally in the Cabinet, in Parliament, and, to an uncommon degree, in the press. As so often was the case, Fisher took upon himself the armour of the great single-minded reformer. Perhaps the age encouraged this sort of superman image, this 'the Navy is safe in Jack's hands' mentality. It is far better to view Selborne as the man who opened the gates for Fisher. As for Fisher, he was never one to give credit where credit was due, instead drawing unto himself the glory of being Britannia's champion and saviour.

The decision-makers knew the quality of the man they were about to place in the supreme assignment. They encouraged his reforms; they welcomed their appearance. The Conservatives, or Unionists, wanted the modernisation of the Navy. They saw in Fisher their man, their instrument. Of that there can be no doubt. What caused concern were Fisher's volcanic nature and his suspicious character. He feared enemies, real or imagined. Thus, according to Esher, Fisher 'fusses because he thinks he will have fights with Selborne, and he wishes for the advent of a new Government.'[4] However, within a few weeks Fisher was saying that the backing of Selborne seemed certain. Esher wrote reassuringly: 'You have captured the first position, and of course you will win all along the line.'[5] Similarly, in a letter from the Prince of Wales, the future George V, who was always lukewarm to Fisher: 'You must be relieved that he [Selborne] has taken it like a lamb, if you have him on yr side it will be all right.'[6]

Fisher need not have feared Selborne, for the latter was fully on side with regards to the impending great and sweeping reforms. Yet Fisher seemed to hesitate, unsure of the politicians' backing at the critical hour. Did he keep Selborne in the dark? The First Lord was apparently not fully conversant with

Fisher's complete programme of reform, and Esher assured Fisher that Selborne did not require details of the programme until 19 October. Balfour seemed satisfied. So what was the problem? Esher further derided Fisher's view that Selborne was of obstinate character and average abilities. 'You will probably find him potter's clay. In fact, you have had experiences of this already.'[7] However, Esher wrote at the end of September that it was possible that Selborne might be appointed to a post in India, meaning that Fisher might find the going even harder under a new First Lord.[8] Selborne was to leave in good time, and he went to South Africa, as High Commissioner. In point of fact, Fisher had misjudged Selborne. Had a less progressive force been First Lord at that time, Fisher's demanding agenda might have been stalled. Fisher's misjudging of Selborne we might regard as symptomatic of the Fisher point of view in regards to any who might stand in his way or otherwise upset his plans. He loved to tilt at windmills. He loved to contrive the dramatic effect.

As to future plans, Fisher put it this way to the King's secretary, Lord Knollys: 'Vast changes are indispensable for fighting efficiency and for instant readiness for war. We have neither at present! And we have got to be ruthless, relentless and remorseless in our reforms!' and 'I hope to reduce the Navy Estimates by many millions with an increase of 30 per cent in fighting strength and instant readiness for war, but it will be a FIERCE fight! And I may "go under", but I think NOT!'[9] He wrote to R B Haldane, Minister of War: 'Even the King and both Houses of Parliament are powerless to work any great reform in the Navy! ... The First Sea Lord is the only man in creation who can effect the reduction of the income tax to three pence in the pound!'[10] And Fisher again: 'My sole object is PEACE in doing all this! Because if you "rub it in" both at home and abroad that you are ready for instant war with every unit of your strength in the first line, and intend to be "first in" and hit your enemy in the belly and kick him when he's down and boil your prisoners in oil (if you take any) and torture his women and children, then people will keep clear of you.'[11]

On 13 and 14 May 1904, Selborne travelled to Portsmouth to extend the formal invitation to Fisher to become First Sea Lord. Fisher accepted on the 16th.[12] The great future lay before him, and the ultimate challenges. No naval administrator of the first rank had faced such challenges, and at such a critical hour. He had the weight of British naval pre-eminence on his shoulders. He faced the most formidable challenge that Britain and the British Empire had been presented with up to that time. There was not a moment to lose.

Fisher took up his appointment on 20 October. He always claimed he arrived at the Admiralty on Trafalgar Day, 21 October. In fact, his eagerness got him there on the eve of the anniversary of that great victory. A delightful cartoon of the day, published in the *Daily Express*, shows Fisher approaching the Nelson monument in Trafalgar Square. Nelson is seen clambering back onto his column at the sight of Fisher entering the Admiralty. The caption reads: 'I was on my way down to lend them a hand myself, but if Jacky Fisher's taking on the job there's no need for me to be nervous, I'll get back on my pedestal.'[13] A French commentator noted that Britannia was safe in Fisher's hands: 'The naval power of Great Britain to-day does not reside solely in the number of crews and of her ships: the British Nation possesses the inestimable virtue of believing, with an intimate and profound conviction, that in trusting to Admiral Fisher she has nothing to fear as regards her destiny.'[14]

With the glittering appointment came a London residence, 16 Queen Anne's Gate, SW1. It was a short walk to the Admiralty Building and equally close to Westminster Abbey. The house had been occupied in the late eighteenth century by William Smith, pioneer of religious liberty, and nowadays is home to the Museums and Galleries Commission. Nearly opposite stood the residence of the Foreign Secretary, Sir Edward Grey, and a few doors away that of Haldane, the Minister of War. It is not far from the Two Chairmen public house, and an easy walk to St James's Park or to all the great ministries of state and the Houses of Parliament. Here Sir John and Lady Fisher could entertain as they wished, and when it suited Jacky to be on neutral ground, so to speak, he could venture across St James's Park, up the Duke of York Stairs, and be at his preferred retreat, the handsome club, the Athenaeum: stiff with literary, scientific, and medical personages and many a bishop. A Service club membership would only have brought him quarrels about the Navy and the Services, but companionship with statesmen and bishops was altogether more pleasant. Not far away, too, was St James's Square, where the Duke and Duchess of Hamilton had a grand house at No. 19, important in later days for our story.

The sole difficulty that Fisher had in accepting the proffered post of First Sea Lord was financial. As C-in-C, Portsmouth, he earned £4,000 per year; at the Admiralty he would get only £2,400. The burgeoning engineering and shipbuilding firm Armstrong, Whitworth of Elswick, Newcastle upon Tyne, wanted him as a director so as to facilitate naval contracts. This would have paid £20,000 annually and was alluring, but Fisher wanted the power of naval office. Having to run his affairs solely on his official income, Fisher desired an extra £800 to supplement his income, arguing that he needed the funds to entertain fellow officers. This being refused, on 21 October 1904 he was made First and Principal Naval Aide-de-Camp (ADC) to the King, an appointment that not only provided him with an extra £365 a year but also secured for him privilege of personal access to the monarch, Edward VII, who became his great friend. Fisher remained bitter at the government's parsimonious treatment: 'Behold! This is the house of my friends ... The Prime Minister, the Chancellor of the Exchequer and the First Lord of the Admiralty all swearing eternal friendship to me and see me d—d before they give me a shilling! And bring me up from the plum of the service at Portsmouth to penal servitude at the Admiralty to suit their convenience!'[15] These fulminations, full of wild exaggerations (for at root Fisher was a patriot above all else), were typical of the man as portrayed in his private correspondence with friends, in this case Lord Esher.

Fisher may have barked about the money, but it was the political connection with the King that was the key matter. Selborne had arranged Fisher's appointment as ADC, but Fisher, who desperately needed the royal ear, had doubtless prodded him. From the moment he became ADC, Fisher's influence on the King in all matters naval was paramount. That connection was not without difficulties, and in one noteworthy case Edward VII charged Fisher with keeping back essential information, with the terrible result, as the monarch saw it, of allowing British naval preparations in dreadnoughts to fall behind those of rival Germany. But the nimble Fisher weathered that storm, and his explanations were accepted.[16] The King's love of his own Navy and his own ships meant that Fisher had to accept the managerial role; indeed, during most of this period Fisher bowed to only one authority other than Parliament, and that was the King, his friend. As a sounding board, Fisher was blessed with Esher, himself a court favourite and conversant with state affairs. As Lieutenant and Deputy Governor of Windsor Castle since 1901, Esher also had direct access to the sovereign.

Edward VII relished Fisher's friendship and company, and approved of his collaboration in making the Navy stronger and the Empire more secure. The King battled against Fisher's enemies. And he made sure Fisher got to meet the important people of the age. So, for example, it was at Biarritz, a small French town on the Bay of Biscay, that Fisher met Churchill for the first time, in April 1907.[17] Perhaps the King could imagine a beneficial partnership that might develop from this preliminary encounter. There were also trying times. Many were the vexatious moments between Edward VII and the headstrong Fisher. Fisher enjoyed the royal association, and a lovely anecdote is told of their relationship and how Fisher rejoiced at being in the presence of His Majesty. The story goes that on one occasion the King, accompanied by his naval ADC, was driving in the royal carriage in London. The crowd was uproarious in support. The King gave the royal wave by way of appreciation to his humble subjects. Fisher could not resist. He also waved to the crowd. 'Don't wave at the people,' Edward VII scolded, 'they are my subjects not yours.' Another account has Fisher standing up and waving his umbrella at a lady he knew. Such antics by Fisher were bound to make the King angry with him. When King Edward VII died on 6 May 1910, in his sixty-ninth year, he left the admiral without his most influential friend. One of the most poignant photos of Jacky Fisher shows him walking behind the casket of the late sovereign in the funeral procession: between them, these two men had largely rearranged the diplomatic, imperial, and naval world. Fisher proclaimed, 'He had the Heavenly gift of Proportion of Perspective!' 'He was a noble man and every inch a King!' 'He conquered all hearts and annihilated all envy.' He had unfailing intuition in doing the right thing at the right time, thought Fisher, and saying the right thing at the right time.[18]

Shaking up administration and education

Prior to Fisher's earthquakes, the previous major reform of the structure of the Board of Admiralty had occurred under George Goschen's tenure as First Lord of the Admiralty in 1872. The supremacy of the First Lord was recognised, as was the principle that members of the Board were individually responsible to the First Lord while at the same time having the collective right, as the full Board, to render advice to the First Lord. It is questionable on constitutional grounds whether the First Sea Lord was first among equals; however, Fisher's domineering instincts, combined with his behind-the-scenes activities, established him as *primus inter pares*. This enhanced authority derived from his personality, not his office. The role of First Sea Lord included serving as the principal adviser to the First Lord, as well as being in charge of operations. The First Sea Lord could also recommend appointments and thus influence the patronage capabilities of the Admiralty. The First Lord, on the other hand, shouldered responsibility in the Cabinet and Parliament for the Navy's fighting effectiveness and its deployment.

Of the reforms that Fisher launched upon coming to the Admiralty, it should be remembered that he did not unleash them alone. Nor were they a piecemeal effort. 'I told Lord Selborne and Lord Knollys that all these reforms were based on years of careful consideration and discussion with the best brains of the Service,' he wrote to Lord Tweedmouth, First Lord from 1905 to 1908, in 1906, adding, in reference to the reforms of the previous two years, 'EVERY SINGLE ITEM IS PART OF ONE HARMONIOUS WHOLE!'[19]

His weapon was economy, more for less. The national political climate had changed between the time Fisher became Second Sea Lord, mainly in charge of personnel and training and education, and his appointment as First Sea Lord two years later. The Liberals, though in opposition, were resurgent, and economy in naval and military matters was the order of the day. The Conservatives faced rising naval estimates each year, and controlling these became the absolute requirement in order to retain public support (which was already sinking fast). When Selborne invited Fisher to become First Sea Lord, he had attached to his invitation this chilling memorandum: 'It is quite certain that the Navy Estimates have for the present reached their maximum ... In 1905–1906 not only can there be no possible increase, but it is necessary, for the influence of the Admiralty over the House of Commons and for the stability of national finances, that we should have a substantial decrease.'[20]

The engine behind the Fisher reforms was his ability, for the present year at least, to secure significant savings from the upward-spiralling naval estimates.[21] When in action, Fisher was not a conventional senior admiral, forever seeking more money for the Navy so as to uphold its supremacy. But Fisher also recognised the limits on naval spending:

> Why did we prior to 1905 spend five million sterling annually in excess of the fighting requirements of the Navy? ... Answer. – Because it is indelibly imprinted in the average, stupid, unthinking mind, just as it is imprinted in that of the average out-of-date retired Admiral and in the 'stupid party' in the Navy League, that fighting efficiency is inalienably associated with big estimates! The exact opposite is the real truth! Parasites in the shape of non-fighting ships, non-combatant personnel and unproductive shore expenditure must be extirpated like cancer – cut clean out![22]

The Report of the Estimates Committee of 26 November 1904 bore out Fisher's aim, as it reported that the navy estimates had been reduced by £4,362,100.[23] For the moment Fisher had fulfilled the mission entrusted to him.

Two years later, Fisher argued that the Admiralty should not be responsible for maintaining the Coast Guard and the Royal Observatory Greenwich, both then under Admiralty control. Technological advances had rendered obsolete the Coast Guard's role in detecting unfriendly vessels in home waters, and while its role in enforcing custom duties and lifesaving was crucial, it was not, according to Fisher, something the Admiralty should be paying for, especially when it diverted Admiralty funds from more important uses.[24] He did not get his way.

Fisher thought that the Navy no longer benefited from the Observatory's technological advances as it once did. And why should the Navy pay for it, when the merchant marine, the railways, the post office, and even the water companies all relied on the work of the Observatory? Fisher pointed to this case to illustrate that those who criticised the naval estimates, and blamed the size of them four-square on the Admiralty, often did not closely examine the estimates to see just what expenses the Navy was responsible for.[25]

Fisher campaigned for a reduction in army estimates as well. He advised Esher on 17 June 1904 that the army estimates needed to be reduced to £23 million, 'and unless some such figure can be arrived at for the Army, I do not think the British Public will face the reduction in the Navy Estimates *which I see to be possible with the increased efficiency*; because they will rightly argue that the Navy is the 1st, 2nd, 3rd, 4th, *ad infinitum* line of defence, and it is simply monstrous therefore that the bloated Army should starve the essential

Navy ... That N.W. Frontier of India is the bug-bear which has possessed the whole lot of our present rulers.'[26]

With this attitude toward expenditure and the naval lobby and press, it was no wonder that Fisher was bound for stormy seas. Enormous pride had been built into the Royal Navy of the late Victorian period as it gave Britain global pre-eminence at sea. Fisher was early in recognising that such primacy – 'showing the flag' – was unsustainable in the long run. He had no use for Pax Britannica. The concept seemed irrelevant, and he had seen its abuses in the Navy, which he recognised was an instrument of national policy, not an imperial yacht club: 'The time will come when the majority of the voters – our Masters – will say "you can agree upon nothing: you are never satisfied, however much you spend you are always discovering new dangers; we prefer to accept risks rather than fling more money into the pit which – on your own showing – is bottomless."'[27]

In contrast to the rising expenses, the growth of the Fleet had not been accompanied by a growth in bureaucracy, leading to over-centralisation of control and information.[28] From the outset, what Fisher wanted in the way of a naval staff was inextricably intertwined with a naval war college. The Royal Naval College, Greenwich, had been established in 1873, but Fisher wanted something else. Thus, while in the Mediterranean, Fisher had written to Selborne on the issue of a naval staff:

> We want the Naval War College *very*, *very* badly, and we want a Naval Von Moltke [Helmuth von Moltke, chief of staff of the Prussian Army in the mid-1800s, is credited with modernising the direction of armies in the field] at the head of it. I hope it is not trespassing too much on your time to glance at (A) in the enclosed print: 'To expect that any one man can devote his attention equally to matters so essentially different as the practical details of peace administration and the theoretical development of war policy and war preparations is described by the eminent German writer (General Bronsart von Schellendorf, late Minister of War in Germany) as nothing less than a terrible mistake "if only for the reason that it would be impossible that a man would be found who was equally master of the art of military administration and of handling armies",' etc. *This applies with tenfold force to the Navy!* An inept General has been saved by his Staff. An Admiral has no Staff to save him![29]

On 25 February 1902 Fisher had sent Selborne his memorandum 'On the Increasing Necessity for a General Staff for the Navy to Meet War Requirements'. In it he argued that the needs of the Navy required a bigger and better administration, and fighting admirals needed to be thinking admirals and have a better tactical and strategic understanding. As indicated above, he thought there should be a General Staff like the great German General Staff, and he offered details, such as the instruction of torpedo experts and the selection of flag captains and signalling and communications specialists. A member of the Board of Admiralty 'must direct this Brain Power of the Navy'. The Navy needed a Moltke who would give his mind and time to the task, who 'must be unfettered and untrammelled by any administrative & executive functions whatever', and who should not be a subordinate but rather a member of the Board. Finally: 'It is positively alarming that we should be dependent for victory on the idiosyncrasy of an Admiral.'[30] That same day, Prince Louis Battenberg, commanding the battleship *Implacable* in the Mediterranean, and a rising officer in Fisher's estimation in consequence of his squadron-handling abilities, sent Fisher a memorandum along the same lines.[31]

Again Fisher did not get his way: his concept of a naval staff was but a will-o'-the-wisp – without serious intent. Although the Royal Naval War College came into existence in Portsmouth in 1906, it did not resemble a naval staff. Rather, it provided a place for the making of plans (or scenarios) for a future war and advanced understanding of torpedo warfare. It was thus a thinking establishment, as well as a professional training establishment, and mirrored what Fisher had done during his time in the Mediterranean command, when he liked to get officers under him to write and converse about strategical and tactical matters; this was continued at Portsmouth. Truth to tell, his essential idea of naval strategy was to keep the war plans bottled up in his own head. Paradoxically, he could write flippantly on this matter, and could be dismissive of a naval staff system. As he wrote, 'a Naval War Staff is an excellent organisation for cutting out and arranging foreign newspaper clippings.'[32] In military colleges to this day, a portrait of Fisher can often be found on notice boards or office doors with this sardonic caption beneath the bright visage of old Fisher and all his glittering medals: 'So far as the Navy is concerned, the tendency of these "Thinking Establishments" on shore is to convert splendid Sea Officers into very indifferent clerks.'[33]

Sir Julian Corbett, prominent historian, student of British maritime strategy, and commentator on strategic questions, was critical of the study of strategy in the Navy 'as revealed by the amateurish rubbish that appeared in official Admiralty papers'. He knew how much opposition existed in the Service to theoretical study of naval matters. He had Fisher's ear, and used the Service's opposition to the study of strategy to edge Fisher further in support of Captain Edmond Slade's work at the Royal Naval War College at Greenwich (it had been moved there from Portsmouth): 'It is your supposed neglect of what you are now devoting yourself to that is their strongest line of attack,' he warned Fisher.[34]

At this time, Corbett, well-known authority on Drake and the Tudor navy, and an exponent of combined operations (that is, the necessity of army and navy working together to sustain the interests of the state), was preparing his lectures for Greenwich, eventually published as *Some Principles of Maritime Strategy* (1911). As an aside, Corbett's book influenced the historically minded Churchill. Most statesmen and political figures, as well as those persons who ought to be interested in history as a guide to the present, ignored the subject at their peril. Lord Esher, writing to Colonel Maurice Hankey at the Committee of Imperial Defence some years later (just as the Dardanelles campaign was meeting its greatest crisis) observed that only Churchill seemed interested in the past and its lessons: 'Why, my dear Hankey, do we worry about history? Julian Corbett writes one of the best books in our language upon political and military strategy. All sorts of lessons, some of inestimable value, may be gleaned from it. No one, except Winston, who matters just now, has ever read it ... Obviously history is written for schoolmasters and armchair strategists. Statesmen and warriors pick their way through the dusk.'[35]

Corbett differed mightily from the American admiral and naval writer Alfred Thayer Mahan, for the latter believed in the concentration of force and decisive battle at sea. Corbett advanced the argument that control in 'theatres of war' or 'theatres of operations' sufficed for the limited objectives in waging war leading to victory. Indeed, he was the originator of the idea of 'limited warfare'. To some degree, this idea perfectly matched Fisher's idea of, say, a Baltic project, though Fisher also clung to the Mahanian view of a decisive battle, which he saw would develop in the North Sea. Some years later Corbett admitted that his leading theme was 'the deflection of strategy by politics'. Here it may be mentioned that Slade, a rising star in in both Admiralty intelligence-gathering and Navy education reform, stood close to Fisher and shared Corbett's interest in combined operations. He had Fisher's full support in extending the work of the War Course and, in consequence, had Corbett's support as well. Slade was conscious of the fact that he was not to teach forty or fifty naval officers 'their work', for that would have been presumptuous. Rather, he was to assist the First Sea Lord 'by establishing a board [or corps] of officers whose function it is to thrash out systematically all sorts of war problems, quite independently, and unhampered by the routine of an Admiralty department.'[36] Here is evidence of the development of Fisher's 'brains trust'.

Rather than a naval staff, Fisher had a 'brains trust'.[37] He liked to gather officers and civilian advisers, such as Corbett, into his confidence. He deplored bureaucracies. But there was more to it than that: he needed to maintain secrecy about what he imagined to be the next war at sea. After 1906 he did not want his plans slipping into the hands of Admiral Lord Charles Beresford and the 'Syndicate of Discontent' (see Chapter 3). Beresford could not keep secrets and made all sorts of ill-advised pronouncements in the drawing rooms of the nation. Fisher was good at developing a 'brains trust', but the processes and the results were often contradictory or ill defined. As we will see, Churchill was appointed to the Admiralty to institute a naval staff, but, like Fisher, he preferred to keep matters much within his own grasp. Churchill's views on the Naval War Staff, dated New Year's Day 1912, were that such an organisation was to be 'the means of sifting, developing, and applying the results of history and experience and of preserving them as a general stock of reasoned opinion available as an aid and as a guide for all who are called upon to determine, in peace or war, the naval policy of the country.' As Marder says, Churchill's appreciation of history remains one of his endearing traits. He adds correctly that few naval officers of that time could have taken the First Lord seriously.[38]

As for the Royal Naval War College, it virtually disappeared with the outbreak of war in 1914, for instructors could not be found and all officers were needed in sea or shore commands. As well, the 'brains trust' passed into another phase. By 1917 it was a shell of its former self. However, the pre-1914 changes were significant. Fisher had energised the Navy into thinking about the sublime aspects of the naval profession, and his revolution in naval education, largely unappreciated, made mighty contributions to readying the Service for war.

Scrapping of obsolete vessels and fleet redistribution

Fisher was a champion of decolonisation, and was a proponent of bringing home the imperial squadrons that were the guardians of empire. His error lay in the fact that he was too far ahead of the times, too quick in taking action. British dominions, colonies, and dependencies had the right of naval protection in shifting and uncertain circumstances. Overseas trade and investment needed protection. The British merchant marine was the largest in the world, and the Navy was its guardian. The German threat was known. Fisher hated sentimentality, but he underestimated the sentiments of empire expressed by the colonies. He thought they were a drain. And his advice generally reflected his own narrow view of imperial defence and naval obligations.

At the same time, while it is true that relentless fleet redistribution occurred under Fisher's watch at the Admiralty, he was not the first to see the desirability of such a policy. In 1901 Selborne sent a memorandum to the First Sea Lord, Admiral Walter Kerr, on the naval balance of power in the Far East and the need to redistribute naval units. In response, Kerr noted, 'The course you propose would be from the Naval side a very great relief ... our hitherto followed policy of "splendid isolation" may no longer be possible and that great as the disadvantages in other ways may be, an understanding with other Powers may be forced upon us.'[39] That same year, Kerr also commented, 'The very fact of the great naval superiority of the U.S. Squadron in the Pacific should show us how impossible it is for us in view of the requirements elsewhere to maintain a

Squadron in the Pacific coping with it ... It is impossible for this country, in view of the greater development of foreign navies to be a superior force everywhere.'[40] In the Caribbean the situation was much the same, and the completion of the Panama Canal in 1914 would turn that ancient British sea into an American lake.

In 1902 Fisher drew up plans for the redistribution of the Fleet. Building on the concept of the flying squadron of the early 1870s, he proposed squadrons that would be 'detached' – that is, mobile – which would make periodic cruises under senior officers, who would command the squadrons in war. Such squadrons were intended to produce a much greater effect than the continued, enervating stay of solitary ships at various ports. When Fisher wrote to Battenberg on the subject of abolishing foreign stations, Battenberg replied: 'I agree that the appearance of a squadron is more effective than a single ship kept tied to the place ... Per contra, local knowledge and mutual understanding between Admirals and others must count for something.'[41]

The Atlantic Fleet of twelve or more cruisers would be the skeleton of the commerce-protecting fleet, and was thus to have a different mission from other cruiser squadrons.[42] The Admiralty, under Fisher's early advice, was now realising that in a future war, protection of shipping in the sea-lanes of the Atlantic would be critical. In that future, such a concentration of cruisers would be dispersed to provide coverage for convoys.

Redistribution was facilitated by the continuing evolution of the submarine cable. They provided two things desperately needed in wartime: accurate information of an enemy's activities; and the quickest, most reliable means of transmitting this information to its place of need. During periods of strain, such as the Fashoda crisis of 1898, the value of the submarine cable had become obvious, and by 1902 the Admiralty was making further energetic advances to ensure that submarine cables could be laid, and cable-laying ships could be sent with reconnoitring forces, to extend the range of communications.[43] Another communications revolution was occurring: wireless was instituted very early in the century, and by 1908 warships sailing across the Atlantic, say from Portsmouth to Quebec, could be in daily communication with 'operations central', the Admiralty.

To Fisher, fleet redistribution also made strategic sense. As of 1904 the Admiralty was concerned that it might face a combination of enemy naval powers, whether it was Russia and Germany or Russia and France. To deal with such a possibility required greater force and mobility in the Home and Channel commands. Withdrawing units from overseas, especially from the China station, would allow a greater concentration of force in the key sea zones and boost the British presence in the Mediterranean.[44]

Finally, Fisher objected to warships 'too weak to fight and too slow to run away'. As early as 1902 he had written to Beresford: 'Just look at the small craft we have in commission all over the world. They can neither fight nor run away. It is fearful to contemplate this fearful waste of men and money. Burn them all at once and damn the Consuls and the Foreign Office!'[45] Two years later he told Selborne, 'Nothing can possibly bring an "OUT-OF-DATE" ship "UP TO DATE"! You simply can't do it!'[46]

In the summer of 1904 Fisher hinted to the Prince of Wales about the plans he intended to bring forward when First Sea Lord. The Prince of Wales generally agreed with Fisher's comments on ship design. However, the intended fleet redistribution caused him worry: 'I don't think, however, you will get the Foreign Office to accept the merchant ship with the White Ensign and the Maxim gun. Why not build a very large destroyer with good speed for this kind of work, which also would be useful with your fleet. Of course the Snail and Tortoise classes ought to be abolished; they are utterly useless for anything.'[47] As to the argument that ships on Pacific station were out of date, the royal response to Fisher was that he should build new ones suitable to the job. But economy was driving the agenda.

The new line of thinking appeared in the Report of the Estimates Committee of 26 November 1904, which stated that redistribution would be a financially beneficial reform, via the expurgation of ships that would be useless in war. There would also be a reduction of 21,000 active service ratings via this scrapping of obsolete vessels. Ascension (South Atlantic), Halifax (Canada), Jamaica (Caribbean), Trincomalee (Sri Lanka), and Esquimalt (Canada) no longer needed to be manned and equipped, and the stores at these locations ought to be freed up. Bermuda, Bombay (India), and Simon's Bay (South Africa) could be materially decreased, permitting considerable savings.[48] According to the naval estimates of March 1905, the elimination of obsolete vessels would decrease the total number of officers, seamen, boys, and Marines by another 2,100. It was also announced in the naval estimates of 1905 that expenditures on the dockyards at Esquimalt, Halifax, and Trincomalee would be greatly reduced in peacetime, although they could be developed in wartime as necessary.[49]

In a memorandum dated 6 December 1904, Selborne informed his Cabinet colleagues that the Home Fleet would be renamed the Channel Fleet and would consist of twelve battleships. What had been the Channel Fleet would be known as the Atlantic Fleet, which would be based at Gibraltar and consist of eight battleships. The Mediterranean Fleet would remain as it was, consisting of eight battleships. The Atlantic Fleet was to undertake manoeuvres with the Mediterranean and the Home Fleets every year. The extra-European squadrons were to be combined into three groups: the Eastern Squadron, which would incorporate the China, Australia, Pacific, and East Indies stations; the Cape of Good Hope Squadron; and the Western Squadron, which would incorporate the North American and West Indian stations (the South Atlantic Squadron was to be abolished).[50]

The specific repercussions of the redistribution policy can be seen in the case of the naval base at Esquimalt, British Columbia, the fulcrum of British maritime authority in the eastern Pacific. In the years leading up to Fisher's tenure at the Admiralty, commanders on the spot, such as Rear-Admiral A K Bickford, had complained of both the weakness of the Pacific squadron and the great risk that Esquimalt could not be defended and hence could easily be seized by ships of the US Navy. There were quarrels over the Alaska boundary and the pelagic fur seal fisheries in the Bering Sea. However, the end of 'splendid isolation' meant that the British found themselves in an alliance with Japan; as well, war with the Americans became increasingly unlikely, especially due to the dominance of the US Navy in the Pacific after the Spanish-American War, the annexation of Hawaii, and the construction of the Panama Canal. At the same time, improvements in wireless telegraphy and submarine cables put admirals in much closer contact with the Admiralty, and therefore greatly increased the speed with which the Admiralty could respond to a naval threat anywhere on the globe. Strategists and planners were quick to point out that technology was replacing 'showing the flag' (much as it is said nowadays that computers and sensors make keepers of lighthouses redundant). The advantages of the telegraph, wireless telegraphy, crack cruisers, trans-Pacific cable, and Canadian Pacific Railway were such that troops could be sent from eastern Canada to British Columbia in six days, or from Great Britain in twenty-six days, including seven for preparation, while warships could be sent from Hong Kong in twenty days. These advancements probably provided British Columbia with more potential defence than it had had before.[51]

As a result, in the redistribution of the Fleet, the Pacific station was closed at sunset on 1 March 1905, when Commodore J E C Goodrich, HMS *Bonaventure*, lowered his pennant and sailed for Hong Kong. The victualling depot and hospital at Esquimalt were closed, the munitions and stores transferred to Hong Kong. Only the dockyard and certain bunkering facilities remained operational at the base. Shortly thereafter, the garrison of Esquimalt (as well as the one at Halifax) was transferred to the Canadian government, followed after a few years by the dockyard and the base as a whole. The Admiralty calculated that it would save £6,940 annually at Esquimalt. By 1908, only the sloops *Algerine* and *Shearwater* and the survey ship *Egeria* remained based there, which obviously were scarcely sufficient for coastal defence. Commander A T Hunt of *Shearwater* remained as Commander-in-Charge for Station Duties on the West Coast of America. The Pacific Ocean was also allotted four unarmoured-class cruisers, second-class, which were to be under the command of the Commander-in-Chief of the Eastern Fleet.

At the Foreign Office, Sir Charles Hardinge complained to the King of the imprudence of the Fisher retrenchment: British interests could be damaged in those places where men-of-war had previously shown the flag. Fisher, monopolist on naval wisdom, cheekily told the King that the gunboat commander knew better than the Foreign Office the nature of affairs on the spot. He put it to His Majesty thus:

> The absolute fact is that the Admiralty always know better than the Foreign Office, and more wisely than the Consuls, when vessels are likely to be required, because the Naval Officer on the spot is invariably a better and more reliable judge than the frightened or gun-boat desiring Consuls, who one and all pine for the prestige of the presence of a Man-of-War within signalling distance of the Consular flagstaff and for the Consular salute of seven guns!

He pointed out that British warships still remained in place protecting national and imperial interests, and that the Admiralty had not defaulted on its duty: it had always met Foreign Office requirements.[52] He reiterated this two years later, telling Tweedmouth that little account should be placed on the concerns regarding fleet redistribution and scrapping:

> I have it all at my fingers' ends, and trust to convince you and also Sir E. Grey [Foreign Secretary] and Lord Elgin [Secretary of State for the Colonies] that their subordinates quite unduly magnify any want of Admiralty attention to their requests, but we cannot possibly get the Naval Estimates down to the figure which I think the House of Commons will insist upon sooner or later, unless we strictly confine our naval expenditure to *absolutely necessary services*, and it can be incontestably proved that any reasonable requirement of the Foreign Office or the Colonial Office has never yet been resisted by the Admiralty.

Fisher further argued that there was no justification for having an immense naval force when the only likely foe was Germany, which was 'many times weaker' than England.[53]

In an essay on the use of the gunboat, Fisher wrote: 'Doubtless it would be convenient, as a temporary emergency arises here or there over the surface of the globe, if at that very spot some British cruiser or gunboat promptly appeared ready to protect British interests, or to sink in the attempt. Indeed, for some time this was the ideal at which the Admiralty aimed.' But the old order was passing, and in its stead came a new one: 'Since the redistribution of the Fleet the Empire has had to do without the ubiquitous gunboat, and, if the truth be told, scarcely seems to have missed it.' The decisions to use the gunboat on distant seas had often been political, and the Empire and the great offices, the Colonial and Foreign, could no longer call on the Admiralty to put out a fire. The Navy, thought Fisher, had scored a victory on this important point of administrative autonomy.[54]

Rear-Admiral Hedworth Lambton (later Meux), a personal friend of the Prince of Wales, also sounded opposition to redistribution early on, but from an imperial point of view as much as a naval one. After the Prince had shown Lambton the proposed fleet redistribution scheme while they were hunting in Speyside, Lambton thought the question had to be looked at again. The scheme did not display what politician Joseph Chamberlain called 'thinking imperially'. In particular, Lambton focused on the abolition of the Pacific squadron. He argued that this would be disastrous for British Columbia's loyalty and for British trade on the west coast of the Americas from Cape Horn to the Bering Strait. American interests in the region were in the ascendant, and there was a danger of further annexation by the United States. While a superior fleet could not be kept in the Pacific, a small squadron headquartered at Esquimalt was essential. In his view, a large difference existed between withdrawing the squadron completely and keeping up a shadow force. He argued that the Navy was more than just a force for war: 'Although the ultimate aim and business of the Navy is War it is not its sole raison d'être. It has its peace duties and utilities and these should never be forgotten ... Have the squadron as small and weak as you like but let there always be one. Why banish our Flag – why take the responsibility of order away from the Commodore [?]' Lambton believed that once stations and depots were relinquished, 'they cannot be renewed. Above all why hasten desperately. Precipitancy is weakness.'[55]

The Prince of Wales shared Lambton's concerns, familiar as he was with British Columbia's and Canada's concerns, and he forwarded the admiral's letter to Fisher on 10 November 1904 along with his own comments:

> If you are going to remove the squadron in the Pacific because the ships are obsolete, you ought to send some new ones to take their place ... I consider that this question is much more than a naval one and that the whole thing should be carefully considered from every point of view, and that the Colonial Secretary and Prime Minister should both be consulted, and also the Defence Secretary. But no doubt you will bring it up before the Defence Committee. Forgive me for having brought up this question, but I feel rather strong on it, and, of course, it applies to the other squadrons you talked of removing.[56]

Lambton also appealed to Selborne: 'I have sent him [Fisher] a long and melancholy wail on your proposed abolition of foreign minor stations – especially British Columbia. I can't help thinking that in years to come when you are aspiring to be Prime Minister it will be very unpleasant for you to have it thrown in your teeth that you flouted the colonies and lowered the prestige of every British merchant in S[outh] E[ast] America and the whole of Pacific littoral.'[57]

The withdrawal of small non-effective vessels did not diminish British prestige, said an unrepentant Fisher at the Admiralty; rather the reverse. And in October 1906 he continued with further alterations to the Fleet. As it currently stood, there were three divisions of reserve vessels in the home ports, all of which fell under the overall responsibility of the Commander-in-Chief, Channel Fleet. These three divisions were to be reorganised into an independent Home Fleet. Thus the reserve ships would train together and be under a single commander-in-chief, which it was believed would increase their efficiency. The Commander-in-Chief, Home Fleet, was also to be given a fully manned division, the Nore Division, composed of six battleships, to be used as a deterrent against a sudden naval attack on the Fleet. Two battleships were to be withdrawn from each of the Channel, Atlantic, and Mediterranean Fleets to compose the Nore Division. There was, again, an immediate outcry against the plan. Opponents declared that the Nore Division was woefully inadequate to defend against the entire German fleet, and it was suggested that the entire plan was driven by party politics and the desire to save money.[58]

Fisher vigorously defended the plan. He wrote to Tweedmouth that the fleet redistribution would not result in any decrease in overall fighting strength; rather, he claimed, '*I don't know anything that we have done which will add more to our fighting efficiency*!' He dismissed out of hand all agitation against redistribution, he wrote: 'The silly cry (which I am assured on most excellent authority has fallen perfectly flat on the Country) that the fighting efficiency of the Navy is being reduced and our naval supremacy impaired will be met in the most conclusive manner by the British Public seeing a new Fleet emerge into being, complete in all its parts, instead of the present disconnected and organically incomplete Reserve Divisions.'[59]

At a meeting with Fisher in October 1906, Edward VII informed the First Sea Lord that the King's sailor son, the future George V, still had serious reservations about the formation of the Home Fleet, and that many naval officers shared these concerns. In response, Fisher drafted a letter for the Prince of Wales, outlining the reasons for the formation of the Home Fleet, and sent it to the King for his approval:

These are the absolute facts of the case: –
Our only probable enemy is Germany. Germany keeps her *whole* Fleet always concentrated within a few hours of England. We must therefore keep a Fleet twice as powerful concentrated within a few hours of Germany.
   If we kept the Channel and Atlantic Fleets *always* in the English Channel (say in the vicinity of the Nore), this would meet the case, but this is neither

feasible nor expedient, and if, when relations with foreign powers are strained, the Admiralty attempt to take the proper fighting precautions and move our Channel and Atlantic Fleets to their proper fighting position, then *at once* the Foreign Office and the Government veto it, and say such a step will precipitate war! ...

('Your battle ground should be your drill ground.' said Nelson!) ...

This new 'Home Fleet' thus called into being by Mr. Balfour's famous 'stroke of the pen' almost admits of more seagoing work being given to ships in Reserve, *together with the essential fighting training they do not get in Battle Practice and other important Fleet exercises.*

I beg you, Sir, to note especially the following facts: – By this new distribution of the Fleet not a single ship will be paid off, nor is there the reduction of one single man serving on board ship, and the Fleet, AS A WHOLE, will have more sea work than at present ...

Pure party feeling solely dictates the present 'Press' agitation ... Reduced Navy Estimates are no sign of reduced naval efficiency.[60]

The letter was approved without change. The same day as the letter, Fisher met with the Prince of Wales, and afterward commented that the Prince 'is cordially in agreement with all the Admiralty are doing.' In a written reply dated 21 December 1906, the Prince of Wales assured the First Sea Lord that he would consider Fisher's notes to be 'absolutely secret'.[61]

Redistribution of Britannia's assets sent strategic tsunamis rolling around the world. The effect on the old dominions was mammoth. In Vancouver, British Columbia, and Halifax, Nova Scotia, cries went up that 'cutting the painter' signified imperial abandonment – a familiar scenario to Canadians. Fisher dismissed such complaints out of hand. His correspondence speaks of 'the old women of Halifax', an obvious reference to those who objected to withdrawing men-of-war and shutting down bases. He contended that if Canadians were left to their own devices, they would soon learn to get along with their rambunctious American neighbours. This view, taken up by various statesmen since 1815, frequently was shown to be wrong, for Canada never boasted military forces or defences sufficient to repel any American force in strength. But Fisher hated to think that imperial forces should be used for colonial policing. And he saw the Navy's use for philanthropic and humanitarian duties as a secondary line of work. The Navy he wanted was a fighting instrument, a sharp sword. The Navy he objected to was the one posed by certain newspapers – in one instance the Toronto *Globe*, making the case that two cruisers loaded with tents and provisions be sent to the Caribbean in January 1907 – which thought the Admiralty ought to have, in Fisher's words, 'an ambulance corps of cruisers and gunboats distributed over the earthquake areas of the globe!'

How could the philanthropic match the belligerent? It could not. 'The Navy Estimates would be a hundred million if everyone had everything!'[62] Fisher was reductionist, and the Navy he was shaping was to be reductionist too: much more belligerent, much less philanthropic. Fisher had his eye firmly fixed on the rising German fleet based on Wilhelmshaven, Jade Bay, in the North Sea.

The redistribution of 1906, and the means by which the Home Fleet was created, not only provoked concern and disapproval. It also figured prominently in the crisis soon to emerge between Fisher and Beresford. We return to this matter presently.

Dreadnought, Invincible, *and technical matters*

We turn now to the story of Fisher's epoch-making HMS *Dreadnought*, from conception to commission. The concept of this capital ship – and its remarkable development – continues to be a subject of research and reappraisal.[63] When Commander-in-Chief, Mediterranean, Fisher had begun considering what the design of such a ship might entail. The Italians and Americans were studying the effectiveness of larger, more mobile ships with great guns. Fisher may have developed his plans irrespective of foreign advances, but this is unlikely, attuned as he was to Britain's pre-eminence at sea. The French, he knew, were of little threat; in the wake of the Fashoda crisis they had removed themselves from the big power naval race with their decision to limit their naval requirements to cruiser warfare – *guerre de course* – and to littoral and torpedo-boat operations. Fisher's requirement was altogether different. He had to advance on two fronts. The revolution he undertook in battleship design was predicated on having not only the biggest capital ship, the battleship, but also a larger and more powerful ship than the armoured cruiser. This resulted in the dreadnought armoured cruiser, known, beginning in 1912, as the battlecruiser. Sir Philip Watts, Director of Naval Construction, who was appointed in 1902 and compiled a masterful report on 'Ships of the British Navy on August 4, 1914', makes clear that when Fisher became First Sea Lord he brought with him from the Mediterranean command several designs of warships, among them a design for an 'all-big-gun' battleship having six pairs of 12in guns all mounted on the middle line: three pairs were at each end of the vessel, in steps, one close behind another, so that six guns could fire directly ahead and six directly astern. Those behind fired over those in front, and all twelve guns could fire on either broadside. The speed of the ship was 21 knots.[64] Gunnery exercises arranged by Fisher in the Mediterranean had revealed big-gun ranges of 6,000 to 7,000yds.

For the task at hand, Fisher had gathered around him some of the best scientists and engineers then available. He had shown an ease of talking to these persons with technical knowledge since his fruitful days at the weapons establishments *Excellent* and *Vernon*, gunnery and torpedoes respectively. The advance in weaponry – bigger guns, greater range, and more rapid fire – signified corresponding progress in ship design. Developments in metallurgy, engineering, lubrication, and electrical arrangements were swift and revolutionary. Admiral Sir Percy Scott, at one time the Inspector of Target Practice, helped Fisher immensely, and his fascination with improving accuracy of fire at precisely the same time that speeds and ranges were increasing was invaluable. All of these persons, naval officers of influence, scientists, and engineers (as well as industrialists), were working in an ethos of tremendous material change, the likes of which had not been seen to that time. Daily there were improvements and daily, too, old ways of doing things became obsolete.

These newfangled devices caught the old guard off balance. It was all too much for some of the breezy aristocrats and not a few admirals of the Old Navy. Prime Minister Gladstone, looking at certain great guns of the 1880s Navy, thought it unfathomable to appreciate their prodigious power. He was not alone in his disbelief. Another prime minister, Salisbury, lampooned Fisher and his cohorts at the Admiralty, who, according to him, 'follow the progress of science at a respectful distance, always arriving at an appreciation of each successive invention just soon enough to find that it is obsolete, and never yielding their adhesion to anything new until the time has come to defend it against the claims of something newer.'[65] Fisher did not have to be immersed in all the technical details to be conversant with the generalities, and he did not invade the realms of the technical specialists. But he could see the rapidity of change. He could see what might come in the way of naval armaments and thus ship designs. For the moment, therefore, there was no sense in laying down any battleships along old patterns, and Fisher got the First Lord's agreement not to commit to constructing any more battleships before he assumed the post of First Sea Lord and had a chance to discuss design matters in detail with him. Always with a view to rival navies and with a view to economy, he told his political counterpart (then Selborne) that 'Russia's naval decline permits us to wait a bit', and that a delay in new construction would do wonders for the estimates.[66] For the moment, a pause in naval construction increases might bring political favour in Parliament.

Selborne's handling of the secret measures for the construction of *Dreadnought* place him among the finest of the First Lords of the Admiralty to hold that post at a critical hour. He knew what Fisher was doing in the backrooms and corridors of the Admiralty. He gave Fisher all the freedom he needed to undertake his grand design. He was good, too, at keeping the new battleship then being designed and not yet approved out of the public eye, for, when launched, *Dreadnought* was finally released to public view, a hitherto secret weapon of naval power. During his speech on the naval estimates of 1905, Selborne stated that one of the reasons for the formation of the special committee on designs was to 'ensure to the Navy the immediate benefit of the experience which was to be derived from the naval warfare between Russia and Japan and of the resultant studies of the Naval Intelligence Department.'[67] The Battle of Tsushima (1905) had revealed many tactical lessons and made it clear that in future naval combat (ship to ship and fleet to fleet), gunnery efficiency in rapidly changing tactical circumstances would be of the essence. Selborne also noted that the quality of the admiral, officers, and men was more important than the quality of the ships.[68] Nelson would have approved – and many another admiral besides.

Selborne had backed Fisher at every turn. He had even led him in the social reforms of the Navy. He had been his closest confidant and working partner. The Conservatives, or Unionists, who held the profit and the power of the British Empire as a central tenet of policy, now needed Selborne elsewhere, and he sailed for South Africa to succeed Lord Milner in the reconstructionist post of High Commissioner. Taking his place at the Admiralty on 6 March 1905 was a person with perhaps even more abilities, especially in business. This was the 3rd Earl of Cawdor, a sometime backbencher but now fresh from the progressive chairmanship of the Great Western Railway, and a person with strong influence among the Unionists.

Lord Cawdor, who took a keen interest in British naval matters, was similar to Fisher in that he had the instinct to look ahead. The future he saw appeared dangerous. With Fisher, he backed the redistribution of the Fleet and the laying down of the revolutionary battleship *Dreadnought* and its equally remarkable counterpart *Invincible*, one of three battlecruisers of the same general specifications. The projects were simultaneous, and they were prototypes of the battleship and battlecruiser that became so common in the First World War. Together they came to be called dreadnoughts.

Although we have already noted the political and strategic motives for the introduction of the new dreadnoughts, the primary motives were actually technical. Vast advances had been made in the engineering, design, and manufacture of torpedoes. This weapon had been largely ineffective when used by the Imperial Japanese navy against the Russians in the Russo-Japanese War of 1904–1905, but startling improvements in steel, steering gears, gyroscopes, and methods of launch and discharge had given it a new lease on life. With improved accuracy, a torpedo could now speed to a range of five or six miles carrying an explosive charge three or four times more powerful than anything previously known. This mandated a complete change of naval tactics, 'with torpedo craft now possessing a weapon that could seriously challenge the proud superiority of the battleship.' Up to this point a battleship might carry four big guns, a number of light quick-firers for repelling small craft at close quarters, and a large number of 6in quick-firing guns (a secondary armament) to be used on enemy battleships at middling ranges. Because the torpedo could match the range of this secondary armament, Fisher argued that the 6in guns were hardly necessary. To engage the enemy, therefore, meant fighting at big-gun range only, which put the ships outside torpedo range. By 1914 the 21in-diameter torpedo with a 200lb charge had a range of 3,000yds at 20 knots. Even this range and accuracy were soon exceeded, which called for enhanced underwater protection in surface ships.[69] Such was the state of affairs at the time *Dreadnought* was designed.

Dreadnought, 17,900 tons, set new standards for gun power and range, armour, and speed. So advanced was this vessel that suddenly all the rest of the British Fleet was placed in a position of technological inferiority. There was really nothing new to this; since the mid-nineteenth century, new ships had been built for the purpose of giving the Fleet an advantage over rivals. What made *Dreadnought* so remarkable was that it was an 'all-big-gun' battleship, with suitable armour, unexcelled speed as a capital ship, and tremendous mobility. The great guns would be able to fire at a hitherto unimaginable 17,500yds. For a nation accustomed to thinking in Nelsonic terms – 'Engage the enemy more closely' – *Dreadnought*'s gunnery capabilities were mystifyingly peculiar. With its service speed of 21 knots, and its heavy 9in armour, it was a ship, and a class of ship, of immense and commanding power.

It is undeniable that *Dreadnought* deprived Britain of her lead in existing ships, but it hit Germany far harder: it required the reconstruction of the Kiel Canal before a single one of the new type, 17,000 tons, could transit it. Within two months of *Dreadnought*'s launch, the German Naval Law of April 1906 authorised the Kiel Canal widening, a job that was not completed until the summer of 1914, mere weeks before the outbreak of the European war. Once completed, Germany could shift her battleships at will from Wilhelmshaven to Kiel, allowing her to retain critical control of the Baltic during the coming war.

Fisher had told the naval writer Arnold White that what he wanted in a ship was 'oil fuel, turbine propulsion, equal gunfire all round, greater speed than any existing vessels of their class, no masts, no funnels, etc.'[70] But above all, and this was typically Fisheresque, he wanted speed and punch. Tactics would determine all in combat, and speed was the most important component for a ship. The side with superiority of speed could force the battle when desired. Similarly, it could avoid battle whenever confronted by a superior force. At this stage Fisher considered firepower as secondary, provided it was at least equal to the gunnery of the enemy.[71] The key factor was to ensure that the Royal Navy was never 'out-classed' by an opponent: 'we must go one better.'[72] Fisher got what he desired.

Throughout this period of rapid change, Fisher was dismissive of those who argued that the shipbuilding policy of the Admiralty was endangering British naval supremacy:

The consistent policy of the Board of Admiralty since October 21, 1904, is to have a *yearly* programme only. '*Sufficient unto the year is the shipbuilding thereof.*' We are not going to be frightened by foreign 'paper programmes' (the bogey of agitators!). But when foreigners, and especially Germans, actually build, *then* we will double!! But no houses of cards for us! Our present margin of superiority over Germany (*our only possible foe for years*) is so great as to render it absurd in the extreme to talk of anything endangering our naval supremacy, *even if we stopped all shipbuilding altogether*!!![73]

Various First Lords of the Admiralty during his tenure – Selborne, Cawdor, and Tweedmouth – must have wondered where Fisher's schemes would take the nation and the Empire. But they managed the change with firmness and equanimity, though with different styles on account of their respective characters and personalities. Many members of the press were content with Fisher's prognostications, believing British naval pre-eminence was secure in Fisher's hands. As long as the Conservatives remained in power, a firm footing could be established in naval construction.

Fisher exploited his connections with James Thursfield and Arnold White, as noted, but his new favourite newsman and editor at this time was James Louis Garvin, at the *Outlook* and, as of 1908, the *Observer*. Garvin was a genius as a publicist, and a colossus among Tory editors and journalists. Most influential as well as partisan, he flew the flag in the national interest on all matters of defence and never shied away from exaggerations and half-truths. Balfour had found him useful in CID matters. Fisher did likewise. Garvin reduced the complexities of any international situation to a simple thesis – that Germany's aims cut across the bow of British intentions, that Germany's naval challenge was the near and present danger, that only the Royal Navy stood in Germany's way, and that British naval supremacy must be sustained at all costs as the sole means of the security of the nation, the Empire, and seaborne commerce upon which the lifeblood of the whole depended. Fisher never played to sentimentality, and Garvin made sure that showed itself in print. The admiral's argument that the freedom of the world best rested in the ships of the Royal Navy became Garvin's mantra, but left in its wake many backwaters of dissent and cavil.

Take the views of Leopold Maxse, a Unionist, who edited *The National Review*. He thought Fisher a man of exceptional ability but a person who had gone wrong since becoming a courtier and social figure. 'He has lost the touch with the Service afloat,' Maxse confided to Garvin. 'He is so cunning in nobbling the press ... including of course the Liberal press who do not care a twopenny damn about the Navy. He has done all this by nauseating flattery ours being the vainest of all professions.' Fisher's dominance at the Admiralty gave Maxse anxiety: 'His detestable spirit of bluster and bounce is our besetting sin as a nation ... Against such forms of insanity the Gods fight in vain.'[74] Not all Unionist-minded presses thought this way, and in fact many backed the pro-Navy faction. Dealing with the Beresford question, which is a main topic of the next chapter, was another matter. The Unionist or Conservative press backed Beresford on grounds of his social standing. Indeed, press agitation against Fisher in the feud against Beresford left Jacky alone and isolated. On that issue *The Times* was lukewarm, and the Liberal Cabinet, which had replaced Balfour's Conservatives in December 1905, hardly supported Fisher. He exploited the press out of necessity, and to his own advantage, but in doing so sowed the seeds of his own destruction.

In Fisher's early years as First Sea Lord, the concentration on the politics of the dreadnought – how many, how many building, and how many in potential enemy hands – had its costs and deflected much attention away from secondary but essential naval requirements in the public eye. The capital ship: that was the thing. No one was better 'at buttering press parsnips' than Fisher, but soldiers were as concerned as naval personnel about the future and acted accordingly. This played to the hand of Colonel Repington, the military correspondent of *The Times*. All the same, both Services were paranoid about military secrets leaking into enemy hands, and a system came into being that was the precursor of the 'D-notice' system, and the Official Secrets Act of 1911. It is the view of A J A Morris, author of *The Scaremongers*, that this tight-lipped system actually made the press hostile to the public interest. Such co-operation as might have been established between the Services and the press was stalled by over-regulation and fear of prosecution. *The Times* favoured the balance of power over the Tory-minded concepts of the 'imperialist faction', and was thus a modernising force. As for the Foreign Office, its reluctant ministers and secretaries held back information, and it was only after the war that Grey realised the disadvantages of not informing the public more generally of critical issues affecting Britain's war effort on behalf of its interests and those of the Allies.[75]

Cawdor and Fisher, with numerical precision reassuring to their political masters, developed a clear plan to outdistance any German response to *Dreadnought*. They intended to lay down four dreadnoughts (one battleship and three battlecruisers) in 1906, four in 1907, and any number required to retain the advantage thereafter. The Cawdor–Fisher calculation was magical. The Royal Navy would have had a fleet of a dozen or so dreadnoughts afloat before a German vessel of those types could be completed. Germany would not be able to close the gap. There was a political intent, too, for it was contended by these sea kings that Germany, if sensible, would renounce the naval race. That, as we know, would be the most likely alternative to war. (One thinks of

President Ronald Reagan's 600-ship US Navy, designed by Secretary of the Navy John Lehman to outbuild the Soviet Navy, as a contributor to the waning of Soviet power.) In any event, the first German dreadnought was laid down in 1906, and by that time the British had a commanding and comfortable lead in the building of battleships and battlecruisers.

Dreadnought, laid down at Portsmouth on 2 October 1905, built in secrecy and also with unprecedented speed, attracted the greatest interest and the most flattering accolades. She was launched on 10 February 1906 by Edward VII and completed in December 1906. She was commanded by the clever Captain Reginald Bacon, and was attached to the Home Fleet 'for special service' – that is to say, for close watching of performance. Stringent tests were required, including a long run at an easy 17 knots across the Atlantic to Trinidad, then back at high speed. Prolonged day and night firings at Trinidad proved effective. So did turning-circle trials, as well as ordinary evolutions with torpedo-net defence. Much depended on the test results, since Fisher already planned to lay down the first three dreadnought battlecruisers of the *Indomitable* class, and *Bellerophon*, the first of three improved dreadnought battleships of 18,600 tons, with a secondary armament of 4in guns to counter the increasing range of the torpedo. 'With four 12-inch turrets bearing we could fire four gun salvoes every fifteen seconds, a loading interval of thirty seconds for each gun being obtainable with good drill,' wrote the Experimental Gunnery Officer, Lieutenant Frederic Dreyer.[76]

As flagship of the Commander-in-Chief, Home Fleet, *Dreadnought* met all expectations. Rear-Admiral F S Inglefield, commanding the 4th Cruiser Squadron, glowingly reported to Fisher: 'She is a *grand* fighting ship, and there is nothing afloat [that] can come anywhere near her.' And to the First Lord of the Admiralty, Lord Tweedmouth, he wrote similarly, adding some tactical observations: 'She merits all the praise that experts have bestowed on her, and in my humble opinion she is a *long way* in advance of any fighting ship now afloat, and I go so far as to say that a Squadron of *Dreadnoughts* would be such a formidable force that any Fleet now in existence would ponder well before venturing within range of their 12-inch guns.'[77] Fisher had no difficulty in imagining the resistance to be faced within the Navy concerning the introduction of this great ship and others of her class. He wrote to Tweedmouth: '[*Dreadnought*] certainly has been a *phenomenal* success, and perhaps in nothing more than in her marvellous handiness. As Bacon well put it, he imagined himself back in a torpedo boat! I suppose the "Syndicate of Discontent" will say the Admiralty as usual is having the Devil's luck! The rejoinder is that the Devil's invariable good luck is consequent on his unfailing attention to every petty detail in order to gain his object!'[78]

Much could be written on this revolutionary vessel, but the essential points of interest are: (1) she introduced all-big-gun armament for long-range firing; (2) she was the first large warship to have turbines; (3) she was the first British battleship to steam at 21 knots; (4) her officers were berthed forward, men aft; and (5) she was built in a year and a day. The authority Oscar Parkes wrote:

In designing the *Dreadnought*, extraordinary steps were taken to ensure that she should embody all requirements on the smallest dimensions and at the lowest cost, so that the anticipated opposition should not be founded on her excessive size and expense. In every way, she proved an epoch-making warship. Brilliant in conception: the cynosure of naval interest during construction and of controversy afterwards; a magnificent success in every way structurally and mechanically; and the finest looking fighting ship of her day ... In appearance the *Dreadnought* with her grim, awe inspiring sense of efficiency was something essentially British, outclassing anything else afloat, and unique in contrast to any other battleship. Her successors although bigger and better armed could never strike the same note of novelty and overwhelming power. The first sight of her completing in dock was an unforgettable experience, and as flagship in the Home Fleet she dwarfed her consorts to an extent that mere difference in tonnage would never suggest. Although accepted as a basis for future battleship development, in 1906 it was difficult to realise that we should one day possess her like in squadrons and that the mighty would in due course pass into obsolescence and the sale list.[79]

And sure enough, in 1922 she was sold for £44,000.

The Cawdor–Fisher combination would have ensured Britain's naval security without limit. Their year-by-year construction of capital ships would have given the nation a sure lead against Germany. But when the Liberals came to power under Sir Henry Campbell-Bannerman (the Cabinet was formed in December 1905), the great scheme completely disappeared, and the Cawdor plan was abandoned, thrown aside. One of the reasons – a strange one – was an about-face taken by the Sea Lords, who contended that the British lead in dreadnoughts was sufficient unto the day and that the construction plans of the future could be scaled back. The Sea Lords were on thin ice, as the newspapers soon proved. Thereafter, the Admiralty began to press the politicians to build more ships to maintain the strong edge possessed against the German challenge. Despite the vacillations at the Admiralty, however, it was the essentially anti-militaristic Liberals who threw away the commanding lead that Fisher had accorded the nation and the Empire. This encouraged Germany to draw level again.

A signal factor in the destruction of the Cawdor plan was Winston Churchill. His rise to influence and office from the time the Liberals took office in 1906 until the outbreak of war in August 1914 discloses one of the great turnabouts in personal political history. Early in those years he fought strongly against building an excessive number of dreadnoughts, and in this regard he had a ready ally in David Lloyd George. Churchill's inconsistency with regards to naval construction can be explained by the fact that once he found himself in power, he always fought from his corner – that is, he defended the interests of his administration and its needs. He was not strictly anti-Navy. At this early stage he was an outsider to the Admiralty and its politics, and it served his political interests to harp against naval expenditures. When he was at the Board of Trade (1908–1910) and the Home Office (1910–1911) he had other obligations, but it did not stop him from sending memos on any number of defence matters to the prime minister and to members of Cabinet. He was never short on opinions and was usually careful to garner the facts, though his judgements were not always sober.

At the start of 1906 a new warship design was considered to deal with the issue of French cruiser warfare. The primary demand was for greater speed, and while armed mercantile cruisers were contemplated, the primary focus was on a new vessel, a 'fusion' class that would be a parent vessel for a new class of coastal destroyers.[80] Torpedo-boat destroyers were already in existence. Fisher's fruitful mind was looking for something different, never realised.

In gunnery, it was similar. In April 1906 Fisher indicated to Sir Andrew Noble, chairman of the armament firm Armstrong, Whitworth & Co Ltd, his thoughts on the direction of gunnery post-*Dreadnought*:

> I must discourage you about 20 12-inch guns at present. I suppose that never has such thought been given to fighting considerations as in designs of *Dreadnought* and *Invincible* class. Well, we are going further next year, in a quite new design, and the tendency will be to reduce the ten 12-inch guns of the *Dreadnought* to the 8 of the *Invincible* as getting the most fighting work for the money, because of absolute independence of blast, and CHIEFLY because with the 8 guns differently arranged than in *Invincible*, you will get 100 per cent of them on the broadside, and a battleship action will be a broadside action, for inevitably and surely the faster fleet will assume this formation in the crowning moment of victory.[81]

Speed meant mobility, and Fisher's maxim was to hit hard, hit often, and then get out of the way. He was grateful that others were noting the importance of speed for warships. He wrote to maritime strategist Sir Julian Corbett: 'I am so delighted to have just seen you are going to give a lecture on the value of speed in Battleships. You have probably got the matter more digested than anyone living, but a mouse once helped a lion (*vide* Aesop's Fables) so if I can be of any help I hope you will command me.'[82] In June 1906 Captain Mahan published an article in the *Proceedings of the Naval Institute* casting doubt on the entire dreadnought policy. He argued that gun power should never be sacrificed for speed, that the all-big-gun ship was a mistake, and that the size of ships should not be increased. Such comments obviously displeased Fisher. A paper defending the dreadnought policy, sent to him by Lieutenant-Commander William S Sims, US Navy, heartened him. Sims stated that the paper was written at the request of President Theodore Roosevelt, and that Roosevelt had been entirely convinced by Sims's case.[83] More difficult were Mahan's objections; his arguments found a ready audience in *The Times*. To counter this, Fisher told the First Lord, Tweedmouth, 'as a Yankee officer told me lately, he is *passé*, and has become a second Brassey and equally a bore!'[84]

The Committee on Designs that produced *Dreadnought* also considered possibilities for an armoured cruiser, similar to *Invincible*, but the naval writer Lord Brassey, with an uncanny eye to the future, summed up the problem this way: 'Vessels of this enormous size and cost are unsuitable for many of the duties of cruisers; but an even stronger objection to the repetition of the type is that an admiral having *Invincible*s in his fleet will be certain to put them in the line of battle, where their comparatively light protection would be a disadvantage and their high speed of no value.' In the end, *Invincible*, the lead ship of the battlecruiser design, had a large expanse of unarmoured side and light deck protection. She was the first large cruiser to steam at 25 knots and had the highest horsepower yet installed afloat (Parsons turbines of 41,000hp, driving four screws) and the highest freeboard of any warship to that time. She carried eight 12in guns. The naval annuals credited the *Invincible*-class ships with 7in belts and up to 10in turrets in 1914; their real protection was slightly less, and from the outset one anxiety existed. Admiral Mark Kerr wrote that when *Invincible* was completed, he expressed concern that a descending shell in an action fought at 15,000yds was sure to penetrate the deck and go straight down to the magazine. In response, Sir Philip Watts, the naval constructor, told him that he knew of the danger but he had orders to protect the vessel from a projectile fired at a range of 9,000yds and he was not allowed sufficient weight to put on further armour.[85] In other words, the ship would have to fight at a certain range from the enemy and not otherwise get in harm's way. Three were built of this class: *Invincible*, *Indomitable*, and *Inflexible*. They were good sea vessels but not particularly steady gun platforms. These greyhounds of the sea were prototypes of others, and the battlecruiser continued to enlarge in size and speed, HMS *Hood* being the supreme model. Of *Invincible*, however, we may note here her triumph and her tragedy: she fought in the action of Heligoland Bight, 28 August 1914; was flagship to Admiral Sturdee in the 2nd Battle Cruiser Squadron; and was in action with von Spee's squadron on 8 December of that same year, and with

Inflexible sank *Scharnhorst* and *Gneisenau*. At Jutland she was struck in 'Q' turret, when the magazine blew up and the ship sank in two halves. Two officers and three men were saved; 1,026 perished.

Fisher in 1906 was enthusiastic about Arthur Pollen's fire control system, as he told Tweedmouth: '*Pollen's invention is simply priceless*, and I do hope we may hesitate at nothing to get ITS SOLE USE. We shall NEVER be forgiven hereafter if we do not! Jellicoe's [Admiral John Jellicoe, Director of Naval Ordnance] arguments are so cogent and convincing that it's useless my enlarging on them!' And again, in a later letter: 'I am specially obliged to you about Pollen. The case is marvellously like the introduction of the Whitehead torpedo [1866]. We could have had the absolute monopoly of that wonderful weapon (and Mr. Whitehead body and soul into the bargain!), but the Admiralty of that day haggled over £80,000. But thanks to you, I hope we shan't make such an idiotic mistake over Pollen!'[86] But the Admiralty did: it made its own arrangements for fire control. Therein lies another sad story for another day.

Even before becoming First Sea Lord, Fisher placed great importance on the submarine, the potent offensive weapon that altered the strategic and tactical conditions under which the Royal Navy would have to operate. 'I don't think it is even *faintly* realised – the *immense, impending revolution which the submarines will effect as offensive weapons of war*.'[87] These proved to be prophetic words. Fisher had little optimism that the Admiralty would come around to his views on the submarines: 'Satan disguised as an Angel of Light wouldn't succeed in persuading the Admiralty or the Navy that in the course of some few years Submarines will prevent any Fleet remaining at sea continuously either in the Mediterranean or the English Channel.'[88]

Earliest inventors of underwater craft contended that they had conceived of a weapon of great importance. In 1805, realising the danger of a submarine to the pre-eminent sea power, Lord St Vincent thought those who commanded the sea ought not to possess it and those who got it would deprive them of their command. Even before the British adopted the submarine, Arnold-Foster had warned in the House of Commons that the weaker power possessing submarines would no longer be an inferior but a superior power. And Admiral Sir Arthur Wilson, in 1901, cautioned that submarine warfare as developed would be detrimental to a nation depending on navigation on the surface for its supplies and necessaries of life. It was the private sector that developed the submarine: Irish engineer John Holland, the Electric Boat Company, Vickers, and other private concerns, mainly American, were the proponents and leaders in the field of underwater warfare. On the whole, writes one authority, 'civilians had been more far-sighted than the admirals'.[89]

Herein lay Jacky Fisher's challenge. He turned to his ally in torpedo development, Captain Reginald Bacon, and in January 1903 appointed him to the new post of Inspecting Captain of Submarine Boats. Bacon was given a free hand to experiment, develop, and organise the infant service. This was a giant step forward, and after months of experience with the five American *Holland*-class submarines at Portsmouth, Fisher pronounced the submarine to be the principal weapons platform for keeping big surface ships away from enemy harbours, even though he thought the submarine a daylight craft only. Bacon recommended the organisation of submarine flotillas to watch and guard passages of large ships through narrow channels such as the Dover Channel, Straits of Gibraltar, and waters between Scotland and Norway. The Admiralty took up Bacon's advice, and henceforth submarines gradually replaced mines at such bases as Portsmouth, Sheerness, Plymouth, Malta, Hong Kong, and Pembroke. Ten submarines were to be built each year, the maximum that Vickers could turn out. Manoeuvres of 1904 confirmed Bacon's affirmations, and Fisher's: 'I have not disguised my opinion, in season or out of season, as to the essential, imperative, immediate, vital, pressing, urgent (I can't think of any more adjectives!) necessity for more submarines at once ... or we shall be caught with our breeches down, just as the Russians have been [by the Imperial Japanese Navy]!' he wrote in 1904.[90] Fisher was far ahead of others at the Admiralty in his views. 'I don't think anyone at the Admiralty in those days, or indeed for some years to come, realised the immense possibilities which lay in submarine warfare,' wrote Roger Keyes, who later became commodore of the submarine service.[91] In any event the building programme had begun, one of immense importance.

Bacon, we imagine, saw the defensive merits of the submarine against cruiser raids. But the range of the submarine was rapidly increasing, with better propulsion systems and larger hulls with oil-bunkering capacity. Fisher could imagine the face of a new underwater warfare. In early 1904 he wrote to Rear-Admiral Louis Battenberg, the Director of Naval Intelligence, concerning his unequivocal faith in the submarine. He stated three deductions: (1) 'the submarine is coming into play in Ocean Warfare almost immediately'; (2) with a Whitehead torpedo (18') the submarine will displace the gun and revolutionise naval tactics; and (3) no single submarine will ever be obsolete. He contended that he would stake his reputation on these three deductions:

Drop a battleship out of the programme [if it is necessary on account of financial necessities] but at any cost double the output of submarines ... If we don't double our output of submarines and go ahead with the Whitehead [torpedo] there will be such an uprising in the Country bye & bye as never yet known in the British Empire! This is big talk but it's coming! I've been living with submarines lately or would not say this![92]

In April 1904 Fisher pressed the Controller of the Navy on the importance of submarines as offensive weapons. 'Had either the Russians or the Japanese had submarines the whole pace of the [Russo-Japanese] war would have been changed for both sides,' he pointed out. The Japanese launched eight separate attacks on Port Arthur, and one submarine would have frustrated these attacks. Japanese transports could never have been employed if the Russians had submarines. He argued that both torpedoes and submarines had greatly increased in effectiveness, but he lamented the lack of concern exhibited by the Admiralty: 'It's astounding ... how the very best amongst us absolutely fail to realise the vast impending revolution in naval warfare and naval strategy that the submarine will accomplish! ... It's the d—d cautious old age spirit that actuates and always had actuated and will actuate the Board of Admiralty ... "Caution is the curse of old age," said Nelson.' The strategic implications of the submarine were enormous: 'When you calmly sit down and work out what will happen – the narrow waters of the Channel and the Mediterranean – how totally the submarine will alter the effect of Gibraltar, Port Said, Lemnos, and Malta, it makes one's hair stand on end!' In a postscript Fisher said 'Our leaders think there is going to be time to get the submarines when war is imminent! ... The supreme feature of sea war is its abrupt, its dramatic suddenness!'[93] In 1905 he predicted that within three to four years the English Channel and the western Mediterranean would become uninhabitable for fleets, due to the threat posed by submarines. As a result, Alexandria would surpass Malta as the key base for the Mediterranean Fleet, although Malta would remain important as a submarine base.[94] And in a letter to Esher, Fisher paraphrased the Controller's response to his demand for more submarines: 'Yes, I fully admit all you say, but we are very busy now perfecting the type of submarines! Just you *wait* patiently till we get our new "B" type, and *then* we'll order submarines in shoals! *Don't* hustle us! Plenty of time!'

The Controller might well have been correct, for if the German experience is anything to go by, many of their early designs proved poor and inadequate, as well as being bad sea boats. It was not until *UB-48*, the precursor of the Type VII of later fame, that a powerful, long-range, and stable submarine came into production. Fisher, impatient fellow that he was, was unsurprisingly indignant at the Controller's response: 'We forget that "half a loaf is better than no bread"! We don't realise that even "pre-adamite submarines are better than no submarines at all"! (And, remember, no submarine of any type, even the pre-historic, ever becomes obsolete.) Our rulers think there is going to be time to get the submarines when war is imminent. Some people think you can go round the corner and buy a submarine like a pound of sugar! *There will be no time for anything*!'[95]

The Admiralty then daringly authorised the first 'A'-type boat, 105ft in length with surface displacement of 185 tons, followed by the 'D' boat in 1910, with displacement of 400 to 500 tons. Still regarded as merely a weapon for local defence, the submarine took on new strategic value when a daring young commander took a 'D' type on a solo mission as part of the 1910 manoeuvres, departing Portsmouth and 'sinking' two cruisers of the hostile fleet in waters off the west coast of Scotland. This exploit gained the attention of the new First Sea Lord, Sir Arthur Wilson. Now aware of the offensive value of the submarine, he decided that the Submarine Service 'should be placed in the hands of a young sea-going Captain of forceful character and modern ideas, imbued with the offensive spirit.' This was Roger Keyes, who had no unique knowledge of these underwater warfare matters or any specialist attainments. Even so, his reputation was one of initiative and dash when in command of light cruisers, scouts, and destroyers. He assumed his new duties in the autumn of 1910, and found, to his dismay, that Fisher's submarine construction programme was tied up in the hands of one supplier – 'a virtual monopoly which Lord Fisher, when First Sea Lord, had obtained from one civilian firm for the construction of submarines and periscopes.'[96] The construction of the larger boats was painfully slow, and Keyes had the monopoly revoked. He realised by 1911 that the Navy had only seventeen seagoing boats, though by then the 'E' boats (600 tons, surface speed 15 knots) were being built. 'The military value of a submarine lies in the skill of her captain and in his powers of leadership,' wrote Keyes, 'If you can add the "hunter's" instinct to a first-class eye and steady nerve, you will probably have a first-class submarine captain.' Having the confidence of his crew was also a necessity: 'They knew in whose hands their fate lay, and one could soon assess the military value of an individual submarine.'[97]

An unintended result of Fisher's technical innovations in the destroyer and the submarine, as well as in torpedoes and gunnery, was that naval tactics became more conservative, less adventuresome. The all-big-gun battleship lent itself to traditional line-ahead tactics, in which each individual captain took up station behind the ship in front of him and blasted away at his counterpart in the opposing line of battle. Little premium was placed on individual initiative. The introduction of the wireless also led to tactical restraint, as the Admiralty could effectively maintain watch over a naval battle in real time, leaving the admiral on the spot with little leeway in the face of Admiralty orders. This was to have significant consequences in the First World War – especially, as shall be seen, during the escape of *Goeben* and *Breslau*.[98] As for the Home Fleet, later named the Grand Fleet, the Battle Orders were drawn up so that a fleet at sea in close formation could make complicated moves when the weapons of the enemy posed real and imminent danger or when an opportunity to exert offensive power against the enemy's fleet presented itself.

The dangers of the torpedo, the submarine, and, to a lesser extent, the mine spun a powerful web of fear among the great commanders at sea. One of the supreme ironies is that it was not until 1905 or 1906 that the Imperial German navy began to consider the submarine a formidable weapon of sea warfare, beneficial to their intended aim of wresting the trident of Neptune from the British. Until then the all-big-gun ship had been their preoccupation in naval construction. Perhaps Fisher's building of *Dreadnought* put the Germans off the scent. And though Germany was one of the last powers to take up the submarine, so sweeping was the German underwater naval revolution that this category of naval weaponry just about ended British naval mastery in 1917 and nearly brought the British Empire to its knees.

Fisher did not exaggerate. Only Bacon, Keyes, Battenberg, Balfour, and Churchill took up his views, and none too soon.

Personnel and other reforms

Fisher's reforms continued in whirlwind fashion, and now included an innovation allowing more ships to be in a state of reserve readiness for any emergency. Again Fisher's genius had an opportunity to demonstrate itself. In a memorandum to Cabinet dated 6 December 1904, Selborne outlined Fisher's new 'nucleus crew' system. Each fighting ship of the Fleet Reserve was to have its own captain, a second in command, and a proportion of other officers. Each ship would have a nucleus crew of two-fifths normal complement, but included in this number would be the more expert ratings, especially in torpedo and gunnery specialisations. Each ship would practise manoeuvres and gunnery, and would form a homogeneous grouping at each of the three home ports: Chatham, Portsmouth, and Plymouth. This system would ensure that such ships would be accustomed to working together, and could be brought up to strength and made ready for action with minimal delay and little worry of damage from ratings unaccustomed to their duties.[99]

Fisher was essentially a democrat. He did not speak or argue as a man of privilege but, rather, the reverse. Some must have seen him as a leveller of the Cromwell age, smiting down the aristocracy and the conservative order of the self-selecting naval governing class. While First Sea Lord he turned to the age-old status of the lower deck, both in terms of conditions at sea and the possibility of promotion. In the course of the nineteenth century, the promotion of men from the lower deck to commissioned rank had all but stopped. From 1890 onwards, the Warrant Officers' Society had sought reform, lobbying for regular commissions to be given to its members. In 1903, 100 chief warrant officers were elevated to the rank of lieutenant. This was entirely thanks to Fisher, then Second Sea Lord with responsibility in the matter.[100] That same year, Fisher also improved the pensions of chief petty officers,[101] and instituted warrant rank for stokers with the creation of the new grade of mechanician.[102] More generally, from 1905 onward Fisher never tired of pressing for more commissions to be awarded to warrant officers.[103]

The number of disciplinary offences, which had been declining until the early 1880s, began to rise in 1893 and hit a twenty-year peak in 1900. This can be attributed to the fact that the number of enlisted personnel increased 90 per cent from 1889 to 1904, an increase that necessitated lower standards in order to attract sufficient personnel.[104] In 1902, though, Fisher told Selborne that there had been improvements in the lower deck in recent years, partly on account of reforms to disciplinary measures. In November 1906 there were disturbances amongst stokers under training at Portsmouth. In a secret telegram sent to the King at Sandringham, Fisher stated that the press had exaggerated the incident. He also argued, 'The men concerned are young Stokers who have recently joined the Navy and are unaccustomed to discipline but it is of course possible that want of judgement has been shown. If so it will be elicited by Court of Enquiry and will be promptly dealt with.' While some, like Beresford, condemned the disturbances, the court of inquiry found that Fisher's suspicion of mishandling was correct.[105] By 1909 the number of disciplinary offences was less than a quarter the number of a decade earlier, a decline that can be attributed to the stabilisation of the number of enlisted personnel from 1904 onward.[106] In October 1909 it was announced that detention quarters would be built at each of the three main naval ports.[107]

Championing lower-deck reforms was Lionel Yexley, who as Petty Officer James Wood had served in the Navy for nineteen years. After purchasing his discharge, Yexley began publishing a monthly, *The Fleet*, that was aimed at the lower deck and raised its concerns.[108] Such actions were radical and, when seen from above, even treacherous. Among the issues for which he lobbied were the reform of victualling and the problem of canteen irregularities, whereby ships' commanding officers would award canteen tenancies to whomever they saw fit, with the result that seamen paid high prices. Yexley also focused on matters of punishment. He had the support of certain members of Parliament, including Gibson Bowles, who would raise questions in the House on such issues, as well as the support of James Thursfield, naval correspondent of *The Times*. In 1906 Fisher asked Yexley to meet with him so that he could acquire background information on the issue of canteen corruption. The first meeting ended icily over a question of providing free paint supplies for ships, but a second meeting resulted in Fisher supporting Yexley's position on the need to eradicate corruption in the canteens.

Out of this support came an inquiry, launched in July 1906 under the chairmanship of Rear-Admiral Spencer Logan. During the autumn it heard evidence from many sources, including many ratings, and presented its report in January 1907. Logan recommended a standard ration and messing allowance as proposed in *The Fleet*; that enlisted men be allowed to purchase additional supplies from the paymaster, who was to be present whenever rations were issued; that centralised catering be created aboard *Dreadnought* as an experiment; and that an inspectorate of canteens be created, and the process of awarding contracts be standardised and overseen by the Admiralty. In June 1907 the government announced its acceptance of Logan's report, and over the next nine months the recommendations were implemented. Not only did the reforms ensure that the lower deck was better fed, but they resulted in a significant financial gain to the individual sailor. He now found himself with a monthly surplus on his messing bills. The reforms were equivalent to a pay raise of 3d a day, which is especially notable considering that there had been no general increase in pay in fifty years.[109]

In 1907 *The Fleet* suggested a new arrangement under which young petty officers could be raised to the rank of acting lieutenant, which would thereby avoid the problem that the only petty officers who were commissioned were often on the eve of retirement. This proposal formed the foundation of Churchill's 'mate' scheme of 1912, although not to the extent Yexley argued for. In 1909 Fisher indicated to Yexley that he was having trouble convincing his Admiralty colleagues of the benefits of promoting warrant officers to lieutenants, and it was only on the eve of his own retirement in 1910 that he was able to widen the effort.[110]

On 13 January 1910 Fisher reassured Yexley that he would continue to champion their causes in retirement. He frankly doubted whether his successors would have the same enthusiasm for causes of the lower deck. He also told Yexley that he had left a memorandum on the subject for his successors.[111] That year, the issue of commissioning petty officers came to the fore, accompanied by some officers' fears that it would mean the democratisation of the Navy. This issue was another of those left to the new First Sea Lord, Sir Arthur Wilson, by Fisher on his retirement, and in August 1910 Fisher wrote to Yexley to say that if Yexley were to draft a realistic scheme for commissioning petty officers, Fisher would push it.[112] He added, 'You cannot in a democratic state go on drawing 99% at least of your officers from the Upper Ten! *It won't last and it ought not to last.* I have just had [First Lord Reginald] McKenna here on his second visit to me and he sees all this but no one [in Cabinet] to back him.'[113] Two days later Fisher echoed these sentiments to Esher: 'It's amazing to me that anyone should persuade himself that an aristocratic Service can be maintained in a Democratic State ... The pressure won't come from inside the Navy but from outside – an avalanche like A.D. 1788 (the French Revolution) – and will sweep away a lot more than desirable! It is essentially a political question rather than a Naval question proper. *It is all so easy*, only the d—d Tory prejudices stand in the way!'[114]

In 1905 the Admiralty appointed a committee under Captain Montague Brown to investigate pay differentials between junior ratings and petty officers. The committee's proceedings had no net impact on the pay received by most seamen.[115] However, that same year, certain changes announced in the Cawdor Memorandum meant that a provision allowance would be paid to men on leave, and in place of the current practice of retaining part of a rating's allotment for his dependants as a security against desertion or death on foreign service, the authorities would henceforth pay the full amount.[116] Prior to this time there had not been significant agitation for pay raises, as most sailors felt that they were better off than their civilian counterparts; but from 1907 onwards the annual loyal appeal of the lower-deck societies included a call for a general but unspecified pay increase.[117] Within a few years the agitation for pay increases grew exponentially. During 1910 and 1911 the country experienced an unprecedented wave of strikes over pay and work conditions, with many of these strikes resulting in pay increases. The lower deck became more aware of the fact that it had not had a pay increase in sixty years, with the common sailor living in much the same world as his grandfather had done if at sea in the royal service, and in 1911 the loyal appeal included, for the first time, a request for a specific pay increase that would average 20 per cent for all ratings. In early October 1911 Fisher told Yexley that he continued to warn the First Lord that he would be wise to anticipate the 'irresistible coming agitation' of the rank and file of the Navy for greater recognition of their legitimate aspirations.[118] Fisher also urged Yexley to forge an alliance with the Navy League, which could potentially raise lower-deck concerns in the House via the Tories.[119] In autumn 1911 Yexley published a book, *Our Fighting Men*, that criticised the current system of discipline in the Navy, especially on the issue of disrating.[120] Fisher ensured he got good coverage and good reviews.

When Churchill became First Lord of the Admiralty in October 1911, he allied himself with Fisher and Yexley on matters of reforms for the lower deck. They found themselves opposed by officers who resisted any changes to the King's Regulations, the so-called drive and punish school. But the trio of Yexley, Fisher and Churchill brought to an end the dark age of naval discipline. The first general pay rise in sixty years was effected. And a real path of promotion from the lower deck to commissioned rank for young men of ability opened up. In other words, when taken in the aggregate, the work of these three was revolutionary.

In these matters, Churchill's challenge had been to convince the Sea Lords of the wisdom of reform. He met particular resistance from Prince Louis of Battenberg, Second Sea Lord from 1911 to 1912 and then First Sea Lord. His

Serene Highness was apathetic to 'lower-deck commissions'. A necessarily emasculated scheme was announced in Churchill's speech on the navy estimates on 18 March 1912. Improvements, such as they were, fell short in the way of pay, discipline, promotion, and food. What marks him out as different from his predecessor (McKenna) and, indeed, his successor (Balfour) as First Lord was his awareness of injustice and discontent in the Navy and, in times of social unrest, the difficulties in the country at large, notably in regards to coal miners and the Minimum Wage bill.

Churchill sympathised with Fisher's concerns for free education for cadets but was unable to get further than the provision of a number of scholarships. It was not until after the Second World War that fees were abolished at Dartmouth, and students were chosen on merit and not on their parents' ability to pay.[121] Fisher disliked this system, with its inbred privilege, and wanted fees to be paid by the state. He knew he would face immense opposition, and he gave this as an analogy, allowing his rhetorical skills full play:

Bows and Arrows died hard in the Navy so did masts and sails; water-tube boilers were going to boil our stokers! To do away with the special navigating class of officers was to ruin the Navy; yet it has reduced wrecks and groundings of ships 30 per cent and a vessel can go to sea now even if the usual Navigating Officer is sick! Salt beef is gone, and the Service is going to the devil! Snuffboxes were made out of it. Boarding pikes have only just left us. Greek is dead, but, alas, Latin still lives! as the shore-going schoolmasters apparently can't teach anything else, and we must have some test for boys entering the Navy; but they learn it no more after entry, which gives Lord Goschen sleepless nights!

The opposition was simply prodigious to Lord Kelvin's compass and sounding machine, perhaps the two greatest because the most life-saving of human inventions. A distinguished Admiral, when First Sea Lord, objected to torpedoes because there were none when he came to sea, and to midshipmen having baths, because he never washed! Yes! the Bow and Arrow party are still with us, and we are 'a retrograde Admiralty'! They can't bear the *Dreadnought* – she is too fast! – and they hate big guns. They'll hate Heaven, probably, because there's no more sea there, and they won't like all the harps playing the same tune. Fancy! Complete interchangeability! Admiral Lambton and a Lieutenant (E) exchanging harps! It will be Hell!

But this new scheme will be much more Hell to the 'Bow and Arrow' party than is Interchangeability, and the making of every Naval officer into an Engineer. Public opinion is the only force able to effect this reform. This is a free country, where everyone can do as he likes, and, if he doesn't he is made to! This is a case![122]

We get another indication of Fisher's revolutionary thinking in his letter to journalist J A Spender on 8 August 1910, in which he argued that this 'democratic country isn't going to stand an aristocratic Navy any more than a non-elective House of Lords! ... We must have State-paid education for the Navy and sufficient pay for the boy to live on besides till he is a Lieutenant.'[123] Later that month Fisher discussed naval issues with Lloyd George, emphasising that the issue of state-paid education would have to be addressed.[124] He continued to agitate for state-paid education after his retirement, writing to Esher in December 1911:

> I enclose you a letter from —, received a little time ago. He is a very eminent Civil Engineer. There is a 'dead set' being made to get the Midshipmen under the new scheme to rebel against 'engineering'! —, — , & Co. are persistently at it through their friends in the Fleet, and calling those Midshipmen who go in for engineering – 'Greasers.' The inevitable result of the present young officers of the Navy disparaging and slighting this chief necessary qualification of engineering in these engineering days will be to force the throwing open of entry as officers in the Navy *to all classes of the population* and adopting State paid education and support till the pay is sufficient to support![125]

Grand strategy and the challenge from Germany

With the close of the nineteenth century came the realisation that Britain's strategic and diplomatic position was evolving in a not entirely desirable manner, and that adjustments might be necessary. Captain C L Ottley, the British naval attaché in Paris, and one of the sharpest brains in the Navy on the subject of shifting international relations, advised that the Fashoda crisis of 1898 had provided the best possible object lesson as to why Britain should maintain a powerful navy. 'We are of course a great naval power, the trouble is we are not also a great military power, and can never become so.' He also noted: 'Captain Mahan's new gospel of the value of Sea Power has penetrated deep into the minds of our Continental Naval rivals.' Russia, Italy, and France were learning lessons:

> The explanation of the universal craving for Sea Power is, I believe, that all nations now see that so long as England holds it unchallenged, she commands the situation in the world. How can we expect Russia, for example, and still less Germany, to acquiesce in such a condition of affairs as that? This leads to a further enquiry – What right has England to suppose that she, alone in Europe, is to for ever stand aside and apart from entangling alliances. The idea of such alliances is hateful, but in the scheme of the Balance of Power a century hence, is it not clear that of two things one [must prevail] – Either

Britain must stand for a confederation of vast Colonial States, or her existence will depend on alliances.[126]

These changing circumstances, so well outlined by Ottley, were of pre-eminent concern to Fisher. No one in the Navy saw it as clearly as he did. During his tenure as C-in-C, Mediterranean, Fisher had turned his mind from France to Germany as the future foe: 'Personally, I have always been an enthusiastic advocate for friendship and alliance with France. They never have and never will interfere with our trade. It's not their line and, really, we have no clashing of vital interests. Newfoundland might be settled in 5 minutes. But we have not been politic toward them. The Germans are our natural enemies everywhere! We ought to unite with France and Russia!'[127] Fisher might write privately to a naval correspondent on such a matter as this, but official policy did not derive from Fisher. Rather, it came from Cabinet, largely led by the Foreign Office. Fisher foresaw the situation as it developed in the run-up to 1914, and because the naval situation was so compelling to Britain's future, he understood it more clearly than most of his contemporaries, notably those outside the Services. That he was often at loggerheads with the Foreign Office is understandable. A future continental war was to be avoided at all costs. A limited war, however, was another matter, and one Fisher did not oppose in theory.

'Splendid isolation' was at an end, and a letter Fisher wrote to journalist Arnold White, dated 6 August 1902, provides an appreciation of Fisher's thinking about the unravelling and shifting international circumstances, and his views on the major powers in Europe. First, on Germany: 'The German Emperor may be devoted to us, but he can no more stem the tide of German commercial hostility to this country of ours than Canute could keep the North Sea from wetting his patent-leather boots! It's inherent. Their interests everywhere clash without, and their gratitude for all our astounding beneficence to them is nil!' On France: 'In absolutely nothing do we clash, *and never can clash* ... Does the French nation realize, do you think, what the German Mercantile Marine in its advancing leaps and bounds means? It means another million of French soldiers required in the vicinity of Cherbourg, where a landing is easy.' On the United States:

> We think of the United States as our friend. (*I don't say so in public, but it's all bosh!*) New York only just comes after Berlin in being the largest German city in the world. There are scores and scores of American cities like Milwaukee where there is hardly anyone but Germans! Only 25 per cent of the United States population are American-born, the rest are chiefly Germans, and what are not Germans are Irish, who hate us only a little less.

And on Russia:

1. Winston Churchill, First Lord of the Admiralty, with Lord Fisher in 1913, when the latter was a regular and welcome visitor to the Admiralty.

2. Churchill as First Lord of the Admiralty. Appointed in 1911, he began energetically to prepare for the clash with Germany that he believed inevitable.

RT. HON. WINSTON CHURCHILL
1ST LORD OF THE ADMIRALTY.

3. Fisher in December 1915, six months after he resigned as First Sea Lord after bitter arguments with Churchill over the Dardanelles campaign.

4. HMS *Renown*, launched in 1886, was Fisher's flagship on the North American station and in the Mediterranean. Fisher was particularly appreciative of this compact and powerful ship's greatest attribute, her speed. She also served as a Royal Yacht and took the Prince of Wales, the future George V, to India in 1905.

5. Young Fisher as captain of *Inflexible*. Perceived as able and competent, Fisher was appointed to the new battleship *Inflexible* in 1881, and it was during this period that he became a good friend of Edward, Prince of Wales.

6. 'The dauntless three.' Fisher in 1903 at Portsmouth, where he was appointed Commander-in-Chief in order to personally supervise the inauguration of his new education scheme at Osborne College. Seen here with Viscount Esher, president of the Committee of War Office Reconstruction, and Sir George Sydenham Clarke, fortifications engineer and strong believer in the Royal Navy's role as the main line of defence against invasion.

7. HMS *Dreadnought*, often perceived as Fisher's radical answer to the rising threat of Germany, was designed in 1904 when war between Britain and both France and Russia was still a possibility; only by the time of her launch in 1906 was the threat of Germany the more real.

H. Lawson M.P

Ivor Herbert M.P

The Navy supported by both Parties!!

8. Fisher in 1913, expounding on the Navy's future requirements while promenading on Kreuzbrunnen-Kolonnade, in the famed spa Marienbad, Bohemia. He is flanked, left, by the Hon Harry Levy-Lawson, Liberal Unionist MP for Mile End, and, right, by Major-General Sir Ivor Herbert, Liberal, Monmouthshire South.

9. Battlecruisers at full speed. The *Invincible*-class battlecruisers, a merger of the battleship and the armoured cruiser, and the subsequent development of the type, both in the Royal Navy and other navies, came about through Fisher's belief in the need for fast ships that could force action on the enemy or withdraw swiftly if necessary.

10. Herbert Asquith, Liberal prime minister from 1908 to 1916. The setbacks of the war, notably the failure of the Dardanelles campaign and the stalemate on the Western Front, combined with the difficulties of mediating between such fractious Cabinet ministers as Churchill and Lloyd George, led to his eventual overthrow in December 1916.

11. Admiral Lord Charles Beresford, Commander-in-Chief of the Channel Fleet in 1907, whose bitter quarrels with Fisher and later clashes with Churchill over the latter's perceived autocratic interference in the conduct of naval operations spanned the early years of the century.

12. A youthful-looking Churchill shaking hands with Kaiser Wilhelm II in 1909 during German military manoeuvres.

13. 'Aye Ready!' A contemporary postcard extolling Churchill's appointment as the First Lord of the Admiralty in 1911. His dismissal from that office in 1915 was a bitter pill.

14. Fisher with Churchill as First Lord of the Admiralty at Devonport dockyard for the launch of HMS *Centurion* in November 1911. She was the third of the four *King George V*-class battleships and the longest lasting. Churchill would see her again in 1944 when she was used as a breakwater off the Normandy beaches.

UNDER HIS MASTER'S EYE.

SCENE—*Mediterranean, on board the Admiralty yacht "Enchantress."*

MR. WINSTON CHURCHILL. "ANY HOME NEWS?"

MR. ASQUITH. "HOW CAN THERE BE WITH YOU HERE?"

15. 'Under his Master's Eye'. A *Punch* cartoon of 1913 pokes fun at Churchill's great fondness for the elegant Admiralty steam yacht *Enchantress*, in which he visited hundreds of ships and naval establishments both in home waters and the Mediterranean.

The Empress of Russia has complete control over the Tsar. She is English through and through. Her favourite sister is Princess Louis of Battenberg, who I know intimately, her husband [being] my best Captain in the Mediterranean Fleet. Whatever people may say to the contrary, our Russian policy of alternating bluster and mistrust with an occasional gleam of confidence thrown in has been stupid beyond measure. Russia does not affect our trade and commerce in any degree whatever, and the Afghan bogey has become ludicrous, simply because we can overrun the country far sooner than the Russians can.[128]

The alarm bells were ringing in the Admiralty in regards to Germany's rapid rise as a naval power. Balfour knew that Foreign Office attempts in 1901 had failed to bring an accord with Germany, but, invariably reluctant to take an alarmist view, he could not yet bring himself to fall in line with the Admiralty. His mood changed from acceptance to alarm. To Selborne in 1902 he commented on the possibility of rivalry with Germany: 'I find it extremely difficult to believe that we have, as you seem to suppose, much to fear from Germany – in the immediate future at all events. It seems to me so clear that, broadly speaking, her interests and ours are identical. But I have sorrowfully to admit that the world, unfortunately, is not always governed by enlightened self-interest.'[129] Balfour was one of the first to take the alarmist view. The Foreign Office sprang into action. During 1902 successive attempts to reach an understanding between Britain and Germany, mainly initiated by Joseph Chamberlain, had failed.[130] This led to an atmosphere of suspicion on the part of Germany. There was growing hostility, too, between the presses of the respective powers, and altogether a thinly veiled hostility between the two countries. Once those in London realised an alliance with Germany was impossible, they turned their attention to solving British strategic problems elsewhere: Britain signed a totally defensive arrangement with Imperial Japan in 1902, and soon, too, overtures were made to France and to Russia. Partly in consequence of the emerging entente between France and Russia, Britain was drawn into an alliance, formal or informal, that sought to counterbalance Germany's dominance on the Continent and its growing influence on and over the seas. Before long, the War Office was engaged in secret discussions with its intended ally, France.

Always concerned with the interlinking of profit and power, the British state remained anxious about the security of the British merchant marine in time of war. In the decades leading up to the First World War, naval men were divided as to the proper means of defending England's merchant marine. All agreed with Mahan's argument for the necessity of a superior battle fleet but were divided as to whether they should police zones and lines of communications or concentrate cruisers at focal points. Opinion was also divided on the question of close escort of convoys. By 1905 everyone agreed that Britain was vulnerable in a maritime war. Not only did they need a great battle fleet, but they also required a force to protect the merchant marine in all possible circumstances. By this time, opinion had hardened against escorting convoys and in favour of concentrating forces at the decisive points. As one MP, a representative of the ship owners, stated: 'Today the convoy system was impossible. Under modern conditions it could not be expected that steamships would collect in large numbers and wait until a convoy had been prepared. They must look to other means for the protection of the mercantile marine, there was one system and one system only ... and that was the proper patrolling of the great sea routes.' Concentration was proclaimed official policy by Fisher in 1905, as embodied in the War Orders to Commanders-in-Chief of that same year, and was adopted in 1914.[131]

Fisher was no sooner at his desk as First Sea Lord than a pair of events concentrated the mind of the Admiralty wonderfully and brought into sharp focus the new state of naval rivalries. Each of these unrelated events – the Russo-Japanese War of 1904–1905 and the First Moroccan Crisis of 1905–1906 – played a crucial role in the development of British naval strategy, and they provide a useful illustration of the flexibility of Fisher's strategic thinking and war-planning capabilities. Britain's and Fisher's responses are what hold them together as revolutionary events in diplomatic history and naval readiness. The Kaiser's Germany loomed larger on the troubling horizon: the unwelcome advent of crises over which Britain could have no control posed the alarms. Britain was bound to be embroiled in these crises, if only indirectly, given the greater stakes and the rising temperatures in the great chancelleries and admiralty boards.

The Russo-Japanese War broke out over the issue of which power was to dominate in Manchuria, and which would benefit from the decline of Imperial China. Imperial Japan, fearing Russian intentions in Korea, started the war by launching a successful surprise attack on the Russian fleet anchored at Port Arthur. This and other early Japanese successes came as no surprise to Admiral Sir Cyprian Bridge, Commander-in-Chief of the China station, as he related to Selborne on 14 February 1904. Bridge, a former Director of Naval Intelligence, informed the Admiralty that the Imperial Japanese navy had an excellent grasp of strategy and tactics, and their spirit and willingness to die to get at the Russians was without parallel in the annals of history. He believed that the Japanese dockyards were second to none, and that the British had 'a great deal' to learn from the Japanese. He also made a comment that would prove prophetic not just for the course of the Russo-Japanese War, but for the rest of the century: '[Japanese success] justifies the view which I have often expressed and which I am disposed to think is worth the attention of statesmen and diplomatists – that Asia is not going to allow itself to be treated by Europe in the twentieth century as it was in the eighteenth and nineteenth; and that Japan is going to make sure of this.'[132]

By the end of 1904, the Russian navy operating in the Pacific had been bottled up in Port Arthur, and its base and fortification there had fallen after a long and murderous siege. In these desperate circumstances, the Russians deployed their 2nd Baltic Squadron from bases near St Petersburg all the way to the Far East. The voyage of this fleet – dubbed by one wag as 'the fleet that had to die' – became a source of mounting tension between Britain, France, and Russia. Britain had been in an alliance with Japan since 1902, so was diplomatically aligned with Japan against Russia and, by extension, France.[133] The terms of the treaty stipulated that if one of the signatories were at war with two other powers, the other would enter the war in support. Thus, while Japan was at war with Russia, Britain was not obligated to help, but if the French violated neutrality in aiding the Russians, and Japan attacked the Russian fleet at a French anchorage, Britain could easily find itself obligated to go to war with both Russia and France.

The 2nd Baltic Squadron, commanded by the redoubtable Admiral Zinovy Rozhestvensky (who Fisher liked to dub 'Roji'), purposely sailed from the Baltic under cover of false information. The Russians feared there were enemy torpedo boats, presumably Japanese, in the area, but that too was misinformation. Russian warships bumbled into some Hull fishing steamers, and in a night action under searchlights raked them with shot and shell without warning. Two English fishermen were killed and others wounded. The Foreign Office launched a flurry of diplomatic protests, and an international commission was set to examine this 'Dogger Bank incident'. All the lies and misconceptions were revealed by the inquiry, and Russia was obliged to pay heavily in compensation.

In the meantime, Beresford, based with his fleet near Gibraltar, worked up his own contingency plans for dealing with the Russian naval units should they threaten, but one by one the Russian battleships and cruiser passed the danger points and shaped their courses for the Sea of Japan. At the Admiralty the cipher clerks were pressed into overtime, receiving regular and accurate intelligence briefings reporting the progress of the Russian fleet toward its impending collision with the Imperial Japanese navy. In particular, the Admiralty knew that the Russian fleet, by arrangement with France, used the French base at Kamranh in Indochina to refuel.[134]

Fisher believed it imperative that the French understand that such usage of the base was unacceptable. It was only through such usage that the Russian Baltic Fleet would be able to engage the Japanese fleet, as Fisher warned Lord Lansdowne at the Foreign Office. Fisher put it this way: if French assistance to the Russian fleet continued, the Japanese Navy 'may take such action as I suppose will involve us in war, for I imagine there is a limit even to their forbearance!'[135]

News of Fisher's concerns reached No. 10 Downing Street. Prime Minister Balfour attempted to calm the First Sea Lord. He argued that France was in a difficult position vis-à-vis the Russians in the Far East, and had done what it could in stretching the limits of neutrality to help its allies. 'I hope the incident will pass without any immediate trouble, ... though if it ends in a maritime reverse for the Japanese, its ultimate results will be most serious.' Fisher remained unconvinced: the French actions seemed to be 'the most flagrant and outrageous breach of neutrality possible to conceive! ... Suppose the Japanese attack Roji in Kamranh Bay, as they are justified in doing. Will France fight Japan? If so, we fight France! What pickings for the German Emperor.'[136]

On 27 April 1905, acting on Fisher's letter, Lansdowne sent instructions to the British ambassador in Paris, Sir Francis Leveson Bertie. He was to inform the French that the Japanese government would be closely watching France on how neutrality was to be maintained in the Far East, especially considering that a third Russian squadron appeared likely to use Kamranh Bay. 'Intense exasperation which repetition of these incidents would produce in Japan might have the most inconvenient results[.] Nor can we ignore effects in this country in which an outbreak of indignation was averted only by action of French government in ordering Rojestvesky's departure ... We earnestly trust that instructions given by French government have been such as to preclude possibility of any further misunderstanding. Speak in this sense but in the most friendly and considerate manner to M. Declassé.' Bertie replied that the French minister had assured him there was no reason to suspect that there would be any repetition of the Kamranh Bay proceedings in French waters. But he said that he would make immediate inquiries and take measures to ensure there was not another incident. Lansdowne subsequently informed Fisher that the French claims that the Russians were not inside Kamranh Bay were weak.[137]

On 1 May 1905 a confidential report from the Director of Naval Intelligence, Admiral Sir Charles Ottley, landed on Fisher's desk. It provided an update on the Russo-Japanese War and, more to the point, detailed its implications for Britain. Ottley, a force to be reckoned with and a seasoned naval attaché with an unparalleled grasp of foreign navies and foreign policy, was then a key member of Fisher's planning elite. In the report, Ottley wondered how much the Far Eastern situation could affect the summer's planned grand manoeuvres of the British Fleet in home waters. It was apparent from all the sources that had come to hand that Russian admirals Rozhestvensky from the Baltic and Nebogatov in Asian waters would soon join their fleets, a surprising fact given that no one had imagined the Russian Baltic Fleet would ever arrive east of Singapore: 'Once more the unexpected has happened, and it behoves us to take measures that prudence demands to meet a situation ... [previously thought improbable].' The political situation was that Britain was bound by treaty to Japan's interests, and at the peace table France, Germany, and Russia would be hostile to Japan and Britain. In the circumstances, Ottley recommended that the British Fleet be reinforced, and that Britain should back Japan and be prepared for war against the three most powerful European nations. He noted the astonishing personal gifts of King Edward VII, who might be important as a diplomat and peacemaker. He suggested curtailing, if not stopping, the planned manoeuvres, as the highly unstable international situation necessitated caution. The next day the Board of Admiralty, after discussions with the prime minister, cancelled the Baltic manoeuvres scheduled to begin on 13 June.[138]

Even as the crisis over Kamranh Bay was at its height, another – the second to cause alarm bells to ring – developed in Morocco. There the Sultan was under pressure from foreign interests. France, for strategic reasons, had its eyes on the geographical prize. The British Admiralty, however, was opposed to seeing the southern shore of the Straits of Gibraltar in the hands of any rival power. Soon the French and the British patched up their quarrel about North Africa, with the French acknowledging British rights in Egypt, and the British, in return, giving the French a free hand in Morocco. However, now it was the Kaiser's turn, and he decided to challenge French claims in Morocco. On 31 March 1905 he paid a personal visit to Tangiers. He made flamboyant speeches to the effect that all powers must have equal rights under the free sultanate, and that Germany had great and growing interests in Morocco. This ploy drew a frightened France closer to her ancient rival, Britain. Before long, rumours of joint talks and joint preparations actuated in the form of scheduled talks. Anglo-French staff conversations began in 1906, though the new prime minister, Sir Henry Campbell-Bannerman, stressed his aversion to the thought of British troops being employed on the Continent in the event of war. Georges Clemenceau, his opposite, was appalled by Campbell-Bannerman's response and chuckled that the conversations could take place without the prime minister's knowledge. The fact was that the Service departments (the War Office and Admiralty) did not agree on how Britain would be involved in a war on the Continent.[139] An intermediary, Lieutenant-Colonel Repington, military correspondent of *The Times*, had taken an informal sounding of French opinion and brought word to London that if war with Germany occurred, France looked for the immediate dispatch of a British force to serve in co-operation with the French army. The French, perhaps predictably, maintained that the British force would be under French command, whether it was acting in direct contact with the French army or not. Here we see the beginnings of an unwanted scenario, of Britain being dragged into continental affairs – anathema to Fisher and to the Navy.

The greatest resistance to what became known as the Continental Commitment came from Fisher. That Britain would be subservient to any other nation's continental campaigning was out of the question. His idea for the proper utilisation of the British Army was that the Navy should throw an expeditionary force ashore in some unexpected place where it could fulfil its duty, perhaps attacking the enemy army in flank or rear. Thus surprise would be achieved through the mobility that the Fleet provided. Fisher credited Sir Edward Grey with the idea but it was actually his own. The CID Secretary, Colonel Sir George Clarke (later Lord Sydenham of Combe), one of the most highly regarded military strategists of his time, favoured this Admiralty policy. However, Grey's consent to the commencement of staff talks was leading down an irreversible path of obligation. Grey acted on his own account; as Clemenceau had suggested, the talks between British and French generals proceeded largely without the knowledge of politicians in London or the Admiralty. Grey bypassed the CID, which did not see the proposal until five years later.

Meanwhile, the British Director of Military Operations, J M Grierson, learned from his French opposite that the French regarded a war with Germany as necessarily involving Belgium. If a German advance through Belgium were to occur, what the French desired most was a British Army sent to give aid to Belgium. Thus it was that the Grierson plan called for a British expeditionary force to proceed via Calais and Dunkirk across northern France to Belgium, there to secure the French left flank. Fisher, fearing submarines or fitful raids by German cruisers in the southern North Sea and in the English Channel, refused to guarantee the direct shipment to Belgian ports until 'command of the sea could be gained' – a correct appreciation of the situation, for troop convoys had to have complete security. Once such sea command was achieved, the base could be shifted directly to the prized harbour of Antwerp. The scheme imagined the British expeditionary force acting independently of the French army, and although Grierson was hostile to Fisher's conception of the Army's role, the plan for operating in Belgium demonstrated one of Fisher's concepts: from Belgium a British force would be in a position to threaten the flank or even the rear of a Germany army advancing into France. In short, Fisher always sought to retain Britain's independent action in a future war – he was right to state these opinions and was correct in his judgements on this matter. But he could not hold back the tide, and the fateful Continental Commitment was born. It was not the Navy's doing.

At this juncture, Whitehall became worried about what the Germans might do in Morocco. The complication was that Britain could be drawn into a war in the Far East if Russia became embroiled in a dispute with France and French interests there, even as it supported France in a fight with Germany over

Morocco. Could the British fight a two-front war? The Foreign Office rightly wanted to know. It wondered about the Admiralty's response to the Moroccan crisis in light of developing difficulties in the Far East: 'If we tell the French we will back them up over Morocco, we cannot tell them at the same time we will fight them [over Russian use of the French base at] Kamranh Bay ... Has Sir J. Fisher a way out of this? Could we say, if you clear the Russians out of K. Bay & maintain a real neutrality we will fight Germany for you?' So wrote Louis Mallet, Lord Lansdowne's private secretary, who attached to the communication the Admiralty's concurrence with his views.[140] It is unclear if the proposal was ever transmitted to Paris and passed to the French, but it is an indication of British priorities in the two crises.

With war clouds steadily gathering, Fisher commanded the Fleet to be ready at short notice to descend on the German coast,[141] and he told Esher and Grey, among others, that this was so. According to Grey, 'It appears that Sir John Fisher has long ago taken the French Naval Attaché in hand, and no doubt has all naval plans prepared.'[142] Here was a perfect Fisher scheme, Nelsonic in audacity but surely to cause a major war. He reasoned that if Germany acquired a port on the Moroccan coast, it would be detrimental to the Royal Navy and, as such, the issue ought to be considered a *casus belli*. A port like Mogador would give the Germans the ability to raid British commerce to eastern seas, which in wartime would necessarily be travelling via the Cape. Fisher argued that the time was ripe for war:

> This seems a golden opportunity for fighting the Germans in alliance with the French, so I earnestly hope you may be able to bring this about. Of course I don't pretend to be a diplomat, but it strikes me the German Emperor will greatly injure the splendid and increasing Anglo-French Entente if he is allowed to score now in *any way* ... All I hope is that you will send a telegram to Paris that the English and French Fleets are *one*. We could have the German Fleet, the Kiel Canal, and Schleswig-Holstein within a fortnight.[143]

At the Foreign Office, Fisher's plans sent shivers up the back of Lord Lansdowne, who was then considering an appeasement line with Germany. Lansdowne sent Mallet to see Fisher on the subject of ceding a port to the Germans. Could the admiral's views be softened? Fisher would hear nothing of it, and Mallet returned to the Foreign Office with a favourable opinion of Fisher, whose belligerence he had come so abruptly to admire. Mallet reported to Lansdowne: 'He [Fisher] is a splendid chap and simply longs to have a go at Germany. I "abound in his sense" and told him I would do all I could with Lord Lansdowne.'[144] Lansdowne was ever more on his guard. In his office, however, the tide of opinion was fast flowing against him. By and large, undersecretaries were decidedly anti-German and did little to improve the tone of Anglo-German relations.[145] In particular, Sir Charles Hardinge watched the enormous build-up of the German fleet with alarm, and saw German naval power more as a power of coercion than an instrument for invasion. He acknowledged Tirpitz's risk theory and concluded that the best way to deal with it was to accelerate Britain's naval programme.[146]

In the worrying circumstances, Fisher, who believed that 'surprise was the pith and marrow of war', conceived of a plan in 1905 – he strengthened it three years later – to wipe out the German navy by one swift stroke. The plan was to 'Copenhagen' the growing German fleet at Kiel – that is, to destroy it as it lay at its moorings without a previous declaration of war, just as the spirited Admiral James Gambier had wiped out the Danish fleet at Copenhagen in 1807. At the same time he proposed to land an army on the Pomeranian coast, less than a hundred miles from Berlin, where the Russian army had arrived in the time of Frederick the Great. The whole thing depended on suddenness and unexpectedness. At first Fisher wished to keep his plan under wraps and concealed it from Prime Minister Campbell-Bannerman. The only person who knew of it was Admiral Sir Arthur Wilson, though Fisher also shared his scheme to 'Copenhagen' the German fleet with his friend Edward VII. Fisher takes up the story: 'It seemed to me simply a sagacious act on England's part to seize the German fleet when it was so very easy of accomplishment in the manner I sketched out to his Majesty, and probably without bloodshed. But, alas! Even the very whisper of it excited exasperation against the supposed bellicose, but really peaceful, First Sea Lord, and the project was damned.' That was Fisher's recounting. 'My God, Fisher, you must be mad!' the King retorted.[147] But the admiral loved to shock. These exuberant words, uttered in jest by the First Sea Lord over brandy and cigars, were often repeated in British wardrooms.[148]

Word of Fisher's bold assault plan reached the Kaiser. In a memorandum to the King on 18 January 1906, Esher related the comments of the financier Mr A Beit regarding his recent audience with the Kaiser, and in particular the Kaiser's views on Fisher:

He [the Kaiser] said that Sir John Fisher thought that because the fleet was in perfect order and more powerful than the German Fleet, it was the moment to provoke war. Mr Beit told the Emperor that he had seen Sir John Fisher in Carlsbad and that although Sir John did not conceal that the Fleet was ready for an emergency, he had not used language like that imputed to him. The Emperor replied, 'He thinks it is time for an attack, and I don't blame him. It is quite human, I can quite understand it, but we are also prepared, and if it comes to a war, it depends on the weight you carry into action, namely, a good conscience, and I have that.[149]

Fisher also related this story to Esher, and in doing so attributed the following comments to the Kaiser: '*Fisher remains*! *that's the vital fact*! I admire Fisher. I say nothing against him. If I were in his place I should do all that he has done (in concentrating the British Navy against Germany) and I should do all that I *know* he has in his mind to do.'[150]

Fisher lacked credibility with the Committee of Imperial Defence and, in fact, did little to encourage it as a useful organisation for analysis of future needs or the planning for a future war. The result of Fisher's unwillingness to 'play' was that the CID moved ahead regardless of the Admiralty. So it was that in February 1906, in keeping with the Anglo-French military conversations, the CID drew up a plan to send British divisions to France in case of a war between France and Germany. Fisher dug in his heels: the plan had to be dropped in the face of Fisher's refusal to guarantee safe passage of the troops across the Channel. This showed Jacky Fisher's petulance and blind devotion to naval matters. In fact, Fisher was upset with the CID for rejecting his own Baltic plans and interfering with his dreadnought policy. He also retained a personal animosity toward Sir George Clarke,[151] going so far as to tell Tweedmouth that he wished Clarke would 'die of yellow fever as governor of some West Indian Island.'[152] In summary, Fisher was not willing to accept any military, or for that matter any French, interference. He did not believe in an expeditionary force for the Continent, while the French and British generals regarded his plans for a joint attack on Schleswig-Holstein as impractical. As a result, Haldane, the Secretary of State for War, went one way and Fisher the other, and there was no real co-operation between the War Office and the Admiralty. This was to be of fateful importance in the years ahead.[153]

On 11 May 1906 the CID proposed that military action should be taken against the Ottoman Empire in order to prevent it from threatening Egypt. Again Fisher intervened: he declared that he was against risking ships or undertaking any further responsibilities in the Mediterranean. Fisher's position remained the same when the CID proposed a similar policy in November 1906. The Admiralty became distanced from the CID, which was to have held a co-ordinating role at the apex of the defence establishment. Fisher wanted to maintain the Navy's freedom of action – to go where and when it pleased.

All this time the German rival increased in strength: as of September 1906, Fisher contended that Germany was England's 'only possible foe'. He was correct in this view but wrong in others: he believed that Austria–Hungary and Italy would not join Germany against England, that France would do nothing, and that Japan posed a grave risk to German interests throughout the Pacific region, especially along the Chinese coast. Germany's only hope came from an association with the United States, but Fisher stated that this 'hope will *never* be fulfilled'.[154] Fisher would not show his hand; he would not disclose his war plans, and this infuriated the war planners and the press. Clarke and Repington in particular were furious with Fisher's reticence, but Esher put up a stout defence: 'The Navy is always on a war footing, and a telegram can send a fleet to the other end of the earth. So why disclose ideas, if there are any!'[155] Esher always kept on side with Fisher, writing reassuringly in the same vein, arguing that strategic control would always rest with him, and that nothing should induce him to disclose his war plans.[156]

Additional advice and support came from Admiral Sir Arthur Wilson, Fisher's confidant, who wrote to Fisher in March 1906 on possible options in time of war. He confirmed Germany as the likely aggressor and argued that the best British warships ought not to be used against ports; instead, older ones should be utilised. What he wrote must have warmed the cockles of Fisher's heart. Wilson urged the destruction of Cuxhaven and the forcing of the Kiel Canal to Hamburg. Old and expendable Admiral-class ships, twelve in all, could be used for this, leaving his fleet at the entrance to the Elbe if the German fleet chose to come out to do battle. Under this bold plan, once the canal was under control, Schleswig-Holstein would be cut off from Germany, a siege of Kiel could be undertaken from the rear, and Hamburg would be at their mercy. River patrol vessels would also be needed. A speed of 8 knots would be enough, but their armament would need to be in good order.[157] However, this forward thinking was made redundant by the German naval build-up. In all things Fisher favoured a close blockade, bringing war to the enemy on its shores, but as weapons development, especially development of mines and torpedoes by potential enemies, began to affect plans, the concept of distant blockade replaced that of a close blockade. (Prince Louis of Battenberg had done much to demonstrate the impossibility of blockading an enemy fleet in a port furnished with torpedo boats and destroyers.[158]) Nor could Fisher's idea of 'Copenhagening' the German fleet at anchor be realised. Pre-emptive strikes had gone out of fashion. The British government would not have sanctioned any such policy. Fisher's plan was unravelling.

Once again the international agenda was determining the Navy's response. By June 1906, naval aspects of the Anglo-Japanese alliance, which was up for renewal, were being discussed in greatest confidence. Russian, French, and German interests and aspirations in Asia were reviewed. The Navy was lukewarm about renewing the alliance, viewing it as neither advantageous nor disadvantageous. Ottley, the Director of Naval Intelligence, in a postscript to the memorandum, commented: 'If the view be accepted that Great Britain and Japan must safeguard their mutual interests by acting in alliance, it follows that the victory of Tsushima no more affects the solidity of that alliance than would a great accession to a wife's fortune affect the validity of her marriage to her husband.'[159] With Russia removed from the board and France in growing entente, the need for Japan's military power was lessening in British eyes.

The reordering of affairs in East Asia and the changing circumstances of France in regards to Morocco highlighted the rising power of Germany in Europe. The German threat was now the one driving the British agenda, and Fisher had already shown his hand by sending the British Fleet into the Baltic on exercise in July 1905. Some saw this as provocative. It was Esher's view that Fisher never lost a chance to irritate the Kaiser.[160] As Fisher wrote to Sir Julian Corbett at that time: 'With great difficulty I've got our Channel Fleet up the Baltic and cruising in North Sea. "Our drill ground should be our battle ground." Don't repeat that phrase, but I've taken means to have it whispered in the German Emperor's ear!'[161]

Fisher had worked up his own plans for the prospective war with the Kaiser, which he shared with Lord Esher. Esher listened to Fisher with a growing fear of the catastrophe he knew might result from a man with such precipitate powers. He tried to influence Fisher. 'They are too secret to write down,' Esher wrote to a friend about these plans. 'He sits still under calumny, because to reply would necessarily entail revelation of our strength and the main strategic idea. In point of fact, our power is six times that of Germany at the given point of battle. He discussed with me his own position, and the difficulties raised by his enemies, and his danger from their animosity.' Esher also told Fisher that only four members of the government mattered, and that the King had stuck to Fisher 'wonderfully'.[162]

In consequence, Fisher appointed a committee to draw up naval war plans. The new Secretary of the CID, Colonel Maurice Hankey, RM, later to play such an important role as Secretary to the War Council, contributed papers to the committee. These focused on four main themes: (1) secure the homeland against invasion; (2) protect shipping against *guerre de course*; (3) blockade the enemy; and (4) use sea power to deliver forces against the enemy.[163] Corbett, at Fisher's bidding, crafted a scholarly introduction to the war plans. These plans concluded that a close blockade was not feasible in the face of the dangers of mines and torpedoes. For the same reasons, coastal invasions were also discounted. Instead, a distant economic blockade was recommended. The committee also investigated plans for blockading Kiel, the easterly German Baltic ports, and the German North Sea ports, but concluded that such operations should only be undertaken in conjunction with the French.[164] In other words, the hazards of amphibious and combined operations in these narrow seas and littoral waters were clearly identified. At the Naval War College, Captain Slade laboured under Fisher's general instructions to draw up plans for operations against Borkum and the Scheldt. As Slade saw it, British strategy should be to prevent Germany from seizing either Holland or Belgium. Slade succeeded Ottley as Director of Naval Intelligence in 1907, and he continued to advance strong plans for coastal operations for the Baltic and the

North Sea. But against this stood the General Staff, which opposed any notion of combined operations.

Once again Fisher met with his political confidant Esher. They talked long and hard on naval strategy. Fisher told Esher how Sir Arthur Wilson, in case of war with Germany, was determined not to locate his battle fleet in the North Sea. The rendezvous would be in the Orkneys, and there would be only cruisers and destroyers in the North Sea.[165] Here was early evidence of the importance of Scapa Flow.

During these crucial years, the Royal Navy was greatly feared in German naval circles. In Berlin it was widely believed that the British would not hesitate to launch a surprise attack against the nascent High Seas Fleet. An anonymous German pamphlet of 1906 reflected these fears: 'They fear Sir John Fisher particularly, who they look on as the strongest man in England, and they think he is bent on crushing Germany's Navy before it proves too strong. It was stated that the Emperor shares this opinion.'[166]

There were sufficient indications from the British side to keep these fears alive. In 1905 Arthur Lee, the Civil Lord of the Admiralty, took the occasion of a public speech to announce that 'the Royal Navy would get its blow in first before the other side had time even to read in the papers that war had been declared.' These wild and irresponsible statements received wide attention in German circles and fed the obsession about a surprise British naval attack.[167] The German navy took the matter seriously: Arthur Marder found in the German records that the High Seas Fleet, when it passed through the English Channel overnight early in 1908, en route home from a cruise to the Canaries, was in full combat readiness.[168] All the same, it might have been just a drill in preparation for some future event.

The Kaiser never failed to argue that Germany had been denied opportunities of imperial expansion (a misreading of history, for since the Treaty of Berlin 1880 Germany had acquired at least a full share), and he claimed that Germans could trade happily and agreeably under the protection of the Union Jack overseas, as indeed they did. At the same time, the Kaiser never lost an opportunity to twist the British lion's tail. For instance, he drew for Captain Kerr of *Implacable* a fearsome plan of what the German navy would amount to in the far-off year 1920. Then he would quickly change his message. He offered the olive branch. The Kaiser stated that he had no intention of going to war: 'We are conquering the world peacefully,' he told Kerr. It was under these circumstances that the Kaiser viewed the Liberal election victory in 1906 as a force for peace.[169] He saw the destinies of the British Empire and his own marching hand in hand. That is only half the story. The Kaiser can be counted among the ranks of Fisher's opponents, although his view of Fisher was ambivalent at best. Doubtless there was a degree of begrudging respect for

Fisher and the threat he posed to the naval ambitions of the Kaiser. Wilhelm viewed Fisher as a mischief-maker. As much as he admired the Liberals in power, he had no illusions about the British court, which he contended was terribly anti-German.[170]

The Kaiser, as we have seen from the occasion of Queen Victoria's funeral, when he boorishly breached protocol by beginning a political conversation on sensitive international questions, had an uncanny ability to stir up trouble between nations, even those with which he desired to be friendly. There was a unique satanic quality to the man. While he might reaffirm his goodwill to Britain on the occasion of a state visit, in the next moment he might be writing to his cousin Tsar Nicholas of how he looked forward to trouble between England and Japan. He could irritate his diplomatic friends with his publicity-seeking actions. Edward VII concluded that the more he saw of the Kaiser the less he liked him, and when another invitation came his way, he declined. Observers looked for the next turn of events and did not have to wait long. As one watcher of the day put it, 'So great an adept in exasperation as the Emperor could never be at a loss for long, and he soon found an opportunity.'[171]

Throughout these furious, eventful years at the Admiralty as First Sea Lord, Fisher kept his strategic ideas and plans to himself, or certainly as much as he could. This was first displayed during the Kaiser's ill-judged Morocco escapade. While issuing blustering messages describing what he would do if Germany acted precipitately and seized a harbour there, Fisher kept his grip on planning and held the cards close to his chest. He did not want to lose any initiative by consulting with the War Office or the CID. He knew his plans would soon be public if the issue were discussed at some council or other. To his confidant Esher, Fisher put it this way: 'I rather want to keep clear of the Defence Committee till Morocco is settled as I don't want to disclose my plans of campaign to <u>any one</u> not even <u>C[harles] B[eresford]</u> himself.' (Beresford was then a trusted ally.) Apparently Fisher had shared his plans with only Sir Arthur Wilson. Even Charles Ottley, of naval intelligence, was kept in the dark. Fisher had his reasons, worth repeating: 'The whole success will depend upon <u>suddenness</u> and <u>unexpectedness</u> and the moment I tell any one there's an end of both.'[172] Here was the Fisher touch, and here was his courage in action. If the War Office got its hands on the project, all would be ruined. In all things, Fisher would run the line on his own hook if he could. That was the essence of the man, and his charm and his danger. Here, too, lay his power and his reputation – and, in the end, his undoing.

3

Dissension in the Navy

Fisher and his opponents

Fisher was particularly pleased by the hatred with which he was viewed in Germany.[1] As he revealed in a letter to Tweedmouth, 'Personally, I am absolutely delighted with and revel in hostile criticism. I know nothing more intensely gratifying than placarding your enemy as a fool.'[2] This aspect of the personality of 'Radical Jack' often served to make implementation of the Fisherite reforms more difficult than they needed to be. Fisher could be immensely charming when he wanted, but he could also be profoundly threatening and hostile when prodded with an unfriendly stick. Another primary characteristic was Fisher's zeal, which produced his often-violent advocacy of concepts, ideas, and reforms, and which also opened him up to derision. The Conservative prime minister Lord Salisbury thought he suffered from 'professional "hallucination"' of the most profound kind.[3] The zeal and hostility combined to limit Fisher's patience for explaining his reforms. He did not suffer fools gladly.

Early in his tenure at the Admiralty, some suspected that Fisher's zeal and the feverish pace of work were having an impact not only on his health but also on his increasingly short temper. One friend cautioned Fisher that he had heard from all sides about this effect of the workload; the friend advised self-control to avoid reaching the breaking point: 'In your case this would be a calamity not only for yourself but for the Country and Empire.'[4] At one critical juncture, when the volume of work was unrelenting, the King had ordered Fisher not to be at work on Sundays and commanded his presence for a weekend visit to the country house of Chatsworth.[5]

Even those in sympathy with his aims became alienated by Fisher's methods. Many regretted, even despised, his dictatorial rule at the Admiralty. This was the case with that outstanding admiral Rosslyn Wemyss: 'I am afraid he is suffering from what the bluejacket calls swelled head, and having got an enormous (too much) power into his own hands, he has taken the bit between his teeth and nothing seems able to stop him in his mad career of perfectly unnecessary reforms.'[6] Wemyss had an axe to grind, as Fisher put unsatisfactory conditions on his employment when the former was to be offered the post of Naval Secretary. Of an ancient Scottish landed family, Wemyss was no doubt considerably put out by Fisher's less than gentlemanly ways, and Fisher left himself open to this sort of criticism. He constantly refuted, out of hand, arguments that were contrary to his convictions. As he wrote to Lord Knollys: 'I am personally accused of never looking at *the other side of things. Well, I don't! It's a waste of time*, because I have been looking at the other side for 51 years last July! And I have no need to look any more.'[7]

Viscount Esher always gave sage advice. In avuncular style he chided Fisher for his methods and his attempt to run the Navy as a one-man show. 'Your pitfall is that you want to carry your <u>one man rule</u> from war into Peace, and all history shows the fatal track along which <u>one man</u> has walked to disaster.'[8] Esher also exhorted Fisher to be careful of using devious methods of dealing with opposition. When Fisher had dismissed the widely accepted Mahan as out of date, passé, Esher admitted that this might well be true, but that was not the perception held by the public at large. Mahan was what counted for the moment. If Fisher really intended to ignore or bypass Mahan, then he had better take appropriate steps. He suggested, particularly, using the stable of journalists to refute Mahan's arguments.[9] But Fisher did not take up the challenge of countering Mahan's points of view, and, truth to tell, he lacked the fine mind that would have allowed for such perspectives to be mounted in opposition to the historian whose arguments about sea power were on everyone's lips. The Fisher tactic was simply to ignore Mahan – or to wildly praise him as he did once when the American had pointed out that 88 per cent of British naval guns were pointed at Germany. As noted earlier, Fisher liked to contrive the dramatic effect.

Fisher reserved the press for his own hobby horses, his own pet schemes. Although he was not alone in this practice, right from the start he made full use of press contacts to further his reforms and reduce the influence of those ranged against him. His modus operandi was to keep his name out of the news. He preferred the battle in print to be waged through surrogates. In 1903 Fisher wrote to Esher regarding his friend and press ally W T Stead. He believed Stead to be a keen observer, and commented that he also believed that press, Parliament, and public would not resist any major reforms. In this he was largely correct, though he misjudged the infighting that would ensue. With respect to the role of the press in advancing the cause of reform:

I pointed out to him [Stead] that my [progress] was that of the mole! trace me by upheavals! When you see the Admirals rise it's that d—d fellow Jack Fisher talking the rise out of them! So I implored Stead to keep me out of the

'Magazine Rifles' or he will interfere with my professional career of crime. So please use your influence in the same direction.[10]

As a further example of Fisher's use of the press, Fisher fixed it so that the naval writer and maritime strategist Julian Corbett would write a return salvo against what he liked to call the 'croakers' in response to the varied criticism of his regime at the Admiralty. Corbett duly did his bidding. His article, 'Some Recent Attacks on the Admiralty', which appeared in the influential *Nineteenth Century* with ammunition quietly supplied by Fisher, was important in countering the critics. It was especially well received by those in authority.[11]

Leadership under stress: standing on the edge of a precipice

The points of dispute and the dissensions that wracked the naval officer corps were fought in several quarters. While the most important aspect of this struggle was the Fisher–Beresford controversy, discussed later in this chapter, their battles were symbolic of larger issues. Fisher was the son of a colonial army officer while the flamboyant Beresford was the second son of the 4th Marquess of Waterford. Their struggle epitomised, in some respects, the last attempt by the aristocratic/landed classes to maintain control of the naval establishment. In the nineteenth century the Navy became increasingly a refuge for the scions of genteel families who needed a respectable career. Throughout the nineteenth century, in contrast to previous eras, it was virtually impossible for officers to be promoted from the lower deck. Military and naval officers were regarded as gentlemen first, and a commission was a form of entrée to society. This was especially the case in areas outside Britain, where military rank bestowed a great deal more respect and influence. The military services represented the last 'legitimate' reason for the existence of the landed aristocracy as the traditional leadership of the nation in arms. One member of the elite in the 1890s told a former petty officer that while he had 'the greatest sympathy ... in your desire to rise ... you have chosen the wrong service. The Navy belongs to us, and if you were to win the commissions you ask for it would be at the expense of our sons and nephews whose birthright it is.'[12] Put differently, the officers formed a self-selecting class; they intended to keep it that way. However, the challenge to the old guard was imminent.

Much of the legitimate concern with the Fisher reforms became tied up in this wider struggle. Tired of being derided as an upstart rogue and a 'half-caste Asiatic', Fisher became increasingly strident and belligerent toward his critics; increasingly secretive, even paranoid; and reluctant to support the legitimate avenues of dissent via further sponsorship of an effective naval staff system. In an attempt to consolidate his efforts, Fisher disillusioned his most ardent supporters and failed to appease the 'dinosaur admirals'.

From 1902 and the outset of his tenure at the Admiralty, Fisher attracted severe criticism. A person of lesser strength and constitution would have caved under such pressure. Many within the Navy expressed deep reservations about the speed, scope, and essence of the proposed reforms. The Selborne Scheme, which Fisher had sponsored during his time as Second Sea Lord, attracted heat early. Fisher contended that a hard core was plotting against him. As he told a friend, 'I believe a Syndicate of old fossils has been formed to attack the scheme, and if they do I hope you will fire a broadside at them between wind and water!'[13] Nearly everyone was forced to take a stand for or against the Fisherite reforms.

Fisher might have been on amiable terms with Edward VII, but he had an unsteady relationship with Prince George, the Prince of Wales (known as PG in the Navy), and in later years Fisher became an embittered enemy of King George V.[14] Fisher's sweeping aside of criticism, his violently hasty and invariably ill-considered response to some questions, and his casual treatment of concerns did not endear him to Prince George. On one occasion the Prince of Wales wrote to Fisher regarding the condition of the Navy's heavy guns. Apparently, according to Carlyon Bellairs, a retired Navy officer and at that time an MP, the heavy guns cracked easily and were unsuitable to modern conditions. Fisher dealt with the letter in an offhand fashion, insulting Bellairs and being rather forward in his response to his future sovereign. 'The retired Naval Officer who is writing these articles in the "Daily Scrap-heap" [*Daily Graphic*] was utterly useless as a sailor, so has taken to the pen and politics – the usual refuge of naval duffers! He wants to get in as a Radical member for King's Lynn ... A nice pair [Bellairs and Gibson Bowles] of them, Sir, in Your Royal Highness's neighbourhood!'[15] Fisher defended himself from the critiques of the Prince of Wales, in particular over the results of the Selborne Scheme. Following these difficulties, Prince Louis of Battenberg, the admiral, wrote reassuringly to Fisher: 'Let your detractors do their worst. No one pays any attention to their yelping.'[16] Battenberg may have come to regret how far Fisher went with his reforms, but he backed Fisher without any public disclosure to the contrary.

Esher attempted to moderate his friend's outbursts. The task was immensely trying, even for a man with such smooth and soothing ways as Esher. Fisher, Esher knew, was his own worst enemy, and on that score Esher often had to call him to account. The issue of the moment was inter-Service co-operation, and Fisher refused to discuss with the War Office matters such as transport of army units to France, the development of combined operations, and the evolution of the Committee of Imperial Defence (CID). On 3 September 1906 Esher confided to his son, 'Fisher has promised to be good, and to come back to the Defence Committee. The King took him to task, and for the present he has buried the hatchet – Clarke and he, however, are bound to fall out again, and especially as Clarke is all agog against the "Dreadnoughts" ... Still, it is no affair of Clarke's ... The Defence Committee might just as well take up a new type of Field Gun. In point of fact, Clarke *did* meddle with that question too!'[17] Shortly thereafter, Esher put it clearly to Fisher, saying there was no point getting angry about Clarke, but that it was good for him to be contradicted, as 'you have things too much your own way'.[18] Esher wrote to Fisher again on 21 October 1906 to say that it was Fisher who was a national asset, not his opinions. Once again he urged caution: Fisher should moderate his tone with respect to his critics:

> *But*, I deprecate, if you will allow me to say so, your *method* in dealing with these opponents ... In a country like ours, governed by *discussion*, a great man is never hanged. He hangs himself. Therefore pray be Machiavellian, and play upon the delicate instrument of public opinion with your fingers and not with your feet – however tempting the latter may be.
>
> In any case condescend to convert the 'six men who count.' As for what you say about the Defence Committee, let me suggest this consideration. The best way of preventing that body from meddling with things which do not concern it is *to give it plenty to do*! ...
>
> *In War*, it played the devil, because *in war* you want a *Man*!
>
> *In Peace*, you want a *Party* behind the Man ...
>
> No Englishman ought to be Sir John Fisher's 'enemy'. Every Englishman should be his Lieutenant. It depends on the First Sea Lord himself![19]

Esher reproved Fisher for his lack of diplomacy. He noted that Earl St Vincent, the great sailor-administrator, for all his good work, fell in the end, and that the 'birds of prey' were circling Fisher closely at this juncture. Esher also pointed to the examples of Richard Haldane and John Morley, who both, taking a customary and civilised route, had referred their particular schemes to the CID and had, by carrying their plans there, in spite of Clarke's opposition, made their positions unassailable.[20] Esher was blunt and to the point. Fisher, by showing mistrust and dislike of the committee, had lost the opportunity to convert it to his uses: 'During the past week or so, the forces ranged against each other have been Fisher versus Beresford. They should have been Fisher plus Defence Committee plus Cabinet versus Beresford, and the odds would have been overwhelming ... *You* invent a policy and you get the Defence Committee to *stereotype* it.'[21] Fisher did not listen.

Fisher was beginning to feel the pressure. His is an example of leadership under stress. Not only was he dealing with the retired 'old fossils' and naval officers still on active service, but there was also growing agitation in the press.

By early 1907 this had reached fantastical proportions unheard of in the Service. Fisher's natural tendency was to fight back, so he champed at the bit, wanting to go after the 'Syndicate of Discontent' – most of the Conservative press and a number of senior officers. In a letter to a friend, Fisher wrote:

> We pander to traitors in our own camp; we subsidize our critics at the Royal United Services Institution, and we fawn on our foes and give them barley sugar instead of a black eye! Again, it is utter rot to talk of *what will the Service think?' Who is the 'Service'?* Nobody can ever answer! You can never get names in reply to that question! It is really the unsuccessful and the discontented! Those who are disloyal to the Admiralty![22]

It was time for him to seek wider counsel among those close to the seats of power. Thus it was that on 3 January 1907 Fisher lunched with his minder, Esher, and with the King's secretary, Sir Francis (later Lord) Knollys. They were on his side. According to Esher, who recounted the events to his son, 'Jackie feels that he is standing on the edge of a precipice to which all great reformers are led, and over which they ultimately fall. But, in spite of the numerous enemies whose darling wish is to hurl him down, it is essential that for a while he be kept up. If he survives another year, the Navy is safe.'[23]

Even so, Esher continued to keep a watch on Fisher's outbursts, and he wrote to Fisher strongly, hoping that he would climb down from putting forward the Admiralty's unbending attitude toward the CID on some point or other.[24] Esher was referring to Fisher's opposition to the War Office and what he regarded as the blocking capabilities of the Committee of Imperial Defence. But Fisher faced many more issues than just army reform or co-operation with the War Office in regards to war planning. Having defined and then attempted to implement so many reforms in so few years (going back to 1902, even before he became First Sea Lord), he was the target for many snipers and on any number of issues. Revolutionaries have to live with the world they are creating, and they have to sleep in beds of their own making.

It was a wonder that Fisher did not go under altogether or walk away from his job, or was not forced out by his political superiors, but he was a fighter of unusual strength and persistence. This characteristic, taken together with his superiors' realisation of the necessity for reform and regeneration of the Navy in this great hour of need, explains the support he was given. Esher and Knollys were but vestigial heads of power who had no constituted office or influence with the press or Parliament, but at this time they were Jacky's main props. And Fisher was not without wider support, for the Liberal press was on his side, and so were certain Conservative journals, notably *The Times*, *Daily Telegraph*, and *Observer*, and two Service journals, *Army and Navy Gazette* and *Naval and Military Record*.

Smouldering volcano: the quarrel with 'Charlie B'

Admiral Lord Charles Beresford (afterwards 1st Baron Beresford), already introduced as second son of the 4th Marquess of Waterford, was flamboyant, dashing, and self-promoting. He might have been classified as one of the great swells of his age had he not also been preoccupied, as was Fisher, with the efficiency and strength of the Navy. In professional matters he had none of the heft of Fisher, though because of his attractive personality and breezy ways – officers and men loved 'Charlie B' – he commanded wide respect. He was quite capable of fighting from his own corner, in defence of himself. He moved in high places. Beresford was also a sometime member of Parliament, and that gave him an additional platform for expressing his views.[25]

Churchill, observing 'Charlie B' in action in the House of Commons, thought him boastful and an empty-headed parliamentarian: 'He is one of those orators of whom it is said that "before they get up they do not know what they are going to say, when they are speaking they do not know what they are saying, and when they have sat down they do not know what they have said."'[26] Beresford was initially a great friend of the Prince of Wales, the future King Edward VII, until they fell out over Beresford's mistress, Lady Brooke, who was also a friend of the Prince. In the course of this squabble, the Prince ostracised Lady Beresford from the highest social circles, and Beresford called the Prince a blackguard. Prime Minister Lord Salisbury had to intervene. Salisbury's opinion of Beresford, whom he had taken on as Junior Naval Lord in 1886, was that he was 'an officer of great ability afloat; but he is too greedy of popular applause to get on in a public department.'[27]

Beresford had a high opinion of himself, believing that he could be a better First Sea Lord than Fisher. He had been second in command under Fisher in the Mediterranean, and they got on well together initially, despite periodic embarrassments caused by Beresford's gossiping and bluster. By late 1906, however, when Fisher's fleet-redistribution scheme became the source of a rift that rent the Navy in twain, Beresford was on the opposite side. He was vocal in his criticism. Malcontent allies and segments of the press rendered him wide support. What Fisher called the 'Syndicate of Discontent' had powerful backing. Beresford's popularity, and the reluctance of the government to sack him, caused innumerable and long-term problems for the Navy that should never have occurred. The dispute came to dominate business at the Admiralty and preoccupy the press, leaving Fisher exhausted.

Admiral Bacon, in his biography of Fisher, suggests that the dispute escalated dramatically after Fisher was promoted in December 1905 to be an additional Admiral of the Fleet in order to remain on active duty until he reached the age of seventy.[28] In other words, Fisher was now ensured another four, possibly five, years at the Admiralty. Beresford had been waiting impatiently for Fisher's tenure to end so he could take the final step to that pinnacle of service, but now Beresford believed Jacky was intentionally blocking his path to the office of First Sea Lord. However, Beresford deluded himself if he thought he could become First Sea Lord, and it was Prime Minister Balfour who had seen to Fisher's final step in rank, thereby giving him an additional five years on the active list.

It would a mistake to dismiss the Fisher–Beresford dispute as merely a personal tug of war between two powerful individuals fighting for supremacy. In a strictly personal dispute with the First Sea Lord, an individual commander-in-chief would be forced to submit. The majority of Service opinion would condemn an individual for subverting discipline for personal satisfaction. The Fisher–Beresford feud was fought simultaneously on several levels that are buried deep in the available evidence and require a thorough immersion in the available political and social literature of the period. First, the most readily apparent point of contention was the clash of two strong personalities from two diametrically opposite bearings. Both men were not shy about using press contacts or aggressive self-promotion. However, Fisher can be regarded as completely professional in his approach, whereas Beresford regarded his naval career as something of a hobby to be indulged. Beresford was bluff, hearty, and, frankly, had not much between his ears. Fisher's intellect and depth far exceeded Beresford's.

Secondly, there was a political element to the dispute bearing on the question of Irish Home Rule. Beresford, who early in his career held one of the Marquess of Waterford's family seats in Ireland, was a leading example of the Anglo-Irish aristocracy and a staunch Unionist (a faction that dominated the House of Commons from 1886 until 1906 and was associated with the Conservatives).[29] The Unionists had made their mark in the late 1800s by their opposition to Home Rule and their support for British imperialism abroad. At the time of the dispute, Fisher was closely associated with key members of the Liberal establishment, especially Esher and, later, Churchill, and was the chief naval adviser to the Liberal government after 1905. It could be argued that Beresford was not only targeting Fisher, but was also going out of his way to embarrass the Radicals and 'Little Englanders' (those opposed to British involvement in international affairs) in the Liberal government, and their moves to limit naval expenditure. Beresford was forgetting that the Navy's financial crunch arose under a Conservative Cabinet. This was the first time naval affairs became a party issue.

Thirdly, social controversy surrounded the professionalisation of the Royal Navy. Fisher was striking at the heart of the old naval officer class, which was essentially self-selecting, by attempting to open up the quarterdeck to those of less than patrician – or landed or clergy – descent by offering further opportunities for engineers, improving the lot of the lower deck, and imposing stringent professional standards. As a social reformer, Fisher was seeking to break down the naval caste system, unique in English and possibly world history. Rank and station had been acquired in battle and was enshrined in legend.[30] Under Fisher this would have to change.

Fourthly, an intellectual and strategic debate was going on behind the scenes. In this struggle, Beresford was largely a figurehead for the ideas and arguments of Admiral Sir Reginald Custance, sometime Director of Naval Intelligence, and his 'Victory School'. These individuals were steeped in a caricature of Mahanian battle fleet doctrine and eschewed the value of a strategic defence at sea, believing the offensive capacity of the Fleet should not be impaired. On the opposite side, the strategical views of Julian Corbett, which emphasised the value of defence and the security of maritime communication, underwrote Fisher's efforts.[31]

The quarrel had profound effects on the operations of the Admiralty and the Navy. Important decisions were taken based not just on the relevant facts, but also in light of the personal disputes between Fisher and Beresford. For example, the rejection of Arthur Pollen's system of director firing control (meant to improve the speed and accuracy of naval gun firing), in favour of Frederic Dreyer's inferior model, was partly due to Fisher's belief that Pollen was backing Beresford. Also, at the end of Fisher's tenure the Naval Intelligence Department was emasculated due to the belief that it was rife with Beresfordians, led by Custance, with the result that Admiral Sir Arthur Wilson's position was strengthened.[32]

When Fisher was Commander-in-Chief, Mediterranean, he had already had certain difficulties with Beresford. The latter's position as an MP gave him a ready-made reason to communicate over the C-in-C's head, which added a political problem to the difficulties of command. Fisher was rather irked when his subordinate's correspondence served 'to aggravate instead of smoothing and facilitating',[33] but he attempted to level out Beresford's rough spots and encouraged him to bounce his speeches off J R Thursfield of *The Times*.[34] Fisher knew Beresford could be useful in promoting his agenda. To Lord Spencer, a former First Lord, Fisher wrote: 'There is a great deal in what Beresford urges, but he exaggerates so much that his good ideas become deformities.' Fisher attempted to get Beresford to be more circumspect in his writings. However, when that failed, Fisher was forced to disavow him on several occasions. Nevertheless, the C-in-C rated Beresford an exceptional fleet commander, going so far as to say that 'no better exists in my opinion.'[35] And for the most part Beresford was co-operative in the general thrust of Fisher's efforts.

According to Churchill, the quarrel began with what are known as the Bacon letters, and the printing and circulation of same. On 12 April 1906 Fisher received a private communication from Captain Reginald Bacon, who commanded a ship in the Mediterranean Fleet and was a solid supporter of Fisher, a fact no doubt known by Beresford, who was then C-in-C, Mediterranean. Both the King and the Prince of Wales had visited Malta, Mediterranean Fleet headquarters, and there were bombarded with the complaints of both Beresford and Admiral Sir Hedworth Lambton. Their main grievance was that they were not being consulted about the changes that were taking place at the Admiralty. Bacon managed to have a talk with both the King and the Prince of Wales in regard to the reforms and emphasised that the Navy was an ultra-conservative organisation that did not take well to change. Then Bacon went further. He reversed the charges, telling the King that the chief problem lay in the want of loyalty to the Admiralty of certain admirals afloat (that is, his superior officers on station): 'They may, while scheme[s] are being initiated, behave like David – clothe themselves in sackcloth and ashes, fast and pray – none of these are they likely to do literally, but the modern alternative is to become friends and correspond with [various senior officers such as] Bridge, Custance, Fitzgerald, Bellairs, and Co.;[36] but when the fiat has gone forth from the Admiralty they must rise, wash, and eat, and accept the superior ruling!'

Bacon wrote to Fisher about this, and three days later wrote again, outlining the chief grievances of the 'croakers'. He went point by point over them, with the most serious being the misunderstandings many officers had of the Selborne Scheme. He advocated that Fisher publish an Admiralty paper outlining the goals of the Scheme, and revealed that both the King and the Prince were worried about the dissension in the Fleet.[37] Fisher's mistake was to print in the Admiralty, for office circulation, the Bacon letters, a breach of protocol and sure to expose Fisher, as it did, to accusations of partisanship in the Navy and the subversive nature of Bacon's actions against his immediate superior officer, Beresford. This was dynamite. Fisher was about to be hoist by his own petard.

All the same, Beresford, an exhibitionist of a different sort from his rival (who played the backrooms rather than Parliament and the press openly), was constantly snubbing the Admiralty and questioning decisions made in London. At one time, contrary to convention and good sense, he even canvassed his captains in the Mediterranean on whether they approved or disapproved of Admiralty policy. News of this was sure to reach Fisher, who went on to report Beresford's unwarranted criticism of the 'short service men' directly to the First Lord of the Admiralty, Lord Tweedmouth.[38] Other admirals were aware of the dissension. Rear-Admiral F S Inglefield, for one, warned Fisher: 'There can be but one undisputed authority to govern the Navy, and that authority must be the Admiralty. Drastic measures become necessary when those in high command are disloyal or insubordinate. Serious trouble must arise in our Service if disloyalty and insubordination are permitted to exist. I am sorry to know these troubles continue – Their continuation is an evil fraught with danger.'[39]

The Bacon letters, as printed, backfired on Fisher. Beresford enlarged the battlefield of dispute. In early March 1907 Esher wrote: 'Fisher has been in stormy waters during the past week, owing to the pointed attack by C. Beresford, and the flank attacks from his various enemies, on the redistribution of the Fleet. The Prince of Wales wrote an excellent Memo. on the "policing of the seas," which the Fisher policy neglects, and making suggestions which the Admiral has now accepted.' Esher also wrote that he, Fisher, Charles Hardinge of the Foreign Office, Knollys the King's secretary, and the Prince of Wales had dined at Marlborough House to discuss it, and that Fisher was 'in excellent spirits'.[40] Beresford was by no means the only opposition in regard to the reorganisation. Even Battenberg, hitherto a Fisher ally, characterised splitting the command of the Home Fleet and redeploying ships as required as 'criminal'.[41] A powerful figurehead had joined the Fisher opponents. Prince Louis was entitled to his opinion, but the fact that he had written an extended critique of Jacky Fisher's Fleet reorganisation and sent it to the naval correspondent of *The Times*, J Thursfield, registers under the heading of disloyalty to a senior officer. 'I am very sorry to go against J.F. but can't help it.'[42]

Shortly after Beresford became Commander-in-Chief, Channel Fleet, Fisher invited him to London to discuss issues in person so as to 'avoid friction and undesirable correspondence'. The letter is noticeably icy compared to the usual run of Fisher's letters, and it seems he could not resist a barb at Beresford and his second in command, Sir Reginald Custance. Fisher indicated that a good working relationship was difficult 'if your Staff are always preparing ammunition for you to fire at the Admiralty'. Not content with suggesting that Beresford did not know how to control his staff, he implied that Beresford had no idea what his immediate subordinate was up to. 'I see something about Custance navigating his Fleet at night in the centre of the line. I hope we are not going to have any changes from the custom of the Service without Admiralty authority.'[43] One suspects that Fisher had been placed under considerable pressure to write a conciliatory letter and was probably as mad as a hatter about it. Beresford responded by agreeing to a face-to-face interview, but his obvious attempt to cover his insubordination with meek letters to the Admiralty ('When the friction begins, I am off. If a senior and a junior have a row, the junior is wrong under any conceivable circumstances, or discipline could not go on.'[44]) must have made Fisher snort with anger, especially considering that at an earlier interview with Beresford, Fisher 'had as a preliminary to agree to three things: – I. Lord C. Beresford is a greater man than Nelson. II. No one knows anything about the art of naval war except Lord C. Beresford. III. The Admiralty haven't done a single d—d thing right!'[45]

After the April interview, Fisher again wrote to Beresford. He made an attempt to inform the C-in-C as much as possible on critical matters, giving him complete access to the Director of Naval Intelligence's office. Fisher, however, decided that it would not be wise to send the full war plans at that precise moment because of changing climatic conditions according to season.[46] This explanation of Fisher's seems disingenuous. He had no intention of sharing secrets with Beresford. Perhaps he had plans to change force structure? Or, more to the point, there was no proper war plan at all? Beresford fired another salvo at Fisher: 'I am loath to appear discourteous, but I cannot see why you ask me not to write a letter for the plans and orders extant' for the Channel Fleet in case of war.[47]

Fisher, furious with Beresford's latest outrages, demanded that the First Lord order him ashore and strike his flag. Tweedmouth failed to back Fisher, and proceeded to admonish Fisher for so readily seeking Beresford's dismissal and not appreciating the C-in-C's good qualities. 'But we all knew those bad qualities of his, no one better than you, when you very wisely recommended his and Sir Reginald Custance's appointments.' Tweedmouth further advised: 'I am the last person in the world to abrogate one iota of the supremacy of the Board of Admiralty, but I do think we sometimes are inclined to consider our views to be infallible and are not ready enough to give consideration to the views of others.'[48]

Tweedmouth, taking the initiative, arranged for Beresford to come to the Admiralty for a three-way conference of the First Lord, the First Sea Lord, and the C-in-C, Channel Fleet, to hammer out an arrangement that would close the growing rift between Beresford and Fisher. The conference failed. According to an Admiralty memo, 'The answers to the questions put to the Commander-in-Chief are a series of clumsy fencings, evasions, and dodgings, and are often contradictory. As a concession, two armoured cruisers and two divisions of destroyers were attached to the Channel Fleet, and as a result Beresford informed the Admiralty on 16 July that he could now create definite war plans. These plans were only submitted to the Admiralty a year later.'[49]

It was not traditional for the Admiralty to disseminate war plans to individual commanders. Indeed, an Admiralty minute of August 1907 asserted the Board's absolute discretion over strategy and war plans, and noted that the job of individual commanders was to train their forces to the best of their abilities, and in war to use the forces placed at their disposal.[50] This statement, circulated to all the respective C-in-Cs, especially those in home waters, was a remarkable development. Although Fisher pestered the Admiralty when he was in the Mediterranean, he did not presume to act in the name of the Admiralty, nor did he attempt to force his way in by exploiting the indecision in the Admiralty's political leadership.[51]

In late September 1907 the Admiralty received another impertinent remark from Beresford at the Channel Fleet, which Fisher complained about to Tweedmouth. Fisher recalled Beresford's wholly improper response to the 15 August minute: 'I note their Lordships consider that the Admiral who in war is responsible for the Fleet in Home Waters should not press his opinion as to its efficiency in time of peace.'[52] According to Fisher, Beresford had committed fresh excesses by stating that he was *responsible for the Fleet in Home Waters*'.

In early October, after the Fleet Review, some of Beresford's associations with the press also backfired. Apparently he had arranged to make a dramatic resignation, which would be coupled with a concentrated assault on the Admiralty to force Fisher's dismissal. However, after receiving the armoured cruisers and two divisions of destroyers from the Admiralty, Beresford did not resign as his journalist friends, particularly Howell Gwynne at the *Standard*, believed he had promised to do.[53] From an unidentified source, Fisher heard that Beresford had written to these friends and 'told them that having got his 2 armoured cruisers etc. he can take no further part in the business because of his official position!!!! (Isn't that a joke? The chief admiral afloat acknowledges to an organised agitation against the Board of Admiralty and when he thinks he can – he chucks them over! What a world we live in !'[54] Fisher vowed to haul Beresford before the Board of Admiralty 'and flatten out Beresford once and for all'.[55]

In fact, the issue was far beyond Fisher's control, and the matter now went to Windsor Castle. Soon thereafter, the King and his secretary, Sir Frederick Ponsonby, summoned Beresford to an audience. Ponsonby reported to Fisher that they found Beresford 'hard to pin down', and when they attempted to steer the talk, Beresford shifted target. When they asked him directly what he would do if he was First Sea Lord, they could get a satisfactory reply on only one point: that Fisher should have taken the public into his confidence regarding the condition of the Fleet. 'It strikes me,' wrote Ponsonby admonishingly, 'that this would have been better than to allow your opponents to bring up these blemishes and call the whole fleet a fraud and a delusion.'[56]

In November 1907 the first of two Scott–Beresford incidents occurred, raising the temperature of the Fisher–Beresford conflict. Rear-Admiral Sir Percy Scott, then commander of the 1st Cruiser Squadron of Beresford's Channel Fleet, was unimpressed with his chief. His resistance to Beresford's attempts to recruit him in the C-in-C's campaign against the Admiralty resulted in Scott's becoming an outcast in the Fleet.[57] On 11 November the Kaiser was scheduled to inspect the Fleet at Spithead, and Beresford wanted everything to be in the best shape. On 4 November, accordingly, Beresford issued an order that exercises would be cut short to allow enough time to paint the ships and tidy them up. Scott's squadron was at that time conducting gunnery exercises, and Scott, whose obsession was gunnery, was upset. When the cruiser *Roxburgh* asked for more time to complete its gunnery exercises, Scott signalled in reply: 'Paintwork appears to be more in demand than gunnery, so you had better come in, in time to make yourself look pretty by the 8th instant.'

When Beresford learned of the signal, he flew into a fury. He viewed it as personally insulting and flouting his authority. He called Scott to his flagship and, in a rage, put his junior in his place. The rear-admiral was stunned and left 'silent and white-faced'. Beresford also sent an embarrassing signal to the Fleet, describing the offending signal as 'contemptuous in tone and insubordinate in character', and ordered that it be expunged from the signal logs of *Roxburgh* and *Good Hope*, Scott's flagship. Not satisfied with this rebuke, Beresford wrote to the Admiralty that the incident was a 'public insult'. The Board of Admiralty informed Scott of their 'grave disapprobation' but took no further action, suggesting that the public censure of Scott by Beresford was sufficient punishment. Not surprisingly, Beresford was enraged that the Admiralty would take no further action. Meanwhile, the incident found its way into the press, becoming public knowledge.[58]

The Fisher–Beresford dispute was waged against the backdrop of a deep-seated fear of invasion and concern about the necessary defence of the British Isles, a concern that had preoccupied British statesmen over the centuries. In the past, France had been the potential threat. In 1797 the French had invaded Ireland in an attempted liberation, but had failed; Napoleon had assembled boats for an invasion that was called off in 1805; and in the mid-1800s Palmerston worried that 'steam had bridged the Channel', and he erected Martello towers in defence. The rise of Germany as the principal military power on the Continent posed the newest threat.

In 1907 the fear of German invasion, which had begun a few years earlier, intensified. The Conservatives' departure from power in December 1905 offered an opportunity to the fear-mongers; they were quite capable of startling the Liberals, who had little experience in defending, or articulating concepts on the defence of, the British Isles. At the National Service League, a powerful pressure group, Field Marshal Lord Roberts, widely popular in the country, called for a large home army to guard against a 'bolt from the blue', a reference to an unexpected German invasion attempt. At the same time, Colonel Charles Repington, military correspondent of *The Times* and the crusading pioneer of journalists on this theme (he commenced his series of articles on the invasion threat in his column of 29 August 1906 and continued them through 1907),[59] advanced the case that Germany could invade the British Isles by a sudden descent on the coast, and the Royal Navy would be insufficient to guard against the threat. Repington fed into the larger fear of invasion within British society, as did a surge in popular fictional accounts of invasion. One of the most prominent was William Le Queux's *Invasion of 1910*, a work in which Field Marshal Lord Roberts had a hand.

Former prime minister Balfour, a guiding and powerful member of the Committee of Imperial Defence, was convinced that Roberts had made a sufficient case to warrant an investigation, and on 20 July 1907 he forwarded his findings to the CID, which proposed that a subcommittee should look into the issue.[60] Up to this point the CID had always backed the Admiralty against the War Office, and Balfour had always supported Fisher. But now Balfour was in opposition.

The King shared these concerns. He feared that the Kaiser might have a plan to 'throw a *corps d'armee* or two into England, making proclamation that he has come, not as an enemy to the King, but as the grandson of Queen Victoria, to deliver him from the Socialistic gang which is ruining the country.'[61] The concern over invasion coincided with the criticisms from Beresford and his associates regarding the proper deployment of the Fleet, and by the autumn of 1907 Beresford and the rest of the 'Syndicate of Discontent' had found common cause with Roberts and the 'bolt from the blue' disciples.

Fisher dismissed the threat, arguing that the Royal Navy was more than strong enough to repel any serious invasion. Findings had shown the Germans had insufficient 'sea lift' to accomplish such a mission, and as long as the British Fleet retained its supremacy, no invader could long remain in the British Isles. Fisher defended the naval estimates and the naval building programme. He believed that the current agitation had as its fundamental goal the idea of universal military service, *'which the Country will never swallow'*. An over-large army would cost the taxpayer millions: 'Spend money on submarines, destroyers, etc., but don't waste money on an armed mob. You might as well arm all the caretakers in London houses with a revolver instead of supplying a police force!'[62] He marshalled his supporters for a counteroffensive, and he drew on his heaviest artillery thus far, Julian Corbett, to deliver his customary broadsides 'between wind and water', as the admiral liked to say. Fisher, while speculating that an article dispelling the invasion bogey would aid the profile of Corbett's *England in the Seven Years' War*, commented that it would be very appropriate for an article to appear in the November issue of *Nineteenth Century*: 'At all events, Repington & Co. will assuredly be at it again soon, and anyhow it's the sort of subject dear to the British Public to get a sort of shiver of the German Host upon them and then feel the returning warmth of security in finding that 40 million Pomeranian Grenadiers can't be landed in five minutes!'[63] He also praised John Leyland's efforts in *The Times* to refute Repington's arguments, but worried that another commentator, 'Navalis', placed too much emphasis on Beresford's role when attacking the invasion bogey.[64]

Fisher dreaded having a subcommittee of the CID investigate the invasion question. He viewed any such inquiry as a direct assault on the Navy and a personal affront,[65] and he suspected the CID was attempting to supersede the Admiralty's role in the development of strategy and would attempt to force its decisions on an unwilling Navy. Fisher argued that the Navy alone, and more particularly the Admiralty, was competent to deploy naval forces. 'For a military officer, however able, to pronounce a categorical opinion upon this maritime question is therefore not less absurd than it would be for the First Sea Lord to write for Mr. Balfour's perusal a note criticizing in a similar strain the adequacy of the British military dispositions against invasion on the North West Frontier of India.'[66]

Esher, Fisher's normally patient minder, now fumed about the admiral's obstinacies. He disliked reductionist thinking and decided to give Fisher a piece of his mind – and a lesson in constitutional matters. He argued that the Defence Committee had a responsibility to the prime minister, representing the Crown, and the Commons, which was the same responsibility the Admiralty had, nothing more. Therefore, the Admiralty could not take responsibility for an issue that precluded its examination by a body appointed by and reporting to the prime minister. The Admiralty was a department of the government, just like any other. Finally, the Admiralty would have to recognise, as the War Office had, that the Defence Committee was now part of the administrative system.[67]

Fisher responded: 'I quite expected to get "slated" by you and *I've got it.* Also I fully expected you would have your wicked way and *you've got it!*'[68] Esher, trying to put a better face on it with his friend, wrote again several weeks later in mollifying words, arguing that the invasion scare was beneficial for the nation and for the Navy. He contended that a nation that felt itself secure was doomed: 'An invasion Scare is the mill of God which grinds you out a Navy of Dreadnoughts, and keeps the British people war-like in spirit.'[69] Fisher bore no grudge to Esher. He replied cordially that he knew that everything Esher said was due to his desire to keep him 'in the straight and narrow way', and that he would take things from Esher that he wouldn't from others.[70] Esher continued to remind Fisher that during peacetime, one-man rule, as Fisher appeared to desire, was unacceptable, and that the Defence Committee was a necessary institution.[71] In this, however, Esher's advice fell on deaf ears.

Colonel Charles à Court Repington, military correspondent of *The Times*, cut a broad figure in the world of journalism, which he considered a form of warfare by other means. A notorious bounder and womaniser, he delighted in exposing the military follies of his age. He backed Beresford against Fisher, spreading false rumours and misinformation. The proprietor of *The Times*, Lord Northcliffe, found in Repington a useful tool to undermine the government and its naval and military commands. (In 1915 it was Repington who exposed the so-called shells crisis just at the time when Fisher was feuding with Churchill over naval assets for the Dardanelles, thus dragging Churchill out of office and bringing down Asquith's government.) Repington's several histories of the war furthered his interests, but he is now regarded as a despicable figure in British journalism, irresponsible in his writings and lacking in judgement. Jacky Fisher was fair game to Repington. The latter loved to shock, and he took it upon himself to contend that England was not free from invasion, that this was Fisher's fault, that Beresford was correct, and that the Admiralty was rotten to the core.

In any event, Prime Minister Campbell-Bannerman, taking into account the views of his ministers, the Opposition, and the press, accepted the CID proposal and created a subcommittee to look into the question of the possibility of a German invasion of the United Kingdom. The subcommittee began its inquiry in November 1907.

Fisher seethed. He wished to reply by means of an Admiralty statement and leave the inquiry at that. Esher warned of the necessity to make use of the inquiry to justify Admiralty policy: 'I said to him [Fisher] that he was fond of quoting Mahan's famous passage about Nelson's storm-tossed ships, upon which the Grand Army had never looked, which stood between it and the dominion of the world; and it should remind him that the Defence Committee, upon which he wished he had never looked, stood between him and a Royal Commission to enquire into the state of the Navy.'[72] Corbett, too, advocated moderation, while offering assistance, and argued that Fisher must find a role for the Army in naval defence and try to find common ground with the War Office: 'You can never get on with any body of men if you begin by taking the attitude that they are no use. Begin by telling them they are indispensable & they cannot deny ... you are a very reasonable person with sound ideas.'[73] Fisher was unmoved and unrepentant. He had no intention of changing course.

At the inquiry's first meeting, 27 November 1907, Roberts and Repington gave testimony which led to their subsequently being cross-examined in a confrontational atmosphere.[74] That the inquiry did not reject Repington's ideas out of hand upset Fisher: 'What fascinates me is that the Committee as a whole don't seem to take in the point that the whole case of Roberts & Repington rests on an absolute Naval Surprise which is really a sheer impossibility in view of our organised information.'[75] Fisher pointed out that a 'bolt from the blue' invasion was an impossibility, for Britannia ruled the waves and was strong everywhere, or could be easily strengthened in geographical areas when circumstances required. This was irrefutable to the naval mind. When Fisher cross-examined Repington, Esher concluded that *The Times* correspondent 'has gone off his head. His judgement seems to have deserted him.'

Beresford, meanwhile, sought to use the inquiry to discredit Fisher and advance his own interests. Fisher believed that Repington's object was to call Beresford as a witness, and that Beresford wished to use the inquiry as 'a splendid platform ... to resign on!'[76] Esher also noted that Beresford had met with General Sir John French the week before the first meeting of the inquiry, had laid out the arguments of the 'bolt from the blue' school of thought and his criticisms of Admiralty policy, and had seemed eager to appear before the inquiry.[77] Asquith, though, ruled that Beresford could not appear.

Esher was confident that the Admiralty would be exonerated: 'The days of intrigue and want of touch with the First Sea Lord are over!'[78] Fisher echoed Esher's confidence: 'As you promise annihilation of the whole d—d lot I won't say more.'[79] On 9 November 1907 Fisher made a speech at the Lord Mayor's Banquet in London, publicly stating that the British could sleep quietly in their beds because the Navy was more than capable of defending the British Isles. He also had his supporters among the inquiry members. Both Haldane and Balfour strongly agreed with Fisher's stance on the importance of the Navy, and General French believed that Roberts's case was 'absurd'.[80] (The final report, released in October 1908,[81] supported the naval case and thus backed Fisher. It concluded 'that so long as our naval supremacy is assured against any reasonable probable combination of Powers, invasion is impracticable' and 'if we permanently lose command of the sea ... the subjection of the country to the enemy is inevitable'. The report resembled an Asquithian compromise, though, as it also recommended the establishment of a home defence force to number 70,000. Not satisfied, Roberts and his supporters continued their agitation over the perceived risk of invasion.[82])

It was in these circumstances, with Fisher reassuring the British populace, and his opponents predicting an easy victory for a German invasion force, that an amendment to the German Navy Law was announced on 18 November 1907, just as the British naval estimates were being prepared. The German amendment provided for an acceleration of capital ship construction. Germany was now to lay down four capital ships a year starting immediately, in 1908/9, instead of the previously stated three. The Admiralty took this in its stride. Their Lordships recognised that Britain continued to have an enormous lead in dreadnoughts, and there was no need to respond immediately to the news from Germany. Indeed, the proposed UK naval estimates called for one battleship and one battlecruiser to be built for the 1908/9 programme year, plus smaller vessels.

However, the German announcement and the naval estimates gave Beresford another opening to attack Admiralty policy and war readiness. The costs of British naval supremacy were rising steeply: the initial draft of the estimates had called for an increase of £2.15 million over the 1907/8 estimates, which had shocked Asquith (the Chancellor of the Exchequer) and prompted Campbell-Bannerman to insist on reductions. At the Admiralty, Tweedmouth sent directions to find places to slash expenditure or at least find something to defer to the next fiscal year.[83] In the event, and although the proposed increase was trimmed to about £1.25 million, the Sea Lords insisted to Fisher that ship construction not be affected. It was this strong stand taken by the Sea Lords that prevented further reductions at this period, and Fisher was initially reluctant to back their position. He subsequently stood by the Sea Lords, perhaps partially in fear of the rising tide of Beresford's agitation and the possibility of support flowing to his rival.[84]

Even the reduced increase provoked a serious Cabinet crisis. The Liberals had come into office on the promise of sweeping social reforms and were now faced with the problem of how to pay for them. There were heated discussions over the estimates at Cabinet meetings from 21 January to 12 February 1908, with several threats of resignation. By 4 February, the government faced a hostile Radical motion on the estimates that was supported by the Tories. Many in government feared defeat. That evening, Lewis Harcourt, First Commissioner of Works, informed Fisher that the Cabinet had decided to trim the estimates by a further £1.34 million. When Fisher stated that the irreducible minimum had been reached, Harcourt replied that either five Cabinet ministers (probably himself, Lloyd George, McKenna, Burns, and Crewe) or the Board of Admiralty would have to resign, and suggested that Beresford was prepared to become First Sea Lord. Later that evening Lloyd George, then the President of the Board of Trade, affirmed this communication in more conciliatory tones, suggesting that Beresford had promised to reduce the estimates by £2 million. Fisher replied that Beresford would 'sell' the government in three months. The next day, Lloyd George attended a meeting of the Board of Admiralty to review the estimates. The Board decided to stand by the proposed estimates. Campbell-Bannerman, the prime minister, considered the Admiralty's case and then sent for Asquith. The prime minister informed the Chancellor of the Exchequer that he had been convinced of the Admiralty's position, and that Haldane would have to trim the army estimates by £300,000 instead. In the end, the increase in the naval estimates was trimmed to £900,000, with construction not being affected.[85] This was perhaps Campbell-Bannerman's last great act of statecraft, and it was taken mere days before he was stricken and confined to his bed in 10 Downing Street on 12 February, and just two months before his resignation and death. He had saved Fisher's job. Asquith became prime minister and formed his first Cabinet in April 1908.

But Beresford would not go away, and like an unwelcome mosquito he made approaches and then escapes, all the while playing to political partisans and the press, who would gladly listen to his inflated views. In November 1907

Ernest Pretyman, a former Civil Lord of the Admiralty, had paid a visit to the Channel Fleet and found Beresford 'in a state of almost open mutiny'. Around the same time, Beresford had met with Campbell-Bannerman and threatened to resign from the Navy, saying if he did so, he would seek a seat as a Radical, on the government's side of the house. This would help achieve his aim of forcing another inquiry into Admiralty policy. Fisher had put both the prime minister and the First Lord on notice that the entire Board would resign rather than submit to such a humiliation.[86]

In January 1908 Admiral Sir Francis Bridgeman, C-in-C, Home Fleet, wrote to tell Fisher that Beresford had issued a memorandum for the North Sea manoeuvres that had severely criticised Bridgeman, his senior officers, and the Admiralty in terms that were 'most damaging to their authority and reputation'. The document was widely available even to the most junior officers, and Bridgeman noted that this would make it difficult to maintain discipline. He ascribed the harsh comments to Custance, even though the memo appeared under the authority of the C-in-C.[87] Fisher responded with the greatest sympathy to Bridgeman: 'His reflections are totally uncalled for, and the First Lord told me to tell you privately that he is astonished at the moderation of your reply, and would have told Beresford "to go to Hell".'[88]

Fisher was irked that Tweedmouth and several Cabinet ministers had met with Beresford, and he accused them of 'coquetting with mutiny & dealing an irreparable blow to Naval discipline.'[89] On 23 January he met with Sir Edward Grey at the Foreign Office and stated his concerns. He followed this up with a strongly worded letter in which he argued that the simple fact of the Cabinet investigating war plans 'would be *prima-facie* evidence of the Cabinet being disquieted and shaken in its confidence in the Board of Admiralty generally and the First Sea Lord in particular, as he is the Member of the Board specifically charged with the organisation for war.' Fisher then took the liberty of sending the 'Board Minute of a former Admiralty' when Lord Hood, in 1795, was ordered to strike his flag after he 'criticized the policy of the Board – not to others but in respectful language to the Board itself'. Fisher also enclosed a copy of the war plans that he had given to Beresford personally over a year earlier. Fisher noted that Beresford was continually asked for his own war plan, which had never been sent. Instead, the previous week Beresford had written to the First Lord asking that the Director of Naval Intelligence should meet him at a hotel to '"*fog out*" a skeleton idea he had!' This was tantamount to subversion of policy. As Fisher noted: 'That is to say that the Admiralty should "*fog out*" a scheme of war in opposition to their own plans which they know and believe to be the best!' Specialised war plans were the preserve of the Admiralty as long as it retained confidence, as Fisher argued, and 'if you have any doubts, get rid of the Admiralty and get fresh members in whom you have implicit confidence; but for God's sake have no Aulic Council for directing the War Policy of the British Navy.'[90]

In the House of Commons, Grey made it clear that he opposed the idea of an inquiry as injurious to the national interest. Shortly thereafter he dined with Fisher and put forward the possibility of coming to terms with Beresford. In his report of the exchange to Esher, Fisher wrote: 'I told him we had once done so very much to the disadvantage of the public service and to glorify his [Beresford's] *amour propre* and he had written officially to say how greatly he appreciated it, etc., and was going to be good ever after ... but it only lasted a few weeks before he was at it again.' Fisher added that he was hearing through the grapevine that Beresford and his wife were making desperate moves to secure editorial support throughout London, and Grey had told him that Beresford had the whole Navy behind him. Fisher disputed this, and added that if it were true, 'so much the more ought the government to be firm in supporting the Admiralty against [a campaign] by Beresford in inciting the Service to mutiny'. Fisher also told Grey, 'it was scandalous this parleying with mutiny by persons in high position giving encouragement to Beresford by seeing him and discussing mutiny with him'. Fisher complained to Esher, 'These politicians are a flabby lot.'[91]

Esher prepared a full memorandum on the Fisher–Beresford tangle for the King. In it, he examined the authority of the Board of Admiralty, which was the supreme naval authority and wielded both royal and executive authority over fleets and their distribution, and admirals. As such, serious insubordination was a punishable event. The First Sea Lord was primarily responsible for strategy and intelligence, but his authority did not relieve the Board of its responsibility as a whole. If a public inquiry were made into the policy of the Admiralty, it would evolve into an inquiry into the government. Since the government of the day was responsible for all policy, it must either support the Board or ask for the current Board's resignation.[92]

At first Esher thought Fisher had time on his side, and he encouraged Fisher by arguing that Beresford would be forced to strike his flag in the near future, as the situation was intolerable. He told Fisher to sit tight and give Beresford a lot of rope with which to hang himself.[93] Then Esher took a harder line. He told Fisher that none of the conspiring would stop 'except [with] the removal of Beresford and Custance. The sooner the better.' In regard to the upcoming estimates, the discussion of which gave opponents every opportunity to stir up difficulty, he advised Fisher to do what he could to get the moderates in Cabinet to defect from Beresford. He added that it was of key importance to detach Haldane, the Secretary of State for War, from the Beresford camp, and then 'there will be no fear for this year or next.'[94]

The state of the Navy and its future strength had become a national preoccupation far in excess of anything to date – and a major subject for party controversy. On one side, the ruling Liberals had convinced themselves, a little naively, that the Kaiser's assurances regarding his fleet could be accepted at face value – in short, it was not intended to challenge Britain's control of the seas. On the other, the Conservatives warned that the Germans had accelerated their naval building and that the German ships would be completed ahead of schedule. In this era of growing anxiety, various disaffected, retired admirals (more than a hundred of them within a few years) had formed an association known as the Imperial Maritime League, an offshoot of the Navy League. Their mission was to protect the Navy and guard the trade and possessions of the British Empire. They fought against withdrawal of gunboats from colonial outposts, opposed the closure of overseas stations, promoted imperial defence consolidation, and sought protection of belligerent rights on the high seas to protect commerce and examine neutral shipping in wartime. The League's immediate objective was Fisher's removal from the Admiralty and with it an inquiry into Admiralty measures to meet the German challenge. When F E Smith (later Lord Birkenhead), a Unionist MP who was friendly to Fisher, joined the League, he wrote to the First Sea Lord to explain his actions. Smith did not advocate an inquiry but felt it was important to defeat the Radicals (or 'economists', as Churchill called them), who wanted no increase in the naval estimates. He assured Fisher that 'the Conservatives are with you to a man.'[95]

In late January 1908 the League invited Esher to join, claiming that Fisher was the most dreaded man in Germany and a trouble to his own country. Esher rejected this overture and counter-attacked in a powerful letter. He rigorously defended Fisher's record and that of the government, and admonished the 'croakers' with a quotation of Liberal MP John Morley from 1893: 'Everybody knows, Liberals as well as Tories, that it is indispensable that we should have, not only a powerful Navy, but I may say, an all-powerful Navy.' He argued that the reforms made by Fisher were done on strategic grounds, not economic ones, and the personnel reforms were backed up by the entire Board, with each one discussed and approved. Esher stated that an inquiry into Admiralty policy was not required and proceeded to equate advocacy of such an inquiry with treason. On 6 February *The Times* published his letter, which contained this explosive sentence: 'There is not a man in Germany from the Emperor downwards who would not welcome the fall of Sir John Fisher.'[96] Sir Francis Knollys, Edward VII's private secretary, told Esher that both the King and the Prince of Wales believed that Esher was right to agree to publication of the letter.[97]

This may well have been true, but when news of the letter reached the Kaiser, as it was bound to do, he decided to take matters into his own hands. Annoyed by insinuations that he was responsible for the naval arms race, he wrote a nine-page letter, in his own hand, directly to Lord Tweedmouth, a breach of protocol and diplomacy. In it, he attempted to allay British fears about German naval construction, and he expressed himself unable to understand those fears of Germany. He turned to Esher's letter:

> In the letter Lord Esher caused to be published a short time ago he wrote 'that every German from the Emperor down to the last man wished for the downfall of Sir John Fisher.' Now I am at a loss to tell whether the supervision of the foundations and drains of the Royal Palaces is apt to qualify somebody for the judgement of Naval Affairs in general. As far as regards German affairs Naval the phrase is a piece of unmitigated balderdash, and has created immense merriment in the circles of those 'who know' here. But I venture to think that such things ought not to be written by people who are highly placed, as they are liable to hurt public feelings over here.[98]

He was at pains to emphasise that the Imperial German navy was designed to protect trade only. He thought it galling that the British press always viewed the German fleet as a challenge and 'the sole danger' to Britain's naval primacy. The Kaiser's response stemmed from his opinion that it was unfair of England to question Germany over naval armaments. It had been a long-standing convention that European states did not question each other about their respective armaments. The Kaiser could not see how the same would not apply to their respective navies. Inasmuch as he viewed the German navy as his personal creation, his pet project, he considered British inquiries about it to be a personal affront.[99]

The Kaiser's petulant letter broke precedence. That a foreign monarch should write directly to a minister of the Crown, without informing the prime minster, let alone the King, was unheard of. 'What would he say,' asked the Prince of Wales, 'if the King wrote to von Tirpitz a letter of this kind?' The King outlined his annoyance in a restrained note to his nephew: 'Your writing to my First Lord of the Admiralty is "a new departure" and I do not see how he can prevent our press from calling attention to the great increase in building of German ships of war which necessitates our increasing our Navy also.'[100] Until he read about it in *The Times* on 6 March, Asquith knew nothing of the correspondence between the Kaiser and Tweedmouth. Senior German ministers were equally in the dark. Prince von Bülow thought his monarch's letter 'childish' – though he did not tell the Kaiser that to his face. He was particularly upset that the Kaiser had sent with his letter a 'whole set of false statistics which the English promptly recognized as such.' Von Bülow knew that such a patently transparent effort to mollify the British would only backfire.[101]

On 19 February Esher learned of the Kaiser's intemperate letter. He told Fisher: 'You have had the greatest compliment paid you that was ever paid a man. The German Emperor has written to Tweedmouth nine pages in his own hand, full of abuse of you.' The King, Esher wrote, 'hates a fuss', but he told Fisher he was confident the episode would blow over.[102]

The matter did not blow over. Now it was the First Lord of the Admiralty's turn to act the fool. Tweedmouth was indiscreet, and after receiving the Kaiser's letter showed it proudly to many people. Esher thought Tweedmouth 'seemed rather flattered at getting a letter from so Imperial a source, and was inclined to treat it as a personal compliment. He talked about it everywhere.'[103] Tweedmouth committed a further indiscretion: he replied to the Kaiser and, as the press alleged, divulged some details of the forthcoming naval estimates.[104] This was a breach of state secrets.

The story, too good to be kept quiet, found its way to the press. *The Times* military correspondent, Repington, exposed the story on 6 March.[105] Next day the press in both England and Germany were 'in full cry' over the issue. There was much collateral damage. In his journal, Esher wrote that Repington had ruined his standing with the government by blurting out the details and that, according to Fisher, Tweedmouth was blaming Esher for the indiscretion. Not to be outdone, Esher noted that he had heard that the Kaiser had put all responsibility for the episode on Tweedmouth.[106]

Now it was Fisher's turn. He protested to the King on 8 March that Esher did not leak the letter to *The Times*: 'Repington, the Military Correspondent of *The Times*, I know to be absolutely unscrupulous ... He is extremely clever and most able with his pen, and Mr. Haldane finds him very useful.'[107] Fisher observed that Tweedmouth was 'frightfully excited about it all – and probably will make a fool of himself.' Esher also noted that the whole affair indicated the necessity of putting England's military forces in perfect order against the obviously aggressive Germans. As a result of it, Balfour had been able to extract from Asquith a promise to lay down enough dreadnoughts over the next three years to ensure superiority: 'So good has come out of evil, if evil it was.'[108]

Asquith all at sea

Herbert Asquith, who became prime minister in April 1908 at the age of fifty-six, was a classics scholar by inclination and a lawyer by profession. A strong Liberal, but of the old school, with a distinct vein of conservatism in his character and habits of thought, he regarded change as inevitable but something not to be sought. He left innovation to others. His natural instinct was compromise, and he disliked the melodramatic in politics. He never courted the press. He never sought publicity. Upon becoming premier, he led a Cabinet of exceptionally able as well as experienced ministers, some of whom had prickly characteristics and were prone to self-advertisement. Many of them were ambitious, awaiting better opportunities and grander departments of state. He managed a team with cool judgement. Peacetime, with all its problems, favoured him. But when peace gave way to war, Asquith did not inspire. Many thought him naturally indolent, as evenings were for bridge or girlfriends (to whom he divulged state secrets). The fortunes of war did not bring out any higher form of executive energy and, as we will see, the forces of time and circumstance overcame him. For the moment, however, he had a chance to choose his own team. It had never been his bent to face issues promptly, and that caused problems for Fisher.

Within a week of succeeding Henry Campbell-Bannerman, Asquith replaced the First Lord of the Admiralty, Tweedmouth, who was deemed mentally unstable or otherwise incompetent. In one of his gossipy letters to his twenty-six-year-old confidante and lover, Venetia Stanley, Asquith recalled:

> The first thing I did was to put 'Cousin Reggie' [McKenna] in Tweedmouth's place at the Admiralty – not a moment too soon, for within a month or six weeks T. was raving mad, & so continued until his death. His was a tragic case, for he was one of the sanest & most high-spirited of mankind. I shall never forget my bewilderment when, in the course of a longish tête-à-tête in the Cabinet room, it gradually dawned upon me that he was off his head.[109]

In 1919 Fisher was to say of this unique interlude that 'Tweedmouth, by a divine help, became a lunatic, and no one knew it but myself but I knew he was going to become a maniac.'[110] Churchill was considered as a possible replacement of Tweedmouth, but only Fisher backed those long odds. As for Reginald McKenna, who was forty-five when he took up the post, a Cambridge rowing blue and an experienced administrator (though an angular and difficult character), he proved an able head at the Admiralty, but events not of his own making eventually brought about his undoing and brought Churchill to the fore in that post. Asquith found in Pamela McKenna, the First Lord's wife, a new source for his political indiscretions; she was also a confidante of Fisher's.

Fisher was necessarily under close watch when Asquith decided to get rid of Tweedmouth, for this could have been the prime minister's rare opportunity to oust the First Sea Lord too, should that be in the national interest. When the change came, the King, on accepting a new First Lord, insisted on Fisher's retention, as he wrote to Fisher: 'When I agreed to Mr. McKenna's appointment it was on condition that you kept your present post. The Prime Minster never made the *slightest* difficulty – on the contrary, was most desirous that you should remain.'[111] And in a curious fashion, the affair – and McKenna's appointment – stopped the agitation for further reductions in the naval estimates.

Fisher's relationship with McKenna began on a hopeful note from Fisher in which he laid down the basis of the authority of the Board of Admiralty vis-à-vis serving admirals:

> If complete confidence cannot be given to the Sea Lords, they ought to be changed, but there is an end of all things if, taking the instance you gave me,

Lord C. Beresford is to dictate to the Admiralty what particular destroyers he should have, or what should be the constitution of his Fleet: 'Se soumettre ou se démettre' – that's the plain answer to give him; or, as Mr. John Burns put it more graphically:

'*The Quarterdeck and Silence,*
or *Westminster and Gas,*'

... In the meantime I am confident, from what you have kindly said, that you will give no encouragement to Lord Charles Beresford that he will receive any sort of countenance in his disloyal ... conduct towards the Admiralty because a new First Lord has arrived.[112]

Fisher's confidence in McKenna was short-lived. He soon found out that the First Lord, doubtless under considerable political pressure from Cabinet colleagues, was making subterranean overtures to the Beresford camp. To counter what he thought was McKenna's 'double-dealing', Fisher – who always could smell a rat – provided his political boss with a complete account of the war plans imbroglio with Beresford. He laid out his defence of the Admiralty's conduct toward the C-in-C, Channel Fleet, indicating that everything had been done to accommodate Beresford despite the abuse endured. As well, despite the attempts of the Admiralty to supply him with war plans, Beresford had not communicated any plan to the Board over the previous ten months.[113] More generally, as Fisher related to Esher: '*It's impossible*! You can't let authority be flouted as he [Beresford] continuously flouts the Admiralty. Daily he is doing something traitorous & mutinous.'[114]

To McKenna, Beresford complained of the resources at his disposal as well as the Admiralty's shipbuilding policies. McKenna wrote firmly in reply, with a copy to Fisher. The First Lord rejected Beresford's comments on construction, since this was beyond his purview, but on the former he stated that the naval units assigned were sufficient and that war plans were under Admiralty authority. McKenna chastised the C-in-C, reminding him that close co-operation with Whitehall was necessary in view of 'the unhappy personal position in which you have placed yourself in relation to the First Sea Lord.'[115] McKenna was on Fisher's side even if Fisher doubted McKenna's loyalty and questioned his motives.

Fisher followed up by having the Admiralty Secretary provide a memoran-dum to Beresford, again reiterating the authority of the Board of Admiralty and the responsibilities of the Commander-in-Chief. At Fisher's behest, the Secretary laid out the uncertainty of war situations, stating that day-to-day conditions could not be counted on: 'While their Lordships will always ensure a largely preponderant force being localized in the North Sea, the exact disposition and plan of action must depend upon the attendant conditions and political and other circumstances of the moment. Nevertheless it is of great importance that every probability should be thought out and provided against, and accordingly no one single plan of action, however perfected, can be accepted as final.'[116]

The Fisher–Beresford relationship continued to deteriorate. In early May, at the Academy dinner, Beresford tried to avoid Fisher, but Fisher insisted on shaking hands with him.[117] However, at the levee on 11 May, the King, ministers, and naval officers were witness to a remarkable scene. As Esher stated in his journal: 'I saw Jackie to-day. He was publicly cut by Beresford at the Levee. In full view of the King and before the Ministers and C.B.'s naval officers. Jackie tried to shake hands, and C.B. turned his back. It is all over the fleet.'[118] Then on 1 July 1908 the second Scott–Beresford incident occurred. Beresford signalled an order for ships under Scott's command to make a turn that would have led to a collision. Scott allowed the ships to disobey Beresford's command, which infuriated Beresford, who requested Scott be court-martialled. The Admiralty and the First Lord were reluctant to do this, as the inquiry needed to prepare for the court martial would dredge up scandal, and the process would make it appear that Beresford was acting vindictively.[119]

Fuel was added to the fire when Arthur Lee's 6 July letter in *The Times* exposed damningly the extent of conflict between Fisher and Beresford: 'It can no longer be denied that the Commander-in-Chief of the Channel Fleet (who is presumably the Admiralissimo designate in the event of war) is not on speaking terms with the admiral commanding his cruiser squadron on the one hand [Scott], or with the First Sea Lord of the Admiralty on the other.' The full extent of the infighting was now public knowledge.[120] In mid-July, press editorials demanded the resignation of both Beresford and Fisher.[121]

In these increasingly alarming circumstances, those close to the centre of power were beginning to express deep reservations. When the King learned of the difficulties, Esher wrote to His Majesty's secretary, Lord Knollys, assuring him that quarrels in the Navy were no new thing. He noted in particular that St Vincent and Nelson were on bad terms in 1803–1804, and that Nelson was writing and speaking in a highly subordinate manner. He also stated that only the King could solve the dispute.[122]

As the accusation that Fisher had leaked word of this latest Beresford–Scott incident to *The Times* gained credibility, Fisher was forced to deny the charges more vigorously and stridently. Even the King had to be circumspect about meeting with his principal naval ADC, Fisher. Instead, the King sent Knollys as his envoy to review with Fisher the whole business. The King wanted peace in his navy – and no further fuss. Fisher blamed 'all the Dukes and Duchesses being worked up by Beresford and attacking the King, so much that His Majesty thought it wise not to see me personally, as he wished to.'[123]

Political problems raised by the dispute with Beresford would soon force Asquith's hand. Esher, with his appreciation of the complexities of the issue, advised Fisher in September 1908 that there was no doubt Fisher would not remain at his post if there was a change of government – an early election was possible as the Conservatives were blocking Liberal legislation in the House of Lords – and that it would be much more dignified for him to make the first move and announce his intention to resign at some distant time.[124] Fisher found such sage advice unacceptable on principle. Besides, he feared impotence if he gave such a sign of weakness. On 3 November 1908 Fisher telephoned Esher to say that he was 'having qualms at the idea of leaving the Admiralty next year.' Undaunted, Esher urged Fisher to write to McKenna and say that he would resign on 9 November 1909. The First Sea Lord replied by stating that McKenna had told him that he hoped not to lose Fisher, and that he would act on Esher's advice. Six days later, Fisher told Esher that he had thought better of his resolve to write McKenna and had put away the relevant letters. Esher believed that Fisher could not bring himself to leave the Admiralty, even within a year.[125]

And so the Fisher–Beresford problem continued, with the antagonists more deeply entrenched in their views, more definite in their actions. The naval problem of high command became a political one. Fisher's authority was being threatened, and in a fight he was unlikely to back down. Given his pugilistic nature, he was probably looking forward to the inevitable final and decisive battle.

4

Fisher's Fall

'We want eight and we won't wait'

The year 1909 began quietly. Parliament was preoccupied with the customary nagging issues – prospects of Home Rule for Ireland, debates on education, duties on spirits and tobacco, licensing of drinking houses, and, not least, the progress of the suffragists and their growing hostility to Asquith and the government. Always in the background was concern about the strength of the Royal Navy against the ascent of the German navy. A sizeable section of the Cabinet, thinking they had satisfied the Admiralty's 1906 demands for laying down new naval units, stood against any further acceleration of the armaments race. David Lloyd George at the Exchequer and Winston Churchill at the Board of Trade (and as of February 1910 at the Home Office), newly in their posts in consequence of the reshuffle of the Cabinet when Asquith became prime minister, joined forces, taking a prominent position on this side of the issue of naval security.

Those following the matter of Britain's superiority at sea were led to believe that Lord Cawdor's 1906 building programme – four dreadnoughts to be laid down per year – as guided by Fisher, would suffice. Churchill understood the importance of a supreme navy – and the importance of preparedness. All the same, he and Lloyd George concentrated attention on social reform rather than naval armaments, and in December 1908 they exerted strong opposition to McKenna's naval estimates.

At this precise juncture, McKenna and Fisher found themselves presented with the gift of strategic and industrial intelligence. Alarming news from Berlin, admitted by Tirpitz before the Reichstag's committee, made clear Germany's potential, if not its actual and muscular intention, to use naval power to fulfil worldly ambitions. It was widely believed that the Germans were in a position to accelerate their construction programme and that, as a result, by 1912 the German navy might actually possess more dreadnoughts than the Royal Navy. British public opinion held that this would jeopardise British security. And who knew what real German intentions might be? Certainly the shipbuilding capacities of the Germans had been disclosed. That was the key to the British appraisal of the darkening situation as 1909 opened and progressed. As Lloyd George understood it, however, and the view he expressed to Churchill, was that obtaining reliable information about German shipbuilding and intentions was not only difficult but was likely to be exaggerated by Fisher, who, when he needed more alarming information, wired British intelligence in Berlin and got 'something more panicky'.[1]

The Admiralty, in its narrowest calculations made for the 1909 naval estimates (to be brought before Parliament that March, as customary), had concluded that eight dreadnoughts should form part of the 1909/10 programme. The four Sea Lords, of whom Sir John Jellicoe was Third Sea Lord and Controller, in charge of the essential gun and turret contracts requiring advance and long-range planning, made this determination. They considered six dreadnoughts, as a minimum, of utmost importance, and sent a memorandum to the First Lord to this effect. Radicals and economisers within the Liberal government put up dogged resistance to this proposal. Even six dreadnoughts seemed too much to bear. For three days the Cabinet roiled in crisis on the issue. In particular, Lloyd George,[2] Churchill, and Haldane came out in favour of only four dreadnoughts, which put them in the 'little-navy faction'. Churchill told Esher to tell Fisher that, as fond of Fisher as he was, he would resign from the Home Office rather than agree to six dreadnoughts, and he insisted he was not bluffing.[3] At this stage of the running crisis, four dreadnoughts seemed the maximum possible.

Fisher, who might have expected in Churchill an ally at least on grounds of friendship, was furious at his opposition. He wrote sharply to Churchill of the betrayal:

> I appreciate your kind motive in writing me your long letter of today's date. I confess I never expected you to turn against the Navy after all you had said in public and in private. (*et tu Brute!*) I am sure that you won't expect me to enter into any discussion with you, as there can be only one exponent of the Admiralty case – the First Lord. As to lack of foresight on the part of the Admiralty, the Sea Lords expressed their grave anxiety in a memorandum presented to the First Lord in December 1907. The Cabinet ignored that anxiety and cut down the estimates. You want to do the same again. We can take no risk this year – last year we did. We felt then that there would be time to pull up – the margin is now exhausted.
>
> I reciprocate your grief at our separation. I retain the memory of many pleasant duets.[4]

Throughout the crisis McKenna, the First Lord, backed Fisher wholeheartedly, and at one time threatened resignation from the Cabinet. His reasoning was that in the year previous, 1908, Germany had laid down four all-big-gun ships to Britain's two. He contended that Britain should now lay down two keels to every German one: that was the new margin of superiority in his view. In the circumstances, he was bitter at the opposition from his colleagues Lloyd George and Churchill, who were distrusted in the Cabinet, and he deplored Asquith's weakness in not resolving the matter in favour of security of the state. At considerable risk to himself he held his ground, though at times he was as exposed and alone as any First Lord of the Admiralty had ever been in British history. Fisher, too, was under extreme pressure at this time, increasingly independent and arbitrary in his actions, which some observers regarded as sure signs of megalomania. The battles over the 1909 naval estimates began in Cabinet in December 1908 and carried on through the following spring.

Churchill's leading role in the attempt to block the laying down of any more than the customary four dreadnoughts per year was first disclosed by Fisher's biographer Reginald Bacon. The battle had been fought out in Cabinet, with McKenna standing practically alone against Churchill's onslaught. 'Mr. Churchill opposed him vehemently, disputing the figures and treating the Admiralty arguments as mere figments of an alarmist brain.' It was at this point that McKenna threatened resignation, and indeed, for all intents and purposes was out of the Cabinet. It seemed as if Churchill had brought about his downfall and discredited Fisher and the Sea Lords.

At this point in the drama, Sir Edward Grey, Secretary of State for Foreign Affairs, stepped in to support the Admiralty. The Foreign Office shared the Admiralty's appreciation of the rising German menace both in number of dreadnoughts and in rate of shipbuilding. Berlin had ordered extra supplies of nickel for the toughening of metals for guns. This, too, triggered alarm. Asquith convened another Cabinet meeting and the whole process was reversed: McKenna resumed his post, the Sea Lords were sustained in their view, and Churchill was defeated. Fisher's biographer thought Churchill reckless in his attack and his intentions: 'Mr. Churchill ... took the leading part in opposing the Admiralty proposal, and he gave no thought to the certainty that, if his views were wrong and the figures quoted by the Admiralty were right, as in fact they were, the Empire would be placed in a position of grave peril.'[5]

When the naval estimates came to the House of Commons, McKenna disclosed that the German government and the German Navy League were working together to complete the aggressive programme of naval shipbuilding by 1912 instead of 1917. It was this acceleration of building that caused alarm bells to sound in Westminster. In spite of official pronouncements from Berlin, some meant to counter Social Democrat opposition to the naval programme, that the idea of an Anglo-German war could not be entertained by sensible people in either country, these reassurances were appearing more threadbare as naval intelligence from Berlin confirmed every fear. The conclusion drawn in England was that Germany might indeed establish equality in the newest types of battleships. McKenna emerged as the champion who saved the day for British naval primacy.

The Cabinet could agree to four dreadnoughts as prearranged. The opposition at first demanded six as the minimum, then went for two more. The Admiralty wanted eight – but how would this be paid for? At the end of February, Asquith gingerly came up with an acceptable compromise. He recommended that four dreadnoughts be laid down immediately as part of the 1909/10 programme. A further four dreadnoughts would be laid down no later than 1 April 1910 if it were judged necessary, and Cabinet would make that determination in November 1909.[6]

Now a new problem arose: just how 'conditional' were those four extra dreadnoughts? And this put the Admiralty back in the limelight. Had the Admiralty fudged the estimates, trumped up the needs of the day? Churchill contended later that this was the case.[7] For its part, the Admiralty rightly demanded a definite statement of the government's intentions and, with it, the requisite authority to stockpile guns, turrets, and other materials for the intended capital ships. Fisher dug in his heels; the Opposition, which in the circumstances proved his strangest bedfellow and closest ally, adroitly aided him. The Unionists led the attack with the belligerent cry of a music-hall refrain: 'We want eight and we won't wait.' The press – aided and abetted in backstairs fashion by Fisher – played to the hand of the big-navy faction, and backed McKenna and Fisher. This was the deciding factor. And thus it was that the Admiralty confidently proceeded under the assumption that the four extra dreadnoughts would be authorised. Orders were made for eight dreadnoughts all at once. Here was an example of the politics of naval supremacy working to the advantage of Fisher and the other Sea Lords.

Some years later, Austen Chamberlain, former Civil Lord of the Admiralty (1895–1900) and Chancellor of the Exchequer in Balfour's Cabinet, recounted that at the time he was unsure what the Admiralty had been asking for. But he was certain that it would get what it wanted if it stood by its demands. During the crisis he had sent encouragement to Fisher, reminding him: 'If the Naval Lords stand firm, and are prepared to resign together, they will get their way now as they did over the Spencer programme [in 1893–94].' Shortly thereafter, Chamberlain chanced upon Fisher in Westminster Palace Yard. 'At the top of his voice, but with great insistence on the need for absolute secrecy, [Fisher] declared that the Prime Minister was behaving abominably, that the Government did not want to resign, and that he himself consequently had the whip hand.' What had transpired was not all Fisher's doing, for with the threat of McKenna's resignation, Sir Edward Grey at the Foreign Office had thrown his weight into the Admiralty scale. This, in turn, convinced Asquith. Chamberlain, a little unkindly given the circumstances, said this about Asquith and his administration: 'Asquith jumps about like a parched pea in a frying-pan, and doesn't know which way to face, the Liberal Party is divided and all sections of it dissatisfied and uneasy, and confidence in the Admiralty has received a rude shock.'[8]

When the dust settled on this amazing turnaround, with Lloyd George and Churchill outfoxed by McKenna, Grey, and Asquith, Fisher could hardly contain his delight. He wrote to Churchill that he thought that the four extra men-of-war ought to be named 'No. 1 "Winston", No. 2 "Churchill", No. 3. "Lloyd", and No. 4. "George". How they would fight! Un-circumventable.' And how did Churchill consider this situation in later years? In all it had been a great crisis; the actual points never came to an issue; the press got involved; the parties traded barbs. The Admiralty exaggerated the claims. The German menace got great attention throughout Britain. 'In the end,' wrote Churchill (who had his own and incomplete explanation of events), 'a curious and characteristic solution was reached.'

> The Admiralty had demanded six ships; the economists offered four; and we finally compromised on eight ... But although the Chancellor of the Exchequer and I were right in the narrow sense, we were absolutely wrong in relation to the deep tides of destiny. The greatest credit is due to the First Lord of the Admiralty, Mr. McKenna, for the resolute and courageous manner in which he fought his case and withstood his Party on this occasion. Little did I think, as this dispute proceeded, that when the next Cabinet crisis about the Navy arose our roles would be reversed; and little did he think that the ships for which he had contended so stoutly would eventually, when they arrived, be welcomed with open arms by me.[9]

And so, with a good naval margin for the present and future, the British faced the rising crisis over which they had no control. In 1912, when Germany had thirteen capital ships completed, the British had twenty-two. Without the full eight decided upon as a result of this crisis the Germans would have had fourteen in August 1914 and the British only sixteen. The eight ships provided for in 1909 marked, according to battleships historian Oscar Parkes, 'the greatest accession to our armoured forces ever undertaken in a twelvemonth.'[10] They gave Jellicoe's Grand Fleet the superior margin in capital ships at the outset of the war.[11]

By April the naval hysteria had blown away, but the naval estimates badly upset the financial calculations. The extra dreadnoughts meant a total of £15 million added to the budget. Another consequence of the naval scare was heightened criticism of the Admiralty in general and Fisher in particular.

Opponents accused Fisher of starving the Navy with his economies. News reports charged that the Admiralty had ignored the warning signs of a massive German naval expansion and had taken insufficient steps to address the problem. They also alleged that the Admiralty lacked effective strategic plans to deal with the German threat, and that the disposition of the Fleet left the Navy vulnerable to a sudden attack. Naturally, the anti-Fisher claims of Beresford and his supporters resonated during this period. Near the end of March 1909, in compliance with orders, Beresford struck his flag as Commander-in-Chief, Channel Fleet, and had come ashore to rapturous applause and enormous crowds at Portsmouth and, later, at London. He had never been so popular, and it appeared that many agreed with his accusations of incompetence at the Admiralty.[12] He began to hold forth in every drawing room in London. 'The Duchesses', as Fisher dubbed the fashionable ladies of London, who hosted dinner parties for Lord Charles Beresford so as to devour the gossip he fed them, did their work. The drawing rooms of London were no field of action for Fisher, who eschewed such circles and venues. He was not in these social circumstances and did not play to the aristocratic circles of Beresford and his friends. Indeed, throughout this whole crisis Fisher kept a low public profile, worked the backrooms of politics and press, and let McKenna carry the arguments successfully. The result was McKenna's triumph, one of the greatest gifts to the Navy in the lengthy annals of British sea power.

The Fisher–Beresford feud and the Committee of Imperial Defence inquiry

We now come to late spring and summer 1909, when another battle for power and influence in the Navy raged in Britain, reaching right to the apex of influence. At this juncture, Fisher had been First Sea Lord for four and a half years, and there was some weariness with the constant feuding and uncertainty that had arisen during his tenure, particularly the quarrel with Beresford that had been building since 1905. The Service was wracked with dissension. Fisher was seen more and more as a dictator. Esher, who understood the matter completely, noted, 'Politicians sicken of prolonged conflict and are apt to blame those who (as they think) have been the protagonists of the policy which is stiffly contested.'[13] Naval officers also came to believe that Fisher's time was coming to an end. Sir David Beatty, a commander in the Atlantic Fleet, confided to his wife: 'That old J.F. [Fisher] has not a bed of roses in front of him, and C.B. [Beresford] intends to stir him up properly before he has finished with him. And I think, in consequence J.F. will very likely go before it gets too hot.'[14] Similarly, Prince Louis of Battenberg, ordinarily a great friend of Fisher, reluctantly recognised that the First Sea Lord would probably have to leave that coveted post, and placed considerable blame on Fisher's shoulders. While acknowledging Fisher's contribution, he observed: 'He has started this pernicious partisanship in the Navy – there is no denying it. Anyone who has in any way opposed J.F. went under. His hatred of C.B. has led him to maintain for the past two years an organisation of our Home Forces which was indefensible.'[15]

Lord Charles Beresford, 'Charlie B', could count fifty years in the Service. He had powerful friends in Parliament among the Conservatives and Unionists. His impulsive nature and zest for action made him attractive to some in the Service. But whereas in the Navy he was regarded as a politician, in the House of Commons, where he sometimes sat as an MP, he was seen as a sailor. On 30 March 1909, an admiral afloat no more, Beresford met with Asquith and explained his case against Fisher, following this up with a letter on 2 April outlining in detail his main charges.[16] Beresford clearly meant to take his case to the people if his concerns were not addressed. He forced Asquith's hand in what amounted to a form of political extortion. Asquith consulted the First Lord. Then, with McKenna's acquiescence, Asquith agreed to Beresford's demand that his charges be investigated by a subcommittee of the CID. This was not to be a general inquiry into the conduct of the Admiralty, but, rather, specific to the charges raised by Beresford.[17]

Exposed and vulnerable, Fisher was infuriated by the decision to launch the inquiry: 'Imagine what a state of affairs when a meeting of Naval Officers on the active list in a room in Grosvenor Street is able to coerce the Cabinet and force the strongest Board of Admiralty to totter to its fall! ... The Country must indeed be in a bad way if so governed!'[18] He was upset with Asquith's initial lethargic replies to the calls in the House for an inquiry, and the prime minister's silence when given a golden opportunity to praise the Board of the Admiralty on the occasion of a supplementary question.[19] Only for a moment did he consider resignation. Strong supportive letters from the King and Esher stiffened Fisher's resolve, and he decided that he would dig in his heels and fight the accusations.[20] He was confident of the outcome of the inquiry, as 'the case is impregnable against Beresford'. However, he believed that Beresford had stacked the committee against him, as both Esher and Sir Arthur Wilson, recommended by the prime minister for appointment, were, on Beresford's objections, not appointed, or, in Wilson's case, appointed but released from this duty.[21] Churchill was not involved. Fisher, ever on the lookout for some intrigue, suspected that Beresford was somehow blackmailing the prime minister.[22]

The CID committee met on fifteen occasions from 27 April to 13 July.[23] It began as expected, with McKenna, the First Lord, acting as inquisitor. Barrister that he was, he led the examination of Beresford competently and thoroughly. Bereford performed in elusive fashion, dodging questions, pleading ignorance or inability to remember dates and other particulars. At every turn he sought to discredit McKenna and the Board of Admiralty and, by implication, Fisher and his regime.

Fisher was bound to remain silent, and bit his lip from time to time. Early stages of the inquiry brought him much disappointment. Beresford was clearly flailing about and was defeated on nearly every point, but he showed resilience. Time and again Asquith would rescue him. Fisher, with a note of nostalgia, put it this way to the king's private secretary: 'the disquieting aspect is the obvious desire of the Committee to get him out of his mess ... It's abundantly clear to me that what the Cabinet thinks of just now is the happy time they all had in that junk when Jonah was chucked overboard – there was calm and peace!'[24] And to the journalist W T Stead: '(*It's cunning to get rid of me on Beresford and not on "two keels to one"!*)'.[25] The only option was to stay the course: 'If I had resigned, I should have done exactly what my enemies wanted and what would have suited the political situation ... So there is no alternative but to hang on.'[26] And so he did, in painful silence. He could not fault McKenna but he was confirmed in his view that Beresford was not competent for the sea command he had held in the Channel Fleet. What Fisher wanted was McKenna and the Cabinet, led by Asquith, to dismiss Beresford.

For the 24 June session, Asquith announced that he was calling Sir Arthur Wilson as a witness, but then, according to Fisher, knuckled under to Beresford by calling in a Captain H H Campbell, Naval Intelligence Department, who happened to be a friend of the Prince of Wales, to discuss trade defence. This topic lay beyond the terms of reference for the committee,[27] and Fisher stated that Captain Campbell 'had been doing "Judas"! perpetually at my house, and selling me all the time to Beresford!'[28] In reading the testimony of this inquiry, one is struck by Beresford's deviousness and his wizard-like ability to avoid censure by changing the subject or diverting the issue raised. Asquith, quite familiar with such shenanigans from a legal point of view, perhaps found it entertaining. Nothing went specifically Fisher's way, and Asquith took no steps to bring clarity to the issue of discipline in the Navy. He was quite willing to leave Fisher high and dry.

Fisher suffered another blow at this time when the journalist Sir George Armstrong, a strong ally of Beresford and then seeking election to Parliament, publicly revealed the existence of two letters Captain Reginald Bacon had sent to Fisher in 1906, when Bacon was in the Mediterranean Fleet under Beresford (see the discussion of these letters in Chapter 3). McKenna said the letters were for internal Admiralty consumption. All the same, the revelation created a sensation, and it bolstered the Beresford syndicate's allegations that Fisher used a system of espionage by his supporters to keep track of and punish those who opposed him.[29] There was a modicum of truth to these allegations, but Fisher was unrepentant: 'However "hot" they may be, I don't regret a word I ever wrote, and I believe my countrymen will forgive me. *Anyhow I won't be blackmailed! ... I am going to fight to the finish!*'[30]

The committee's final report appeared in print as a Parliamentary Paper dated 12 August 1909. It dealt specifically with the accusations of Beresford. With respect to the distribution of the Navy, it stated that the creation of the Home Fleet in March 1909 satisfied Beresford's objections on this issue. They also concluded that there was no deficiency of small craft and destroyers during the period that Beresford alleged there was. The report further concluded that no grounds existed for Beresford's claims with respect to war plans, but did note with approval the steps being taken to establish a War Staff at the Admiralty. Crucially, the report also took a middle ground on the Fisher–Beresford controversy: 'The Board of Admiralty do not appear to have taken Lord Charles Beresford sufficiently into their confidence as to the reasons for dispositions to which he took exception; and Lord Charles Beresford, on the other hand, appears to have failed to appreciate and carry out the spirit of the instructions of the Board, and to recognize their paramount authority.'[31]

That insider Esher was cynical about the final report, as he wrote to Balfour, who knew the politics of the CID better than anyone: 'I wonder what you think of Asquith's Report? It is couched in his usual cold judicial language, and, as you will note, contains no words of appreciation of the value of the naval reforms introduced by Selborne, which lie at the root of the policy which C.B. [Beresford] attacked. I imagine Jackie [Fisher] will be hurt at the want of direct support given to him, and C.B. will be furious. So I suppose the Report fulfils all "political" requirements.'[32]

Esher was not mistaken about Fisher's reaction. After reading the finished and signed report, Fisher was furious and wrote bitterly to McKenna. 'BUT *it's a cowardly document!* ... No downright words for discipline, and a clear lead given for Beresford to pose as having accomplished his ideas and sacrificed himself in so doing! I am bitterly mistaken in the 5 men who signed the Report. I *thought* they were great men – they are great cowards! ... Luckily there is a Hell, where all things are compensated for! Sometimes the Hell is on earth. I hope the 5 will have it here instead of waiting!'[33] He greatly resented the implicit censure that both sides were equally to blame.[34] Fisher went even further when writing to Esher. He was particularly bitter about the fact that no attention had been paid to Beresford's griping from the beginning: 'How could we [take him into our confidence] when he abused that confidence within 24 hours of assuming command?' He also resented the charge of a lack of strategic thought in the Admiralty despite the foundation of the Naval War College and the concentration of the Fleet. Fisher feared that McKenna was now basically powerless, as 'the whole Cabinet want to get rid of him – *Lloyd George is now supreme.*' Fisher considered the politicians 'damned fools not to squash Beresford'.[35] Who was to blame? He pointed the finger at Haldane, Secretary of State for War, for fixing the Beresford Report; in Fisher's view he had always stood against the Navy. From that moment on, Fisher counted Haldane among his enemies.[36]

Fisher had grounds for feeling betrayed. The footings had been cut from beneath him. His future seemed in doubt. Esher, who knew Fisher as well as anyone, suggested to J S Sandars, Balfour's private secretary, on 9 September, that some sort of encouragement ought to be sent to Jacky, some sort of kind word. He added, 'I do not say that he [Fisher] has not made mistakes. Who has not? But he is a great public servant, and at the end of a long life, devoted to his profession and to the state he is the victim of Asquith's want of moral courage.'[37] This was a correct assessment of the matter. Fisher had thought Beresford insubordinate to naval authority, and he was right. Fisher was in effect left high and dry by the Beresford inquiry, which was a preliminary to Fisher's downfall.

Resignation

Instead of squashing Beresford, the inquiry had wounded Fisher, and the question was now whether he would remain at the Admiralty beyond the end of 1909. Moving him out of his pre-eminent job would not be easy. The politicians might bribe him, cajole him, or even threaten him, but by regulations he was entitled to serve another year, and he would leave on his own terms. In early October 1909 Asquith talked with Esher and told him he could make Fisher a peer if he retired. Esher passed the message to Fisher, adding that his time was up: if Fisher did not retire, McKenna or some other minister would turn him out. This was fair warning. Fisher, with all his immense power and popularity, held his ground. He remained obstinate, but he could not stay.[38]

It was announced in November that Fisher had been created a peer – Baron Fisher of Kilverstone – in recognition of his long and distinguished services. He chose as his motto 'Fear God and Dread Nought'. He might have expected to be made a viscount. That was not to be, but, as Esher wrote to the admiral, Fisher got his peerage 'to the great disgust of his foes'. The true rewards were flattering letters from Asquith and the King: these were worth more than the honour.[39]

One contemporary described Fisher's five years and three months as First Sea Lord as 'the most active and pregnant years of his life. Though politicians and others might try to lull the public into the belief that war with Germany was impossible, Sir John had adopted the view first put forward by the Naval Intelligence Department in 1900. He had come to realise that war with Germany was inevitable. Every one of his reforms was carried out in direct preparation for the struggle he saw looming up over the eastern horizon, and often in the face of the most strenuous opposition.'[40]

Many fine appreciations were given Fisher on his retirement as First Sea Lord. Among the best is that of Arthur Balfour, who had watched him closely from the days when the Committee on Imperial Defence was established in 1902, with the intent of making Britain ready for war by increasing the co-operation of the Navy and the Army:

> I have been in closest touch with the Admiralty since he became First Sea Lord, and I have discussed with him many of the schemes which the Board of Admiralty have since carried into effect, even before he belonged to it. The policy began with Lord Selborne, and carried on by Lord Cawdor, has been a revolutionary one; and if the revolution be beneficent (as I am confident that it is), there can be no doubt that the part played by Sir John Fisher differs not in degree only, but in kind, from the majority of First Sea Lords. This, of course, *does* not mean that the latter have fallen short of their duty; we do not want revolutions every five years. But it does so happen that at the very moment when the changing conditions of naval sea-power rendered administrative revolution necessary, in Sir John Fisher was found a man of genius particularly fitted to aid in its execution.[41]

And what did Fisher think of his exit from the heights of naval Olympus? He put it this way, with a customary amusing touch: 'It certainly is a relief to be free of having to run the British Navy all over the world! It makes me think of St. Paul! "And besides all this, there came upon me daily the care of all the churches."'[42]

When Fisher's retirement became public knowledge, speculation mounted as to who would replace him as First Sea Lord on 25 January 1910, the date announced for Fisher's retirement, and what role Fisher would play in the choice of his successor? Beresford was out of contention. But Admiral Sir Arthur Wilson, who had kept himself entirely aloof from the squabbles about Beresford that had led to the Cabinet inquiry, and who had distanced himself from the administrative complications at the Admiralty, was in an independent position that favoured his selection. Highly regarded in the Service and in the country, Wilson was known for his firmness and sense of justice. Self-restrained, reserved, and thoughtful, his sound and independent judgement made him the ideal candidate. He was no manipulator, and he had few connections with the press. Of modest height, athletic in build and disposition, attentive to all around him, he was sixty-six when he took up the post. He had won the Victoria Cross in 1883 in the Battle of El Teb. He could pour oil on troubled waters. In many ways, then, he differed from his friend Fisher. But he was approaching his sixty-eighth birthday and had abandoned all thoughts of serving again.[43]

Fisher probably recommended Wilson to the King as best fitted to succeed as First Sea Lord, if he could be persuaded. Fisher wanted to keep opponents from that top spot. The King came to Kilverstone and there met with Wilson and Fisher, and then commanded Wilson's presence at Sandringham on 6 November, when he asked Wilson to accept the post. Always unassuming, 'Old 'Ard 'Art' was reluctant to take on such an immense obligation, but the King could not be dissuaded. On 20 November the formal offer of appointment from the First Lord, McKenna, reached him. On 25 January he assumed office and moved into the First Sea Lord's house in Queen Anne's Gate.

News of Wilson's appointment passed throughout the Fleet (it was gazetted 2 December). From Gibraltar, in HMS *Queen*, Beatty, who followed the changes at the Admiralty as best he could, wrote to his wife, 'I don't hear any news beyond it being officially announced that Fisher goes on Jan. 25th, relieved by Wilson. It is actually settled at last and the Service will breathe again, I trust, a true, honest and straightforward atmosphere. I wonder what the old rascal will do with himself in his declining days?'[44] Many afloat and ashore would have asked the same question. What indeed was to become of the naval revolutionary?

It was the social dissension in the Navy, among the officers, that was the prime reason for Fisher's fall. 'The duel between Fisher and Charlie Beresford overhung the Navy like the smoke of a constant manoeuvre,' Shane Leslie wrote in his unpublished biography of Beatty. The two admirals had lunged at each other, Leslie said, like a couple of angry, exhausted prizefighters. Each had been convinced that the Navy was wrong and could only be reformed on their principles and theirs alone. In the circumstances, the Navy passed through perilous times. The material changes and strategic reordering that Fisher had guided or put in place had been effected. Fisher had added an inch and a half to the formidable 12in muzzles of the Fleet. His dreadnoughts had taken the place of all the distant cruisers and gunboats of yesterday. 'The day of the broadside had gone. He realised that one crashing salvo should be enough.'[45] As Beatty also knew, when Fisher passed out of his office in the Admiralty, a sigh of relief went up in the Service. Neither he nor Beresford would command in the coming day of battle.

The Admiralty after Fisher

Edward VII died on 6 May 1910. That day marked the end of an era, for the King had exhibited great strength in his royal and personal functions. He was the high guardian of Britain and the Empire, an all-knowing force for consolidation and protection of national and imperial interests. His death cast a pall over future affairs of state. He had always given Fisher advice and counsel, and gave his confidence unreservedly. This, in turn, inspired devotion, and Fisher was devoted to the monarch. Fisher grasped the fact of Edward's unerring judgement of men and women when he wrote: 'I don't mean to urge that King Edward was in any way a clever man. I'm not sure that he could do the rule of three – *but he had the heavenly gift of Proportion and Perspective.*'[46]

The death, though long expected, brought heaviness to Fisher's heart. Gone now were the lovely days of happy association with his royal friend, Edward VII. The social whirl of the Marlborough set came to an end, and even the habitual dinners that Fisher had at the Marlborough Club, where he had customarily gathered with old friends to talk long and late on affairs of state and international rivalries, held no charm for Jacky. He could not shake off the sense of loss at the King's death, he told Esher, and the latter, who had been constantly in the royal presence, similarly noted that others close to the late monarch would never get over their loss.[47] 'There never was such a break up. All the old buoys which marked the channel of our lives seem to have been swept away.'[48]

In the funeral procession for King Edward VII, Fisher walked alone, behind six Admirals of the Fleet.[49]

George V, who came to the throne on the death of Edward VII, lacked the magnetism of his father. A former naval officer, he knew a great deal about the Service, particularly its senior officers, and was not partial to Fisher, given his unsettling ways and reforming zeal. A stern fellow, he was no less dedicated to the security of the state and the Empire than his father. Whereas Fisher said that Edward VII had been his finest friend in regards to naval and other matters, he could not say the same about George V, who eyed him with understandable suspicion and treated him with strict formality.

Now, with Fisher gone, would McKenna be next? Esher imagined this battle would soon come. Such a manoeuvre would be over the estimates, but could also include an inquiry into the dreadnought type of warship.[50] Intelligence from Berlin indicated that the German building programme had not progressed as quickly as feared in 1909. Instead of having nine dreadnoughts, Germany had only five. The little-navy faction wanted a corresponding reduction in the British shipbuilding programme, with equivalent cuts in the estimates. Questions were raised: had Fisher and McKenna inflated the evidence about German naval construction? How would Wilson guide McKenna in the next round of naval estimates?

In fact, Wilson undertook no initiatives; he lacked Fisher's fire, his daemonic character. Haldane at the War Office lamented the lassitude that had engulfed the Admiralty. As Esher wrote to Balfour in September, 'Haldane – who is not a Fisherite by any means – was lamenting yesterday the change that has come over the Board of Admiralty. No doubt the "service" may have benefited, but the doors of the Admiralty are closed to all new ideas and new developments.'[51]

Fisher's exit created a vacuum. Would his absence provide the opportunity the economists and little-navy faction had been waiting for? Esher feared the worst. On 7 February 1911 he wrote to J S Sandars, Balfour's private secretary, that he wanted Balfour to attack McKenna in the House of Commons. Esher believed that a strong attack from Balfour would actually help or shield McKenna against those who wanted him removed, and would also help to ensure that the number of new ships being ordered wouldn't be cut down: 'You see, what Jackie would call the "low cunning" of this manoeuvre!'[52]

Throughout 1911 Esher kept Fisher apprised of developments. In April he wrote that the great hope for the future was that the new King grasped the Imperial idea. He also reassured Fisher about the Navy: 'That remains the one care of all who care for their country. Haldane and Henry Wilson and all the Generals in the Empire cannot deflect the mind and hearts of the people from their elemental love for the British Navy. Instinct tells them that the sea is their dominion and their only sphere of safety.'[53] Again, at the end of the year:

> May you grow in power and influence, and do many more good strokes for our country which you have served so splendidly. I think we are getting on here fairly well. Winston is on right lines now. But the navy does not stand where it did a few years ago. It is all your fault. Everyone naturally compares you with your successors, to their detriment. Some of the younger men seem able. They ought to be pushed to the front. Winston is clever – but he is young. I think it would be better if he had you always at his elbow.[54]

By the time Esher wrote this in December 1911, Churchill had undergone a change of heart. In the autumn of 1909 he went to Germany as a guest of the Kaiser to witness German army manoeuvres. He returned convinced of Germany's peaceful intentions. He was certain that no profound antagonism existed between the two countries and so continued to oppose substantial increases in military expenditures. It is remarkable that within two years he became the political head of the Admiralty and a big-navy man. He always fought from his own corner, so to speak, and it was the circumstances of the day that gave opportunity for his character to demonstrate itself. Another crisis in Anglo-German naval relations brought him to the supreme position at the Admiralty to continue Fisher's reforms and to undertake some of the largest naval expenditures in Britain's history. Such were the twists of fate as the European continent continued to move toward the great catastrophe of 1914, and it is to Churchill that we now turn.

PART TWO

'Ruler of the Queen's Navee'

5

The Most Glittering Post

Young man in a hurry

Winston Leonard Spencer Churchill, already introduced but now our companion character of abiding interest and merit, was the first son of Lord Randolph Churchill and his American wife, the former Jennie Jerome. Churchill was born at Blenheim in 1874. This Vanbrugh palace was a gift from the nation to Winston's illustrious ancestor, the soldier, John Churchill, 1st Duke of Marlborough. The location of Winston's birth was accidental, as his family did not live at Blenheim, but he was a child of aristocratic privilege.

Young Winston cut a romantic and impulsive figure, one adventurist in outlook, with a sense of *Boy's Own Annual* heroism. He inhabited the age of great imperialism and imbibed the ethos. He was a self-absorbed man of destiny.[1] His schooldays at Harrow were difficult ones, particularly for his teaching masters. After Harrow, Churchill went on second application to the Royal Military College, Sandhurst, and then was commissioned in the 4th Hussars. He was a war correspondent in Cuba during the guerrilla insurgency against Spanish rule, and filled the same role on India's Northwest Frontier, again in the Sudan, and then in South Africa during the Boer War. He told his mother 'this is a pushing age', and he was right. He sought the limelight and danger, and the record shows he was in pursuit of campaign medals.[2] In South Africa he was a prisoner of the Boers but escaped. He showed early an extraordinary capacity as a writer, and this became his principal means of livelihood. He was among the top-paid journalists of the epoch.

Early on he also demonstrated indomitable courage, and this has been linked to his depressive personality. His lifelong depression, or 'Black Dog', originated in parental neglect – as a child, Winston was starved of parental affection. Only his nanny, Mrs Everest, provided comfort: as he revealed at the time of her death, she was the dearest, most intimate friend for his first twenty years, and she became to him a symbol of the poor and the needy – as well as a family predisposition to melancholy. His father had what nowadays are called mood swings. To counter this malady, young Winston developed extreme ambition and a pugnacious will. It is a remarkable fact that from his depressive personality he exerted the powerful force to command the affairs of state. We have it on the authority of Anthony Storr, one of Britain's foremost psychiatrists, that Churchill, the visionary hero of Britain's darkest hour, crafted a strategy against this malady, escaped into a make-believe world, and by the strength of his convictions inspired the world to stand up to Nazi tyranny when civilisation's fate hung in the balance. 'He remained hungry – hungry for fame, for adulation, for success, and for power; and although he gained all these in full measure, the end of his life showed that he never assimilated them into himself, but remained unsatisfied.'[3] The iconoclastic historian A J P Taylor, whose history of England in the first half of the twentieth century has Churchill as a central figure, came to much the same conclusion without resorting to psychoanalysis. He proclaimed Churchill 'the saviour of his country', which is undoubtedly true.[4] When Churchill became First Lord of the Admiralty in 1911, Britain's finest hour, and his, lay far in the future. Many failures were to stare him in the face, but always that indomitable courage, extreme ambition, and pugnacious will drove him forward.

By the time he entered Parliament, no one could ignore Churchill, and no one did. He attracted attention. His name was on the lips of everyone of any importance. He always seemed to be in the newspaper columns. Some persons might think ill of him, while others cut him considerable slack. He was vocal, even outlandish, and undeniably vulnerable. He had few close friends, and these were of highly individualistic character, F E Smith (Lord Birkenhead) and Max Aitken (Lord Beaverbrook) being examples. Asquith, a noted student of character, thought Winston admirable on paper but a fellow who tended to think aloud – a good assessment. Churchill had many enemies, not least in the Navy. David Beatty, later a famous admiral and First Sea Lord, commented to his wife on the matter shortly after Winston's election to Parliament. 'You are quite right, Winston Churchill is not nice, in fact he is what is generally described as a fraud, and to use a naval expression, all Gas and Gaiters.'[5] He spoke too soon, for when he next met Churchill, Beatty was much struck by him. Their first encounter had been on the Nile, before the Battle of Omdurman, when Beatty, a junior lieutenant, commanded a gunboat. A bottle of champagne was tossed toward shore, where Churchill was, and he retrieved it from the water where it had safely fallen.

Churchill entered Parliament in the election of 1900 as a Conservative. He was just twenty-six years old. He lived in the shadow of the memory of his father, Lord Randolph Churchill, who had died at age forty-five. Fresh from the life of a soldier and a journalist, Winston wanted to make a career in

Parliament. He prepared his speeches with care. His natural instinct was based on his experience in the fields of war. He fought against increases in War Office and Army expenditure, arguing that the strength and power of the British Empire rested in seaborne matters. The Army ought to be considered an adjunct of the Navy, he said, and the first priority in defence spending must be the Navy. He was not alone in his views. He was a Liberal imperialist, and in 1903 he crossed to the Liberals. The Conservatives never forgave him for this defection. Churchill became one of the Radical Liberals alongside David Lloyd George. Though strange bedfellows, these two found common cause because they were the 'thrusters'. They differed from H H Asquith, R B Haldane, Edward Grey, Reginald McKenna, and others who dominated Liberal parliamentary matters after the party came to power in 1905. Observers noted that he was exceedingly ambitious, and imagined that therein lay the fatal flaw. Churchill disliked being in subordinate positions. As a young man, he had dominated all his cousins at Blenheim.[6] (He had also had a penchant for getting into scrapes and was prone to accidents.)

The Liberals took power in late 1905, and in early 1906 several ministers were given new positions in the Liberal Cabinet. According to Esher, Prime Minister Campbell-Bannerman would not hear of appointing Churchill to the Cabinet: 'He [Campbell-Bannerman] is, like Mr. G. [Gladstone], old fashioned and disapproves of young men in a hurry.'[7] Others near and far saw Churchill as indeed a young man in a hurry. Against the grey panorama of Edwardian statesmen and ministers, he stood out in bright relief, a self-described 'glow worm'. In April 1908 Esher wrote that although the calibre of Cabinet ministers had declined in recent years due to the size of Cabinets, 'Winston, on the other hand, has very nearly, if not quite, a first-class intellect.'[8]

Churchill's first appointment after the Liberals took power was as Undersecretary of State for the Colonies, and one of his main concerns was the reconstruction of South Africa. In 1908, after Asquith became prime minister, he gave thought to putting Churchill in charge of the Local Government Board, but the young man did not wish to be 'shut up in a soup-kitchen with Mrs. Sidney Webb'. Well, what about the Admiralty? asked Asquith. Churchill declined that too. Sir John Fisher, the First Sea Lord, reproached him for not taking up a heaven-sent opportunity. What wonderful work they could have done together at the Admiralty was Fisher's enduring thought. Instead, Reginald McKenna became First Lord. Churchill was placed in the Cabinet as President of the Board of Trade, replacing David Lloyd George, who became Chancellor of the Exchequer. Lloyd George saw in Churchill a tool to do his bidding in Trade. To Esher it appeared that Lloyd George had managed to get Churchill to lead a frontal attack on R B Haldane, Secretary of State for War, on the army estimates. Such an attack, however, was 'bound to be repulsed with heavy losses. This is not a very auspicious move for a young Minister. Haldane will remain in position. But where will Winston be? Not in such force as before.'[9] Four days later, Asquith asked Esher to talk to Churchill to attempt to fix the quarrel: 'I then went over to the Board of Trade, and had two hours' talk with Churchill. He was clever and ingenious, but wild and unpractical. I think, however, that he realises the difficulty of forcing Haldane's hand, and the undesirability of breaking up the Government.'[10] Esher saw this episode as an example of Churchill's thrusting desire to be at the centre of affairs and to increase his power and influence: 'My idea is that Winston wanted to push to the front of the Cabinet. He thinks himself Napoleon. But then we are not governed by a Directoire. Men of the Grey, Crewe and Asquith type (notably the former) are so unlike the adventurers whom Napoleon swept out of his path. Our rulers have roots which go deep down into political soil.'[11]

During Churchill's preliminary years in the Cabinet, Grey and Esher weighed his merits and considered his faults. Then and later Churchill was compared to Lloyd George. During the naval scare of 1909, for example, Lloyd George appeared as an imperialist at heart and picked up the whole case adroitly; Churchill, though he worked hard, got involved in subtleties. While Lloyd George realised the danger England could be in by 1912, Churchill could not see it. Esher commented with worry in April 1909: 'Yet there are people, headed by Winston Churchill, who see no dangers ahead, and would stint the Navy!'[12] Observers noted how Lloyd George gained in popular opinion, and Esher remarked on this during the crisis over the 'People's Budget' in 1909–1910: 'Ll. George seems to be establishing a firm position for himself at the expense of Winston. He appeals strongly to "the man in the street".'[13] Grey, for his part, thought Churchill a genius. 'His fault,' Grey concluded, was 'that phrases master him, rather than he them. But his faults and mistakes will be forgotten in his achievements.' Esher, too, concluded, 'Winston has the real political fire.'[14]

Lloyd George said laughingly that he had never met anyone with such unbridled passion for politics; even at his wedding, Winston talked politics with Lloyd George in the vestry. George Riddell, the powerful pressman, thought Churchill a unique phenomenon, and he learned with interest that Winston had his valet wake him every morning at 5 or 6 o'clock, whereupon he sat up in bed and wrote speeches, articles, etc. News got around that the editor of *Strand* magazine had paid £150 per article for serial rights to his Ugandan adventures. There is no doubt that Winston was preoccupied with his career advancement as a member of Cabinet, but he also intended to continue to be a name in the news on account of his brilliant writing of tales of adventure. There were costs that he did not realise. H H Asquith expressed sorrow that he did not always find the young statesman as attentive as he should be, though Winston was always loyal and devoted to his chief.[15] And his other colleagues did not find him constant, or reassuring.

As to the wedding referred to, the occasion was his marriage to Clementine Hozier at St Margaret's, Westminster, on 11 September 1908. It was a packed house, and the words of Bishop Welldon of Manchester (Winston's old headmaster at Harrow) did not go unnoticed: 'There must be in the statesman's life many times when he depends upon the love, the insight, the penetrating sympathy and devotion of his wife. The influence which the wives of our statesmen have exercised for good upon their husband's lives is an unwritten chapter of English history, too sacred to be written in full.'[16] How true this was.

The courtship had been brief, happy, and intense; the engagement was announced on 15 August. She was ten years younger than he, a tall and striking beauty, second of four children of Sir Henry Hozier and Lady Blanche Ogilvie, daughter of the 10th Earl of Airlie. Like Winston, she came from what is nowadays called 'a broken family', for Sir Henry was a womaniser and of no wealthy means. Clementine later doubted that Sir Henry was her father, but leaving that aside, it may be suggested that Winston and Clementine were much the same in the way of odd family circumstances, similarly deprived of affection. Accordingly, they recognised how precious were the bonds of affection that had brought them, and would keep them, together.[17] As Winston said in the final words of *My Early Life*, 'after September 1908 he married and lived happily ever after.'

From Clementine's perspective we know the marriage to have been a periodic trial. She was his minder and guardian, and she sought gallantly to save him from all sorts of perils. But truth to tell he did not always listen and take sagacious advice. It was not in his nature. He was too headstrong. He tried his colleagues, and his superiors in station and age found him perplexing. In that brilliant book of Ronald Hyam's, *Elgin and Churchill at the Colonial Office*, we are told repeatedly that Churchill presented 'a curious combination of magisterial statesman and mischievous schoolboy'. He had a tendency to exaggeration. The work of one department was not enough: he was fruitful in producing schemes for other departments. On holiday he was incapable of relaxing. He had 'the unhappy gift for putting people's backs up by an apparently gratuitous offensiveness of matter'. Suspicion and hatred of him grew in Liberal circles, adding to similar feelings already solidly fixed among the Conservatives and Unionists. In 1908, at the time of his marriage, few of his colleagues could have predicted a brilliant future for him. All the good work he did in the Colonial Office, admired by his colleagues there, could not overcome the disapproval of his pugnacity and obstinacy, his powerful arguments and emotions, his flourishing journalistic tendencies, and his inability to show complete loyalty to Lord Elgin, the Secretary of State for the

Colonies. Sir Francis Hopwood, the Permanent Secretary, thought Churchill 'most tiresome to deal with, and will I fear give trouble – as his Father did – in any position to which he may be called. The restless energy, uncontrollable desire for notoriety, and the lack of moral perception, make him an anxiety indeed!'[18] These are powerful words from one who had worked with him closely, a person universally admired and respected.

There was talk of Churchill going to the Admiralty, which caused shudders in the Navy. Beatty remarked on this just prior to the first 1910 election: 'I see in the papers that if the Radicals come in after the Election that Winston Churchill will become 1st Lord of the Admiralty. No greater blow could possibly be delivered to the British Navy.'[19] After that election, Esher met with Sir Edward Grey and Lord Crewe, noting in a letter: 'They both agree that Winston Churchill has shown marked improvement during the elections, in grasp and tone.'[20] Churchill did not get the Admiralty. Instead, Asquith offered him the post of Irish Secretary. On advice from John Morley, Churchill refused this and asked instead for the Home Office, to which Asquith consented.[21]

It was during his tenure at the Home Office that a celebrated incident occurred which, for some, was a portent of his future actions and methods of leadership. At the end of 1910 a gang of burglars killed three police officers; several members of the gang were arrested, and two holed up at 100 Sidney Street in the East End of London, firing on any officers who attempted to approach. Churchill, as Home Secretary, agreed to authorise the use of a detachment of the Scots Guards to deal with the murderers. Unable to learn any further news at the Home Office, he travelled to the scene and made an inspection of the area. The house soon caught on fire, and he confirmed the police decision not to send any firefighters against the blaze for fear of being fired upon. The house burned to the ground, and the bodies of two individuals were discovered. Churchill later claimed that his presence on the scene had not interfered with the authorities' handling of the situation. However, his actions were greatly criticised by the press and by the Opposition. They wondered why the Home Secretary needed to be present when such an incident was much better left to the professionals in charge of the operation. For many, the Sidney Street affair symbolised Churchill's desire to be not just an administrator, but to take an active role in the execution of the orders he drafted, as well as his willingness to interfere in matters better left to the professionals. As shall be seen, this impression was only reinforced in the years to come.

At the Home Office, Churchill played a role in the evolution of the modern British intelligence system, which had its origins in the aftermath of the Boer War and in the Anglo-German rivalry of the first years of the twentieth century. The frequent invasion scares of this period were accompanied by fears of infiltration by spies. Such fears were heightened by widely read novels, such as

Erskine Childers's *Riddle of the Sands* (1903) and William Le Queux's *The Invasion of 1910* (1906). In March 1909 Asquith requested Haldane to examine the threat from foreign espionage and to recommend means to combat it. In a matter of weeks, Haldane became convinced that the danger was real, and soon thereafter the CID approved the formation of the Secret Service Bureau. The Bureau quickly evolved into two separate branches: MI5, or the Security Service, and MI6, or the Secret Intelligence Service (SIS).[22]

In his first years in Parliament, Churchill often spoke of the deficiencies of British intelligence. These comments arose out of his experiences in the Boer War. Although as president of the Board of Trade he did not play any role in the initial creation of the Secret Service Bureau, he was overawed by the German military prowess he saw displayed during a visit to that state. Haldane took the opportunity to have the War Office intelligence chief, John Spencer Ewart, meet with Churchill and impress upon him the espionage threat. Churchill responded by offering any aid he could give, and replied to Ewart's questions with a sixty-page document. Not long afterwards, Churchill was promoted to the Home Office, which included responsibility for internal security. For instance, the Secret Service Bureau had no executive authority of its own, and therefore required the closest contact with the local police and the chief constables, who reported to the Home Office. At the same time, Asquith appointed Churchill to two CID subcommittees to continue to carry out Haldane's recommendations on intelligence.[23]

At the Home Office, Churchill worked on several bills that were then held back until the appropriate moment. For example, he approved the draft Aliens Restriction Bill, which empowered the government to use Orders in Council to remove aliens from any sensitive area, register them with police, and severely restrict their movement. The bill also allowed for the deportation of aliens. Concerned about Parliament's response to such a bill, Churchill held it back until 1914. The day after the declaration of war, the Aliens Restriction Bill passed through Parliament and received Royal Assent.

Leading intelligence officers pressed for immediate peacetime measures to deal with spies, and a bill designed to establish an effective press and postal censorship system, as well as to strengthen the Official Secrets Act, was approved at a meeting chaired by Churchill in July 1910. Again, due to concerns about the parliamentary response, Churchill withheld the bill until the crisis over Agadir in the summer of 1911 (see the section on Agadir later in this chapter). At that time, Haldane presented the bill in the House of Lords as nothing more than a minor change in procedure. After approval there, it moved to the House of Commons, where it was rushed through second and third readings on a Friday afternoon when the House was sparsely attended. Never before had a bill passed through all its stages in a single day without a word of explanation from the responsible minister, and Colonel Maurice Hankey, Naval Secretary to the Committee of Imperial Defence (CID), stated that the affair was 'a masterly example of Parliamentary strategy.'

Intelligence officers also requested a registry of suspicious aliens, and Churchill ordered the county police services to comply. Thus was born MI5's famous (or infamous) registry. Churchill waited until the same Agadir crisis to approve close surveillance of aliens. No outcry followed, and soon the entire country, except London, was covered by the surveillance scheme, with 29,000 names in the registry. As well, during his tenure at the Home Office, Churchill gave increased powers to the intelligence services to search the public mail, and he played a role in ensuring that stocks of naval cordite, as well as railways transporting crucial South Wales coal, were adequately guarded from attacks by saboteurs. By the time he left the Home Office for the Admiralty, Churchill had played a significant role in the augmentation of Britain's secret service.[24]

The chatterers

Churchill knew of Admiral Jacky Fisher, for the latter's name was on everyone's lips. He first met Fisher in 1907, when Churchill was the new Undersecretary of State for the Colonies. They instantly hit it off and spent hours in each other's company. Conversing with Fisher energised Churchill, as he later related: 'He was then First Sea Lord and in the height of his reign. We talked all day long and far into the nights. He told me wonderful stories of the Navy and of his plans ... I remembered it all. I reflected on it often ... At any rate when I returned to my duties at the Colonial Office I could have passed an examination on the policy of the then Board of Admiralty.'[25] Fisher had his own recollections. He told the journalist Arnold White: 'I had a two hours *tête-à-tête* with Winston Churchill, wanting to do battle on my behalf, but I told him "silence" was the watchword ... Winston said he felt a great fellow-feeling with me, as I always painted with a big brush!'[26] They met again at Biarritz in early April, where the admiral was a guest of King Edward. There, as Fisher told Lord Tweedmouth, he 'fell desperately in love with Winston Churchill. I think he's quite the nicest fellow I ever met and such a quick brain that it's a delight to talk to him.'[27] The King found Fisher and Churchill 'most amusing together. I call them the "chatterers".'[28] While at the Colonial Office, Churchill had limited contact with Fisher in the course of his official duties, but Fisher did write to him in regard to the suppression of disturbances on the Caribbean island of St Lucia: 'For God's sake don't send British bluejackets inland amongst sugar cane on this job or we shall have to set up a War Office inside the Admiralty & goodness knows one War Office is enough!'[29]

In January 1908 Fisher sent a message to the fast-rising Churchill that he wished to see him. In view of the Beresford situation, Fisher said, '[I would] feel safer with you at hand for advice and counsel'. Almost in the same breath, Fisher, with an eye to the future, urged Churchill not to 'overdo yourself as I want to be First Lord when you are Prime Minister.'[30] Later that month they had lunch at the Admiralty when Churchill came by unexpectedly. According to Fisher, 'he is very keen to fight on my behalf and is simply boiling with fury at Beresford & Co.'[31] Churchill was on his way to becoming part of the pro-Navy faction in Parliament, and one of its strongest supporters in the Cabinet. Fisher's influence in this is entirely clear.

There was a rocky patch in the Churchill–Fisher relationship in 1909 when Churchill joined the ranks of the 'economists' of the Liberal Party. He had hounded Lord Haldane, the Secretary of State for War, in regards to the army estimates. This brought him closer to Lloyd George, the Chancellor of the Exchequer, and together they also attacked Reginald McKenna, the First Lord of the Admiralty, on the building of dreadnoughts, as related in Chapter 4. McKenna held firm, earning Fisher's everlasting respect. Churchill and Lloyd George seemed paired in harness as internal critics of the government; the infighting was extensive and carried on for months.

However, in the summer of 1911 Churchill's fortunes took a remarkable turn. His hostility to naval and military expenditure, while still conspicuous, was lessening. Something was in the wind, and circumstances beyond Cabinet's control brought about a revolution in thinking that provided, if just for the necessary moment, a unanimity of opinion around which Asquith and Grey could formulate a direct response to Germany's rise. This development, and this change, would in the next few months deny Haldane a move from the War Office to the Admiralty, sweep McKenna out of the Admiralty against his wishes, and bring Churchill into that supreme post, with all its glitter, its national pride of place, its historic associations, and its unusually independent position in national affairs. The revolution would enhance Lloyd George's position, and Grey's opinion about Germany's intentions would be steeled.

The power of a German gunboat: Agadir and repercussions

'How wonderfully Providence guides England! Just when there is a quite natural tendency to ease down our naval endeavours comes AGADIR!' So wrote Fisher to Lord Esher on 1 August 1911.[32] He was speaking of the major naval crisis before the outbreak of war. As of July of that year, Cabinet had taken no specific position as to a future war policy. The CID had been at work, it is true, and many position papers had been printed. But the War Office and the Admiralty vied for predominance, while foreign dangers had not yet fortified the national will or jolted the Cabinet. In July there arose a unique challenge to British policy in regards to German ambitions, this time in North Africa. Fisher, as we have seen, had prepared the Fleet to deal with a North Sea threat. He had largely met

Beresford's charge that the Navy was not ready to fight. Now the problem presented itself in a new guise. Rival colonial ambitions lay at the root of insecurities, as all the great powers were pegging out new anchors of empire – some for coaling stations, others for harbours of supply or refuge, others as places from which cruisers, submarines, or torpedo boats could venture forth to prey on a future enemy's shipping. A port in North Africa might be a feather in the hands of one power but a sword in the hands of another.

To this point, the Foreign Office had dealt with German colonial claims through accommodation and delay. At the same time, the British, who had their own imperial interests to guard, viewed the steady French advance in Morocco with suspicion. The French sought, so they said, to prop up the Sultan of Morocco at the capital, Fez. At the Foreign Office, Sir Edward Grey and his undersecretaries were dismayed by the French decision to send a military expedition to Fez on 21 May 1911 on a pretext of safeguarding European citizens. Grey, who anticipated a negative German reaction, worried that some sort of Franco-German agreement might arise, one detrimental to British interests. In all, it was a diplomatic tangle of the first order.

German commercial interests were divided on the wisdom of their government making an intervention, but Chancellor Theobald von Bethmann-Hollweg and Foreign Minister Alfred von Kiderlen-Waechter, who saw in the imbroglio the makings of a possible diplomatic triumph that would compel a French retreat, took the hard line. Put differently, they thought a German triumph in Morocco might disrupt the Entente Cordiale between France and England. To force the issue, the Germans dispatched the gunboat *Panther* to Agadir, on the Atlantic coast of Morocco, arriving on 1 July. The vessel was lightly armed and carried no landing party, but her appearance radically altered the European situation, causing a flurry of excitement in London and Paris. Even a single German gunboat posed a worrisome menace in those times when insecurity haunted every British imperial position.

For its part, the Admiralty expressed anxiety that with Germany in possession of Agadir, the rival would have a base near the vital Strait of Gibraltar; moreover, this would be a likely place for cruisers and U-boats to be based, or refuelled, astride the Atlantic and Mediterranean sea-lanes. Agadir was a poor harbour, said the Admiralty, and the worry would have been amplified if the Germans had their eye on a base on the Mediterranean shore.

The Foreign Office immediately interpreted the situation as not just another colonial squabble but a direct challenge to the Entente. It mattered little if the issue was more an imperial and Foreign Office concern and less a naval question from the British position: the shadow of war nonetheless appeared. Sir Eyre Crowe, a leading figure in the Foreign Office, declared the German challenge 'a trial of strength, if anything ... Concession means not loss of interests or loss of prestige. It means defeat, with all its inevitable consequences.' Crowe, along with his colleagues Sir Francis Bertie and Sir Arthur Nicolson, advised Grey to take a hard line with Berlin, with Crowe and Nicolson urging Grey to send a gunboat to stand off against *Panther*. Grey demurred, and the Admiralty took its cue from the Foreign Office.

On 4 July the Cabinet, taking Grey's advice, decided on a moderate course that did not oppose, in principle, colonial concessions to Germany. The object was appeasement – to reach a compromise agreement. Grey sent Berlin a warning message. When the French informed the British in mid-July that the Germans were demanding practically all of the French Congo in return for recognising France's position in Morocco, the Foreign Office was further outraged and accordingly hardened its position. The government decided to warn the French that it did not consider a decision to resist German territorial demands in Morocco as a *casus belli*.

In Whitehall, worries mounted. Grey had received no comment from the Germans to his warning of 4 July. Long days of summer passed. Still no word came from Berlin. In response to Germany's ominous silence, the Cabinet authorised Grey to inform the Germans that the British government would not recognise any settlement in Morocco in which it had not had a say. This further strengthening of the official line was backed up by a warning speech by Lloyd George at the Mansion House banquet, City of London, on 21 July. Lloyd George had conferred with Asquith and Grey as to the precise terms of his speech, and in it he declared:

> I believe it is essential in the highest interests not merely of this country, but of the world, that Britain should at all hazards maintain her place and her prestige amongst the Great Powers of the world. Her potent influence has many a time been in the past, as may yet be in the future, invaluable to the cause of human liberty. It has more than once in the past redeemed continental nations, who are sometimes too apt to forget that service, from overwhelming disaster and even from national extinction.

Nothing should justify a grave international disturbance; Britain would not surrender her position that had been 'won by centuries of heroism and achievement'. In short, Britain was not to be treated 'as if she were of no account in the Cabinet of Nations ... peace at that price would be a humiliation intolerable for a great country like ours to endure.' Grey and Churchill may have seen Lloyd George's speech before it was delivered. The speech signified Lloyd George's abandonment of pacifism and therefore of his Radical pacifist colleagues, like Lord Morley, who were dismayed. This immediate crisis, as A J P Taylor rightly says, had turned a Radical such as Lloyd George into a person strongly resisting German aims of aggrandisement.[33]

Lloyd George had ventured forth as tribune, and such a new-found station in foreign affairs was bound to give Grey anxiety. Lloyd George courted Lord Northcliffe, proprietor of *The Times*. Asquith's worries mounted, for of all his difficulties, relations between Lloyd George and Grey were potentially the most explosive.[34] Press publicity was abhorrent to the Foreign Secretary. Then, as later, Churchill did not court the press.

However, Lloyd George did wake up the German chancellery. At last the Foreign Office heard from Berlin. The German ambassador, Metternich, protested strongly to Grey on 24 July. The next day Grey told Churchill and Lloyd George that he had just received a communication from the German ambassador 'so stiff that the Fleet might be attacked at any moment. I have sent for [First Lord of the Admiralty] McKenna to warn him.'[35]

During August, as fear of war heightened, most of the Cabinet scattered to the country, as was normal for summer months. The grouse season started on 12 August. Only Asquith, Grey, Lloyd George, Churchill, and Haldane remained in London, carrying the direction of policy, a rump group, a shadow war Cabinet. Grey attempted to restrain the rising bellicosity of his colleagues. At the same time he had his hands full keeping negotiations continuing between the French and the Germans.

Haldane, fearing the Kaiser's military advisers were pushing Germany toward war, halted the 1911 manoeuvres in order to save money to complete mobilisation arrangements, if necessary. More importantly, he informed the German government, via their military attaché in London, that the British Army was prepared for any eventuality, including the deployment of six infantry and one cavalry division along the Belgian frontier. The German General Staff attached no importance to this communication, as they considered the British Expeditionary Force (BEF) to be of no significance in a future continental war. At the same time, they discounted the idea that the BEF could be safely conveyed across the Channel by British naval and merchant ships.[36]

Churchill, then at the Home Office, had, as stated, invariably opposed increased military spending, though he always preferred supporting the Navy over the Army. To that point he had contended that war with Germany was not inevitable and, further, that Germany's intentions were not necessarily aggressive. *Panther*'s steaming into Agadir had changed his view. Of Churchill, Grey wrote: 'his high-mettled spirit was exhilarated by the air of crisis and high events.' (Late each afternoon Churchill would call for Grey and take him to the Royal Automobile Club, Pall Mall, where after a weary, anxious day 'he would cool his ardour and I revive my spirits in the swimming bath.'[37]) Churchill now saw Germany in a new light – as a bully – and, in contrast to his earlier assessments, became convinced that Germany would exert its military might to acquire hegemony. He also concluded the outbreak of war to be only a matter of time.

From then on, Churchill became one of the warlords of the Cabinet, one of the few who took formidable positions in favour of readiness to do battle and to be prepared for any eventuality on the seas or on the Continent. He stood apart from so many of his colleagues. Even at the Board of Trade or the Home Office he concerned himself with such things as national security and readiness for war. He was not only a war man; he had the remarkable ability, as did Fisher, to see the current trends and imagine the unfolding prospects of the darkening scene. This explains why he was distrusted by his party and by most of his fellow members of Cabinet, all of whom were pacifists and non-interventionists, all of whom opposed a Continental Commitment, and all of whom were desirous of maintaining a position of neutrality. Along the way, Churchill had written his wife, Clementine, that Lloyd George's intervention had been of great value. 'Today [2 August] the news about the big thing is that the bully is climbing down & it looks as if all would come out smooth and triumphant.' And again, on 6 August, 'There is no doubt that the Germans are going to settle with the French on a friendly basis. They sent their *Panther* to Agadir & we sent our little Panther to the Mansion House: with the best results.'[38]

Churchill's rise to become First Lord of the Admiralty stems directly from the Agadir crisis. The manner of the appointment, and Churchill's thrusting role in securing it, has some interesting though loose parallels to how he became prime minister in 1940. The crucial moment of both the crisis and Churchill's career to that point came on 23 August 1911, when Asquith secretly convened a meeting of the CID. In order to bypass those in the government opposed to a hard line against Germany, Asquith and General Sir Henry Wilson, Director of Military Operations of the Imperial General Staff, invited only the supporters of an aggressive stance. Churchill was among them on account of his recently written paper 'Military Aspects of the Continental Problem'. Asquith, Grey, Haldane, Lloyd George, McKenna, and the Service chiefs were also present. Morley and others who were opposed to war had not been invited. The two Service chiefs were both Wilsons, though unrelated: Sir Henry Wilson, already mentioned, and Admiral Sir Arthur Wilson, the First Sea Lord.

Urgency commanded the day, for what aid was to be given to France if it was attacked by Germany? The War Office presented detailed plans for transporting an expeditionary force to France to fight the Germans alongside the French. This, as explained, would be in accord with discussions with the French. So closed the long morning session; a recess followed. Came the afternoon and, in contrast to the War Office's detailed and well-thought-out plan, Admiral Wilson refused point-blank to commit to transporting the BEF across the Channel. Moreover, he presented an alternative, announcing that the Admiralty planned that the BEF would be landed piecemeal in the Baltic at various points on the shores of Prussia. Haldane says that this plan derived from Fisher's reading of the events of the Seven Years War, evidently agreed to by Sir Arthur Wilson. Haldane and Churchill ridiculed the Navy's plan to use the BEF as little more than a landing party in a series of amphibious raids. The hard-headed Sir William Nicholson, Chief of the Imperial General Staff, asked Admiral Wilson bluntly if the Admiralty had studied maps of Germany's strategic railways. The admiral responded that it was not their business to do so.[39]

Admiral Wilson could not match the Director of Military Operations' clarity or persuasiveness. 'In this battle of the Wilsons the grim old First Sea Lord was no match for the witty and debonair Director of Military Operations.' Hankey, the CID Naval Secretary, who was more sympathetic to the Baltic strategy than most of those present, observed that 'Admiral Wilson had filled me with dismay' and that 'the Senior Service on this occasion had sustained a severe defeat.'[40] Churchill noted that secrecy was Admiral Wilson's security: 'He did not reveal the Admiralty war plans. Those he kept locked away in his own brain, but he indicated that they embodied the principle of a close blockade of the enemy's ports.'[41] The War Office had clearly got the better of the Admiralty, as there was general unease about the state of the Admiralty's war plans or, more precisely, the lack thereof. As Haldane put it, the Morocco crisis had led to a severe shock at the CID, and he soon took it up as his personal mission to do something about it. Having (or so he thought) successfully reorganised the War Office, he now intended to do the same at the Admiralty, the next goal of his ambition – though his long-term aspiration (in keeping with his legal expertise and interest) was the Chancellorship. The spotlight had shone starkly on the Admiralty and the War Office, and the former's performance was glaringly exposed. McKenna, the First Lord, would have to pay for this, his days at the Admiralty numbered.

Churchill saw matters coming to a crisis. He wrote to Grey on 30 August: 'Perhaps the time is coming when decisive action will be necessary. Please consider the following policy for use if and when the Morocco negotiations fail.'[42] Wide-ranging matters of European security now commanded his attention, and he was ahead of most of his colleagues in this line of thinking. He recommended a triple alliance with France and Russia so as to safeguard the independence of Belgium, Holland, and Denmark. Churchill was never reluctant to advise other ministers of government on policies that ought to be pursued. By this time Grey already had matters in hand, and Asquith, who was never quick to act, had them under consideration. Position papers and draft plans were circulating quickly around the offices of state in Whitehall.

By no means was the Cabinet united on how to deal with the German threat in Morocco, as many members opposed strong action. Compromise was reached by the end of September, however. Lloyd George, like Churchill, had urged Grey to give stronger support to the French and reassurance to the endangered Low Countries. Grey informed the French that British support was conditional on a genuine French effort to reach a settlement with the Germans. His position was that Britain should support the French if the Germans forced a war on them, but that everything must be done to prevent that situation from occurring. Negotiations continued between the French and the Germans, though early meetings were futile. However, a financial panic in Germany, the result of the prospect of war, weakened German resolve. On 11 October the initial draft of the Moroccan Convention was signed. In exchange for a de facto French protectorate over Morocco, Germany received about a hundred thousand square miles of territory that had formerly belonged to French Congo. This gave the German colony of Cameroon access to the Congo and the Ubangi.

Nevertheless, the end result was a setback for Germany. France had achieved its goals in Morocco, while the Germans had received much less of a slice of central Africa than they had demanded or expected. The nationalist press in Germany expressed outrage. Even worse, the crisis had shown that Germany could not break the Entente. While the British had urged the French to reach a reasonable compromise with the Germans, they had also shown that if the French believed they were faced with unreasonable demands, the British would back up their ally. Within the British government, the crisis helped supporters of a hard line against Germany make their case, and brought Lloyd George, the leading Radical Liberal, into the camp of those opposed to Germany.[43] The crisis passed, but the Grand Strategy had been determined: if war came, an expeditionary force would be sent to France's aid, and it would be situated on the left of the French armies, along the Belgian frontier.

At the Home Office, Churchill lobbied incessantly for greater war-readiness. He vowed to do everything possible to prepare Britain militarily for the inescapable day of reckoning. On 13 September he wrote to McKenna on naval policy in the event of war. German warships prowling the seas in wartime worried ship owners, and in response to their concerns about the cost of ships lost to the enemy in any forthcoming war, he told McKenna that the British government should guarantee to pay full indemnity for all British or neutral ships sunk or captured by the enemy in the course of bringing essential foodstuffs and manufactures to British home ports. In the end, the British government would guarantee 80 per cent, the balance to be paid by private insurers. This measure calmed the waters, so to speak, for it reassured the private sector. Churchill did not stop there. He continued to criticise existing naval policy. For instance, he doubted if the naval force now based at Cromarty, in Scotland, was sufficient to defeat the whole German High Seas Fleet. He imagined that a concentration of force would be needed in the decisive battle. He urged reinforcement if necessary. 'Are you sure that the Admty realise the serious situation of Europe? I am told they are nearly all on leave at the present time,' he wrote to Asquith in September 1911.[44] Churchill prepared his own memorandum for the CID on the present situation and future prospects. Although it had no effect on the outcome, it is worth noting that he predicted with uncanny accuracy the course of a war between France and Germany.

In regards to the preparedness of the British Fleet, the Agadir crisis had important side effects. Like Churchill, Hankey thought there was apathy in the Admiralty and said, with justification, that the Fleet lacked sufficient readiness for battle. It was dispersed to various home ports, with the Atlantic Fleet located at distant Cromarty. McKenna, apparently oblivious of realities, had gone off shooting in Scotland. Haldane, as irate as he was flabbergasted by what had transpired at the CID meeting already referred to, informed Asquith that he could not continue to be responsible for military affairs unless there was a sweeping reform at the Admiralty. Haldane wanted to bring about that reformation. But a nagging concern was how far he would go.

And so it was that a change was required at the Admiralty. The story of this episode in the shuffling of Cabinet is worth the telling. It has been said that Churchill's appointment to the Admiralty was fixed up during a game of golf. Even if true, this is only half the story of the remarkable course of events that unfolded over a weekend in Scotland.

Asquith had the loan of Archerfield House on the East Lothian coast. It was not far distant from Cloan, Haldane's estate. Asquith, brooding over the recent difficulties in defence planning and co-ordination and alarmed by what had transpired at the famous meeting of the CID, asked Haldane to meet him at Archerfield. Haldane motored over as soon as he could. He was full of optimism that the Admiralty would be his. Haldane was Asquith's oldest and closest political friend. He had done great work in War Office reforms. He was hungry for further action along the same lines, this time at the Admiralty. But he was a member of the House of Lords.

The Secretary of State for War, while driving up the tree-lined approach to the house, spied Churchill standing at the door, an odd and perhaps ominous form of greeting. Churchill's presence came as a surprise, and the uneasy Haldane soon learned that Churchill had been pressing Asquith heavily for the key post at the Admiralty. Asquith, as it turned out, found it difficult to deal with Churchill's importunities. He was well aware of Haldane's desire (and his reformist's skill and experience) to do at the Admiralty what he had done so admirably at the War Office. But – and this was the issue – would Churchill be suitable for the post? The discussion ranged far and wide. Churchill argued that the First Lord should have a seat in the Commons; Haldane, that a seat in the Lords was no less important in the critical circumstances. The discussion extended to the next day (Churchill stayed overnight; Haldane motored over again). Asquith had Haldane and Churchill closeted alone in a room to discuss matters. Haldane, who took the lead role, was blunt and to the point. He told Asquith that he did not think his opposite possessed the capabilities to reform the Admiralty by putting in a war staff, and he contended that for a man of Churchill's instincts, the War Office might well be a better fit. When his turn came, Churchill listened and apparently waited out the counsel and advice, and in the end Asquith gave the nod to Churchill, but not before Churchill had extracted the odd promise from Haldane that in the making of plans for a war staff, Haldane would give guidance. It is not beyond the realm of possibility that Asquith put Churchill in the Admiralty because he did not want Haldane to go there and establish a super ministry. (When Churchill became prime minister in 1940, he again outwaited his rival, Lord Halifax, at the critical juncture in a private meeting in the presence of the third person, the one who would make the final decision, or recommendation, to the King.)

Violet Asquith, the premier's daughter (who met Winston at a dinner party in 1906 when she was a mere nineteen and was transfixed by him) became one of his closest friends and adoring admirers. In her memoir, written as Lady Violet Bonham Carter, she described how she discussed the Admiralty situation with her father.

> I felt sure that the alternative candidate in his mind was my own and he admitted it. 'Why don't you ask my advice about it?' I asked him teasingly. He teased back: 'Because though in many situations I rate your judicial faculties high I know that in this particular instance they are in abeyance and I could not expect a cool, dispassionate verdict. Between Haldane and Winston you are not a judge – you are a barefaced partisan. Your scales are loaded by gross favouritism and emotion. You are not thinking of the chances of a Naval War Staff being born or of the reactions of the sensitive Admirals. You are thinking how much Winston would enjoy it.'

And it is true that Violet Asquith reported Winston Churchill, after a game of golf with the prime minister that weekend at Archerfield, had in his face 'radiance like the sun'. She offered him afternoon tea. 'I don't want tea,' he replied. 'I don't want anything – anything in the world. Your father has just offered me the Admiralty.'[45]

In late September 1911 Asquith began to rearrange his Cabinet, but he left Haldane at the War Office. On 27 September came Winston's great chance, when it was confirmed that he would go to the Admiralty to replace McKenna. McKenna would be shifted to Churchill's old post at the Home Office.[46] It was the changing of the guard, but more than that. Churchill was a rising star, and

Esher thought that only Asquith and Lloyd George were of his capacities and political calibre. All the same, some believed his arrival at the Admiralty boded poorly for the Navy. Esher again: 'I fear Winston as a First Lord of the Admiralty. Will he play up? He has one eye undoubtedly on the navy, and to be a popular First Lord. But the other not unnaturally is on the radical tail.'[47] The appointment worried the press. The Conservative journals, invariably pro-Navy, had little faith in Churchill's appointment, fearful that his rhetorical style and changeable moods, as they saw it, were unsuitable to that pre-eminent administrative post. 'We cannot detect in his career any principles or even any consistent outlook upon public affairs,' remarked the *Observer* on 29 October 1911, to which was added: 'His ear is always to the ground; he is the true demagogue, sworn to give the people what they want, or rather, and what is infinitely worse, what he fancies they want. No doubt he will give the people an adequate Navy if they insist upon it.'

The episode at Archerfield had exposed Churchill's jockeying for position and advancement, his reaching for something more compelling than the Home Office and the rooting out of German spies. This thrusting characteristic seemed unusual to many observers of British politics. In Haldane's reactions we sense disquiet about the young man on the make. Asquith, by contrast, could not stem the tide of opportunism, so McKenna, who did not give up easily, was sent away, and Churchill brought up in his place. In the end, could it have been more about getting rid of McKenna and bringing in a replacement, not the best solution but one of political expediency? If this is the case, then Reginald McKenna paid dearly for his inability to provide Admiral Sir Arthur Wilson with a clear mandate to disclose naval war plans at that famous CID meeting. Even if he had been able to do so, Wilson might not have provided any revelations, for there may not have been any naval war plans in place to disclose. As said, Haldane remained at the War Office but was eventually swept from office by the rising tide of anti-German feeling; of all members of Cabinet, he was the most Germanophile by inclination and education.

And so all was fixed, with Churchill destined for the Admiralty. He had aspired to the post. It offered great prospects. All eyes would now be on him. The back alleys of the Colonial Office, Board of Trade, and Home Office opened to the broad streets and boundless seas of the Admiralty, where he could hope to fulfil his ambition of developing imperial navies and strengthening British global interests. And, possibly, it might lead to the premiership.

Where did Fisher stand in all of this, and what roles did he play? Asquith was making his Cabinet dispositions with shattering effect. The Admiralty was a troubled department. War was possible. Fisher was in Lucerne in early October when he received an urgent summons from his old chief McKenna begging him to return and 'put the gloves on again'. McKenna wanted Fisher back when Sir

Arthur Wilson 'vanishes early next year!' That was months away. In the meantime there were other critical matters needing attention, including appointments, contracts, and future directions.

Churchill wrote to Fisher on 25 October, the same morning he actually departed from the Home Office: 'I want to see you very much. When am I to have that pleasure? You have but to indicate your convenience & I will await you at the Admiralty.'[48]

Churchill desperately needed guidance. The Navy was the biggest department of state. Churchill was known as its critic. A new Board of Admiralty would soon be sworn in. In the interim, the awkward matter for Jacky was how to give professional advice but not become embroiled in relations between Churchill and Wilson, and to do so in such secrecy that Churchill would not be exposed. It was in these shifting circumstances that Fisher, with extreme reluctance, answered McKenna's call to meet with Winston and half his Cabinet colleagues. The task of educating Churchill on naval affairs was daunting. Usually, Churchill was the one in the room doing most of the talking.

On arrival in London Fisher met with Reginald and Mrs McKenna (she was one of his favourite correspondents) at Charing Cross. Anxious conversation extending over three hours sufficed as a briefing from the then departed First Sea Lord. Churchill arrived; the McKennas said their goodbyes (Fisher observed that they were terribly upset at having to leave the Admiralty). Fisher motored with Churchill to Reigate Priory, Surrey – a great house with many royal and naval associations – where, beginning on 28 October, the talk was all about the good of the Navy. For three days Fisher answered questions, contributed to discussions, wrote position papers. Churchill recounted:

> I plied him with questions, and he poured out his ideas ... My intention was to hold the balance even [on account of the feuds], while adopting in the main the Fisher policy, to insist upon an absolute cessation of the vendetta [with Beresford] ... I began our conversations with no thought of Fisher's recall. But by the Sunday night [29 October] the power of the man was deeply borne in upon me, and I had almost made up my mind to do what I did three years later, and place him again at the head of the Naval Service ... All the way up to London the next morning I was on the brink of saying 'Come and help.'[49]

Reading between the lines of Fisher's correspondence we learn that it was on this occasion that Fisher pressed upon Churchill that Sir John Jellicoe should be brought to the fore as the great commander-at-sea; this was his sole object. There were discussions about a proposed war staff, too, and the Royal Naval War College. Fisher advanced plans for the revolutionary and formidable 15in gun for a supremely fast super-dreadnought (what became the *Queen*

Elizabeth class). Arrangements for transport of the BEF were considered, but when they were discussed, Fisher became extremely agitated. Sir Arthur Wilson's alleged lack of war plans was dismissed by Fisher as preposterous. War might well come in October 1914, predicted Fisher. The old admiral did come round to accepting the innovation of a naval war staff and at one time even offered to head it up. Such was his mercurial nature, a nature that charmed Winston.

Winston and his Cabinet colleagues were grateful for Fisher's advice. In the months ahead Jacky met secretly with Winston. In retirement he was guiding the naval destiny of the nation. It was the patriotic McKenna who had brought Fisher back into the inner circle; he had been badly abused by his colleagues in consequence of the notoriously poor performance of Sir Arthur Wilson at that infamous August war plans meeting. On Christmas Eve Fisher wrote that he had had a hectic time with four hurricanes crossing the Channel en route to Naples and 'balancing on the tight-rope with one end held by Winston and the other by McKenna.' And as to Winston, Jacky had found him tremendously receptive as well as brave. 'And as 16 Admirals have been scrapped I am more popular than ever!!'[50] Fisher found himself in the middle of the whirlpool again, as he put it delightfully. He would have had it no other way: that was the essence of the man.

First Lord

The ex-lieutenant of Hussars arrived at the Admiralty on 24 October 1911, five weeks before his thirty-fifth birthday. Though a widely read student of military history, he was not a naval expert. Upon arrival at the Admiralty, he, in many ways, wore the mantle of the naval cult of personality that Fisher had created around himself. His instincts had been sharpened by the events of Agadir. Churchill insisted on being at the centre of every decision, of being fully informed on all matters. He was full of self-confidence, with inexhaustible vitality. His willingness to ignore the traditional chain of command helped ensure that while he was at the Admiralty, events revolved around him.[51] He visited every big ship; he met every senior officer, though he often bypassed senior officers, inquiring of a more junior officer particulars of some technical matter. In these actions he offended many. He was unconventional, his questing desire to know about the Navy, its ships, and its men without limits.

The Navy had not seen anyone of this sort before. Many were unnerved when Winston walked the halls of the Admiralty. 'I can see him now, stepping impatiently along the Admiralty corridor, his short, thickset person immaculately clothed in morning coat and top hat, his little eyes screwed up with hidden purpose,' wrote Vice-Admiral Usborne in recollection.[52] What was Winston up to? Many wondered and they waited.

Churchill took to the Admiralty with relish. He held a 'big navy' view but was by no means an uncritical admirer of the Royal Navy. As Vice-Admiral Sir Peter Gretton wrote, 'He retained a sense of proportion and this is well illustrated by his reply to the senior officer who criticized one of his proposals on the grounds that it was against naval custom: "Don't talk to me about naval tradition. It's nothing but rum, sodomy and the lash."'[53] Churchill thought tradition no reason to continue a policy, and Rear-Admiral S S Hall, who served on the oil commission, liked his upsetting ways: 'I hope Mr. Churchill may remain long, I admire his disregard of tradition.'[54] For every Hall, though, there were ten who thought otherwise.

Churchill inherited Admiral Sir Arthur Wilson, VC, as First Sea Lord. Wilson may have been at one time a bold and masterful tactician with a fleet, and it is true that the Fleet loved him, but he had no political instincts. He had been brought to the Admiralty by Churchill's predecessor, Reginald McKenna, in order that Fisher's reforms would not be overturned by other senior admirals who were in the 'Syndicate of Discontent'.[55] Taciturn to a fault, 'Old 'Ard 'Art', as he was called, was a great contrast to Jacky's ebullience. He was opposed to any newfangled staff at the Admiralty and, like Fisher, preferred to have, as Churchill put it, a state of affairs where 'all plans were locked up in the mind of one taciturn admiral'.[56] Wilson was due to retire in the spring of 1912.

Churchill's enthusiasm for the Admiralty was suspect on both sides of the professional divide, as naval officers were less than impressed with Churchill's interference in everything, which sometimes verged on the subversion of discipline and the traditional place of professional members of the Board of Admiralty.[57] Naval officers were used to First Lords who had enough knowledge to present and defend the estimates but deferred to the professionals on everything else. By contrast, Churchill exhibited profound interest in all naval matters.[58] His Cabinet colleagues chuckled about his newly won interest. Lloyd George complained that 'Winston is less and less in politics and more and more absorbed in boilers,'[59] and he told Churchill, 'You have become a water creature. You think we all live in the sea, and all your thoughts are devoted to sea life, fishes and other aquatic creatures.'[60]

Churchill's amazing capacity to out-argue opponents became well known at the Admiralty. The highly intelligent Reginald 'Blinker' Hall noted:

Once I remember, I was sent for by Mr. Churchill very late at night. He wished to discuss some point or other with me – at once. To be candid, I have not the slightest recollection what it was: I only know that his views and mine were diametrically opposed. We argued at some length. I *knew* I was right, but Mr. Churchill was determined to bring me round to his point of view ... I distinctly recall the odd feeling that although it would be wholly against my will, I should in a very short while be agreeing with everything that he said. But a bit of me still rebelled ... I began to mutter to myself: 'My name is Hall, my name is Hall ...'

Suddenly he broke off to look frowningly at me. 'What's that you're muttering to yourself?' he demanded.

'I'm saying,' I told him, 'that my name is Hall because if I listen to you much longer I shall be convinced that it's Brown.'

'Then you don't agree with what I've been saying?' He was laughing heartily.

'First Lord,' said I, 'I don't agree with one word of it, but I can't argue with you, I've not had the training.'[61]

In April 1912 Churchill made various senior appointments. He designated Admiral Sir Hedworth Meux [formerly Lambton] as C-in-C, Portsmouth, and Admiral Sir Reginald Custance to review the system of entry and education of naval cadets. He also appointed Admiral Sir Berkeley Milne to the Mediterranean as commander-in-chief. All of them had fought against Fisher on one matter or more. Churchill's appointments smacked of giving satisfaction to Beresford and 'the Syndicate of Discontent'. An outraged Fisher denounced the appointments, fearing both that they would undo his reforms and return to haunt England in wartime. Also, he wanted to put his own favourites in place and line them up for future command. Sending Milne to the Mediterranean, for instance, might scupper his cherished plan to appoint Admiral Jellicoe, the navy's gunnery expert, to be Commander-in-Chief of the Grand Fleet. Furious, he wrote privately to Churchill to say that he felt he had betrayed the Navy and had bowed to court influence: 'Anyhow, all I can do is to avoid any further communication with the Admiralty. The mischief is done. "*Vestigia nulla retrorsum*" [I never retrace my steps]!' To Esher he vented his frustration: 'Nevertheless, he [Churchill] has sold his Country for a mess of pottage, SO I'VE DONE WITH HIM! ... *The mischief is done*! Milne, an utterly useless Commander ... is now the Senior Admiral afloat, and Hedworth Lambton's appointment to Portsmouth renders him eligible to be First Sea Lord ... The Providence of God may take both Milne and Lambton into another world any day! *I believe in Providence*! Nearly all my enemies have gone to Hell!' To his son he wrote that he blamed the King for putting the pressure on Churchill that led to the three appointments.[62] Milne, cautious to a fault, had been a former groom-in-waiting to Edward VII. Fisher regarded him as a 'backstairs cad'. In any event, Milne went to the Mediterranean and was not a candidate for the position that Jellicoe later attained on the eve of the war.

Others tried to calm Fisher. They did so on the grounds that it was shipbuilding that mattered, and would Jacky please leave his animosities about who got this command and who got that alone? Esher, well connected at court, tried to smooth matters over. He wrote to Fisher on 29 March 1912 with respect to the naval estimates then being steered through Parliament by Churchill: 'You must have been mightily pleased with Winston. He has done splendidly. It was a hard job for him too. What a tragedy it would be if this Government were to be displaced by Bonar Law & Co. I wonder what Charlie Beresford's friends think of him now.'[63] The Liberals were augmenting their naval power in ways unimagined by the Conservatives. Truth to tell, Winston had weathered the storm, and his naval estimates for 1913, as those of the year before – larger than any others previous – were rapidly augmenting the British Fleet with plans for ships of all designs, capabilities, and measurements. It was 'big ship time', and it was Churchill's.

6

Preparing for War

Naval staff and war plans

Churchill had been brought to the Admiralty in 1911 to force a naval staff structure on the Navy. He eagerly turned to this task and crafted a long and well-reasoned memorandum on the requirements of a naval staff. It shows all the capabilities of his expansive mind. He might have imagined that any such scheme would meet with opposition. Certainly it put up the backs of the admirals in Whitehall, who were always suspicious of their political masters.

'Old 'Ard 'Art' let fly when he wrote his response to this memo, sent to Churchill in early November 1911:

> It is often suggested by advocates of a War Staff that special officers should be selected and trained for duty on the Staffs of the Admiralty and Admirals at sea ... The service would have the most supreme contempt for any body of officers who professed to be specifically trained to think. There is no service where there is more thinking done, but officers are judged by what they can do when they are afloat ... [unlike the Army] naval policy is based almost entirely on experiment and the result of actual practice at sea.[1]

In his view, and this was Fisher's as well, the work that a staff would do was best kept in the mind of the First Sea Lord; war plans were to be prepared by the First Sea Lord with regard to such circumstances as were then developing. The remaining Sea Lords shared his views. Wilson also made clear that he, as First Sea Lord, had all he needed in the way of advice: his own naval assistant, a director of naval intelligence, and a director of naval mobilisation were the key personnel to assist him.

These were not the words that Churchill wanted to read. He had to keep in mind the expectations of the Cabinet wishing such reform. Faced with a recalcitrant Board of Admiralty opposed to his scheme, Churchill decided to make a clean sweep of it and reconstruct the Board. He kept Asquith informed of developments, and he moved quickly and quietly. Here was an early indication of 'Action this Day'. Time had come to brush away opposition.

Churchill contemplated bringing back Fisher. They had never worked there together, and the prospect seemed glorious. But then, as before, political expediency ensured the impossibility of such a course. Churchill looked elsewhere. Gradually the pieces fell into place. Admiral Wilson was moved aside two months before his time, and a very reluctant Admiral Sir Francis Bridgeman brought in as his successor as First Sea Lord. Fisher had lost his arch-defender in the highest professional office at the Admiralty, though Bridgeman privately assured Fisher that he would not lie down in the face of Churchill's demands. Prince Louis of Battenberg (who Churchill would have preferred as First Sea Lord but who was deemed unsuitable by Asquith on grounds of his German ancestry) was appointed Second Sea Lord. Churchill appointed Ernest Troubridge as Chief of the Naval Staff. Thus, by his own manipulations of talents available, Churchill got his own man in place (one who 'is "my man" and knows my whole mind and wishes'). Troubridge reported directly to Churchill, thereby subverting Bridgeman and the Board.[2]

At the same time, Churchill arranged the appointment of Sir John Jellicoe – Fisher's anointed one – to the key command of the Atlantic Fleet. He sought out Rear-Admiral David Beatty (at thirty-nine the youngest admiral since the age of Nelson) and made him his Naval Secretary, a position that came with unimagined influence in bestowing promotions and guiding appointments, and he did so over the objection of other Sea Lords, who opposed giving the silver-spooned prodigy such a task. There was no denying Churchill, whose star continued in the ascendant and was now carrying Beatty's with it.[3] There was a clean broom at the Admiralty. Churchill pushed through many appointments. The times and the darkening horizons produced by war preparations on the Continent favoured him, and in his earliest days at the Admiralty he accomplished much.

Not until Wilson retired was a 'Naval War Staff' announced, but even then it was a cut-down version of what Churchill (and those who admired Haldane's reforms at the War Office) had imagined. Given the circumstances, it seems not at all surprising that Churchill managed to create a staff that combined the worst aspects of the old and new. Wilson's main objections proved to be well founded. 'The idea that Winston Churchill created a proper Naval Staff is a myth,' writes authority Nicholas Lambert. 'Effectively, all he did was to rename the old Naval Intelligence Department, add three extra clerks, and place a different officer in charge with the title Chief of the War Staff.' The Naval War Staff remained advisory not administrative, an arrangement that played into Churchill's hands, giving him autonomy and thus authority. On the declaration of war, Churchill instituted a War Group and did not establish clear lines of responsibility between the First Lord and the First Sea Lord. Politically this was not a problem under Bridgeman and Battenberg, who tended to defer quietly. But under Fisher it was a disaster. Admiral Sir Herbert Richmond, observer to these events and others, condemned the whole system as operationally and intellectually corrupt. Such structural defects as remained in the Admiralty were still there when Churchill left in May 1915. Shortly thereafter the positions of First Sea Lord and Chief of Naval Staff (the War Staff, so called) were merged into one.[4]

Some years later, Churchill observed that it took 'a generation to form' a naval staff. In his words, 'at least fifteen years of consistent policy were required to give the Royal Navy that widely extended outlook upon war problems and of war situations without which seamanship, gunnery, instrumentalisms of every kind, devotion of the highest order, could not achieve their due reward.'[5]

The naval staff, such as it was, came into existence in January 1912. Esher congratulated Churchill on 'the most pregnant reform that has been carried out at the Admiralty since the days of Lord St. Vincent.' He was overstating the case. To Fisher, Esher wrote soothingly that a naval staff was necessary to restore confidence in the Admiralty. That was undeniably true. As a palliative he added that nothing could 'ever prevent *the man* taking hold of the tiller, if there happens to be *a man* about at the crucial moment. I do not see one just now.'[6] He kept in the back of his mind the idea that Fisher could be recalled to the Admiralty and the supreme command.

Churchill exploited the naval staff, using it to serve his own political ends. It allowed him to bypass the Sea Lords in the acquisition of professional advice and information, and thereby gave him a greater degree of independence and latitude of action than he might otherwise have had. However, the staff remained small up to the outbreak of war. In August 1914 there were only thirty-three officers on the staff, and twenty-eight more had to be drafted, including three from half-pay and fourteen from retirement. The naval staff did little to stimulate discussion in the Admiralty prior to 1914 on economic warfare against Germany and the possible effects of a blockade. Hankey alone kept alive the idea of economic war.[7]

As the prospect of war with Germany grew more certain, the Admiralty hastened its preparations for better basing of the Fleet in northern waters. The matter was of fundamental concern to Beatty, Churchill's private naval secretary. On 24 March 1912 he met with Churchill for two hours. Afterwards, and apparently reassured, he wrote to his wife, Lady Beatty, 'Matters are better & my mind is not so perturbed about the questions of great importance I told you of, & we see things from the same point of view.' Beatty drafted for Churchill a paper on the subject of naval dispositions in the North Sea in case of a war against Germany.[8] Strategic concerns were shifting to higher latitudes.

The War Office, anxious to guard the English Channel against any enemy intrusion, expressed reservations regarding new bases or watchtowers on the North Sea, and Esher told Fisher on 4 August that it was useless to throw away millions on fixed defences that turned out to be impractical. He noted in particular the new base at Rosyth, near Edinburgh, where a hurried decision to establish a base (for the battlecruiser force) had recently been made to stave off a debate in Parliament, where action on this had been demanded. Esher preferred some sort of mobile defence and noted favourably Fisher's old idea of having cruisers – the eyes of the Fleet – on the lookout for any hostile German naval move.[9] Haldane at the War Office wanted a subcommittee of CID to investigate the Admiralty's proposals for fixed defences at landlocked Scapa Flow and Cromarty, eastern Scotland. Churchill defended his office: he made abundantly clear in reply that the proposals were a Navy matter, and he accordingly opposed the creation of such a subcommittee. This would have been Fisher's response too. It evoked this private assault by Esher on Churchill: 'Winston, brilliant as he is, does not listen to the opposite side, and is impatient of opinions that do not coincide with his own. This is a fatal defect in a civilian minister who has to consider the initial moves in a great war. If Winston is going to wield the armed forces of the Empire he should cure himself of this grave fault.'[10]

Churchill, therefore, had to hold his own against the old pretenders who thought they knew better where ships should be deployed from and how harbour installations should be fortified and protected. He did so handsomely. Esher was heart and soul with Fisher, but he was at odds with Winston. For instance, Esher believed that Churchill's 'naval holiday' speech in 1913, in which the First Lord offered to stop building capital ships in England if Germany would do the same, was silly and motivated by a desire to play to the Radical gallery.[11] This may be true. The 1913 estimates provoked a crisis in politics equivalent to that of McKenna's 'We want eight, and we won't wait.' Lloyd George, Chancellor of the Exchequer, saw in Churchill's vast shipbuilding programme and enhanced naval estimates a demand from the Admiralty for an extravagant margin in ships that was both burdensome and provocative. The Chancellor believed that smaller vessels should be built for protection of trade; that England should seek an arrangement with Germany; and that Germany was now concentrating on her Army rather than her Navy. Churchill had gone through a complete turnabout, said Lloyd George: 'In my first protest against what I conceived to be panic demands from the Admiralty I received the zealous and energetic support of Mr. Winston Churchill. Unfortunately, by 1913 he had become caught by the fascination of the monster ship. The fight against "bloated armaments" – to use the old Disraelian phrase – was weakened by so formidable a defection.'[12] Many

Liberal pacifists, economists, and Radicals – the 'Little Navy' men – saw in Churchill's naval build-up abundant cause for alarm. Such political disaffection as Churchill inadvertently brought on himself through these measures of preparation and readiness during his period at the Admiralty before August 1914 distanced him from the rank and file of the Liberal Party at the same time as it distanced him from many in Cabinet. As was observed by the staff of the CID, Churchill was the most difficult member of Asquith's team that the prime minister had to handle.[13] But a grateful Navy never forgot his contributions to the building up of the Fleet for the critical moment that seemed to come inexorably upon the blackening and deepening scene. 'I love my work at the Admiralty,' Winston told a friend, and he had never worked so hard nor been so happy. To this he added 'that he had knocked Germany "sprawling" in the matter of naval construction.'[14]

All about oil: 'Wake up, England!'

The forward-looking Churchill was among the first to realise the essential strategic benefit that oil would bring to the British Fleet: notably, greater speed and range for ships, and more efficient use of officers and men. 'To commit the Navy irrevocably to oil was indeed "to take arms against a sea of troubles",' he remarked. But against the domestic coal lobby and naval opponents who continued to champion coal, he pushed forward. In the future, Britain would have to base its 'naval supremacy upon oil'. This became an overriding passion with him. As he put it, there was really no choice: 'Mastery itself was the prize of the venture.'[15]

Although Churchill could proclaim oil as the basis of naval primacy, it was Fisher who, long before others, had a consuming passion for oil. He saw that the oil engine would revolutionise war and peaceful commerce. As early as 1886, when Fisher was Director of Naval Ordnance, high-level officials described him as oil-crazy. Marcus Samuel of Shell Transport, brother of Samuel Samuel, called him 'the God-father of oil'.[16] Even as Fisher paved the way for rapid shipbuilding, overseeing completion of the coal-burners *Royal Sovereign* in two years and *Dreadnought* in a year and a day, he knew that the ships of the future would be revolutionary, based on 'revolutionary principles', which included 'oil fuel' and 'turbine propulsion'. At the end of a letter he wrote in 1901 he said, 'Oil fuel will absolutely revolutionise naval strategy. It's a case of "Wake up, England!" but don't say anything about it, or they will certainly say that I have been writing to you on the subject.'[17] Oil, Fisher stated, settled half of the Navy's manning difficulties, as ships would require only half as many stokers. 'Someone called me an "Oil-Maniac" the other day,' he wrote in 1902, 'but I am absolutely confident I am right and tremble at the thought of being forestalled by another nation.'[18]

In 1904 Fisher advanced the suggestion of substituting oil for coal, only to receive from the First Lord, Selborne, the laconic and not ill-informed reply: 'The substitution of oil for coal is impossible, because the oil does not exist in this world in sufficient quantities. It must be reckoned only as a most valuable adjunct.'[19] Still, some British warships were being built to use oil only. During Fisher's first tenure as First Sea Lord, thirty-six torpedo boats – the 'oily wads' – were launched between 1906 and 1908. So, too, were the Tribal-class destroyers of 1906/7 and the *Acorn*-class destroyers of 1909/10. By the time of his retirement, the plans were well advanced for the *Arethusa*-class cruisers to use only oil.[20] As well, the first British 'overseas' submarine, *D.1*, came into service in 1909 and was diesel-driven, the first of many.[21]

While taking the cure at the spa in Marienbad, Fisher got to know one of the moguls of black gold, the London socialite William Knox D'Arcy, who helped get the British and Admiralty concessions in southwest Persia (now Iran). It was through this early connection that Churchill was able to advance the policy to ensure the supplies by which oil boilers provided the propulsion of His Majesty's ships.

On 5 August 1910 Fisher explained to the influential Esher the 'two immense episodes [that] are doing Damocles [forecasting impending doom] over the Navy just now': oil engines and the democratisation of the Navy. In Fisher's view these were essential issues to be dealt with successfully for the well-being of the Navy, the nation, and the Empire. He then turned to the usual obstructions he faced. He noted that he had apparently 'bored' Esher with the issue of oil engines at a recent dinner, and that since then the German company of Blohm & Voss had received an order to build an oil-driven liner that was to have no engineers, no stokers, no funnels, and no boilers – only 'a d—d chauffer'. He told Esher that he had been prepared to 'shove [his] colleagues over the precipice about both of them, but ... left hurriedly to get in Wilson.' He had advised McKenna to '"Shove 'em over the precipice! *Shove!*" But he's all alone, poor devil!' He also commented with the usual bluster that he was greatly inclined to resign from the Defence Committee and campaign out in the open on these two issues.[22] Three days later, Fisher sent a similar letter to the Liberal pressman J A Spender, arguing that the supreme power of the recently launched battlecruiser *Lion* – 'The Dreadnought is a flea-bite to her!' – was overshadowed by the announcement from Blohm & Voss, which presaged motor battleships that would revolutionise naval strategy. He finished by declaring that 'these sanguinary asses want to tie the Admiralty hands with an act of Parliament to build dozens – shoals of obsolete vessels before they are launched! Dear Garvin [editor of the *Observer* newspaper and a Fisher supporter] says, "Oh! give the Sailors a blank cheque," but Parliament won't!'[23] In a postscript to a letter of 31 January 1911 to naval writer Arnold White,

Fisher stated, 'The one absorbing anxiety is, shall we go ahead as we ought to in the development of submarines and internal-combustion propulsion! *These are the two burning naval questions of the day*; all the rest, ROT!'[24]

The German announcement and Fisher's own visions of a future naval war led him toward designing and constructing a new fast battleship that would burn oil. It would have prodigious advantages: 'the reduction of personnel and the increased radius of action and no going into harbour to coal'. He pushed all of these arguments on rising admirals, notably Jellicoe. He also noted that one British company, Shell Transport, had 'over *two hundred thousand tons of oil ALWAYS in transit on every ocean*', and he urged Jellicoe to 'ram this down Winston's throat'.[25]

In April 1912 oil-fired super-dreadnoughts of the *Queen Elizabeth* class, which would form a fast division in battle, were included in the annual naval estimates (see the next section for further discussion of these ships). Churchill had taken Fisher's guidance on bringing these forward. Churchill said the 'fateful plunge' had been taken, for 'the supreme ships of the Navy, on which our life depended, were fed by oil and could only be fed by oil.'[26]

Once the decision had been taken that the *Queen Elizabeth* class would be oil-fired, the question of oil supply and storage became a crucial issue for Churchill and the Admiralty, and he recommended that a Royal Commission be appointed to investigate.[27] Oil had begun to rule world politics. The Navy shifted its strategic needs accordingly. While speaking on the naval estimates on 18 March 1912, Churchill made clear the coming importance of oil as an ingredient in sea power:

The adoption and supply of oil as a motive power raises anxious and perplexing problems. In fact, I think they are among the most difficult with which the Admiralty have ever been confronted. Oil as a fuel offers enormous advantages to ships of all kinds, and particularly to the smallest kind. In speed, convenience, cleanliness, economy, and in the reduction of personnel oil is incontestably superior to coal, and if internal combustion engines of sufficient power to drive warships could be perfected, as may be hoped for within a very reasonable time, all these advantages of oil will be multiplied, and some of them will be multiplied three or four times over. But, on the other hand, can we make sure of obtaining full supplies of oil at reasonable prices in time of peace and without restriction or interference in time of war? Can we accumulate and store a sufficient reserve of oil to meet our ever-growing requirements, and can we make that reserve properly protected against attack either by aeroplanes or sabotage? All those matters are receiving continuous attention.[28]

The cruise of Enchantress

It was against this background of new and further dreadnought design considerations as part of the naval construction race between Britain and Germany, fuelled by the venture of a German gunboat to Agadir (which upset all calculations of equipoise), that Churchill planned a voyage in the Admiralty yacht *Enchantress* to give the prime minister, Asquith, an on-the-spot indication of the Mediterranean state of affairs, and to invite Jacky Fisher to discuss with the premier the prominent issues of the day. If Fisher would not come to London, Churchill would go to Naples, where Fisher was wintering in a modern Pompeian villa, pleasantly far away from the chatter of Whitehall and Fleet Street. In the sunshine, and with the memories bright of Nelson and Sir William and Lady Hamilton, the world's problems could perhaps be seen from a different angle and in a clearer light. The First Lord of the Admiralty, facing a multiplicity of challenges, decided that Asquith ought to meet Fisher, and vice versa, for the former held the supreme political power and the latter the supreme professional naval expertise. Oil was the big issue – and Fisher was its greatest champion.

The other questions on Churchill's mind were no less potent. For one, what force of naval strength needed to be kept in the Mediterranean? Churchill hinted that naval war plans were now afoot for the evacuation of the Mediterranean as the first step in preparing for a war with Germany. No one knew the Mediterranean naval situation better than Fisher; no one knew the German rivalry in the North Sea better than the same old sailor. Asquith's world was Oxford, Whitehall, and Westminster. Would a little travel to the world of the ancient Romans and Greeks enlarge his understanding? Perhaps this was Winston's ploy. He also hoped to get the two men together in quiet conversation, and to bridge certain gaps of understanding that existed. Fisher believed that Asquith had never properly defended him in the Beresford feud inquiry and report. Another factor was that the Admiralty was still in disgrace, in Asquith's view, because of the appalling statements Sir Arthur Wilson had made at the famous 23 August 1911 CID meeting. And Winston needed a chairman for his oil commission, on which so much depended for the future of British sea power. Such were the underlying demands of a pleasant cruise to the wide reaches of the Mediterranean Sea, that great cockpit of empires, and the corridor of British power to Egypt, India, and beyond. Britannia's might needed strengthening. Churchill saw the urgency. He needed to bring Asquith and Fisher onside.

In May 1912 *Enchantress*, almost 4,000 tons, a magnificent yacht and Churchill's much-used floating office (outfitted like a West End London club, though rather than leather the chairs were upholstered in chintz), steamed to the Mediterranean. Churchill and members of his party embarked at Genoa.

The premier brought along his daughter Violet (later Lady Violet Bonham Carter, afterwards Baroness Asquith). The Second Sea Lord, the pleasant, blue-bearded Prince Louis of Battenberg, accompanied the party, as did Churchill's private secretaries, Eddie Marsh and James Masterton-Smith. David Beatty was along as Naval Secretary to the First Lord. Clementine Churchill and her sister Nellie Hozier were part of the entourage, as was Winston's brother's wife, the kind and remote Lady Gwendeline Churchill, known as 'Goonie'. For the passengers, this cruise seemed an interlude of delight.

Fisher declined Churchill's initial invitation, but Winston was not deterred: he told Fisher of the yacht's intended call at Naples on 23 May. And so it was that *Enchantress* made a fast and serene passage to Naples, where Fisher came on board the Admiralty yacht just before lunchtime. The startled Beatty recounted Fisher's arrival in a letter to his wife:

> That old rascal Fisher arrived on board directly we got here [Naples] looking very well and young, never stopped talking and has been closeted with Winston ever since, wasn't that something to come to Naples for? Do not mention in conversation to *anyone* that Fisher is in close confidence with Winston. It would be most injurious to the Service if it ever got out and the Navy would hate it. I took the opportunity to bolt to the shore and send you a wire, but found them together still on my return and they are spending the afternoon together. Prince Louis hates it and keeps out of the way also as much as possible.[29]

Beatty was disturbed by this turn of events, for he thought that Churchill's direct discussions with Jacky were subversive to Admiralty administration and could undercut relations with the Board of Admiralty.

The social scene on the yacht equally distressed Beatty. He found the company unbearable, and told his wife so. 'Old Asquith very debonair and round, Prince Louis magnificent. Myself and two Secretaries make up the party with Winston and Lady Gwendolyn, the latter queerer to look at than ever. Not very exciting is it? How I am going to bear with them for another fortnight is more than I can understand.'[30] Asquith occupied himself reading Thucydides or studying Baedeker travel guides to antiquities. In the evenings there were games, notably bridge, with Winston showing dangerous flourishings in bidding and execution, to partner Asquith's dismay.

Violet Asquith sensed the tension between Fisher and Churchill – Fisher's awkwardness, and his accomplished desire to show the party some antiquities ashore; Winston's necessarily deferred discussion of the main question – oil. Winston's mind was far away, but at last when they returned to *Enchantress* Fisher and Churchill were, as in old times, 'locked together in naval conclave ... I'm sure they can't resist each other for long at close range.'[31] Next morning, before breakfast, she danced with Jacky for a very long time. Violet provides this delightful snapshot of Jacky:

I examined him minutely and tried to diagnose his mood and his potential placability. His eyes, as always, were like smoldering charcoals – lighting up his own jokes. He was very friendly to Father and Prince Louis but glowered a bit, I thought, at Winston. To me he retained the stock of anecdotes, puns, chestnuts, and riddles which might have come out of crackers. (I expect that all 'great men' of action talk like this – at least to women?)[32]

By the time the yacht sailed from Naples on the 26th, it appeared that Fisher had agreed to be chairman of the Royal Commission on oil.[33] In his memoirs, Fisher recounted that 'oil is the very soul of future Sea Fighting. Hence my interest in it, and though not intending to work again, yet my consuming passion for oil and the oil engine made me accept the Chairmanship of a Royal Commission on Oil and the Oil Engine when Mr. Churchill and Mr. Asquith found me at Naples in May, 1912.'[34]

Soon after his meeting with Churchill, Fisher changed his mind for reasons unknown. He would have to quit retirement and sunny climes. Duty called. He could not resist. The ever-grateful First Lord wrote persuasively and flatteringly to Fisher on 11 June 1912:

The liquid fuel problem has got to be solved, and the natural inherent, unavoidable difficulties are such that they require the drive and enthusiasm of a big man ... No one else can do it so well. Perhaps no one else can do it at all ... But this means that you will have to give yr life & strength, & I don't know what I have to give in exchange or return. You have got to find the oil: to show how it can be stored cheaply: how it can be purchased regularly & cheaply in peace, and with absolute certainty in war. Then by all means develop its application in the best possible way to existing and prospective ships. But on the other hand yr R. Commission will be advisory & not executive ... Its report must be secret ...

I recognise it is little enough I can offer you. But your gifts, your force, your hopes, belong to the Navy, with or without return; as your most sincere admirer, & as the head of the Naval Service, I claim them now – knowing full well you will not grudge them. You need a plough to draw. Your propellers are racing in the air.[35]

Upon receipt of this letter, Fisher accepted, and on 19 June he returned to England. Churchill may have played to Fisher's vanity. Even so, there was urgency in Churchill's words. Fisher had found a partner to his cherished enterprise. When Fisher accepted the post (and so as to avoid conflict of interest), he immediately sold his Shell oil shares, though at 'great prospective loss'.[36] Had he retained those shares, a fortune would surely have come his way. He now began to work solely in the national interest in oil, an essentially imperial story vital to the Empire and to commerce and to security.

Fisher was now in Churchill's bag. The cruise continued to Malta, with its grand harbour and battlements. Here Sir Ian Hamilton, the general, and Kitchener of Khartoum, consul of Egypt, came on board for consultations about defence measures in the Mediterranean corridor to eastern empire and to comment on British and rival naval strengths. All very quietly but yet assuredly the Mediterranean Sea was being reordered.

All about oil redux

It lay with Churchill to announce the new arrangements. During consideration of the naval estimates in Parliament on 22 July 1912, Churchill commented on the soon-to-be-announced Royal Commission. He stated that there was nothing sensational about the inquiry and that it did not portend any sudden changes in the methods of Navy construction. However, the issue required intensive study,[37] and on 30 July 1912 the appointment of the Royal Commission on Fuel and Engines, with Fisher as chair, was announced. *The Times* noted that the terms of reference were 'to report on the means of supply and storage of liquid fuel in peace and war and its applications to warship engines, whether indirectly or by internal combustion.'[38]

Fisher got to work immediately in an evolving scheme for fast ships of the future, both for war and commerce, and he hauled in two experts, Sir Trevor Dawson and his coadjutor, James McKechnie, to see his outlines. Fisher preposterously wanted a ship capable of carrying enough fuel to go around the Earth. Conversation that day led to the establishment of a special government research department. *Incomparable*, described that morning of 17 September 1912, would have ten 16in guns on a light hull powered by 150,000hp (the engines secured in a diamond-shaped citadel), quadruple screws, and a speed of 32 knots minimum. Imagined also was a turtle-backed armoured hull, twin conning towers, eight broadside torpedoes, and ammunition service by hydraulic power. Fisher resurrected this concept – his last battlecruiser proposal – in late spring 1915, at which time he increased all its planned dimensions and expectations (for instance, 20in guns and speed of 35 knots). Fisher's dream surface ship, perhaps intended for Baltic operations, remained only an idea.[39]

On 20 September 1912 Fisher wrote to Esher: 'The one *all-pervading, all-absorbing* thought is to get in first with motor ships before the Germans! Owing to our apathy during the last two years, they are ahead [with internal combustion engines]! *They have killed 15 men in experiments* [with oil engines] *and we have not killed one!* And a d—d fool of an English politician told me the other day that he thinks this creditable to us!' He also noted the construction by the Germans of an oil-driven cruiser, and insisted that it was necessary to continue to push forward, although progress was hindered by 'boneless' politicians like 'Laurier in Canada and W.C.'s enemies in the Cabinet over here', whose imagination couldn't picture that a revolution bigger than *Dreadnought* was upon them. He also noted the importance of motor torpedo boats and the havoc they could wreak on an enemy fleet. *'I've worked harder over this job than in all my life before!'* he wrote. '3 months since I came over and I've left no stone unturned!'[40]

Fisher spent November 1912 putting the finishing touches to his memorandum 'Oil and the Oil Engine'. He then turned to the great propulsion engineer Sir Charles Parsons, of steam turbine fame, and urged him 'to associate the turbine with the principle of internal combustion propulsion'.[41] Fisher believed the diesel turbine was a crucial factor if battleships were to attain higher speeds, and that the 'oil engine' was essential on grounds of its endurance, requirement for fewer personnel, and economy. However, when Parsons appeared before the commission at Fisher's request, he was not quite so sure. He outlined some difficulties in regards to large diesel units, though his testimony did not deflect Fisher's plans, now in initial formation.[42]

On 12 December 1912 the commission heard evidence about German companies producing diesel engines for the German and other navies. The accuracy of this intelligence was revealed in 1913 when, true to expectation, the first four diesel-driven U-boats came into service. These were essentially designed for long-range cruising. This constituted a chilling development in Anglo-German naval rivalry. While the German High Seas Fleet would be deployed in the North Sea, the U-boats could range to distant seas and coasts, an alarming challenge to British surface shipping in time of war. Meanwhile, British plans for diesel engines were being drafted by J W Reed, engine manager at Palmers Shipbuilding and Iron Company. Noting that similar engines for marine use were being designed by German firms, Reed argued, 'We must all get into the thick of the fight starting away with well-proved units and going on.' He believed that British firms could face the challenge successfully.[43]

Financial limitations were a 'major factor' in what one authority called the 'technological backsliding in the choice of fuel'. In February 1913 the Director of Stores reported that the adoption of oil for all new vessels would mean a substantial increase in expenditure for fuel and storage, while the adoption of oil for only light cruisers and destroyers would require less expenditure because large reserves, needed for battleships, would not be required for smaller vessels. The subsequent decision in 1913 to fit oil propulsion in smaller vessels but not battleships is proof of the role of financial considerations in the decision.[44]

On 3 March 1913, after the Dutch oil baron Henri Deterding testified before the Royal Commission, Fisher drew up a memorandum for Churchill on 'Oil and its Fighting Attributes'. In it he cited Deterding's statement that 'Oil fuel when stored, does not deteriorate as coal does. The stocks would therefore constitute a national asset, the intrinsic value of which would not diminish', and he repeated Deterding's plan to 'raise every penny I can get and build storage, and even when I have built five million tons of storage I am still going on building it and filling it ... It is always so much condensed labour stored for the future.' Deterding had commented that the only limit to oil was its production, as there would be consumption no matter how much was produced. He also argued that because of the long-term unreliability of oil wells, the Royal Navy needed to get its oil from someone who could draw oil from many different sources. Fisher described Deterding as 'Napoleonic in his audacity and Cromwellian in his thoroughness', and therefore someone to be listened to. He concluded: *'The British Empire "has the long purse;" build reservoirs and store oil. Keep on building reservoirs and buy oil at favourable rates when they offer.'*[45] By 7 December the whole scheme had crystallised. On that date a secret memorandum was completed outlining the arrangement for supplying oil fuel for the Navy. This private state document ranks among the great strategic statements of the British imperial edifice.[46] Among its features: a four months' supply of oil to be on hand; inexpensive means of storing oil; protection of oil storage vessels from air attack; and an assurance of supply in time of war. The main work had been done. All else was elaboration.

For technical advice, Fisher drew on specialists. For example, he acquired the services of Captain S S Hall, a past Inspecting Captain of Submarines, as one of the secretaries of the Royal Commission. Hall duly fed Fisher pertinent information on submarines, which had direct influence on Fisher's important paper 'The Oil Engine and the Submarine'.[47] Then there was Dr George T Beilby, a Glasgow expert in fuel economy and low-temperature distillation. He explained all the details of the then present practices and experiments in making fuel from coke. Beilby knew a good deal about the Scottish oil-shale business and refining expertise, and he argued, as Churchill was arguing in the House, that homemade fuel would be advantageous to the country and particularly to the Admiralty. What was needed was an apparatus to produce it. He was given permission to build a new research facility at East Greenwich and to conduct experiments with engines in this regard.[48] It was on the basis of Beilby's ingenuity and experimentation, plus his conviction, that the Royal Commission reported the way ahead in the development of a new carbonising industry, founded on the distillation of coal at a temperature well below that used in gas retorts and coke ovens.

On 10 February 1914 the third and final report of the Royal Commission was released, championing the belief 'that the perfected oil engine will be the future source of power of fighting ships, because the radius of action of the fleet will thus be so greatly increased, its fighting efficiency so largely added to, and its instant readiness for action provided.' The third report also emphasised the need for storage and reserves.[49] When late that month the commission was dissolved, its members paid the highest tribute to Fisher: 'We, the undersigned, members of the Royal Commission on Fuel and Engines, desire to place on record at this, the final meeting of the Commission, our deep sense of the dignity, conspicuous ability, and impartiality with which you have presided over the sittings of the Commission and conducted the proceedings, as well as the national value of the services which you have rendered in facilitating the discharge of the responsible duties to the Commission by His Majesty the King.'[50]

The Foreign Office had no difficulty accepting the view that a sufficient oil field had to be secured for the British Navy. The Secretary of State, Sir Edward Grey, was aware that diplomatic assistance alone could not secure it; only pecuniary assistance could lock down the arrangement. Thus it was that the government itself became a shareholder in the Anglo-Persian (later Anglo-Iranian) Oil Company.

Churchill was the fixer in all of this. On 17 July 1913 he announced to the House of Commons that oil would be replacing coal. A commission sent to Persia confirmed this. Admiral Edmond Slade, former Director of Naval Intelligence and head of the commission, advised that the supply could be assured if the Admiralty had control of the operation at its source. When he warned that it would be a disaster if the Persian concession were allowed to pass into foreign hands, the arguments were sealed and the rationale demonstrated. After the backroom arrangements were completed, the Treasury insisted that Parliament be informed, and thus it fell to Churchill, who rose in the Commons on 17 June 1914 to introduce a historic measure, that the government would invest in and control 51 per cent of the Anglo-Persian Oil Company and have directors on the company board: 'If we cannot get oil, we cannot get corn, we cannot get cotton and we cannot get a thousand and one commodities for the preservation of the economic energies of Great Britain.' The Admiralty, Churchill explained, had 'to retort, refine ... or distil crude oil.' Left confidential was the secret twenty-year contract the deal provided to ensure the Admiralty had fuel oil. Churchill faced the challenges of other oil interests, arguing that price fixing and rival contenders did not allow the British to have a secure supply. That was the issue. Churchill's advocacy of government ownership of a private company was indeed unprecedented, as Daniel Yergin, expert on intentional oil politics and history, has said (though he reminds us that Disraeli had purchased shares in the Suez Company, also on strategic grounds). Churchill's attack on monopolies and trusts allowed him to carry the House but so, too, did his assault on foreigners and 'cosmopolitans'.[51] Elsewhere Churchill would explain that the profits from the British shares in this firm more than sufficed to pay for the dreadnoughts and super-dread-noughts commissioned in subsequent years. Admiral Slade, who had led the Admiralty's investigation to Persia, was rewarded with an appointment to a seat on Anglo-Persian's board of directors.

Bringing together the Scottish oil-shale business and the refining expertise of Beilby laid the basis for what became the modern giant British Petroleum. Meanwhile, Deterding, the 'Napoleon of Oil', developed a tanker fleet that revolutionised the requirements of naval strategy, and as early as 1914 assured the Royal Navy of oil for its fuel bunkers. On 30 July 1914 Fisher wrote to Churchill: 'I have just received a most patriotic letter from Deterding to say he means you shan't want for oil or tankers in case of war. GOOD OLD DETERDING! How these Dutchmen do hate the Germans! Knight him when you get the chance.' Deterding, a Dutch citizen, was awarded an honorary knighthood in 1921.[52]

In all, a vital new chapter of the naval annals had opened. The combination of Fisher and Churchill in the oil business may be said to be the most important element that secured the British Empire at the moment of its supreme peril. It gave the Navy's battlecruisers the mobility they needed on distant operations, including that of the Falklands, in 1914. It allowed for the immense fuel requirements needed to deal with and contain the U-boat threat. It provided an essential means of protecting convoys that provided the foodstuffs and supplies upon which the United Kingdom depended. The conversion to oil, and the commitment to pursue it so vigorously in a new venture of state/private interests, had begun with Fisher's enthusiasms and foresight but was carried in the end by Churchill's parliamentary and ministerial influence. Yergen provides an authoritative summary:

> Quite simply, the decision was driven by the technological imperatives of the Anglo-German naval race. Even as the Germans sought equality, the British Navy was committed to maintaining naval supremacy, and oil offered a vital edge in terms of speed and flexibility. The deal assured the British government a large supply of oil. It provided Anglo-Persian with a much-needed infusion of new capital and a secure market. It spoke directly to the need for survival of Anglo-Persian, and indirectly, to that of the Empire. Thus, by the summer of 1914, the British Navy was fully committed to oil and the British government had assumed the role of Anglo-Persian's majority shareholder. Oil, for the first time, but certainly not the last, had become an instrument of national policy, a strategic commodity second to none.[53]

In mid-1917 Fisher commented on oil reserves in a letter to Churchill. After Fisher stated that he had introduced oil as the sole fuel, he noted that Churchill had 'splendidly backed up ... the all-oil vessels in your regime.' Fisher went on to say that the Navy should have stored up to the three million tons of oil which had been recommended by the Royal Commission on Fuel and Engines, and he noted, 'Some day before this war is over this will be deeply regretted.'[54] Until the war's end, Fisher maintained that oil was the very soul of future sea fighting, and that the Royal Navy was often too late in its technological innovations in this regard, and its ships outdated. The whole tendency of the British during the war was to acquire a reliable and assured source of oil for their military and commercial purposes, and this had remarkable effects on the shaping of foreign policy toward the Ottoman Empire and the Middle East. Fisher, in later years, followed developments closely.

The British empire of oil spread eastwards after 1918 with remarkable speed. But it is noteworthy that in Fisher's time, for he was there at the inception of it, he always looked at the naval requirements; the imperial acquisitions were only of importance to him to assure supply – and that often meant keeping the Germans out. It was Admiral Slade who, beginning in 1916, championed the naval-imperial reach to the oil fields of Mesopotamia, Kuwait, Bahrain, and Arabia, and the Admiralty position was especially aggressive in the pursuit of formal empire.[55] This was a position that Arthur Balfour, then the Foreign Secretary, could not accept, worried, as he was, that the extension of formal empire ought not to be a war aim taken to a conclusion at the peace tables. Further details need not concern us here, but what is clear in the recounting is that the revolution in the marine engine and the need for oil to serve it had its genesis in Fisher's great fighting ship. As to the maintenance of such formal empire or mandates, the Royal Air Force would police it, with the Navy covering the water approaches and securing the broad common over which tankers would have to pass.

The Mediterranean naval revolution

We left *Enchantress*, with Churchill, Asquith, and Battenberg aboard, in Malta, that key fulcrum of British naval authority in those seas. Kitchener and Hamilton came on board. A tour of the dockyard followed, and then it was on to the main event, a conference on 'the Mediterranean Question'. Should the British withdraw their naval armament in the Mediterranean and concentrate on a deployment in the North Sea? That was the burning issue.

In the two years before the outbreak of war in 1914, the dynamic and unstable naval arms race was not in the North Sea, but in the Mediterranean. Both the Italians and the Austrians committed themselves to dreadnought construction programmes, and although these programmes were as likely aimed at each other as at anyone else, there still existed the possibility that the Italian and Austrian dreadnoughts could combine against French and British naval forces in the Mediterranean.[56] The state of British naval capabilities in the

Mediterranean and the state of the French navy in an informal and undeclared alliance with Britain were other matters on the minds of Asquith, Churchill, Battenberg, and their sometime companion Jacky Fisher. Above all was the question of how could Britain remain paramount in the North Sea against the vaulting ambition and rising naval capabilities of the Kaiser's navy? Here was a complex scenario, with many tortuous acts or smaller scenes. Churchill and Asquith may well have solved the big problem of getting Fisher to lead the Royal Commission on Oil for the Royal Navy, but how were they to deal with the radical reorganisation of the Fleet so that the Mediterranean would not be denuded of power, British interests would not be sacrificed in that sea and in imperial lands beyond, and intemperate cries would not rise up in Parliament heralding the imminent fall of the British Empire? These were the interlocking issues, strategic and political.

At the Admiralty, the First Sea Lord, Admiral Wilson, must have wondered what Churchill, Asquith, Battenberg, Beatty, and the others were deciding on board *Enchantress*. He stood strongly opposed to any weakening of the Mediterranean Fleet. That sea, he and almost all other admirals then on the active list knew, had been the centrepiece of British naval strategy, for not only did it serve as a deterrent against any rival nation's navy trying to test Britannia's influence there, but it also guarded the approaches to Egypt and the Suez Canal. British statesmen regarded the Mediterranean Fleet, based on Malta and deployed on missions to show the flag, as an expression of British foreign policy. The British naval armament in that sea was one that other states could not ignore.

However, Fisher foresaw the North Sea as the place of pre-eminent need. He supported Churchill's contention that 'the first necessity was the certainty of victory in the North Sea.' Churchill could not make this shift in strategy by himself, particularly as his critics, though admiring his brilliance and resourcefulness as Esher did, thought concentrating all available ships in the North Sea was madness. The question of saying 'adieu to the sea command of Great Britain' in the Mediterranean could not be Churchill's decision alone,[57] and resistance to this shift in strategy would continue for months. The ever-sympathetic Esher cautioned Churchill not to take this resistance personally. Almost overnight, however, there came a change, and it seemed as if the strong men of the Cabinet, including Foreign Secretary Grey and Prime Minister Asquith, were behind Churchill. But the former First Lord, Reginald McKenna, dug in his heels. McKenna insisted on the Mediterranean being protected with an adequate British naval armament. There were many heated moments, but after a long drawn-out fight it was decided a British naval presence would remain in the Mediterranean[58] – a fleet there was symbolic as well as actual in its might – but its force strength was cut back severely.

The new Admiralty policy for the Mediterranean, as urged by Churchill and Fisher, would be a battle fleet equal to a one-power Mediterranean standard, excluding France. Malta would continue as a base at existing strength, but Gibraltar would grow in stature; the ships based there would be able to swing into the Mediterranean as required. In other words, the British armament in these seas would match that of Italy, or Austria but not a combination of these powers. Thus it was that all battleships were withdrawn from that sea in the summer of 1912, replaced by battlecruisers. Churchill never recommended that the Mediterranean be abandoned, but he said that the battleships or battlecruisers needed there to protect British interests did not exist, needed as they were elsewhere, though they could be built given time and increased naval estimates. There the matter rested. The result was that France was now obliged to shoulder a greater burden.

The North Sea was calling forth Britannia's major naval assets. In a long, cogently stated memorandum to Cabinet on the Mediterranean naval situation, the German naval situation in the North Sea, and 'The Time Table of a Nightmare', Churchill made clear to his colleagues his comprehensive, wide-ranging views on the unfolding scenario which seemed to lead to the most unwelcome of states in human affairs. For the moment, he reasoned, the Mediterranean was safe to British interests. France was not an ally, though conversations with the leaders of the French navy had begun, a consequence of the revolution in deployments away from the Mediterranean. By this stroke, Churchill's strategic understanding of the state of European affairs, pressed upon him by the importunate Fisher, was given effect. As long as Gibraltar, with the 4th Battle Squadron based there, was safe, the Mediterranean was secure for British interests. Gibraltar could deploy its naval weight into the Mediterranean as required, giving additional muscle to the strong force of battlecruisers to be stationed at Malta. With a suitable complement of destroyers and submarines, the Navy could deal with any threat posed by enemy battleships there. Sea power was flexible, Churchill knew, and naval assets could be sent into the Mediterranean as required. In consequence, Gibraltar received a new lease of life, its strategic position changing with the times and circumstances. The note that firmed up this policy also suggested that the Mediterranean 'could never be a true war route' – it was therefore, by definition, a cul de sac – and that 'Aden and the Cape are the main naval points for maintaining the road to India and the East.'[59] It is fascinating to note that Churchill, and those advising him on this shift, made clear in 1911 – and this is of general interest and for later consideration – that it was no longer possible to force the Dardanelles; further, no modern fleet ought to be exposed to such perils.

Technical advances: superdreadnoughts, torpedoes, and mines

When on 13 December 1911 Fisher commended Jellicoe for his 'splendid pushing' of submarines, he waxed eloquent about his newest ship design. He outlined his vision of a new oil-burning battleship that would have eight 15in guns, ten submerged torpedo tubes, a speed of 30 knots, and a cost of £1,995,000. He argued that speed was crucial, as 'that great preponderance of speed ... enables you to fight WHEN you like, WHERE you like, and HOW you like!'[60] Fisher continued to press upon Churchill that the key factor was speed. Jellicoe's '*one, one, one* cry is SPEED! *Do lay that to heart!* Do remember the recipe for jugged hare in Mrs. Glasse's Cookery Book! "*First catch your hare!*"' And, by way of repetition: 'Sea fighting is pure common sense. The first of all its necessities is SPEED, so as to be able to fight – *When* you like, *Where* you like, and *How* you like.'[61]

The *Queen Elizabeth* class, sometimes called the super-dreadnoughts, ordered as part of the 1912/13 building programme, represented a significant evolutionary, if not a revolutionary, step forward in the development of warships. One reason for this was their gunnery. They were the first to carry the prodigious 15in gun, which represented a leap forward as each shell weighed 1,920lbs, compared to 1,400lbs for those of the 13½in gun or 850lbs for the 12in gun. The disposition of the main armament gave a right ahead and right astern fire as well as broadside fire, a great increase over all earlier designs. And the weight of the projectiles fired in a broadside of the 15in guns of a *Queen Elizabeth* was 15,360lbs. Fisher was ecstatic about the prospects for these guns, writing to Churchill: 'I've been looking up what the 15 inch gun will do! It will "stagger humanity"! Just glorious!' Fortified by Fisher's encouragement, Churchill ordered four *Queen Elizabeth*s (a fifth was later added),[62] based on the usage of 15in guns, before these guns had even been tested. In British terms they were the high mark in naval architecture and design for some time. It was only after hurried prototype guns had been built and tested that Churchill knew his gamble had paid off. The good performance of these guns on an excellent hull influenced the design not only of later First World War battleships, such as the new *Royal Sovereign* class and Germany's *Bayern* class, but even Second World War battleships like *Bismarck* and *Tirpitz*.[63]

Even so, the radical character of the *Queen Elizabeth*s did not stop with their great guns, for they were the first capital ships fitted with boilers for burning oil only, and their design raised the possibility that all future vessels would be oil-fired. Therefore, they had a crucial influence on the adoption of oil for the Royal Navy and the creation of the Royal Commission on Fuel and Engines. Another unique aspect of the *Queen Elizabeth*s was their speed. Initially there was wild talk, which began with comments from Fisher in November 1914, that the new ships were capable of 28 knots. They were clearly incapable of achieving this speed once they joined the Grand Fleet: in a pinch they could achieve 26 knots. Their design speed was 25 knots, and it turned out that *Warspite* could do little better than 23½ knots. Nevertheless, their speed was unprecedented for a battleship and set them apart from the rest of the battleships that formed the main line of battle for the Grand Fleet.[64] In consequence, these super-dreadnoughts took up station as a battle squadron – the 'Fast Division', Churchill's personal achievement – within Beatty's battlecruiser force.

Taken all together, the *Queen Elizabeth*s broke the mould of capital ship design since *Dreadnought*. Heretofore, all capital ships were either slow, heavily armoured battleships with the largest armament available, or faster battlecruisers with less armour and slightly fewer main guns. On the one hand, a vessel of the *Queen Elizabeth* class had the same number of guns as a battlecruiser and was faster than a battleship. On the other hand, it was as heavily armoured as a battleship, if not more so. After construction there was serious discussion over just which category they fell into.[65] However, their significance is that they were a hybrid of both types, combining the best of the battleship and the battlecruiser. By the same token, they effectively supplanted the true battlecruisers, as they had all their advantages without their most significant drawback, which was the inability to survive in the face of the enemy's main fleet. As a result, after the *Queen Elizabeth*s, no more battlecruisers were built of that size. By early 1914 the Admiralty had decided that the *Queen Elizabeth*s would form the fast division of the battle fleet, taking over this role from the battlecruisers. The battlecruiser squadron was to have been broken up in May 1915, and the units distributed in pairs to four squadrons of the most modern light cruisers, tasked for reconnaissance. The outbreak of war intervened, however, and the battlecruiser squadron continued to grow until it became a fleet of its own.[66]

The super-dreadnoughts did not come into service until 1915. On 14 July 1914, the eve of the war, Jellicoe sent a prescient and apprehensive memorandum to the First Lord describing the 'very striking' inferiority of British battleships' protection against guns and torpedoes as compared to their German counterparts, with their 'far more complete [German] inner armour protection against torpedoes'. He summed up by stating that it was 'highly dangerous to consider that our ships as a whole are superior or even equal fighting machines.'[67] This was a fair assessment, and it demonstrated the doubts that had begun to enter Jellicoe's mind.

Advances in submarines (which we will examine in the next section), torpedoes, and mines were continuing to revolutionise naval warfare, limiting the power and mobility of surface ships. To a service dominated by gunnery considerations, these technological changes posed unwelcome challenges, and the British were ill prepared to deal with them. All the old assumptions of maritime warfare needed to be re-examined in the face of these new weapons and weapons platforms.

Great advances were made in torpedoes prior to the First World War. From the Russo-Japanese War to the First World War, torpedo ranges increased prodigiously from 5,000 to 11,000yds. The speed of torpedoes climbed from 19 knots if set for 4,000yds or up to 33 knots at 1,000yds to as much as 45 knots if set for 7,000yds. The diameter of torpedoes went from 14in to 21in. As well, the introduction of the gyroscope in the 1890s allowed the torpedo to stay on the course it was launched on.[68] While no more torpedo boats were built after 1909, destroyers underwent an increase in size, speed, and endurance. The notable 'M' class of destroyers, built in 1914, was 1,200 tons, capable of a swift 34 knots, and stoutly armed with four 21in torpedoes and three 4in guns.[69]

As for mines, Fisher knew of their offensive value, and so did others at the Admiralty. Thus, in 1913 the War Staff drew up schemes for mining the Heligoland Bight and the Straits of Dover. Only Churchill was interested in the plan, until he learned the prohibitive cost of 50,000 mines. As a result, when war came, Britain had no mining policy,[70] and the efficiency of the 4,000 spherical mines in stock was questionable.[71]

Leaving aside the cost of mines, more fundamental issues presented themselves to the First Lord of the Admiralty, who now changed his mind and opposed mining measures. Churchill instituted distant blockade. More, he wanted wide seas for the operations of Royal Navy ships, and he thought the laying of mines hazardous to those prosecuting that policy and not likely to bring the desired result of sinking enemy shipping. Kitchener, who saw a greater chance of a German invasion, was alarmed by Churchill's policy. He viewed mines as a defensive measure protecting the approaches against German inshore operations.

As to the dangers faced by a fleet in major action against an enemy, Jellicoe, Commander-in-Chief, Grand Fleet, expected the Germans to fully deploy minelayers and submarines in a fleet action. For this reason, defensive considerations dominated his thinking. Minesweeping could only proceed at painfully slow speeds, 10 knots maximum, and the areas to sweep were vast. Jellicoe determined that he could not put his capital ships and escorts in harm's way unless he was assured that the areas likely to have mines had been cleared. He had thought through all aspects of the problem that bore on tactics, and in October 1914 he issued instructions as to future forays that would be made by the Grand Fleet into the North Sea. His policy was that the British would not be drawn into the fray or drawn over mines and submarines, and, accordingly, this meant deploying British naval units at 'a very high speed to a flank before deployment takes place or the gun action commences. This will take us off the ground on which the enemy desires to fight, but it may, of course, result in his refusal to follow me.'[72] This became the Jellicoe rule, and early in the war the rules were set that would be followed by the Commander-in-Chief at Jutland in 1916.

For the time being, however, it is noteworthy that Fisher did not share Churchill's anti-mining policy, which the latter had brought before the Cabinet on 12–13 October 1914. On this occasion Kitchener raised his objections, but the First Lord was not moved: 'We have never laid one we have not afterwards regretted,' Churchill told Jellicoe later. Fisher, by contrast, saw the mine as an offensive weapon in British hands that would hamper the enemy minesweepers' movements, serve as a blockade of the German ports, and protect British east-coast trade. In this tug of war at the Admiralty, professional opinions eventually surfaced with success. Some modification to Churchill's embargo against British use of mines occurred when Fisher again became First Sea Lord. Thus in January 1915 the British minesweepers sowed mines off Amrum Bank, Heligoland Bight; they did so nearby twice again in May 1915. The Foreign Office was worried about the reactions of neutral states should their shipping be affected, so an aggressive mining policy was set aside until 1917. 'Returning to the autumn of 1914,' concludes Arthur Marder, 'we find that Admiralty mining policy enraged the many mining enthusiasts among the naval writers and officers, who wanted to see the enemy mined into his ports. It was one more count in the indictment against the First Lord.'[73]

Submarines: 'The days of the dreadnoughts are numbered'

Like the debates about the use of mines, discussions of the value of submarines for offensive and defensive purposes dragged on at the Admiralty and among politicians. Fisher was one of the first who understood the menace posed by enemy submarines. As mentioned earlier, on 12 December 1912 Fisher's Royal Commission on oil heard evidence about German companies producing diesel engines for the German and other navies. It was advertised that in early 1913 the first four diesel-driven U-boats – essentially the big long-range overseas submarines (of the minelaying variety) – would come into service.[74] There were a variety of responses to this alarming prospect, some showing awareness of the danger, while others displayed lassitude and professional negligence. Although Fisher was now out of the mainstream of naval administration, he undertook a new crusade in the face of the submarine revolution, and he never tired of alerting others to the danger.

Given the paucity of anti-submarine measures at the time, Fisher's alarm is understandable. He told journalist Arnold White that submarines were the next dreadnoughts. He also said that aviation would supplant cruisers, but that hardly anyone, with the exception of Balfour, was able to grasp these concepts.[75] All of this was true, as subsequent events were to prove. White, connected closely to the Navy League, might have been in a position to help Fisher, but his credibility was largely curtailed given his previous interventions in the press in favour of 'Copenhagening' the German fleet in harbour.

Fisher believed that British submarines, and sound flotilla defence, could halt any projected invasion of the British Isles.[76] Submarines would be based at harbours such as Harwich, there to set forth on missions, usually in company with a cruiser as command-and-control ship. Torpedo-boat flotilla defence also would act from a base of operations, spreading influence across the sea in a tactically developed way designed to find the enemy and bring it to account. Fisher's enthusiasm for the submarine while he served on the oil commission infected Churchill, but only to a degree. The First Lord was slow, as we will see, to accept the U-boat as the new danger. On 24 June 1912 Fisher wrote a memorandum to Churchill entitled 'Battleships and Trade in the Mediterranean', which dealt with proposals to redistribute British naval strength away from the Mediterranean in response to Tirpitz's new Navy Law. With respect to submarines, Fisher argued that the 'immense development of the submarine precludes the presence of heavy ships of war or the passage of trade through the Mediterranean Sea.' He noted:

> If it be observed that Christian nations ... would be shocked by the murder of defenceless trading vessels carrying our food from the Black Sea, would anyone hesitate to send to perdition some two thousand soldiers packed in a transport trying to invade England, as compared with only the dozen men forming the crew of the grain ship? *The essence of war is violence and moderation in war is imbecility!* Nor would it be waste of torpedoes to use them to sink these valuable cargoes of grain and merchandise. A line of submarines and destroyers across the [Strait] of Gibraltar or the Malta Channel or other narrow spaces need only sink a few ships to stop the trade effectively.[77]

On 4 July 1912 Fisher attended a plenary meeting of the CID, the subject of which was dear to his heart: the proposed withdrawal of large warships from the Mediterranean. The views Fisher expressed were hard for others to grasp. His understanding of how a war at sea would be fought challenged the old concepts of engaging the enemy's fleet in action. He seemed to expect discursive warfare and fitful raids by the enemy on British installations and ports, and he advocated flotilla defence in response. With respect to the potential for an invasion of Malta, Fisher argued that 'the danger to transports from submarine and torpedo attack was so serious that any idea of invasion anywhere in face of them was out of the question.' Asquith was unconvinced that submarines were the sure line of defence. In response, Fisher stated that he 'had absolute confidence in the power of the submarine' against heavy warships, and that if Britain provided 'adequate flotillas of submarines and destroyers at Malta, Gibraltar, and Alexandria no [enemy] battleship could move in the Mediterranean.' Significantly, Fisher also noted that he did not expect trade to pass through the Mediterranean in wartime. McKenna observed, 'If this estimate of the power of the submarine [is] correct the North Sea [is] equally unsuitable for battleships.' Fisher responded by stating that the British battle fleet would not be in the North Sea but, rather, off the northern coast of Scotland or outside the Straits of Dover, and that British submarines and destroyers would be used to weaken the German fleet if it should sortie into the North Sea. On this point there was no response from the First and Second Sea Lords, Bridgeman and Battenberg. Many were unconvinced. Shortly afterward, Churchill observed, 'The Board of Admiralty did not entirely accept Lord Fisher's views on submarines.'[78] Indeed, the established hierarchy of the Navy looked down on the young, adventurous submariners who risked their lives in dangerous contraptions of then unproven value, and Fisher's friend Sir Arthur Wilson, former First Sea Lord, considered the submarine 'underhand, unfair, and damned un-English'.[79] Fisher was ahead of his time, and clear in this thinking. Experience would show others the merits of his views.

By March 1913, after the second report of the oil commission had been completed, Fisher was thinking through problems of ensuring the country's supply of food and oil. Simultaneously, his interest in submarines was further stimulated by the CID's renewed investigation of the invasion problem. Not only did Fisher feel that submarines had made invasion impossible; he also saw that the submarine question could be used as an argument against the British Expeditionary Force, as German U-boats could discourage the transport of the BEF to France.[80] Until his departure from the oil commission's office in February 1914, Fisher worked vigorously on the final draft of his submarine paper. He consulted widely and made influential gains among politicians.[81] One of Fisher's most demanding critics was former prime minister Arthur Balfour, whose dialectical logic was the wonder of onlookers. He was no fool. He wrote to Fisher to say that the troubling question was not whether British submarines could render an enemy's position intolerable, but vice versa. If it were true that a large submarine could blockade a hostile port for long periods of time, and if it could not be driven off by any known method of attack, he wondered, 'What is to prevent the Germans sealing up every port, military or commercial, round our whole coast – and this whatever our superiority in battleships and cruisers might happen to be? That's the question *I* want answered!'[82]

The original version of Fisher's memorandum on the submarine menace, dated 15 May 1913, was sent to Balfour and Maurice Hankey, Secretary of the

CID. It began alarmingly: 'No means exist of preventing an enemy's submarines from coming out of their harbours and cruising more or less at will, short of mining and blocking operations on a very large scale.' The advantage lay with the likely future enemy: 'a close investment' of the British North Sea ports by German submarines would be five times as difficult as a similar blockade of the German exits by British boats. For the moment, Germany lacked a sufficient number of boats. However, he continued, as the number and capability of submarines grew, and they became increasingly powerful, it would be all but impossible to obtain and maintain naval supremacy, especially in enclosed waters like the North Sea. This would make any invasion of England, as well as the dispatching of any expeditionary force, a very hazardous affair. Therefore, the rise of the submarine, provided that Britain had a number equal to or greater than her enemy, would result in increased national safety.[83]

Attention now turned to how the enemy's submarines could damage the surface ships of the Royal Navy. Information reaching Fisher from the Naval Intelligence Division, as well as from submarine builders and contractors, painted a horrific picture of potential damage. Captain Reginald Hall predicted the 'extermination of surface war vessels by submarines of 2000 tons'. From other sources Fisher received details of submarines then under construction, including an overseas type of 1,694 tons being constructed by the dominant submarine builders Vickers, Britain's preferred contractor. Fisher needed no further convincing. He summed up his disquieting views on a small sheet of paper that was justifiably and liberally underlined in red:

> The Submarine of 1,700 tons displacement is now
> the dominant factor of Naval War.

NO ONE HAS DISCOVERED HOW TO DESTROY A SUBMARINE!
A SUBMARINE WILL KEEP THE SEA LONGER THAN A DREADNOUGHT!
No Invasion or Raid is possible.
No Expeditionary Force can leave these shores.
So don't worry about Conscription or Territorials.
But German submarines will blockade our commercial Ports so you had best agree to Channel Tunnel and Private Property at Sea immune.[84]

Fisher ranged far ahead of the politicians on the matter of a future war at sea in which the submarine would play a prominent part. Balfour was normally conscious of defence matters and priorities, but on 20 May, in an attempt to dampen Fisher's ardour, he reiterated his belief that Britain would not likely benefit from the development of the submarine, and that the neutralisation of neighbouring waters meant a worsening of Britain's relative position, as not only would the British become useless to Continental allies, but they would also have great difficulty in keeping themselves alive. Therefore, it was necessary to reconsider existing views on the capture of private property at sea, or, rather, its destruction, as submarines could not capture property.[85] Balfour and, indeed, the Foreign Office were still wrestling with the many legal matters regarding a future enemy (Germany) trading with neutral powers, something subversive to British survival. No answers had yet been found to this puzzling problem.

In June, Fisher produced a second version of his paper, entitled 'The Oil Engine and the Submarine', which ran to eight pages of print. It bore the unmistakable Fisher hallmark. It was much more dramatic than the later versions that appeared in *Records* and the *Jellicoe Papers*. The memorandum opens with Fisher declaring that, due to submarines, a blockade as close as fifty miles would be impossible without a gradual loss of surface ships. Nevertheless, he stated that 'English blockade of the German outlets is vitally essential', and 'the larger submarines are the only type of vessel capable of maintaining any form of blockade, *they have sea-keeping qualities far in advance of any surface vessel*, and by reason of their internal combustion engines they can remain on their beat ready for full speed without any expenditure of fuel.' Meanwhile, older and smaller types of submarines remained useful in countering enemy raids, as they could start their engines immediately 'from "cold" like a taxi cab'. Acting 'in conjunction with the destroyers and torpedo boats of the patrol flotillas, they form a most valuable second line of defence, and the most bigoted conscriptionist will allow that they would be a formidable hornet's nest' for an invading enemy. There followed a section on 'The Enemy's Submarines', which developed in more detail the points made in the original paper of 15 May. The idea that the development of the submarine would afford Britain increased safety, given British numerical superiority, was maintained. Clearly, Fisher's strengthened arguments were designed to bring Balfour on side, and they were largely effective.

The most striking result of Fisher and Balfour's collaboration was the section on 'Submarines and Commerce'. This begins even more alarmingly than the version that subsequently shocked both Churchill and Asquith: 'The suggestion that Germany, by stationing submarines off our principal commercial ports, may occasion greater damage than we can effect by means of our whole sea power is perhaps open to argument.' If Germany fought in an alliance with Austria and Italy against Britain, France, and Russia, she would find herself 'in a very tight place' commercially, while Britain's position – excluding submarines – would be reasonably secure. However, 'when it is realised that the enemy's submarines may be met off all our own commercial ports', there would be an impact 'on freight and insurance rates', and it would not be long before this fact would become known to the public, and the question of diverting trade to less vulnerable western ports would have to be examined. He also reiterated that it would be 'impossible for submarines to deal with merchant ships in accordance with international law. Is it presumed that they will disregard and sink any vessel heading for an English commercial port?' Then comes the crucial part of the memorandum:

> It must be admitted that this submarine menace is rather desperate business for British commerce, for no means can be suggested at present of meeting it except by reprisals. All that would be known would be that a certain steamer did not arrive or that some of her boats [had been] picked up with a few survivors to tell the tale.
>
> It would be an altogether barbarous method of warfare, but if it is done by the Germans, the only thing would be to make reprisals. Many of these reprisals suggest themselves which might cause the sinking of our merchant-men by German submarines to be stopped.
>
> One is inclined to think in this light the arming of our English merchant-men is unfortunate, for it gives the German submarine an excellent excuse (if she wishes one) for sinking her, namely, that of self-defence against the gun of the merchant steamer.

In the margin, Jellicoe wrote in terms that now seem naive: 'I cannot conceive that submarines will sink merchant ships without warning.' Elsewhere he remarked, in reference to Fisher's wish to substitute twenty large submarines for a dreadnought, 'But I would not cease building Dreadnoughts.'[86]

Sir George Clarke, fortifications analyst and a stout believer of 'the blue water school', had received a copy of 'The Oil Engine and the Submarine' and had agreed with Fisher's criticism of the arming of merchantmen, while believing that surface vessels without the assistance of submarines could easily defeat an invasion. Having formerly opposed Fisher's dreadnought plans, he could not resist remarking that the paper provided 'the most destructive argument against large battleships' yet. He agreed that submarines would pose a significant menace in the North Sea, but an admiral could 'carry through his task without much loss.' On the most crucial point he wrote (and here he was not alone) that he could not believe that submarines would sink unarmed merchant shipping, and he reckoned that modern sentiment would not stand such proceedings. He also suggested the use of aeroplanes as a weapon against submarines. Fisher was always frosty when it came to Clarke, whom he thought rough and a bit of a bully. He took no action on these suggestions; in consequence, Clarke's valuable insights were not sufficiently represented in the revised version of the paper printed in November.[87]

By the summer, Churchill's curiosity about Fisher's promised 'upheaval' on submarines had been sufficiently aroused. He acquired a copy of the final (unsensational) section of the June print from Commodore Roger Keyes.[88] Churchill was now a convert, as was the ever reluctant Balfour. The latter wrote to Fisher with respect to submarines and recent naval manoeuvres, saying, 'I am more than ever convinced that the days of the Dreadnoughts are numbered; but how soon the end will be I know not!'[89]

In November the paper was nearly ready to be given to the First Lord. At this point Fisher wrote to Corbett to ask for his assistance to 'make it a work of art, *as the subject deserves it*!' He also noted that the oil engine was the thread that ran through every aspect of naval fighting, and that everyone had thought him a lunatic when, as First Sea Lord, he advocated developing submarines. However, due to his efforts, Britain had the lead on Germany with respect to submarines.[90]

The next day Corbett expressed his immediate reaction: 'This is immense. It makes me feel as if I had a flash of lightning by the tail.'[91] He criticised the idea that Britain should reconsider her views on the capture of private property at sea, writing: 'You show that given all you anticipate from the submarine, we by the advantage of our geographical position can entirely stop German oversea trade while she will have difficulty in making any *effective* impression on ours.' He saw aircraft as a possible antidote to submarines, and wondered how many torpedoes would be needed to sink a large ship with watertight compartments. As well, he asked, 'Do you really think that any Power now-a-days would incur the odium of sinking merchant ships out of hand?'[92]

Fisher did not give way on this last point, and his view (supported by Balfour and Esher) proved devastatingly accurate. He did defer to Corbett, though, by adding a note on 'captures at sea'. This policy, he wrote, should be retained due to Britain's geographical position, the uncertainty concerning the effect of aircraft, the limited range of vision from a submarine's deck, the consequent inducement for it to attack trade as this converged on a port, and the increased possibility of counter-attack by aircraft in such an area. He also expressed doubt as to whether 'powerful neutrals' would recognise 'blockade by submarines only'. As a further improvement, food and oil were designated as the chief prey of U-boats. In early November, Fisher had included in the paper the idea of building a Channel Tunnel as a partial solution, but he removed it by the end of the month due to his concern that it would help transport the BEF to the Continent. Therefore, on 6 December 1913, when the paper was sent to Churchill, the development of the west-coast ports stood as the main remedy to the submarine menace.[93]

Churchill acknowledged receipt of Fisher's 'epoch making Memo about Submarines'. He promised to communicate further once he had thoroughly 'digested it'.[94] On 1 January 1914 Churchill wrote regarding what he called 'the brilliant and most valuable paper' Fisher had drawn up. However, there

were a few points on which he was not convinced. In particular was the
question of the sinking of merchant ships by submarines. He suggested that 'if
there were a nation vile enough to adopt systematically such methods, it would
be justifiable and indeed necessary, to employ the extreme resources of science
against them: to spread pestilence, poison the water supply of great cities, and,
if convenient, proceed by the assassination of individuals. These are frankly
unthinkable propositions and the excellence of your paper is, to some extent,
marred by the prominence assigned to them.'[95]

In response to Fisher's submarine paper, Jellicoe wrote to Churchill in support
of Fisher's argument that Britain should build large numbers of submarines.
Jellicoe was largely alone in support of Fisher. Both Battenberg and Keyes were
unconvinced of the likelihood of enemy submarine attacks on commerce.[96]

Dissatisfied with the reaction of the Admiralty, Fisher sent his paper to Prime
Minister Asquith on 8 May 1914. 'IT IS REALLY MOMENTOUS,'
commented Fisher in his covering letter, adding that he himself would drop a
dreadnought for twenty submarines instead. He continued:

> There are a lot of idiots who lecture at the Naval War College and write in
> the papers that Tirpitz won't use his submarines to sink merchant ships! The
> civilized world they say would execrate him! Skobeleff exterminated the
> Turcomans (man, woman and child!) Was he recalled? Was Russia banned?
> General Nogi had no prisoners in Manchuria till some European busybody
> asked where they were! The Mexican Generals murder ad lib.! The Essence
> of War is violence and moderation in War is imbecility![97]

Fisher's paper, not surprisingly, failed to galvanise the prime minister into action.
Asquith was the last in the Cabinet to take an aggressive or advanced view,
preferring largely to await the course of events. Fisher, however, took satisfaction
in what he had done, and he was able to report to Jellicoe on 25 May that he had
at least inflicted a degree of trauma on Asquith: 'The Prime Minister has asked
me to dine with him, but I've declined. I let fly at him about submarines, and he
is evidently *greatly moved! but he entreated me to say nothing! Burn this!*'[98]

In retrospect, against many detractors, Fisher had advertised the utility and
influence of submarines in war of the future. Carrying torpedoes as well as deck
guns, and powered by diesel-burning engines, the submarine would replace the
dreadnought as the paramount weapon. Air power, too, would place the
dreadnought's future in doubt, and we take a brief look at that next. But at
this early stage, and even before the great 'castles of steel' had contested for
control of the North Sea (even if in hit-and-miss fashion), the submarine's future
had been proclaimed. This had been Fisher's doing, and Churchill had been
reluctantly brought into the discussion, readily accepting the oil-burning engine
but unwilling to believe that the submarine could become the dominant

weapon. Prescient though Churchill was, he could not imagine German 'unrestricted U-boat warfare' against unarmed merchant traffic or comprehend that the U-boat war would bring Britain to the brink of starvation in 1917. Churchill was not alone: few of his fellow countrymen, save for Fisher and the submariners in the Navy, foresaw the vast changes that the submarine would bring to future naval combat and to merchant shipping in time of war.

Air power

Churchill was always an enthusiast for flight and air power, and when he came to the Admiralty he was much attached to the naval aviation pioneers who were to form the Naval Air Service of the Royal Navy. From 1912 onwards there was constant lobbying for a strengthening of Britain's air power, led by the Aerial Defence Committee of the Navy League.[99] Fisher believed that 'aviation supersedes small cruisers & Intelligence vessels', and that Churchill was right to push aviation, though he cautioned that he shouldn't 'take away our splendid young Naval Officers who have been suckled on Gunnery and sea fighting to do what civilians can do better.'[100]

At this point there was a debate whether aeroplanes would be of more value than airships – the latter being lighter-than-air craft, with or without a rigid supporting structure, that fly by their own power. Jellicoe, who had become Second Sea Lord in December 1912, was keen on airships for their potential value in naval scouting, as he felt that aeroplanes were unsuitable for the role. He had been to Germany in 1911 and had actually flown in a Zeppelin. However, the rest of the Sea Lords did not share his enthusiasm.[101] Meanwhile, the Navy's first rigid airship, the 'Mayfly', built by Vickers at Barrow-in-Furness in 1910, was launched in May 1911 but was destroyed a few months later when a violent crosswind broke her in two.[102]

At a meeting of the CID on 6 December 1912, Churchill made clear his 'great anxiety' at the threat posed by German airships. He spelled out the importance of the problem, 'both from the point of view of airships as auxiliaries to the Fleet and from that of defence against their attacks ... Our dockyards, machine shops, magazines, and ships lying in the basins, were absolutely defenceless against this form of attack if an enemy airship were to succeed in reaching a position whence it could attack.' He asked for the development of a suitable type, as the Admiralty needed to know the capabilities of airships if it was to defend against them. Admiral Sir Arthur Wilson thought the value of airships greatly exaggerated: they could carry only a limited amount of explosives, and they were quite vulnerable to being shot down by land-based guns, ships at sea, or other aeroplanes. Asquith sided with Wilson, and thus a recommendation by the Technical Sub-Committee on Aerial Navigation to build a fleet of airships superior to the German fleet was set aside.[103]

When the CID resumed the airship discussion in February 1913, the Technical Sub-Committee put forward an amended recommendation that requested the development of an airship that was in no way inferior to those possessed by other countries, for naval purposes and for the training of airship personnel. The question of the number of airships was set aside until the prototype could be evaluated. While Jellicoe argued the merits of airships in comparison to aeroplanes, Wilson argued the limitations of airships. In the end the recommendation was adopted, although Wilson remained unconvinced. Colonel Seely, the Secretary of State for War, declared that the Army was leaving airships to the Navy to develop. The Army would focus on aeroplanes.[104] In early 1914 the Admiralty ordered eight airships. None of these were ready when war broke out: in fact, only two Royal Navy airships had any operational value at the outbreak of war, the Astra-Torres No. 3 and the Parseval, which had been purchased in France and Germany.

Meanwhile, in 1913 *Hermes*, a cruiser built in the 1890s, was recommissioned as the world's first aircraft carrier, carrying three seaplanes that could not return to the ship once launched. She was used in trials throughout 1913, but when war began she was used only to transport aircraft and supplies until she was sunk by a torpedo in October 1914.[105]

In the House of Commons on 17 March 1914, Churchill declared that aeroplanes would be valuable for coastal defence, for scouting at sea, and for defending military assets such as oil tanks and docks. He emphasised their scouting role. As scouts, aeroplanes could locate the enemy fleet, whether it was in harbour or on the sea. They could find the enemy fleet when it was hidden from the Home Fleet by a fog bank, and could indicate where guns should be aimed. They could spot and destroy submarines, mines, and torpedo craft, and also warn merchantmen of danger.[106] Still, the favourite theory was that they would be used to attack and repel invading forces. 'Any hostile aircraft, airships, or aeroplanes which reached our coast during the coming year would be promptly attacked in superior force by a swarm of very formidable hornets,' Churchill assured the Commons brazenly.

That air power was revolutionising war at sea was without question. Among the champions of air power was the gunnery expert Admiral Percy Scott, known widely in the Service as 'Shoot Straight'. He always held strong opinions. On 5 June 1914 *The Times* published his letter announcing that the submarine and the aeroplane had 'revolutionised naval warfare', and that so far as cruisers were concerned, it was no longer the seaman's business to find the enemy as that role had been assumed by aeroplanes.[107] But the naysayers so often held the day, and aircraft had not been proven in wartime. Nor had anti-aircraft guns been developed. The Navy was at the leading curve of so many changes, and in these circumstances it is not surprising that we find one officer believing the 15in gun to be the dominant weapon, another the submarine, and a third the Zeppelin or tactical air bomber that could destroy a ship sailing the surface of the North Sea or the English Channel.

The shadow of war

In comfortable retirement on Long Island, Admiral Alfred Thayer Mahan, distinguished commentator on the influence of sea power on history, watched with alarm the rise of German naval might. His recent articles on the war between Russia and Japan that had left the Asian power triumphant, and his studies of the Caribbean and the Hawaiian Islands as significant strategic choke points, were in 1910 pushed aside by more urgent matters, and his main focus became the rise of the German Navy. He followed the British press on the problems of the Admiralty, and he found error in the fact that *personality* was dominating the Board of Admiralty – and by this he meant Jacky Fisher. Only one power had the capacity to check Germany's rise to supremacy at sea, and that was Britain. 'The power to control Germany does not exist in Europe, except in the British navy; and if social and political conditions in Great Britain develop as they now promise, the British navy will probably decline in relative strength, so that it will not venture to withstand the German on broad lines of policy, but only in the narrowest sense of immediate British interests.' With an eye to the future, he thought British national life was declining in force at the same time that Germany, with traditions of two centuries, possessing a system of state control, and with a populace accustomed to it, was increasingly the note of the times. By way of warning, he observed that, as an organic body, the German empire was greatly superior to that of Great Britain, and he even began to speak in ominous tones of the future in which Germany might become the pre-eminent sea power and the predominant world empire.[108]

In these strained circumstances, war seemed inevitable, and the great powers lurched toward catastrophe. Although Wilhelm II wished to bring Fisher and Tirpitz together in conversation, he pushed simultaneously for greater German naval armament. He refused to accept the undeniable fact that he himself was one of the principal ingredients in the naval arms race. He did nothing to appease an alarming scenario then developing. In London, pacifist sectors of the Liberal party naively tended to take at face value the Kaiser's statements about keeping the line of peace. But if the Kaiser was a man of peace, did it mean Britain was responsible for the naval armaments race? Parliament and the press became a battleground for divisive positions. The Cabinet lacked unanimity on what, if any, hard line should be taken against the Kaiser and Tirpitz, with some members suggesting that a form of 'soft diplomacy' – private visits or representations, or even 'naval holidays' in shipbuilding – could be tried as last-minute expedients.

The great challenge facing British statesmen was how to convince their German counterparts of peaceful intentions. For his part, Haldane, at the War Office, came to believe that his opposite, Theobald von Bethmann-Hollweg, was sincere in desiring peace, and that he viewed the issue of naval rivalry in much the same light as did counterparts in England. To Haldane's alarm, however, he found that Bethmann-Hollweg lacked the stature of a Bismarck: thus when Bethmann-Hollweg expressed his views to the Kaiser, they were not given the same weight. Haldane also came to the reluctant conclusion that although the Kaiser seemed to desire peace, he failed to understand that constant sabre-rattling was not the preferred method of promoting that state of affairs. Haldane concluded correctly that the Kaiser's military advisers, especially Tirpitz, were pushing the Kaiser toward further naval expansion. Though Haldane informed the Germans that their continued naval construction would lead to renewed British efforts to out-construct them on a rough ratio of 2:1, the Germans would not budge. A copy of the forthcoming Navy Bill given to Haldane indicated that the Germans had no intention of slowing their naval construction, and so it was that the Admiralty had no choice but to continue its counter-preparations.[109]

Could the British outbuild the Germans in ships of war? By 1912 it had become clear that the Royal Navy retained a significant margin of superiority over the High Seas Fleet, and that such a margin could be maintained indefinitely. The British government had firmly committed itself to a 16:10 ratio in the North Sea, and the Germans realised that they did not have the resources to exceed this limit. Tirpitz himself publicly declared that he accepted the 16:10 ratio. It became apparent that a continental power like Germany, surrounded by strong and hostile land powers, could not have an army strong enough to take the offensive against France and Russia as well as a navy large enough to rival the Royal Navy. By 1912 the German army command had had enough. They had watched for years as the naval budget skyrocketed – with no obvious benefit as the German navy still lagged far behind the Royal Navy. They demanded that attention revert to the army, and that a line be drawn on further naval expenditures. Tirpitz, conceding that Germany would not exit the zone of danger of his risk theory for years to come, was powerless to resist. By 1914 the naval arms race in the North Sea had brought Germany, not Britain, to the brink of bankruptcy.[110]

On the diplomatic front, on 20 May of that year, Churchill suggested to Grey at the Foreign Office that he meet with Tirpitz to discuss prospects of a 'naval holiday' and other measures, such as limiting ship sizes, deploying naval strengths overseas (rather than concentrating them in home waters), and reducing naval espionage. This was an alluring idea, Churchillian in audacity. In the end, Grey dismissed it on the grounds that it might cause more harm than good.[111] Emissaries such as Sir Ernest Cassel, the businessman, might make an appearance in Berlin in a peaceful effort, and Haldane went under Cabinet instructions. Nothing eventuated. These measures were seen as ploys, last-ditch attempts, well meaning, naturally, but in the circumstances doomed to failure and even to ridicule.

Churchill, seizing the initiative and exerting his influence, made Service appointments in order to prepare the Navy for the coming war. He had indicated to Fisher that the highest positions in the Fleet would not be controlled by seniority. The Navy's future rested in the hands of men who had his confidence and that of Fisher, he said.[112] Fisher, when he was Director of Naval Ordnance in 1889, had chosen Jellicoe, then a lieutenant, as his assistant on the grounds that he was 'far the best officer in my opinion'. Long before any appointment of the kind could be made, Fisher (as disclosed in *Memories*) was manoeuvring with Churchill to dispose the list of admirals so that Sir John Jellicoe was bound to be Commander-in-Chief when war came. On Christmas Eve 1911 Fisher predicted that Jellicoe would be Commander-in-Chief, Home Fleet, in December 1915. He was off by a year. Early in 1914 Jellicoe was appointed C-in-C designate of the Home Fleet. He could hoist his flag in December, when Sir George Callaghan's term expired. As Correlli Barnett puts it so grandly, 'Fisher had unrolled the carpet; Jellicoe stepped neatly along it.'[113] Jellicoe was vaulted into the greatest sea command at precipitate speed.

'In the spring of 1913,' wrote Churchill's cousin Shane Leslie, in an unpublished biography of David Beatty, 'Destiny began moving pieces on the board. Squadrons of the Fleet were being given their commanders in case of war. Two incomparable positions remained uncertain in the future. All other commands were as pawns to King and Queen compared to the Commandership in Chief (held by Sir George Callaghan) and the Battle Cruiser Squadron held by Sir Lewis Bayly.'[114] Jellicoe was to replace Callaghan, first becoming his second in command. And when Bayly's tenure came to an end, Churchill shot Beatty into that vital position. Churchill had decided, with Asquith's concurrence, that Beatty would command the 1st Battle Cruiser Squadron. It was all arranged by the close of *Enchantress*'s Mediterranean cruise. Beatty accepted on 14 November 1912. The subsequent public announcement aroused great jealousy in the Service. Beatty's professional merits were at first misjudged by his naval contemporaries. Luck and his independence, derived in part from his wife's wealth, had favoured him, given him preferment. Fellow naval officers noted how the Service was only a convenience for him. 'It was in this atmosphere of whispering jealousy,' wrote one sailor of great merit, 'that Beatty was given command of the famous Battle-cruiser Squadron by Churchill, whose unerring judgment picked out the very man we needed at sea.'[115]

Beatty's new command was a swift one in every sense. 'The Battlecruisers combined speed, armour and guns of the utmost qualities ... They were the mobile and protective shield which could be wielded over the North Sea while the invisible Trident of the main Fleet remained poised for the annihilating blow.' On 1 March 1913 Beatty, with acting rank of vice-admiral, hoisted his flag in HMS *Lion*. His force consisted of a bevy of giant cruisers, including *Invincible*, *Indefatigable*, and *Indomitable* – ships that bore names 'which seemed to infringe on the Divine Attributes ... To a cautious Admiral they were armoured elephants. To the daring they were the hounds of war spreading havoc at high speed. From the beginning they indicated the strategy of luring larger ships than themselves into inescapable situations.'[116]

Beatty took to the assignment with relish: he trained his squadron in close order to manoeuvre at highest speeds, and he arranged target shooting accordingly. The great ships trained in preparation for war. Churchill relied on him from time to time to advise on strategic matters. In his many discussions with Churchill, Beatty had cleared up essential points. He seems to have been correcting or modifying Churchill's administrative measures. In Beatty the First Lord had someone he could not only trust but who could render professional advice. He never shared that closeness with Jellicoe, who was Fisher's man.

That same spring of 1914, Grey at the Foreign Office authorised the Admiralty to begin discussions with the Russian naval authorities similar to those that began in 1906 between the British and French general staffs. That summer Beatty took the squadron on a courtesy visit to Russia, intended also as a cover for an extensive investigation of Kronstadt's defences.[117] *Lion* led the naval units to the Baltic. With them sailed the United Kingdom ambassador Sir George Buchanan and various rising officers, including 'Flags' R Seymour, Ernle Chatfield, Walter Henry Cowan, Reginald Plunkett (Drax), and Reginald Hall of naval intelligence – all notable persons in the evolving drama of war. Here was fleet diplomacy on the grandest imaginable scale, with Beatty as the quarterdeck admiral carrying out the wishes of Grey and the Foreign Office. He was good at diplomacy and Churchill knew it. Kronstadt had been specially dredged and buoyed for the British battlecruisers before they anchored as guests of the Imperial Russian Navy. Tsar Nicholas II and the Tsarina came on board *Lion*, along with two thousand more guests. Champagne supplies ran low, and the dancing on the main deck of *New Zealand*, lashed alongside *Lion*, went on well towards midnight. Ashore the hospitality was even more lavish. Caviar and vodka were plentiful. Luncheons were laid on. Photos of the grouping exist, views of an age soon to pass from view. Beatty made a trip to Moscow, where he was warmly received. The Tsar was impressed with the battlecruisers and watched admiringly as they manoeuvred at 25 knots. He, too, expected war. Meanwhile, another squadron led by Sir George Warrender was dulling all suspicions of the German fleet by joining in the Kiel Regatta.

At the precise hour that the Tsar was being entertained aboard *Lion*, Archduke Franz Ferdinand and his wife were assassinated at Sarajevo. The heir to the Austro-Hungarian Empire had been removed from the board, and although it seemed impossible that Serbia would light the long-dreaded flames of world conflict, that, indeed, is what was occurring. Vienna's calculated ultimatum to Serbia was sent. A time bomb was ticking. The British squadrons made their respective exits from Kronstadt and the Kiel Canal, unaware that they were returning to take up their battle positions. The days of review and manoeuvre passed quickly in the next month. The North Sea began to consume all attention.

Churchill's speeches on the 1912/13 naval estimates had earned him a brilliant place in naval administration – had brought him to the fore in Parliament, in the press, and in the country. Besides promoting a larger navy that would be the sure shield of the Empire and protect its global trade and interest, Churchill was championing the profit and the power of the United Kingdom in the face of growing and uncertain rivals. All the same, these positions had raised much anguish among his Cabinet colleagues, reinforced the hatreds against him in the Opposition, and made him a figure of praise, critique, and ridicule in the press. But he had also come forward to champion the Fleet – its ships, its officers, and its men. At the CID, the Secretary, Maurice Hankey, watched his actions closely and wrote to Fisher that Churchill's speech introducing the 1912/13 naval estimates 'made a profound impression in the country. He is a really great man, but I expect he got his inspiration from you. He is far more brilliant than McKenna, but probably has not such solid qualities. *A bit impetuous, but extraordinarily hard working.*'[118] Hankey had a long and sometimes tempestuous relationship with Churchill, but his earliest impression was that Churchill was the Navy's champion, which indeed he was.

Churchill worked strenuously to bolster the Fleet, to give it a clear margin in the North Sea and a commendable armament in the Mediterranean. Fate intervened at a vital hour; imperial defence proved a chimera.[119] Canada, the senior dominion, gave Winston his greatest disappointment, for the three dreadnoughts that Sir Robert Borden's Conservative government in Ottawa said it would pay for came to grief on the rocky shoals of that dominion's politics. Careful planning that had made these three ships the sure margin of safety fell victim to an axing measure by the unelected upper chamber in Ottawa, dominated by the cagey Liberals. It was a cruel blow. There was no time for recriminations. Churchill had a good memory. In Admiralty calculations (as requested by him), fortunes had been spent to protect Canada from American invasion over the past century, and now, when the centre of Empire urgently needed help against its greatest challenge at the supreme moment, Canada had removed itself from the equation. Churchill could not say how bitter he was at this, and the shameful matter passed.

Churchill faced many challenges in Parliament in regards to the naval estimates. Aware that many 'economists' and anti-militarists within his own party fought vigorously to keep the costs of British naval supremacy in line with what the nation could afford, he stood resolute. The worry existed, too, that 'bloated' estimates would only play into the hands of German statesmen, admirals, and those in the press calling for an even larger navy. There were quarrels in Cabinet and many heated exchanges, particularly between Churchill and McKenna. Churchill also had to contend with his old friend Lloyd George, the Chancellor of the Exchequer. In a strange reversal of his Agadir speech of warning to Germany, Lloyd George put up strong resistance to the estimates Churchill considered necessary to outdistance Germany in capital ships. They fought doggedly over the estimates, and not until the final moment, when the details were finally agreed, was peace made between them. The Admiralty Board stood firmly behind the First Lord, and the supreme crisis passed when Asquith and Grey sided with Churchill. In the face of a possible division in Cabinet and the necessity of holding a general election, all matters were finally settled. This was Churchill's biggest political challenge to that point, and with the Irish crisis looming, he rose to the occasion. He had proposed a 'naval holiday' but without success. His biggest problem was not sending the Kaiser and Tirpitz a strong message about British naval preparations and readiness; it was dealing with his own party colleagues who fought for retrenchment and holding the line. Churchill had become a big-navy man only out of necessity. The security of the nation and the Empire was his sole concern, and he knew the power of the British Empire rested on the profit and well-being of commerce. He had always backed blue water concerns; he knew the value of British naval supremacy. His opponents saw the matter more narrowly. When the war finally came it was a relief to Churchill, who, like Fisher, had prepared the Navy to face one of its greatest challenges, perhaps the greatest, in its long and celebrated history.

'Was war coming? David Beatty bet me a "fiver" it would not,' the Admiral's chief of staff, Ernle Chatfield, wrote years later of Beatty's views in June 1914.[120] But Chatfield thought differently: 'He longed for it. We had not fought for a century; it was time we repeated the deeds of our forefathers. It would not last long, the financiers told us, and they must know; they had lectured to us as had the economists in our war courses. Besides, at sea we were overwhelmingly strong; well-trained, the sons of our forefathers, longing to prove we could repeat their deeds.'[121]

PART THREE

Misfortunes of War

7

'Commence Hostilities against Germany'

Week of decision: 'We had the drawn sword in our hands'

On 17 and 18 July 1914 'incomparably the greatest assemblage of naval power ever witnessed', as Churchill later described it, lay at anchor at Spithead for review by the King.[1] Here was gathered in the historic anchorage the power and the prestige of the British peoples, and here, too, the essential security to British and neutral seaborne trade and the protection of the outworks of the British Empire. There had been many such naval rendezvous before, but none like this. Fifty-seven battleships and battlecruisers, and many more of various classes and descriptions, tugged at their anchors and moorings in the Solent. Five lines of warships stretched to the horizon. The First Fleet was fully manned, the Second partly so, with crews brought up to full strength, and the Reserve Fleet was specially commissioned for the occasion. Faith in the warships as well as the sailors was unbounded, and if the naval challenge from the Kaiser's Germany amounted to war, as seemed likely, British expectations ran high and were unqualified.

Fisher visited Churchill on board the Admiralty yacht *Enchantress* and had a first-class view of the armada. Next day, to close the review, the royal yacht *Victoria & Albert* anchored off the Nab Lightship, and then the whole Fleet weighed and passed out into the Channel in single line ahead, with bands playing. The scene was memorable, bringing to everyone's attention Britannia's unqualified might. Each ship's company gave three cheers as their ship steamed past the new sailor king, George V. It took six hours for all the ships to process past *Victoria & Albert* doing 15 knots. There was some magnificent ship and squadron handling in the exercises that followed. There were night exercises too, and at other times the great new warships – all shipshape and with brass gleaming, all hands to stations – were on show to politicians, statesmen, and soldiers alike. And when it was all over, 'Britain's bulwarks' retired to anchorages at Portland, Isle of Wight.

209

'This fleet,' observed Admiral Sir Lewis Bayly, 'was the result of many years of building new ships of all classes, in order to have a fleet strong enough to fight against any enemy that might be brought against it. And for years we had all known that a war must come sooner or later.' This was the fleet that Jacky Fisher had built, and several commanders-in-chief, such as Admirals Sir Francis Bridgeman and Sir George Callaghan, had trained it. Admiral Bayly, a senior flag officer at the time, had it right when he wrote years later, 'And great credit is due to Mr. Churchill, who fought the political battle for this end as First Lord of the Admiralty.'[2] Churchill had added to its strength by the great contributions of the 1912/13 naval estimates, the insurance for the future that supremacy at sea would be sustained against all foreseeable naval rivals. For the moment, as Jacky Fisher had assured them in a speech at the Lord Mayor of London's Banquet in 1907, the British could sleep peacefully in their beds. The ships and men of the Royal Navy were their mighty and invincible shield. They were '*nulli secondis*,' he said proudly. 'Our object has been the fighting efficiency of the Fleet and its instant readiness for war; and we have got it.'[3] That was the rosy view from 1907 but a more pronounced claim could be made in 1914. To the Navy's air of invincibility had been added the material and personnel requirements to assure supremacy.

In those same last weeks of July, the paramount issue on the minds of British politicians was the Irish question. Three times the House of Commons had passed a Home Rule bill, which would have given Ireland the right of self-government in its domestic affairs while remaining within the United Kingdom; twice the House of Lords had rejected it. The Parliamentary Act 1911, however, barred the upper chamber from vetoing the measure a third time, thus making Home Rule an apparent reality. Unionists in Ulster, a province in the north of Ireland, were apoplectic at the possibility of Home Rule, and under Sir Edward Carson, their zealous leader, made urgent preparations to proclaim a provisional government for the province that would separate it from the rest of Ireland and retain close ties with Britain. Their harsh words were backed by a quarter of a million guns that had been smuggled into Ulster in the previous twelve months. Meanwhile, Irish Nationalists looked on the prospect of this partition with horror, and they began, with sinister German connivance and gun-running, to arm themselves. The Curragh incident of March 1914, when several officers in a British Army unit in Ulster resigned to avoid taking military action against the Unionists, raised serious doubts about the loyalty of the Army if it were called upon to enforce Home Rule in Ireland. At this juncture, Asquith became Secretary of State for War to keep a firm hand on the situation. A last-ditch conference held at Buckingham Palace on 24 July broke down, and civil disorder in Ireland appeared imminent. Indeed, in those last desperate days before the outbreak of international hostilities, Britain was closer to civil war than at any point since the days of the Jacobites. Churchill decided to deploy the 3rd Battle Squadron within striking distance of Belfast Lough, and spoke of putting 'grave matters to the proof'. Asquith, fearing the consequences of this escalation, took steps to rein in Churchill: the naval orders were cancelled. Other measures aimed to 'coerce' Ulster. But then all of these preoccupations and muddled measures of policy were swept away by a new and sudden reality: the assassination of Archduke Franz Ferdinand was drawing Britain into a continental war.

The timetable had its own fascinating logic. The murder of Archduke Ferdinand and his wife on 28 June at Sarajevo led Vienna to send Serbia an ultimatum on 23 July. The Serbian government sent an unacceptable reply. Within the space of a week, Europe stumbled into war. Austria mobilised against Serbia. Russia mobilised. The German war plan was already in motion. On 24 July Churchill wrote to his wife, Clementine, that Ireland had now become 'a humdrum affair'.[4] In *The World Crisis* he memorably related, 'The parishes of Fermanagh and Tyrone faded back into the mists and squalls of Ireland, and a strange light began immediately, but by perceptible gradations, to fall and grow upon the map of Europe.'[5]

On Saturday, 25 July, Prince Louis of Battenberg, the First Sea Lord, was at the Admiralty reading the papers for the latest news and sifting the intelligence. Cabinet ministers were long accustomed to going to the country at the weekend. Asquith, Grey, and Churchill were all out of London at 6pm on Saturday when the Austrian ultimatum to Serbia expired. Alone in the Admiralty, Battenberg read all the fearful telegrams as one by one they arrived from British embassies abroad. As he wrote on 28 July: 'Ministers with their week-end holidays are incorrigible ... On Monday morning [the 27th] the big fleet at Portland had orders to disperse, demobilize, and give leave. I took it upon myself to countermand everything by telegraph on Sunday afternoon. When the Ministers hurried back late that evening they cordially approved my action, and we had the drawn sword in our hands to back up our urgent advice.'[6] Battenberg reported to the King the action taken.

Churchill, who liked to command centre stage, was not prepared to give Battenberg credit for this pre-emptive action. He contended that he had given the latter instructions over the telephone not to let the Fleet disperse.[7] Battenberg was never one to make public any complaint against his political superior, and his story was not known until a letter in his private correspondence was published in his authorised biography.[8]

That Sunday evening, when Churchill returned to London, it was agreed, in consultation with Grey, to issue a notice that the Fleet had not been dispersed. Churchill hoped that the Kaiser would notice the announcement, and take it as an indication that England was ready for any possible situation.[9] The next day,

Churchill and Battenberg decided they must send the First Fleet, still anchored off the Isle of Wight, to the North Sea. If that fleet were caught off guard in the event of a sudden outbreak of war, it would have been a strategical nightmare. The North Sea would be the next parade ground, as Fisher had forecast. Churchill worried about bringing the matter before the Cabinet, so went directly to 10 Downing Street to reveal his plans to Asquith. The ever-reluctant premier wanted to keep his options open. On other occasions around this time he thought Churchill very bellicose. Now he treated Churchill with almost silent acceptance. Churchill recounted, 'He [Asquith] looked at me with a hard stare, and gave a sort of grunt. I did not require anything else.'[10]

Churchill's primary responsibility was to ready the Navy for any eventuality. As he wrote to Clementine in these last days of July: 'Preparations have a hideous fascination for me ... yet I would do my best for peace, and nothing would induce me wrongfully to strike the blow. I cannot feel that we in this island are in any serious degree responsible for the wave of madness which has swept the mind of Christendom.'[11] In keeping with other intentions and schemes to check the onrush of war, including his proposed but ill-fated 'naval holiday', Churchill made one last try for peace. At the 27 July Cabinet meeting he suggested that all the kings and other heads of state of Europe meet to resolve the problems besetting the nations. Nothing came of his call for a 'Kingly Conference'.[12] Peace was slipping away.

Mobilising the Fleet was not all that was on Churchill's mind in these desperate hours. That same day, Churchill called Admiral Sir George Callaghan, C-in-C of the First Fleet, to the Admiralty. There he told Callaghan that he was to be superseded by Sir John Jellicoe, his second in command. It seems likely that Fisher had a role to play in this, for he had long wanted Jellicoe to have that ultimate sea command in the face of Armageddon. Callaghan was on the eve of his sixty-second year; Churchill thought him too old for the requirements of the Service. Another more indeterminate factor was that Churchill and Battenberg, who did not question Churchill's decision, had concluded that Callaghan's health and apparently diminished physical strength made it doubtful that, should war come, he would be equal to the great strain. Thus it was that the gallant Sir George Callaghan, last of a long line of old admirals since Nelson, was set aside. The matter remained one of secrecy.

Clementine Churchill pressed on her husband to let Callaghan down gently, even offer him a post at the Admiralty. She worried that the various wives of the admirals would prove troublesome in their gossip and subvert the Service. She reminded him of their evil, wicked ways, these women behind the Fleet. In the end, Churchill was too busy or unmindful to attend to Clementine's importunities. However, Callaghan was made C-in-C, The Nore, an important shore-based appointment responsible for trade protection and security of the Thames Estuary.

When the change was in the wind, Vice-Admiral Sir David Beatty, in command of the Battle Cruiser Squadron, who answered directly to Callaghan, launched forth in fury and in warning at Churchill: 'Private – contemplated change rumoured would cause unprecedented disaster. I beg of you to reconsider. Moral effect upon Fleet at such a moment would be worse than a defeat at sea – it creates impossible position for successor whose difficulties would be incalculable. At present confidence of Fleet is high, morale magnificent which would be destroyed by this step.' A copy was telegraphed to the First Sea Lord, Prince Louis of Battenberg, with this additional wording: 'I am sure you will realise national gravity of the question which alone makes me write. Other Flag Officers would be overwhelmed if they knew.'[13] Beatty's advice, predictably (for Churchill was unmoved), went unheeded.

Churchill may have been the main agent of change in this paramount sea command, but the story runs deeper than this: others in high places were accessories. On the evening of 28 July, recounts Jellicoe, who was there, a dinner was given by Lord Morley at the United Services Club, Pall Mall. It seems that Jellicoe was unaware of the underlying motive for the dinner, for, given the company present, it could not be merely a social affair. Churchill and Kitchener were there, and others, including Lord Bryce, recently ambassador to the United States. Jellicoe, who was then Second Sea Lord, does not say what subjects were discussed. But Austria's recent declaration of war on Serbia had brought immediacy to discussions about the future of Europe, and Germany's war aims. All the great powers were readying for war, and those present at the dinner were likely to be wondering if all was as ready as it might be in Britain. In any event, the next day Jellicoe, in a long conversation with Churchill and Battenberg, was told that under 'certain circumstances' he might be appointed commander-in-chief instantly in succession to Admiral Sir George Callaghan.

That very night Jellicoe found himself on a lonely night train speeding north for Wick and the water connection to Scapa. In his possession was a sealed envelope, given him by a naval officer, with instructions not to open the envelope until ordered to do so. He must have wondered what destiny lay in wait. He was a gunnery expert, like Fisher and Sir Percy Scott, and had done well in every assignment and every command. Fisher had praised him to the skies and told Churchill that he would be the next Nelson.

Of short stature and of pleasant disposition, Jellicoe had entered *Britannia* in the customary way and had risen quickly to the top in everyone's professional estimation. He had no enemies in the Service; in fact, quite the opposite. He was much admired by the lower deck. He had been wounded in a shore action during the Boxer Rising, and had been decorated. He commanded the Atlantic Fleet and then was Second Sea Lord for a time, in charge of personnel and appointments. He was aggressive on shipbuilding policy, was familiar with torpedoes and mines, and was at the forefront of the dreadnought revolution. He moved easily in political circles, too, and was respected by Kitchener, Churchill, and others.

Jellicoe showed great confidence on the surface but this hid insecurities from which he could not escape. He was not a Fisher, not a Nelson, and not a Beatty. There was never a more reluctant British admiral in command of a fleet. Unlike Nelson he had no ambitions to take charge and seize the day. Technological innovation had made him conservative in his thinking, so that defensive positions seemed to be more paramount to him than taking the offensive. Then again, he had everything to lose. He knew that one enemy torpedo or mine could sink any British dreadnought. He disliked independent-minded and dynamic admirals, and made his appointments accordingly. A compulsive worrier, he had a deep streak of pessimism. He was cautious to a fault, circumspect in all his activities, and anxious for the well-being of the nation and Empire, and the future of the Navy, but he lacked the essential capacity of risk that every great commander must exercise at the hour of demand.[14] Nelson has said that in combat some matters must be left to chance. Jellicoe sought to control every situation, to minimise risk.

This fault was disclosed early on. From 1 to 3 August, telegrams passed back and forth between Jellicoe and the Admiralty. Jellicoe insisted that moving him from second in command to Commander-in-Chief of the new Grand Fleet would be 'fraught with danger', especially considering how important it was for this gigantic conglomeration of battle units (battle squadrons, cruiser squadrons, destroyer flotillas, minesweepers, and units of naval aviation) to operate smoothly at the outbreak of war. He worried that the officers, petty officers, and lower deck would feel that their high admiral had somehow abandoned them. He also insisted that his opinions were based on national, not personal, reasons, though he was a friend of Callaghan. Throughout 3 August he continued to insist that his replacing Callaghan was inappropriate and potentially disastrous, and also he emphasised the long experience of Callaghan and the loyalty of the Fleet to him. As one of Jellicoe's biographers puts it, Jellicoe's last message to Churchill and Prince Louis Battenberg was 'close to impertinence'. This read: 'Quite impossible to be ready at such short notice. Feel it my duty to warn you emphatically that you court disaster if you carry out intention of changing before I have thorough grip of fleet and situation.'[15] However, Jellicoe's use of the telegraph was in vain. At last an exasperated Churchill told him that he had forty-eight hours before his fleet would set to sea and that at such a juncture, personal feelings could not count.[16] That settled the matter. At the time, Churchill must have wondered about the decision to appoint Jellicoe to the supreme command afloat. Further, he may have doubted Fisher's prescience in believing that Jellicoe would be the best of the British sea kings with war threatening. However, Jellicoe now had his orders, and Churchill wrote to Lady Jellicoe, 'We have absolute confidence in his [Jellicoe's] services and devotion. We shall back him through thick and thin. Thank God we have him at hand.'[17]

When, after joining the flagship *Iron Duke*, Jellicoe met Callaghan in the commander's quarters, Callaghan did not yet know he was being relieved of command, though he took it all in good grace, and retired as conveniently as possible. There was a war on. Some days later, Jellicoe still regretted having to replace Callaghan. To a fellow admiral at the Admiralty he wrote: 'I hope never to live again through such a time as I had from Friday to Tuesday. My position was horrible. I did my best but could not stop what I believe is a grave error. I trust sincerely it won't prove to be so. Of course each day I get more into the saddle. But the tragedy of the news to the Commander-in-Chief was past belief, and it was almost worse for me.'[18]

Had Fisher misled Churchill about Jellicoe? That is the burning question. There will be discussion of that for time immemorial. From this historian's viewpoint, Jellicoe was not the man for the job, though the additional question arises: who would have been better? Beatty? I am not sure; nor was Professor Marder. As that distinguished historian of sober judgements put it half a century after Jutland's terrible unravelling of events and consequences, 'Montagues and Capulets still abound.'[19] No easy answers are to be found.

Sir John Jellicoe remains a fascinating but conflicted figure. In his life there is the element of Greek tragedy. So much was expected of him but he delivered so little. Jellicoe biographer John Winton writes, 'Jellicoe was the right choice undoubtedly. Churchill had made the right decision, but it took a man of real moral courage to do it.'[20] Correlli Barnett's description is on the mark:

> In a service dominated by social life, Jellicoe was a keen and clever professional; in a service that truly regarded guns as objects that made ships dirty when they fired, he was profoundly knowledgeable on gunnery and shells. Jellicoe was the modest son of a master of the merchant marine. His mind was a well-ordered filing system of detail, reflected by his small neat person, the tight mouth, and the watchful, calm brown eyes that looked out steadily past the prominent nose. His manner was cool, controlled and always polite. This self-containment rested on profound self-confidence. Above all, like Fisher, he believed in the supreme importance of big guns.[21]

We can venture farther than this: Jellicoe was reluctant to take the supreme sea command at the critical hour and was forced into an obligation he did not seek. He wanted to assume that obligation on his terms only, and therein lay the problem. As great an administrator as he certainly was, and as great a sailor (much adored by the officers and men of the Fleet), in this historian's opinion he was not the right man for the tasks at hand. Everything that he faced made him cautious, timid, or fearful. Fisher had to keep propping him up. This did not inspire confidence, as we shall see.

The removal of Callaghan came as a great shock to the Fleet. Senior officers talked of making a formal protest, one that would have gone eventually to the King, though nothing came of it. In any event, Fisher and Churchill now had their supreme sea commander in his post and perhaps none too soon. Jellicoe was left to do his work, to prepare the Grand Fleet for action.

In the meantime, at seven on the morning of 28 July, one by one the ships of the British First Fleet under Vice-Admiral Sir George Warrender had slipped from Portland and steered in majestic procession for a destination known only to the flag officers. It is said that the column of ships stretched for eighteen miles. Each of the ships sailed that morning in misty conditions, and a course was made southwest, out of sight of land, so that no one could spy out the intended direction of the Fleet. Nightfall came late in these summer latitudes. The Fleet then altered course to the east, into the English Channel, keeping toward the French coast. But the movements of the dreadnoughts could hardly go unnoticed, so massive was the armada hastening north at high speed. A German mail-carrier, steaming vigorously up the Channel and chancing upon the scene, stood by while the long line of ships passed by. Only then did it continue its voyage home, bearing the news that the British Fleet was at sea. This was not the only strange occurrence. During the night, while passing Dover with all lights out and ships darkened (and presuming to be going undetected), the Fleet was lit up by searchlights from shore – an omen. These 'gigantic castles of steel', Churchill wrote later, bore with them into the broadening North Sea 'the safeguard of considerable affairs'.[22]

The next day the great armada moored at Scapa Flow. On the morning of 30 July the Admiralty received a signal that the First Fleet had arrived at its war station. That day, Fisher happened to be in the Admiralty building. Churchill heard that he was there and invited the admiral into the War Room. There he told him that the First Fleet was now at its battle stations in the North Sea. Fisher's face must have brightened in anticipation at the news. Churchill later wrote: 'I told him what we had done and his delight was wonderful to see.'[23]

On 1 August Churchill asked the Cabinet for full naval mobilisation. That meant the Fleet would not be dispersed and the Reserves not stood down. The Cabinet refused to accede to Churchill's request. Perhaps this was a response to Churchill's apparent warmongering. According to Asquith, at that meeting Churchill had been 'very bellicose'. Even so, all around Whitehall the mood darkened quickly. Hour by hour the international situation passed through violent convulsions. That same day the Great Powers mobilised their armies.

Later that evening, Churchill returned to Admiralty House to relax with friends, including Max Aitken (later Lord Beaverbrook) over a hand of bridge. Recent intelligence had indicated a postponement of the German ultimatum to Russia. Churchill brushed this aside. The German menace, he said, had to be faced. His logic, in Beaverbrook's words, was that 'it would be impossible for British statesmen ever to plan out a peaceful progress for the nation until it had been settled once and for all if Germany was going to control the German Ocean. You were not really avoiding a war – you were simply postponing it.' This formed Churchill's clear view. The game continued. A clerk brought in a huge dispatch box, and Churchill instinctively reached for his key to open it. A single sheet of paper was produced, which seemed far too big for the message written on it: 'Germany has declared war on Russia.' Churchill had been right, and a war against Russia was a war against France. The triple entente – Britain, Russia, and France – was now forged in iron. Churchill passed this sombre news to his guests. He then asked his servant for a lounge coat, taking his dress coat from his back. He said not another word. Beaverbrook was instructed to take over his bridge hand, but, as he says, it was hard to concentrate on the game at hand.[24] Churchill hastened to Downing Street and asked Asquith for full naval mobilisation. Asquith would take no position. Churchill interpreted the prime minister's lack of comment as an indication that he would not stop Churchill.[25]

'Churchill makes a picture for me at this critical moment when he got the message which meant war,' recounted Beaverbrook, who provided this vital witness of history unfolding:

He left the room quickly, as in duty bound, and forthwith the Navy was mobilized in defiance of the decisions taken by the Cabinet early on that day. History has recorded the dramatic directions given by the First Lord that night.

For my own part, I simply saw a man who was receiving long-expected news. He was not depressed; he was not elated; he was not surprised. He did not put his head between his hands, as many another eminent man might well have done, and exclaim to high heaven that his world was coming to an end. Certainly he exhibited no fear or uneasiness. Neither did he show any signs of joy. He went straight out like a man going to a well-accustomed job.

In fact, he had foreseen everything that was going to happen so far that his temperament was in no way upset by the realisation of his forecast. We have suffered at times from Mr. Churchill's bellicosity. But what profit the nation derived at that crucial moment from the capacity of the First Lord of the Admiralty for grasping and dealing with the war situation![26]

At 1.25am on 2 August, a Sunday, Churchill sent the order to mobilise the Navy. This had untold advantages in putting in place, and certainly not too soon, the means of strangulation – a denial of the sea on which the outcome of the war would, in the end, be determined. As military historian Basil Liddell Hart put it, if the historian of the future were to select one day upon which the future course of the war could be decided, it would be 2 August, when Churchill readied the Fleet and ordered it to its war stations.[27]

Churchill, with his keen strategic sense, had long recognised that war could not be averted and raced well ahead of his colleagues in seeing the necessity of readying for war. His seals of office alone demanded it. He faced the obvious, doing so more realistically than the prime minister and many others in the Cabinet, who were slow to accept the realities. Perhaps they were hopeful the scenario then developing would quickly enter some ameliorative end state. But when war is imminent, fleets usually go to sea, to their war stations. Although many diplomatic triumphs can be achieved when the Fleet is lying at anchor, in this case the close geographical proximity of the British Isles to Germany necessitated positioning the Fleet in the most effective place to meet challenges from the enemy. Complete control of the English Channel was the requirement; coupled with this was the need to hold the North Sea against German raids on England and Scotland. While these objectives were being pursued, the Navy had to ensure the safe and timely passage of merchant ships coming to and from its shores. The security of the British Empire rested on this complex and difficult set of requirements. The Navy and Churchill stood at the centre of the whole scheme.

If we praise Churchill and Battenberg for readying and mobilising the Fleet at this momentous hour, we must not fail to understand that Churchill's colleagues, except Grey at the Foreign Office, whom Churchill consulted on the matter of mobilisation, had no clear view of the distant horizons from their same vantage point. Each of his Cabinet colleagues expressed reservations about what seemed to be a rush into war. None of them wanted war with Germany. It was natural that those sitting around the Cabinet table reflected the cautiousness of the country. They knew of the great perils then facing the Continent, and they were mindful of how such a calamity might draw their nation into a general war. In consequence, in an atmosphere of high stress, when it seemed as if the political organisation of the country might rupture, they unsurprisingly held out to the very end before the fatal decision had to be taken. War might bring down the government, for its whole rationale was based on the maintenance of peace and prosperity. This was a war not of Britain's choosing.

One of the few interventionists, Sir Edward Grey at the Foreign Office strongly believed that Britain must support France in any European conflict. He alone knew how deeply engaged the British had become as a result of his conversations with the French. As a result of military discussions, the French believed that Britain had a moral responsibility to enter the war. When Grey told the distraught French ambassador Cambon that the British would be staying out of a continental commitment, he received the stark reply that according to 1912 arrangements between the Admiralty and the French navy, the British were morally obliged to keep the German navy out of the Channel. The French had denuded their ports of naval defences and were trusting to the Royal Navy. Next day, Cambon asked David Lloyd George all about the military and naval conferences between the two powers. 'All our plans have been arranged in common. Our General Staffs have consulted. You have seen all our schemes and preparations,' he exclaimed.[28] These representations led to a change of British official heart. Grey had stated privately that he would resign if Britain stood aloof. Asquith supported his Foreign Secretary, deciding that he would not preside over a Cabinet that did not live up to its obligations. The question of protecting the frontiers of Belgium was then of lesser importance than the compelling naval obligation to France.

Most members of the Cabinet had no idea of the extent of the obligations that Britain had entered into just two years earlier. Many believed that they retained complete freedom to decide their role in any European war, and some used that belief to argue that they should remain neutral. As Hankey told Esher on 31 July, 'The great question as to whether we shall do what our War Office friends want or not is, I believe, quite undecided, and it must be settled at the Cabinet and not here (C.I.D.).'[29] Leading the anti-war faction was Lord John Morley, practically the last free trade, non-interventionist Liberal in politics, who had inherited from W E Gladstone a disdain for power politics. In this Cabinet conflict, the position of Lloyd George was crucial. If the Welsh Radical sided with the anti-war faction, the government would be likely to fall. If, however, he sided with Grey, enough of the Cabinet might hold together to allow it to enter the war relatively united. Churchill attempted to convince Lloyd George of the latter necessity. In Cabinet meetings he passed a series of notes to the Chancellor of the Exchequer, using a variety of arguments to gain his support. Relentless, Churchill also sent Major Alfred Ollivant, RE, a staff officer with wide appreciation of current difficulties (he was then the War Office liaison officer at the Admiralty), to Lloyd George to 'lecture' him on the European situation.[30] Forming a coalition government would have solved this matter, although not all problems, and Churchill was at the forefront of urging such a reconstitution of authority in July and August. The lack of trust for him on both sides of the House stymied his efforts.

'Mr. Churchill was the leader of the War party in the Cabinet,' recounted Beaverbrook, and the reason for this was that his position at the Admiralty had 'long inured him to regard Germany much as a man of business regards a rival who is always cutting his prices.' He was uneasy with his pacifist colleagues in Cabinet. They eyed him with suspicion and disdain, and watched warily for any unauthorised action on his part. They feared his overreaching powers and his vaunted ambition.

Churchill would have been a natural ally of the Conservatives and their leader, the sober-minded, clear-thinking Andrew Bonar Law, but that was not to be, for Churchill and Bonar Law were personal opposites and rivals. Moreover, Churchill's defection from the Conservatives could not be forgotten. If there were Cabinet colleagues who looked for Churchill's misstep and undoubted fall in consequence, there were many on the Conservative benches who had already decided that he must go. They despised him on grounds of disloyalty and his opportunistic disposition. They thought of him as a wild card and a turncoat, not to be trusted. Some hoped that his actions would bring about the government's downfall. It was a vain hope. For the present they, under their leader Bonar Law, were prepared to bide their time, and went about upsetting Churchill's plans whenever opportunity offered. Churchill showed rancour in his relations with Bonar Law, and was patronising in his comments up to the outbreak of the war. 'Churchill never did justice to Bonar Law's intellect and Bonar Law always underrated Churchill's character.' Bonar Law never wanted Churchill as an ally and preferred him only as an antagonist. He was suspicious of Churchill. Thus when Churchill sent F E Smith (Lord Birkenhead), as an agent to try to effect a coalition on the eve of the war, Bonar Law refused Churchill's invitation to dinner. Churchill thought that if some Liberal Cabinet ministers resigned on the question of intervention in the war, their positions would have to be filled, and he contended that the Conservatives might be interested in forming this alliance. Bonar Law had now to consider the prospects of this, and having consulted Lord Lansdowne and Arthur Balfour on the matter, determined to tell Asquith that they would be ready to see him whenever convenient. Asquith was not to be moved: the meddling Churchill had failed in the attempt to reconstruct the government, and whatever administration he had in mind with himself as its leader had to be set aside. His jockeying for influence did not endear him to Asquith and made him a source of greater suspicion to Bonar Law and his colleagues.

Into this complicated scenario arrived the most eminent British soldier of the age, Field Marshal Horatio Herbert Kitchener, 1st Earl Kitchener, on annual leave from his post as consul in Egypt. At lunch at the Admiralty on 31 July, when news came of Russian mobilisation in response to Austria's moves against Serbia, Kitchener told Churchill that if France fell, Britain's power would never again be sustainable. If Germany controlled the Continent, British power and influence would be terminated. Asquith, who was present, said little but his distress was apparent.[31]

At Churchill's urging, Asquith appointed Kitchener Secretary of State for War, the first general in the Cabinet since the Duke of Wellington. His reputation as a soldier, administrator, and proconsul was unexcelled. His magic lay in his success in the field – in the Sudan, South Africa, India and Egypt – and also in his being little known at home, for when he arrived at Dover he had been away for four decades. Born and schooled in Ireland, a Royal Engineer by training, he had defeated the Mahdi in the Sudan. Then he had suppressed the Boer insurgents and ended their quest for autonomy. Something of an eastern mysticism hung over him, which, with his shyness and reticence, gave him a distant and private persona. This, with his elusive charm and immense reputation as the most famous of all Empire soldiers, made England seem safe in his hands. Arrived at his desk, he scratched out 50,000 as the suggested number of men to be immediately called up and wrote in 300,000. Alone among his military colleagues, he added to his prestige by his pronouncement that this would be a war of many years, not over by Christmas. He was also prophetic on the matter of the scope of the war. It was to be a war of siege. As Secretary of State for War he had three powers: overseeing normal wartime operations in the War Office, raising the 'New Armies' and taking measures for the supply of military material, and supervising actual operations in the field. Here we note, in advance of our narrative, that these obligations increased with time. Kitchener was unable to delegate. Press agitation by late 1914, and certainly in early 1915, was hurtful to Kitchener (unlike Fisher and Churchill, he despised the press) and spelled office reorganisation and diminished duties for the great field marshal.[32] But he was in on the planning of the Dardanelles, as we shall see, and also was the gatekeeper for sending out British divisions. Asquith gave him little succour, and eventually Lloyd George became Minister of Munitions, a new portfolio hived off from that of the Secretary of State for War. As with Fisher and Churchill, the shadows were forming around Kitchener, the political darkness deepening with the days and weeks. Kitchener, Fisher, and Churchill all suffered the catastrophic shift of the May 1915 Cabinet reorganisation, and although we are pre-empting our narrative here, it bears keeping in mind that the ground was quickly shifting under all these powerful leaders.

With Britain on the brink of war, it was natural for the Cabinet to waver; a war against Germany, so long avoided and so little sought, had to have a legal and thus a moral purpose. On 3 August Germany declared war on France. The argument for intervention steeled once it became crystal clear that Germany intended to violate Belgium's neutrality as part of its offensive against France. Here was an issue to rally the undecided to the war banner. Britain had a long tradition of ensuring that a hostile power did not occupy the opposite Channel shore. From the eighteenth century, if not before, the continental balance of power – checks and balances – had been the watchword of British foreign policy-making. Britain had a written pledge that guaranteed the independence of Belgium, something far more concrete than the nebulous assurances to France. Almost everyone in the Cabinet believed that Britain must intervene on Belgium's behalf. Significantly, Lloyd George took the lead in attempting to persuade the anti-war ministers to remain in Cabinet. He pointed out that if the German army proceeded with its great sweeping plan, its far, outside arm must pass through the neutral territory of the King of Belgium – in violation of a sacred treaty to which Britain was signatory and guarantor. In the end, Lord Morley, almost alone in his protest, resigned. Later that day, Churchill received from Asquith and Grey permission to begin full Anglo-French naval collaboration, especially for the defence of the Channel. The Cabinet was not consulted. As Churchill wrote in *The World Crisis*, 'the King's ships were at sea'.

On 3 August the King of the Belgians appealed to the great powers to uphold Belgium's neutrality. That afternoon Grey spoke in the House of Commons. He made clear that there was no technical reason requiring Britain to go to the aid of France but that Britain had guaranteed Belgium's borders by treaty. Grey detailed the prospects should Britain not declare war: the subjugation of Belgium and Holland, the fall of France, and the domination of Western Europe by one great and hostile power. Britain ought not to run away from its obligations and its interests, he said. Once he had finished, he sat down. The House greeted his speech with cheering, and all of a sudden the public will of Britain backed the future war effort. It was Grey and not Churchill who was the deciding force in the making of war. Larger measures than sea-power predominance were at stake.

Germany drew the sword. National ambition was determined by military command. Of all the nations and empires that geared up for war, some instituting conscription, only Germany had a war plan with specific details and requirements – the Schlieffen Plan, described later in this chapter – and as the clock advanced toward the British deadline of 11pm GMT on 4 August, the scheme had already and automatically been put in place. Even at this late hour, Germany could have halted its progress but it did not do so. Its armies were in motion as the trains trundled out of the many garrison stations and assembly points, crossing through into Luxembourg and then headed for Belgium and the frontiers with France. The juggernaut rolled on to Armageddon.

On 4 August all Britain waited expectantly for word of whether Germany would violate Belgium's border. Asquith, Grey, McKenna (the Home Secretary), and Lloyd George were in the Cabinet room as the minute hand of Big Ben approached the fatal hour. 'In the War Room of the Admiralty, where I sat waiting,' Churchill recalled, 'one could hear the ticking clock tick. From Parliament Street came the murmurs of the crowd; but they sounded distant and the world seemed very still.' Churchill waited a seeming eternity for the reply to arrive from Berlin. Nothing came. At last the hands of the clock moved to 11pm. The deadline had been reached.

The windows of the Admiralty were thrown wide open in the warm night air. Under the roof from which Nelson had received his orders were gathered a small group of Admirals and Captains and a cluster of clerks, pencil in hand, waiting. Along the Mall from the direction of the Palace the sound of an immense concourse singing 'God Save the King' floated in. On this deep wave there broke the chimes of Big Ben; and, as the first stroke of the hour boomed out, a rustle of movement swept across the room.

From the Admiralty, Churchill's telegram 'Commence Hostilities against Germany' was flashed to Royal Navy ships and establishments across the globe. Churchill went outside into the warm summer night. 'I thank God I could feel also in that hour that our country was guiltless of all intended purpose of war.'[33] From a newsman's point of view it had been 'a difficult business to disentangle', as Geoffrey Dawson of The Times wrote in his diary, 'things moved so quick at the last ... W[inston] in v[ery] good form – a cheering crowd outside the Adm[iralty].'[34]

Churchill at last had his war. He hurried across Horseguards Parade to 10 Downing Street. Lloyd George recalled Churchill's striking appearance: 'Winston dashed into the room radiant, his face bright, his manner keen, one word pouring out on another how he was going to send telegrams to the Mediterranean, the North Sea, and God knows where. You could see he was a really happy man.'[35] Lloyd George was not alone in witnessing Churchill's excitement at the outbreak of hostilities. Churchill is said to have remarked, recounted Margot Asquith, 'Oh, this delicious war!' His ardour did not dampen: in February 1915 Violet Asquith recorded him as saying, 'I think a curse should rest on me – because I love this war. I know it's smashing & shattering the lives of thousands every moment – & yet – I can't help it – I enjoy every second of it.'[36]

As the Admiralty flashed its signal to the Fleet, bases, dockyards, and all outworks of the British Empire, Sir Edward Grey, the Foreign Secretary, watching from his windows in the Foreign Office as the lights were springing out in the gathering dusk, said to a friend, 'The lamps are going out all over Europe; we shall not see them again in our lifetime.'[37] Indeed, in the days leading up to the British ultimatum to Germany, Asquith wrote that he heard a 'distant roaring', and that 'war or anything that seems likely to lead to war is always popular with the London mob.' To which he added: 'You remember Sir R[obert] Walpole's remark, "Now they are ringing their bells; in a few weeks they'll be wringing their hands."'[38]

It is a fact that Churchill had forecast this war and how it would unfold. Fisher had done something similar, and he reminded Churchill of his own prescient memorandum of three years previous that had accurately foreshadowed the course of the first forty days of the war: 'Your memorandum of AUGUST 1911 is both astonishing and exhilarating! *It makes one trust your further forecast!* I also have a minor coincidence! A friend sends me a letter of mine also written in *August 1911* saying that Armageddon would begin in August 1914 and that Jellicoe would be our Admiralissimo!'[39] We return to this matter in due course.

The Navy's first act upon the declaration of war was to establish a presence at the two gateways through which trade reached Germany. The Germans, so strong in torpedo craft, did not hazard those smaller vessels any more than they would their capital ships. Tirpitz, overruled, could not send the fleet to sea to pursue its great aim and object. Thus the English Channel, in British control, offered safe passage for the intended British Expeditionary Force.

As shadows of war fell across the British Empire, Churchill's immediate attention was not consumed by the dispositions of the Grand Fleet, lying at its war station, and its new if reluctant commander, but was necessarily drawn to the unfolding Mediterranean situation. He had a prominent part in the scenario developing there even before the outbreak of hostilities. His unwitting role in the decision taken by the political leadership of the Ottoman Empire, notably its powerful centre, Turkey, with its rising national aspirants, 'the young Turks', owes much to Churchill's actions in snatching away from them two dreadnoughts destined for Ottoman ownership. This is our next subject of interest and concern.

'The most damnable episode of the war': the escape of Goeben *and* Breslau

In waging a naval war, Churchill's hands were tied until hostilities were declared. Gone were the days of Fisher's madcap scheme to 'Copenhagen' the German fleet lying at its moorings in German lairs. In the circumstances, he had to await the unfolding of events or turn his mind to other possibilities and concerns. For some months, as First Lord of the Admiralty, he had been considering the state of naval rivalries in the Mediterranean. He was particularly worried about the Ottoman Empire and its fulcrum of authority, Turkey, with its major city at Constantinople (later Istanbul) on the Bosporus, reached from the Mediterranean via the narrow and difficult Dardanelles, and linked within the Eurasian continent by the Sea of Marmara and the Black Sea. Germany had made a bid for influence here, with the Berlin to Baghdad railway and many other concessions and gifts. In the circumstances, Churchill was already conniving to upset these existing arrangements, and his position at the Admiralty gave him a unique and independent advantage to do so. Austria–Hungary had three dreadnoughts and an assortment of lesser vessels, a danger to British and French navies, particularly if Italy could be brought on side (in the event, this proved impossible).

As the Great Powers moved inexorably toward war, Germany and Britain vied for the allegiance of the Ottoman Empire. The British expressed optimism, for already there existed significant spheres of Anglo-Turkish co-operation. After the Ottoman defeat in the First Balkan War in 1912, Admiral Sir Arthur Henry Limpus, who headed the British naval mission to Constantinople, undertook to reorganise and retrain the Ottoman navy. This friendship was to have been further cemented with the delivery, in 1914, of the modern battleships *Reshadieh* and *Sultan Osman I*, ordered and constructed in British shipyards. The pair had been completed by July of that year, and at the end of that month Ottoman sailors were in Britain waiting to take control of their ships. These powerful instruments of sea power would guarantee them a newly exalted status in the Mediterranean and Black Seas. And they were precious symbols of Anglo-Turkish friendship, dear to the Ottoman Empire.

Churchill had other ideas – with unintended but disastrous consequences. On 29 July, under a carefully calculated scheme devised in advance of Cabinet assent, he ordered the builders to prevent the ships from leaving their shipyards. He had previously asked the Foreign Office if any objection existed to holding the ships in British waters. The Foreign Office replied conveniently that it was an Admiralty matter. In consequence, Churchill had a free hand. On 31 July the Cabinet accepted Churchill's arguments that the two dreadnoughts should be taken over by the Royal Navy. Under the circumstances it was deemed unsafe to release two powerful battleships to a still neutral state that could end up in the hands of possible enemies. The ships were quietly added to the strength of the Grand Fleet, with *Reshadieh* being renamed HMS *Erin*, and *Sultan Osman I* renamed HMS *Agincourt*.[40] In Constantinople, however, the Ottoman government was rightly infuriated by what seemed a hasty and insulting British action. Raising money for the battleships had been a great national cause, and all plans for legitimacy as a new naval power had vanished by the single stroke of Churchill's action. Churchill had perhaps underestimated the Ottoman response. However, British security on and over the seas against the German challenge now trumped all other considerations. The die was cast. And another urgent matter commanded the attention of the First Lord of the Admiralty and the Admiralty staff.

In the days leading up to the outbreak of war, Churchill's focus turned to two powerful warships comprising the German squadron that had been at Pola, the Austrian naval base on the Adriatic, since the outbreak of the crisis. These were the battlecruiser *Goeben* and the light cruiser *Breslau*. *Goeben*, a modern vessel mounting ten 11in guns and a powerful secondary armament of 5.9in guns, could make, with boilers in excellent condition, 26 knots.[41] In Rear-

Admiral Wilhelm Souchon the German squadron possessed an energetic and imaginative leader. This pair of German warships had an importance even beyond their actual strength due to the threat they posed in the Mediterranean. The Mediterranean theatre was crucial to Entente operations. Not only was it the British lifeline to India and the Middle East; it was also essential for the French war plans on the Western Front to transport the XIXème Corps from Algeria to metropolitan France. Vice-Admiral Augustin Boué de Lapeyrère, commander of the French fleet in the Mediterranean, had as his primary task the escort of these important transports.

The French fleet, largest in the Mediterranean, consisted of one dreadnought and fifteen older battleships, six cruisers, and two dozen destroyers. However, none of these could match the firepower or the speed of *Goeben*. The British force – in two squadrons – consisted of Fisher's three powerful battlecruisers, *Inflexible* (flag), *Indefatigable*, and *Indomitable*, under Vice-Admiral Sir Archibald Berkeley Milne, C-in-C, Mediterranean, and four armoured cruisers, four light cruisers, and sixteen destroyers, the 1st Cruiser Squadron, all under command of Rear-Admiral Sir Ernest C T Troubridge. Each of the British battlecruisers was inferior to the German quarry in firepower, though each sported eight 12in guns and could do 28 knots at a pinch, thought sufficient to overhaul the Germans in a stern chase. Despite the convention between Britain and France of 1912, in which the British Mediterranean Fleet had been greatly reduced in strength, only the British naval units possessed the firepower and expected speed to prevent German attacks on British shipping and French troop transports.[42]

In the circumstances, it might reasonably be expected that these forces had the capability to track down and destroy two less powerful enemy naval units. This was Fisher's assumption. Churchill had no doubt that this task must be effected and was prepared for an intervention on the eve of war. He was hungry for instant action. But who were the British commanders, and did they have the instinct to trap and engage the enemy? Some judged Milne, the senior British admiral in the Mediterranean, a lightweight. As noted in Chapter 5, Fisher was shocked and outraged when Churchill gave Milne this command in 1912. Milne, Fisher suspected, had backed Beresford. Troubridge stood higher in estimation, but in the days ahead, Fisher's reservations would be borne out not just for Milne, but for Troubridge as well.

New communications technology favoured Churchill's instincts of command and control. Whenever possible he took up his place in the War Room so as to direct the naval units as required. Through coded messages sent by cable or wireless transmission, he was directly in contact with admirals afloat. He sent a stream of these messages to Milne. However, they were so changeable as time and circumstances unfolded that the Commander-in-Chief, Mediterranean, may have withered under the assault, or was otherwise unable to respond quickly. And it must be remembered that because Troubridge answered to Milne, messages to him had to be relayed to, and new commands issued from, Milne's flagship.

On 30 July the Admiralty learned that the two German warships had sailed from Pola. Churchill immediately signalled Milne:

> Should war break out ... your first task should be to aid the French in the transportation of their African Army by covering, and if possible, bringing to action individual fast German ships, particularly *Goeben*, which may interfere with that transportation ... Do not at this stage be brought to action against superior forces except in combination with the French as part of a general battle. The speed of your squadrons is sufficient to enable you to choose your moment.[43]

At the same time, Milne was told to husband his forces. Churchill later explained that, as 'superior forces', he had in mind the Austrian fleet, with its heavily armed ships. Churchill was exaggerating this difficulty, for the Austrian fleet hardly entered into the Admiralty's calculations at this point. On 2 August, acting on advice from the British consul at Taranto that *Goeben* had been seen there heading southwest, Churchill again telegraphed Milne: '"Goeben" must be shadowed by two battle-cruisers. Approach [to] Adriatic must be watched by cruisers and destroyers. Remain near Malta yourself. It is believed that Italy will remain neutral but you cannot yet count absolutely on this knowledge.'[44]

Churchill, during these darkening hours, clearly intended by these instructions that the two battlecruisers should hunt down and engage *Goeben*. Another vessel, *Chatham*, was deployed from Malta to search the Strait of Messina, but too late: six hours before this *Goeben* had already left. 'Follow her and shadow her wherever she goes and be ready to act upon declaration of war which appears probable and imminent.'[45] That was Churchill's third and last order to Milne. As for Milne, he had no idea where the German ship was, where it was sailing to, and what its ultimate destination might be. It never crossed anyone's mind that it could be going to Constantinople, via the Dardanelles.

As the hours passed slowly towards the expiry of the British ultimatum to Germany on 4 August, Churchill's hands were tied. He and Battenberg were eager for action, painfully powerless to act. Afloat, the British naval commanders were similarly restrained. All they could do was shadow the enemy – if they could find the German cruisers.

In the circumstances, all initiative lay with the German commander, Admiral Souchon. On 2 August *Goeben* and *Breslau* arrived at Messina, Sicily. A narrowing window of opportunity presented itself. Late on the 3rd he made a lightning dash from Messina. On the 4th *Goeben* shelled Philippeville, and *Breslau* targeted Bône, both on the Algerian coast. As the ships returned to

Messina to coal, they passed within range of the British battlecruisers *Indefatigable* and *Indomitable*. These two ships had been detached from Troubridge's force to sail to Gibraltar to bar exit from the Strait. The British, necessarily observing strict neutrality, could not open fire. Thus, the two squadrons passed each other on reciprocal courses at 8,000yds, guns manned but still trained fore and aft. Once past, the two big British ships swung around and shadowed the Germans as they steamed back to Messina.

When word of this encounter reached the Admiralty, Churchill telegraphed: 'Very good. Hold her. War imminent.' Later, Churchill wrote expansively of these tense hours:

> Throughout this long summer afternoon three great ships, hunted and hunters, were cleaving the clear waters of the Mediterranean in tense and oppressive calm. At any moment the *Goeben* could have been smitten by sixteen 12-inch guns firing nearly treble her own weight of metal. At the Admiralty we suffered the tortures of Tantalus. At about 5 o'clock Prince Louis observed that there was still time to sink the *Goeben* before dark.[46]

Believing a German attack on French transports could happen at any time, Churchill issued new instructions to Milne to engage *Goeben* if she attacked the French transports. Seeking assurance, the First Lord asked Asquith and Grey to approve his action. This was authorised but then met complications. At a Cabinet meeting, the First Lord explained why he believed immediate action was necessary. Faced with the obviously belligerent position of Churchill, who wanted pre-emptive rights in a war against Germany, the prime minister had to take a resisting, legalistic position. Britain would act by the book in the international law of war. Thus it was that the Cabinet refused to grant permission to attack *Goeben* until the ultimatum had expired. Grey backed Asquith on this. The heated nature of that Cabinet meeting, the last held before the old order of Europe came to a crashing halt, is hinted at in Asquith's memoir:

> We had an interesting Cabinet, as we got the news that the Germans had entered Belgium and had announced that if necessary they would push their way through by force of arms. This simplifies matters. So we sent the Germans an ultimatum to expire at midnight requesting them to give a like assurance with the French that they would respect Belgian neutrality. They have invented a story that the French were meditating an invasion of Belgium and that they were only acting in self-defence, a manifest and transparent lie. Winston, who has got on all his war-paint, is longing for a sea-fight in the early hours of the morning to result in the sinking of the *Goeben*. The whole thing fills me with sadness. The House took the fresh news to day very calmly and with a good deal of dignity, and we got through the business by half-past four.[47]

In the face of the Cabinet's decision, Churchill had no power. He informed all the King's ships at sea that no action was to be taken until after 11pm GMT on 4 August. To Milne, he signalled that his latest instruction cancelled his authorisation to engage *Goeben*. He also informed Milne that as Italy had declared neutrality, this was to be respected, and no British warships were to sail within six miles of the Italian coast. Battenberg pleaded with Churchill to allow an attack before nightfall. He did so in vain. The First Lord's hands were tied.

Thus it was that the German ships returned safely to Messina, arriving early on the 5th, in part because the order forbidding a belligerent's violation of Italian waters precluded any pursuit through the strait separating the Italian mainland from Sicily. In any event, Milne, believing that his primary objective was to cover the French transports, deployed his battlecruisers to the west of Sicily, leaving them completely out of position to chase Souchon's vessels should they attempt to sail eastwards. Thus the Germans made good their escape. The British squadron could not follow, hamstrung, as it was, by inappropriate and hastily composed orders. International law only restrains belligerent vessels from fighting in neutral waters. Milne should have immediately protested that restriction. Churchill stated in *The World Crisis* that if the Commander-in-Chief had questioned the order, it would have been immediately rescinded. Milne, in his authority as Commander-in-Chief, Mediterranean, should have either questioned the order's wisdom or, *in extremis*, have had the moral courage to disobey it. The fact that he did neither showed serious weakness in the administration and command system upon the outbreak of war.[48] Blind obedience to orders curtailed any risk-taking. Milne played strictly by the book.

Meanwhile, the German admiralty staff in Berlin in the early hours of 4 August sent Souchon orders to sail from Messina to Constantinople with all dispatch. The British Admiralty intercepted this intelligence but, strangely, had no capacity to decipher the communication. In the circumstances, it relied heavily on the advice and knowledge of the British ambassador to the Porte, Sir Louis Mallet, and on a former consular officer in Constantinople, Gerald Fitzmaurice, who knew more about the intrigues of that city than any other Briton. However, when Fitzmaurice was ordered back to London in 1914 in consequence of stern representations from Berlin (the German government had argued that his activities were not conducive to Anglo-German friendship, and the Foreign Office, with nary a whimper, obliged), the Admiralty was cut off from a vital source of military intelligence. Had this information been available, it would have been possible to intercept the German warships and possibly shatter the German-Ottoman alliance before it took root.[49] On 4 August Berlin also advised Souchon by wireless message that an alliance had been concluded with the Ottoman Empire two days earlier (the Allies did not know this until much later).[50] And to add to the potent pressures to proceed eastwards, the Italian government warned Souchon that, in view of its neutrality, it would intern the two cruisers if they did not leave harbour when coaling was completed.

At 5pm on 6 August Souchon, having signed his last will and testament, cleared for action and, with his bands playing, slipped out of Messina.[51] He sailed into uncertain seas. He was alone, having discretionary powers as to what passage to take or when he should arrive at Constantinople – if the Ottomans should let him in. Berlin nervously expressed concern over the reception he might get from the Ottomans if he arrived prematurely at the Dardanelles. Austria might yet remain neutral in the coming war, which would make Pola an unacceptable destination for *Goeben* and *Breslau*. After apprising Souchon of the state of affairs, the German Admiralty gave him freedom to make the choice. He concluded that the addition of his two ships to the Austrian fleet would make little difference in the Adriatic, but his arrival at the Dardanelles could have a decisive result. He decided to proceed east toward the Aegean. The latitude given Souchon stands in obvious contrast to the detailed and often contradictory orders received by the British naval commanders on the spot. The initiative lay with the Germans. It would be cat and mouse.

In London a strange quietude descended over high affairs of state. 'Oddly enough,' remarked the placid Asquith on 5 August, 'there is no authentic news either by land or sea. All that appears in the papers is invention.' At the Admiralty, Churchill's resolve had not relaxed. His desire to get at the German cruisers caught Asquith's attention. 'Winston's mouth waters for the *Goeben*,' he noted, adding, 'but so far she is still at large.'[52]

Even so, other matters concerned Churchill, and on the afternoon of 5 August a critically important War Council was held. Strategic issues were reviewed and the question of what was to be done with the British Expeditionary Force (BEF) raised. Churchill was there with Asquith, Haldane, and Grey, and the great generals of the day: Sir Ian Hamilton, Sir John French, and Sir Douglas Haig – 'a rather restless gathering,' said Asquith. The next day they reconvened, this time with a French army officer in attendance. That day Cabinet sanctioned the dispatch of the BEF's four divisions, and not six as some had hoped. Asquith states that the decision was embraced with 'much less demur' than he expected. Smaller schemes for attacking German ports and wireless stations in East and West Africa and the China Seas came up for discussion. A rough cast had come over those who were now in control of the national war direction. The politicians had sat down to their martial work. Upon their doing so, Asquith made this observation: 'Indeed, I had to remark that we looked more like a gang of Elizabethan buccaneers than a meek collection of black-coated Liberal Ministers.'

Kitchener joined the Cabinet that day and took over the War Office reins from Asquith, who thought it would be amusing to see how the powerful hero of Khartoum, an imperial soldier par excellence, would get on in Cabinet. Here was the warrior among the essentially pacifist Liberals. We can imagine that Asquith may also have thought Kitchener would watch Churchill warily and guard against young Winston's enthusiasms and desires for adventure in fields of war. (Kitchener had met Churchill in the Sudan in 1898 and was irritated that Churchill, who was covering the Sudan expedition as a journalist, had insinuated himself into the 21st Lancers through family connections. Churchill, for his part, remarked on the 'vivid manifestation upon the senses' produced by Kitchener's appearance, his 'sunburnt and almost purple cheeks and jowl', just before the Battle of Omdurman in Sudan.[53])

Meanwhile, on board *Goeben*, Souchon made his calculations. When he departed Messina, only the light cruiser *Gloucester*, commanded by the redoubtable Captain Howard Kelly, was so situated as to report on German movements. *Gloucester* was no match for the enemy, and Kelly knew it. Souchon decided on a feint toward the Adriatic. *Gloucester* doggedly shadowed Souchon and even on one occasion exchanged fire with *Breslau*, but a shortage of coal obliged her to break off pursuit on the afternoon of 7 August. Now the calculations narrowed. This left the 1st Cruiser Squadron under Admiral Troubridge as the only force able to intercept Souchon. Prudent but undoubtedly timid, Troubridge declined to intercept the German force, believing it to be superior to his own.[54] This left Souchon a clear run to the Aegean. Milne's three crack battlecruisers had wasted a day attempting to combine with Troubridge's cruisers due to a faulty message from the Admiralty on 8 August that indicated a state of war between Britain and Austria. In response, Milne had adhered to pre-existing war orders to combine his forces in the face of a threat from Austria. In fact, Austria was deliberately attempting to evade hostilities with Britain, and war was not declared for several days more. Obedience to the pre-existing plan failed to take into account the pressing need to intercept the German vessels. Again, neither Milne nor Troubridge had the independence of thought to pursue the essential object at that moment. And even though the mistaken message was cancelled several hours later, the second message advised Milne that the situation with Austria was 'critical', thereby implying that Milne should still consider combining his forces against any threat from Austria. The confusion gave Souchon time to make for Ottoman waters. He coaled unmolested near Naxos and sailed eastward.[55] Any vision of snatching the enemy ships was fading quickly.

As the affair unfolded, the Foreign Office remained in the dark about true Ottoman sympathies and about the possibility of Souchon arriving at the Dardanelles. The messages of H Beaumont, the British military attaché in

Constantinople, showed a lack of understanding of the intentions of the Ottoman Empire. On 6 August he had telegraphed that the Ottoman minister of marine was acting like a 'spoiled child' over the two seized British battleships, and he suggested that a telegram from Grey to the Ottomans would have a soothing influence. He also asserted that the British declaration of war against Germany had 'already calmed pro-German ardour artificially created and unscrupulously encouraged by [the] German ambassador.' Beaumont's message of the next day indicated that Ottoman mobilisation was limited to Thrace, was unpopular and not as thorough as originally intended, and appeared to be meant primarily to secure payment by Christians of fines for exemption. In another message of the same day he gave his opinion that the 'unreasonable attitude' of the minister of marine was 'only partially shared by his colleagues'.[56]

Nevertheless, evidence available to the Foreign Office indicated that the Ottomans were beginning to associate themselves with Germany. In the ruling circles in Athens the destination of *Goeben* was common knowledge. The British naval officer at the head of the Greek navy, Rear-Admiral Mark Kerr, kept the secret to himself and did not warn London until it was too late to act.[57] On 3 August the Kaiser had bragged to the Greek minister in Berlin that the Ottomans had decided to ally with the Germans. This news was quickly passed to the Greek prime minister, who on 5 August informed William Erskine, the British chargé d'affaires in Athens. However, Erskine's report of the conversation, received at the Foreign Office on 6 August, offered the opinion that the Kaiser had deliberately misled the Greek minister in Berlin in order to frighten the Greeks into an alliance with Germany.[58] Next day the Russians emphasised to the British their fear of the ambiguous position of the Ottoman Empire, and the possibility of the Austrian fleet sailing to the Black Sea, perhaps in conjunction with Ottoman and German vessels. On 9 August the Russians told the British that they suspected *Goeben* was proceeding to the Dardanelles.[59] However, the same day Beaumont related a conversation with the Grand Vizier in which the latter informed Beaumont that additional mines had been laid in the Dardanelles at the request of the Russian ambassador. Beaumont did not view the laying of these mines as an act directed against the Entente, and thought the question of Ottoman connivance with the Central Powers was out of the question. He believed that if the Austrian fleet were to attempt to transit the Dardanelles, they would not be welcomed, hence casting doubt on the Russian idea that the Ottomans were about to welcome Austrian, and by implication German, ships. Beaumont also stated his opinion that the Grand Vizier's views reflected the views of the majority of his colleagues.[60]

Such information as was available did not find its way to Churchill at the Admiralty. Apparently the Admiralty was also decrypting the signals between Souchon and Berlin, but did not pass this intelligence to Milne. As late as 10

August, Milne had no indication from the Admiralty that the Ottoman Empire was even a possible destination of the two German ships. He believed the Dardanelles to be mined and barred to all warships.[61] Instead, mere hours before *Goeben* and *Breslau* passed into the quiet waters of the Dardanelles, Milne signalled Cairo to warn about the possibility of the German ships entering the Suez Canal!

At five o'clock in the afternoon of 10 August, the scope of this intelligence failure dramatically revealed itself when *Goeben* and *Breslau* entered the Dardanelles untouched, reached Constantinople, and held that city under their guns. The consequences of the Mediterranean Fleet's failure to intercept the German ships now became apparent. Nine days earlier, Enver Pasha and two other members of the Ottoman cabinet, operating without the knowledge of most of the Ottoman leadership, had negotiated a secret treaty with Germany. It sounded the death knell of the Ottoman Empire. Under Article II of this treaty, the Ottomans undertook to side with Germany and Austria–Hungary if those powers became involved in a war against Russia. Germany was eager to gain the Ottoman Empire's accession to the Central Powers. The arrival of *Goeben* and *Breslau* at Constantinople on 10 August seemed to affirm in Ottoman minds what they imagined to be the duplicity of Britain (in the loss of their dreadnoughts) as well as the strength and friendship of Germany, and helped Enver Pasha's pro-German policy win more support among the Ottoman leadership.

When *Goeben* and *Breslau* reached Constantinople, Germany promptly offered to sell them to the Ottomans as replacements for the two dreadnoughts Churchill had 'requisitioned'. The Ottomans accepted. Milne telegraphed the Admiralty confirming that both German ships had been sold as a formality into Ottoman service and renamed *Yavuz Sultan Selim* and *Midelih*. This deception was discussed at the 12 August Cabinet meeting. London decided to insist on the replacement of the German crews with Ottoman crews. Churchill wrote to Grey that same day to elaborate the Admiralty's position, which was that the sale or transfer of the two cruisers to the Ottoman Empire should be allowed, as long as it was 'bona fide and permanent'. Churchill attached as an 'essential condition' that the German officers and company of both ships had to be returned to Germany immediately and without exception. Only if this were met would the British naval mission remain in Constantinople. Churchill also stated that the Admiralty would be willing to negotiate with the Ottomans with respect to the two requisitioned ships after the war. Churchill had lost his grip on the matter; the world was unfolding in a fashion quite beyond his control. Asquith's comment on the affair was that 'the only interesting thing is the arrival of the *Goeben* in the Dardanelles and her sale to Turkey. The Turks are very angry at Winston's seizure of their battleships here.' However, he did not feel that the Ottoman acquisition of the warships would be significant: 'As we shall insist that the *Goeben* should be manned by a Turkish instead of a German crew, it doesn't much matter: as the Turkish sailors cannot navigate her – except on to rocks or mines.'[62]

However, not even the Germans believed that the 'sale' of *Goeben* and *Breslau* was 'bona fide and permanent'. On 20 September Admiral Souchon defiantly informed the Turks via a member of the German ambassadorial staff that he did not consider himself bound by their decisions, regardless of the fiction of his incorporation into the Ottoman Navy. Later that day he led *Breslau* on a brief sortie into the Black Sea, ignoring Ottoman orders forbidding such action.[63]

In faraway Whitehall there was much talk about what should be done with the renegade cruisers. Churchill insisted on strong diplomatic action.[64] He continued to sound the alarm. On 17 August Asquith wrote: 'Turkey has come to the foreground, threatens vaguely enterprises against Egypt, and seems disposed to play a double game about the *Goeben* and the *Breslau*. Winston, in his most bellicose mood, is all for sending a torpedo flotilla through the Dardanelles to threaten and if necessary sink the *Goeben* and her consort. Crewe and Kitchener very much against it.'[65] Of the Cabinet meeting of that same day, Asquith reported to the King: 'The most pressing question was the attitude of Turkey, which during the last few days has become more unsatisfactory. The *Goben* [*sic*] & *Breslau* are now flying the Ottoman flag, but the German crews do not appear to have been got rid of. Both Lord Crewe & Lord Kitchener were anxious that Moslem susceptibilities in India & Egypt should be carefully considered, and that if possible the aggressive should come from Turkey & not from us.'[66]

On 17 August Churchill informed Grey that the situation with the two vessels was 'extremely unsatisfactory', that the condition of repatriation had not been met, and that the naval mission had been banished from the Ottoman ships committed to their charge. He stated that the uncertainty over the fate of the two vessels meant that a pair of British battlecruisers, urgently needed elsewhere, had to lie in wait outside the Dardanelles.[67] This got the attention of the Foreign Office. Efforts were now made to recover from the consequences of Souchon's escape. With Grey's concurrence, Churchill attempted direct mediation with Enver Pasha, whom he had met several years earlier. He offered full compensation for the Ottomans at the end of the war. Further, on the advice of the Foreign Secretary, he offered to guarantee Ottoman territorial integrity if she remained neutral in the war. In a letter of 17 or 18 August to Grey, Britain's ambassador to the Ottoman Empire, Sir Louis Mallet, wrote, 'I am getting in touch with Ministers. Minister of War is delighted with Mr. Churchill's message, and told Admiral Limpus [head of Britain's naval mission] that he realised force of his arguments, and would answer it.' Churchill was too late in all of this, and such diplomatic manoeuvring could not check the course of events or counter German pressures. All along, Enver Pasha knew that his country's destiny lay with Germany. The arrival at Constantinople on 22 August of the sailors who were to have taken control of the two battleships in Britain added further fuel to the fire. By the end of August it had become apparent that the Ottoman Empire was co-operating fully with the Germans and did not intend to comply with Britain's injunction that Ottoman crews man *Goeben* and *Breslau*. For Churchill, still unaware of the German-Ottoman treaty, this could 'only have one significance'.[68]

In the months that followed, efforts were made to establish what went wrong and who was responsible. Churchill attached the following comment to a minute by himself and Battenberg on Admiral Milne's report on the *Goeben* chase: 'The explanation is satisfactory, the result unsatisfactory.'[69] On Troubridge fell the blame for failing to carry out the instructions of the Commander-in-Chief. Milne was instructed to strike his flag, come home, and report to the Admiralty. Initially, the Admiralty officially sanctioned Milne's deployments and actions. However, Churchill informed Milne that he would not take up the Nore Command, as had been announced. Milne languished on half-pay for the remainder of the war.[70]

The Admiralty's opinion of Troubridge's conduct was distinctly critical. Battenberg vented his anger in a minute of 7 September, calling for Troubridge to return to England forthwith and proceed to Portsmouth for a court of inquiry. In the First Sea Lord's estimation, Troubridge had failed to carry out his duty, and in all tactical circumstances failed to bring the German ships to account or bring them to battle with Milne's forces. Battenberg wrote: 'The armament of the British force was 22 9–2 in, 14 7–5 in. and 20 6 in. That of the opponent 10 11 in. and 12 6 in. The Trial speed of the slowest British ship was 23 knots ... that of the Goeben 27 knots ... Superior speed ... in a single ship can be nullified by proper tactical dispositions of four units.' He concluded: 'The Escape of the *Goeben* must ever remain a shameful episode in this war. The Flag officer who is responsible for this failure cannot be entrusted with any further command afloat and his continuance in such command constitutes a danger to the State.'[71]

On 5 November a court martial was convened on board HMS *Bulwark*, at Portland, to try Troubridge. The charge, under the Naval Discipline Act, was that Troubridge did, 'from negligence or through other default, forbear to pursue the chase of His Imperial German Majesty's ship *Goeben*, being an enemy then flying.' Admiral Sir George Egerton, C-in-C, Plymouth, was president of the court, which also included eight other flag officers and captains. Rear-Admiral Sydney Fremantle served as prosecutor, and Leslie Scott, KC, ably defended Troubridge. In his defence, Troubridge referred to a standing order of 30 April, a message in Churchill's own hand, in which the Admiralty had advised Milne that on no account were his forces to be drawn into action with superior forces except in conjunction with the French. He asserted that the two German vessels constituted such a superior force.[72] Battenberg refused to accept this assertion by Troubridge. Although Souchon had 11in guns, they were not greatly superior to the British 9.2in guns. And Battenberg knew that a squadron of lesser ships could harry those of greater firepower and bring them to destruction. His tactical knowledge far exceeded that of Milne or Troubridge. (The details of the Troubridge court martial were kept under lock and key until the tenacious Arthur Marder obtained access. Even then, his account faced the closest scrutiny but was eventually published after a dust-up with the Board of Admiralty. Naval and family reputations had to be preserved. Referring to those looking after confidential documents, Marder wrote, 'These chaps are extraordinarily sensitive about scholars seeing and quoting papers in their custody.' In fact, said the Admiralty, Marder should never have seen the court martial record proceedings of November 1914 as they were embargoed by the hundred-year rule on such records. However, Marder had seen them and had acted in good faith, and his second volume of *From the Dreadnought to Scapa Flow*, which provided the revelations, finally appeared after numerous lengthy delays.[73])

In the end, the charge was not proved and Troubridge was acquitted, although he never again had a command at sea. In 1915 he was employed in commanding the Danube flotilla and British heavy guns on the Serbian front. He was made vice-admiral 9 June 1916 and rose no further. Troubridge and Milne were joined in this disgrace. They became political scapegoats even though, in the end, they were absolved of their actions.

Fisher also had his say on Troubridge's court martial:

> This most disastrous event of the escape of the *Goeben* and lamentable blow to British Naval prestige would never have occurred had Sir B. Milne been off Messina with the three Battle-Cruisers (*Inflexible*, *Indefatigable*, and *Indomitable*) – even if short of coal – at the time *Goeben* was in Messina Harbour for then the *Goeben* could not possibly have escaped – observing that notwithstanding the Admiralty telegram 'to respect Italian neutrality' ... yet nevertheless Sir B. Milne had rightly decided ... 'to ignore any question of Italian territorial waters if necessary to get at her (the *Goeben*).'[74]

Though Troubridge's argument that he faced a superior force helped ensure his acquittal in his court martial, Churchill's view can be inferred from the following letter, dated 11 January 1915, from the Admiralty to Rear-Admiral, 2nd Light Cruiser Squadron. Churchill himself drafted this letter and indicated that he lauded Captain Kelly of *Gloucester* for doing precisely what Troubridge would not:

It is clear from a perusal of the report in question that the *Goeben* could have caught and sunk the *Gloucester* at any time had she dared to turn upon her. She was apparently deterred by the latter's boldness, which gave the impression of close support at hand. The combination of audacity with restraint, unswerving attention to the principal military object, viz. holding on to the *Goeben*, and strict conformity to orders, constitute a naval episode that may justly be regarded as a model.[75]

Churchill also believed that the British force had been sufficient to engage the two German vessels. In a letter of 20 September from the Admiralty to the French, requesting two battleships of the *Démocratie* type to assist in covering the two German vessels in the Dardanelles, Churchill made the following notation: 'Although I approve this telegram, I must record my opinion that the British force was ample to engage alone, and that the French ships are not needed.'[76] The Admiralty, though criticised for the proceedings and conclusion, would admit no errors on their part.

Years later, Troubridge remained critical of Churchill, stating that, as a politician, his account of the episode in *The World Crisis* might have been subconsciously motivated by a desire to deny any personal fault. He contended that Churchill, after having a brilliant idea and giving orders for its execution, ignored the matter afterwards: 'Such for example was the detachment of the two battle-cruisers from my flag to watch the *Goeben*, the telegrams urging them to "hold" her and the subsequent complete detachment of the Admiralty from the affair which allowed of their non-return to the original Admiralty directed disposition with my flag but on the contrary their attachment instead to the flag of Sir Berkeley Milne and their being frittered away in a superfluous and unnecessary and faulty strategic position.' Troubridge charged Churchill with ignoring evidence that would have shown that he was wrong in the *Goeben* affair. He dismissed Churchill's criticism of his change of mind, and argued that his assertion regarding the range of his guns versus those of *Goeben* had been confirmed 'in responsible quarters'. Troubridge also argued that, in Churchill's calculations of ships available to him, he included all vessels between Greece and Malta, including those low on coal or those too slow to catch the German ships. Finally, Troubridge concluded: 'Can I not imagine Mr. Churchill saying [if Troubridge had engaged *Goeben* and suffered a Coronel-like defeat], "I particularly telegraphed orders that the ships of the Mediterranean Fleet were *not* to allow themselves to be brought to battle by a superior force of the enemy until we were able to reinforce the Mediterranean Command."'[77]

After the war, Churchill wrote the following unpublished note critical of Milne:

It must be admitted that the orders to respect rigidly Italian neutrality & to keep six miles from the Italian coasts, issued without any idea of the *Goeben* being at Messina, seriously complicated the task of the British forces. Had this point been referred to the Admiralty by Sir Berkeley Milne the prohibition w[ou]ld at once have been cancelled. The prize was worth the risk. In fact permission to chase through the Straits was given unasked by the Admiralty as soon as it was realised that the *Goeben* was escaping unblocked to the Southward.

He could at any moment after he first suspected that the *Goeben* was at Messina have telegraphed to the Admiralty in the following sense: – 'I believe *Goeben* is at Messina. Submit since she has entered Italian territorial waters I may follow her, observing that otherwise I shall be much hampered in my operations.' It would not have been unreasonable to expect a Commander-in-Chief to ask the Admiralty a simple vital question like this. One would have expected him to do so, if only for his own protection. He said nothing.[78]

The escape of *Goeben* and *Breslau* raised questions about the conduct of operations directed by the naval war staff and Churchill. How the ever-powerful, ever-victorious Navy, so strong in the Mediterranean, had allowed *Goeben* to escape continued to puzzle the critics. No matter what reasons and explanations were forthcoming, nothing substantial was ever produced. Historian Sir Julian Corbett noted that although many excuses could be made to explain the failure in those crowded growing days of the war, the episode would remain forever 'a shadow in our naval history'. Another analyst, Rear-Admiral Sir Eardley-Wilmot, writing after the war in regards to what he rightly called 'one of the most ghastly mistakes of the whole war', got in a sly dig at Churchill when he stated: 'When an autocrat professionally ignorant takes control of a Service anything may happen. We see this with the Kaiser, when he resisted advice to send auxiliary cruisers to sea before war broke out in his desire to avoid any act which might precipitate war with England.' He also probably gave the order to *Goeben* that sent her to Constantinople. 'Our Naval Administration,' Eardley-Wilmot warned, 'is not without similar dangers.'[79]

What contributed to the failure? Several factors. Although much blame may be placed on the commanders on the spot, Milne and Troubridge, the combination of poorly composed orders and over-centralisation of command at Admiralty headquarters played a significant role. The naval staff system, a very recent development, had been imposed on an unwilling naval establishment. Battenberg, the First Sea Lord, exerted no independent influence against the domineering and overbearing First Lord, and the Board of Admiralty fell completely under the domination of Churchill. In such circumstances, the naval staff, having no institutional standing, was ill-equipped to examine events critically or to rein in the exuberance of the First Lord.

Moreover, the unpractised use of wireless and the temptation of central authority were fatal flaws that allowed London to dictate specific dispositions to commanders afloat, often on the basis of intelligence of uncertain quality. The role of the staff and the First Sea Lord should be to give the respective commanders-in-chief specific objectives, but Milne was given a whole series of constantly changing objectives, from protecting the French transports to preventing the Germans from escaping to the Atlantic. He also received the erroneous message about a state of war with Austria. When such orders are transmitted without benefit of adequate intelligence, a commander is left in difficulty. In Milne's case, the Admiralty was also ordering his ships about, constantly interfering with the Admiral's disposition of his men and ships. Admiral Dewar made this the basis of his criticism of the episode in a 1956 article in the *Naval Review*.[80] The German commander was given considerable leeway to determine specific courses of action; by contrast, both Troubridge and Milne were not similarly favoured. No one in the Admiralty machinery was keeping track of orders being dispatched to the Mediterranean, and no one seemed to have a concrete grasp of the essential military objective of Milne's operations. That being said, an officer of Milne's stature (an obvious require-ment to become Commander-in-Chief, Mediterranean) should have had the intelligence and the moral courage to question orders from London, or at least should have queried Battenberg about the specific objective of his operations.

Doubtless, too, an intelligence gap existed between the Foreign Office and the Admiralty about the possible avenues of escape open to Souchon. The Foreign Office neglected to see that the Ottomans might come into the war on the side of Germany, or the degree to which the seizure of the two Ottoman battleships had turned opinion in that country against London.

Churchill understandably had a desire to appear decisive in command at the outset of hostilities. This was his show. Making and directing war was his natural inclination. However, with no effective staff to restrain him, there was no check on his exuberance. He might well have overridden his staff, or tried to, but if there had been a First Sea Lord and a naval staff that could restrain Churchill's energies and channel them, Souchon might have had a very bad day. Thus we may say that the most critical failure was the Admiralty machinery, which did not have a systematic view of the situation in the Mediterranean. Decisions were made off the cuff without due consideration of their impact.

Fisher's final indictment of the affair cast harsh condemnation of those involved: 'We also had a d—d fool as Chief of the Staff at the Admiralty [Frederick Charles Doveton Sturdee], and a very silly telegram he sent gave the poltroon the excuse for running away and pretending his ship wanted coal at

Malta. It is perhaps the most damnable episode of the War, and no one punished, and the truth never known.'[81] (In October Sturdee was replaced by Henry Oliver as chief of staff.) Fisher's words ring true. The escape of the German cruisers had long-term consequences. As Churchill was to say after the fact: 'For the peoples of the Middle East SMS *Goeben* carried more slaughter, more misery, and more ruin than has ever before been borne within the compass of a ship.'[82] Within months, the escape would also come back to haunt both Churchill and Fisher, drawing them into a distant and logistically difficult theatre of operations that harmed Churchill's reputation and ended Fisher's career. And it showed Battenberg in a poor light, casting a pall over his administration.

Only Admiral Souchon, the German commander, survived this cauldron of conspiracies. He effected the escape of *Goeben* and her consort. He ran free to the Dardanelles and thence to Constantinople. He crowned the achievements of the Young Turks. He brought teeth to the jaws of the German alliance with the Ottomans. He thereafter caused a good deal of havoc in the Black Sea. His immense achievement, perplexing to the Admiralty, the Navy, and the Foreign Office, knows few parallels in the history of naval warfare and international diplomacy. 'I have thrown the Turks into the powder-keg and kindled war between Russia and Turkey,' Souchon wrote to his wife on 29 October.[83] He alone forced the pace, disregarding even Berlin's occasional hesitations. His was the sweet turn of events. Others were left to ponder the might-have-beens of history. None did it better than Churchill. 'In all this story of the escape of the *Goeben*,' he says in *The World Crisis*, 'one seems to see the influence of that sinister fatality which at a later stage and on a far larger scale was to dog the enterprise against the Dardanelles. The terrible "Ifs" accumulate.'[84] The escape of *Goeben* and *Breslau* at the beginning of the war made a close blockade of the Dardanelles entrance necessary to prevent these ships breaking out again into the wider Mediterranean. A mixed British and French force carried this out, including six submarines, three from each country. One of the British boats, *B11*, Lieutenant N D Holbrook, passed through the Dardanelles, avoided minefields, rose to periscope depth, and, at 800yds, fired a torpedo that sank the Ottoman battleship *Messudieh*, at anchor off the Asia Minor shore. More submarines were sent to exploit the possibilities of a passage of the Dardanelles. After it was determined that no further attempt should be made by surface ships to force the Narrows because of heavy guns ashore, the submarine showed how great damage to the enemy could still be done.

Before we close our examination of the accumulations of 'ifs' attendant on the escape of the two German cruisers to Constantinople, it is instructive to note that another scenario, equally ineffectual but part of the story, had been working itself out in a quiet wing of the Old Admiralty Building in Whitehall, in a room known as OB 40.

Initially, 'Room 40', as it was known, was dedicated to intercepting German strategic intelligence, but soon it changed focus to German naval tactical traffic, which promised to render great service in combating the High Seas Fleet. Heading up the Admiralty's intelligence efforts was the Director of Naval Intelligence, Captain Reginald 'Blinker' Hall, who earned his nickname from his habit of screwing up his eyeballs and blinking furiously as he talked. He embraced the dark world of deception and espionage, and soon became one of the most powerful men in Whitehall. His job was to find out all he could about the German navy and to do so by whatever means were expedient. He worked with Scotland Yard, with the War Office Intelligence Department, and with the head of counterespionage. He augmented his staff with men who might be called a 'dirty-tricks brigade'. Among them was ex-diplomat Gerald Fitzmaurice. While Hall had German prisoners interrogated; German messages intercepted, decrypted, and analysed; and spies hunted down, he employed Fitzmaurice in an audacious attempt to bribe the Turks to allow the British Fleet safe passage of the Dardanelles, a marvellous escapade with financial operations of a covert nature. Ian Fleming, of James Bond fame, would have approved.

Hall worked up his scheme in early February 1915. He did not know that the Ottoman Empire was now allied with Germany, and he believed there to be a fair chance of obtaining peaceful passage of Allied warships through the Straits to Constantinople. In order to do that *Goeben* and *Breslau* had to be eliminated as a threat. Why not make the Ottomans an offer they could not refuse? To negotiate with them, he sent Gerald Fitzmaurice and Griffin Eady, a principal in the naval constructing firm of Jackson that had built the promised (but 'requisitioned') dreadnoughts. Hall took upon himself that the emissaries should offer the Ottomans considerable sums – up to £4 million for safe passage through the Dardanelles, and the removal of all mines, as well as *Goeben* and *Breslau* – but the initiative, done entirely on Hall's will, was never brought to fruition. A pity. Schemes and dreams have the great calamity of being directed, or derailed, by bolts from the blue.

In this case, the bolt was a German telegram to Constantinople, deciphered on 13 March, which indicated that the Ottomans were short on ammunition and that Germany was doing everything it could to overcome the problem. One of the intended measures was to send a German or Austrian submarine to the Straits. Hall took this potent message down the passage to Fisher, now back at the Admiralty as First Sea Lord. Hall knew that Fisher was lukewarm about diverting the war effort to the Dardanelles, but the particulars of this message heightened the First Sea Lord's optimism at the same time they diminished his opposition to diverting forces. 'This quite unexpected news that the Turks were short of ammunition,' Admiral Sir William James states, 'had an immediate, if temporary, affect on Fisher's attitude to the operations. Indeed, he seemed as enthusiastic as the members of the Cabinet, whose views he had hitherto bitterly opposed.'[85] By then the die was cast, and the Dardanelles adventure (dealt with in Chapter 9) had many adherents, but none so hot for success but so poorly equipped or supported as Churchill and Fisher.

Hall was about to return to his room when Churchill (who was perhaps having second thoughts) turned and asked for the latest news from the British agents in Constantinople. Hall continues, 'it was then that I told him of the large sum of money I had personally guaranteed. He stared at me. "How much?" "Three million pounds," I replied, "with power to go to four millions if necessary," and as I mentioned these figures they did seem to be extraordinarily large. He was frowning. "Who authorised this?" he demanded. "I did, 1st Lord." "But – the Cabinet surely knows nothing about it?" "No, it does not. But if we were to get peace, or if we were to get a peaceful passage for that amount, I imagine they'd be glad enough to pay."'

Churchill turned to Fisher. '"D'you hear what this man has done? He's told his people they can go up to four million to buy a peaceful passage! On his own!" "What," cried Lord Fisher, starting up from his chair. "Four millions? No, no. I tell you I'm going through tomorrow, or as soon as the preparations can be completed." He turned to me [recounted Hall]: "Cable at once to stop negotiations. No, let the offer for *Goeben* remain. But nothing else. We're going through."'

Thus the necessary cables were sent. These rendered future discussions useless and, as Hall suggests, destroyed the 'belief in Turkish minds of our good faith … Ironically enough, when the gallant attempt of March 18 had proved unsuccessful, the Cabinet were asking me to spare no expense to win over the Turks. Unfortunately, it was then too late.'[86]

'The Crown jewels': Admiral Jellicoe and the Grand Fleet

At distant Scapa Flow, on board *Iron Duke*, Vice-Admiral Sir John Jellicoe had assumed command of the Grand Fleet (the 'Crown jewels', Churchill called these great dreadnoughts). That he had done so reluctantly has been described, but he soon took the great armada to sea and out toward the Norwegian coast, then back to the anchorage. On his shoulders rested the future of British naval mastery and the security of the British Empire.

Jellicoe could not put in place a blockade of German ports, sealing the German fleet in its harbours, because enemy mines, torpedoes, and shore artillery made such inshore action impossible. Instead, a 'distant blockade' was instituted. The interception and destruction of German shipping proceeded as an act of belligerence. Interdicting neutral shipping to Germany posed other difficulties. Dutch, Swedish, and Norwegian shippers found

British methods of search irritating, but the British sought to curtail trading with the enemy in war materials. This was part of the long, slow process of sea denial.

Jellicoe soon set to work drafting Battle Orders for issue in printed form to all ships. Many helped prepare these orders, but as one officer in the Fleet, Sir Frederic Dreyer, recounted of those furiously busy days, Jellicoe was the mainspring. 'His labours in harbour were prodigious. His brilliant mind was stored with knowledge of his profession and its history. He was full of ideas, and encouraged all in the Fleet not only to strive to perfect a great fighting machine, but also to make suggestions.' At sea he was recognised as a master seaman and fleet handler and a great leader. Sailors soon became aware of the competence of those in command: they all had unbounded confidence in Jellicoe. 'Jellicoe is the Grand Fleet.'[87]

Jellicoe was a centraliser, a not uncommon characteristic of great commanders. But if that was a fault, another factor in obtaining successful results against the enemy in battle was the never-ending strain of the almost solitary office he held as supreme commander at sea in those distant high latitudes, facing all the perils, real and imagined. Long hours at the desk brought fatigue and haemorrhoids and possibly megalomania. Dependent on confidential, private letters from Fisher giving encouragement and advice, he was otherwise in a state of loneliness of command, increasingly isolated from Whitehall. He was also far from his wife, Gwendoline, Lady Jellicoe, 'the woman behind the fleet', a faithful guardian of his reputation. This reinforced his centralising tendencies, which would eventually consume him, a story to be told later. For the moment every expectation, and Churchill's unqualified backing, had given Jellicoe his moment of destiny. Churchill, with unrivalled capacities as an assessor of those who held such supreme commands, put it best: Jellicoe was the only man on either side who could lose the war in an afternoon.

Insights into the strain of command are given in Jellicoe's letter to 'My Own Darling Mother' on 7 August about what he regarded as the Admiralty's drastic decision:

I hope you have not been anxious about me, but I have of course been simply without a moment [to write to you]. I was sent north as Second-in-Command, and at the last moment was told I might have to take command. I protested most strongly against the folly of changing the Commander-in-Chief on the eve of war, and after arriving up north telegraphed twice a day imploring the Admiralty not to do it, as I was sure it was a fatal error. I put on one side my strong objection of superseding a very old friend at such a moment, the idea of which distressed me that I felt quite ill, and could not sleep at all. It was so utterly repugnant to my feelings. But the Admiralty insisted ... poor Sir George Callaghan left her [*Iron Duke*] utterly broken down. It was a cruel and most unwise step. I really wonder that I kept my head at all when I think of what I went through. But I am all right, Mother dear, and every day makes it easier ... You won't be anxious about me I hope, Mother dear. God will protect me and I look to Him to help me to do my duty to my country. I feel that our cause is just. The war has been forced on us, and that right will prevail in the end.[88]

Jellicoe never forgot that the Grand Fleet, in its conception and implementation, owed much to Fisher, especially for the preparation of dreadnought battleships and battlecruisers. However, peacetime operations and manoeuvres were never a substitute for war experiences. Consequently, 'it was the conditions under which war broke out that made it necessary for us in the Grand Fleet to build up what was almost a new organisation.' Among these conditions were the now-formidable submarine, the new use of the airship as a scout, the mine ('neglected by us [but] highly developed by [the] enemy, both defensively and offensively'), enhanced ranges of guns and torpedoes, and the use of wireless telegraphy in ways 'undreamt of'. Jellicoe also noted with satisfaction the concentration of the Grand Fleet immediately before the war: 'Fortunately, the Admiralty in the last days of July, 1914, placed us at once in a strong strategic position. For this action the nation should be grateful to the First Lord and First Sea Lord.'

The British public expected that Germany would be prepared to make sacrifices on the sea and that a great fleet action would at once be fought. As Jellicoe recollected, 'Most people found it difficult to imagine that the High Seas Fleet (built at vast expense, and rightly considered by the enemy to be an efficient weapon of war) would adopt from the outset a purely passive role, with the inevitable result that German trade would be swept from the seas.' Jellicoe noted two reasons for this passive stance by the Germans. First, they worried that the Baltic might pass into enemy hands. Secondly, they realised that the defensive role of the Fleet 'created by far the most difficult situation for' the Royal Navy. As long as the German fleet remained 'in being', it pinned down the British, although its enforced idleness did create German morale problems.[89] The necessarily defensive British posture favoured the enemy. Cruiser hit-and-run raids on the eastern coast of England, the sowing of mines in English and Scottish harbour mouths and estuaries, the deployment of submarines to lie in wait for British warships and merchantmen – all of these could be undertaken by the enemy from across the Narrow Seas. The Royal Navy kept the English Channel inviolate, but farther north on the Belgian coast, all the way north to Norway, the German navy ranged wide and at will.

British naval minds now turned to ways to engage the German navy. This is the story leading up to the battle known as Heligoland Bight, 28 August, considered below.

At the time Jellicoe assumed command, the new super-dreadnoughts of the *Queen Elizabeth* class were about to come into commission – five of them in all. They were creatures of Churchill's 1912 naval estimates and boasted powerful 15in guns, first of their size. Fisher exaggerated their operational top speeds, and trials proved that they did not have the speed to run in company with the battlecruisers. Jellicoe arranged for the commands to go to safe hands who would pose no trouble to him. Beatty wanted the five vessels attached to the Battle Cruiser Squadron, and this was done, but when he shared his private correspondence with Jellicoe on this with the Admiralty, the C-in-C was furious.[90] Jellicoe's rigidity of command reflects his desire to control all communications, and while Fisher tended to mollify him, Churchill left well enough alone or showed sympathy with Beatty, who had been his Naval Secretary from 1911 to 1913. Just as the Fisherites and those who had supported Beresford had feuded and caused dissention, so too did the gap begin to grow between those supporting Jellicoe and those favouring Beatty. Jellicoe had his loyal supporters, including his brother-in-law, Admiral Sir Charles Madden, sent by Churchill to give help in all the paperwork at Scapa. Beatty, however, developed a strong 'band of brothers', not the least of whom was Ernle Chatfield, captain of Beatty's flagship *Lion*. 'About the only things Jellicoe and Beatty had in common were scars from Chinese bullet wounds, and the unshakeable loyalty of their respective followers,' writes Andrew Gordon in *The Rules of the Game*, 'Yet in spite of their differences in age (56 and 45) and temperament, and the infrequency of their meetings, they got on serviceably well, as their considerable correspondence shows.'[91]

Among Jellicoe's great problems was his lack of secure bases. Scapa Flow was indeed a great sheet of water with good anchorage in northern latitudes. But it had many faults that geographical location could not overcome. The disingenuous Fisher later claimed credit for 'discovery' of Scapa Flow as main fleet anchorage. He described himself locked up in a room at the Admiralty one day in 1905. Fisher, according to Taprell Dorling, a naval officer and writer, who must have got the story directly from him, was 'looking at the chart of the North Sea while making up his mind upon a safe and properly-situated anchorage for the British fleet in the event of war with Germany. His eye fell upon "a large inland land-locked sheet of water."'[92] As of 1910 the Home Ports Defence Committee, an offshoot of the recently formed Committee of Imperial Defence, took no notice of Scapa Flow. No one thought of it as a war station. It was too far distant, so reasoning ran, for a blockade to be undertaken against Germany. Prevailing wisdom suggested that the Firth of Forth would be the main operational base of the Fleet in a war against Germany, and a dockyard at Rosyth was under construction. Churchill says in *The World Crisis* that the First Sea Lord at that time, Admiral of the Fleet Sir Arthur Wilson, intended to employ a close blockade of the German Bight and by this means check German ventures into the North Sea. No plan was ever put on paper by Wilson, and he had no intention of telling others, save Fisher, what was sealed in his brain. In fact, while the War Office pressed the Admiralty on the state of defences of the Orkneys (as well as the Shetlands), the Admiralty replied in clear terms that Cromarty Forth and not the Orkneys would probably be selected if a move north of Queensferry (the approach to the Firth of Forth and Rosyth) were ever required. There may have been urgency in these strategic decisions but nothing of the sort shows up in the documents of the day.

However, in early 1912 an internal Admiralty paper reported that Scapa Flow offered advantages found nowhere else. There was worry about German spies making observations there. Further, if safeguards were put in place to prevent a night attack by torpedo craft operating from Norway, 300 miles distant (it was suggested that such a strike would occur *before* the outbreak of hostilities), then the place was inviolate. Even submarine attack was unlikely, according to this report, given the sea conditions of the approach to the anchorage. If certain narrow channels leading into the Flow through Holm Sound on the east could be blocked, all surely would be well. Never was an Admiralty report on sea defences so riddled with error and false assumptions, and never were the stakes so high, as they concerned the safety of the grandest fleet ever assembled. The fact was that urgency stalked the halls of the Admiralty, and the best-case scenario had to be worked out to find a northern base in these fateful times. A German naval visit to the Shetlands highlighted Admiralty fears that German torpedo craft would be deployed as required, and the advent of torpedo craft and submarines made it impossible to fulfil Sir Arthur Wilson's reassertion of the ancient maxim of close blockade: the Royal Navy must plan for a war not on the immediate sea approaches to Germany.

In September 1912 Churchill took up the position in favour of Scapa Flow, and the Sea Lords began to refer to this location as a site of high strategic significance – though, for security reasons, Scapa Flow was spoken of only as the 'Northern Base'. This inland sea, as the Admiralty Pilot described it, offered safe anchorage to the largest fleet. Before 1914 only nature provided its sure defences. Frequent bad weather, strong tides in the approaches, and almost no communications rendered this location in the Orkneys theoretically secure. No action had been taken to provide gun defences. Almost as an afterthought, Scapa Flow had been thrust into strategic prominence.

The Grand Fleet arrived at this forlorn northern anchorage in the latter days of July 1914, on the very eve of the war. Fear of a 'bolt from the blue' attack on the Grand Fleet still remained, and the Navy went there partly because they had to keep the Fleet out of German hands and partly because it served as the rendezvous point for the main units of fighting ships, nearly one hundred of all classes. On the morning of 4 August Admiral Sir John Jellicoe arrived to assume, if reluctantly, the chief command and to lead the Fleet to sea at once on its first war mission. 'The defenceless condition of the Base, both against destroyer attack and submarine attack, was brought very strongly into prominence by the presence of so valuable a Fleet at this Base,' recounted Jellicoe. He pointed out that Scapa Flow lay 450 miles from the German naval bases, and was therefore open to attack by enemy destroyer flotillas as well as by submarines.[93] In all previous wars, Britain had been advantaged by geographical position, lying athwart the great sea-lanes and capable of mounting blockades on enemy shores. But technology had changed all that. The fast destroyer powered by turbine engines, and the submarine prowling under cover of darkness and acting as a surface raider, had made the capital ships capital targets. The enemy was armed with torpedoes and mines. Therein lay the British weakness, and therein lay Jellicoe's greatest and insurmountable difficulty.

On 6 August came news of the sinking of the light cruiser *Amphion*. The day before, a flotilla of destroyers patrolling off the Dutch coast in the northern approaches of the English Channel had found the German minelayer *Königin Luise* (a converted liner), and after a hot chase had sunk her by gunfire. *Amphion*, returning from this sweep and changing her course so as to avoid the minefield sown by the enemy, thought she was clear but struck a mine. Most of the ship's company was saved but the explosion killed 130 outright. Here was the first indication of the kind of warfare that lay ahead in these waters. This was not unexpected, as the Russo-Japanese war had demonstrated the extensive use of mines on both sides, and the British had ordered both minelayers and minesweepers. To meet the new reality, the Admiralty ordered that coastwise patrols be instituted day and night to put a stop to further enemy minelaying operations in these seas. This replaced the original nucleus-based flotilla operations that had been responding to enemy threats as they arose. The loss of *Amphion* was chilling, as indeed all ship losses are, but this was a new kind of mine warfare, in which the British had only theoretical knowedge. 'It was the first opening of our eyes to the kind of enemy we had to deal with,' reflected Corbett in the official history. 'The incident, moreover, could only add to the Commander-in-Chief's anxiety for his base, especially as by the second day of the war it was fairly clear the enemy had located him.'[94] The lethality of the mine was now brought home to the British Fleet.

The loss of *Amphion* was potentially political dynamite. The public demanded an explanation. Next day Churchill spoke in the House of Commons on the enemy's use of mines. Churchill decided to disclose fully the loss and, in consequence, his speech had important implications about the role of the press in wartime. He argued that the indiscriminate use of mines against peaceful merchantmen was new in warfare and deserved to be considered by 'the nations of a civilized world'. Churchill wanted open disclosure of such tragedies, as he thought that the papers were too full of gossip and untrustworthy information. He also announced the formation of a Press Bureau, to be headed by the clever lawyer F E Smith, an MP and friend of Churchill, which would ensure that there would be a steady stream of trustworthy information from the Admiralty and the War Office to journalists, and hence remove from newspapers scurrilous and possibly damaging rumours. He also applauded the press for its restraint during the initial mobilisation period.[95] (Smith did not last long in this post, which was quite unsuitable to his nature, and within a few weeks Sir Douglas Brownrigg became the official censor of Admiralty information.)

Fisher wrote to Gwendoline, Lady Jellicoe, reassuringly on 16 August 1914:

A few lines to cheer you up! I went to London and had my *tête-à-tête* with Winston [15 August], and afterwards saw all the war arrangements. All seemed to me first class and most satisfactory. He was full of admiration and regard for 'J. R. J[ellicoe].'! (*and well he may be!*), and he felt and spoke so nicely of the fearful strain of nightly going out to sea, etc. *Burn this.*

Give J. R. J. my best love when you write and say he is always in my thoughts, but I have no misgivings of the final result. Every day that goes by makes it worse for Germany on the sea. Our policy should be that of the serpent, not the lion![96]

In distant Scapa Flow a lonely Jellicoe pondered how to deploy the Grand Fleet in mine-infested waters. His woes never diminished. In a letter to Battenberg, Jellicoe enumerated the dangers facing the Grand Fleet in the North Sea. He warned of considerable risk from mines during a sweep of the North Sea. As he pointed out, the use of minesweepers sent out in advance was bound to slow the battle fleet to a dangerous 10 knots and make it vulnerable to enemy submarines and torpedoes. If the mines did not get the dreadnoughts, the torpedoes might. In future naval warfare a calculated risk had to be taken; this he realised. He bravely argued that the risk, and even the possible loss of several dreadnoughts, would be worth the price – in ships and men – of catching the German fleet at sea.[97]

Jellicoe maintained his composure in the face of all these challenges. Churchill, ever mindful of Jellicoe's difficulties, had the measure of the situation when he wrote, retrospectively, on the potential posed by mines and torpedoes and how this affected strategy and tactics:

16. Churchill inspecting a guard of honour at the launch of HMS *Warspite* at Devonport by Mrs Austen Chamberlain in November 1913. Churchill was also to be present at her gunnery trials in 1915 when he was suitably impressed by her 15in armament.

17. Churchill, the First Lord of the Admiralty, and Prince Louis of Battenberg, his First Sea Lord, cross Horse Guards Parade in 1914 at the outbreak of the war. The latter was dismissed at the end of October that year, partly as a result of the press campaign against all things German.

18. HMS Audacious listing to port after striking a German mine off the north coast of Ireland on 27 October 1914, photographed here from the deck of the White Star liner *Olympic*, which stood by to take off the crew. Not wishing to fuel a debate about the value of battleships, Churchill insisted on a blanket news ban. The press abided by this and the loss was not announced until November 1918.

19. Churchill and his wife Clementine pictured relaxing on the beach at Sandwich, Kent, in about 1912.

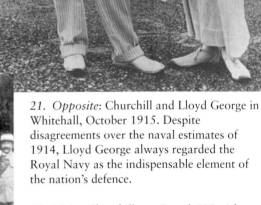

21. *Opposite*: Churchill and Lloyd George in Whitehall, October 1915. Despite disagreements over the naval estimates of 1914, Lloyd George always regarded the Royal Navy as the indispensable element of the nation's defence.

20. Major Churchill at a French HQ. After falling from grace and leaving the Admiralty in May 1915, Churchill found a battalion command on the Western Front later that year. He was forty-one but his training as a soldier allowed him to make a success of his new role and his experiences gave him an insight into aspects of warfare denied to other leaders.

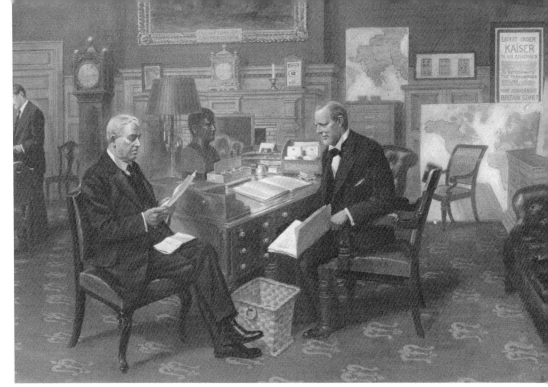

22. A drawing of Churchill with Fisher at the Admiralty in 1914, which appeared in *The London Illustrated News* and was intended perhaps to depict the two working together in complete accord.

23. *Right*: Churchill leaving his London home for the House of Commons on 7 March 1916 to speak in the debate on the naval estimates, at the end of which he urged the First Lord of the Admiralty to recall Fisher and provoked, to his dismay and humiliation, derision across the House and beyond.

24. Admiral of the Fleet John Jellicoe, onboard *Iron Duke* with ships of the Grand Fleet astern. Reluctant to take on the command of the Grand Fleet when war broke out, it took the intervention of Churchill finally to persuade him.

25. Admiral of the Fleet David Beatty was a favourite of Churchill, who admired his swashbuckling style, appointing him as his Naval Secretary in 1911.

26. Kaiser Wilhelm II, the driving force behind the expansion of the German navy.

27. Grossadmiral Alfred von Tirpitz, creator of the High Seas Fleet.

The four principal architects of the German navy.

28. Admiral Reinhard Scheer, commander of the High Seas Fleet at Jutland.

29. Admiral Franz von Hipper, commander of the German battlecruisers at Jutland.

30. The Grand Fleet at sea, led by *Iron Duke*. Its role as a deterrent was essentially a passive one, but in May 1916 it found itself facing the prospect of a major sea battle.

31. Rear-Admiral Sir Douglas Brownrigg, the chief naval censor throughout the war, worked closely with Churchill while he was at the Admiralty and found himself in daily contact during the Dardanelles campaign.

32. Jellicoe bidding farewell to Kitchener onboard *Iron Duke* on 5 June 1916 as the latter prepared to board HMS *Hampshire*. Later that day observers on the Orkneys witnessed *Hampshire* explode and within minutes she was sinking by the bows. Kitchener's body was never found.

33. British battleships, photographed from a naval airship and led by HMS *Queen Elizabeth*, lead in the German High Seas Fleet on 21 November 1918 prior to their internment at Scapa Flow.

34. Sketch drawn by Oscar Parkes of Fisher's proposed HMS *Incomparable*, shown here alongside HMS *Dreadnought*. She was designed to mount six 20in guns, which would have fired shells weighing 2 tons.

35. Fisher died on 10 July 1920 and on the 13th his body was borne in solemn state to Westminster Abbey, passing Nelson's column, and flanked the whole way by, as *The Times* reported the following day, 'crowds upon crowds of the English public, bareheaded, still, silent, reverently paying their inarticulate homage to the great man.'

First and foremost, last and dominating in the mind of the Commander-in-Chief stood the determination not to hazard the Battle Fleet. The risk of under-water damage by torpedo and mine, and the consequent destruction of the British battleship superiority lay heavy upon him. It far outweighed all considerations of the results on either side of gunfire. It was the main preoccupation of Admiralty thought before the war. From the opening of hostilities the spectacle of great vessels vanishing in a few moments as the result of an under-water explosion constantly deepened the impression.[98]

Churchill's comment has often been called up in reference to what transpired at Jutland. The truth is that it obtained in respect to the naval war from beginning to end.

War in the Narrow Seas

Meantime, the Kaiser's great fleet, known as the German High Seas Fleet, rode easily at anchor at the mouth of the Jade. The ships, officers, and men were doubtless prepared for war. So they remained for a tantalisingly long time. Ships' companies waited for a command that never came. Rust set in. No order arrived from Berlin to venture into the English Channel to pounce on transports carrying the BEF to French ports. Such a somnolent interlude had not been imagined, but the Kaiser had determined that his ships should not be hazarded in an action. The 'fleet in being' was what mattered most, and this brought strong objections from the Secretary of the Navy, Admiral von Tirpitz, who grumbled that it was 'simply nonsense to pack the fleet in cotton wool'. He thought that continual activity and minor successes would force the Grand Fleet to seek out the German fleet in its own waters. We have it on the fine authority of Admiral Scheer that, to a man, German admirals assumed that at the outbreak of war, in keeping with British tradition and lore, the Grand Fleet would attack the German High Seas Fleet as soon as it showed itself and wherever it did so.[99] But Tirpitz and the admirals were wrong: in London the Admiralty had no such intention, prepared as it was for the waiting game.

And so began the game of cat and mouse. Who would make the first move? At war's outset the Admiralty had no designs for ordering a rapid sortie into German inshore waters, notably the well-defended Heligoland Bight; better to keep a distant blockade (the policy adopted in 1912) and await the enemy's appearance in the broader waters of the North Sea. The Admiralty had no intention of entering the Baltic, either (though Churchill and Fisher flirted with the prospect). Fisher's idea of 'Copenhagening' the German fleet along Nelsonic lines was dead.

Passivity became the order of the day on both sides. Meanwhile, in numbers the British dreadnoughts grew in superiority over the German counterparts. In the circumstances it was natural that the British public had an expectation of battle that was never realised; they had been misled by the Nelson tradition and other heroic episodes of naval combat that decisive battles were the main features of a war. They were therefore ill-equipped for the long and tedious struggle of strangling German commerce and throttling the German populace by blockade. 'Although unseen and unheard,' noted *The Times* on 25 August 1914, 'the Fleet is exerting continual and progressively stringent pressure upon the vitals of the foe.' Such reassuring views were small comfort in the British Fleet, where impatience grew.

In the circumstances, or perhaps in spite of them, Churchill was restless. He must await the first German move at sea. The great dreadnoughts of the Grand Fleet found themselves caught in circumstances beyond control, and as long as the Kaiser held on to his warships and embargoed any sortie, Jellicoe and Beatty could do little. Thus the naval war in the Narrow Seas settled down to ambushes and counterstrokes. The effect on Churchill was clear to Captain Herbert Richmond, working as the assistant director of the operations division in the Admiralty, who had Churchill to dinner in late October. Richmond found the First Lord in:

> low spirits ... oppressed with the impossibility of doing anything. The attitude of waiting, threatened all the time by submarines, unable to strike back at their Fleet ... and the inability of the Staff to make any suggestions seem to bother him. I have not seen him so despondent before ... I urged mining their coast, but he won't have it. I suggested a raid ... upon these confounded intelligence [gathering] fishing craft [under neutral flags]. He liked that ... He wanted to send battleships – old ones – up the Elbe, but for what purpose except to be sunk I did not understand.'[100]

Then, as earlier, Churchill was anxious to get the Germans out of harbour somehow.

This state of affairs changed when a forty-three-year-old commodore, an expert in destroyer and submarine tactics, finally got the attention of the Admiralty by requesting an interview with Churchill, then four years his junior. The push for an action in the dangerous waters of the Heligoland Bight originated with Roger Keyes, in command of the submarines at Harwich.[101] He found an able accomplice in Commodore Reginald Tyrwhitt, who led the destroyer flotillas also based at Harwich. Keyes and Tyrwhitt brought a scheme audacious in intent, something along the lines of Nelson's 'Engage the enemy more closely'. In a meeting at the Admiralty, Churchill heard Keyes out and gave support – to which Battenberg gave concurrence. The plan was made and put in motion. Thirty-one destroyers, including flotilla leaders in light cruisers, plus eight submarines and two battlecruisers would sail from their respective British ports at midnight on 26 August. In the early morning of the 28th, in patchy visibility, most of the units came on the scene where, as events proved, single-ship engagements were the rule. Meanwhile, from his base at Scapa, Jellicoe had wisely ordered three battlecruisers and six light cruisers in support. He did so on his own initiative, fearing Admiralty meddling. It was a good thing he sent the battlecruisers. In fact, the British submarines and destroyers, the latter led by Tyrwhitt in the light cruiser *Arethusa*, were approaching the jaws of death. The submarine and destroyer flotillas steamed into the German Bight. Alarm bells sounded. German light cruisers were sent out to engage, but without help from heavy units. Three German light cruisers and a destroyer met their fate, and more than a thousand German officers and men were casualties on the day. In the hot action, *Arethusa* suffered much damage. No British ships were lost, but there were seventy-one British casualties. Post-mortems continue on this battle, and it is clear that the combined force would not have extracted itself had Beatty not arrived with a force of two powerful battlecruisers and scattered the enemy with heavy gunfire. The appearance of three German light cruisers, and three more in the offing, had led Tyrwhitt to call on Beatty for aid. Churchill's description in *The World Crisis* of the British 'rampaging about' is hardly accurate.[102] It was very nearly a British naval disaster.

After the Heligoland Bight action, Tyrwhitt was made a Companion of the Bath, and he recorded that Winston 'fairly slobbered over me'.[103] Beatty's report of proceedings of the action off Heligoland gave much satisfaction to Their Lordships, who sent an appreciative letter to him, proclaiming 'the resolution and promptitude shown by him in bringing his Squadron into action with decisive effect notwithstanding the risks which he had to face from submarines and floating mines.' Jellicoe, who forwarded this message to Beatty, concurred fully in Their Lordships' appreciation.[104] This has its fascination, for it reveals in the early months of the war the acceptable risks that battlecruisers could take against enemy cruisers, destroyers, submarines, and mines. Had, however, one of these great greyhound racers been stopped by any such obstacles, we wonder what the Admiralty might have sent in reply. In the circumstances of success, all they could do was send approbation.

Beatty knew that the loss of even a single battlecruiser would have been a catastrophe, and that the whole operation was fraught with danger. In the event, he had arrived in overwhelming force, changing the tide of battle. Churchill had minuted on the report of proceedings: 'It was a fine feat of arms, vindicated by success.'[105] That was the Churchillian touch. However, there had been disasters in signals intelligence. For example, at 8.53am, Keyes saw four light cruisers in the area and assumed they were German. He ordered his destroyers to go west and extricate themselves from a perilous situation. The cruisers were in fact British, commanded by William Goodenough. Keyes signalled him: 'I was not informed you were coming into this area; you run great risks from our submarines ... Your unexpected appearance has upset all our plans.' Goodenough replied tartly: 'I came under detailed orders. I am astonished that you were not told.'[106] Admiralty blunders continued. In truth, Keyes contended privately, the Heligoland Bight action had been an 'awful muddle', and they could have sunk several German vessels if the submarines had been deployed early enough.[107]

Thoughts now turned to the prospects of damage that mines, torpedoes, and U-boats could do.[108] The certainty that Germany, as a defensive measure, had mined approaches to its anchorages and fortifications was a matter of great concern. But it was simply an example of tit for tat in the new naval war. Just as German Admiral Franz von Hipper complained, privately, of 'a damned dangerous lack of information on where the British have laid mines' in waters near Scarborough and Hartlepool, where a bombardment was to take place in December, so too the British did not know what they might expect in waters mined by the Germans.[109] Fisher was guided by history. In his view, the British should make much better use of mines by mining the exits of the German ports, as Japanese Admiral Togo Heihachiro had done to the Russians at Port Arthur. Such a move would let the British know when the Germans were about to sortie, based on their minesweeping efforts.[110]

There was added concern about torpedoes. Churchill knew that the Germans were wise to decline battle, for doing so automatically secured to them the command of the Baltic. A conference was held aboard Jellicoe's flagship *Iron Duke*. In attendance were Churchill, the Chief of the War Staff, and various senior commanders. Operations in the Baltic were discussed, but due largely to danger from mines, it was decided to be inadvisable to risk any forces in 'eccentric movements'. Vice-Admiral Sir Lewis Bayly, commanding the Channel Fleet, however, had advocated an attack on Kiel. Jellicoe, our authority for what transpired in these discussions, stated that once it was possible to field two strong fleets, one in the North Sea and one in the Baltic, the question of policy would be investigated once again.[111]

Even as the British were making their inquiries and calculations, Hipper, the flag officer responsible for defence of the German Bight, with several flotillas of minesweepers in his command, was recommending more sophisticated measures for underwater attack and, indeed, for underwater defence. He needed more seaworthy, larger, and speedier vessels for minesweeping and torpedo work. He wanted U-boats that were capable of laying mines (ten U-boats were added to these operations in 1915/16). Later he advocated a complete net defence of German Bight and harbours. For each net barrage a watch ship was appointed. He wanted, too, wire-controlled speedboats that could go out in advance of any force sent to sea. They were built, but not in time for the war.[112]

The first months of the war also saw the first use of signals intelligence, or SIGINT, by 'Blinker' Hall and the men in Room 40, mentioned earlier. German naval codebooks had come into the Admiralty's hands, and wireless direction-finding equipment was aiding the reading of German actions and intentions. By mid-November, Churchill, with Fisher's concurrence, had taken a significant step by ordering that all intercepted intelligence – the raw data – was to be interpreted by a specially assigned expert in order to ensure the credibility of the intelligence reports and to fit them into the broader intelligence picture. This ensured that the intelligence received underwent a rigorous examination to ensure its utility, and made it much more valuable in terms of combating the tactical moves of the German fleet. Intelligence acquired by Room 40 was also kept extremely secret. An intelligence report, of which only one copy was to be made, would be sent to the Chief of Staff who then forwarded it to the First Sea Lord. Members of the Cabinet or the War Council were not informed of the existence of such intelligence, and only the prime minister, among those outside the Admiralty, was routinely informed of the latest intelligence coups of Britain's most important intelligence organisation. Unfortunately, commanders at sea were also excluded from the intelligence reports. The lack of a full and effective naval war staff also militated against the effectiveness of Room 40.[113] All in all, however, the British possessed an advantage over the Germans that was to have a profound impact on the outcome of the war.

Winston's little war: the Dunkirk circus and the Antwerp adventure

On 1 August the Kaiser authorised the mobilisation of the Field Army of the German Empire, commanded by Colonel-General Helmuth von Moltke. Germany planned to strike first against France with full force. Moltke told the chief of the Austrian General Staff that France would be routed in six weeks; then the army could shift to the east to smash Russia in turn. General Count Alfred von Schlieffen, Moltke's predecessor, had first sketched this plan in 1905. It involved railway timetables, unit deployments according to schedule, supply arrangements worked out in advance, and a victory that would be won by a wide flank march around the powerful French fortresses between Verdun and Belfort. However, the German high command miscalculated: the German armies kept up the offensive, but at terrific cost. Moltke collapsed and had to be replaced: he was horrified by the civilian casualties inflicted.

Beginning on 6 August and lasting for nearly two weeks, the German army deployed in a great methodical sweep to envelop France. On the north, the ring fortress of Liège guarded the Belgian plain, but the soon-to-be-famous staff officer Erich Ludendorff took the town, then awaited the arrival of monster howitzers to complete the destruction of the defences. The Liège forts soon fell to heavy bombardment, and the Belgian army withdrew to Antwerp for the desperate last stand. German army units had already begun reprisals against thousands of Belgian civilians, utterly destroying the famous university city Louvain.[114] These first several months of German actions made clear that German military strategy included the concept of frightfulness, and in England the image of the Hun came into gruesome, sharp relief. It now seemed certain that Belgium would be occupied, making the possibility of German military posts on the English Channel a formidable prospect.

On 7 August, under the safe cover of British cruisers and naval aircraft, the Admiralty set about the massive task of transporting the British Expeditionary Force across the English Channel to France. Between then and 27 August the Royal Navy, without the loss of a man or damage to the ships, safely deployed 120,000 men across the English Channel. It had been a wonderful operation of a scale previously undreamed of, and it had been conducted in such secrecy that the German Supreme Command confidently told its army command in Belgium that no landing of British troops on a large scale had yet taken place. This was on the eve of the first shot fired by the British on the Continent on 22 August. Fisher liked to say that the Army was a projectile to be fired by the Navy. Here lay proof of that.

The BEF commenced its concentration, taking up its intended position on the north and west flank of the French army. The great clash occurred at Mons, followed by a British withdrawal to reposition. The German army's push to defeat the French army was halted at the Battle of the Marne. The day of the Schlieffen Plan had ended. Then, in consequence of a whirl of flanking and counter-flanking movements, the front shifted north and into Belgium, leaving the exposed and, for the Allies, vitally important Channel ports alone. If Germany could get possession of Antwerp, it would gain immeasurable power in waters opposite the River Thames. German staff knew that Antwerp must be taken to safeguard the right rear of their armies swinging down into France. After Mons, when the officer commanding the BEF, Sir John French, recommended that Le Havre needed to be reinforced, the Board of Admiralty advised that precautions should be taken at Cherbourg and St-Nazaire, even farther west and south. Churchill also signalled Jellicoe to contemplate the proper positioning of the Grand Fleet if the Germans were to control the Channel coast.

Churchill grasped the realities of the German sweep toward Paris by way of Luxembourg and the Belgian frontier. He had the instincts for making war, and instincts for taking the initiative. He had his pet schemes, and the Admiralty gave him almost unlimited scope to carry them out. On 2 August the Admiralty authorised the formation of the 'Flying Column' Royal Marines, from which developed the Royal Marine Brigade, something of a private army for Churchill, and he had his own air wing, the Royal Naval Air Service (RNAS); he could do very much as he liked with these resources. At the outset of the war he had established a naval air station at Ostend, where he deployed aeroplanes and an airship crossing the Channel. This was seen as critical in matters of surveillance and communications, as it was designed to keep a watch out for any German naval movements, including submarines, and to give early warning. Under Wing Commander C R Samson, aeroplanes made reconnaissance flights daily over the area between Bruges, Ghent, and Ypres. Samson made a motor-car reconnaissance as far as Bruges in two cars, one of them fitted with a Maxim gun. Churchill considered it essential to deny Zeppelins the use of space within a hundred miles of Dunkirk. On 3 September Kitchener asked Churchill to take responsibility for the aerial defence of the United Kingdom. Churchill agreed, and so was in charge of all Royal Flying Corps aircraft engaged in the defence of the home islands, plus searchlights and anti-aircraft guns, as well as the RNAS.[115]

Churchill was the apostle of the offensive and soon began considering landing forces on other coasts. All this ran counter to wisdom at the highest level in the Admiralty. Sir Julian Corbett, the historian who knew the lessons of history in amphibious and combined operations, and who was then working at CID offices at 2 Whitehall Gardens, was shocked to hear proposals for amphibious strikes coming from the First Lord. As early as 11 August, he noted in his diary, some important people began to promote swift offensive measures. Corbett was appalled: 'Our position at sea gives us all we want.' Later dubbed the father of limited war, Corbett thought it absolutely reckless to send small, slightly trained amphibious attacks to the Continent. They were not viable substitutes for intensive combined operations. Corbett, powerless to give direct advice to Churchill or Battenberg, nonetheless began to prepare a memorandum for the naval staff on the inadvisability of attempting an offensive against '[a] skulking enemy'.

But within a week Churchill was advocating formation of a naval brigade, using naval reservists, that would be built around the existing Marine brigade and under Admiralty control, which would serve alongside the Army, occupying advanced naval bases.[116] At this early stage the best Churchill could get from the Board of Admiralty was approval for a naval demonstration – in an effort to distract the Germans, the Marine Brigade was landed at the port of Ostend, Belgium, on 26 August, where it stayed for a week.[117] This was half a loaf. A modified Churchill plan was later carried out, but it was of too small a scale to have any dramatic effect on German movements. This episode showed how Churchill 'could overrule his naval experts, that he hungered for action, and that he ignored naval advice.'[118] All the plans, schemes, and rules for the conduct of war that had been worked out for years at the Naval War College in Greenwich, where Corbett had been the leading exponent of maritime strategy, and of limited, combined, and amphibious warfare, were now dead. Political expediency had supplanted sound military thought and practice. Politics deflected strategy. Churchill proceeded with his designs.

On 7 September *The Times* announced formation of a force of 15,000 men called the Naval Brigades. These grew into the Royal Naval Division, consisting of the 1st Brigade (Battalions: Benbow, Collingwood, Hawke, and Drake) and 2nd Brigade (Battalions: Howe, Hood, Anson, and Nelson). 'Mr. Churchill, with characteristic genius and energy, has decided to take advantage of this patriotic feeling [of young men wanting to join the Navy] ... the nucleus of which will be found in existing reserves for the naval services which cannot be given employment afloat at present.' The Royal Marines, which had been at Ostend, formed a third brigade.

Fisher was drawn into the scheme. On 6 September he wrote to his son to say that Churchill had called him. 'Winston Churchill got me on the phone this morning and wants me to be the head of something – some sort of Naval Brigade, I think ... but the telephone not very clear. He said he had written, but I had never got the letter. Probably some German spy postman has sent it to Berlin!' A lunch at the Admiralty was set for discussion of it, and Fisher told Churchill that he was 'ready to do any mortal thing, *even to co-operating with Beresford!* if any good for the War.'[119] Fisher was made the honorary colonel of the 1st Royal Naval Brigade. The first thing he did was send the following letter to its commander, Commodore Wilfred Henderson:

> Tell them to look forward to splendid duty both by sea and land.
> Our island history is full of glorious deeds of Sailor's Brigade in every war.
> Let us beat the record!
> A fight to the finish![120]

The formation of the Naval Brigades came as a stopgap, for the BEF did not have the force in strength that had been anticipated (two divisions were held back in England for territorial defence). Four divisions of infantry plus the cavalry division were despatched to the Continent. Churchill's argument was that if the sailors were not needed at sea, they could be employed with effect on land. With haste they were gathered together and drilled as best they could be, but it is generally agreed that they were poorly trained and ill-equipped. Churchill had asked Kitchener for artillery, and had even suggested that units in India be brought home to support the Naval Division. Kitchener replied that he had no officers or guns to spare. It was said at the time that these new and largely untrained units would not be used on the Continent until the naval situation was entirely favourable to the Allies. However, as the days of August advanced, and as German successes became manifest, it was clear the Naval Brigades would soon be deployed.

Our story now shifts to the left flank of the Allied armies and to the double and interlocking story of the 'Dunkirk circus' (or as Churchill renamed it 'the Dunkirk guerrilla') and Churchill's Antwerp adventure, the whole forming a chapter in British military operations that has always been on the margins of history. It has unerring attraction for us, as it is an episode in which Churchill played a conspicuous part. As events proved, it did him little credit, engulfed as he was in the tumultuous events of those early months of the war. Fisher later wrote that the BEF ought to have gone to Antwerp rather than to the Ypres salient, and he may have been right.[121] But in the circumstances of the unfolding war, the requirement to come to France's immediate aid did not allow for a Belgium operation, and so the die was cast.

On 16 September Kitchener received a telegram from General Joffre of the French high command asking for reinforcements to be sent to Dunkirk to confuse the Germans as to the strength of the defences and to otherwise threaten their lines of communication. Churchill later maintained that the 'Dunkirk circus' did not originate with him but was the result of other factors. This is correct: Kitchener consulted Churchill. What was needed, besides reinforcing the Dunkirk garrison, were mobile forces that could display power by mobile arrangements and create diversions. Churchill sent the Royal Marine Brigade and insisted that a force of yeomanry also be sent. Thus it was that the Oxfordshire Hussars, mobilised on 4 August and in which his brother Jack Churchill was a major, came to be part of the operation. A charming sidelight on the Churchills' own regiment was recounted by General J F C Fuller, the noted historian of war:

> I remember when the Oxford Hussars embarked, they brought with them a vast quantity of kit: tin uniform boxes, suitcases and cabin trunks, as if they were on their way round the world. Someone questioned the loading of this baggage, whereupon a red-faced Major burst into my office in a towering rage: 'This is simply damnable!' he shouted. 'Winston said we could take 'em, and now one of your prize B.F.s says we can't ...' 'All right! All right!' I cut him short. 'What is the trouble about?' And having ascertained what the First Lord of the Admiralty had sanctioned, I telephoned down to the A.E.S.O. in charge to load the officers' trousseaux – a word which did not seem to please my furious friend. All were loaded, and, I believe, a week later were unpacked by German hands.[122]

It was also arranged that fifty London motorbuses would be sent with them to make them as mobile and conspicuous as possible as they rumbled through Ypres, Lille, Tournai, and Douai. The whole business constituted a demonstration, or a feint, designed to give an ostentatious display of a British Army arriving and thereby warding off a German approach to Belgium and the adjacent French coast. Using air reconnaissance and cover, and employing mobile squads, the intention was to give an appearance of something greater than it actually was. Churchill could supply the naval air support as required. The Royal Marines were disembarked at Dunkirk on the night of 19/20 September. They gave aid to the RNAS unit that had a squad of fifty armoured Rolls-Royce motor cars. These mounted Vickers machine guns, and some of them carried mounted armoured plate slung in such a way that they could bridge cuts in the road deliberately excavated by German units. (A hint of the development of the tank shows itself here.) Jack's company of Oxfordshire Hussars acted as an escort to the naval air squadron commanded by Captain C R Samson. The ranging sorties of these cars with armour plating discomfited the Germans, causing them to withdraw, but at the same time attracted the attention of the German higher command. Three squadrons of RNAS bombarded German defences from bases in northern France. And from its base at Dunkirk the naval air wing soon began to take the war to the enemy's air power. Twelve aircraft stationed at Dunkirk flew missions of destruction against Zeppelin bases, and put advance German air bases and refuelling depots being constructed in Belgium out of commission.

Churchill took an active part in directing these operations, crossing the Channel frequently in the cruiser *Adventurer* to confirm the force's needs were adequately provided for, and at one stage intervening to make sure that heavy lorries and additional buses were sent. It was a successful operation, but the Royal Marines were withdrawn three days later, and were embarked in the 7th Battle Cruiser Squadron, the same units that had ferried them across the Channel. Worries that the cruisers posed too tempting a target brought the amphibious operation to an end. From this early episode we find the genesis and evolution of the 'Dunkirk circus' – with Churchill at the centre of operations and decision-making.

Asquith, said his daughter, referred to Churchill's Dunkirk force as 'his own little army', which is true.[123] It was rather clear to his critics (sitting more comfortably in London) that he was engaging in what might be called 'Winston's little war', and he waged it with intensity and imagination. While many of his Cabinet colleagues recoiled at thoughts of a continental war and others sought alliances to serve the interests of the nation, Churchill plunged right in and proceeded to act strongly and independently, a tendency supported by his powerful office at the Admiralty. The Battle of the Marne, already mentioned, checked the German race to the sea and took the pressure off Dunkirk, but now the worrying scene shifted north along the coast to Antwerp. Napoleon had seen this Belgian city as 'a pistol pointed at the heart of England',

and Churchill, fully conversant with Napoleon's thinking on these matters, realised that the coast and the Channel ports in enemy hands would threaten the security of the British Isles. At the outset of the war he had pressed on his Cabinet colleagues the necessity of guarding against German domination there; however, no independent action was possible as there still was no Allied military strategy in this regard. Meanwhile, events were unrolling rapidly. With Kitchener's nominal support, Churchill's immediate scheme was to keep the Channel ports in Allied hands.

From the British perspective, precious Antwerp had to be held, and the King of Belgium and his army kept in the field against rising German numbers. In 1914 the Belgian army comprised six divisions and a cavalry division, with fortress troops stationed at the 'national redoubt', Antwerp, which was intended to serve as the last defence and rallying point of Belgian forces. Its defences consisted of an inner ring of fortifications and an additional outlying girdle of posts. Farther beyond were barrier forts and bridgeheads on the Meuse River and at Liège and Namur, designed to guard approaches to Antwerp. By virtue of Belgium's avowed neutral status, Belgian military dispositions guarded against all comers, including the French, the British, and even the Dutch. The Belgian government's policy was to await the course of events. Reorganisation of the army had been ordered in 1912, though the implementation was incomplete. Not only was Belgium less ready than most nations, but it was also in the throes of reorganisation and incapable of putting as many men into the field as even the British regular army.[124]

By early September the tide of events had overwhelmed Belgium. The fate of Antwerp, the last refuge of the gallant little Belgian army, hung in the balance. The situation declined daily. The Germans were masters of northern France, and their advance had left only a narrow and insecure land corridor to the west of the city. The Belgian army, vastly outnumbered, had fallen back on Antwerp. From whence should aid come? To the north, the Dutch, defending their own neutrality, resolutely insisted that no military vessels use the River Scheldt to move reinforcements to Antwerp, which fronted on that river. Churchill, though, insisted that the city must be held, and he sent both naval guns and ammunition, and pressured Grey, unsuccessfully, to more strongly assert to Dutch authorities the British desire to traverse the Scheldt.[125] Daily the pressure mounted: Zeppelins bombed Antwerp. Krupp howitzers – the great tactical innovation of the war – pounded the outworks of the city. By midnight on 2 October the situation in Antwerp had become critical. The fall of the city seemed imminent. Word reached Grey at the Foreign Office that the Belgian government might soon capitulate. If that occurred, and the Belgian army surrendered, the BEF would be further imperilled, to the point of complete withdrawal or even surrender.

What measures could be taken in these desperate hours? In London, Kitchener, Grey, and Sir William Tyrrell, an official of the Foreign Office, were holed up at Kitchener's residence in Carlton Gardens, trying to decide how to deal with the situation. Asquith, on political business, had left the capital for Cardiff and was largely out of touch. The burden fell on the shoulders of Kitchener, who seemed to have grown older since becoming Secretary of State for War, time and anxiety having taken their toil. Not many days before, Churchill, sensing the growing danger, had burst into his room, pleading for Kitchener's permission to leave at once for Antwerp. Now the situation had changed, and Churchill was on a train bound for Dover, en route to Dunkirk on some naval business. Kitchener and Grey decided they must consult Churchill in person. Accordingly, they sent an immediate message halting his train (then passing through Kent) and calling him back to London. Before very long Churchill was at Victoria Station, and shortly thereafter he entered Kitchener's drawing room accompanied by Battenberg, the First Sea Lord. Kitchener gave his explanations. Churchill developed a plan, while the others listened and reserved opinion. Antwerp must be propped up. He announced that he would go there at once himself and would also send the Royal Marine Brigade to the city. When he was on the spot, he said, he would be able to send back an immediate report on the situation.

Kitchener voiced opinion in favour of Churchill going. For his part, the Foreign Secretary was not at all sure that Churchill ought to undertake this adventure, not because it seemed foolhardy or undesirable in itself, but because 'the risk of having the First Lord of the Admiralty shut up in Antwerp was startling.' He nonetheless thought that the energy, resourcefulness, and courage of his colleague might save the situation. Accordingly, he set aside his reservations and Grey acquiesced.[126] In the circumstances, as all three realised, Battenberg would remain alone at the Admiralty to deal with whatever might arise in Churchill's absence. No fears or reservations seem to have been expressed. Perhaps Churchill would be back in London in a few days? No one knew.

The First Lord, charged with new, perhaps even hoped-for, duties largely of his own design, started off again at midnight for Victoria Station. By 1.30am he was comfortably back on his specially waiting train, outward bound not for Dunkirk, as was customary, but for Antwerp. When Asquith learned of the discussion the next day, he wrote to Venetia Stanley: 'I was of course away, but Grey, Kitchener & Winston held a later meeting, and (I fancy with Grey's rather reluctant assent) the intrepid Winston set off at midnight ... I cannot but think that he will stiffen them [the Belgians] up to the sticking point.'[127] Asquith, amused by the whole adventure of intended rescue, wondered how fluent in French Churchill was, 'but if he was able to do himself justice in a foreign tongue, the Belges will have listened to a discourse the like of which they have never heard before.'[128]

Churchill's plan was put into operation. Two brigades of the Royal Naval Division, already landed at Dunkirk, were dispatched toward Antwerp on the night of 3/4 October. With the 3rd Brigade, the Royal Marine Brigade, they came under the command of Brigadier General Sir George Aston, RMA. Among the tasks of the Marines was securing any possible naval bases of use to the Allies. In the air, reconnaissance by naval pilots aided progress and security on the ground.

Chaos and pandemonium reigned in and around Antwerp when Churchill's motor car arrived in a cloud of dust at the *hôtel de ville*. Roads and intersections were jammed with carts, lorries, motor cars, and buses. There was disorder among the troops. The prospect of enemy shells landing at any moment added to the confusion and the fear. There was, said an English observer, the *Daily Mail* correspondent J M N Jeffries, 'no-one to direct, no-one to disentangle the jumble.' He continued:

No-one, that is to say, till a man jumped from a car and, hoisting himself to vantage upon some unseen pedestal or other, began to cry out at the mob in Anglo-French, and to point with vigorous, imperative gestures to this or that centre of the maelstrom. He was a remarkable and in that places an inexplicable figure, clad in a flowing dark blue cloak, clasped at the neck with silver lion-heads or something of that sort, after the fashion of the cloaks worn by prelates in Rome, and this cloak fell in great folds from this stretched oratorical arm. But there was purpose in his gestures, and power in his voice, and under his direction cars and carts were unlocked from each other, and the traffic gradually sorted into streams.

The car in which I was fell into its own channel and went past with the others, but as I looked back he was still at his post, poised like a statue, watching till the order he had created was installed with durable momentum. It was Mr. Winston Churchill.

It is hard to imagine the First Lord of the Admiralty directing traffic in a Belgian city. Yet the tale is true, for Churchill was in a hurry to get to his destination, his intended command headquarters. Jeffries sent news of this characteristic and valuable piece of work to London in his telegram. However, censors forbade it to be printed.[129]

Another correspondent, an American, recorded Churchill's flamboyant arrival at his designated headquarters:

At one o'clock that afternoon a big, drab-coloured touring-car, filled with British naval officers, drove down the Place de Mer, its horn sounding a hoarse warning, took the turn into the March-aux-Souliers on two wheels, and drew up in front of the hotel. Before the car had fairly come to a stop the door of the tonneau was thrown violently open and out jumped a smooth-faced, sandy-haired, stoop-shouldered, youthful looking man in undress Trinity House uniform ... As he charged into the crowded lobby he flung his arms out, in a nervous characteristic gesture, as though pushing his way through a crowd. It was a most spectacular entrance, and reminded me for all the world of a scene in a melodrama where the hero dashes up bare-headed on a foam-flecked horse, and saves the heroine, or the old homestead, or the family fortune, as the case may be.[130]

While meeting with the Belgian high command on 3 October, and hoping to stiffen their resolve, Churchill offered as direct aid to send the Naval Brigades in addition to the Royal Marines Brigade. Afterwards, Churchill sent a detailed account of the discussions to Kitchener and Grey: 'If you clinch these propositions, pray give the following order to the Admiralty: Send at once both naval brigades, minus recruits, via Dunkirk, into Antwerp, without tents or much impedimenta, but with five days' rations and 2,000,000 rounds of ammunition. When can they arrive?'[131] Churchill never got any sizeable artillery to support his forces, but ammunition was supplied generously to the Belgians. The Naval Division was sent as Churchill requested.

For his headquarters he chose one of the principal hotels. Rear-Admiral Henry Oliver, the Naval Secretary, took Churchill's dictation while the First Lord was in bed in the forenoon. In the afternoon of 4 October, Churchill toured Antwerp's defences, often under German gunfire, taking note of enemy dispositions, giving advice on trenches, suggesting places for reinforcement, and rather blatantly taking direct charge of the search for available men and equipment. Walking stick in hand, he thumped the ground with it, seizing command of a deteriorating situation. He telegraphed the Admiralty for specific supplies and ordered entrenching tools, 4in guns, and duffle suits for the crews of the armoured trains being readied for action.[132] Such items as he could command he did, and he made the best of them. On one occasion he called for air support, and four planes of the RNAS from Ostend agreeably came on the scene to deal with a Zeppelin dropping bombs on the city.

The situation for the defence grew increasingly grim, and the next day, 5 October, Churchill had become less sanguine about the prospects of holding Antwerp against the relentless German assault. He came to believe (as only he could) that continued resistance had come to depend on his leadership. He therefore proposed to take formal military charge of British forces in Antwerp. He telegraphed Asquith offering his resignation from the Admiralty:

If it is thought by HM Government that I can be of service here, I am willing to resign my office and undertake command of relieving and defensive forces assigned to Antwerp in conjunction with Belgian Army, provided that I am given necessary military rank and authority, and full powers of a commander of the detached force in the field. I feel it my duty to offer my services, because I am sure this arrangement will afford the best prospects of a victorious result to an enterprise in which I am deeply involved ... Runciman [President of the Board of Control] would do Admiralty well.[133]

(It may be mentioned here that Churchill had no copy of this telegram sent from Antwerp. When he read proofs of Beaverbrook's *Politicians and the War* in 1927, he found the text of the telegram there, and asked the author how it had come into his possession. Beaverbrook answered: 'I have the original message annotated in Kitchener's own writing. It would bother me greatly to explain how the telegram reached me under the Official Secrets Act. But I fear it would bother other people more. And this is a world of bother.'[134])

In any event, Churchill's brave request astounded Asquith and perhaps even amused him. The prime minister politely declined the First Lord's offer. It was 'a patriotic offer to resign his office & take command of the forces at Antwerp,' Asquith responded, but he told him his services could not be dispensed with at home. To Venetia Stanley, recipient of the prime minister's most intimate confidences, he reported the reception he and the Cabinet gave the offer:

Then comes in a real bit of tragi-comedy. I found when I arrived here this morning the enclosed telegram from Winston, who, as you will see, proposed to resign his Office, in order to take the command in the field of this great military force! Of course without consulting anybody, I at once telegraphed to him warm appreciation of his mission & his offer, with a *most decided* negative, saying that we could not spare him at the Admiralty &c. I had not meant to read it to the Cabinet, but as everybody, including K, began to ask how soon he was going to return, I was at last obliged to do so, carefully suppressing the last sentence, in wh he nominates *Runciman* as his successor!

I regret to say that it was received with a Homeric laugh. W is an ex-Lieutenant of Hussars, and would if his proposal had been accepted, have been in command of 2 distinguished Major Generals, not to mention Brigadiers, Colonels &c: while the Navy were only contributing its little brigades.[135]

In contrast to Asquith and others in the Cabinet, Kitchener was not unmoved by the appeal from this whimsical genius, his opposite in the Admiralty. Rather than make an issue of it, however, he noted in the margin of Churchill's telegram that he was willing to commission Churchill as a lieutenant-general to supervise the operations in Antwerp.[136] Asquith pointed out to Kitchener that Churchill would have had to leap over seven ranks and over many senior officers awaiting appointments, and that was only asking for trouble.[137] And in regards to Antwerp and Belgian defences, Churchill's attempt was given a poor chance, for as Field Marshal Sir John French, commanding the BEF, later commented, not even the Guards Division could have effected the relief of Antwerp.[138]

Churchill remained in Antwerp until 6 October, leaving the Admiralty without a political boss. Asquith, growing impatient and trying to save Churchill from himself, reported to Venetia Stanley:

> Winston persists in remaining there, which leaves the Admiralty here without a head, and I have had to tell them (not being, entre nous, very trustful of the capacity of Prince Louis & his Board) to submit all decisions to me. He (ie Prince Louis) is coming here directly (5 pm) to see me. I think that Winston ought to return now that a capable General is arriving. He has done good service in the way of starching & ironing the Belges.[139]

Hourly the situation deteriorated. That evening, Churchill left the beleaguered Belgian port for England.

On 7 October, having returned to London, Churchill talked with Asquith. Churchill loved the sharp end of war and the excitement of the firing line. His desire to be at the front had not abated. He told Asquith that he had 'tasted blood' and desired sooner rather than later to take a command in the field. In particular, he desired command of one of the new armies Kitchener was raising.[140] He was prepared to give up office for the battlefield. Asquith would have listened to his political colleague and friend with interest and perhaps amusement. As to Antwerp, now in peril, help was desperately needed to assist the left flank of the Allied forces on the Continent. On 5 October, responding to Churchill's urgent appeals, Kitchener had dispatched the 7th Division and the 3rd Cavalry Division. The French agreed to send marines and infantry. This aid came too late, and on 9 October German General Hans von Beseler demanded Antwerp's capitulation. Continued resistance was impossible. The German army entered the city. Zeebrugge and Ostend also fell into German hands. The Belgians retreated to the south and held their ground to the end of the war, and the Western Front was established, with the great opposing armies embedded in trenches from the Channel coast all the way to the Swiss border. No flanking movement by sea or land could dislodge the Germans. Nor could the Germans advance farther along the coast.[141] The military experts were perplexed. 'I don't know what is to be done,' Kitchener confessed to Grey, 'this isn't *war*.'[142]

Men of the Naval Division faced an unexpected war, for almost a thousand were interned in Holland, having mistakenly crossed the frontier into that neutral country. About two hundred were killed in action. Great was the consternation in Britain at the loss of these men, and clouds over Churchill darkened in consequence. The Royal Naval Division suffered heavily, and the division's own history describes the two Naval Brigades as 'a slender asset from the military point of view'.[143]

Churchill's role in the Antwerp affair irritated his colleagues and increased the numbers of his critics. Above all, it unleashed the hostile press and strengthened the power of the Opposition. One of the chief criticisms was that the Naval Brigades were sent with untrained and unprepared recruits directly into the battle lines. The Opposition cries against the government found full voice in H A Gwynne at the *Morning Post*. In a leading article on 13 October he advised the government 'to keep a tight hand upon their impulsive colleague ... to see that no more mischief of the sort is done', adding that 'the attempt to relieve Antwerp by a small force of Marines and Naval Volunteers was a costly blunder, for which Mr W. Churchill must be held responsible ... We suggest to Mr Churchill's colleagues that they should, quite firmly and definitely, tell the First Lord that on no account are the military and naval operations to be conducted or directed by him.'

On 16 October Gwynne wrote to Asquith, Lloyd George, Grey, McKenna, and others that Antwerp showed 'that Mr Churchill is unfitted for the office which he now holds, and I am firmly convinced that the country will be in a state of considerable disquietude, if not panic, unless a change is made at the Admiralty.'[144] He threatened to publish the true facts of the enterprise unless Churchill were removed from the Admiralty. Northcliffe's *Daily Mail* joined the chorus, and his most influential paper, *The Times*, referred to sending the Naval Brigades to the fighting line as 'deliberate murder'. The *Observer* came to Churchill's support but the hostility of the press stood strongly against Churchill. When remnants of the Royal Naval Division returned on 18 October, he took the opportunity to defend himself. He argued that the troops were sent not by oversight or personal quirk, but because they were the nearest troops available, and the need was immediate and pressing.[145] Churchill's arguments could not hold back the flood of rebuke, and in a moment of despair he told Haldane that he might resign.

Though Asquith had supported Churchill during the Antwerp enterprise, by 13 October his opinions had changed: 'I can't tell you,' he wrote to Venetia Stanley, 'what I feel of the *wicked folly* of it all. The Marines of course are splendid troops & can go anywhere & do anything: but nothing can excuse Winston (who knew all the facts) from sending in the two other Naval Brigades.' (Asquith's views appear to have been coloured by the experiences of his son Arthur Asquith, 'Oc', who served with one of the Naval Brigades in Antwerp.[146]) 'I trust that Winston will learn by experience,' Asquith confided, 'and now hand over to the military authorities the little circus which he is still running "on his own" at Dunkirk – Oxfordshire Yeomen, motor-buses ... armoured cars &c &c. They have really nothing to do with the Admiralty, which ought to confine its activities to the sea & the air.'[147]

Inside the Navy there was much grumbling about the Antwerp siege and capitulation. Admiral David Beatty assessed Churchill's actions with the sharp precision that was his special feature: 'The man must have been mad to have thought he could relieve [Antwerp] ... putting 8,000 half-trained troops into it ... If we only had a Kitchener at the Admiralty we could have done so much and the present state of chaos in naval affairs would never have existed.'[148] Fisher, too, had strong views. He linked the Antwerp affair with the sinking of the three cruisers of the 'live-bait squadron' (discussed in the next section) – and blamed Winston. To Pamela McKenna, wife of a former First Lord of the Admiralty, now a confidante, he wrote concerning a matter raised in *The Times*, the very subject he had been telling her about. 'The whole point is that Winston has surrounded himself with third-class sycophants, and so is autocratic! and is taking charge of Dunkirk instead of the Navy!'[149]

Fifty years later, A J P Taylor assessed the Antwerp adventure this way: 'The affair brought Churchill much discredit. He had operated a bold strategy with inadequate means, and thus laid a first stone in the reputation for impulsive irresponsibility which was to dog him for many years.'[150] However, Churchill's distinguished biographer Sir Martin Gilbert correctly points out that Churchill came under attack for undertaking responsibilities that Kitchener had requested, and for giving aid that the French, or at Antwerp the Belgians, had called on the British to provide. In the absence of British-French co-operation in that exposed coastal area, where a daily breakthrough by the Germans was possible, communications with the front lines were fluid, and the shortage of men and materiel 'added to the difficulties of anyone who undertook such responsibilities.' As mentioned above, the 'Dunkirk circus' helped halt the German advance at the mouth of the Yser,[151] and the role the Naval Division played in the defence of Antwerp was of great importance. Not least among its successes, it enabled most of the Belgian field army to be withdrawn to the west in a condition suitable for reorganisation and refit. This subsequently allowed that army to earn immortality in the operations on the Yser river. Doubtless the role of the Allies and of Churchill was significant in that matter. As well, the enemy was prevented from taking the Channel ports.

In November 1915, as he prepared to take up a command on the Western Front, Churchill again defended his actions. He stated that he had sounded a warning about the threat to Antwerp in early September 1914, but nothing was done about the situation until 2 October. Regarding the use of the Naval Division, he argued that he was completely justified in sending the force, and that their training and equipment were more than sufficient to defend the city. He also suggested that though Antwerp had fallen, the delay caused by the arrival of the British troops severely disrupted the plans of the German General Staff, slowed the enemy advance, and ensured that the decisive battles were fought more to the north than otherwise would have been the case.[152] This was confirmed by the King of the Belgians in 1918: 'You are wrong in considering the Royal Naval Division Expedition as a forlorn hope. In the case of Antwerp the delay the Royal Naval Division caused the enemy was of inestimable service to us. Those three days allowed the French and British Armies to move northwest. Otherwise our whole [Belgian] Army might have been captured and the northern French ports secured by the enemy.'[153]

Ten years after the events, in his memoirs, Churchill's colleague Sir Edward Grey gave this more tempered perspective on the origins of the Antwerp adventure:

> The action has been much criticized. I am not competent to pass a military judgement upon it, but, as I acquiesced in it and was one of the four persons present, it is right that I should give my independent recollection of the circumstances in which the decision for Churchill to go to Antwerp was taken. It was indeed his own idea and initiative, but it was part of a concerted plan, and not the mere madcap exploit of a passion for adventure, which it was for some time afterwards assumed to be.[154]

And in an essay, 'Second Choice', published in *Thoughts and Adventures* in 1932, Churchill admitted that he had erred in confusing the role of the statesman for that of a commanding officer in the field; the two could not be done jointly. The supreme command had escaped Churchill at Antwerp and after, and the lesson was not lost on him. And there, for the moment, we leave the matter. It was, however, marching hand in hand with yet another incident involving Churchill.

'The live-bait squadron'

With the BEF safely in France by 19 August, the nation waited impatiently for some promised action with the German fleet. After all, just such a main event had been expected and forecast. Nothing transpired except raids and counter-raids in the Narrow Seas. Throughout these preliminary months of the war, when the struggle to control the Channel ports was critical to Allied objectives, the Admiralty sent various classes of warships to patrol the coast and provide firepower on the littoral – in support of the British and French armies and to keep the German armies at a distance. Admiral Alexander Bethell had some older battleships employed on this service, and light cruisers were periodically brought south from 'the Broad Fourteens' on similar duties. Possessing command of the sea, the Navy needed monitors (essentially powerful shallow-draught gunboats) for ship versus shore operations. No need had existed for the type in the days of 'blue water' warfare, and in the new circumstances the Navy found itself without any of this kind, so contracts were let for various sizes of monitors, most carrying 6in guns and capable of 9.6 knots – 'cheap and nasty' men-of-war, though lightly armoured. These vessels were first used on the Channel coast, and then found themselves at Gallipoli and later in North Russia. Churchill's administration was responsible for building at least forty monitors, one of which, *M.33*, survives from the 1914–1918 war.[155] The building of monitors accorded completely with Churchill and Fisher's Baltic schemes, of which more below.

Unexpectedly, in the early months of the war, the Navy suffered a series of embarrassing setbacks; Churchill's competence as head of the Admiralty, and his judgement as to naval decision-making came under attack. Lying deep in the recesses of concern were matters relating to the respective roles of the statesman and the professional sailor – the age-old business of political-military relations, or, as some would later have it, problems of 'supreme command'. Churchill, then largely inexperienced in the conduct of war, was unsettled on this question because he found working with admirals and others at the Admiralty difficult. They doubtless held similar views of him. His natural tendency to seize the day and to command the scene rankled in the well-ordered, conservative Service, with its ancient and august Admiralty. During these early months of the war he had a compliant First Sea Lord, Battenberg, who allowed Churchill full rein and did little to check the enthusiasms and military thrusts of his political superior. Battenberg's nickname at the Admiralty was 'Quite Concur'. Nature abhors a vacuum, and Churchill filled it.

At the same time, he was quite capable of getting himself into mischief. On 21 September he made a grievous error: he boasted at Tournament Hall, Liverpool, that the Navy enjoyed complete command of the sea, as if the German navy had been defeated. The British Navy could not fight while the enemy remained in port, he said. That brought laughter. Nor could he resist an attractive turn of phrase. He stated roundly: 'Although we hope that a decision at sea will be a feature of this war, although we hope that our men will have a chance of settling the question with the German fleet, yet if they do not come out and fight in time of war they will be dug out like rats in a hole.'[156] Arthur Marder's after-action report rings true: 'There was a sixteenth-century ring about the statement, which might have been made by an Elizabethan seadog. Unhappily for Churchill, the digging-out operation was hardly feasible, the "hole" being heavily defended by shore guns, mines, destroyers, and submarines.'[157] Churchill's bombast exasperated the Fleet: Admiral Lewis Bayly, commander of the 1st Battle Squadron, wrote, 'How very annoyed and angry the senior officers (and possibly juniors) in the First [Grand] Fleet are [at Churchill's remarks] ... we all pride ourselves on keeping from any bombast, and remaining quiet and ready ... we feel that we have been dragged down to the level of bombasting and breathing bombastic defiance, and we hate it.' Churchill himself came to regret the expression. As Marder explains, when he was heckled in the House of Commons on 7 March 1916, Churchill admitted, 'digging them out [was] a very foolish phrase, and I regret that it slipped out.'[158] The King complained to Asquith, pointing out that Churchill's words were hardly dignified for a Cabinet member, and besides, the rats were coming out of their own holes at the cost of losing British cruisers.[159] He was referring to the loss of the *Cressys* the very next day, 22 September, to which we now turn.

We begin by noticing the warning that had been given to Churchill about just such a possible disaster. During a recent visit to the Grand Fleet, one of the admirals, Sir Roger Keyes, in the presence of Churchill, had spoken of 'the live-bait squadron'. When Churchill inquired as to what Keyes meant, the admiral replied that a number of old cruisers of the *Bacchante* class – *Aboukir*, *Hogue*, and *Cressy* – were patrolling dangerously near the Dogger Bank and were believed to be vulnerable to German attack. This alarm was supported by Tyrwhitt and Jellicoe. Appalled, Churchill wrote to Battenberg on 18 September, ordering that the patrols be discontinued, but it was too late.[160] Normally these cruisers would have been accompanied by protective destroyer flotillas, but given the gales that had swept the Narrow Seas for days, they had been confined to harbour. When the storms passed and the waters reverted to a silky smoothness, the cruisers were unsupported and dangerously exposed. Changes in the weather dealt the British a terrible blow.

Early in the morning of 22 September, *U-9*, skippered by young Lieutenant Otto Weddigen, prowled the coast of Holland in what the Admiralty referred to as the Broad Fourteens, an area south of Dogger Bank with a fairly uniform depth of 14 fathoms. *U-9* sent torpedoes, one after another, into the unsuspecting British cruisers: the first victim was dead in the water at 6.30am and sinking; the second thought the first had struck a mine and chivalrously stood by to take on survivors, and the third followed suit. The total loss of life is estimated at 1,459 of total ships' complements of 2,200. From the British point of view, this marked one of the catastrophes of the naval war. Never again would a warship stop to take on survivors. Churchill and Fisher were consciously aware that the loss of officers and men was the essential matter of concern, and Fisher believed crews were more important than ships. As he wrote to Jellicoe after further loss of great ships, 'Still war is war and we are bound to have big disasters and must steel our hearts and minds – for if only we can save the crews (which are irreplaceable) we can afford great losses in vessels of war of all natures.' Churchill issued a Confidential Interim Order, 'Employment of

Large Ships for Rescue Work', containing the following instructions: 'In war the preservation of important & irreplaceable units with their crews, for the duty of fighting the enemy, must be the primary consideration and the proper precaution & disposition of war must not be neglected in any circumstances.' Rather typically, Churchill sent this out without final knowledge shared with Admiralty staff officers, or even the First Sea Lord.[161] The rear-admirals responsible for the patrol, Arthur Christian and Henry Campbell, were placed on half-pay. Of Campbell, Fisher wrote, 'It was *pure murder* sending those big armoured ships into the North Sea! and [Rear-Admiral] H.H. Campbell [commanding the Cruiser Force] (like the d—d sneak he is!) stays in harbour when he ought to have hoisted his flag in one of the other ships of the Squadron, and been at sea with them, and taking his responsibility.'[162]

The lamentable chronicle of British difficulties and disasters at sea lengthened through September and increased in October. On 15 October the British protected cruiser *Hawke* fell victim to the same German submarine, *U-9*. In this case *Hawke*, caught in the lethargic act of picking up mail from a delivery boat, was torpedoed amidships off Aberdeen and sank without even sending a radio report. Nearly 523 officers and men were lost. Fisher rued the loss of highly trained, and not easily replaced, officers and men. 'Seldom has a ship sunk so quickly and carried so many men to the bottom of an icy sea,' says the German report. The loss revealed how warships without adequate 'bulges' (to guard against torpedoes) were vulnerable to torpedo attack. The unexpected range of the U-boats from their bases was also clear. Jellicoe shifted to temporary bases at Loch Ewe, Isle of Mull, Scotland, then Lough Swilly on the north coast of Ireland. The British had been chased out of their supposedly safe lair at Scapa Flow. German spies were thought to exist there, another source of serious danger. The British received some grim satisfaction when they learned that *U-9*'s commander Weddigen, the first of the German submarine aces, finally met his death when the submarine he was commanding was sliced in two by HMS *Dreadnought*.

As commander of the 1st Battle Cruiser Squadron, and given his previous association with Churchill as his Naval Secretary, Vice-Admiral Sir David Beatty had freedom to advise Churchill on naval matters and, indeed, to press him to deal with urgent matters. On 17 October Beatty, in a state of alarm, laid clear in plain language to Churchill the critical state of affairs in the North Sea. 'At present I feel that we are working up for a catastrophe of a very large character. The feeling is gradually possessing the fleet that all is not right somewhere.' Beatty contended that the British had been lulled into a false sense of security because they had not yet been attacked. But the dreadful day might soon come, he warned. The menace of mines and submarines increased daily, without the means of countering them. Submarine nets, sea gates, torpedo nets, piles or concrete blocks, sunken ships, wire hawsers, booms, and mines as passive defences, plus artillery manned by trained artillerymen (not Territorials), were needed. So were strengthened seagoing patrols. Beatty was alarmed that the British were giving up the North Sea, and carrying on patrols and the protection of shipping from distant bases. He noted, 'The situation as it is, we have no place to lay our heads.' No base existed for adequate coaling, replenishing, refitting, and repairing. Scapa Flow, Cromarty, and Rosyth were not adequately defended, and hurried arrangements had been made for the Fleet. All the steaming done by the warships since late July was now taking a toll; repairs were needed. The remedy was to fix upon a base and make it impervious to submarine attack. Cromarty was Beatty's preferred place. The boom defences there, a novelty, had just been completed. A reorganisation of forces was also needed, along with the appointment of some great naval leader who could meet the submarine menace with well-organised patrol flotillas under competent, determined, and energetic command. As for possible nominees, Beatty liked John de Robeck (later to emerge prominently in the Dardanelles difficulty): 'He might not have been a genius, but with guidance from you at the Admiralty he is a born leader of men of great energy and determination; in fact with those qualities which come to the front only in war. I am sure that if he had been there he would have curtained the depredations of the minelayer and the submarine.' Beatty also recommended better measures to locate and counter enemy submarines and minelayers, avoiding permanent patrols, which were hazardous owing to the enemy submarine. But of all his concerns, none ranked higher in importance than making entrances to bases secure. The enemy's submarines needed to be kept out:

> I trust, First Lord, you will forgive this long bleat ... I think you know me well enough to know that I do not shout without cause. The fleet's tail is still well over the back. We hate running away from our base and the effect is appreciable. We are not enjoying ourselves. But the morale is high and confidence higher. I would not write this if I did not know that you with your quick grasp of detail and imagination would make something out of it.[163]

The menace of the U-boat was reordering the disposition of the British heavy units. 'Even then the battlecruisers lay at anchor with their torpedo nets out, in doubtful security.' So wrote Filson Young, a reporter on board Beatty's *Lion*. Beatty was suspicious; he disliked having a nosy newspaperman aboard his ship, but he was still generous in conversation. From such discussions, Young came to some revelatory observations on the state of affairs: 'It was the old story ... of the unaccountable indefinite gap between the Admiralty and the Navy, which no one in the history of either has ever yet bridged.' The Admiralty seemed indifferent to the views of officers and regarded the equipment of the

Fleet as suitable to the needs of the day. 'The Admiralty as an organisation was partly unworthy of the great trust reposed in it ... [and there] the spirit informing the whole was a narrow and lifeless spirit, expressing itself everywhere in the policy that the means were more important than the end.'[164]

On 27 October Jellicoe sent Churchill the unwelcome news that the battleship *Audacious*, one of the recent *King George V* class, had been lost after striking a mine off the Donegal coast of Ireland. First of the dreadnoughts launched during Churchill's term at the Admiralty, she had been conducting gunnery exercises. Thankfully there was no loss of life. It was not a torpedo from an enemy submarine that had done the damage in this case, but a mine sown by an enemy minelayer, and here again was an indication of how sea warfare had changed and would change. The chief naval constructor later assumed that *Audacious* was finally lost from the action of the sea in very bad weather or the violent explosion that occurred just before she sank – in short, a single mine did not destroy her.[165] Like all of the dreadnought battleships and cruisers, from the original *Dreadnought* to the *Queen Elizabeth* class, she had been carefully designed to be safe against the explosions of two torpedoes in any position. In the calculations of operational risk commanders, British and German alike, the lethal mine as well as the torpedo now had to be considered.

But for the moment the matter of 'damage control' and media spinning raised its head. Jellicoe emphasised to Churchill that the loss of one of the great capital ships should be kept secret so that the Germans would not know of their success and the diminution of the strength of the Grand Fleet.[166] Fisher, too, demanded silence on the matter. Although he sought to protect the First Lord, there was more to it than this. At a Cabinet meeting on 28 October, it was decided, in conformity to policy already adopted for such cases, not to make the news of the loss public at that moment. All of the Cabinet favoured withholding the news, except for Lloyd George and Asquith, who nevertheless acquiesced to the majority view.[167] Shortly after the British euphoria engendered by the Navy's confident success in defeating von Spee's East Asiatic Squadron at the Battle of the Falkland Islands in December, Churchill resolved to make a statement in the Commons regarding the loss of *Audacious*. The timing seemed propitious, for the House was soon to adjourn until mid-January, leaving no possibility of endless questions and challenges being raised in Parliament. However, on the appointed day, and just as he was about to leave the Admiralty to make his statement, he was intercepted by Fisher. The admiral cajoled, threatened, and browbeat Churchill until he agreed to remain silent about the incident. Jellicoe reasserted keeping silent about the issue, at least as long as the main force remained weakened, as he did not want the Germans to realise that the Grand Fleet had lost a capital ship. (Later Jellicoe added a long list of damaged, vulnerable, or not fully operational dreadnoughts to the *Audacious* loss.) By contrast, Sir Douglas Brownrigg, the superintendent of the Admiralty's censorship department, argued that the suppression would cost the Allies prestige once the Germans learned the truth and, more, would give the Germans a useful bit of propaganda to use against Britain. Even if the Admiralty were abused for a day or two, Brownrigg reasoned, the matter would pass. He was right: the Admiralty lost a degree of public confidence in terms of accurate war reporting that it did not recover until Jutland.[168] Even then, attempts at damage control proved ineffective.

As it turned out, the loss of *Audacious* could not be kept quiet. At some considerable risk to his vessel, the captain of the White Star liner RMS *Olympic* had arranged a rescue of the ship's company. There were many American passengers on board the liner, some with cameras. One by one, reports found their way to the press. The Admiralty communiqué, produced a day or two after the Armistice, eventually announced the vessel's loss some four years before. The drawing up of that message, done by Brownrigg with tongue in cheek, brought measured enjoyment to the Admiralty censor. Asquith believed that the loss of *Audacious* was 'cruel luck' for Churchill. Indeed, it was cruel luck but it represented matters of deeper merit: the Admiralty and the Navy had underestimated the enemy's capabilities in the use of mines, torpedoes and submarines. Technological innovation was changing the nature of war at sea. Staff work had not kept up with these changes. The North Sea was becoming the German Ocean. The loss in officers and men had been prodigious.

The Titans at the Admiralty

'Here comes Jack'

A storm was gathering over the Old Admiralty Building. The First Sea Lord, Prince Louis of Battenberg, an outstanding sailor who had been named to that position in 1912, was being made the scapegoat for German successes in the opening months of the war.[1] The press grew increasingly virulent, concentrating on Battenberg's alien origins and possible German sympathies and his alleged treachery (these latter outrageous falsehoods).[2] King George V, in receipt of many letters abusing Battenberg, was alarmed by the unwarranted attacks on the First Sea Lord. Once the campaign started, it gathered momentum. Asquith and Churchill did not share these views of Battenberg, but Asquith kept a close watch on the furore, for it had become a matter of Cabinet concern.[3] This is but half the story. The tide was running strongly for a change at the Admiralty for other reasons. Battenberg was too easy-going, or perhaps in a state of depression: he spent mornings at the Admiralty reading *The Times* and sending forth remarkably few minutes or memoranda. Asquith recalled how he had little confidence in Battenberg during the Antwerp episode, when the First Sea Lord was alone at the Admiralty; he had found working with Battenberg difficult and unsatisfactory.[4] He had no intention of getting rid of Churchill; the prime minister saw him as one of the strongest MPs in the Cabinet – energetic and forthright, a fighter. What could be done? Were new admirals needed at the Admiralty? Certainly drive and spirit were lacking in the professional leadership in the Admiralty Building. Others in Cabinet shared the prime minister's views, and the nasty and rising press campaign soon gave Asquith the opportunity – one is tempted to say the excuse – he needed.

On 19 October, from the War Office, Haldane wrote handsomely to Churchill that if Admirals Fisher and Sir Arthur Wilson were recalled it would 'make our country feel that our old spirit of the Navy was alive and come back.'[5] This would be a desperate measure, but action was required in the darkening circumstances of the third month of the war. Next day, Churchill took up the matter with Asquith. He stated that, given public pressures, Battenberg would soon have to bow out, and he wanted to bring back Fisher and Wilson. Asquith displayed no opposition, though the concern existed that the old running sore with Beresford and the 'Syndicate of Discontent' might be inflamed. Churchill confidently told Asquith that he was content to be happily reinforced by two 'well-plucked chickens' aged seventy-four and seventy-two.[6]

At this juncture Battenberg made his own decision to resign, though on Churchill's suggestion. His letter to Churchill makes for painful reading. The minor reverses at sea meant that the public was in no mood to tolerate further setbacks. He had been accused of faulty dispositions of naval units. Critics charged him with treachery. Knowing that the public confidence in the Board of Admiralty had to be restored by his resignation, he wrote accordingly to Churchill on 28 October.[7] A second letter followed the day after: 'I beg of you to release me. I am on the verge of breaking down & I cannot use my brain for anything.'[8]

And so the wheels were put in motion for the exit of Battenberg and the return of Fisher and, by extension, Wilson. The first hurdle had been overcome, and broaching the matter with the King presented itself as the next challenge. In the event, the King could do nothing but accept the painful reality that Battenberg must go. On 29 October, a day of anxiety and unhappiness, the monarch committed the details of the unfolding scenario to his diary:

> Spent a most worrying and trying day ... At 11.30 saw Winston Churchill who informed me that Louis of Battenberg had resigned his appt. as 1st Sea Lord. The Press & Public have said so many things against him being born a German, & that he ought not to be at the head of the Navy, that it was best for him to go. I feel deeply for him: there is no more loyal man in the Country.
>
> Churchill then proposed that Lord Fisher shd. succeed him as 1st Sea Lord. I did all I could to prevent it & told him he was not trusted by the Navy & they had no confidence in him personally. I think it is a great mistake & he is 74. At the end I had to give in with great reluctance ...
>
> At 3:15 I saw the Prime Minister. I used the same arguments as I had to Churchill with regard to Fisher, but had to approve. At 4.0 I saw poor Louis, very painful interview, he quite broke down. I told him I would make him a Privy Councillor to show the confidence I had in him, which pleased him.[9]

After Battenberg's resignation, Churchill wrote to his late colleague: 'The Navy of today, and still more the Navy of tomorrow, bears the imprint of your work.'[10] How right this was, for Prince Louis, first as Second Sea Lord (1911–12), and then as First Sea Lord, had worked wonders to prepare the Fleet for its battle stations. Relieved of duties at the Admiralty, Battenberg remained on the active list but was never employed again. At the King's suggestion he changed his name: His Serene Highness Prince Louis Battenberg was transformed into the Marquess of Milford Haven, and in due course Battenberg became Mountbatten. He was made Admiral of the Fleet, and he died in 1921 in the inauspicious surroundings of the annexe of the Naval and Military Club. How the mighty had fallen.

George V swallowed the bitter pill of seeing the exit of Battenberg. Now he had to swallow another as he saw the potentially troublesome Jacky Fisher return. We know, from a memorandum by the King's secretary, Lord Stamfordham, that George V appealed to Asquith to prevent Fisher's appointment. Stamfordham told Asquith that the King had an 'unconquerable aversion' to Fisher, which Asquith attributed to the King being a Beresfordite. According to Stamfordham, the King proposed the names of individuals like Meux and Jackson for the post, which Asquith believed Churchill would never allow. The prime minister, in turn, stated his full support for Churchill and his promotion of Fisher's return, and said – and this is the central point – that the person chosen to become First Sea Lord in Battenberg's place would have to be congenial to the First Lord.[11]

Asquith attended on the King to advise on this matter of bringing Jacky back to the Admiralty. On 29 October, after meeting with the King, Asquith wrote, tellingly: 'He gave me an exhaustive & really eloquent catalogue of the old man's crimes & defects, and thought that his appointment would be very badly received by the bulk of the Navy, & that he would be almost certain to get on badly with Winston.'[12] The prime minister replied that he gathered from what the First Lord, Churchill, had told him that there was no one else suitable for the post. Besides, the Admiralty Board was, at the present, weak and incapable of initiative. The Navy had failed to fulfil the hopes and expectations of the country. In Asquith's view, anything that had been done successfully to date, even the readying of the Fleet on the eve of the outbreak of war, was due to Churchill. There was another factor, no less important. He believed that Fisher's appointment would be welcomed by the public. The King declared, with obvious resignation, that he could not oppose his ministers in this selection but felt obliged to register his protest. Eventually the word 'protest' was replaced by 'misgivings', and thus the King's letter to the prime minister, dated 'Buckingham Palace, October 29, 1914', read:

Following our conversation this afternoon, I should like to note that, while approving the proposed appointment of Lord Fisher as First Sea Lord, I do so with some reluctance and misgivings. I readily acknowledge his great ability and administrative powers, but at the same time I cannot help feeling that his presence at the Admiralty will not inspire the Navy with that confidence which ought to exist, especially when we are engaged in so momentous a war. I hope that my fears may prove groundless.[13]

Fisher may have known of the King's distrust of him, and his view that with Fisher as First Sea Lord only trouble would come, or reappear, among the senior officers of the Navy. However, with customary bravado, Fisher told the prime minister that when he met with the King they 'had got on like "a house on fire", and [had] come to an agreement that they should regularly meet once a week!'[14] The King wrote in his diary:

October 30. Received Lord Fisher (whom I had not met for six years) on his appt. as 1st Sea Lord. He is now 74. He seems as young as ever. I only trust he will do well at Admiralty.[15]

In advance of the pending changes, Churchill summoned Fisher to the Admiralty. On 28 October they reviewed the proposed arrangement.[16] That same day, Churchill received Battenberg's conforming letter which stated his preference that Fisher should succeed him as First Sea Lord, with Wilson as Chief of Staff.[17] All this was brought about on 1 November.

Thus did Jacky Fisher make his return to Whitehall. Politicians and press praised the appointment, but there must have been many expressions of caution, and even regret, also. As for himself, Fisher could not contain his delight, and to his old friend Esher, the fixer, he wrote on the day of his return to his old desk at the Admiralty:

Thanks for your dear letter! Isn't it fun being back?

Some d—d fools thought I was dead & buried! I am busy getting even with some of them! I did 22 hours work yesterday but 2 hours sleep not enough so I shall slow down!

SECRET. The King said to Winston (I suppose dissuading!) that the job would kill me. Winston was perfectly lovely in his instant reply: 'Sir, I cannot imagine a more glorious death!' Wasn't that delicious? but burn please![18]

Churchill now had as his professional colleague the most distinguished admiral since Nelson, a person with originality of mind and spontaneity that set him apart from the ordinary. 'His genius was deep and true,' Churchill wrote later. 'Above all, he was in harmony with the vast size of events. Like them, he was built upon a titanic scale.' He and Wilson had outlived their contemporaries and had a position far above the next naval generation. Churchill refers to them as 'great old men and weather-beaten seadogs', and that they were. They had 'braved the battle and the breeze, and were Captains afloat when I was in my cradle.'[19] Changes were needed at the Admiralty: Fisher, at Churchill's suggestion, became Chief of Staff, and Wilson took a place in the reformed War

Group. In *The World Crisis*, Churchill makes great play of the fact that Fisher was of advanced age, and the strain of the work made it necessary for him to live a very careful life. He went early to bed, after 8pm, and arose refreshed between 4 and 5am. He did his work in the morning, completing his tasks in such a way that Churchill was filled with admiration and reassurance. For his part, Churchill slept till perhaps eight, with a customary one-hour sleep after lunch. He could work well into the evening without fatigue. Thus Fisher and Churchill operated in tandem; they could deal with incoming communications, or leave messages for the other as required. They thus worked around the clock, adhering, Churchill says a little brazenly (for the pact would be broken), under mutual agreement that neither would take a significant action without consulting the other. 'I had not previously seen the pulse of the Admiralty beat so strong and regular.'[20] Fisher was back.

'There had probably never in any Ministry before been such a combination of genius and driving power as when Mr Churchill and Lord Fisher were at the Admiralty, but it was always doubtful whether the harmony that in the early months gave such promise that the war at sea would be conducted with great vision and immense vigour would endure.' That was the view of Sir William James, then working in the Admiralty as publications censor. He explained further: 'Mr Churchill was not the man to be content with the passive role of leaving the First Sea Lord and Chief of Staff to issue all strategical orders, when he was responsible to Parliament and would have to accept blame for failures, and he expected [Room 40's Captain] Hall to bring him all important news of the German Fleet, which would normally be sent only to the naval staff.'[21] James understood that Winston wanted to continue his primacy in running the war at sea.

Despite the First Sea Lord's advanced years, Fisher's return to the Admiralty brought a flurry of activity and a reinvigoration of the workings of that institution. 'I knew his methods and fully appreciated that things had to move with a "snap" and that in order to keep on terms with him one had to remember the maxim, "Get on or get out,"' wrote Rear-Admiral Sir Douglas Brownrigg, the naval censor. He clearly remembered 'the chronic hustle and bustle in the passages.'[22]

Fisher demanded that things be done immediately. Long before Churchill developed 'Action this Day', Fisher had enshrined it. He had always despised Admiralty red tape. Admiral Sir Percy Scott has related an example of this. Early in 1915 the Admiralty ordered monitors, a type of shallow-draught warship with big guns, to be built with 15-, 14-, and 9.2in guns. However, the initial design called for only 13.5 degrees of elevation instead of the required 30 degrees. Scott brought the problem to the attention of Fisher, who allowed Scott to contact the manufacturer, Messrs Armstrong, Whitworth, and Co. Scott sketched out an improved design, had it approved by Fisher, and sent it off. All this was accomplished in a mere twenty-two hours. As Scott attested, under normal Admiralty conditions the error would have taken a month to fix, if it were fixed at all.[23]

As to Sir Arthur Wilson, 'Old 'Ard 'Art' had always been useful in the Admiralty – quiet and unassuming, and a sound thinker in terms of naval tactics and strategic dispositions. He posed no problems to Fisher, and vice versa. Wilson agreed to his new role as special adviser on condition that he render his services without appointment or pay. He was what Fisher called one of the 'charity admirals'. Already a member of the Committee of Imperial Defence, he now took his place in the Naval War Staff, where from time to time he was joined by Churchill, Fisher, and others in the war work. Asquith liked to refer to Churchill, Fisher, and Wilson as the naval trinity. Wilson focused on enemy intelligence gathering, the perfecting of mines, and the use of nets to catch submarines.

Thus it was that early November 1914 found a renewed and more vibrant administration in place at the Admiralty. On 4 November the all-seeing Esher, reviewing recent events, confided to his journal about the changes:

It has been felt for some time that the Board of Admiralty required renovating; the personal attacks upon Prince Louis, grossly unfair as they are, have brought the matter to a head. Prince Louis is not only a fine sea-officer but also one of the most high-minded and loyal subjects of the King. I remember him since his youthful days, and from the time onward he has borne himself high in the esteem of the profession he loves and that has always honoured him. But undoubtedly the country will benefit by having Fisher and Wilson back again at the Admiralty. More driving power was required, and they will supply it.[24]

Commenting on this revolution in the administrative affairs at the Admiralty, David Beatty contended that Battenberg's German origins were only the excuse for his dismissal, as the politicians had to sacrifice someone after the Antwerp debacle, and Battenberg was the one to go. He also believed, a little unkindly (for he did not know Churchill's overbearing ways), that Battenberg did not keep a proper check on Churchill. But the new broom would be beneficial for the Service. Beatty contended that Fisher's energy, ideas, and low cunning were what the Navy needed just then. Fisher's age did not count in Beatty's analysis. He also believed that Fisher would rightly believe his position secure, and rule the Admiralty and Churchill with a heavy hand, and that Churchill would have to conform to Fisher's ideas. At the same time, and with prescience, Beatty feared that Churchill and Fisher could not long work in harmony, and would soon quarrel. Beatty also hoped that Beresford would remain quiet, and not stump up and down the country the way he had done the last time Fisher served as First Sea Lord.[25]

In *The World Crisis*, Churchill wrote of Fisher, 'I backed him up all I could. He was far more often right than wrong, and his drive and life-force made the Admiralty quiver like one of his great ships at its highest speed.'[26] But more than personal preference was involved when Churchill invited Fisher back to his old haunts. Many misfortunes had attended the Navy since the outset of war, and Churchill was politically vulnerable after the loss of the three *Cressys*, the adventure of Antwerp, the dispatch of the Naval Division to the Continent, and his ill-timed speech regarding forcing the German dreadnoughts into a sea battle by digging them out like rats. *Hawke* had been lost to a German torpedo, and the super-dreadnought *Audacious* to a mine. Fisher's recall would buttress Churchill's hold on the Admiralty and deflect criticism he was bearing personally. Ironically, and most optimistically, both men were seen as ideal in the sense that one could check the excesses of the other. Churchill could keep a lid on an autocratic old man; Fisher, viewed as the essential elder statesman, could restrain the impetuosity of the young politico. Others, more presciently, saw it differently. Churchill himself believed he would not have to cede any real authority to the new First Sea Lord. As he told Violet Asquith during the May 1915 crisis, 'I took him because I knew he was *old* and *weak*, and that I should be able to keep things in my own hands.'[27] In the words of Beaverbrook: 'Churchill co-opted Fisher to relieve the pressure against himself, but he had no intention of letting anyone else rule the roost. Here, then, were two strong men of incompatible temper, both bent on an autocracy. It only required a difference of opinion on policy to produce a clash, and this cause of dissension was not long wanting.'[28]

Now, with his new authority in place, Fisher felt able to curb the encroachments of the War Office into naval matters, including the building of ships. In November, Fisher went to Kitchener to protest in the strongest language the recruitment of valuable shipyard workers into the Army. Fisher told Kitchener that he would resign at 6pm that very day if the recruitment was not immediately halted. Kitchener consented to Fisher's demand, but such methods did not augur well for the new duo at the Admiralty.[29]

It was not long before other difficulties began to appear. As soon as Fisher was reinstated at the Admiralty, ancient vendettas came to the fore. Herbert Richmond, at the time assistant director of operations on the Admiralty's naval staff, wrote in his diary: 'Fisher, unfortunately, at this supreme juncture, seems more busy in getting at his enemies than at those of the country. He is after "Sir Berkeley Goeben," as he calls him, at this moment, and also [Sir Doveton] Sturdee ... It is rather pitiable to see this curious passion of his so ruling even at this time.'[30] Fisher had personal scores to settle. As Richmond forecast, Fisher dismissed the Chief of War Staff, Sturdee, who was furious and humiliated at this ill treatment. His name will surface later in the victorious Falklands battle, but even then Fisher could not accord a successful fellow admiral (who had once opposed him) the common recognition of good manners. Fisher never forgave those who had stood in his way. To his discredit, a deep vindictive streak ran through him. He also used the power of his position to favour his own ends, personal and professional. Newly ensconced in the Admiralty, Fisher set about extracting his daughter and son-in-law from detention in Germany, where they had been 'taking the cure' when war broke out. He succeeded.

One of the most difficult matters of this sort involved the capable Commodore (later Admiral of the Fleet) Sir Roger Keyes, in charge of the submarines, and a man whose tempestuous relationship with the First Sea Lord entered a new phase when Fisher returned to the Admiralty. Keyes admired Fisher's abilities and ruthless energies, and expressed this in a letter to Fisher written shortly after Fisher's recall. Fisher responded to this 'beautiful letter' by stating that he had no designs on Keyes and had faith in him. Keyes, though, still could not believe that Fisher was not scheming against him for some past wrong.[31] When Fisher returned to the Admiralty, Churchill mentioned to Keyes that he would have to keep the two apart. Perhaps Winston sensed their combative natures. For months Keyes came under Fisher's observation and censure. Keyes put it rather whimsically when he wrote that he believed he would be up against the Admiralty as much as the Germans.[32] By early December, Keyes was convinced that Fisher was attempting to remove him from his command. Writing to his wife, Keyes complained that he had 'thought J.F. was going to start fresh with me – but no – he is determined to knock me out!' And again, Fisher 'really is a ruthless unforgiving old villain and he *is* so vindictive, he never forgives.' Apparently Fisher was complaining that Keyes would not go to sea, despite the fact that Keyes had been ordered not to go to sea, and nevertheless had managed to circumvent the order on several occasions.[33] Even after a meeting in early January at which Fisher 'was very civil', Keyes complained to Churchill at the start of February that 'I am up against a very wicked vindictive old man who was absolutely determined to jab a knife in to me on every possible occasion.' Thanks to Churchill and Sir Henry Francis Oliver, Churchill's secretary, Keyes was able to maintain his position against Fisher, for the time being.[34] Keyes was in every instance courageous. He would not shy away from a fight. He was forthright and, when necessary to his way of thinking, would say his piece. In this sense he was unusual. Churchill found this trait in Keyes attractive; Fisher regarded it as professional independence bordering on insubordination. Keyes did excellent work in the organisation of submarine flotillas, though he was not a submariner. As a seagoing officer and commander he was denied a victory in battle on one occasion because the Admiralty muddled signals and delivered them to him hours late. Still, he had seniority on his side, and he would have been given command of a battlecruiser except that he was needed as Chief of Staff to Admirals Carden and de Robeck in the Dardanelles campaign. And there he rose with all the fire and enthusiasm that were his hallmarks to success.

Fisher seems to have been the last person to realise the damage he was doing to himself, to others, and to the Service with all the old posturing and conniving. His professional expertise in shipbuilding, propulsion systems, gunnery, and weapons platforms had given him his high authority, and with that authority he had brought about a naval revolution, but the power had gone to his head. He had not learned a lesson from the feud with Beresford. He was selfish to a fault, an egoist, and even, as Asquith began to see, a megalomaniac. He liked conspiracy and encouraged conspiracies. Churchill later commented that for one who was charged with 'so much secret and deadly business', Fisher was 'voluminous and reckless in his correspondence ... The buoyancy of his genius alone supported the burden.'[35] There would be victories ahead but there would be many tragedies, too, and ultimately disaster, contempt, and scorn. He could not see his own downfall. Nor, for that matter, could Churchill.

Tragedy and triumph: Coronel and the Falklands

In the fiery furnace of war, human character tends to show its truest self, and so it was in the case of Fisher and Churchill. In this connection, at this stage of our narrative, it is Fisher who particularly attracts our attention, for in the great and decisive battles in the South Pacific and South Atlantic the actions of naval commanders – German and British – showed remarkably well the capabilities as well as limitations of both navies. Here was a real test of war, and a triumph of naval technology. Sadly, as will be recounted, Fisher could not allow his personal animus against the victorious commander-in-chief to pass, even though this was 'his show', as Churchill put it. Rather, Fisher remained shackled to old personal dislikes and prejudices, disclosing his true tragic character along Shakespearean lines. Truth to tell, it lessens our appreciation of him and heightens appreciation of Churchill, who worked to check this flaw. This account of sea warfare far away from home waters shows Churchill in charge of ship deployments, sending out messages as required, and determining how to bring a successful conclusion to events. He made terrible miscalculations,[36] and he also fought later to salvage his reputation at the expense of those in command at sea. All these facets need to be kept in mind as we enter a remarkable chapter in the annals of war at sea.

At war's outset, the days of the small but powerful German East Asiatic Squadron, based on Tsingtao, in the German colony in China (but then on a training cruise in the German Caroline Islands), may have been numbered given British superiority at sea. All the same, Admiral Graf von Spee, its forthright commander, received instructions from Berlin to do as much damage as possible to enemy communications and shipping, and then run for the security of home.[37] His actions bear a strange resemblance to those of Captain David Porter of the United States commerce-raider *Essex*, a frigate, a hundred years earlier. On 28 March 1814 Porter passed Cape Horn from the South Atlantic and did immense damage to British whaling ships before two British men-of-war chased *Essex* into Valparaiso, blockaded her, and eventually sank the ship in Chilean territorial waters.

Von Spee's squadron consisted of the powerful armoured cruisers *Scharnhorst* (flag) and *Gneisenau* and the light cruisers *Leipzig*, *Nürnberg*, and *Emden*. *Scharnhorst* and *Gneisenau* were newer and more powerful than the British cruisers then in those seas. They were manned by long-service ratings, as opposed to the reservists who were the majority on the British ships. They were also better protected at the waterline and gun casements. Von Spee detached *Emden* to cruise the Indian Ocean and effect what damage she could. This lone raider, under the command of Captain Karl von Müller left a sunken trail of 100,000 tons of merchant shipping and two warships before being run aground on North Keeling Island after an engagement with the cruiser *Sydney*, the first great victory of a ship of the Royal Australian Navy. This showed the formidable power of a single warship to cause damage on the high seas, the very force in action that Fisher feared so greatly and took efforts to counter.

In London, the Admiralty was unsure of von Spee's intentions and worried about the possible threat to troop convoys from Australia and New Zealand. Isolated reports indicated that von Spee was making for South America, where he could expect to find colliers and supplies, so the Admiralty sent a warning telegram, dated 5 October, informing the British commander, Rear-Admiral Sir Christopher Cradock, to 'be prepared to meet them in company.' Although the British warships on the South America station had been sent to protect trade, the new reality was that they must meet the German warships in battle.

Cradock flew his flag in the armoured cruiser *Good Hope*. With him were the armoured cruiser *Monmouth*, the light cruiser *Glasgow*, and the armed cruiser *Otranto*. Altogether Cradock's squadron was no match for the German squadron, and the Admiralty noted that it was sending the pre-dreadnought battleship *Canopus* to bolster his forces, though this was an ageing ship of slow speed and doubtful fighting value. Churchill optimistically assumed that if *Canopus* were present with her powerful 12in guns, the other vessels would be shielded from harm. The German cruisers would not dare come within range of what Churchill described as 'a citadel'. This was a great miscalculation. The slower *Canopus* was well astern when Cradock gave the order for the units of his squadron to spread twenty miles apart and seek out the enemy.

When Fisher arrived back at the Admiralty in Battenberg's stead on 1 November, Churchill took him to the War Room. Scanning the charts spread before them, they assessed the current dispositions of British naval units. The British appeared outmatched. Speaking of Cradock's force, Churchill said, 'You don't suppose he'll try to fight them without the *Canopus*?' Fisher did not give any decided reply.[38] It is likely the scenario then unfolding alarmed him, and he immediately detached the armoured cruiser *Defence* from the Mediterranean to bolster the South American squadron. The Admiralty sent other messages of a confusing and conflicting nature, all of them known to Churchill (he was presumably running the show in the Admiralty War Room and sending those messages). Churchill took pains to distance himself from any knowledge of the stream of messages when the truth of this deployment came out.

On 3 November, after firm news of the German squadron's location had arrived, but before it was known that battle had already taken place, Cradock was informed by signal that *Defence* was to join his flag, and he should concentrate his squadron, including *Canopus*. Fisher's decisive action was for naught; as Churchill said, 'We were already talking to a void.'[39]

At 4.30pm on 1 November the British spied the smoke of the German ships. Rather than running for safety, Cradock made plans to engage. He breathed the Nelson dictum of engaging the enemy, and yet there exists the distinct possibility that he knew he was sailing to his doom. Corbett writes in his official history of naval operations of the Great War:

> It is not without emotion that one contemplates the feelings of so fine an officer when suddenly he found himself face to face with the hopeless situation in which, against all his protests and better judgment, he clearly believed himself to have been forced. A cloud that can never be lifted has fallen on one of the most tragic moments of our Naval history. All we can ever know is the silver lining. For whatever he thought and felt, Admiral Cradock did not flinch.[40]

In engaging the German squadron from a position of inferiority, Cradock may have been conscious of the blame placed on Admiral Troubridge for the escape of *Goeben*. He wrote to a senior officer: 'I will take care I do not suffer the fate of poor Troubridge.'[41] He would not let the Admiralty blame him for not fighting.

The Germans had a tactical advantage; they were east of the British ships, and as the sun set could fire at the silhouettes of the enemy on the dazzling horizon. Von Spee opened at 12,300yds and closed to 5,500yds. By dark the British ships had been destroyed – 'humiliated to the depths of our being' is the way that one officer put it – save for *Glasgow* and *Canopus*. 'We hardly spoke to one another for the first twenty four hours. We felt so bitterly ashamed of ourselves for we had let down the King. We had let down the Admiralty, we had let down England.'[42] Two second-rate cruisers and 1,600 British sailors were lost. On the other side, the Kaiser, jubilant at this victory, awarded three hundred Iron Crosses to officers and men – though they were never to receive these medals.

The loss of Cradock reverberated through the Fleet. In the North Sea the news flashed out that *Good Hope* and *Monmouth* had been sunk with all hands. 'It was blowing hard when I went to report this to [the commander of HMS *Orion*, Sir Robert] Arbuthnot in his sea-cabin. I shall always remember his comment. "Poor Kit! Poor Kit Cradock!" he said; "he always hoped he would be killed in battle or break his neck in the hunting-field."'[43]

In London there were many recriminations. The recently departed First Sea Lord, Battenberg, took the blame for Coronel according to his official biographer, Mark Kerr.[44] The same authority has defended Battenberg's decision to send *Canopus* as reinforcement for Cradock's squadron, arguing that the low speed (14 knots) of the outdated battleship would not be a problem, as the enemy would have to go past the squadron if it was in the Straits of Magellan.[45] From the outset, Churchill sought to avoid blame, to put Cradock in a bad light. He told Kitchener: 'Admiralty orders were clear ... It is vy disappointing. We had 7 separate forces awaiting them at different points, each of wh properly handled & concentrated cd have fought them well. A good many moves are necessary in consequence of this contretemps.'[46] Churchill was not alone in this view. Asquith wrote to Venetia Stanley that 'I am afraid the poor man has gone to the bottom: otherwise he richly deserves to be court-martialled ... As I told Winston last night (and he is not in the least to blame) it is time that he bagged something, & broke some crockery.'[47] Kitchener wondered, 'What could the Admiral have been thinking of to take on such a vastly superior force in guns.'[48]

All the same, Churchill could not avoid some blame for the defeat. Lloyd George was critical of his role according to his private secretary and mistress, Frances Stevenson, who kept a diary: 'Churchill is too busy trying to get a flashy success to attend to the real business of the Admiralty. Churchill blames Admiral Cradock for the defeat in South America – the Admiral presumably having gone down with his ship & so unable to clear himself. This is characteristic of Churchill.'[49] However, the First Lord worked at damage control and did so effectively. As explained earlier, he always had the advantage of being not only a participant in war but also his own chronicler of these same great events. Corbett, in the official history, argued strongly against the Admiralty, quoting telegrams Churchill sent to Cradock, and then outlining alternatives of action facing the admiral on the spot. For his part, Churchill disparaged any hint of ambiguity expressed in his instructions in the spirited defence of the Admiralty he wrote in *The World Crisis*. His discussion of the threat, the deployment of vessels to counter all possible German moves, and his appreciation of the speeds and armaments of all ships involved makes for a powerful case in defence of his administration – and, indeed, Battenberg's. 'The first rule of war is to concentrate superior strength for decisive action and to avoid division of forces or engaging in detail. The Admiral showed by his telegrams that he clearly appreciated this. The Admiralty orders explicitly approved his early assertion of these elementary principles. We were not, therefore, anxious about the safety of Admiral Cradock's squadron.' He concluded, 'I cannot therefore accept for the Admiralty any share in the responsibility for what followed [at Coronel],' which he described as 'the saddest naval action in the war.'[50] Here was a denial of responsibility.

The brilliance and vividness of his narrative shields the true story of the confusion at the Admiralty, the mixed messages sent by Churchill and others at the headquarters in London, and the failure to understand the difficulties of waging a war at sea in such far-off waters, where distances were immense, seas often high, and navigation and wireless communications complicated. When Corbett's official history, cited above, was being finished, Churchill objected to the treatment given to Coronel, but in the end the volume was passed by a vote of one, and thus it went to press. The first volume of *The World Crisis*, published three years later, was intended to avoid further censure for the difficulties of naval war in that preliminary year of the war, 1914, when hardly anything went well for the Royal Navy. Then and later Churchill sought to shield himself from charges of incompetence by massaging the narrative and selective recall.

Fisher, who, it is interesting to note, spoke of Cradock in 1906 as 'one of our very best officers',[51] assumed the office of First Sea Lord twenty-four hours before news of the Coronel disaster arrived at the Admiralty. The first full report, in the days after the battle, came from the British consul in Valparaiso, who gave von Spee's version of events. British naval communications encountered delays. Captain John Luce, of *Glasgow*, reported the outcome of the action by cable ten days after the engagement.[52]

After Coronel the British were uncertain as to where von Spee would go. It was clear in London that the enemy commander had a couple of options: transiting Panama and operating in the West Indies or rounding Cape Horn and steaming for home. After Berlin heard word of Coronel, von Spee was secretly ordered to proceed home to Germany via the South Atlantic. His ships were low on ammunition and there were no reserves available to him.[53] Unbeknown to the British, he shaped a course for Valparaiso, and there he and the German navy were splendidly welcomed by the German community.

We leave him now, for a moment, and turn our attention to the Admiralty in London.

Upon learning of the Coronel disaster, Churchill and Fisher acted quickly. This was in sharp contrast to the indecision and lack of clear thinking that had predominated at the Admiralty and had led to the melancholy tale described above. Fisher promptly made plans to deal with von Spee. Within six hours of learning of Coronel, Sir John Jellicoe received orders to coal at once the speedy battlecruisers *Inflexible* and *Invincible* and prepare them to sail for the South Atlantic, 7,000 miles distant. The avengers had first to steam for Plymouth, there to be fitted out and provisioned for distant duty, and Fisher issued a deadline by which the ships were to sail. Jellicoe protested at this weakening of the Grand Fleet, but Churchill wrote to him personally by way of explanation. Despite protests, several dockyard workers were taken along to finish up last-minute work. A third battlecruiser, *Princess Royal*, was deployed to the Caribbean to cover the West Indies and watch the Panama Canal. In the event, their water-tube boilers and turbine machinery performed magnificently. As Admiral Sir Herbert Richmond, at the time a serving officer but later an outstanding historian, commented, it took a calculable risk on Fisher's part to make such a bold and decisive decision – and it was to his credit.[54] Detaching units from the main fleet in being carries danger with it. And the tough decisions are the hardest to make (as was seen when the Admiralty dealt with the *Bismarck* in the next war).

In home waters, meanwhile, the effect of the diminution of the Grand Fleet by three of its dreadnoughts was immediate. Jellicoe was obliged to grudgingly accept the sending of two of his battlecruisers. But losing *Princess Royal*, one of the 'magnificent cats', to the Caribbean rankled. It left Beatty, commander of the 1st Battle Cruiser Squadron, tremendously vulnerable. Jellicoe believed that *Princess Royal* would only be needed if she were fighting German battlecruisers, and he believed that none were likely in the Caribbean.[55] He was also sore over how the Admiralty had treated him during the episode, implying that he had delayed the sending of the ship. Fisher wrote back that no snub was intended, and that it was only the press of business that caused the misunderstanding, coming as it did in the first days of his return to office.[56] No doubt Beatty and his staff complained to both Jellicoe and the Admiralty regarding the diversion of the three battlecruisers to deal with von Spee. And as we shall see, the Germans deduced that the battlecruiser numbers were down and prepared for their own sortie against English coastal towns.

Command of the force fell to Admiral Sir Frederick Charles Doveton Sturdee, previously chief of the War Staff. Fisher despised Sturdee, but Churchill apparently convinced the First Sea Lord to send Sturdee out with the two battlecruisers to find von Spee's cruisers and destroy them.[57] Sturdee took his time in sailing to the deep South Atlantic. He stopped to examine merchant ships en route, did not hurry his coaling, and even planned a two-day rest at the Abrolhos Rocks. Fortunately Captain Luce of *Glasgow* persuaded him to sail a day early, and they arrived at East Falkland with no time to spare. Meanwhile, Fisher had sent his own instructions: *Canopus* was to be beached so as to make her a stable gunnery platform, her guns trained to sea to guard the approaches to Port Stanley and to open fire when the opportune moment presented itself. Lookouts were posted, and it was assumed, quite correctly, that von Spee would soon make his appearance. The success of British preparations is a triumph for those who claim synchronicity as a factor in the outcome of great events. All transpired miraculously, in the nick of time, so that the British were awaiting the German arrival. They did not have to wait long.

Meantime, von Spee and his squadron had been feted by the German colony at Valparaiso. A man of honour, he replied to an unwelcome toast to the damnation of the Royal Navy, 'I drink to the memory of a gallant and honourable foe.' Setting to sea shortly thereafter, he shaped a course for the Falkland Islands, expecting to destroy British wireless stations, coaling bases, and merchant shipping, and anticipating no major obstruction to his tasks. As he rounded Cape Horn, false messages emanating from British sources led him to believe that no warships were at Port Stanley, the Falklands' main harbour and coaling base.

On 8 December the sea was calm and the season midsummer. At 8.30am the lookout in *Gneisenau*, sent to investigate Port Stanley, sighted the wireless station and an unwelcome cloud of coal smoke. Describing the moment when *Gneisenau* came in sight of Port Stanley in *The World Crisis*, Churchill wrote, 'A few minutes later a terrible apparition broke upon German eyes. Rising from behind the promontory, sharply visible in the clear air, were a pair of tripod masts. One glance was enough. They meant certain death.'[58] Only dread-noughts had tripods, and the lookout passed the news to the control room: von Spee must flee the scene.

In Port Stanley harbour, meanwhile, the lookout in *Glasgow* spotted the approaching German cruiser (and an accompanying smaller warship) and raised the alarm. The bugle sounded the urgent call to quarters. The British ships, then coaling, hurriedly raised steam and sailed as soon as they were able. One by one they cleared harbour in pursuit of the fleeing enemy. At 12.47pm *Invincible* and *Inflexible* came within range and opened fire on the slowest enemy ship, *Leipzig*. Von Spee ordered his supporting ships to scatter, while *Scharnhorst* and *Gneisenau* steamed in relative company and as fast as they could. A long, hard stern chase ensued. Heavy black smoke drifted across the waters, interfering with British gunnery prospects, and, wonder of wonders, a full-rigged sailing ship (French but wearing the Norwegian flag) passed, wraith-like, between the great men-of-war then unleashing their gunfire. The British hunters kept outside of the gunnery range of their quarries – the perfect tactical advantage. One by one, under British gunfire, the German warships went to the bottom, all except *Dresden*, which escaped to a remote Chilean bay at Mas á Tierra, Robinson Crusoe's island. Fisher wanted a Nelsonic annihilation of the enemy, and the elusive behavour of this errant raider infuriated him. He believed the British ships should surely have brought her to account. How easy that was from the purlieus of the Admiralty. Three months later, after much anxiety and a wearying search of many frustrations, *Dresden* was cornered by *Glasgow* and others. Churchill ordered the warships to attack *Dresden*, in spite of the worries of Grey and Asquith that it would embroil the British with Chile and alienate others.[59] Under the British cruiser's superior fire, the captain of the German vessel sank his ship by opening the seacocks. With this, the last of von Spee's cruisers had been swept from the southern oceans. The general opinion of historians who concern themselves with battle at sea maintain that the Battle of the Falklands was the greatest British naval victory of the war. Fisher thought it the most stupendous triumph of the Navy.

To some degree the Navy's victory at the Falklands saved Churchill, and gave him a sense of personal elation close to the end of that horrid first year of the war.

> At 5 o'clock that afternoon [December 8] I was working in my room at the Admiralty when Admiral Oliver entered with the following telegram. It was from the Governor of the Falkland Islands and ran as follows: –
>
> 'Admiral Spee arrived at daylight this morning with all his ships and is now in action with Admiral Sturdee's whole fleet, *which was coaling.*'
>
> We had had so many unpleasant surprises that these last words sent a shiver up my spine. Had we been taken by surprise and, in spite of our superiority, mauled, unready, at anchor? 'Can it mean that?' I said to the Chief of the Staff. 'I hope not,' was all he said. I could see that my suggestion, though I hardly meant it seriously, had disquieted him. Two hours later, however, the door opened again, and this time the countenance of the stern and sombre Oliver wore something which closely resembled a grin. 'It's all right, sir; they are all at the bottom.' And with one exception so they were.[60]

Fisher received news of the Falklands victory with what Churchill says was 'a moderated satisfaction'. A jubilant Churchill sent Fisher hearty congratulations: 'This was your show and your luck. I should only have sent one greyhound [ie, battlecruiser] and *Defence*. This would have done the trick. But it was a mighty coup. Your flair was quite true. Let us have some more victories together and confound all our foes abroad – and (don't forget) – at home.'[61] The victory brought many congratulations, from the residents of the Falklands, from Jellicoe, and from Allied governments.

Within six weeks of being sent to the South Atlantic, Sturdee had completed the task entrusted to him. Surprised by the enemy in circumstances that would have rattled many another man and led him to make serious errors of judgement, he had scored a victory as decisive as any in British history – in his son's words, the last to be 'fought out in the old style, against a worthy foe whose force displayed tremendous courage, determination and efficiency, between ships by gunfire alone, unaided by aircraft, in waters entirely free from minefields and submarines.' Recognising their superiority, the British ships had adopted tactics that enabled them to sink four out of five of the German squadron which for the past four months had cast its menacing shadow over Allied operations in three oceans, without suffering significant damage or casualties themselves.[62]

Certainly, the battlecruiser had exhibited its gunnery in circumstances that Fisher had dreamed of, though with prodigious expenditure of shells. Its speed had been its reason for success. Fisher might have exhibited pardonable pride for the superior material he had sent out to deal with the German ships, but he chose not do so. Why? He was cautious, and it may be suggested that he was probably trying to curtail the overabundant enthusiasm of Churchill. These two were equally familiar with shooting parties, so 'it may have been like shooting pheasants' rings true. There is nothing that breeds success like a successful event, beautifully planned and skilfully executed. And so it was with the Falklands battle.

Churchill, who bore heavily so many disasters at sea to that point, could scarcely contain his enthusiasm about the revenge exacted on the Germans by the Falklands triumph, and he crafted a press release for Christmas Day. He wanted to get the jubilant news out as soon as possible, perhaps to deflect mounting criticisms on other naval matters. Fisher stood in his way: he was adamant that it should not be published. He went further – Fisher warned the First Lord that if that particular communiqué were released he would be obliged to resign: 'I suggest to you to hold your hand about Cradock & the Falklands. No doubt the *Dresden* told all but yet there are always lingering doubts till you hear the other side ... But that is not the point – the point is there is inexplicable folly in the escape of the *Dresden* and the murder of Cradock best left alone ... So let your facile pen have a Christmas rest!'[63] Churchill's communiqué had described in detail the battles of Coronel and the Falkland Islands, including ship names, losses, and even the British strategy for containing von Spee's squadron. According to censor Brownrigg, the report gave too much credit to Sturdee for von Spee's defeat and none to the efforts of the First Sea Lord: 'Nothing can rob Lord Fisher of the credit of having engineered that victory.'[64] This was undeniably true.

In fact, Fisher was not alone in his criticism of Sturdee. Captain Richmond, at that time on the naval staff, certainly had no love for Sturdee and blamed

Sturdee for the dispositions leading up to Coronel and the destruction of Cradock's squadron. Richmond termed him 'a consequential blunderer' and found it ironic that Sturdee was a hero 'when the keels of 5 good ships and some 3500 men lie to his account.'[65]

Fisher demanded explanations of Sturdee; he did so in the old tradition that the Board of Admiralty had done when faced with news of a naval action not completed to satisfaction. An exchange of messages, unedifying to Fisher and at the same time demonstrating Sturdee's determination to answer charges, followed. Sturdee stated in conclusion, 'Their Lordships selected me as Commander-in-Chief to destroy the two hostile armoured cruisers and I endeavoured to the best of my ability to carry out these orders. I submit that my being called upon in three separate telegrams to give reasons for my subsequent action was unexpected.' Fisher barked back, 'Last paragraph of [your signal] is improper and such observations must not be repeated.'[66] Still settling old scores, Fisher examined information about the battle, then decided that Sturdee's tactics during the battle had been wrong. The next day, 11 December, he announced that Sturdee should be kept on the distant South Atlantic station as commander-in-chief, with his flag to be flown in a cruiser, a warship far below a dreadnought in power and prestige, in order to hunt down *Dresden*; until that was done his job was incomplete. For a victorious senior admiral such as Sturdee, now blazoned in glory, what Fisher had in mind promised a sort of penal servitude – a scheme to keep him away from London.

All the same, Fisher was not as all-powerful as he imagined. Churchill, realising the First Sea Lord's motive, vetoed his ploy. Thus it was that Sturdee returned home full of success and, expecting more, was given command of a battle squadron in the Grand Fleet. For his part, Sturdee seethed with resentment and later maintained that as part of Fisher's vendetta against him, his dispatches had been altered so as to paint him in a bad light. There is little evidence to support this, as Churchill only asked that the dispatches be edited in a reduced draft for publication, omitting anything that could be useful to the Germans. Captain Richmond undertook this under the supervision of the Director of Operations, Captain Thomas Jackson.[67]

Fisher treated Sturdee shabbily, and Churchill was not much better. The two sea lords had examined the various reports on proceedings and concluded that Sturdee was dilatory and not on top of the details. One of Sturdee's critics wrote to Fisher, 'No one in history was ever kicked on to a pedestal of fame like Sturdee. If he had been allowed to pack all the shirts he wanted to take ... Sturdee would have been looking for von Spee still!' Sturdee survived it all, was rewarded with a baronetcy, the thanks of Parliament, and a grant of £10,000, and after Fisher's death he was made Admiral of the Fleet. He spent his last days restoring Nelson's flagship *Victory*.[68]

To conclude, Fisher's treatment of Sturdee does not show the First Sea Lord in a good light. His exhibition of spite will always be regretted in so great a commander in the highest naval post. He never succeeded in taking away, as he sought to do, the glory that was due to Sturdee. In almost every other capacity, Fisher's aim had been true.

This was the first occasion when the dreadnought type of armament had been in action with the enemy. The heavy and long-range armament of *Inflexible* and *Invincible* decided the results of the day, and victory was a vindication of Admiralty policy that put such a powerful armament as eight 12in guns in such swift cruisers. It also was a triumph for Fisher's dreadnought design and policy.

In larger measure, the victory at the Falklands and the revenge for Coronel also justified Fisher's return to the Admiralty. In 1917 Fisher reflected that the victory at the Falklands was the 'only substantial victory' to that point in the war. As Fisher was aware at the time of the Falklands victory (and as he recounted later in *Memories*), had von Spee's squadron not gone to the bottom, the consequences would have been terrible. He enumerated them:

1. We should have had no munitions – our nitrate came from [Chile]. 2. We should have lost the Pacific – the Falkland Islands would have been another Heligoland and a submarine base. 3. Von Spee had German reservists, picked up on the Pacific coast, on board, to man the fortifications to be erected on the Falkland Islands. 4. He would have proceeded to the Cape of Good Hope and massacred our Squadron there, as he had massacred Cradock and his Squadron. 5. General Botha and his vast fleet of transports proceeding to the conquest of German South-West Africa would have been destroyed. 6. Africa under Hertzog would have become German. 7. Von Spee, distributing his Squadron on every Ocean, would have exterminated British Trade.[69]

Some believed that British success in the Falklands battle presaged a turn of the tide in naval affairs and, more, in the fortunes of war. However, 'by the 10th December', wrote Frederic Dreyer, flag officer in *Orion*, 'news of the Falkland battle had made it clear that at least two battle-cruisers were absent from the Grand Fleet. So the Germans arranged a raid on the Yorkshire coast.' On 16 December the whole High Seas Fleet put to sea under Admiral Ingenohl, who sent four battlecruisers and one heavy cruiser ahead under Vice-Admiral Hipper. A light cruiser division and two destroyer flotillas sailed in company. Unimpaired, they reached the north Yorkshire coast and proceeded to bombard defenceless Scarborough, Whitby, and Hartlepool with impunity, killing 105 civilians, wounding 525, and causing immense damage ashore. Although the Admiralty got wind of the projected raid from Room 40, it did not know that it involved the whole High Seas Fleet. In consequence, only a detachment of the Grand Fleet, the 2nd Battle Squadron (six battleships, four battlecruisers, plus cruisers and destroyers), under Vice-Admiral Sir George Warrender, was sent to engage the Germans. Hipper ran for home after the bombardment and escaped unharmed. Bad visibility kept Warrender from shooting on Hipper as he came out of the known minefield gap, and even the German cruisers escaped because commanding officers on British dreadnoughts expectantly awaited orders that never came from their superior officer. They took no initiative, and in doing so defied the Nelsonic tradition. Six British battleships missed the glorious opportunity that day and added to the toll of the Navy's blunders. Even so, the Germans had lost their opportunity, too, for they were in superior strength on the day. A distraught Tirpitz regarded the episode as a failure, for Ingenohl, he wrote, 'had the fate of Germany in the palm of his hand. I boil with inward emotion whenever I think of it.'[70]

Fisher was also distraught, for at one moment Beatty had been within twenty minutes' steaming time of the German battlecruisers. 'How unkind was the Heavenly mist!' he wrote to Jellicoe in reference to the very poor visibility of that day, the cover that allowed the German ships to escape virtually unscathed. Misfortune had attended the Royal Navy, and Fisher reflected that perhaps lack of humility in sinking all those German ships at the Falkland Islands had resulted in Providence coming along and giving us a 'nasty knock in allowing the German Bombadiers of women and children at Scarborough and Whitby to escape when they were all actually in our grasp! But Heaven sent down a thick mist, like the cloudy pillar of the Israelites, and they dashed off at right angles at 30 knots speed and we never saw them [any] more!'[71]

George V expressed sorrow and anger. '"Yesterday morning," the King wrote indignantly in his diary, "four large German cruisers, it being foggy, appeared off the east coast of Yorkshire about 8.0 o'clock, & shelled Hartlepool & Scarborough for 40 minutes, doing considerable damage, killing about 40 women, children & civilians and maiming & wounding about 400. This is German *kultur*."'[72]

After the battle, Fisher attempted to clean house – to sack the various commanders – Keyes, Goodenough, and Warrender. Churchill intervened and dissuaded him from this course. Keyes, Churchill wrote, 'has done very well ... All these three years I have watched his work with increasing confidence. Merit, zeal and courage must not be easily overthrown by bad luck.'[73] Churchill and Keyes were bound together in one certain way: both believed in positive offensive action, whether in politics or in war. They also shared contempt for those exhibiting more cautious temperament. Such views brought each of them to the brink of disaster, and their naive views on how to conduct the war at sea were not widely shared by their contemporaries. In the latter category was Jellicoe, the epitome of the fleet commander who guarded his naval assets, materiel, and personnel, to the exasperation of many onlookers but who, in the end, maintained the seaborne security of the state and did not hazard the command of the sea that the British enjoyed and the Germans could never obtain. Churchill, like Keyes and Fisher, wanted 'action this day', to use his famous adage. However, prosecution of the war was not done on a whim, and no victory could come in such a fashion. This war at sea, as it daily proceeded, was one of silent and patient watching and readiness. No individuals on the British side were more impatient than the British sailor, trained and ready to deal with his German opposite.

Jellicoe was 'intensely unhappy' at the results and, from his distant vantage point, laid primary blame for the missed opportunity on the thick weather. This prevented interception. He also was critical of the low numbers of destroyers that were able to accompany the squadron, and argued that a larger number would have allowed a more effective interception of the German forces. Beatty, writing to Jellicoe, was critical of Commodore William Goodenough, to the point where he questioned whether he should remain in command.[74] He declared, 'There never was a more bitterly disappointing day.'[75]

Fisher attempted to reassure Jellicoe after the Scarborough raid:

The great thing is not to be downhearted! Had you heard the Prime Minister last night (at our secret War Council) talking of Beatty missing the German battlecruisers yesterday, you would have thought England's last hour had arrived! It was bad luck for us to be so very close indeed to all the German ships, and in such immense superiority, and for the thick weather to save them from us *in the very jaws of death*! ... But the same thing exactly happened to Nelson in the West Indies, and he also did not take the right turn![76]

This did not keep Fisher from laying blame: 'I agree with you as to Goodenough and the 16th, but I go further and think that all concerned made a mighty hash of it ... But no use crying over spilt milk. Had I only stuck to my own opinion and brought you out, instead of only Warrender.'[77] Again: 'There is of course immense and universal disappointment at the Germans being missed by Warrender, Beatty, and Goodenough ... *We can't possibly have a better chance of catching them, nor ever again such early information of their movements*.'[78]

Nothing to this point in the naval war had demonstrated Britannia's overabundant power at sea. If the distant German cruisers and squadrons had been almost swept from the seas, if their submarine cables had been cut and all their wireless communications upset, if their codes had been broken by naval intelligence aided by good fortune, and if a few German warships had been sunk, as at Dogger Bank and the Falklands, the German navy still held the initiative and to some degree the advantage. As underdogs they benefited mightily from geographical advantage and could choose their moments of attack in what they wanted to be 'the German Ocean'. Their very position on the east side of the North Sea gave them a favourable place from which to mount great sweeps or sudden thrusts to keep the British off balance. Their growing air power, discussed shortly, gave them tremendous psychological advantage. And of all their new means of waging war, the U-boat, whose lethality had only to be imagined, would soon make a dramatic and effective appearance as a principal means of disconcerting British predominance at sea. All the old equations of blue water warfare seemed unsolvable: this was littoral warfare in narrow seas, tip-and-run stuff, blockade and counter-blockade, mine and minesweep. Even the Grand Fleet, the great instrument of Britain's imperial strength, was holed up in Scapa Flow or otherwise relocated to less-exposed locations such as Loch Ewe or Lough Swilly. Churchill and Fisher both had schemes to weaken the German forces (and we will look at these shortly). In the meantime, new difficulties arose and a new, fantastic opportunity presented itself for a naval thrust of British power in the eastern Mediterranean, designed to knock the Ottoman Empire out of the war, secure Constantinople, and aid a sagging ally, Russia. And so one fantastical year of the war had come to a close and another one of equal oddity was about to begin.

Fisher's return to the Admiralty had given that office of state higher credit in the nation. Fisher worked well in harness with Churchill. Their Baltic scheme was maturing, though without Cabinet decision in support. Fisher found Churchill energetic, and his 'power of work' to be amazing. 'Winston has so monopolized all initiative in the Admiralty and fires off such a multitude of purely departmental memos ... that my colleagues are no longer "*superintending Lords*", but only "*the First Lord's registry*"!' Churchill did not like this observation when Fisher said it to him.[79] But it did seem that Churchill had taken over the main features of the Admiralty dealing with the conduct of the war at sea. In the absence of an adequate and efficient staff organisation, the First Lord grasped the need. Fisher, on his return, did not attempt to run the show. He was happy to let Churchill do so and was absorbed in ordering new ships – including 612 for his Baltic armada (discussed in the next section) – and shaking up persons in control of operations.

On 3 November 1914 Fisher presided at a conference on shipbuilding at the Admiralty. First order of business was construction of submarines. Churchill championed the expansion of this arm of the Navy. He wanted more submarines – and when contracts were let for them, insisted on delivery in fifteen months. 'It is indispensable that the whole possible plant for submarine construction should be kept at the fullest possible pressure day and night,' he stated and urged that every effort of ingenuity and organisation should be exerted so as to secure 'utmost possible delivery'. Fisher ordered twenty submarines to be immediately constructed with all speed, and with red tape to be averted by handling any questions himself. He also exploited his connections in the United States, and before long Bethlehem Steel and Electric Boat Company had contracts. Working around embargoes of Secretary of State William Jennings Bryan and further red tape, Charles Schwab of Bethlehem Steel arranged for ten submarines to be built in Montreal at the Canadian Vickers shipyard. The steel was supplied in the guise of 'structural steel for bridges to replace those destroyed in Europe'. By 26 May 1915 the last of the first batch of ten of 'Britain's clandestine submarines' (an American term for them) was sailing to England under its own power to be integrated into the Fleet.[80]

The second order of business was the new building programme of 612 ships of various classes. Included in this number were five battlecruisers, two light cruisers, five flotilla leaders, fifty-six destroyers, sixty-four submarines, and thirty-seven monitors. At the conference, Fisher declared that the vessels were required 'for a special purpose'. A crucial component of the programme was the reassignment of *Renown* and *Repulse* from battleships to light-draught battlecruisers.[81] Fisher brought energy, commitment, and dedication to the shipbuilding tasks. He continued to push for more and faster battlecruisers, and asked Jellicoe and Beatty to send him casual letters stating their preference for battlecruisers capable of 32 knots. As he told Jellicoe: '*I am alone here fighting the battle for more battlecruisers ... None of our existing ships have the necessary FUTURE speed! ... If I don't get these 3 battlecruisers of 32 knots speed, I shall have to leave the Admiralty on January 25 next.*'[82]

Churchill praised Fisher's efforts. Due to the multitude of new ships ordered soon after Fisher's return:

the yards were therefore full of work, and care was needed not to impede current construction by new orders. Lord Fisher, however, brought a very great surge of impulse to this sphere of our activities. It was a moment when megalomania was a virtue ... Fisher hurled himself into this business with explosive energy ... This tremendous new Navy ... was a providential aid to the Admiralty when more than two years later the real German submarine attack began. Its creation on such a scale is one of the greatest services which the nation has owed to the genius and energy of Lord Fisher.[83]

The emergency war construction programme of 1914 was very fortunate because of the massive need for escorts later in the war when 'suddenly the storm burst. Fisher and I had gone, but mercifully there was in existence this immense flotilla of anti-submarine vessels which alone enabled us to get through.'[84]

Fisher, with his customary enthusiasm for heavy guns on light hulls, powered for high speed, ordered three light battlecruisers built around a light cruiser hull. These ships were called *Courageous*, *Glorious*, and *Furious* (though

Fisher's critics gave them other monikers: namely, Outrageous, Uproarious, and Spurious).[85] These ships were capable of 32 knots, had a 22ft draught, and possessed heavy guns, but would have only a 3in main armour belt. The first two vessels mounted twin Mark I 15in naval rifles arranged in two turrets, one forward and one aft, while *Furious* mounted two 18in guns in single turrets. None of these three ships possessed the minimum six guns required for salvo firing to make efficient use of their heavy armament. After the war, all three vessels were converted into aircraft carriers. The four 15in gun turrets were later mounted in the Royal Navy's last battleship, *Vanguard*, which was completed in 1946. These guns remained in service until 1960!

The ill-fated Baltic scheme

Schemes to use superior British sea power to exercise direct action on the German mainland were not new in 1914. Indeed, according to Esher in 1912, Fisher had had in mind as early as 1899 an amphibious attack on the Pomeranian coast ninety miles from Berlin.[86] The Moroccan crisis of 1905 led Fisher to send the Channel Fleet on a 'Baltic cruise' as a useful exercise in naval diplomacy to remind Germany of Britain's capabilities at sea. Fisher would have been happy to fight, says one authority, but this exhibition of naval power sufficed in part to deter Germany from pushing the crisis to war.[87] As early as 1906/7 a committee working in the War College, which included both Corbett and Hankey, drafted plans for a naval war against Germany. These were submitted to Fisher and Wilson, the latter as the commanding officer of the Channel Fleet. They became the basis of the Admiralty War Plans of 1907, which were 'based on the presumption of a war with Germany ... they envisage the massing of overwhelming naval strength on the very doorstep of the enemy, beating in all his naval and coastal defences, and opening the enemy's seaboard to the possibility of a British military descent.'[88] The three possible areas of attack were the Baltic coast, Heligoland, or the ports and islands stretching from the Elbe to the Ems. It need hardly be imagined what local German forces might come out to meet parties of bluejackets and Marines arriving on shore in such shallow waters, where enemy gun emplacements ashore gave full fields of fire. The War Office was rightly sceptical. Any Baltic landing scheme or any attempt to seize any base or fortified island first required dealing with the enemy's naval fleet. But Fisher dreamed on, and he carried many with him in his thinking. He had the power to set naval officers to their planning tasks, and so considerable measures were taken to get the 'best heads' thinking on this project. Of course it would have been better to 'Copenhagen' the German fleet, but that was not possible. And so the planners continued their work.

It seems odd that this particular war plan of 1906/7 remained unchallenged by most senior naval officers. Politicians were ignorant of strategic principles, and Fisher and the Navy kept the plans away from the prying eyes of the CID, but the directors of naval intelligence of the period, Ottley (1905–1907) and Slade (1907–1909), raised no objection, and even Julian Corbett was optimistic that such an offensive would be effective. After all, the Baltic had been one of the Royal Navy's parade grounds up to that time. Despite its shallow waters and other difficulties of navigation, the Baltic posed no major obstruction to British schemes. Such plans, though, were never seriously thought through for detailed staff work. The Army did give some thought to the prospect of amphibious operations in the Baltic. It concluded that nothing could be accomplished by such an enterprise, and any troops landed would soon find themselves defeated and captured by a superior force. This lack of Army support did not seem to dampen the enthusiasm of the supporters of the Baltic scheme. Fisher again suggested landing an army ninety miles north of Berlin at the 23 March 1909 CID subcommittee meeting on the military needs of the Empire. The Army rejected the plan out of hand.[89] The underlying policy of the British at sea was to mount a distant blockade so as to strangle German overseas trade. Any such raids as Fisher intended on harbours or estuaries might oblige German naval units to set to sea in response.

Right from the start of the war, Churchill was looking to the offensive. All his reading of military history suggested this as the best strategy. Churchill's instincts were to go for the jugular, to wipe out the Germans in their nests, and to take the war to the enemy. As early as 31 July he sent Asquith a list of all points on the German, Dutch, and Scandinavian coasts that would be suitable as overseas bases for offensive operations against Germany.[90] On 9 August Churchill proposed to Battenberg to seize one of the East Frisian Islands, which could be fortified and used as a base for further operations.[91] At a meeting of the War Council on 1 December he argued that the best means of providing for the defence of the home islands would be to seize an island off the German coast. He always liked Borkum in this regard. Such a base would allow constant supervision of the German fleet, as well as a base for bombing raids on German ports and facilities. Fisher added his endorsement for such a plan.[92]

Churchill was also keen on an attempt to block up the Elbe Estuary or the Kiel Canal, but with enemy submarines becoming all too active and effective, such a forward action by surface ships faded from view. Instead, Commodore Sir Roger Keyes deployed submarines into the Baltic, setting off all sorts of German naval alarms. Some of the German dreadnoughts at Kiel Bay were withdrawn to safer waters. The next year, 1915, more Royal Navy submarines went into the Baltic, with greater success, and continued to do so until the collapse of Russia as an ally in 1917. The submarine story lies outside our study, but it is a terrific saga of guile, adventure, and great seamanship.[93]

Landing a British army on the German or Russian coast would require transports and surface-ship gun cover. Could such a thing be done? As early as 19 August 1914 Churchill was advocating operations in the Baltic and managed to acquire Russia's preliminary approval for a joint Anglo-Russian landing on the Pomeranian coast. It came to naught after the Russian defeat at Tannenberg later that month, and the Russians were never again in a position to carry out such an operation. When Fisher was made privy to this correspondence he 'rallied enthusiastically to the idea.'[94] Fisher's policy of scrapping outdated ships, however, left the Royal Navy with too few vessels available to act as escorts for troop transports for any landing as part of the Baltic scheme, meaning that the Grand Fleet itself would have to act in this role, risking its valuable dreadnoughts in German waters.[95] But the shape of the war as it was unfolding in the early autumn of 1914 called for a more active role for the Royal Navy against the German navy, which was sitting snugly in harbour. Thus it was that maritime strategist Corbett sent Fisher his assessment of a possible Baltic project: 'The risks, of course, must be serious; but unless we are fairly sure that the passive pressure of our Fleet is really bringing Germany to a state of exhaustion, risks must be taken to use our command of the sea with greater energy.'[96]

Churchill's frustration at the quagmire that was the Western Front mounted. Again we are reminded of his proposition that some better alternative must exist 'to chewing barbed wire' in that theatre. As a student of military history, and now close to the centre of directing the war effort, he favoured peripheral warfare. He wrote to Fisher in late December: 'The Baltic is the only theatre in wh. naval action can appreciably shorten the war.' That accorded completely with Fisher's plans. Churchill also favoured an attack on Zeebrugge – to crush the U-boat menace at its source. He continued to emphasise this point in a letter to General Sir John French, Commander-in-Chief of the British Expeditionary Force, on 11 January 1915 and at the War Council meeting of 28 January.[97] In March, Churchill told Jellicoe that Fisher was making 'extraordinary exertions' to complete six monitors for 1 May, which would be used for an attack on Borkum, then actually scheduled for 15 May. Churchill did not envision requiring the Grand Fleet on the first day of the operation, although the Germans might move on the second. About a week or so after the operation, or so it was planned, a fast division, perhaps made up of *Warspite*, *Tiger*, and *Queen Elizabeth*, accompanied by light cruisers and destroyers, would be deployed to blockade the Baltic ports and shatter German influence in Scandinavia. It was wildly imagined that Holland and Denmark might be brought on side.[98]

Here was Churchill's imagination and insight fully at work. The plan also confirmed Sir Arthur Wilson's pet project, the seizure of Heligoland, the highly fortified and heavily gunned island that commanded the water approaches to Wilhelmshaven: he had strongly advocated such a course when he returned to the Admiralty in 1914 as a member of the War Staff group. However, the War Office regarded such an attack as suicidal. Selborne, former First Lord, believed that Wilson's plan was 'stark, staring madness', and Jellicoe commented to McKenna that 'we one and all doubted Sir A.'s sanity ... Anyone who could put forward the proposition as he put it forward is capable of *anything*.'[99] And so the project lapsed and was, in any event, overtaken by events in the eastern Mediterranean.

In an early post-war critique of the Baltic scheme, historian Thomas Frothingham found it strange that a senior officer such as Fisher should have plunged himself impetuously into an unpracticable plan. As a consequence, his very energy had the odd effect of 'paralysing British naval strategy'.[100] The great irony remains: the British did not take up the Baltic as a theatre of action – a war in the narrowest and most difficult of waters, for littoral warfare is indeed full of dangers. Instead they found themselves in the Dardanelles campaign, with the Gallipoli landings, a high-risk venture far from home against an unknown enemy. That was the tragedy.

War of terror from the air

On Christmas Eve 1914 a German aeroplane hoping to hit Dover Castle dropped a bomb in a nearby garden. This was a warning of horrors to come from above. The German press proclaimed that German genius had at last shown that England was vulnerable because of its insularity. In the circumstance, the German naval airship division made new plans for attacks on the east coast of Britain and the Thames Estuary. The Kaiser authorised these on 9 January 1915, but specified that targets had to be limited to docks, arsenals, and other military targets. Zeppelin attacks on King's Lynn, Yarmouth, Southend, and elsewhere brought war closer to home. It became unmistakably clear to the British that the well-known policy of German 'frightfulness' could do no end of damage as well as incite fear.

Responsibilities for air defence had been given to Churchill as an Admiralty matter. On New Year's Day 1915 he signed a confidential memo to Cabinet reporting receipt of intelligence that the enemy planned to bomb London by airships and to do so on a grand scale at an early opportunity. 'The unavenged destruction of non-combatant life must therefore be considerable,' he warned. He added that the Air Department of the Admiralty had studied the matter closely, with the conclusion that it was quite powerless to prevent such an attack, particularly if good fortune and favourable weather conditions existed. Fisher was alive to the new danger too, and on 4 January he wrote to Churchill on the issue of possible Zeppelin raids on London. He argued that the only defence against these potentially devastating raids was to announce beforehand that if these raids took place, reprisals would be taken by shooting one German prisoner of war for every civilian killed. He continued by stating, '*As this step has not been taken I must with great reluctance ask to be relieved in my present official position as First Sea Lord* – because the Admiralty under present arrangements will be responsible for the massacre coming suddenly upon and unprepared for by the Public. *I have allowed a week to elapse much against my judgment before taking this step* to avoid embarrassing the Government I cannot delay any longer.'[101]

Churchill was blunt in his reply to the admiral. Fisher, he pointed out, had no professional experience with the question of aerial defence. Moreover, the question of reprisals was one for the Cabinet, not the Admiralty, to decide upon. In short, Churchill could not support Fisher's proposals and said so. As to a threatened resignation: 'I hope I am not to take the last part of your letter seriously. I have always made up my mind never to dissuade anyone serving in the department over which I preside from resigning if they wish to do ... But I sympathise with your feelings of exasperation at our powerlessness to resist certain forms of attack: and I presume I may take your letter simply as an expression of those feelings.'[102] Fisher let the matter pass, and Churchill did not receive a written reply from him. As recounted in *The World Crisis*, Churchill saw Fisher later in the day. Fisher did not mention the issue and appeared 'in the best of tempers' and, in fact, their 'work proceeded as usual'.

Churchill's memo cited above had immediate effect. A War Council was held on 7 January with all the senior Cabinet members and military heads in attendance, including Fisher. The matter was reviewed in detail. Churchill explained the defences of London from air attack as arranged. Fisher repeated Churchill's warning, indicating that the enemy craft would come by night, in clear weather, and would navigate by following the Thames from its estuary to London. All naval intelligence indicated a German build-up in the war in the air.[103]

Within months the terror from the air increased to such a degree that it gave Fisher even greater anxiety, and we will return to this presently. For the moment, new measures were being taken at the Admiralty, some by Fisher and others independently by Churchill, to add new equipment to the military capabilities of the Navy. These were dirigibles and the tank, which we take, briefly, in order here.

Throughout all these nervous months the Royal Naval Air Service had been increasing its number of planes (air and sea) and pilots, navigators, and ground staff. Fisher, in February 1915 as at other times, was lobbying for an increase in naval air power and was concerned with a severe shortage of naval air officers in the Air Service, where there were large numbers of civilian aviators instead. Captain Murray F Sueter, a pioneering administrator and leader in naval aviation, commented: 'It is a matter of opinion whether Officers piloting and fighting aircraft are of more value to the Navy when counting the German fleet in the Heligoland Bight, putting submarines out of action with bombs, making raids on Airship Sheds, etc., or in a minor position in a ship.' He argued for a nucleus of fifty commissioned officers and an effective strength of 5,000 in the air service, and not so many civilians.[104] Consideration was also given to barrage balloons and to dirigibles. Fisher was informed by George Holt Thomas, a leading airship designer, about small airships, or as he purposefully called them, 'dirigible balloons'. On 2 July 1914 the Director of Navy Contracts at the Admiralty had sent particulars regarding the design of small dirigibles. Holt Thomas noted that these small dirigibles were more economical to use than seaplanes, and that there was less risk in using them. Also, they could be used for night patrol work against U-boats.[105] At the Navy's Ordnance Department, where Rear-Admiral Sir Charles Ottley was in charge, Fisher's secretary, Captain T E Crease, on 24 February 1915, discussed what he considered to be a brilliant anti-submarine measure: he wanted the Royal Navy to think about building a stationary aircraft – the dirigible – with a two-man crew, a 1pdr gun, and a maximum speed of 25 knots. These small dirigibles could be used as an antidote to the submarine menace. Ten to twelve months would be needed to construct the dirigibles, and a building the size of St Paul's would be required for their erection. He noted that steel wire nets had been proposed but set aside due to costs, and that a submarine detection net, which would stretch from Calais to Dover, was being pondered.[106]

By this time Churchill was considering the concept of the 'land battleship', which ultimately became the modern tank. Churchill was invited to dine with the Duke of Westminster, who commanded a squadron of armoured cars. There Churchill met a Major Hetherington, who spoke persuasively about the concept of having large armoured vehicles as a battlefield weapon. Suitably stimulated, Churchill was determined to pursue this concept and asked Major Hetherington to turn over his plans. On 18 February 1915 Churchill forwarded to Fisher Hetherington's preliminary plans for 'land battleships' and urged Fisher to 'devote his great energies and mechanical aptitudes to getting them carried through.' Churchill also pushed forward a Landships Committee of the Admiralty under the presidency of Tennyson d'Eyncourt, Chief Constructor. The committee came up with concept vehicles, and Churchill ordered eighteen built (six of the wheeled version and twelve as caterpillars). Indicative of his power, Churchill spent nearly £70,000 without consulting the Admiralty Board, the War Office, or the Treasury.[107]

Perils of the Grand Fleet

Meantime, in the North Sea, all the initiative lay with the German navy: the Royal Navy was obliged to respond only when circumstances allowed. From our times, we can now see that this was the defensive phase of the war at sea, but at the time it was a long period of exasperation at not being able to come to grips with the enemy. The U-boat had made its dreaded appearance. German minelayers had sown their lethal tools of destruction. There was fear of invasion, and so, immediately upon Fisher's return, he had Sir Roger Keyes, who was in charge of submarines, prepare a paper on the effectiveness of Britain's submarine defences against invasion. Keyes concluded that submarines were potentially a key weapon in combating an invasion, but there were an insufficient number to cover all of the vulnerable areas.[108] In December Keyes received a letter from Rear-Admiral George A Ballard, who had been harangued by Fisher for what he perceived as the failings of the submarines during the raids on Scarborough and Whitby. Ballard was thoroughly unimpressed with Fisher's views on the proper tactical deployment of submarines, which included the beliefs that they always should work singly, and that they did not need harbours as they could rest on the bottom.[109] It is clear from this that Fisher did not understand the role of submarines in actual war, and that he had a romantic over-appreciation of the capability of the submarine in regards to tactics and force deployments.

Fisher placed the blame on those responsible for protecting the fleets at anchor. In particular, he decried the 'effete inexcusable' state of anti-submarine defences at Navy anchorages. He deplored the unfit state of the admirals in charge of creating such defences, and the fact that work was started at many anchorages instead of concentrating on completing Scapa Flow – the great watchtower – at the outset. Then Fisher changed his mind about Scapa Flow. He told Jellicoe that the 'real strategic centre' that should have been made submarine-proof – and that should have been the base for the Grand Fleet – was the Humber river estuary.[110] It is hard to accept Fisher's reasoning, and Jellicoe was sceptical of the advantages of the Humber. In reply to Fisher he argued that only twelve or fourteen dreadnoughts could use the estuary. Moreover, it could easily be mined, and the weather there had a strong tendency to be foggy.[111] Jellicoe wanted more destroyers to protect his great ships and guard entrances to ports and harbours. He thought defensively about command of the sea. But this raised the question: were destroyers developed for defensive or offensive purposes? Were they for escorting the dreadnoughts, for engaging in tactical deployments, or for defending the ports? The first duty of the destroyer flotillas of the Grand Fleet was to screen the Fleet from submarine attack; coupled with this was the counteroffensive of warding off German flotillas seeking to unleash torpedoes. Equally important was the launching of torpedo attacks against the enemy's battle fleet if the circumstances offered. There were routine patrols around the base, convoys to be escorted, and emergency duties.[112] Jellicoe could never have enough destroyers, the maids of all work.

Fisher sympathised with his cries for more destroyers: 'I will see what can be done about sending you the 'M' class [destroyers] at once, but every one in this building wants them for aggressive action down here at the outset! Nevertheless I believe you are going to have a tough job with the German destroyers accompanying the German fleet.'[113] Fisher encouraged Jellicoe's habit of writing about every problem with the Grand Fleet – 'the whole point is that you SHOULD tell me all these *most exasperating* episodes'[114] – and Jellicoe continued to complain about inferiority in destroyers compared to the High Seas Fleet into December, in particular urging that the 'M'-class destroyers be sent up to him.[115]

It was entirely natural for the Commander-in-Chief of the Grand Fleet to want every scrap of naval material to be at his disposal, but larger issues were at play at this time, with the Germans taking the initiatives on and over the seas, making the North Sea into their field of action, as it were. Thus in mid-November the Admiralty informed Jellicoe that the pre-dreadnought *King Edward*-class ships were to be sent south to Rosyth in order to better protect the east coast from German raids. They were well-gunned and had good speed for the job intended, but in response Jellicoe noted that he greatly wanted to have the *King Edward*s up at Scapa Flow for gunnery exercises and tactics.[116] Jellicoe failed to consider the possibility of a German raid on the east coast. 'I can't believe the Germans will waste their battlecruisers over a bombardment,' he wrote to Fisher on 2 December. 'I should think it is just what our submarines would pray for, and if they got back without heavy loss, I should be pretty surprised. At any rate, I am perfectly certain that it would be the faultiest possible strategy to base our fleet with the idea of preventing a bombardment.'[117]

In the aftermath of the Scarborough raid, and with worries circulating that perhaps the German navy would next strike south toward the Channel and even Portsmouth (Fisher believed that the next raid by the German battlecruisers would be on more distant targets, possibly Folkestone and Portsmouth, and then on to the coast of Ireland),[118] the Admiralty decided that British ships seemed to be stationed in the wrong locations to deal with the near and present danger, and ordered the transfer of Beatty's battlecruiser squadron to Rosyth, to be accompanied by four of the faster light cruisers. In case of a further raid, orders to Beatty would be sent to him directly from the Admiralty, although they would be repeated to Jellicoe as well.[119] Jellicoe doubted that the Germans would attempt to move through the Channel, and if they did he believed the submarines and destroyers could surely engage them.

He also doubted the utility of Rosyth or the Humber as a fleet base, and wrote to Fisher: '*I fear this perpetual idea of raids will affect our strategy. I fully realise it is most difficult to resist the idea that we must be there to catch them*, but, honestly, I don't see how it is to be done. Manoeuvres have shown time after time that you can't do it.'[120]

Fisher reflected Jellicoe's cautiousness.[121] By late December he was urging Jellicoe to keep his vessels out of the North Sea entirely, unless the Germans first sortied. He told Jellicoe that he would make a formal written statement outlining this belief. He argued that the use of large vessels in the North Sea and the Channel made them vulnerable to submarines, as shown by the sinking of *Cressy*, *Hogue*, and *Aboukir*. He bemoaned the men lost in such sinkings ('*More men lost than by Lord Nelson in all his battles*') and argued that the work of such ships could be just as easily carried out by armed trawlers.[122] He also agreed with Jellicoe's protest '*against taking risks for which there is no compensating advantage*', and urged Jellicoe to impress upon Churchill the threat from the new German submarines.[123] (Churchill failed to see the growing danger from the U-boats. He was dismissive of the threat from any use of the Belgian ports by German submarines, and in response to Grey's and Haldane's worries about the Germans using Ostend as a submarine base, Churchill replied that he could, if necessary bombard the port into ruins within twenty-four hours and make it uninhabitable.[124] That demonstrates his bravado.)

In the new year Jellicoe's concerns over the state of the Grand Fleet and Scapa Flow continued. The defences of Scapa Flow and the vulnerability of his dreadnoughts to submarine and mine attack worried him, as did the closeness of the German-British ratio in dreadnoughts, especially with the High Seas Fleet holding the initiative.[125] Jellicoe detailed the loss of capital ships: *Audacious* had been mined and sunk; *Iron Duke* and *Ajax* had leaking condenser tubes; *Orion* and *Superb* had turbine problems; *Conqueror* was refitting; *New Zealand* was in dock; *Erin* and *Agincourt* were not yet fit to lie in the line; and *Emperor of India* and *Benbow* were not properly worked up. There were inadequate numbers of destroyers, and a similar lack of cruisers needed to support destroyer raids or stop and board merchantmen ('BATTLECRUISERS ARE OUR LIFE BLOOD,' he stated). 'It is astonishing how quickly our supposed superiority in dreadnoughts and Battle Fleets vanishes,' Jellicoe wrote to Fisher in January 1915. 'Thank goodness the Germans imagine we have proper defences ... otherwise there would be no Grand Fleet left now.'[126]

Jellicoe's health began to suffer terribly. A case of haemorrhoids was corrected by surgery, and Fisher counselled him to take a good long rest. This was impossible, and Jellicoe continued to attend to mounds of paperwork. He was a centraliser and did not delegate. When he began to exercise with a medicine ball, he hurt a knee and a finger.

At the Admiralty, Fisher read Jellicoe's stream of worrying letters; he shared the anxieties of the C-in-C, Grand Fleet, and no doubt put his own twist on the matter when he wrote to Churchill that Jellicoe 'is not well, and is in consequence suffering from a temporary depression.' He insisted that no effort should be spared in giving the C-in-C what he wanted, since 'such a state of mind is infectious and may easily spread through the Grand Fleet.' Reinforcements for psychological reasons seemed to be the order of the day. He argued that a third light cruiser squadron and more destroyers should be sent to Scapa. Jellicoe also wanted the two battlecruiser squadrons divided, with one based in Cromarty and one at Rosyth, due to the difficulties associated with transiting the anchorage at Rosyth and its vulnerability to mining. Fisher, however, concurred with Beatty's desire that both squadrons should be based together, since they were a tactical unit. Fisher held that no effort should be spared to make Scapa Flow secure, and he talked about the use of monitors, with their mobile, powerful guns capable of fending off any German cruisers that might attempt a fitful raid. He seemed to be flailing about to find a solution for Jellicoe, and was nearly pathological in his desire to do whatever he could to support his fair-haired boy.[127] And he too expressed anxiety over the ratio of strength of the Grand Fleet and the High Seas Fleet.[128] Fisher never forgot that it was Jellicoe who was bearing the weight of naval readiness. On 21 January he wrote to Jellicoe reassuringly that the power of the Grand Fleet had increased enormously since the outbreak of war and that, by all appearances, the Germans had not conducted gunnery exercises in at least three months.[129]

Churchill was dismayed by Fisher's anxiety: 'You seem to have altered your views, since taking office, about the relative strengths of the British and German ... Fleets.' The First Lord saw no reason to worry, since there had been no major alterations in the respective orders of battle since Jellicoe received his recent reinforcements.[130] Churchill believed that Jellicoe's concerns were groundless: 'In these circumstances, his telegram attached is not worthy of him, and ought certainly not to affect our dispositions.'[131] Churchill thought Jellicoe dwelled too strongly on the dark side of things. He deplored any diminution of his fleet, and all his calculations, as Churchill said, always exaggerated the 'deductions', when in fact his superiority over the Germans in number of capital ships was always assured and strong. As Jellicoe biographer John Winton writes with care: '[Churchill] could see that Jellicoe was always magnifying his own disadvantages, however small, and always crediting the enemy with more ships than they actually had. Churchill also tended to fall into his own error of comparing ships solely by the size of their guns; he could not accept Jellicoe's opinion that a ship was virtually useless until she was properly worked up.'[132] Jellicoe's complaints exasperated Churchill, and Fisher sensed the coolness growing between the First Lord and the Commander-in-Chief of the Grand Fleet.

After the war Churchill turned the argument on its head. It was he, he claimed in *The World Crisis*, and not Fisher, who was supremely concerned with the margin of safety in the North Sea. Churchill stated that he thought the number of battleships in home waters was barely enough, but that Fisher felt sufficiently assured of British naval superiority to insist on the transfer of light vessels to the Channel and Harwich, and for the transfer of several battlecruisers to other theatres in the aftermath of Coronel.[133] At the Lord Mayor's Banquet on 9 November 1914, Churchill spoke reassuringly of the power of the Grand Fleet and British sea power. 'The conditions of naval warfare are curious and novel,' he said.

We have a great preponderance in force and numbers, but we have also a task to discharge infinitely greater and more difficult than that which our enemies are called upon to undertake. (Hear, hear.) We are endeavouring to maintain all the seas; we are endeavouring to clear all the highways across the ocean; we are endeavouring to secure the most peaceful commerce of the world against a multitude of new dangers and against methods never before practised in the warfare of civilized nations.[134]

Churchill understood maritime strategy and the dynamics of sea power, and he did so against the large backdrop of British naval experience in war. To the many other demands on the British navy was added the transport of great armies of the Empire to their places of urgent need. Here, and at other times, he was constantly obliged to explain the Navy's responsibilities and, perhaps, the difficulties facing the Admiralty.

The Dogger Bank action

The strange quietude that had descended on North Sea naval affairs over the Christmas period was punctured by an event that occurred on the last day of 1914, which made alarmingly clear the power of the torpedo in enemy hands. The recently strengthened Channel Fleet, commanded by Vice-Admiral Sir Lewis Bayly, who wore his flag in *Lord Nelson*, was making a leisurely 10 knots in a formation unconcerned with the advantage of zigzagging. Off Start Point the pre-dreadnought *Formidable* was sunk by *U-24*, which fired two torpedoes. The ship went down with the loss of 547 lives. When the news arrived at the Admiralty on New Year's Day, Fisher was outraged over Bayly's incautious handling of his force. Bayly had failed to take precautions. He had ignored the threat of submarines. Fisher did not consider Bayly's explanations as being at all satisfactory. Their Lordships decided to remove Bayly from his command, although Churchill was later to write that he agreed to do so only with 'extreme regret'.[135] Bayly asked for a court martial so he could clear his name but was refused. He was soon appointed president of the Royal Naval College at

Greenwich. As Churchill explained to Jellicoe on 11 January 1915, Bayly was appointed 'not for his own sake, but because to terrorize Admirals for losing ships is to make sure of losing wars.'[136]

The quietude was shattered later in January by an event known as the Dogger Bank action. The episode was significant in itself, but it also did nothing to soothe the growing conflict between the First Lord of the Admiralty and the First Sea Lord. Dark clouds continued to gather over the Admiralty and the Fleet.

On the morning of 23 January 1915 Room 40 intercepted a signal from Ingenohl to Hipper ordering him to reconnoitre Dogger Bank in hopes of destroying British fishing vessels suspected of gathering information on German naval movements. The plan called for Hipper's battle- and light cruisers to sortie from the Jade river after dark and return twenty-four hours later. The Germans did not know that British naval intelligence had deciphered his signals; they considered that their actions were known to themselves alone. Thanks to British intelligence, within an hour and a half of Hipper receiving his order, Room 40 knew the Germans were raising steam for the intended operation.

Churchill had just returned to the Admiralty from visiting Fisher, who was laid up with a cold in Archway House, adjoining the Admiralty buildings, when Wilson and Oliver arrived excitedly in the First Lord's room. As Churchill wrote in *The World Crisis*:

> [Wilson] looked at me intently, and there was a glow in his eye. Behind him came Oliver with charts and compasses.
> 'First Lord, these fellows are coming out again.'
> 'When?'
> 'To-night. We have just got time to get Beatty there.'[137]

Churchill was now apprised of the intelligence intercept, and the trap was set to catch the German force. Strict radio silence was to be kept. Beatty's two squadrons would rendezvous at daybreak with Tyrwhitt's destroyer force just north of the Dogger Bank, while the Grand Fleet would conduct a general sweep of the North Sea. (In the event, the Grand Fleet was no nearer than 140 miles from the action, though it was not intended that it would play a role in the impending battle.) Churchill consulted with Fisher as to the developments then unfolding, and he asked Wilson and the Chief of the Staff to take the charts and the draft telegraph over to Archway House so that Fisher could give guidance, if required. 'Lord Fisher was quite content with the decisions which were proposed, and action was taken accordingly.'[138]

In the event, and true to expectations, Beatty, with five battlecruisers (he flew his flag in *Lion*) and a superior force of light cruisers and destroyers, pounced upon three unsuspecting German battlecruisers and an old, slow armoured cruiser (*Blücher*) sailing with some cruisers and destroyers. *Blücher* was sunk and the other enemy vessels were damaged and forced to flee. *Seydlitz*, Hipper's flagship, received a hit near a magazine, and flames spread until the two aft turrets were destroyed. Only prompt flooding of the magazine saved the ship. Thus the Germans learned that their current anti-flash precautions were useless. By contrast, the British did not learn that lesson until Jutland, when it cost the British three battlecruisers.[139]

Meanwhile, in London, the Admiralty waited in suspense. Late that evening news arrived. By 9.50pm a telegram from Beatty had been deciphered. The engagement with German forces had indeed occurred as expected. *Lion* and *Tiger* had taken the greatest blows from the Germans. *Lion*'s port fuel tank had been hit, and she was largely disabled and reported limping for home, guarded by cruisers and destroyers.[140] Her thin plates were punctured by the enemy's smaller 11in shells. Fisher, hearing that Beatty's flagship had been damaged and was obliged to steer for home, supposed that she had hit a German mine. That was not the case. Beatty had shifted his flag to a destroyer and returned to port.

In all it had been a strange reversal of fortunes. As the story unfolded there seemed little to cheer about in the halls of the Admiralty, especially as it became apparent that prized opportunities had been wasted. In fact, a state of gloom settled over the building. Churchill was disappointed in the battle and angry at the results. He wrote to Sir John French on the 24th: 'Today a chance offered, but only one forfeit cd be exacted. I had hoped for more. We hit them vy hard. But their strong armour protected their motive power: & they fled so fast, we cd not obtain a decision.'[141]

Fisher, trying to make an analysis of the battle, realised that the Grand Fleet (and Jellicoe) in Scapa Flow lay at too far a steaming distance to be of any use in such an episode: 'He might as well be at Timbuctoo!' Fisher confided to Beatty. 'He ought to be at Rosyth, as you ought to be at the Humber, now the submarine defence is finished and 8 berths ready.'[142] Out of necessity, German naval movements – raids and minelaying – were drawing British naval forces south. For two days Fisher pored over the telegrams, signals, and in-letters. Dogger Bank failed to meet his expectations and that of others. The more he pondered it, the more he fretted. Why, he asked Beatty, did not *Tiger* and *Princess Royal* press on against the Germans after *Lion* had become incapacitated? Two enemy ships, *Derfflinger* and *Seydlitz*, 'VERY HEAVILY ON FIRE ... and both seriously damaged', were allowed to escape at noon when three or four hours' steaming time remained before German coastal mines could be a matter of concern. These vessels steamed to safety and 'had to scuttle into dock with great urgency and a very great number of killed.' 'You are mistaken about the enemy submarines,' he told Beatty, 'we know from themselves exactly where they were, hours off you.' To him, Rear-Admiral Archibald Moore's discontinuance of action at noon was inexcusable. 'It's quite terrible to me that they should have been allowed to go free at noon. WHAT POSSIBLE EXPLANATION IS THERE? What excuse have we to offer!'[143]

Fisher was devastated. His highly touted battlecruisers had been robbed of a signal and complete victory. The enemy firing had been more accurate, scoring a higher hit rate. This was owing to the system of director-firing of turrets then completed in practically all the modern German ships; the British lagged behind, and only *Tiger* was thus fitted on the British side. Although at the Admiralty there was consolation that the battlecruiser design had been vindicated, much unease existed, brought forth by Fisher and Beatty and shared by others. On 27 January Fisher conversed with Churchill about the Dogger Bank action and other matters. Larger issues made him anxious. Fisher remained worried about concentration of force in the North Sea. That night he received from Jellicoe advice (spontaneous and unsolicited) that Fisher immediately relayed to Asquith: 'The battle cruiser action [Dogger Bank] showed most conclusively the absolute necessity of a BIG preponderance of these ships and I hope will at any rate result in no diversion of any 'Queen Elizabeths' or any battlecruisers from the decisive theatre (the North Sea). Had we lost the *Lion*, the victory would have turned into a defeat.'[144] Fisher also deplored the gunnery of *Tiger*.[145] There was much talk in the Navy under the heading, as Beatty put it: 'We ought to have had all four.'

By 31 January Fisher sought to console Beatty. The old admiral had made up his mind who was to blame for the lost opportunity, as he wrote to Beatty: 'Your conduct was glorious. *"Beatty beatus."* Moore's was despicable. The Captain of the Tiger (I forget his name [Captain Pelly]) was a poltroon. He was a long way ahead, he ought to have gone in, had he the slightest Nelsonic temperament in him, regardless of signals! like Nelson at Copenhagen and St. Vincent.'[146] The unfortunate Moore was removed from his command.

Beatty shared Fisher's disappointment. He criticised Moore and Pelly for their conduct during the battle, as he wrote to Jellicoe:

1st Lord was in a disturbed frame of mind and wanted to have the blood of somebody. I gather this is the First Sea Lord's idea also; they settled on Moore. Well frankly between you and I he is not of the right sort of temperament for a BCS. He is too clever and I fancy his relations in the *New Zealand* were terribly strained after *Lion* fell out … Moore had a chance which most fellows would have given the eyes in their head for, and did nothing … Then Pelly did very badly, first in not carrying out the order to engage his opposite number which had disastrous results and second in running amuck after *Lion* fell out and not attacking enemy's rear … I have said that Pelly has done very well up to then, he has had difficulties to contend with and I don't think he is likely to do the same again, but he is a little bit of the nervous excited type.[147]

As Jellicoe wrote to the Admiralty on 10 February, the two important factors for British ill-success were Moore's discontinuing pursuit of the three enemy battlecruisers to concentrate his fire on *Blücher* instead, and *Tiger*'s failure to engage her opposite number in the German line.[148] There was nothing startling in this appraisal, and the Admiralty agreed with Jellicoe, but Pelly was not sacked from his command, and Moore was transferred instead of disciplined. This was primarily due to the influence of Churchill, who did not wish to stir up any trouble: 'the future and the present claim all our attention.'[149]

However, the Dogger Bank action was more decisive than it initially appeared to the Admiralty. In the highest circles of the Germany navy the outcome of the battle caused heated arguments over the proper deployment and uses of the High Seas Fleet. The losses sustained gave credence to those who argued that the High Seas Fleet simply did not have the strength to challenge the Grand Fleet. The advocates of the offensive were silenced.[150] For a time the Germans retreated to a 'fleet in being' concept of sea power.

After Dogger Bank, Fisher wrote to Beatty that the world was now seeing that battlecruisers were the 'breath of life', and that he had been proven correct. As to urgently raised questions about weaknesses of battlecruisers: 'This is wartime, and we can't have any d—d folly about susceptibilities. Don't you worry about any odium – I will take that and love it.'[151] With respect to the serious damage done to two of the battlecruisers, Fisher wrote that both *Lion* and *Indomitable* would be repaired in northern waters since it was too dangerous to send them south, because of submarines. He also spoke of his two new light cruisers, armed with 15in guns, capable of 33 knots, and with a draught of only 21ft. These ships would join Beatty's force by December 1915 and would be 'a surprise packet for Tirpitz!' Fisher also expostulated on his view of the future of the war. He doubted that the Germans would sortie on their own; rather, they would only conduct raids on the east coast. This would make the role of Beatty even more important: 'I don't believe the Battle Squadrons will be in this war. THE BATTLECRUISERS will finish the job! IF ONLY THEIR GUNNERY IS PERFECTION!'[152]

When talk resumed after 24 January about stationing Beatty's force at the Humber, Jellicoe strenuously objected. He wrote to Beatty: 'I'll be hanged if I can see where you, 3rd BS, 3rd CS, light cruisers and possibly the Channel Fleet are going to find room in the Humber.'[153] To Churchill, Jellicoe restated the problems with Rosyth, such as insufficient room, potential vulnerability to attack, and the tides. Scapa Flow had none of these problems, and the distance differential between the two favoured Rosyth only by sixty to ninety miles, or only four hours' steaming time.[154] Beatty agreed with Jellicoe's concerns: 'I talked to 1st Lord about it and I certainly thought I had made it plain that I did not agree with putting battlecruisers at the Humber. First of all and lastly it is impossible, as there is insufficient water.'[155] Nevertheless, Fisher continued to push the change: 'All you say about the disadvantages of Rosyth makes a great impression on me. Nevertheless at Scapa YOU WILL NEVER BE IN TIME! – ALWAYS 150 *miles too far off*! The same applies to Beatty going to Cromarty. We should not have had Jan. 24 if Beatty had been at Cromarty.'[156] In the end, Fisher conceded that the view of the Commander-in-Chief had to prevail.[157]

The Churchill–Fisher combination at the Admiralty had not yielded a great victory. Dogger Bank was a missed opportunity of heightened proportions. Was bad staff work to blame? No. Was it poor intelligence gathering and use? No. The finger of blame pointed at the commanders at sea, the lack of the Nelsonic touch, Moore's incompetence, and bad signalling by Beatty. The misfortune to his own ship played mightily in the equation leading to failure. His shifting of his flag to the destroyer, correct in the circumstances, had somehow not been understood by the other commanders. No naval exercise before the war had apparently imagined such a scenario. Lack of imagination as to how war might unfold at sea among heavy ships in combat was the self-inflicted wound. 'After the event any fool can be wise,' said Homer. But in the Dogger Bank action a comedy of errors had been acted out.

After the events of Dogger Bank a period of quiet reigned – luckily, as Jellicoe was ill and laid up. His letters continued to bear his worries. Unduly pessimistic by nature, he constantly complained about the size and state of the Grand Fleet. Beatty sensed his despondency. Fisher urged Jellicoe not to worry about the condition of the Fleet,[158] and he worried about Jellicoe's mental well-being, believing that Jellicoe's state of mind would have corrosive impact on those in command who were responsible to Jellicoe. At this stage, in January and early February 1915, Fisher thought that the Grand Fleet enjoyed superiority in strength to its German rival. He was right, but this did not assuage Jellicoe's fears.

By March, Churchill was becoming even wearier of demands from the C-in-C for more and more ships and men. Jellicoe was good at stating his case, but he exaggerated. When he prepared a memorandum in which he made a play to strengthen the Grand Fleet by getting the pre-dreadnoughts of the Channel Fleet stationed at Portland (previously commanded by Sir Lewis Bayly before he was relieved of command), he outlined his warning that if the High Seas Fleet made a move in the North Sea, they would take everything, including seventeen dreadnoughts and eight *Preussen* pre-dreadnoughts, to engage twenty-one Grand Fleet dreadnoughts, with a German superiority in torpedo craft: 'I have purposefully left out the Battle-Cruisers and Armoured Cruisers because you cannot, with summer fogs and low visibility in the North Sea guarantee that they will be in the main action. Our Battle-Cruisers may be drawn off to chase the 5 German Battle-Cruisers.' Jellicoe concluded that the British were outgunned twenty-nine ships to thirty-nine, especially when the German could choose their moment. Fisher questioned leaving out so many ships from the C-in-C's calculations: '*This is a lot to leave out!!!!*'[159] Churchill remained unimpressed with Jellicoe's plea for more ships: 'This paper is full of silliness. If the Germans go at the speed of their slowest ships we can do whatever we like with the head of their line and need not engage the tail ... Fancy ruling out the Battle cruiser fleet & 6 armoured cruiser squadrons.'[160]

In early March, Sir Reginald Tyrwhitt, Commodore of the Harwich Force, saw Churchill at the Admiralty and complained of inaction in the North Sea. He asked if they were waiting for the Germans to 'come and kick us'. Churchill was upset at the suggestion, and Tyrwhitt 'nearly got kicked out'. Apparently even Fisher had reined in some of his enthusiasm for the offensive.[161] It was time to watch and wait. Thus, later that same month, Fisher wrote to Jellicoe about his fears of invasion. He believed that von Pohl might make a dash with transports and conduct a landing at Harwich and in the Thames. He feared that, due to the location of the Grand Fleet in northern latitudes, they would be powerless to intercept for thirty-six hours. He reiterated his belief that warships needed to be based at the Humber, as the defences there were now completed: '[The Humber is] THE REAL STRATEGIC CENTRE! and you won't agree to Beatty going there! Such is life!'[162]

On 9 April Fisher challenged Jellicoe on the matter of the latter's hesitancy. He noted that there were reports of German armed liners about to leave New York, and that *Invincible* or *Indomitable* should be sent there to intercept them. He did not detach a battlecruiser force to deal with them, for 'you and Beatty gave me such an awful time of it crying out about the *Princess Royal* day by day that I decided it really was better to chance it, and that is what I am doing, *against my own better judgement*!' He also criticised the pessimistic views of Jellicoe and Madden: 'I fear you and Madden, whose letters are really terrible, react on each other in your lugubrious forecasts of the gloomy future! ... You and Madden want to bottle up everything up north, and we shall have a disaster. You will never get anywhere in time!'[163] Apparently Jellicoe objected to the tone and content of this letter, for Fisher soon wrote again, saying that at no time had he any doubts about Jellicoe's fitness for his current command, and apologising if his remarks had caused any offence.[164] But this exchange revealed the essential difference between Fisher's idea of what a battlecruiser was – a distant and fast strike weapon – and Jellicoe's concept that vessels of that class must be kept in battle squadrons in proximity to the main battle fleet.

The dispatch of reinforcements to the Grand Fleet, and Fisher's desire to support Jellicoe at every turn were to no avail. From Scapa the C-in-C complained unremittingly that the war group at the Admiralty failed to take into account the slender superiority held in heavy ships; the risks of submarine, torpedoes, and mines; and the problems of fuel expenditure and coaling of vessels. His frustration with the Admiralty is expressed in this letter to a fellow admiral, 'I have been so disgusted of late that I wrote my plain ideas to the First Sea Lord three days ago. What the result will be I don't know, and moreover I don't care. ... Lots of submarines about to-day. The North Sea seems full of them. I *hope* to get in without being bagged, but it is a bit of a lottery in daylight, though 18 knots is my best safeguard.'[165] Jellicoe's problem was of his own making: he could not get enough warships to provide the insurance he thought so very necessary. And the irony was that he was doing so little in an offensive way with what he already had at his disposal. He took no risks. The concept of 'fortune favours the brave' held no charm for him.

Jellicoe's comment about submarines in the North Sea reflected the Germans' new policy. Until February 1915 Germany had acted with restraint: attacks without warning on merchant ships had been few, though the losses were not to be discounted. But now losses to U-boats were rising sharply. What had brought this about? In January senior German naval officers, backed by an anxious press, called for a U-boat campaign against Allied shipping without warning. Higher command gave in. On 4 February, on a pretext of British violations of international law, Germany declared unrestricted U-boat warfare, effective 18 February. This allowed U-boat captains to sink, without warning, non-military ships, even those from neutral countries.

To this point, British intelligence had supplied valuable data that helped combat the nominal threat. Each day, Churchill, Fisher, and others received a current summary of the strength and location of U-boats, gleaned from Room 40 intercepts.[166] But the German pronouncement made waters around the British Isles a war zone. As the official British Naval Staff monograph put it, the Germans were about 'to adopt a procedure hitherto limited to savage races making no pretence at civilisation as understood in Europe.'[167] On 15 February 1915 Admiral Wilson wrote in correspondence:

We are anxiously waiting to see what is going to become of the German submarine threat after the 18th. If they shoot at sight they will, I think, get a good many merchant ships, but not enough to seriously affect trade. Most of the mischief is done by false reports which divert patrols from the proper places ... I think in time we shall keep them out of the English and Irish Channels, but I don't see yet how we can block their ports and keep them out of the North Sea.[168]

The submarines' hunting ground was the Western Approaches, used by shipping entering the English Channel or the Irish sea from the Atlantic or Bay of Biscay. British merchant losses began to rise at an alarming rate, with forty-two ships sunk by U-boats in August. Sharp protest from Washington led the Germans to suspend unrestricted U-boat warfare, but that policy could not hold. Again pressures within the German military command called for measures to defeat the Allies by the end of 1916. Berlin imagined that a much greater toll could be exacted that would bring the war to an end.

The Lusitania *tragedy: 'a damned dirty business'*

Meanwhile, on 7 May the gigantic unarmed Cunard liner *Lusitania*, homeward bound from New York to Liverpool and making a steady course at a reduced speed of 21 knots, was torpedoed without warning by *U-20* at 2.15pm, within fifteen miles of the south Irish coast, in sight of the Old Head of Kinsale. She went down in eighteen minutes with a loss of 1,198 – of whom 128 were United States citizens. The United States was outraged, as were all civilised nations. The State Department protested in the strongest terms to Berlin. The Germans considered the sinking of inestimable propaganda value, duly exploited. Conspiracy theories abound; counterfactual appreciations are rampant.[169] The sinking was proclaimed in some circles as pure aggression against an innocent ship carrying citizens of a neutral country. Others claim the liner was carrying either troops or munitions, and that the explosion of the latter is what caused the liner to sink so rapidly.

Myths die hard. *Lusitania* had no guns mounted. She was not an armed merchant cruiser. Her sinking was in contravention of the rules laid down at the 1907 Hague Convention, which stated that a merchant vessel could not be sunk without visiting her to establish the fact that she was carrying contraband. Passengers and crew also had to be provided for. While *Lusitania* carried 4,200 cases of rifle cartridges as well as other contraband, these could not have caused the explosion that occurred after the torpedo hit. Underwater investigations by Robert Ballard (who also discovered the wrecks of the *Titanic* and *Bismarck*) led to the irrefutable conclusion that an explosion of coal dust followed the fatal torpedo hit.[170] Less likely possibilities exist. Historian Diana Preston has shown that steam-line explosions were the most likely cause of the subsequent explosion, and the torpedo, which had caused catastrophic damage, was sufficient to sink *Lusitania*. This historian finds Ballard's evaluation irrefutable. In any case, it could be said that *U-20* 'mounted the perfect attack'.[171]

At the time Churchill was in Paris on a secret mission to negotiate for Italy's entry into the war. He was ill, suffering effects of influenza. Fisher was at the Admiralty, dealing with the heavy strain of office. The routine passage of *Lusitania* was far from his mind, concentrating as he was on other matters. On

10 May, when Churchill returned from Paris, Lord Charles Beresford fired a barrage of questions in the House of Commons, all implying Admiralty neglect. The loss of the 'live bait' squadron still haunted the Admiralty, casting doubts on matters of command and control. Churchill could not answer Beresford directly, could not disclose classified information, and resorted to evasion. A board of inquiry had been announced that morning, and there for the moment the matter rested.

So what was the Admiralty's responsibility in this tragedy? It did not supply the liner with an escort vessel, although in this regard there is no record that any liner was so escorted. It has been mischievously argued that Churchill and Fisher allowed *Lusitania* to be sunk by a U-boat in order to provoke the United States to enter the war on the side of the Entente. No credible evidence has come to light to indict the British government of having deliberately exposed this ship. Churchill did want the United States in the war as an ally, but goading Germany into taking an action that would require a US Senate response to end neutrality lay beyond his capabilities. He must wait and see. True, George V said to President Woodrow Wilson's personal adviser, Colonel Edward House, 'Suppose they [the Germans] should sink the *Lusitania* ...' But this does not mean that the King was betraying state secrets, for six days beforehand the warning was common knowledge in Britain. Nonetheless, fingers pointed accusingly at the Admiralty. Captain William Thomas Turner of *Lusitania* complained bitterly that the Admiralty failed to provide protection. And that influential figure Lord Esher, for one, wondered why the Admiralty did not send out an escort for the liner.

In fact, the Admiralty believed at the time, and for some time afterwards, that the best defence for fast transoceanic liners lay in their speed and a zigzagging course: thus, attempting to provide an escort would only make the liner more vulnerable as it slowed and awaited the escort's arrival.[172] As past experience had shown, *Lusitania* had outrun a predatory U-boat on her westward crossing. As for who would have protected *Lusitania*, Admiral Sir Charles Coke, Commander-in-Chief, Coast of Ireland Station (based on Queenstown, now Cobh), had at his disposal an overextended squadron of four older cruisers and seventeen small vessels. This force, which became derisively known elsewhere in the Service as 'the Gilbert and Sullivan Navy', was inadequate in speed to give aid to a sleek greyhound of the sea. In fact, in the circumstances, support had been called off based on the belief that a cruiser providing convoy might become a target.[173] In fact, after Admiral Coke received *Lusitania*'s 'Come at once – big list', and estimated her position ten miles south of Old Head of Kinsale, he ordered the cruiser *Juno* to steam to the scene. In sight of the survivors in the water, *Juno* returned to base – for having heard the details, they did not want a recurrence of a 'live bait' scenario. Other rescue vessels, merchant and navy, collected the survivors and the dead bodies. Two precious hours passed from the time of *Juno*'s departure until the rescue began.[174]

Admiral Coke and the Queenstown office did nothing to pass messages to Captain Turner before the attack. The Admiralty had known, through 'Blinker' Hall and Room 40, that U-boats were operating around the British Isles and the south of Ireland. Indeed, three merchant ships along the pathway of *Lusitania* had been sunk recently,[175] and Hall had fed the Germans false intelligence about troop transports, his intention being that U-boats would sortie against fictitious ships.

Neither Fisher nor Churchill was a conspirator in the terrible scenario. They were fixated on other tasks. They were, too, preoccupied with larger operational issues – especially the agonising Dardanelles, as shall be seen – to have conspired over *Lusitania*. In fact, though Churchill and Fisher would have known, quite generally, that the liner was soon expected at Liverpool, neither knew *Lusitania*'s exact location on that fateful day. In any event, the Admiralty gave only guidance concerning a liner's routing in those days; specific control was unheard of. Indeed, ship owners resented any naval interference in the prerogative of ordering their ships to proceed as they deemed appropriate. Of all long shots, Hall makes a more likely agent, with his conspiratorial temperament and his access, through Room 40, to all the relevant facts, but this too is unlikely. Could it be that Admiralty indifference and inaction, in part due to the centralisation of power and information in the hands of Fisher and Churchill, contributed to the disaster? As Diana Preston puts it: 'Far from being the subject of conspiracy, the *Lusitania*, in her last days and hours, was the victim of complacency and neglect. While neither a verdict of wilful murder nor even manslaughter is sustainable on the basis of surviving evidence, a claim of contributory negligence certainly is.'[176]

Churchill and Fisher, neither of whom accepted any share of the blame, now found themselves under even more censure than before and set about finding a scapegoat. Together they laid much of the responsibility on poor Captain William Turner. He had reduced his speed in order to take a sighting so as to fix his position and time his arrival at Liverpool, and then he had gone below. Thus had he erred – and become a target. Captain Richard Webb, director of the Admiralty's Trade Division, set about demonstrating Captain Turner's incompetence. He was selective in his use of evidence and dishonest in his approach. On whose instructions he acted is not known, but his report, accepted by the Admiralty, was that Turner was either a knave or a fool.[177] The Trade Division was seeking measures to dodge its responsibilities in this disaster.

Churchill took up Webb's cudgel. He commented, 'I consider the Admiralty case against the Captain should be pressed before Lord Mersey [Britain's expert on the law of wrecks and now head of the official Board of Trade inquiry] by a skilful counsel ... We shall pursue the Captain without check.' Fisher, to his discredit, was taken in by Webb's duplicity. He was more adamant: 'I feel *absolutely* certain that Captain Turner of the *Lusitania* is a scoundrel and been bribed. No seaman in his senses could have acted as he did.' Five days after the sinking it was learned that German agents had infiltrated Cunard's New York office and learned of *Lusitania*'s intended course. Fisher accused Turner of being a traitor and suggested that he should be arrested regardless of the result of the official inquiry.[178] Captain Webb had all the authority he needed when he sent this memorandum, bearing Sicilian overtones, to Lord Mersey: 'I am directed by the Board of Admiralty to inform you that it is considered politically expedient that Captain Turner the master of the *Lusitania* be prominently blamed for the disaster.' It was a nasty matter all round. As for Lord Mersey, who appreciated this more than anyone, he duly delivered his report and told Asquith that he wished to be excused from further administering His Majesty's justice. To his children he said, 'The *Lusitania* case was a damned dirty business.'[179]

Churchill's and Fisher's separate attempts to blame the unfortunate captain smack of dishonour. Until the day he died, Turner never forgave the Admiralty in general or Churchill in particular. As for Blinker Hall of Room 40, he seized on the opportunity strangely offered by arranging the production of a medal designed by Herr Goetz (intended as a satirical comment on Germany's allegations that the liner carried contraband) and had 300,000 made by the patriotic Gordon Selfridge, the department store owner.

The sinking was indeed a case of 'wilful murder', and no one on the British side of the story comes away from this horrific event unscathed. The victim gets the blame. The undeniable culprit, however, is the U-boat captain, Walter Schwieger, aged thirty, who, using the instrument of destruction at his disposal, executed his plan. That he knew *Lusitania* would be crossing his bow was certain. The liner was an acknowledged target. All he had to do was make his calculations and issue the order to release the torpedo. He did so with cold precision. His decision, and his alone, brought on the terrible result. The *U-20*'s doctored diary, and disingenuous German explanations, only serve to darken the predatory and premeditated action taken by the German U-boat service. And what happened to Schwieger, who necessarily saw his job as following instructions? He was awarded the Iron Cross for sinking *Lusitania*. He undertook no fewer than thirty-four missions, sank forty-nine ships totalling 183,883 gross register tons, and lost his life, age thirty-three, when on the hunt for further quarry off Terschelling, Frisian Islands: his *U-88* hit a British mine and was lost with all hands.

The *Lusitania* tragedy and its immediate aftermath as directed by Churchill and Fisher, aided by Webb and possibly Hall, occurred in that black month in naval affairs – May 1915. Almost concurrent with this – in a strange synchronicity that persons other than historians might unravel in explanation – were, first, the shells crisis and, second, the looming last act of the struggle between Churchill and Fisher over naval units and dispositions, highlighted by the Dardanelles problem and Fisher's eventual and ultimately final resignation (and Churchill's removal from the Admiralty). In short, the Admiralty's blaming of Captain Turner soon yielded to other important matters.[180]

Supreme war direction in disarray

We return now to the last days of 1914 and the earliest of 1915 for a capsulation of the state of affairs on the eve of the momentous decision to take the Dardanelles. Here we pause to review the nature of British war planning and strategy. Those who had opposed the Continental Commitment – and they were many, fearing intractable and growing obligations of the British Expeditionary Force (BEF) – now had proof positive that their forebodings and warnings of danger were valid. The fine British Army sent into the field was now a shadow of its former self, for losses had been unimaginably heavy. As the scope of the war broadened, and it became apparent that the conflict would not 'be over by Christmas', the overall structure of the British war effort began to show strain. The organisational problems within the Admiralty were only a reflection of the larger inability of the British to adjust their governmental and strategic thinking to the realities of modern war. Not least did this bear on the system of Cabinet government and the various political entities vying for power in what turned out to be the last days of the Asquith ministry. The old order was about to be swept away but not without one last gasp of life.

Lord Esher, an original member of the Committee of Imperial Defence, had envisioned the committee operating in peacetime in preparation for war; once war began, its role would be reduced to almost nothing.[181] The CID was replaced by the War Council, which met for the first time on 25 November 1914. Amongst its members, Lord Kitchener and Churchill wielded the most influence over strategy. Churchill's mind was the most active and fertile of any member of the War Council, but the stolid Kitchener held the most power. An imperial legend, he had immense prestige. His reputation ensured that his views on strategy were in the fore. Indeed, Kitchener's reputation was so great that it was a major factor ensuring the Tories remained a quiet opposition during the first months of the war, as they could hardly criticise the living embodiment of the imperialism they embraced. Churchill initiated strategic decisions, but lacked the power Kitchener held to carry them out.

In keeping with the war plan, the British had intended to send only four divisions to the Continent. Meanwhile, they had deployed the Naval Brigades. The Canadian 1st Division had arrived on Salisbury Plain in October and was being employed on the left flank of the besieged French army. But the naval war was one of uncertainty, the enemy more elusive on the high seas than expected. The lack of strategic direction was hinted at in a comment Churchill made to Captain Herbert Richmond in the first days of the war. As Richmond related to his diary, 'As I went away, he [Churchill] stopped me, saying he wished to talk about some matters. Said, "Now we have our war. The next thing to decide is how we are going to carry it on."' This appalled Richmond: 'What a statement!'[182] That the Royal Navy lacked a strategy for the war, defensive or offensive, was to Churchill an opportunity and to Richmond appalling. As Churchill himself acknowledged later: 'We had competent administrators, brilliant experts of every description, unequalled navigators, good disciplinarians, fine sea-officers, brave and devoted hearts; but at the outset we had more captains of ships than captains of war.'[183]

These problems began at the top with the prime minister. Asquith abandoned the strategical in war. He clung to power as a great chairman of the board about to be deposed or otherwise subverted. He may have had an interest in fronts and sideshows, but he left the decision-making and implementation to others. A J P Taylor is correct when he says that Asquith 'did not understand the great issues which the conduct of the war provoked.'[184] Asquith lacked knowledge of how to wage war, and he devoted no energy to the matter. A good parliamentarian and party leader, he was diffident in dealing with the Services. By default, this gave various ministries, committees, and staffs, besides the private sector and industry, a free hand. He was no strategist, as Roy Jenkins puts it, only a materialist for the bloodletting process.[185] He acquiesced to the Service chiefs and to Haldane, Kitchener, and Churchill, and shrewdly went about cultivating for his government and administration whatever public support it could garner and sustain. Asquith took a hands-off approach to government in order to keep everyone happy; nowadays, this would be called decentralisation. As Lord Morley presciently noted in the first days of the war, 'Mark my words, Asquith is not the pilot to weather this storm.'[186]

Asquith's lack of dynamic leadership caused some unrest in the Cabinet. Churchill urged him to take action: 'Plans could be made now for April and May which would offer good prospects of bringing the war to its decisive stage by land and sea. We ought not to drift ... Without your direct guidance and initiative ... a succession of bloody checks in the West and in the East will leave the allies dashed in spirit and bankrupt in policy.'[187] Nor was Churchill the only one to express disappointment with the lack of zip in the naval war. As Hankey at the CID wrote to Fisher in late January: 'Like you I am not quite happy about the Navy, who lack ginger. The root of the trouble is that the whole nation has fixed its eyes too much on the army (which has effected nothing) instead of concentrating on the sea. The same fault goes right through the Cabinet, parliament, press & people, and the people at the Admiralty, being unassertive by temperament, have quietly acquiesced.'[188] As Corbett wrote: 'The soldier square-heads have got hold of the war solid & refuse to do anything except on the Western Front, damn it!'[189] The lack of a naval staff system isolated from the political leadership of the Admiralty did not help matters. Fisher, instead of making himself the head of the naval staff, let Churchill's war group continue, with himself increasingly on the outs with Churchill.

Lloyd George, who favoured more dynamic leadership and a more concerted war effort than Asquith, soon got himself involved in issues far beyond the range of his position as Chancellor of the Exchequer. Munitions in particular drew his interest, but he also found himself active in causes such as the overconsumption of alcohol by factory workers. The net result of all these efforts, though, was neglect of his duties at the Exchequer. After August 1914 he spent almost no time on purely Treasury business, and his 1915 Budget was less than adequate. Worse, he neglected the financing of the war. By early 1915 Britain was fighting the war almost entirely on City credit and a ballooning overdraft at Morgan's in the United States, and the value of the pound was beginning to fall. By May the Permanent Secretary of the Treasury, John Bradbury, was begging Asquith to transfer him to any other post, as he could no longer stand Lloyd George's inattention to financial matters, and could work under him no more.[190]

There was unrest with Kitchener's handling of the War Office. He seemed to have had little grasp of the supply and logistics side of fighting a modern war, and resisted all attempts by outsiders to assist the flow of munitions to the troops in the field. His laissez-faire approach to the issues of supply infuriated those, like Lloyd George and Churchill, who wished for the British nation in general, and British industry in particular, to be fully mobilised for the war. Kitchener was also contemptuous of the Territorials (the active-duty volunteer reserve force of the Army, which was not obliged to serve overseas). However, his immense public prestige made him untouchable. Only death could carry him from the scene.[191]

In the first year of the war, when strategy impinged on foreign policy, as seemed the norm, both Kitchener and Churchill had to accommodate themselves to Sir Edward Grey. Grey had long been used to having complete freedom over British foreign policy without having to stoop to consult his Cabinet colleagues – most vividly shown by his pre-war negotiations with the French. He had little interest in the intricacies of strategy, and did not see any great need to adjust his views or his foreign policy to suit the realities of war. Asquith could have resolved the disagreements that inevitably arose between Kitchener and Churchill, or between the two and Grey; by temperament, though, Asquith was ill-disposed to play such a role, and seldom intervened decisively.[192]

As the months dragged on, an atmosphere of conspiracy and intrigue swirled around the Cabinet. Combinations and counter-combinations, actual and rumoured, of the key players appeared and disappeared with stunning regularity. Almost all felt a general malaise with the war effort, and ideas were discussed for the rearrangement of offices or the infusion of new blood. It may be impossible to know conclusively just how many conspiracies were real or rumoured, but the atmosphere generated by such rumours was hardly conducive to the successful conduct of the war. Not surprisingly, Churchill was often to be found at the centre of the rumours. His second suggestion that a coalition government be formed, made in March 1915, fell on deaf ears – opponents and rivals doubtless saw the idea as a power grab. The Unionists under Bonar Law were by this time chatting about getting Winston, who they saw as the real danger, out of the government and forming a coalition, but only as a last resort. They did not want to bring down the government only to wait until such time as the ministry could be reconstituted. Politically, this was a sound approach, but it took Fisher's actions to set events in motion.

Asquith remained on his guard against the dangerous duo of Churchill and Lloyd George. He received wild reports that these ministers were secretly conspiring with Arthur Balfour and, at the same time, busy undercutting Kitchener, with Churchill also suggesting that Balfour should take over the Foreign Office when Grey was absent on one of his fishing trips. According to Margot Asquith, her husband said that Churchill was a 'young puppy ... let him come and suggest this to me and I'll tell him what I think of him! he really is the greatest donkey! he goes gassing about, abusing K[itchener] to Arthur and I've no doubt abusing me, giving him much too much information. He thinks he knows Arthur Balfour, he has not the foggiest idea of what Arthur really is.' Asquith himself commented:

> It is a pity ... that Winston hasn't a better sense of proportion, and also a larger endowment of the instinct of loyalty ... I am really fond of him: but I regard his future with many misgivings ... He will never get to the top in English politics, with all his wonderful gifts; to speak with the tongue of men and angels, and to spend laborious days & nights in administration, is no good, if a man does not inspire trust.[193]

Churchill had diminished somewhat in Asquith's eyes. In a letter to Venetia Stanley, in which he mused about sending Churchill to India as Viceroy, he commented that 'it is not easy to see what W[inston]'s career is going to be here: he is to some extent blanketed by E. Grey & Ll. George, & has no personal following: he is always hankering after coalitions and odd re-groupings, mainly designed (as one thinks) to bring in F.E. Smith & perhaps the Duke of Marlborough. I think his future one of the most puzzling personal enigmas in politics – don't you?' In another letter Asquith, writing about the War Council meeting of 26 February, said that 'Winston was in some ways at his worst – having quite a presentable case. He was noisy, rhetorical, tactless, & temperless – or – full.'[194] Churchill's political fortunes were already in decline. Not only was his administration at the Admiralty failing woefully to bring forth the results, in the form of successful naval actions, that the world's ranking naval nation had confidently expected, but he was also engaged in another war: the manoeuvrings in Whitehall, in the ministry, and on the opposition bench, that threatened to bring him down. We return to this presently.

The conspiracies and intrigues were not limited to the Cabinet: they spread to the military commanders. Sir John French had early become convinced that Kitchener was out to remove him from his command. He was not entirely mistaken. When Kitchener had been in France for a conference with French generals, he had asked them their opinion of Sir John's leadership and offered to put General Sir Ian Hamilton in his place as commander of the BEF – an offer that was an egregious breach of confidentiality. The French generals, with the agreement of the French president, stated that they could not support a switch of generals in mid-campaign, and hence supported Sir John. When French learned of Kitchener's intrigue, he became very suspicious and sent Captain Freddie Guest, Churchill's cousin, to London to inquire of Asquith if Sir John still had the confidence of the government. Though Asquith assured him privately that he did, French never again felt secure in his command.[195] Kitchener had planted the seed of doubt. French also worried about Churchill's interference. In December 1914 Kitchener became upset with Churchill's regular visits to General French. In particular, he was concerned about Churchill's discussions with French on army strategy and deployment. Kitchener viewed such discussions as fundamentally undermining his authority. He drafted a letter to Churchill outlining his concerns, and ended with a remarkable suggestion: 'I am suggesting to the PM that you should take the WO and let Fisher be 1st Lord then all would work smoothly I hope.' Asquith wisely prevailed on Kitchener to withhold the letter.[196] Churchill never fully grasped the distrust of him that was developing in Kitchener's mind. He knew of tensions existing between French and Kitchener, and even tried to mediate – but to no avail. French's days were numbered, and he relinquished his command in mid-December 1915.

In point of fact, the old Cabinet system was breaking down, the War Council could not hold the centre, and the prime minister, excellent chairman though he was, had not the capacities of a Pitt to make it work. Fisher, pronouncing on the War Council as he saw it, wrote: 'Vacillation is the order of the day and procrastination is the idol of politicians.'[197] Hankey later wrote, 'Fisher put his finger on the spot when he said: "You want *one* man."' But that was not to come until the rise to the premiership of Lloyd George.[198] And the road to Lloyd George's rise led through a disastrous military operation in the East and a Cabinet crisis of the first order that was to have a decisive impact on both Churchill and Fisher.

As to the war at sea, the overall advantage lay with the Germans. They might lose their overseas cruisers, but their powerful High Seas Fleet lay inviolate behind safe and secure harbour entrances near the Jade at Wilhelmshaven. In these circumstances they could pick their time and place of attack, all the while keeping the British off balance. Time and again the Admiralty acted, but only in response to German sorties and initiatives (including those of the Zeppelins). The British might establish a distant blockade so as not to risk ships in enemy coastal waters, but this policy, too, was reactionary. None of this suited Churchill's mindset, or Fisher's either. All the vaunted hype about British superiority at sea, of making a pre-emptive strike, as Fisher had proposed in his suggestion to 'Copenhagen' the Germans lying at anchor or as Churchill had done in his impossible scheme of digging them out like rats from their holes, had come to naught. Month by month, year by year, the Britannic tragedy was unfolding.

Troubles worsened in the Admiralty. Hankey, Cabinet insider and man about Whitehall, got wind of this when he lunched with Fisher and Admiralty heads of department on 29 March 1915. Fisher had learned of a possible German attack on neutral Holland by land and sea, with a demonstration by the High Seas Fleet on the English coast – a deadly combination. Fisher explained to the heads of department his countermeasures then being hastened, and Hankey thought them admirable. The German attack never came but Fisher was alive to the prospect. In Churchill's absence he was seeking to retain the centre of naval affairs. 'Afterwards, he kept me alone in his study for an hour, explaining his difficulties with Churchill, who insists on sending telegrams to the Admirals marked "private", but dealing with public matters with which the Board alone ought to deal.'[199] Fisher, Hankey learned, had threatened again to resign, but Hankey dissuaded him and began his quest for a solution, a matter which escaped even his talented function as Whitehall and Cabinet insider.

PART FOUR

'Damn the Dardanelles.
They will be our grave.'

9

Troubles at the Admiralty

'**D**amn the Dardanelles,' Jacky Fisher wrote to Winston Churchill on 5 April 1915. 'They will be our grave.'[1] Such was the seasoned admiral's prognostication: he had a knack for making forecasts, and he made this one just after the plan to force the Dardanelles by the Navy – 'by ships alone' – had met formidable obstacles on the spot. Fisher was speaking of the fate of the administration at the Admiralty – and by extension the fate of the British government and even the British Empire. He was not far off the mark. In evaluating this pronouncement from these dark days of the war, the reader, just like the historian, ought to keep a photo of Jacky to hand, and observe in his heavy-laden eyes the wisdom as well as the warning, while his turned-down lips seem about to open with yet another cautionary or censorious utterance.

Genesis

The Dardanelles, those narrowing straits leading from the Aegean Sea to the Sea of Marmara, stretch twenty-seven miles eastward through a pinched, mile-wide neck between Chanak on the Asian shore and Kilid Bahr on the storied Gallipoli peninsula. Navigation in these waters is challenging on account of the rush of water pressing through the 'Narrows' from the Sea of Marmara at a rate of 4 to 5 knots. At war's outset, Ottoman defences were nominal: a few well-sited forts mounting artillery on both sides of the straits. Beyond the Sea of Marmara lies the Bosporus, and where the one becomes the other, a river flows in from the north. Here lies the commodious basin known as the Golden Horn, the magical and legendary harbour that lies beneath the Constantinople of old, now Istanbul. Here Asia meets Europe. East again the Bosporus affords a shipping lane to the Black Sea. British warships had passed through these waters on many an occasion, notably during the Crimean War, but safe passage always depended on unrestricted navigation and no interference from shore.

Immediately preceding August 1914, the Ottoman Empire had received many battering blows in the Balkan and Italian wars. Rather isolated from the Central

Powers by communications, the sprawling giant desperately needed munitions and stores. Railway systems were incomplete, giving no material unity to the Ottoman Empire. None of the Central Powers had a common frontier with Turkey. Germany offered attractive commercial and military considerations, particularly against Russian aggrandisement, and Colonel Liman von Sanders, the resourceful and energetic German military adviser, expert in artillery and engineering, made plans for defence as well as for offensive sorties. Six years before war dawned, Turkey, and the Ottoman Empire, were in flux, beset on all sides with problems, and in these circumstances the local nationalist forces in Constantinople saw a great opportunity against the tottering sultanate. Enver Pasha and the Young Turks seized the day. German organisation and investment and von Sanders' forcefulness swung the Ottoman Empire to the side of the Central Powers.

The Ottoman Empire declared war on the Allies on 5 November. This set the whole Middle East in flames, for it made more uncertain the British position in Egypt and the protection of the Suez Canal. That was the vital waterway to the east, the imperial highway. The Ottomans controlled Palestine to the eastern bank of the Canal, and part of the reason for the Gallipoli campaign, a companion of the Dardanelles adventure, was to draw off Ottoman strength. A victory at Gallipoli, it was imagined, would open the way to Constantinople itself; it would bring the Ottoman Empire to ruin.

In the British imperial logic, control of Egypt and the Canal was central to future fortunes, and in the Cabinet the 'Easterners', so called, had history on their side; the 'Westerners', by contrast, were preoccupied with the main theatre, the intractable Western Front. These were irreconcilable positions. Churchill and Fisher can be classified as 'Easterners', because they advanced strategies at the peripheries: they preferred the indirect approach as a means to defeat of the Central Powers. Such adventures were to be their ruination: they would leave both of them in the wilderness by late 1915, and would upset the Asquith administration by bringing the Opposition into the Cabinet. In the immediate term the Dardanelles were the grave of Churchill and Fisher, but the lids on their coffins were never sealed. And in regards to Churchill in particular, his return to a position of power, as Minister of Munitions, in 1918 would announce his resurgence. All of this lay ahead.

The Dardanelles campaign derived from a variety of sources and various reasons; it has never been established exactly what the ends of the operation were, and the objectives that were identified were improperly communicated to the officers on the spot. Command and control were shoddy. The official history of British military operations yields few clues.[2] As early as 1904, in the wake of the Dogger Bank incident (when Russian warships fired on British fishing boats), Fisher was asked about the possibility of forcing the

Dardanelles. He concluded that 'even with military co-operation forcing the Straits would be mightily hazardous',[3] and dismissed the idea as absolute folly. In 1906 he wrote the King's secretary, Sir Frederick Ponsonby, in regard to forcing the Straits: 'So clever a man as Lord Cromer [long time British Controller-General of Egypt] is has lost his head over this business and wants our Fleet to force the Dardanelles! *It all comes of his marrying again when he was 65!* No fellow can stand it!'[4] The General Staff of the British Army agreed with the Director of Naval Intelligence: naval losses would occur going in or coming out. As well, in the Italo-Ottoman War of 1912 five Italian torpedo boats were obliged to retire when attacked during their attempt to penetrate the Dardanelles.[5]

Among the first to attempt to unravel the riddles of the Dardanelles and Gallipoli was Major-General Sir Charles Callwell, a close observer of these fatal events of 1915. He was also among the first historians to pass judgement on the decision-making process. 'By those responsible for setting the campaign in motion,' he wrote in 1919, 'the conquest of the Hellespont was rightly regarded as merely a preliminary to further combinations of war. The real objective that they had in view was Constantinople and the Bosporus – especially the latter.' From this would devolve all sorts of military, political, and strategic benefits: Russia being able to export her abundant agricultural exports and to import war materiel; the Sultan's dominions being split, thereby setting up a barrier against German and Austro-Hungarian pressure; and the Entente's ability to secure benevolent neutrality over the Balkan states. This masterstroke was to have all these benefits and more besides. 'As it turned out,' comments Callwell, 'the project in reality never got beyond its introductory stage. The attempt to win the Dardanelles, first by naval effort and afterwards by the superimposition of a military expedition on a great scale upon the original operation, came to naught. Hence it has followed that the enterprise, in spite of what was contemplated to start with, has come to be looked upon merely as a campaign undertaken for the mastery of those Straits.'[6] Historians ever since have been examining these issues, and the documentation available in the Dardanelles Commission files help tell the true story of great muddling, uncertain leadership, contrary-minded personalities, deceptions, changes of plans in midstream, various plans ill designed to bring success – and numerous after-the-fact 'cover-ups'. The great main plan, 'by ships alone', was Churchill's almost exclusively, for the War Office would not or could not yield assistance.

As much as hindsight and history have showered blame on Churchill, let us turn the debate about the responsibility for the Dardanelles on its head. One individual cannot be blamed for the entire episode since individuals – even persons as influential as Churchill and Fisher – are never free agents but work within the constraints of circumstances and as parts of a system. They are drawn together by force of events. The fundamental failure for adequate planning and co-ordination between the Army and Navy was the weakness of the Committee of Imperial Defence. To this was added at the supreme moment the War Council, whose constitution, functions, and methods of transacting business seem ramshackle. Failures in the conduct of supreme war direction directly impacted the development of the Dardanelles operation. In the event, Fisher found himself increasingly in a hopeless condition.

Warnings from history had been made: politics always tended to deflect strategy. Past advice was set aside. In 1906 the British General Staff concluded that unless a surprise could be effected, any attempt to disembark an army on the Gallipoli peninsula would be too hazardous to be recommended.

The tempting matter was examined again in 1911, and once more in September 1914: a possible Dardanelles adventure had allure and would not go away. At that time, Callwell, then Director of Military Operations and Intelligence (and future author of the contest for the control of the Dardanelles), categorically laid down in a memorandum: 'It ought to be clearly understood that an attack upon the Gallipoli Peninsula from the sea side (outside the Straits) is likely to prove an extremely difficult operation of war.'[7] That same month Admiralty and War Office staff officers met and discussed the possibility of seizing the straits using a Greek expeditionary force. They decided that it was not a feasible military operation. However, a few days later, with the forceful and imaginative Churchill crucially present, it was stated that, though such a military operation would be extremely difficult, it would be possible and justifiable.[8] Admiral Sir Charles Ottley emerged as the proponent of amphibious operations.

Fisher was the stumbling block from the outset. Despite all his pronouncements on how a successful Baltic project might eventuate, he had no capacity for lateral thinking such as might be applicable to the Dardanelles. He was a prisoner of the past. He had been opposed to working closely with the War Office, which he did not respect and disliked intensely. Historian Trumbull Higgins puts it this way: 'Fisher soon made it clear he would have nothing to do with the heresy of joint inter-service planning. He boycotted and thereby aborted Ottley's promising start toward the organisation of effective amphibious warfare.'[9] It was Fisher's disposition to blame others for his failures.

From the outset, he opposed the Dardanelles adventure, but his relations with Churchill on this were hardly consistent. His level of support fluctuated. Christopher Bell writes that 'as First Sea Lord in 1915 his bold words often belied a timid and hesitating disposition.' He shrank from direct confrontation with Churchill, says the same authority.[10] Fisher's correspondence does not disclose these withdrawing or avoiding tactics; rather the reverse. Fisher, as we will see, rose to the challenge presented by Churchill.

In later years, Fisher came to his own curious explanation of how the whole scheme developed. He was cagey and elusive even in his explanation. The Dardanelles came upon the British high command, statesmen, and senior military and naval authorities like a miasma, he wrote in his memoirs. 'Now if anyone thinks that in this chapter [on the Dardanelles] they are going to see Sport and that I am going to trounce Mr. Winston Churchill and abuse Mr. Asquith and put it all upon poor Kitchener they are woefully mistaken. It was a Miasma that brought about the Dardanelles Adventure.' This was indeed that curious miasma 'that, imperceptibly to each of them in the War Council, floated down on them with rare subtle dialectical skill, and proved so incontestably to them that cutting off the enemy's big toe in the East was better than stabbing him to the heart in the West; and that the Dardanelles was better than the Baltic, and that Gallipoli knocked spots off the Kiel Canal, or a Russian Army landed by the British Fleet on the Baltic shore of Schleswig-Holstein.'[11] Churchill had his own explanation for the sordid developments that were to ensue: once the British government decided to concede to Russia the long-cherished and great prize of Constantinople, interest was lost in the enterprise. With one sentence Churchill says all: 'Her infirm action and divided counsels arose from secret motives hidden in the bosom of the State.'[12]

On the morning of 29 October 1914 those troublesome cruisers *Goeben* and *Breslau*, commanded by Admiral Souchon and flying the Ottoman flag, steamed through the Black Sea and without warning shelled the Russian ports of Odessa, Nikolayev, and Sevastopol. This action had been ordered by Enver Pasha in compliance with a German request, and was done without consulting his political colleagues. The Young Turks were in disarray. For Britain, the bombardment offered a clear warning. A week earlier, intelligence had been received that the Ottoman high command was planning an invasion of Egypt. This, coupled with the naval attack on Russian ports, cast the die in favour of war with the Ottoman Empire, and Russia, France, and Britain declared war on 1 November. Immediately thereafter, Churchill expressed interest in an Anglo-Greek assault on the straits. At this time, Churchill also advocated that the best defence for Egypt was an offensive against the Dardanelles. He contended – and this is the critical point – that such an operation would require a large force of soldiers, and that transports ought to be immediately collected in Egypt.[13] For the moment, however, British and French warships took up station in the Aegean in hopes that *Goeben* would emerge. They waited in vain.

On 3 November the battlecruisers *Indefatigable*, flagship of Vice-Admiral Sir Sackville Carden, and *Indomitable* commenced bombarding the forts guarding the entrance to the Dardanelles. While these vessels were shelling the enemy on the Gallipoli side, the French battleships *Suffren* and *Verité* threw shells at forts on the Asiatic shore. Little if any damage was done to the Ottoman defences, and the warships that had opened fire at 13,000yds passed by unscathed. Ottoman fire was wild and undisciplined (not to be repeated three and a half months later, on 19 February 1915, when Carden returned with an enlarged fleet and more serious intent). The events of 3 November brought the Allies no benefit. These preliminary moves to probe Ottoman defences proved pointless and only served as advance warning to the Ottoman high command.

The German high command was similarly undecided what moves to make next. Their blunt appreciation of the failure of the Schlieffen Plan recognised that a quick victory had been denied them in France and Flanders. At headquarters in Berlin, possible future priorities ranged between 'Westerners', who believed the war could be won or lost in France, and 'Easterners', who pressed for a conquest of Russia as a preliminary to a victory over France. The Ottoman entry into the war made the Easterners' plan that much more attractive. Support for the Ottoman army, some argued, would aid Austria–Hungary's stalled campaign against Serbia. Further, it would enable the Ottoman army, estimated at 700,000 strong, to come to grips with the Russian army and even to put pressure on Britain, then so prominent in Mesopotamia, Persia, and India. In Berlin, too, reconsiderations were the order of the day. German planners imagined that Bulgaria would join the Central Powers against Russia, and that Romania would do the same. Thus did the defeat of Russia become a German priority, and support for the Ottoman Empire became a strategic necessity.[14] German High Command and political leadership never resolved the difference between the 'Westerners' and the 'Easterners', but sufficient commitment was given to supporting the Ottoman cause in a timely fashion. The Germans were undertaking their initiative, one designed not just to stop the Anglo-French effort to control the Straits and Constantinople, but also to topple the British Empire in the Middle East and India. At the risk of pre-empting our narrative, it is noteworthy that in the end it was the Russian Empire that fell: thus, had the British and French more urgently prosecuted the forcing of the Dardanelles, a reversal of fortune might possibly have occurred.

Churchill, unhappy with the Navy's apparently defensive posture after shutting down German commerce and instituting a wearying blockade, and mindful that the British Expeditionary Force was confronting siege warfare at such terrible cost in Flanders, turned attention to striking blows elsewhere. In the circumstances, he favoured ex-centric operations, war on the margins. He had at his command the greatest military instrument ever assembled: the Royal Navy. Churchill desired a way of using the superiority of the Navy to support military operations, or, if necessary, to undertake actions 'by ships alone'. The Dardanelles offered a tempting opportunity to use the superior strength of the Royal Navy, raise the profile of the Navy in the public's eye, and bolster Churchill's flagging political fortunes.

Fateful decision

In a critical memorandum of 28 December 1914 Lieutenant-Colonel Maurice Hankey, Secretary to the War Council, amplified and fleshed out the earlier proposals to force the Dardanelles:

> Has not the time come to show Germany and the world that any country that chooses a German alliance against the great sea power is doomed to disaster? Is it impossible now to weave a web round Turkey which will end her career as a European power?
>
> ... Left to themselves [the] Balkan States, all of whom [Greece, Romania, Bulgaria] stand to gain from the ejection of Turkey from Europe and from the dismemberment of Austria, will be unable to realise their overwhelming opportunity, so great is their mutual distrust.
>
> But supposing Great Britain, France, and Russia ... were themselves to participate actively in the campaign and to guarantee to each nation concerned that fair play should be rendered ... It is presumed that in a few months time we could, without endangering the position in France, devote three army corps, including one original first line army corps, to a campaign in Turkey, though sea transport might prove a difficulty. This force, in conjunction with Greece and Bulgaria, ought to be sufficient to capture Constantinople.
>
> If Russia, contenting herself with holding the German forces on an entrenched line, could simultaneously combine with Serbia and Romania in an advance into Hungary, the complete downfall of Austria–Hungary could simultaneously be secured.[15]

This memorandum had an important effect on the members of the War Council, beyond giving evidence of Hankey's increased abilities and importance. It opened up the possibility of great victories with little bloodshed and in a short period of time. Churchill had been anxiously awaiting this memorandum and gave it his support in a letter to Asquith on 31 December.[16]

In time Churchill was to be swept up in the alluring prospects of forcing the Dardanelles, but it must be remembered that at the year's end he was pressing upon Asquith his old favourite, a campaign to seize an island like Borkum, to invade Schleswig-Holstein, and to obtain naval command of the Baltic in order to land a Russian army within reach of Berlin. Here was a grand scenario, in general conformity with Fisher's. Though the prime minister expressed no preference, he was greatly dissatisfied with the stalemate on the Western Front and believed that planning needed to begin immediately on some sort of diversion.[17] Lloyd George also now looked for a way around the stalemate of the Western Front. He cast his eyes eastwards, and focused on operations in support of Serbia against Austria, and on a landing in Syria against the

Ottoman Empire.[18] For the moment Fisher was not embroiled in any alternate schemes beyond his Baltic project. He was overcome by the events of the New Year. Power was slipping from his grasp.

On New Year's Day 1915 news arrived through diplomatic channels of a great change on the Eastern Front. It now appeared, through exaggerated reports, that Russia faced severe difficulties after the crushing defeat of its armies at Tannenberg. On 2 January the Russian Crown Prince requested help for his hard-pressed forces in the Caucasus region. The British ambassador in St Petersburg signified to the Foreign Office the urgency, and when the Foreign Office passed the message to the Secretary of State for War, Kitchener immediately read it and then crossed to the Admiralty to consult with Churchill. The appeal from an ally could not be ignored.

Kitchener could not know the Russian request did not reflect the military need in the field. At that precise moment, Ottoman forces, widely scattered, were being dealt with in the snowy mountains at Sari Kamish. 'Yet out of this grain of mustard seed,' wrote one military historian, 'developed a tall tree. As the British Ministers could not make up their minds whether they would or would not have troops available, it was decided to try what could be effected by naval action alone.'[19] No one knows who coined the term, but Kitchener suggested some sort of 'demonstration' to prevent the Ottomans from sending more troops to the Balkans or the Caucasus. His use of this term signifies the greatest under-appreciation of military requirements ever vouchsafed in the history of modern warfare. What was he thinking? Was this to be another of the small wars of Empire? Was showing the flag enough, or sending a field army to secure some distant outpost?

In fact, although offering not one single soldier, Kitchener suggested to Churchill a naval bombardment of the Dardanelles. The ultimate object, from which all sorts of imagined military benefits would accrue, was to force the Dardanelles and 'ultimately to ... overawe Constantinople.'[20] At first Churchill was dubious that a purely naval assault could bring the desired results of this 'demonstration'. He thus asked Kitchener for troops to make it effective. Kitchener, after consultation at the War Office, found this impossible: 'I do not see that we can do anything that will very seriously help the Russians in the Caucasus ... We have no troops to land anywhere ... The only place that a demonstration might have some effect in stopping reinforcements going East would be the Dardanelles ... We shall not be ready for anything big for some months.'[21]

The project quickly grew in its dimensions, taking on a life of its own. Glittering visions presented themselves. Could the means be found to make the ends possible? Churchill could not back down from this challenge; it was not in his nature. It was in this sunny disposition of strategic consideration that

Churchill summoned his Admiralty war group to look into the feasibility. He then sent a telegram to Vice-Admiral Carden, commander of the Blockading Squadron at the Dardanelles:

> Do you consider the forcing of the Dardanelles by ships alone a practicable operation?
>
> It is assumed older battleships fitted with minebumpers would be used preceded by colliers or other merchant craft as bumpers and sweepers.
>
> Importance of results would justify severe loss.
>
> Let me know your views.[22]

Fisher and Jackson saw this telegram before it was sent. Churchill had framed it in order to elicit a positive response. Carden's reply was keenly awaited.

Vice-Admiral Sir Sackville H Carden, aged fifty-seven, still haunts the margins of British naval history, and much of the slowness of the naval campaign as it developed after being approved can be attributed to him. The admiral superintending Malta Dockyard at the outbreak of war, Carden had been vaulted to command the Mediterranean Fleet. Whether his poor performance can be attributed to inexperience is questionable, for what naval officer afloat had more experience in 'ships versus forts' than Carden? Health was a factor, for psychologically as well as physically he was not the best to hold such a demanding post at the critical hour.[23] For some time he had to contend with an ulcer, and there are rumours of acute mental anxiety at the moment of crisis. He knew that November's action had only given the Ottomans an indication of what might transpire in the future. The strain of command weighed heavily on him.

While a reply from Carden was awaited, Fisher jumped in on 3 January.

> Dear Winston:
>
> I've been informed by Hankey that the War Council assembles next Thursday, and I suppose it will be like a game of ninepins! Everyone will have a plan and one ninepin in falling will knock over its neighbours!
>
> I consider THE ATTACK ON TURKEY HOLDS THE FIELD! But ONLY if it's IMMEDIATE! However, it won't be! Our Aulic Council will adjourn till the following Thursday fortnight
>
> ... We shall decide on a futile bombardment of the Dardanelles ... What good resulted from the last bombardment? Did it move a single Turk from the Caucasus?
>
> ... In the history of the world – a Junta has never won! You want *one* man![24]

Fisher knew that one of the essentials of such an attack was surprise, but had he, too, lost sense of reality? Did he really believe that the Ottomans were not prepared for such an attack? And who was he referring to when he said, 'You want *one* man'?

Fisher cast about for allies. Next day, 4 January, he urged upon Balfour, a member of the War Council, 'the peculiar merit of Hankey's Turkey Plan [of 28 December 1914]. *I do hope you will give it all your support.*'[25] Balfour backed the project. It may be observed that Fisher was leaving the door open for a purely naval attack on the Straits. As Churchill wrote a little disingenuously in *The World Crisis*, this was the first hint that a naval attack on the Straits might be feasible.

Truth to tell, Fisher's plans shifted with the days, and there was no steady thinking in strategic terms about the campaign at this particular stage. He proposed an eastern Mediterranean campaign that would include a joint military and naval assault on the Dardanelles. He argued for taking the British Expeditionary Force out of the line, substituting Territorials, and shipping an expedition out of Marseilles under the command of General Sir William Robertson, then land the troops against Haifa and Alexandretta (his favourite target in these seas), thereby securing a foothold for guarding vital oil supplies. Subsequently, according to Fisher's way of thinking, the Greeks would move on Gallipoli, the Bulgarians advance on Constantinople, and the Russians concentrate on Austria. A British military force would land at Besike Bay on the Asiatic shore, well outside the entrance to the Dardanelles. At the same time, a naval force under Admiral Sturdee (apparently now in Fisher's favour) would force the Dardanelles with ships of the *Majestic* and *Canopus* class (ancient by the standards of 1915 but with good armour, propulsion, and firepower). Visions of success flashed brightly, but Fisher also brought a hard-headed realism to the military planning: such an attack would be feasible only if it was immediate. And Fisher strongly objected to a purely naval attack since it would wear out *Inflexible*'s guns without effecting any changes in the situation. He was mindful of the November attack on the Ottoman forts – 'Did it move a single Turk from the Caucasus? And so the war goes on!'[26] Taken altogether, this multi-headed operation seems preposterous. No such project could be undertaken overnight.

Behind these schemes lay a growing imperial vision of British Empire in the Near East, with Egypt as its bulwark, the Suez Canal as an enhanced passage of trade and therefore power, and India as the continuing Jewel in the Crown. Alexandretta held the key, said Fisher – and he was not alone. Oil had revived the British imperial impulse, and the war afforded opportunities not to be lost. Churchill was one of the architects of a British oil empire, and Fisher was at the heart of the Navy's adoption of oil-fired engines. Here was a natural combination. T E Lawrence, British army agent and imperialist, argued for action. 'Can you get someone to suggest to Winston that there is an oil spring on the beach ... and that it [Alexandretta] is a splendid natural naval base (which *we* don't but which no one else can have without detriment to us). If Winston settles on a thing he gets it, I fancy: especially with K[itchener]'s help.'[27] Lawrence realised the advantages and necessity of seizing Alexandretta so as to keep France out of it in the future and even to discourage Russian intentions in that area. He was advancing a classic rationale for empire, and he seems to have understood it better than most. Fisher shared the vision, but in the end, Fisher's scheme could not be advanced. He could not back a 'by ships alone' scenario. He wanted a joint operation against the Dardanelles.

Now it was Churchill's turn to prevaricate. He attempted to pour cold water on Fisher's enthusiasm: 'I think we had better hear what others have to say about the Turkish places before taking a decided line. I would not grudge 100,000 men, because of the great political effects in the Balkan Peninsula: but Germany is the foe, and it is bad war to seek cheaper victories and easier antagonists. This is, however, a very general question.' Churchill also spoke in favour of a landing against Borkum, an operation close to Fisher's heart, as it would open the avenue to his Baltic project.[28] Churchill wrote similarly to Jellicoe, emphasising the importance of seizing Borkum.[29] On the same day, Fisher wrote to Churchill: 'The naval advantages of the possession of Constantinople and the getting of wheat from the Black Sea are so overwhelming that I consider Colonel Hankey's plan for Turkish operations vital and imperative and very pressing.'[30] But all seemed at sixes and sevens in the Admiralty.

Fisher, caught by new visions of success, was shifting between the northern seas and the eastern Mediterranean. He was casting about, rather uncertain of the two objectives that he came increasingly to see as conflicting. Neither the Admiralty nor the War Office had reached a definite conclusion as to future action at the Dardanelles. Fisher, increasingly anxious, even erratic, offered his resignation on 4 January over a completely unrelated matter. He expressed anxiety over the possibility of Zeppelin raids on London, which it was imagined could cause considerable damage, and offered the suggestion of shooting German prisoners of war as a reprisal for civilian casualties. Nothing had been done with his suggestion, and Fisher was thoroughly put out: 'As this step has not been taken, I must with great reluctance ask to be relieved in my present official position as First Sea Lord.'[31] Churchill was 'offended' by the suggestion of shooting or threatening to shoot German prisoners,[32] but he managed to restrain Fisher; the First Sea Lord elected to stay on. We know that Fisher, on seeing Churchill several days later, did not bring up the matter but continued to work the backrooms and to express his growing dissatisfaction with Churchill. Meanwhile, Churchill still contended that a combined military and naval attack on Borkum was the better plan, and all other considerations were set aside.

Admiral Carden's electrifying response on the morning of 5 January to Churchill's telegram on the question of forcing the Dardanelles was the deciding and compelling factor: 'With reference to your telegram of 3rd instant, I do not consider Dardanelles can be rushed. They might be forced by extended operations with large number of ships.' The admiral stated that he could force the straits by a protracted and systematic assault by ships alone. He detailed four necessary phases: levelling defences at the entrance, clearing the Narrows and providing a safe channel, reducing the Narrows forts, and making the final advance to the Sea of Marmara. This was the first positive expression of success. Upon what basis Carden came to make his recommendation no evidence survives. Did ambition or duty lie beneath it? Did illness weaken his judgement as well as his body? He saw the operation in purely operational terms, and while admitting the object could not be met in a day, did not consider it impossible or overly expensive. It was a vital telegram, as Churchill later testified: 'Here was the Admiral, who had been for weeks sitting off the Dardanelles, who presumably had been turning this thing over in his mind again and again, wondering on the possibilities of action there, who produced a plan, and a detailed plan and a novel plan.'

On receipt of the Admiral's reply, Churchill telegraphed: 'High Authorities here concur in your opinion. Forward particulars showing what force would be required for extended operations, how you think it could be employed, and what results could be obtained.'[33]

Churchill read out Carden's letter to the War Council that same day, 5 January. It was not yet adopted as policy, but Carden's letter and Churchill's action lent support to the Dardanelles option, which was particularly favoured by Kitchener.[34] On 7 January the War Council met again. Churchill again pressed his fancied Borkum plan. He also argued in favour of using the British Expeditionary Force to advance along the Belgian coast and seize Zeebrugge, a sally port on the North Sea used by U-boats and coastal craft based on Bruges. The War Council approved in principle the Borkum attack, and even went so far as to authorise Churchill to begin detailed planning for such an operation. Lloyd George, unsure of that scheme, argued for using troops in some alternate theatre, an argument he raised again at the following day's War Council meeting. Kitchener then declared that the only viable alternative strategy would be an attempt on the Dardanelles, a position vocally supported by Hankey. Discussion still centred on options on the North Sea, including Borkum, Zeebrugge, and Holland.[35]

Nothing was or could be settled. No homogeneity of action existed between the departments of State, particularly the War Office and the Admiralty. There was no supreme command, no way of conducting business systematically. Sir George Riddell, proprietor of the *News of the World* and other papers, followed these affairs closely: 'The P.M. is unrivalled in giving speedy and accurate decisions on matters submitted to him, but he has not got the art of probing into things for himself and cleansing and restoring weak places.'[36] This is fair comment, and for the present the creaking naval and military organisations continued on separate paths. It was in these circumstances that the Admiralty assumed the initiative for the Dardanelles operation.

Admiral Bacon, Fisher's biographer, makes these damning assessments of Churchill's overbearing and forceful measures, and particularly how he had established a system to bypass the First Sea Lord on operational matters:

Now, this telegram [Churchill's reply to Carden] adumbrates acceptance of extended operations. It is reasonable to expect that it would have been sent to Lord Fisher as First Sea Lord, but it was not. Moreover, so far from being sent by Lord Fisher, he did not even see it before it was sent! When this subject was inquired into by the Dardanelles Commission, Lord Fisher told them that, had he seen the telegram, he would have most certainly have asked for it to be altered, as he did not agree with it. Who, then, were the High Authorities? Mr. Churchill explained to the Commission that they were himself, Admiral Oliver, the Chief of Staff, and Admiral Jackson; the latter two having expressed their opinion verbally to him. In so important a matter the opinion of all concerned should have been recorded in writing. Admiral Carden, in the Mediterranean, however, assumed that Lord Fisher had blessed the scheme; for, as he remarked, Lord Fisher was at the Admiralty and, therefore, naturally he assumed that he was one of the High Authorities. This is a good example of the misunderstandings and confusion that resulted from the vicious practice introduced by Mr. Churchill into Admiralty procedure in 1912 of having a Chief of Staff who was not First Sea Lord. The result was that 'Operation' telegrams and orders were at times sent out by him without even the knowledge of the First Sea Lord.[37]

In any event, on 12 January Carden's urgently awaited reply (dated 11 January) arrived at the Admiralty and contained a detailed plan for forcing the Dardanelles. The C-in-C concluded that it was an operation the Navy could execute on its own, without army landings. Here was the first fatal error, followed by a second. Carden stated that such an operation could be commenced within a month. By this time, Admiral Sir Henry Jackson and others at the Admiralty had expressed reservations: Army units would be needed to occupy Constantinople; and if the Ottomans did not cave in, British warships would face the hazards of withdrawal. These were set aside. Carden estimated that twelve battleships, three battlecruisers, and several smaller warships would suffice for the immediate task, though in the course of a month losses would be sustained. Churchill brought the telegram before the Admiralty war group, which included Fisher, and together they drafted a minute on plans for forcing the Dardanelles. According to Churchill in his narrative of events, Fisher approved it. Jackson concurred. The minute declared that the forcing of the Dardanelles 'would be a victory of first importance.' The attacking force, under the command of Vice-Admiral Carden, would consist of *Ocean*, *Swiftsure*, *Triumph*, *Vengeance*, *Canopus*, *Albion*, *Caesar*, *Prince George*, *Victorious*, *Mars*, *Magnificent*, *Hannibal*, *Queen Elizabeth*, *Inflexible*, and *Indefatigable* – fifteen capital ships – and that all of these ships were already on station in the Mediterranean, had already been ordered there for other purposes, or had been scheduled to be dismantled. Operations could begin on 1 February, via long-range fire from the 15in guns of the *Queen Elizabeth* on the forts at the entrance. Finally, Churchill stated that detailed plans would need to be worked out accordingly.[38]

The scheme was building within Churchill's mind, with support in the Admiralty in certain quarters. Could he seize the day? Could he bring the whole scheme into motion, backing Hankey's highly regarded proposal? Political will was still lacking for this project, but broader support was being garnered from outside the Admiralty. On 13 January, for instance, Esher lunched for the second straight day at the Admiralty with Fisher. Balfour joined them. As an expression of the complexities of policy formation at this time, we have the observation of Esher, in imitation of Fisher, that on the War Council every member has his own plan, and that 'it is like a game of ninepins; one plan is knocked over, and, in falling, knocks over the next one, and so on until the board is clear; the result is a total want of initiative of any kind.' He also wrote that the 'Turkish menace' was becoming greater, and that there was 'a strong body of opinion crystallising round the idea of taking the initiative at, perhaps, Gallipoli, instead of holding Egypt on the defensive.' Esher also commented that time was crucial, as the French spirit could waver.[39] Already the Allies were locked in mortal combat with the enemy on the Western Front, and every human and material force was needed for the war effort. What could possibly be deployed to a distant, new theatre in the eastern Mediterranean? And who would take responsibility for this adventure?

That same day, 13 January, the vital meeting of the War Council occurred. It sat to discuss the Dardanelles project. Churchill was powerful in committee and always well prepared. The Admiralty documents were spread before him, including Admiral Carden's most recent appreciation of requirements. If command and control started at the top, it seemed that Churchill was in abundant control. The outlook seemed promising. A glittering prize presented itself. Victory at the Dardanelles could confound the enemy and even knock Germany out of the war. This was the state of affairs in Whitehall.

Opinion coalesced around Churchill's scheme, for the First Lord was now its ardent champion. The resolution as eventually adopted was that the Navy should 'bombard and take the Gallipoli Peninsula, with Constantinople as its objective.' This badly worded resolution led to the gravest error of all, says Arthur Marder: the conception of a purely naval exercise. Many critics at the time and many historians since have held this view, and it need not be challenged here. As Marder notes, the Navy would have preferred to wait until troops were available and a combined assault could be mounted, and he quotes, most tellingly, Lieutenant-Colonel Hankey, in a letter to Balfour on 10 February: 'From Lord Fisher downward every naval officer in the Admiralty who is in on the secret believes that the Navy cannot take [ie pass?] the Dardanelles without troops. The First Lord still professes to believe that they can do it with ships, but I have warned the Prime Minister that we cannot trust this.' Marder's analysis shows that the Navy might well have succeeded by itself in forcing the Straits and knocking the Ottoman Empire out of the war, but goes on to explain the half-hearted nature of the enterprise as directed by naval staff and naval commanders.[40] According to Hankey's memoirs, the idea of the Dardanelles operation was well received: 'The idea caught on at once ... The War Council turned eagerly from the dreary vista of a "slogging match" on the Western Front to brighter prospects, as they seemed, in the Mediterranean ... Even French ... caught something of the tremendous enthusiasm.' Also according to Hankey, both Lloyd George and Kitchener expressed their approval for the plan.[41]

After the War Council meeting, Churchill drew up a minute that, according to him, had the concurrence of Fisher and the Chief of the Naval Staff. He argued that no effective action could be taken in the Adriatic, which had been suggested at the meeting, and any action would certainly incur ship losses. Besides, the French had a large naval force in the area and were in accord with British plans. On the other hand, an attack at the Dardanelles could bring about decisive strategic results in the Mediterranean, and therefore they should focus on 'the methodological forcing of the Dardanelles'.[42] This means that Carden's plan for the bombardment of the Dardanelles forts had been approved. Carden was also promised the resources he requested, including *Queen Elizabeth*, which had just been completed. 'We entirely agree with your plan of methodical piecemeal reduction of forts,' Churchill wrote to Carden on 15 January.[43]

Observers had been watching the growing tension between Churchill and Fisher, sparked by Fisher's resistance and diminishing influence in naval affairs. McKenna, who had become sarcastic about the Navy, told newspaperman Riddell that he could not now understand Fisher: it seemed to him, as he told Riddell, that Jacky and Winston were 'manoeuvring for a spectacular battle on the old-fashioned lines' – in other words, a battle royal about constituted powers and who was in charge.⁴⁴ At this point, Churchill claims, Fisher's opposition came to the fore, and grew when Jellicoe complained about the strength of the Grand Fleet, especially since he was not to have the powerful *Queen Elizabeth*. Jellicoe also bemoaned the decision to send *Inflexible* to relieve *Indefatigable* in the Mediterranean, as, according to him, the French fleet should have been capable of handling the now-damaged *Goeben*, and the two battlecruisers were needed by the Grand Fleet to guarantee a margin of strength over the High Seas Fleet.⁴⁵

Other matters were causing Fisher discomfort and worry. His fertile mind kept generating new projects or reviving old ones. For instance, he held out the possibility of flanking and blockading operations in Holland as meriting attention. In a letter of 18 January to Churchill, in which he stated that he had 'no wish whatever to cold-douche any projects for our being troublesome to the enemy,' he wrote:

> I am not minimizing the coming Dardanelles operation, but I wish to aggrandize the great big fact that 750,000 men landed in Holland, combined with intense activity of the British Fleet against, say, Cuxhaven, would finish the War by forcing out the German High Seas Fleet and getting in rear of the German Armies! The First Lord has twice put before the War Council the Dutch Project and no one 'gainsaid' it! Is it going to be done? Great preparations are involved. The frost so deadly to Holland is over in May. Cannot a definite decision be reached?⁴⁶

Fisher's project had no future.

Churchill ranged far in advance of political and, certainly, Service support, but was in apparent conjunction with Asquith when, on 19 January he sent Grand Duke Nicholas a solemn pledge of support: 'It is our intent to press the matter to a conclusion.'⁴⁷ The effect of a defeat would be serious; Kitchener's view was that there could be no going back. Thus, even in advance of the celebrated War Cabinet meetings (numbers 9 and 10) of 28 January, the matter had been settled. By Churchill's action, the Cabinet was heavily committed.

Despite his apparent support of the Dardanelles project, Fisher made an about-face at precisely this time. On 19 January he wrote to Jellicoe expressing his discontent with Churchill and the proposed Dardanelles operation: 'And now the Cabinet have decided on taking the Dardanelles solely with the Navy, using 15 battleships and 32 other vessels, and keeping out there three battlecruisers and a flotilla of destroyers – *all urgently required at the decisive theatre at home!* There is only one way out, and that is to resign! But you say "*no*", which simply means I am a consenting party to what I absolutely disapprove. *I don't agree with one single step taken.*'⁴⁸ The decisive factor here was the deployment of warships to the eastern Mediterranean in considerable force. Fisher's undeniable preoccupation was backing Jellicoe in his demands to keep the Grand Fleet at optimum strength to deal with its German opposite. Churchill thought Jellicoe's requirements overly exaggerated and believed he had more than sufficient instruments of sea power to deal with the enemy should it venture from its lair.

On 20 January Churchill issued a minute, with Fisher's agreement, that the attack on the Dardanelles should begin as soon as *Queen Elizabeth* was ready. As soon as the attack had begun, Alexandretta should be seized. 'Thus if we cannot make headway in the Dardanelles, we can pretend that it is only a demonstration, the object of which was to cover the seizure of Alexandretta. This aspect is important from an Oriental point of view.'[49] Most likely this was offered as a sop to Fisher who desired assurances that the attack could be withdrawn at any time.

All this time, Fisher regularly poured out his grievances to Hankey, who urged Fisher to make his objections known and also passed this information to the prime minister. Asquith recorded:

> Hankey came to see me to-day to say that Fisher, who is an old friend of his, had come to him in a very unhappy frame of mind. He likes Winston personally, but complains that on purely technical naval matters he is frequently overruled ('he out-argues me'), and he is not by any means at ease about either the present disposition of the fleets or their future movements. Though I think the old man is rather difficult, I fear there is some truth in what he says.[50]

Asquith had, therefore, warning signs of what might happen. Fisher wrote in similar terms to Beatty at Rosyth: 'Diplomacy and the Cabinet have forced upon us the Dardanelles business so damnable in taking away *Queen Elizabeth*, *Indefatigable* and *Inflexible* and a whole lot of destroyers. However the Grand Duke Nicholas sent an ultimatum and we had to cave in. He is the autocrat of the war.'[51] Fisher also wrote to Churchill on the same day to press for the return of the destroyer depot ship *Blenheim* and its destroyer flotilla from the Dardanelles, replacing them with French destroyers.[52] Churchill wrote, 'I could not agree to this, as of course it would have paralysed the Dardanelles Fleet and destroyed the plans which the staff were maturing.'[53] The problems of command and control continued; unity of purpose was absent. Heavy clouds were gathering on the horizon.

Fisher's frustrations increased. He told Jellicoe that he believed the Dardanelles plan would interfere with the needs of the Grand Fleet, and that he had 'fought against it "tooth and nail".' However, the government had decided on the plan for diplomatic reasons, and Grand Duke Nicholas had demanded such a step be taken. He also wrote that he 'just abominate[d] the Dardanelles operation, unless a great change is made and it is settled to be made a military operation, with 200,000 men in conjunction with the Fleet. I believe that Kitchener is coming now to this sane view of the matter.'[54]

Churchill countered Fisher's every position. The First Lord held that from time to time, and since taking office, the First Sea Lord had changed his point of view. The result was a war of wills, and a day-to-day struggle. Fisher steamed on, doing battle with Churchill, writing to friends near and far, courting opposition to his political chief. On 23 January, to Jellicoe, Fisher expressed his dismay that Asquith had asked Jellicoe to attend the next War Council meeting, taking him away at a critical time from his sea command. Fisher also complained that the planned Army attack, to be co-ordinated with the naval bombardment of Zeebrugge, had been precipitously cancelled.[55] Fisher's dire warning to Churchill – that unless the First Lord interfered less in the work of the Sea Lords, Fisher would leave office – first voiced in December, continued. They fell on deaf ears.

At this stage, the two seemed incapable of dealing with matters face to face; rather, they passed notes and memoranda back and forth. The conduct of naval affairs at the highest level was conducted through 'in' and 'out' trays of office mail. With Fisher working early mornings and Churchill late afternoons and evenings, even patterns of work were unusual and unlikely to produce co-operation. The usual meetings of the Board of Admiralty, with resolutions discussed and decided upon, seem not to have happened during January, or if they were held, only occasionally. Churchill took the initiative. The old admiral withdrew from the withering fray. The press followed his doings. When he did not show up at the office, they took note. Fisher's unhappiness with Churchill and the direction of planning was likely a contributing factor to his 'cold' and absence on 23 January. Three days later *The Times* reported that Fisher was in perfect health.[56]

Churchill and Fisher were awakened from their distant and independent positions on the Dardanelles by the stirring events of 24 January, the Dogger Bank action, recounted in Chapter 8. The significance of this event to the larger saga of the Straits leading to Constantinople did nothing to lessen the struggle at the Admiralty. It did nothing to soothe the growing conflict between the titans. That the opportunity offered to Vice-Admiral Sir David Beatty's battlecruiser squadron had been squandered further unsettled Fisher, made him more nervous and agitated, and certainly a less competent chief professional head of the Navy at a critical hour.

Fisher attempted to refocus Churchill's attention on the Baltic. He argued that battlecruisers were the key, as they could go through 'the international highway of the Sound' and defeat all German light cruisers, just as *Invincible* 'knocked out the *Scharnhorst*' in the Falklands battle.[57] On 26

January Fisher supplied a memorandum to Churchill on the fleet distribution. In it, he made clear that the fundamental responsibility of the Navy was to possess the maximum strength in the decisive theatre of operations. Apparently this memorandum was not distributed to the War Council, which disappointed Fisher. He explained in a marginal note that it had been compiled 'in view of my acrimonious attitude against the Dardanelles Operation then being incepted.'[58] Churchill responded to this memo by confirming security in the North Sea was key but that the Navy must also secure trade routes and be available for special services like the Dardanelles.[59] Churchill did submit the memorandum to Asquith, along with a covering paper that showed the secure margin of superiority in the North Sea.[60] He also sent a personal note to Fisher: 'There is no difference in principle between us. But when all your special claims are met, you must let the surplus be used for the general cause.'[61]

Events were now overtaking Fisher, and the initiative passed to bureaucratic action likely designed to solve the problems at the Admiralty. Hankey, the still-powerful Secretary of the CID, arranged a subcommittee on the Dardanelles and invited Lloyd George, Kitchener, Balfour, Churchill, and whoever Churchill wanted as advisers to meet on 26 January. Churchill asked Fisher to come but he did not attend.[62] Perhaps he was ill; perhaps he was walking away. The events of the next few days confirm the latter as a strong possibility.

The all-important ninth meeting of the War Council was scheduled for 28 January. The subject was the Dardanelles operations. Before the meeting, Fisher sent a note to the prime minister telling him he had no intention of attending the scheduled War Council: 'I am not in accord with the First Lord and do not think it would be seemly to say so before the Council ... I say that the Zeebrugge and Dardanelles bombardments can only be justified on naval grounds by military co-operation, which would compensate for the loss in ships and irreplaceable officers and men. As purely naval operations they are un-justifiable.' Fisher went on to explain the importance of the decisive theatre (which he contended was the North Sea and its annexe, the Baltic), and he hinted at resignation: 'I am very reluctant to leave the First Lord. I have a great personal affection and admiration for him, but I see no possibility of a union of ideas, and unity is essential ... The British Empire ceases if our Grand Fleet ceases. No risks can be taken.'[63]

What more did Asquith need to know about Fisher's intended action? But still the prime minister took no action, brushed it aside. Maybe he regarded the matter as purely an Admiralty affair. Perhaps he sensed that Fisher was only the Unionists' tool. After all, Asquith was determined to keep his Cabinet and his government from floundering and being reorganised. Delay was to his benefit. Inaction favoured his position. But events were overtaking him, too.

And thus the matter settled on Churchill, to whom Fisher had fired off a letter of resignation:

I entreat you to believe that if as I think really desirable for a complete '*unity of purpose*' in the War that I should gracefully disappear and revert to roses at Richmond ... that there will not be in my heart the least lingering thoughts of anything but regard and affection and *indeed much admiration* towards yourself.

...

My position is quite clear: –

I make no objection to either Zeebrugge or Dardanelles if accompanied by military co-operation ... Simultaneous Military & Naval actions but no drain thereby on Grand Fleet Margin so therefore *no modern vessels at Dardanelles*.

I shall not as arranged with you attend the War Council and am going down to Richmond.[64]

Fisher was voting with his feet.

On receipt, Churchill sought to stop this breakaway action. He consulted with Asquith and arranged a meeting in advance of the War Council, and insisted that Fisher attend. 'You have assented to both the operations in question and so far as I am concerned there can be no withdrawal without good reason from measures which are necessary, and for which preparations are far advanced. I would infinitely sooner work with you than with Sturdee who will undoubtedly be forced upon me in the eventuality of which you write so light-heartedly.'[65] (This certainly would have riled Fisher; he despised Sturdee, as shown by his attempt to leave Sturdee stranded in the South Atlantic with a lone cruiser in the aftermath of the Falklands battle.)

At 11.10am on 28 January Asquith brought Fisher and Churchill into his study for a chat in order to prevent the obvious and intended absence of the First Sea Lord at the War Council meeting. Asquith now displayed his concern about the schism between Fisher and Churchill. Fisher took the initiative. He argued forcibly against the Dardanelles and the Zeebrugge plan. Instead, he advocated a combined assault in the Baltic or in support of the armies in France. For his part, Churchill told Asquith that he favoured both Zeebrugge and Dardanelles but if he was faced with a choice of one or the other he preferred the Dardanelles.

Asquith, always a bit distant in relations with others, mulled over the difference. Then he proclaimed: 'I am the arbitrator. I have heard Mr. Winston Churchill, and I have heard you [Fisher] and now I am going to give my decision. Zeebrugge will not be done; the Dardanelles will go on.'[66] Asquith did not think Zeebrugge worth an argument, but he held that the Dardanelles scheme was important and ought to be undertaken. The die was cast – by Asquith a political and strategic decision of necessity out of an irresolvable difference of opinion between the political head and Service chief of the Navy. Perhaps Fisher expected that Churchill would honour the views of the professional Service head. He was in for a rude shock.

Asquith chaired that meeting as he did all War Councils. He assumed his decision in regards to the difference between Churchill and Fisher had been resolved. Somewhere down the table from him, Fisher sat in silence. Perhaps he was caught up in the maelstrom of events or still brooding over some point of difference raised at the pre-Council meeting. He was not expecting the Dardanelles matter to be brought up for discussion, so when Churchill did bring up the prospect, Fisher was taken totally aback. Churchill had forced the issue. And Asquith, who could not deny a fellow Cabinet member the right of speaking to the issue, insisted that the matter be dealt with that moment.[67]

Fisher had been forced into a corner. He rose from the table and made to leave the room (though some sources say he went to the window), chased by Kitchener who asked the First Sea Lord what he intended. Fisher confided that he had decided to resign; moreover, he had no intention of returning to the table. Kitchener sought to bring reason to this unwelcome course of events. He pointed out to Fisher that he was the sole person in opposition to the Dardanelles plan. All others favoured it, including himself, and since the Cabinet had taken the decision, it was Fisher's duty to remain at his post. Kitchener called for something of a higher responsibility. He managed to persuade Fisher to stay on.

Fisher's position on this, later explained to the Dardanelles Commission, that he was merely a technical adviser to the War Council, does not hold up since, as Jeffrey Wallin has argued, Fisher did not hesitate to make his objections known before. As well, the importance of his getting up and leaving seemed to indicate that Fisher was more than a mere adviser.[68] Even so, Asquith had failed to make clear to Fisher the certainty of his position as a member of the War Council. Had his opinion been asked – and here's the rub – he would have given a reply. Fisher clearly saw himself as a Service head giving advice and direction to the First Lord of the Admiralty. What Fisher did not want to do was embarrass Churchill. Nor did he want to show a lack of unity at the Admiralty. These are the reasons for his silence.

Among Fisher's papers there survives a strange newsprint item concerning this incident:

The dramatic scene which followed may one day furnish material for the greatest historical picture of the war. Lord Fisher sat and listened to the men who knew nothing about it and heard one after another pass opinion in favour of a venture to which he was opposed. He rose abruptly from the table and made as if to leave the room.

The tall figure of Lord Kitchener rose and followed him. The two stood by the window for some time in conversation and then both took their seats again. In Lord Fisher's own words: 'I reluctantly gave in to Lord Kitchener and resumed my seat.'

Mr. Asquith saw the drama enacted, and Mr. Asquith knew that it arose out of Lord Fisher's opposition to the scheme under discussion. But he allowed his colleagues on the Council to reach their conclusions without drawing from the expert his opinion for their guidance. The monstrous decision was therefore taken without it.

Written after this, in Fisher's hand: 'But they all knew it – such a scene could not occur without everyone knowing the cause.'[69]

Asquith confided to Venetia Stanley many particulars of the gathering storm at the Admiralty:

Another personal matter which rather worries me is the growing friction between Winston & Fisher ... I tried to compose their differences by a compromise, under which Winston was to give up for the present his bombardment of Zeebrugge, Fisher withdrawing his opposition to the operation against the Dardanelles. When at the Council we came to discuss the latter – wh. is warmly supported by Kitchener & Grey, & enthusiastically by A.J. B[alfour], old 'Jacky' maintained an obstinate and ominous silence. He is always threatening to resign & writes an almost daily letter to Winston, expressing his desire to return to the cultivation of his 'roses at Richmond'. K[itchener] has now taken up the role of conciliator – for wh. you might think that he was not naturally cut out![70]

Writing many years later about that desperate and confused day, Asquith concluded: 'I assert unhesitatingly that at this time the whole of our expert naval opinion was in favour of a naval operation. It is true that Lord Fisher disliked it. But his opinion, as he told me the same morning, was not based upon the technical or strategic merits of a Dardanelles operation, but upon the fact that he preferred another and totally different objective in the Baltic.'[71] Hankey held similar views: 'Fisher alone, whose silence had not meant consent as was generally assumed, was beginning to brood on the difficulties of his position which were eventually to lead to his resignation.'[72]

When the council resumed its business, Churchill announced that the Navy's ultimate object was to obtain access to the Baltic. This goal was to be achieved in three stages by clearing the outer sea, clearing the North Sea, and then entering the Baltic. This would expose Germany to attack on its northern flank.

Germany, he said, was and always had been, very nervous of an attack from the Baltic. Churchill also noted that Fisher had designed cruisers for just this purpose.[73] This may have been a concession to Fisher, pure and simple, an attempt to keep him on side. All the same, there is much evidence that Churchill favoured some sort of naval campaign in these waters.

After this agonising if dramatic meeting of the War Council, Churchill, in a long and intense conference with Fisher, convinced the latter to give him his support. Churchill was persuasive. After that, according to Fisher, 'I went the whole hog, *totus porcus*.'[74] A second War Council meeting, the tenth overall, was held later that same day. Churchill announced, with Fisher and Oliver at his side, that the Navy would force the Dardanelles. For Churchill, it was the decisive moment: 'After it, I never looked back.'[75] The last resistance that stood in the way of the action had been overcome. Or so he thought.

Even if Churchill had determined on the Dardanelles as the main event in the eastern theatre, discussion continued on other prospects. Churchill's colleagues did not share his belief that the decisive decision had been made. Discussion continued on various strategic alternatives, and Lloyd George continued to push his plan for a landing at Salonika. It was decided, though, to abandon the proposed assault on Zeebrugge,[76] so one of Churchill's intended adventures had come to a crashing end, giving relief to the First Sea Lord. Oddly, however, the Zeebrugge operation might have been more achievable than the Dardanelles.

Fisher now bit his lip. He began to make what plans he personally could, or was able to do, to advance the Dardanelles scheme. Others at the Admiralty, heeding Churchill's requirements, were also hurrying their preparations. Fisher confided in Lloyd George, who wrote to Fisher that the 'by ships alone' strategy for the Dardanelles was disquieting. He wished he could disagree but did not know enough to do so. 'These views ought to be brought to the War Council. We poor ignorant civilians must necessarily defer in these matters on the guidance of experts like yourself.'[77]

Fisher was in agony, distraught beyond belief. The fruits of independence had escaped him. He was now unable to shape the course of the naval war, but was at the beck and call of Churchill, the War Council, and, by implication, the War Office. On 29 January Fisher talked with his friend and confidant Lord Esher. He sought consolation and advice. The latter recorded in his diary that Fisher 'was in low spirits, and said that for the first time in his life he was a pessimist. At the bottom of this depression lies uncertainty on very material points affecting the functions of the navy. He finds Winston very brilliant, but too changeable; he has a different scheme every day.' With respect to the previous day's War Council meeting, Esher wrote that it 'sat till eight o'clock; Fisher got so irritated that he rose and walked to the window. Lord K[itchener] got up and asked him what was wrong, and he said that he would have to resign. Later on, the Prime Minister had an interview with Fisher and Winston, and acted as arbitrator upon their differences, which are occasioned by the proposed operations at Gallipoli.'⁷⁸

After the 28 January meeting, things seemed back on an even keel at the Admiralty, at least on the surface. As Asquith wrote: 'Winston and Fisher have, for the time at any rate, patched up their differences, though Fisher is still a little uneasy about the Dardanelles.'⁷⁹ As well, after the meeting, Fisher wrote to Jellicoe: 'I had fierce rows with Winston and the Prime Minister, and it was a near thing! I was six hours yesterday with them and [the] War Council and sat till 8 p.m.! They are a *"flabby"* lot! However, a calm has resulted and I go on pegging away.'⁸⁰

As to Churchill and Fisher, the former continued his energetic and often interfering ways, the latter to brood and plot. And in that month of January time passed without action. Opportunities were missed, calculations not made, decisions were deferred. Here the behind-the-scenes observations of Captain Herbert Richmond, then doing operation planning at the Admiralty, provide stark judgements, oft-times verging on hyperbole. He wrote acidly in his diary entry for 16 January:

The reports seem to shew that the Turks have begun their advance against Egypt. If we had done as I proposed and had an expedition ready to drop upon the coast and capture Haifa and otherwise disturb their communications, we should now be in a most favourable position. But our preparations have not been made. Sir Henry Jackson sits & looks at the map of Syria – so I found him this morning – but no one takes the business up seriously as a joint naval and military operation. It is now two months since I recommended sending the Portsmouth horse-boats out to Malta so that they might be ready, and proposed a small force [3000 men] for harrying the Syrian coast to keep their coast garrisons employed. When the time comes for slow-thinking people to realise what there is that can be done, the opportunity will, I fear, be past. I spoke again to General Callwell about it at lunch to-day. He said Kitchener couldn't, or wouldn't, make up his mind. The French Naval Attaché is very keen to do something there – preferably to force the Dardanelles. This Oliver has proposed, and Sir. H. Jackson has, I believe, prepared the outline of a plan. So have I, which I have given Oliver, & he is now busy drafting some remarks upon it. With our modern long range heavy guns we can outrange the Turkish forts, & a useful bombardment can be carried out. If we can force the passage, we have Constantinople open, & the result will I hope be a revolution in Turkey. The two things should come together – an attack on the

Dardanelles & a landing in Syria. The joint effect would be fatal to Enver Pasha & his German advisors.

Meantime, Winston is busy thinking out pinpricks in the shape of air raids, which he seems to think will produce wonderful results, & fails to appreciate that their proper value is reconnaissances & no more. He also has still his silly Borkum scheme in mind & wants [it] worked out. I have made some remarks upon it which I hope may go some way towards damning it.[81]

And on 9 February:

The campaign goes slowly and the Board of Admiralty do little to hustle things. Oliver [in charge of Plans] told me a few days ago that Fisher does nothing, Winston proposes mad things & hangs grimly on to his silly Naval Division, whom he will not allow to be used anywhere, [Sir Arthur] Wilson opposes all suggestions made by anybody except himself & cannot get it out of his head that anyone younger than himself can possibly know anything. He proposes archaic plans of bombardments, which would lead to nothing, but opposes combined operations, which would lead to something. Winston, very, very ignorant, believes he can capture the Dardanelles without troops & that Borkum can be destroyed by bombardment. Strange fallacies! In discussing plans for Dardanelles, I told Oliver I thought the C.-in-C. ought to have 4000 marines for operations of landing & destroying forts which have been knocked out by ships, torpedo stations, mine directors & cables, searchlights & so on. Winston refused to send more than 2000. Oliver [the Chief of Staff] suggested that it was 'about time the Naval Division earned its keep' & should go out *en masse* for the business. They are pretty rotten, but ought to be good enough for the inferior Turkish troops now in the Gallipoli peninsula, & a bit of work would finish off their training properly & make them fit for service on the Continent later. But no, not one of them will the 1st Lord allow to go. It is hopeless trying to make war with men like these.[82]

Richmond chomped at the bit, ever anxious to maintain the strength of the Grand Fleet. He shared Fisher's concept of a strong concentration of force to check the High Seas Fleet but was equally supportive of an urgent expedition to Constantinople, one that would topple the Ottoman government and help end the war. He was most critical of Fisher: 'In reality he does nothing. He goes home and sleeps in the afternoon. He is old and worn-out and nervous. It is ill to have the destinies of an empire in the hands of a failing old man, anxious for popularity, afraid of any local mishap which may be put down to his dispositions.'[83]

Churchill, underestimating the First Sea Lord, also took the view that Fisher was in a less than healthy state to do the demanding work at the

Admiralty. Easy it was for Churchill to write these words in retrospect, years after the events:

> Lord Fisher's age and the great strain to which he was now to be subjected made it necessary for him to lead a very careful life. He usually retired to rest shortly after 8 o'clock, awaking refreshed between four and five, or even earlier. In these morning hours he gave his greatest effort, transacting an immense quantity of business, writing innumerable letters and forming his resolutions for the day ... As the afternoon approached the formidable energy of the morning gradually declined, and with the shades of night the old Admiral's giant strength was often visibly exhausted. Still, judged from the point of view of physical and mental vigour alone, it was a wonderful effort, and one which filled me, who watched him so closely, with admiration and, I will add, reassurance.[84]

Fisher seemed uneasy with the responsibilities of the Admiralty when Churchill was away. Given that Churchill was running the naval aspect of the Dardanelles operations, this is not surprising. Fisher did not have – indeed, had not had – his hand on the tiller. It was Churchill's show. The old admiral seemed particularly nervous and wary. He was out of touch, too, with Churchill's other contributions to the war effort, including diplomatic assignments. Negotiations with Italy were under closest wraps, and Fisher misread the circulated view that Paris was a place for mistresses, when in fact that was a euphemism for doing diplomatic work. This misunderstanding blew up in Fisher's face.

When Churchill was out of town, Clementine often invited Fisher to lunch. One day, in early May, Churchill went to Paris to aid the entry of Italy into the war on the side of the Allies. Churchill's youngest daughter, Mary Soames, takes up the story.

> [Fisher came to lunch,] which passed very agreeably, and he took his leave of her in a cheerful mood. A short while later she herself left the sitting room and, to her astonishment, found the old Admiral lurking in the passage. She asked him what he wanted, whereupon, in a brusque and somewhat incoherent manner he told her that, while she was no doubt under the impression that Winston was conferring with Sir John French, he was in fact frolicking with a mistress in Paris! This took Clementine much aback, and she treated this scurrilous claim with the scorn it deserved. 'Be quiet, you silly old man,' she said, 'and get out.' He went.[85]

Thereafter, Clementine's disdain for Fisher knew no bounds. Mary Soames, as this historian can attest, carried the family's same dislike of the meddling admiral, the man whose actions had dragged Winston from the Admiralty.[86]

The Director of Naval Intelligence, Reginald 'Blinker' Hall, became aware of the change in Fisher in early 1915:

By the time of the Dardanelles campaign Lord Fisher was a tired man. The strain under which he worked would have been terrific in any case, and it was now made more irksome owing to divergence between his own views and those of Mr. Churchill. Hall and his fellow Directors of Divisions gradually became aware that the Fisher they had known and so much admired was no longer with them. In his place was a sorely harassed and disillusioned man who was overtaxing his strength to carry on.[87]

By ships alone

From the time the War Cabinet agreed to the attempt to force the Dardanelles, Churchill firmly took the lead at the Admiralty in directing operations. This was his show. He exerted supreme control over communications, at the expense of his Chief of Staff, Admiral Sir Henry Oliver. Fisher seems hardly to have been involved in the shaping of policy for this campaign. He was largely excluded from the details on account of Churchill's complete stranglehold on communications.[88]

As well, Churchill underestimated the enemy. On 3 February an Ottoman invasion of Egypt, which had reached the Suez Canal, was repulsed. Kitchener distributed reports of the action to the War Council. These reports emphasised the inferior quality and low morale of the Ottoman troops, reinforcing the perception that the Ottomans were not an effective opponent, and that the Dardanelles operation would be relatively easy.[89] These proved to be scandalous oversights.

At the eleventh meeting of the War Council on 9 February, Churchill announced that the naval attack on the Straits would take place on 15 February. This was subsequently postponed to 19 February.[90] Also on 9 February, according to Churchill, Fisher added the pre-dreadnoughts *Lord Nelson* and *Agamemnon* to the fleet for the Dardanelles.[91] Such additions were hardly a contribution to 'grand strategy', but we can see them as a minor support to the unfolding drama as the Navy readied its forces for attack.

By mid February, however, there was growing dissent in the Admiralty. As noted earlier, Sir Maurice Hankey intimated to Arthur Balfour on 10 February the startling news that 'from Lord Fisher downwards, every naval officer in the Admiralty who is in on the secret believes that the Navy cannot take the Dardanelles position without troops.'[92] On 14 February Captain Richmond drafted a memorandum on the current naval strategy and declared 'The bombardment of the Dardanelles, even if all the forts are destroyed, can be nothing but a local success, which without an army to carry it on can have no further effect.' The memorandum was well-received by Hankey and Fisher, the last commenting 'YOUR PAPER IS EXCELLENT.'[93] The effect of this criticism led to discussion of the matter at the War Council meeting of 16 February and the decision to reinforce the naval assault with both British and ANZAC troops, and in particular the 29th Division, an infantry division of the British Army. Three days later, at another War Council meeting, Kitchener retreated on his earlier pledge of the 29th Division. Despite Churchill's cajoling at further meetings on 24 and 26 February, Kitchener remained firm, and it seemed as if the division was not to be made available for the Dardanelles. However, Kitchener changed his position again on 10 March, allowing the 29th Division for the operations, although the delay in authorising its use was fatal to the enterprise.

In accordance with the revised plan, on the morning of 19 February Admiral Carden commenced the bombardment of the outer forts at the Dardanelles. Although no enemy guns were knocked out of action, magazines of two of the forts exploded, and Ottoman communications were severely disrupted. Next day the bombardment could not be resumed owing to bad weather – a pity, for it gave the enemy time to regroup. Could ships be successful against forts? Nelson had counselled otherwise, and the Navy in 1915 had little practice in shore bombardment.

Even at this early moment, critics were gathering against Fisher and his inability to resist Churchill's machinations. Why could he not have stood up to the First Lord and told him that the expedition was doomed to failure? The fact was, as Fisher explained confidentially to Beatty on 26 February, the Navy was being forced into action: 'We are forced against our wills and against all principles of War to send Destroyers and Submarines instantly to the Dardanelles. We pay a heavy price for producing a big political effect. But without a doubt the Dardanelles has brought the Balkan states to our side.'[94]

Fisher had always been keen on immediate action. Now it was too late. By the end of February it was already clear that the British had lost the opportunity. With sad reflection, Esher wrote, 'Three months ago the Dardanelles might have been easily forced, only now attempted too late and inadequately.'[95] During this interval the enemy build-up was prodigious, with the German military advisers and materials bolstering the Ottoman forces at every turn. Vice-Admiral A H Limpus, who had been the British naval adviser to the Ottoman Empire until 1914, and was left to rot at Malta while the campaign was being carried out, considered the scheme 'one of the toughest jobs I can imagine, i.e. the forcing of the Dardanelles which is in German hands.' A military landing would be required, since the British were facing not just the Ottomans but also Germans. According to Limpus, whose opinion smacks of arrogance, if they were fighting against Turks alone, any action would succeed. 'It would be possible to get some destroyers and capital ships into the Marmara without any landing on the Peninsula at all. If *that* be the objective well and good, it can be attained. But my own view of what the objective should be is to open up the Dardanelles first and then the Bosporus to all traffic and oust the Germans from Constantinople; the Turks will be ousted automatically.'[96]

In late February there arrived happy news in London of the piecemeal destruction of the outer forts by Carden's force on 25 and 26 February. This buoyed Churchill's spirits. He sought to spread the happy news far and wide. He wrote encouraging notes to the Grand Duke Nicholas of Russia and Sir Edward Grey at the Foreign Office. It seemed like a turning of the tide. At news that neutral Greece was thought to be leaning toward entering the war on the Allies' side in the wake of Carden's initial success, Churchill was jubilant. 'I was sitting with Clemmie at the Admiralty,' Violet Bonham Carter recalled, 'when Winston came in in a state of wild excitement and joy ... Winston totted up our combined forces ... all determined to play a part in the fall of Constantinople. All these tremendous consequences had flowed from our united naval enterprise ... I went back across the Horse Guards treading on air. Turkey, encircled by a host of enemies, was doomed, the German flank was turned, the Balkans for once united and on our side, the war shortened perhaps by years, and Winston's vision and persistence vindicated.'[97] Word of Churchill's abundant joy spread through Whitehall, with Asquith remarking that Winston was 'breast high about the Dardanelles'; Hankey, that 'the sensation in the Near East is colossal'.[98]

On 3 March Churchill heard that Kitchener had appointed General Sir Ian Hamilton to command the land forces in the eastern Mediterranean. This, too, was a pleasing development, and next day he commented to Kitchener: 'No choice could be more agreeable to the Admiralty, and to the Navy.'[99] In August 1914 Esher had waxed eloquently about him:

He is so brave and gallant that his non-employment against our enemies seems an error of judgement. His Celtic nature, that of the soldier poet, does not appeal to the sober English character. Ian Hamilton is brilliant, and a leader of men, rather than a planner of battles. His genius would have been well suited to the wars of the seventeenth century. Wherever he has served, or wherever he may command, men have followed him or will obey him with ardent affection. Confidence is a plant of slower growth, and I am uncertain of its ever blooming in the sunny atmosphere of his impetuous personality.[100]

While Churchill's spirits soared, Fisher's plunged. Even in these early days of operations at the Dardanelles, Fisher was becoming increasingly sceptical, as he wrote to Churchill on 4 March: '*The more I consider the Dardanelles, the less I like it!*'[101] However, he was not yet prepared to press his concerns to resignation. Instead, he concentrated on certain points of the campaign. In order to get his chief to make up his mind about the goal of the campaign, Fisher wrote another anxious letter to Churchill: '*Are we going on with Constantinople or are we not?* If *NOT* – then don't send half a dozen Battleships to the bottom which would be better applied at Cuxhaven or Borkum. If *YES* – then push the military co-operation with all speed ... Everything points to instant action by a collective vote & decision of the War Council with the Opposition joined in.'[102]

Churchill had no doubts as to the object in view, and wanted to keep it as a purely Admiralty-led operation. Therefore, he replied to Fisher: 'I don't think we want a war council on this. It is after all only asking a lot of ignorant people to meddle in our business. I expect K[itchener] will do what we want about the troops being concentrated at Mudros ... Meanwhile the naval operations are proceeding within safe & sure limits.'[103] Churchill's reassuring words may have calmed Fisher, but not for long.

At a War Council meeting of 10 March, in a bid to further engender and nurture the Russian alliance, it was decided to accept Russian claims to Ottoman territory – specifically, Constantinople, the western shores of the Bosporus, the Sea of Marmara, and the Dardanelles (in addition to other territories) were assigned to a post-war Russian sphere of influence. This decision demonstrated a departure in foreign policy hitherto unimagined in London. It also reflected the politics of expediency. These were desperate days in so young a war. The War Council made this decision primarily to avoid a breach with Russia, and to help ensure that Russia did not sign a separate peace with Germany. If Russia were to exit the war, France would be at the full mercy of the German army and probably indefensible. The enemy would overrun the Western Front. As for the Russian position in regards to these entreaties, Grand Duke Nicholas played a careful hand. He promised Russian forces for an attack on Constantinople, but the rub was that they would not act until the Allied fleet was already off Constantinople.[104]

As mentioned in Chapter 7, Blinker Hall in naval intelligence had been attempting to negotiate with the Ottomans. On 13 March, three days after the War Council meeting, an encrypted message to German military authorities in Constantinople was unravelled at Room 40. Hall, who knew that Fisher was lukewarm about the Dardanelles effort, described what came next – an extraordinary turn of events involving Fisher and Churchill:

On 13 March there was brought to me the German Emperor's telegram [a VB decode by Room 40], and it seemed to me of such importance that I took it at once to the 1st Sea Lord's room. Lord Fisher, I learned, had gone to the 1st Lord's room and there I found him standing with Mr. Churchill before the fireplace. 'First Sea Lord,' I said, 'we have just received this.' [The message read: 'From Nauen (the German high power station) to Constantinople. 12.3.15. Most Secret. For Admiral Usedom [the German Inspector-General of Coast Defences and Mines at the Dardanelles], HM the Kaiser received the report and telegram relating to the Dardanelles. Everything conceivable is being done here to arrange the supply of ammunition. For political reasons it is necessary to maintain a confident tone in Turkey. The Kaiser requests you to use your influence in this direction. The sending of a German or Austrian submarine is being seriously considered. By command of All Highest. v. Muller.']

Of the impact this had on the First Sea Lord, Hall wrote:

Lord Fisher took the message, read it aloud and waved it over his head. 'By God,' he shouted, 'I'll go through tomorrow!' Mr. Churchill, equally excited, seized hold of the letter and read it through again for his own satisfaction. 'That means,' he said, 'they've come to the end of their ammunition.' 'Tomorrow,' repeated Lord Fisher, and at that moment I believe he was as enthusiastic as ever Mr. Churchill had been about the whole Dardanelles campaign. 'We shall probably lose six ships, but I'm going through.' The 1st Lord nodded. 'Then get the orders out.'

Without further consideration, Fisher sat down with Churchill at his table and drafted the orders, but it was Churchill who sent the instructions to Carden. The Admiralty, ran the orders, dated 14 March:

had information that the Turkish forts are short of ammunition, that German officers have made despondent reports and have appealed for more. Every conceivable effort is being made to supply ammunition, it is being seriously considered to send a German or an Austrian submarine, but apparently they have not started yet ... All this makes it clear that the operation should now be pressed forward methodically and resolutely by night and day. The unavoidable losses must be accepted. The enemy is harassed and anxious now. The time is precious as the interference of submarines is a very serious complication.

Two days later, Churchill told Carden that the results to be gained were of sufficient magnitude 'to justify loss of ships and men if success [could] not be obtained without.' He released the Commander-in-Chief to his urgent obligation: 'We wish you now to feel quite free to press the attack vigorously as you suggest.'[105]

Misfortune played its hand at this juncture. Carden's health broke down. On 16 March he was placed on the sick list by order of the medical officer and therefore was obliged to relinquish command. His second in command, Rear-Admiral John de Robeck, succeeded to the command, even though Rear-Admiral Rosslyn Wemyss, Senior Naval Officer at Lemnos, was senior to de Robeck.[106] Wemyss agreeably stepped aside, for he believed the command should go to someone closely engaged in and familiar with the plans of the operations. De Robeck was promoted vice-admiral and soon bore the heavy weight of obligations. Urged on by Churchill, who sent him new instructions, he pressed on with plans for bombardment of the enemy forts, the first phase that would clear the sea road to Constantinople and all its alluring prospects.

On 18 March, the day of the attack on the Narrows, the battleships *Irresistible*, *Ocean*, and *Bouvet* were sunk by recently sown mines laid in unsuspected lines. Moreover, the battlecruiser *Inflexible* was severely damaged after striking a mine and put out of action. The Navy had been wonderfully fortunate in saving life. But the loss of big ships and their formidable firepower was irredeemable. Churchill and the War Council, as well as Fisher and Wilson, were shocked by this turn of events and felt it to be a terrible opening to the campaign.[107] The firepower of the British and French ships against guns and forts ashore had been prodigious, with great results, but the newly sown mines were unexpected. From this point on, Fisher began to get cold feet, but Churchill continued to believe in 'by ships alone'. And so the die was cast for the final dissension in the Admiralty between the titans.

The day after the expensive failure at the Dardanelles, Churchill wanted de Robeck to continue the attack. But Fisher, who was now having second thoughts about the horrors of the day previous, reverted to his old position. At the War Council on 19 March he once again expressed disquiet at the continuation of the naval operations against the Dardanelles forts. The worrying loss of *Irresistible*, *Ocean*, and *Bouvet*, and the near loss of *Inflexible*, was discussed. Naval operations would continue, affirmed the War Council, provided that the admiral at the scene concurred. 'Lord Fisher said that it was impossible to explain away the sinking of four battleships. *He had always said that a loss of 12 battleships must be expected before the Dardanelles could be forced by the Navy alone.* He still adhered to this view.'[108] The War Council did not meet again between 19 March and 14 May. Thus the decision-making passed to the Admiralty and War Office, advised by their men on the spot.

In the immediate aftermath of such heavy losses the Admiralty telegraphed de Robeck: 'We regret the losses you have suffered in your resolute attack. Convey to all ranks and ratings Their Lordships' approbation of their conduct in action and seamanlike skill and prudence with which His Majesty's ships were handled.' Fisher then went on to explain the further reinforcements that de Robeck could expect.[109] On the same day, 20 March, Callwell, Director of Military Operations at the War Office, sent his memorandum on the Dardanelles and expressed concern about the vulnerability of troop transports to U-boats: 'But we, the military, are hardly ready to undertake serious land operations yet and are a good deal concerned at the determined attack of the 18th having been undertaken so early. We had hoped that the fleet would not have been quite so definitely committed until we were in a position to land considerable bodies of men at various points to follow up any advantage gained.'[110]

The events of 18 March had come as a shock to Churchill. He wanted the operation to proceed with vigour and was still confident of success, but was angered by the heavy losses sustained. He was irked that wooden fenders or some such protective device had not been worked out to guard against mines and wrote bitterly to his professional advisers, blaming the inertia of the Admiralty: 'How can you be content to let these great ships, which are your pride and on which so many millions are spent, be ruled off the war path by mine and torpedo without regarding the remedy against these dangers as the first charge on naval inventiveness beats my civilian mind?'[111] Churchill was clearly upset with the Navy's lack of preparedness for war in inshore waters. Had they been too long preoccupied with blue water considerations? Did they know anything anymore of littoral warfare, of which they had been masters in years gone by? Well he might have asked these questions. Sir Arthur Wilson, for his part, asked whether any of the damaged or sunk vessels had been fitted with mine fenders. If they had been, the fenders were obviously not effective, but if not, Wilson suggested that all the remaining ships should be sent back two at a time to be modified. In the meantime, four complete sets of mine fenders were sent out to Malta, there to be affixed to capital ships.[112]

There were still further complications from Admiral de Robeck. He argued that the security of communications from the entrance to the Dardanelles to the Mediterranean could not be guaranteed until all land-based batteries were knocked out of action, and of these batteries only a small percentage could be destroyed by naval artillery fire. A raid to destroy one battery had alerted the enemy. It was apparent that future undertakings would meet organised and well-prepared resistance. Operations inside the Straits, where ships were vulnerable to enemy guns, could result in heavy losses. It was therefore recommended that the tempo of operations be reduced until the Army was ready.

De Robeck was not alone in this view. Vice-Admiral Sir A H Limpus, the Admiral Superintendent Malta, concurred with the decision about the necessity of seizing the Gallipoli peninsula as the first step. He knew of the dangers posed by floating mines in the Straits.[113] Limpus advised the Admiralty that capital ships of sufficient strength to deal with *Goeben* and their auxiliaries could not operate in Marmara without the capture of Gallipoli.[114]

De Robeck met with General Sir Ian Hamilton on 22 March and concluded that a combined operation was essential to obtaining great results. In a retrospective comment to Limpus, the admiral revealed that he was under pressure from Churchill for early action, though he had come to the conclusion that a conjoint action by the services had to be undertaken:

> We were very unlucky on the 18th March in losing ships but were on the contrary wonderfully fortunate in saving life. The actual bombardment went well enough, it is the old story, we suppress the fire of forts but fail to actually destroy guns. My view is to now have a combined attack which should succeed and not throw our ships and ammunition away until both the Army and Navy can strike at once! W.C. is urging one to go on and strike. Much as one may like to obtain one's glorification I prefer to go on my considered opinion and not be hurried![115]

The reader might reasonably ask if de Robeck was laggardly in his approach. Certainly he could only have guessed that Fisher was opposed to inter-Service co-operation.

In talking to Hamilton, it became obvious to de Robeck that the Army would 'not be in a position to undertake any military operations before 14th April.' He sent a telegraph stating that he wished to suspend naval operations until then. As he put it unerringly, 'It appears better to prepare a decisive effort about the middle of April rather than risk a great deal for what may possibly be only a partial solution.'[116]

At this, Fisher performed a volte-face and agreed with Admirals Sir Arthur Wilson and Henry Jackson at the Admiralty that purely naval operations should be suspended pending advice from the respective commanders. Checked by his professional associates, Churchill went to Asquith, and although the prime minister supported Churchill, he would not overrule the three powerful naval figures. Churchill knew that if a further rebuff had come in consequence of the follow-on bombardment, his career would indeed have been finished. In the circumstances, Churchill could not send out instructions to de Robeck. However, he could still send a private letter, and he drafted one that he showed to Fisher. Jacky was infuriated and adamant: 'Although the telegram goes from you personally, the fact of my remaining at the Admiralty sanctions my connection with it, so if it goes I do not see how I can remain.'[117] In a subsequent letter the same day he ended with the postscript, *'Send no more telegrams! Let it alone!'*[118]

Fisher was correct that Churchill's actions were compromising his authority at the Admiralty. It was at bottom a fight between political and Service heads of department, and it is also an example of how personality and character influence policy and deflect strategy. We see, moreover, the fractures in the command structure and the breakdown of control. In essence, Churchill was one of those people who insisted on having his own way, which was to cause him endless difficulties – and many are the occasions when he did not get what he wanted. But in a characteristic statement (dug up by A J P Taylor) he made about himself in such circumstances, Churchill wrote, 'All I want is compliance with my wishes after reasonable discussion.' Churchill was inexhaustible: he wore people down. As Fisher complained, he could not out-argue Churchill. Martin Gilbert later wrote that Churchill wanted to 'drive forward the whole machinery of war-making'. That was as true for the Second World War as it was for the First. He told Admiral Sir Dudley Pound, First Sea Lord in December 1939, 'An absolute defensive is for weaker sources ... I could never be responsible for a naval strategy which excluded the offensive principle.' Or as General Alan Brooke (later Lord Alanbrooke) complained, Churchill suffered from a 'regular disease', to get an attack launched.[119]

Churchill, too, would only with the greatest reluctance accept his share of the blame. In his words at the Dardanelles inquiry: 'Lord Fisher took the line that hitherto he had been willing to carry the enterprise forward, because it was supported and recommended by the Commander on the spot. But now that Admiral de Robeck and Sir Ian Hamilton had decided upon a joint operation, we were bound to accept their view. I do not blame Lord Fisher for this decision.'[120]

Meanwhile, concern mounted that Germany was about to seize Holland. This situation worried Fisher and shaped his responses. He used it as a lever against further extension of the Dardanelles operation: 'It is awful our having at this juncture to send Destroyers and submarines to the Dardanelles and we want *Inflexible* & *Queen Elizabeth* in the North Sea ... There's no doubt the moment is most opportune for Germany to seize Holland.'[121] Again, three days later, Fisher wrote to Churchill, addressing him simply as 'First Lord', using the Holland concern to lever more ships from de Robeck in favour of Home Waters.[122] In Churchill's words: 'But while he [Fisher] welcomed every sign of the despatch of troops, he grudged every form of additional naval aid.'[123] Fisher's various prevarications and his advocacy of slowing down the Dardanelles campaign or replacing it with a smaller show of force against Haifa or an attack on Holland, had brought Churchill to a state of exasperation.

It was at this stage of events that Fisher warned Churchill, 'The Dardanelles will be our grave.'[124]

The tragedy at Anzac Cove: Gallipoli

The shifting circumstances did not favour Fisher, for once it was decided that the Dardanelles would be a joint operation, and that the naval attack could not proceed without landings on the Gallipoli peninsula, the War Office became increasingly responsible for planning the operation, at the expense of Churchill and the Admiralty. Fisher was again being bypassed. In key offices at the Admiralty, among those holding greatest responsibilities and those who were closest and presumably most loyal to Fisher, concern was growing. Perhaps a revolt was brewing. The partisans disliked the developments that were taking the Navy's direction out of the Admiralty's control. On 8 April, a memorandum addressed to Fisher from the three members of the Board of Admiralty – Second Sea Lord Vice-Admiral Sir Frederick Hamilton, Third Sea Lord and Controller Rear-Admiral Frederick Tudor, and Fourth Sea Lord Captain Cecil Lambert – offered reassuring support. At the same time the trio sought clarification of the commitment to the Dardanelles operation and the overriding concern that it would draw off strength from the Home Fleet. 'We will start from ground on which there is common agreement, viz: That the Grand Fleet should always be in such a position, and of such strength, that it can be at all times ready to meet the entire fleet of the enemy with confident assurance as to the result.' They reaffirmed that only one individual, the First Sea Lord, ought to be in overall operational command. They worried that the larger strategy was being placed in jeopardy by lack of one person taking the final decision, based on ample advice. 'That person, subject to the high points of policy which can only be decided by the Cabinet, is, and should be, the FIRST SEA LORD. If, however, he has not the final voice, the result must be that the policy becomes one of compromises, which is obviously unsound, and likely to lead to mistake, and possibly to disaster.'[125]

It is hard to know if this memo came independently of the action of the beleaguered First Sea Lord or was in fact solicited by him. In any event, if this provided comfort to the First Sea Lord, as it was intended to do, no indication is given. Fisher reassuringly replied to his colleagues on the Board that the Dardanelles operation, 'if successful, will certainly shorten the period of the war by bringing in fresh Allies in the Eastern theatre and will break the back of the German-Turkish alliance, besides opening up the Black Sea.' Fisher wrote that he had consented to the operation, with hesitation, since it was decided upon by the Cabinet, and on the understanding that it was 'subject to strict limitation of the Naval forces to be employed, so that our position in the decisive theatre – the North Sea – should not be jeopardized in any one arm.' Fisher went on to say that British strength was at its limit and that he might need the support of the Sea Lords against Churchill if he endangered the position there. 'I have expressed this view very clearly to the First Lord, and should there at a later period be any disposition on the part of the Cabinet to overrule me on this point, I shall request my Naval colleagues to give their support in upholding my view.'[126]

The same day the Sea Lords were heartening Fisher with words of their utmost support, Churchill sent Fisher a letter on a possible delay in the intended location of the land attack at the Dardanelles, even raising the question that perhaps the Army ought to land and take Haifa en route to Damascus. These were breathless proposals, but they were motivated by the prospect that Italy might join the Allies. Nothing came of this. But Churchill's letter also urged his professional colleague to greater resolve. He quoted Shakespeare:

> And thus the native hue of resolution
> Is sicklied o'er by the pale cast of thought,
> And enterprises of great pith and moment
> With this regard their currents turn awry
> And lose the name of action.
> *Hamlet*, Act 1, Scene 3

And Napoleon: 'We are defeated at sea because our Admirals have learned – where I know not – that war can be made without running risks.'[127]

In all his calculations, Fisher had to preserve the strength of the Grand Fleet. Any and all measures that seemed, in truth or imagination, to diminish its power drew from him explosive comment. Beginning in early April his fulminations on this matter grew in intensity. Witness what he told Churchill categorically, by private letter, early morning on 2 April: '*We cannot send another rope yarn even to de Robeck.* WE HAVE GONE TO THE VERY LIMIT!!! And so they must not hustle and should be distinctly and most emphatically told that no further reinforcements of the Fleet can be looked for! *A failure or check in the Dardanelles would be nothing. A failure in the North Sea would be ruin.* But I do not wish to be pessimistic.'[128] In response to Fisher's refusal to accede to de Robeck's request for naval liaison officers for the landings, Churchill wrote:

> Seriously, my friend, are you not a little unfair in trying to spite this operation by side winds and small points when you have accepted it in principle? It is hard on me that you should keep on like this – every day something fresh: and it is not worthy of you or the great business we have in hand together. You know how deeply anxious I am to work with you ... Excuse frankness – but friends have this right, and to colleagues it is a duty.[129]

Preparations for the landings went ahead by fits and start. The date of the landing was set for 25 April. On the 20th Fisher sent Admiral de Robeck a private and personal note, in secret cipher: 'Now that the time is drawing so near I send both Ian Hamilton and you my fervent best wishes and full confidence that you will succeed but settled weather before beginning seems a necessity.' The admiral's response came the next day: 'Many thanks for your message and good wishes which are much appreciated by Sir Ian and myself. We are ready as soon as the weather improves. N.E. wind and heavy rain at present.'[130]

On 22 April, even as the boats were being prepared at Mudros in anticipation of the projected landing at Suvla Bay on the 25th, the first public criticism of the Dardanelles operations was raised in the House of Commons. It came from Lord Charles Beresford, Fisher's old enemy, in the form of a question. Who was responsible for the operation? Implicit in this was the charge that the Navy had erred in attacking the forts before the Army was ready for landings. Asquith replied in measured tones that the Navy and the Army were conducting it jointly, and that he could not comment further. That same day Asquith received a letter from the journalist H A Gwynne. He asserted that the apparent failure of the Dardanelles campaign to date illustrated the faults of the First Lord, Churchill, which, he noted, he had already brought to the attention of Asquith in the aftermath of the misdirected Antwerp episode.[131] (Earlier, Gwynne had written to General Sir Henry Wilson: 'The Dardanelles is the greatest horror of the lot. Antwerp was bad enough in all conscience, but the Dardanelles is worse, for we were given to understand that with the dismissal of Louis of Battenberg the conduct of operations at the Admiralty was altogether changed; that here was a great, strong man, Fisher, coming in, who would stand no nonsense and would insist that the expert's point of view should prevail. Unfortunately, the exact opposite has happened.'[132])

Until that time it had been a matter of conjecture as to what would happen to a sizeable force landed on a well-defended port. Such an adventure was hazardous and most difficult, but the intention was to establish a foothold ashore and advance from there. In the event, the commanders were anxious for quick results. There were many notable and heroic achievements on 25 April at what became known as Anzac Cove. There was disembarkation of 16,000 Australian and New Zealand soldiers in the face of determined resistance and little shelter on land. Troops scrambled ashore and went after the enemy with bayonets, making gains. The assailants suffered a great many losses, and much bitterness developed. National legends were born. There is evidence that Sir Ian Hamilton and his staff underestimated Ottoman grit and capabilities. The fact was that if the Allies were going to be successful in their Dardanelles operation, an extensive and expensive land operation would be an integral part of the war effort.

Churchill's quick response to the 25 April landings was a fear that too few men were available to exploit them and ensure success, as he wrote to his brother Jack, who witnessed the landings, on 27 April. The day before, the First Lord had drafted the following lines to Colonel Fitzgerald, Kitchener's private secretary, but had not sent them: 'A valiant & successful attack like this may go well for a time; but there must be *stuffing* behind & inside it ... Remember every minute of this is history: and every attack requires backing.'[133]

On 3 May Churchill again attempted to stiffen Fisher's resolve: 'It is clear that the favourable turn to our affairs in S.E. Europe arose from the initial success of our attack on the Dardanelles, was checked by the repulse of the 18th [March], & can only be restored by the general success of the operations. It is thus necessary to fight a battle, (a thing wh has often happened before in war) & abide the consequences whatever they may be.'[134] A sardonic note had entered Churchill's call to arms, as if to chide his professional opposite that he was shying away from battle.

Now we come to the events of the second week of May, a decisive moment in the campaign. General Hamilton's army had been checked. That being the case, now the issue was how the Navy was to conduct a littoral war – that is, one along the watery margin of the Gallipoli shore, while on the Asiatic shore, below Chanak, the enemy showed stiff resistance. These dispiriting results in the eastern Mediterranean sped Fisher's already heightened discontent. On the 10th the Vice-Admiral Eastern Mediterranean sent a lengthy telegram to the Admiralty, detailing the state of affairs – a good situation report but full of forebodings. From the naval point of view the issue was how to keep down the fire of the enemy's batteries if the Fleet were to pass into the Sea of Marmara. This following sentence got Fisher's attention, and with his green pencil he highlighted it: 'From the vigour of the enemy's resistance it is improbable that the passage of the Fleet into the Marmara will be decisive & therefore it is equally probable that the Straits will be closed behind the Fleet.' Here was the problem in a nutshell, and it had obvious implications. If the resistance of the enemy could be overcome 'in time to prevent the enforced withdrawal of the Fleet owing to lack of supplies', then this was a matter of slight importance. But it also invited speculation about the prospects of forcing the Dardanelles, and the admiral held the opinion that bringing this off would in and of itself not gain the end result, for 'the temper of the Turkish Army in the Peninsula' indicated otherwise. From all of the above, two points for decision presented themselves: (1) Could the Navy, by forcing the Dardanelles, ensure the success of the operations, and (2) 'if the navy were to suffer a reverse, which of necessity could only be a severe one, would the position of the army be so critical as to jeopardize the whole of the operations?'[135]

Here were deep issues of military strategy demanding the greatest consideration and immediate attention. Clausewitz had noted how difficult war was in a littoral controlled by the enemy, and the passing and repassing of the Straits in this instance gave formidable advantages to the enemy. Wolfe had talked of the making of war as an option of difficulties. To minimise losses the Allies had to use veteran warships, but in a narrow channel many navigational difficulties could present themselves, especially if the enemy had sown mines hitherto undetected. In the eastern Mediterranean the new reality had dawned on the commanders. London's advice was requested. What should be the next step?

Churchill returned from France on 10 May. The next day he had a tough encounter with Fisher. Lines of battle were clearly drawn. Churchill desired de Robeck to attack the Kephez minefield and shell the forts. Fisher was wary that this limited operation might well succeed and force him into the position of expanding the operations further and perhaps have de Robeck break into the Sea of Marmara. Fisher dug in his heels. Now was his chance to reply – and to write a memorandum on the subject. With the admiral on station's intelligence to hand, Fisher exploited Hankey's talents and had him write a memorandum under Fisher's name, dated 11 May, arguing against further attempts with naval action alone. Hankey made Fisher's points with strength.

> Our deliberations on the subject of these operations have been conducted either in personal conference or by the interchange of informal notes, and there is therefore no official record of the views that I have from time to time expressed. Although I have acquiesced in each stage of the operations up to the present, largely on account of considerations of political expediency and the political advantage which those whose business it is to judge of these matters have assured me would accrue from success, or even partial success, I have clearly expressed my opinion that I did not consider the original attempt to force the Dardanelles with the Fleet alone was a practicable operation.

He had always insisted that the North Sea was the proper theatre of operations for the Fleet. There alone could the enemy cause irreparable harm, or allow for a decisive British victory over the German fleet. For the past four months, he explained, he had 'looked with misgiving on the steady drain of our Naval force to the Dardanelles ..., whether the operations were to be conducted in conjunction with the Army or not.' The dribbling away of forces from the North Sea had compelled Fisher, a few weeks earlier, to draw the line. To his cost, Churchill had ignored this caution, and he had gone even further, telling de Robeck that the Board of Admiralty might be prepared to sanction undertaking further operations against the forts even if the land forces were unable to advance beyond their present positions. Churchill had not acknowledged that Fisher had asked for a check on this last position.

> I therefore feel impelled to inform you definitely and formally of my conviction that such an attack by the Fleet on the Dardanelles forts, in repetition of the operations which failed on 18th March, or any attempt by the Fleet to rush by the Narrows, is doomed to failure, and, moreover, is fraught with possibilities of disaster utterly incommensurate to any advantage that could be obtained therefrom.
>
> In my opinion we cannot afford to expose any more ships to the risk of loss in the Dardanelles, since the ships there, though not consisting in the main

of first line units, are the reserve on which we depend entirely for supremacy in the event of any unforeseen disaster.

Fisher buttressed his arguments with details of previous battleship losses, the terror of enemy mines, and the prospect of enemy submarines and the existence of further Ottoman batteries higher up the Straits. Even if the Fleet got into the Sea of Marmara, it could not be supplied there and would be a hostage to fortune. 'A Fleet by itself can effect very little at Constantinople,' Fisher noted, and extricating it would be hazardous: 'We are dealing this time with highly scientific and skilled and trained Germans, and we cannot gamble on any possibility of inefficiency on the part of the defence.' He concluded the 11 May memorandum with this: 'Purely Naval action, unsupported by the Army, would merely lead to heavy loss of ships and invaluable men, without any reasonable prospect of a success in any way proportionate to the losses or to the possible further consequences of those losses. I therefore wish it to be clearly understood that I disassociate myself from any such project.'[136]

If ever a clear warning was given, this was it. Churchill had heard Fisher's points of view on a daily basis. He was not only not listening to Fisher, not taking his professional advice, but was running roughshod over him. Herein lay the root of the unfolding tragedy.

If Churchill was aware of how precarious his relations with the First Sea Lord were, he now told Fisher that there would be no question of forcing the straits by naval action alone.

We are now in a vy difficult position. Whether it is my fault for trying or my misfortune for not having the power to carry through is immaterial. We are now committed to one of the greatest amphibious enterprises of history. You are absolutely committed. Comradeship, resource, firmness, patience, all in the highest degree will be needed to carry the matter through to victory. A great army hanging on by its eyelids to a rocky beach, and confronted with the armed power of the Turkish Empire under German military guidance; the whole *surplus* fleet of Britain – every scrap that can be spared – bound to that army and its fortunes as long as the struggle may drag out: the apparition of the long-feared submarine – our many needs and obligations – the measureless advantages – probably decisive on the whole war – to be gained by success.

Surely here is a combination & a situation wh requires from us every conceivable exertion & contrivance wh we can think of. I beg you to lend your whole aid & goodwill, & ultimately success is certain.[137]

This was written longhand on 11 May. Once again we see that Churchill would not listen, would not budge.

Fisher brushed aside this powerfully worded appeal to close ranks and join in common cause at the critical hour. He did so, in part because he believed he had the prime minister's support to stop Churchill. After writing his memo of 11 May, Fisher had sent Hankey to tell Asquith of his (Fisher's) intention to resign. Asquith dismissed this as 'a very foolish message', or so Hankey recorded in his diary, but in the circumstances, and to calm Fisher, the prime minister sent back a verbal reassurance – Asquith was good at verbal pacification – to the effect that any separate naval action would not be taken without Fisher's concurrence. This was a constitutionally correct position for the prime minister to take, and entirely in keeping with the requirement that the Service head should not be overridden by his political colleague. In fact, the statesmen could not direct the affairs of the Navy without the agreement and support of the Board of Admiralty, including Fisher as First Sea Lord, first among equals of the naval fraternity. This was all well and good in theory, but Martin Gilbert, Churchill's official biographer, says that Fisher interpreted it as giving him a veto over any decision taken by Churchill, although only the prime minister could have such overarching powers over a member of the Cabinet.[138]

Now, in response to Churchill's note, Fisher went to consult Hankey in his office in nearby Whitehall Gardens. Hankey wrote in his diary that Churchill's letter was 'rather a slippery one', and advised Fisher that, rather than threatening resignation, he should first send his own 11 May memorandum to Asquith. 'It was absolutely necessary to bring Churchill to his bearings,' Hankey wrote in his diary.[139]

When this was done, Fisher replied to Churchill:

> Until the Military Operations have effectively occupied the shores of the Narrows &c no naval attack on the minefield can take place. But your letter does not repudiate this and therefore in view of our joint conversation with the Prime Minister prior to March 18 I have sent him a copy of my memorandum to you – With reference to your remark that I am absolutely committed – I have only to say that you must know (as the Prime Minister also) that my unwilling acquiescence did not extend to such a further gamble as any repetition of March 18 until the army had done their part.[140]

Though Churchill did not reply directly to this letter, he did meet with Fisher later on 12 May. By this point, Fisher was increasingly insistent on the withdrawal of *Queen Elizabeth* from Admiral de Robeck's order of battle. The sinking of the Cunard liner *Lusitania* on 7 May by *U-20* had shown the cruel effectiveness of submarines and the tremendous public outcry at the loss of such a grand ship and so many innocent lives. The Admiralty, basing its calculations on naval intelligence, was now reporting that more enemy submarines were headed toward the Dardanelles.[141] The danger mounted. The sinking of *Goliath* on 12 May by an enemy destroyer convinced Fisher that the risk to *Queen Elizabeth* was too great, and that she must be recalled.[142] In order to placate Fisher, Churchill agreed on 13 May to withdraw *Queen Elizabeth*.[143] To add firepower in the equation of 'ships versus forts', the Admiralty sent out *Exmouth* and *Venerable* and also the first two new monitors, *Admiral Farragut* and *Stonewall Jackson*, with two 14in guns (effective range of 20,000yds, firing 1,400lb high-explosive shells), which had special bulges installed on either side of their hull to protect them from mines and torpedoes.

In the Commons, members of the Opposition, who had sensed disagreement in the Admiralty, cross-examined Churchill. In reference to alleged difficulties between the First Lord and the First Sea Lord, Churchill replied: 'With regard to the hon. Member's question, I am sure this House will not approve of this kind of question, which is calculated to be detrimental to public interests of serious importance. The unity and integrity of the Board of Admiralty ought not in time of war to be impugned by any Member.'[144] Churchill was at his best in his own defence but the ground was shifting beneath his feet. He was powerless to stop it.

That same day, Fisher crossed to 10 Downing Street to explain to the prime minister why he objected to Churchill's granting to de Robeck the latitude in operations the admiral had asked for. He was already in a retrospective mood, aware of how history had determined his course up to that moment and how it would guide him in the next few precious hours. He had already made up his mind to go.

He was sitting in the room of Asquith's private secretary, Maurice Bonham Carter (otherwise known as Bongy), when Margot Asquith entered the room. She had the prescience to record their conversation in her diary:

M: How are things going?
LORD F.: As badly as they can, 30,000 casualties in the Dardanelles, 16,000 English, 14,000 French, and 60 per cent of the French engaged. I was always as you know against this mad expedition. The North Sea is the place where we can beat the Germans, we ought to have taken the island of Borkum, landed these Dardanelles fellows there and got into Berlin.
M: You know you have talked too much – all London knows you are against the Dardanelles expedition. Why didn't you resign at the time?
LORD F: It's a lie – I've seen no one, been no where, I'm far too busy.
M: But you've talked to a few – enough for all to know.
LORD F.: … It's Winston that talks to AJB[alfour] and F.E. Smith. You can ask AJB if I wasn't against this expedition – taking all our men out there and our ships will have to go too. It will bleed us white.
M.: Well, we're in for it and *must* see it through.

LORD F.: Oh, yes, it may turn out all right but I doubt it.

M.: It's helped to bring Italy in – Has she good ships?

LORD F.: Mere organ grinders! No use whatever, but it's no good looking backwards. Why, look at Lot's life, she looked backwards!! ... Come along and have a valse.

He seized me by the waist in Bongy's little room and we valsed round. The old boy is a fine dancer. His last words were 'I'm very glad you told me what they say.'[145]

Later that day, writing to Asquith, Fisher stated, '*I feel my time is short.*'[146]

That evening, Kitchener and the Chief of the Imperial General Staff went to the Admiralty and were surprised to hear that *Queen Elizabeth* had been ordered home. Kitchener strongly argued against the withdrawal of the ship. This drew an angry response from Fisher: *Queen Elizabeth* would 'come home that night' or else he would 'walk out of the Admiralty then and there.'[147] Fisher was in a constitutional struggle with the more influential Kitchener. He hated hearing the War Office suggest what should be done with the King's ships. Not convinced by Fisher, Kitchener wrote to Asquith that this redeployment would have a powerful effect on army morale:

Lord Fisher said he would leave the Admiralty if the *Queen Elizabeth* was not at once withdrawn, as he could not stand the fear of losing the ship. I may say that I have had to face the loss of some 15,000 men in the operation to help the Navy ... This desertion of the Army after coming to the assistance of the Navy when they failed to force the passage of the Dardanelles, will undoubtedly have a very unpleasant effect on the confidence that ought to exist between the two Services.

The process had begun and was not to be stopped. Churchill and Fisher moved forward to the crisis, a crisis of unsolvable differences on the method of waging the war using the naval assets available to the Admiralty. Over-enthusiasm had ruled early decision-making. Mistakes had been made in planning. Reconaissance had been incomplete. There was a touch of arrogance as to the capabilities of the defenders. At the Admiralty, age was not a factor, nor the press of work. This was a crisis as to where ships and men should be stationed in readiness to deal with the main threat, always there, the German High Seas Fleet.

PART FIVE

The Sea Kings Depart

10

The Titans Exit the Admiralty

Locked in combat

The growing unrest was not limited to Admiralty business. The Conservatives, or Unionists, lived in a spider's web. Many were increasingly discontented with the overall direction of the war. Since the beginning of hostilities, an informal truce existed between the major parties, but in light of perceived Liberal failings, some on the Unionist backbenches were calling for a reopening of party hostilities and confrontation in the House of Commons. The Opposition formed the Unionist Business Committee in late January to formulate more aggressive tactics, and some backbenchers began to put pressure on the Leader of the Opposition, Andrew Bonar Law, whose leadership was not completely secure. At the same time, he greatly dreaded a renewal of party hostility. He did not see how the Unionists could openly oppose the government while the war was still popular. He was appalled equally by the prospect of destroying the Liberal government and leading a Unionist government. Better to bide his time. He knew the trade unions and significant segments of the population would accept measures like conscription much more readily from a Liberal government than a Unionist one, and if he waited long enough, the Liberal party would succumb to its pacifist elements. Thus Bonar Law was caught between a desire to fully support the war effort, and a need to oppose what he and his party perceived as Liberal misconduct of the war.[1]

While Bonar Law stubbornly waited the course of events, Asquith disclaimed any chance of a coalition government when he was asked in the House of Commons on 12 May about the possibility. His attitude was dismissive; he viewed the French coalition government as weak and afraid of the press and each other.[2] All the same, the seeds had been sown, and the decisive events were but days away.

As the crisis over the Dardanelles approached its climax, the government became embroiled in another controversy. On 9 May the British Expeditionary

Force offensive at Aubers Ridge on the Western Front was repulsed with 20,000 casualties without gaining a yard of ground. Sir John French, commanding the BEF, informed Colonel Repington, military correspondent of *The Times*, that the cause of the failure was a severe shortage of high-explosive shells, and that the politicians in London were mismanaging the war effort. This accusation was in no small part motivated by French's belief that the Dardanelles represented a dangerous diversion of resources and had to be stopped. Repington sent his now-notorious telegram to *The Times* for printing. The story broke on 14 May in *The Times* with shocking headlines: 'NEED FOR SHELLS. BRITISH ATTACK CHECKED. LIMITED SUPPLIES THE CAUSE. A LESSON FROM FRANCE.'[3] The newspaper claimed that British soldiers were dying in vain due to government incompetence, notably at Kitchener's War Office. The news hit like a thunderbolt. A month earlier, Asquith had publicly declared that the supply of munitions was more than sufficient for the military. That declaration now seemed to have been proven hollow.[4] Kitchener was under close examination, his position already weakened. All the same, he held to the view that the clamour for shells was exaggerated.[5]

A case has been made that the shell crisis was part of a conspiracy by Lord Northcliffe, one of England's most powerful press magnates (he was proprietor of *The Times* and other papers), and Sir John French to depose Kitchener from the War Office, and that Lloyd George, Churchill, and Balfour participated in the plot to enhance their own positions in a Cabinet reconstruction that might not include Asquith. Historian Stephen Koss argues this line: he contends that Churchill played a key role in Repington's dispatch, as he, along with Repington, was at French's headquarters on 8 and 9 May.[6] Koss contends that during this stay, Churchill conspired with French and Repington to break a story about a shells shortage, thereby crippling Kitchener and possibly bringing down the government. This would serve the interests of all three, in that French could ensure that he would receive the supplies he desired and would not have to deal with Kitchener; Repington and his boss, Northcliffe, could strike at Kitchener, whom they despised; and Churchill could advance his political career. One of French's 'agents', whom he had sent to London to contact Lloyd George and Bonar Law, as well as major newspapers, about the shells shortage, was Captain Freddie Guest, Churchill's cousin and a bête noire of Clementine's.[7] This theory, however, is supported by circumstantial evidence at best, and is based on the letters of Charles Hobhouse, a minor Liberal Cabinet minister, who was by no means in the inner circle in May 1915. More importantly, no explanation is given as to why Churchill would ally with Northcliffe.[8] The latter had long campaigned against both Churchill and the Dardanelles; indeed, if Northcliffe achieved his goals, not only would Kitchener have been deposed, but the Dardanelles campaign would also have been brought to an end, perhaps along with the career of Churchill. It is unlikely that Churchill would have allied with a political enemy.[9] A more plausible case can be made for collusion between Lloyd George and Northcliffe, as they met regularly in private during the May 1915 crisis.[10] All the same, and as if to deflect the arguments away from his own administration, Churchill later contended that it was the shells crisis that led to the reconstitution of Asquith's government and not the feud at the Admiralty between himself and Fisher.

The War Council met for the first time in six weeks on that same morning, 14 May – the long 'coma', as Lloyd George called it, was over. All the great heads of the government were there, including the Service professionals Kitchener and Fisher. Kitchener was in a particularly foul mood. Churchill described the meeting as 'sulphurous'. There were many ill tidings. The misfortunes of war continued: Kitchener reported a series of reverses on various fronts. As Kitchener discussed *The Times*'s charges in regards to a shells shortage, he became increasingly gloomy. Alan Moorehead writes, 'No organisation, he said, could keep pace with the expenditure of ammunition. No one could foresee what would happen. If the Russians cracked in the east it was quite possible that the Germans would bring back their armies to the west and set out upon the invasion of England.'[11]

Kitchener then moved on to the dreaded Dardanelles. He had sent an army to Gallipoli on the assurance that the Navy would force the Dardanelles. Churchill had proclaimed to him the glorious potentialities of *Queen Elizabeth*. Hamilton's army was now stalled at Gallipoli; *Queen Elizabeth* was being withdrawn at the critical hour. He argued that the Army, fighting with bravery ashore, was being let down by the Navy, which was unwilling to run any risks in hazarding its ships so as to assist the soldiers.

As correct as the gloomy Secretary of State for War might have been in his analysis, Fisher could not let this pass. He was unwilling to allow the honour of the Admiralty to go impugned. He therefore interrupted Kitchener to inform the War Council that he had been against the Dardanelles operation from the beginning, and that both the prime minister and Kitchener were perfectly aware of this fact. There was a stunned silence. As Churchill later wrote, 'This remarkable interruption was received in silence.'

After a moment's pause, Kitchener resumed his pessimistic litany of difficulties. Then it was Churchill's turn, and he defended the Admiralty. He argued that if he had known three months earlier that an army of 80,000 to 100,000 would be available for the Dardanelles in May, he would not have consented to the naval operation there in February and March. He dismissed Kitchener's pessimistic concerns about invasion as unrealistic and improbable, and contended that the Dardanelles operation did not rely on one single ship. Hankey later wrote cheerily, but with exaggeration, that Churchill's spirited defence restored a degree of confidence. But it was readily clear to all present that a deep and even long-standing fissure existed between Fisher and Churchill over the operation.[12] Hankey noted in his diary: 'There is a horrible muddle with all this bickering and intriguing between Churchill and Fisher.'[13]

Now that Fisher had openly declared his antagonism, Churchill's position was weakened. But Churchill was not the only one obstructing his plans to lessen the liability of the Navy in the Dardanelles. The First Lord had the support of Asquith and the Cabinet, and in a second meeting the same day, the War Council decided that Kitchener would ask Hamilton what military force he would require in order to ensure success at the Dardanelles. The operation would continue.

In the circumstances, as Admiral Sir Arthur Wilson put it, Fisher 'was faced at last by a progressive frustration of his main schemes of naval strategy.'[14] Now he sought to distance himself from the measures taken by the war machinery – the Supreme Command, Hankey terms it – by arguing a specifically constitutional point. He was not a member of the War Council, he maintained, and though it was true that he had attended its meetings, there was a distinct difference between the responsibility of a person attending it as an expert and one being a member. Cabinet members alone were responsible for the decisions; this was his view. This was why he believed he could say he had been no party to the Dardanelles operation from the outset. (He repeated this later, in an Admiralty memorandum of September 1916, arguing that he was 'in no way responsible for the decision to attack the Dardanelles.'[15]) Fisher had simply given his advice to the First Lord. Moreover, when Fisher had the matter under first consideration he had made known his opinion to the prime minister at a private interview. This was entirely true. But Fisher's revelation of this was nonetheless a bombshell, for it exposed Churchill and certainly Asquith, who had known that Fisher was against the Dardanelles expedition from the beginning, but had not properly read the warning signs from Fisher, content as he was to let Churchill run the show. Now any accommodations existing among these three were exploded. Fisher's action – his public disclosure, as it were – was a reversal of his form of action of 28 January. He could not bite his lip in silence. Now the fighting was out in the open and potentially lethal to the conduct of British warfare.

Churchill seethed over Fisher's remarks. But he took no public measure. Rather he wrote to Asquith that same day, 14 May, stating unreservedly the stunning revelation that made Fisher's statements a lie: 'The First Sea Lord has agreed in writing to every executive telegram on which the operations [in the Dardanelles] have been conducted.'[16]

Earlier that evening Churchill and Fisher discussed at length how they would resolve outstanding difficulties. They drew up new orders for Admiral de Robeck, and in them Churchill included only those recommendations he knew to be acceptable to Fisher. Fisher took his leave. Churchill then sat down and formally drafted what they had agreed upon. He then went to bed. Shortly after midnight, Captain Crease, his Naval Secretary, sent the memorandum embodying these recommendations to Fisher. According to Fisher, when he saw the memorandum at the beginning of his work day, Churchill had altered the arrangement, adding two submarines as reinforcements for de Robeck, who had requested them, and also accessing from home sources – not from the Grand Fleet – vessels and material for the strengthening of the Dardanelles Naval Force.[17] Fisher had been outflanked.

Abdication

On Saturday, 15 May came the eruption. At that time Fisher received the memorandum which proved to him that Churchill was not paying attention and once again was meddling with naval deployments in contravention of earlier arrangements with Fisher.

This was the last straw. Fisher was unable to acquiesce: he took his decision to resign once and for all. Outdone at last, as he saw it, it was time for him to go. He made the crucial and irrevocable decision.[18] The great office that he held, at the apex of naval and imperial affairs, was about to see one of its most powerful admirals leave under a cloud.

He slept briefly and was up early that Saturday morning. He left his house and walked to the Admiralty. Sometime between 4am and 5am he penned two letters, now legendary. To Asquith he simply stated his inability to continue as First Sea Lord.[19]

Fisher then wrote to Churchill:

After further anxious reflection I have come to the regretted conclusion I am unable to remain any longer as your Colleague. It is undesirable in the public interests to go into details – Jowett [famed master of Balliol] said, 'Never explain' – but I find it increasingly difficult to adjust myself to the increasingly daily requirements of the Dardanelles to meet your views. As you truly said yesterday, I am in the position of continually veto-ing your proposals.

This is not fair to you besides being extremely distasteful to me.

I am off to Scotland at once so as to avoid all questionings.[20]

That evening Fisher took refuge in the Athenaeum Club 'to escape from Winston', as he told Maurice Hankey, who met him there by appointment.[21]

After stopping at the Foreign Office to put final touches on the treaty with Italy for her entry into the war, Churchill was stopped by his private secretary while he was returning across Horse Guards Parade and was informed, 'Fisher has resigned, and I think he means it this time.' Churchill was then handed Fisher's note of resignation.[22]

For Fisher, Churchill's additions to the memorandum of the late evening of 14 May showed irrevocably that, as he wrote, if he remained as First Sea Lord, he would be in the untenable position of constantly vetoing Churchill's proposals, which would not be fair to Churchill. More significantly, Fisher realised that he could do no more himself as long as Churchill was there. As Fisher wrote by way of further explanation to Churchill on 16 May, he had always been extremely reluctant about the Dardanelles operation, but 'YOU ARE BENT ON FORCING THE DARDANELLES AND NOTHING WILL TURN YOU FROM IT – NOTHING.' As such, '*You will remain*. I SHALL GO.'[23] That Fisher was resolved to work with Churchill no longer was the key to events. To Asquith, Fisher wrote, 'I am leaving at once for Scotland so as not to be embarrassed or embarrass you by any explanations with anyone.'[24] It was an odd way of exiting the scene, a disappearing act of unconscionable notoriety, vintage Fisher.

Alarmed that Fisher had left his post (leaving the Admiralty and the Navy rudderless), Asquith put the word out to find the truant. A messenger was sent to the Admiralty. The Admiralty truthfully reported that the First Sea Lord had disappeared, leaving no address. At this juncture, and unimaginably, the Admiralty had no professional head in office, an unheard-of state of affairs, a perilous situation in wartime especially.

Fisher's resignation also presented a major political problem to the prime minister. Asquith was never quick to form independent judgements, preferring collegial decisions, but he knew that Fisher's exit would bring down the government or force a reorganisation or coalition. The old order lay in Fisher's hands.

In an extraordinary act calling Fisher to account and perhaps trying to bring him to his senses, Asquith ordered Fisher to return to the Admiralty.[25] His instruction read:

15 May 1915
10 Downing Street

Lord Fisher

In the King's name, I order you at once to return to your post.
H.H. Asquith

Thinking that Fisher had not escaped to Scotland but had, instead, gone to the Continent, Asquith also apparently had the ferries crossing the English Channel checked. He contacted Lady Fisher to see if she knew her husband's whereabouts.[26] She did not. Asquith thought that Lord Esher might know where Fisher was. At that moment, Esher was with the King, and the King told him, quite mistakenly, that both Fisher and Churchill had offered their resignations, that Asquith had refused to accept Churchill's, and that after a meeting that afternoon between Fisher and Asquith, there was some idea that an arrangement had been made. It was all a muddle. However, Esher noted in his journal, 'The King sees that Fisher's resignation at such a moment is bound to have a deplorable, if not a disastrous, effect upon the public, not only at home, but abroad.'[27]

Many and various are the stories as to where Fisher disappeared. He did not go to Scotland as advertised, or at least he did not go there immediately. One account says that he went to the Charing Cross Hotel and locked himself in his room. There he was found, and it was the command that he return to duty 'in the King's name' that drew him from the locked room.[28] Sir Martin Gilbert had a different view: he believed Fisher sought sanctuary at Balcombe Place, West Sussex, one of the country residences of Nina, Duchess of Hamilton.[29] Balcombe lies on the Charing Cross to Brighton rail line, about twenty miles south of Croydon – easy for Fisher to get to as a refuge. Fisher likely received assurance from the Duchess and her husband that he could indeed escape to Scotland when the time came. And he was quickly able to return to London if circumstances favoured that.

The truth of the matter is made unmistakably clear by Hankey's diary, cited above: Fisher had taken refuge in the Athenaeum Club, where Churchill could not get at him. It has been generally believed that Asquith or his messengers finally tracked Fisher down late on the 15th, and had him come to 10 Downing Street. This is unlikely. Asquith was attending a wedding in the country that day.[30] A quite different (and more plausible) version is found in the memoirs of David Lloyd George. He was one of the few persons to actually speak to Jacky on the volcanic day that Fisher went to see the prime minister. Lloyd George happened to chance upon the First Sea Lord as he waited in the entrance lobby of 10 Downing Street for Asquith's return. This was probably mid-morning on 15 May.

Lloyd George recorded the scene with dramatic, artistic flair: 'A combative grimness had taken the place of his usually genial greeting; the lower lip of his set mouth was thrust forward, and the droop at the corner was more marked than usual. His curiously Oriental features were more than ever those of a graven image in an Eastern temple, with a sinister frown. "I have resigned!" was his greeting.'[31] Asked why, he replied, 'I can stand it no longer.' He would no longer participate in the Dardanelles 'foolishness' and was off to Scotland. Lloyd George tried to postpone his departure until he could place his case before the War Council on the Monday.

> I told him that so far as the Council was concerned he had never expressed any dissent from the policy or the plans for the expedition; that though I was a member of the War Council and had been opposed to that venture from the start I had not heard one word of protest from him; and that it was only

right that we should be given an opportunity of hearing his objections, weighing his advice, and taking the appropriate action. His answer was that Mr. Churchill was his Chief, and that by the traditions of the service he was not entitled to differ from him in public. On being reminded by me that the Council was a Council of War, and that he was bound as a member of that Council to speak his mind freely to all his colleagues around the table, he stated that he had at the outset made an emphatic protest against the whole expedition to the Prime Minister privately, and had left to him the responsibility of communicating or withholding that knowledge. Here he was referring to a conversation he and Mr. Churchill had with Mr. Asquith in advance of the War Council meeting of 28 January. This protest had never been passed on to Council.[32]

Lloyd George, seeking to protect Asquith's government, attempted to keep Fisher in harness, but his arguments, and Asquith's subsequent representations, were to no avail. Lloyd George says that Fisher next went to see McKenna, his former First Lord of the Admiralty and an opponent of the Dardanelles expedition.

At this period Mr. Winston Churchill was Mr. M'Kenna's pet aversion, for Mr. Churchill had supplanted him at the Admiralty. He was, therefore, not in a mood to extricate his supplanter from his troubles. Whatever happened at this interview, the impulsive old sailor left for Scotland that night, his departure producing an inevitable crisis, for political circles in London were seething with disquieting rumours, and there was a general feeling that things were being muddled badly and that the War was therefore not going well for us. The next I heard of the matter was when I saw Mr. M'Kenna that afternoon. Lord Fisher had reported to him the conversation he had with me. Mr. M'Kenna said that the 'old boy' was quite obdurate and was not open to persuasion.[33]

In fact, McKenna, desperate to keep Fisher in his post, informed the First Sea Lord that the prime minister 'holds the opinion that your resignation is void until he accepts.'[34]

In the circumstances, and with Fisher refusing to take his post, business at the Admiralty was reduced to a shambles. At this stage, Churchill, still First Lord of the Admiralty, though his own position was now entirely tenuous, went scrambling for a replacement for Fisher. On the Sunday morning he offered the job to Sir Arthur Wilson, who was already undertaking the work along with the Second Sea Lord. Wilson, after some hesitation, accepted, but only to serve under Churchill. Wilson was rightly miffed at his naval colleague Fisher for his silent exit – they had always been good friends and saw eye to eye – which left him and others holding the bag, as it were. As Wilson confided to his diary, 'Fisher's bombshell has done us more harm than a big defeat and I don't know yet in the least what will come of it. He sent in his resignation and left the Admiralty ... without troubling himself to think how the work would be affected.'[35]

In Fisher's wake flowed many letters of personal support. His private correspondence files tell the story. Wilson, always brief and to the point, urged him to reconsider: 'It would mean a great national disaster and you have no right to consider your private feelings in the matter while the interests of the country are so much at stake as they are now. Do change your mind and see the thing out.'[36] A substantial note of support for Jacky, whose ghost had already begun to haunt the halls of the Admiralty, came immediately from the Admiralty Board. The remaining Sea Lords in collective action, thinking to ensure their enduring loyalty to their old chief, issued a memorandum addressed to Fisher, Churchill, and Asquith, the triumvirate of Britannia's power. In it they vouchsafed their agreement with Fisher in the reasons for his resignation. They were dissatisfied with the operations at the Dardanelles, and stated their opinion that the dispositions necessary to carry out that offensive 'jeopardize the crushing superiority of the Grand Fleet which is essential to the successful prosecution of the war.' Further, they disagreed entirely with the methods taken by the First Lord in ordering fleet movements: 'We associate ourselves with Lord Fisher, and are of opinion that the present method of directing the distribution of the Fleet, and the conduct of the War by which the orders for controlling movements and supplies appear to be largely taken out of the hands of the First Sea Lord is open to very grave objection.'[37]

This vote of confidence in Fisher as against Churchill's domineering ways had no effect. Nothing could budge Fisher. His mind was narrowing now, selfishly concentrating on his personal, as opposed to the Service's or the nation's, requirements. He was falling from grace, tumbling from the greatest office a British admiral could hold ashore. Wounded by events and too proud to reconsider, he thanked the Sea Lords for their memorandum. Never at a loss for words, he added, 'if you knew as much as I did, I AM SURE you would not wish me to remain.'[38] To his faithful private secretary, Captain Crease, Fisher commented, 'I hope the Sea Lords clearly understand my undoubtedly correct reason for not entangling them, but I *grieve they allowed themselves to be made use of to send me advice which I did not require*, AND IT WAS EXCEEDINGLY BAD ADVICE.'[39] Megalomania had taken control of Fisher. The stress had been too much, and perhaps his age had something to do with it. Certain it is that he had acted all alone, and had not taken the counsel of others. He exhibited the problems of solitary command.

Fisher's action shocked the King. It was irresponsible at a time when it was thought the German fleet was about to put to sea. Esher, Fisher's closest friend in such matters, learned from the King that Fisher had definitely resigned, that the decision was irrevocable. According to Esher, the King was 'very much disturbed and worried, but wonderfully sensible.'[40] Esher had his own opinions on the conduct of naval administration, and to Fisher he irresponsibly suggested that in view of the fact that these quarrels could never permanently be patched up, the only thing to be done was to revive the office of Lord High Admiral. Jacky should take it himself. 'Otherwise we are beaten presently at sea; and unless Lord K[itchener] takes the war into his hands ... ditto on land.'[41] Esher was foreshadowing the concept of a supreme commander, something quite imponderable in the present circumstances.

On 16 May Churchill met with Asquith in the country at Wharf House, Sutton Courtenay. He informed the prime minister that Fisher's resignation appeared final, and offered his own resignation. Asquith declined Churchill's offer. He clearly wanted Winston to remain at the Admiralty and in Cabinet, but, wondering how secure Churchill stood among the senior admirals, he inquired whether the First Lord could indeed, if he remained, still assemble a Board of Admiralty – that is, one loyal to him. Churchill replied that he could do so, with Wilson as the new First Sea Lord, and the other Lords retaining their places. Asquith's private secretary mentioned to Churchill that the prime minister believed that, in light of Fisher's resignation and the shells crisis, the Unionist leadership might have to be consulted.[42] In short, Asquith could not protect Churchill completely; he was sensing his own political lifeblood draining from him.

That astute observer of events Max Aitken (later Lord Beaverbrook) says that Churchill did not realise just how fragile his position was, for he was quite unaware of what was transpiring with the Opposition. Now more than ever the Tories and Unionists were out to get him, as Churchill might have imagined, but he somehow did not sense the acuteness of the danger. He was, in the circumstances, still working mightily to save his relationship with Fisher – that was the cardinal requirement at this stage as he saw it – and he summed up the history of his relations with the admiral in a letter to Jacky that showed his historical appreciation of the demands of the then current circumstances:

Our friendship has been a long one. I remember how in 1908 you tried to bring me in to the Admiralty as First Lord. When I eventually came in 1911 I proposed to the Prime Minister that you should return to your old position, and only the difficulties which your enemies were likely to make at that time prevented the accomplishment of my first wish. As it was I followed your guidance in the important decisions which have given us the 15-inch gun and Jellicoe to-day.

Six months ago in the crisis of this great war you came to my aid; since then we have worked together in the very closest intimacy. One difficulty after another has been surmounted; vast schemes of new construction have been carried through; and tremendous reinforcements are now approaching the Fleet. Over the whole range of war-policy and Naval administration there is nothing that I know of on which we are disagreed – except the series of events which have led us into the 'Dardanelles'. Even then we are agreed upon the immediate steps, for I shall not press my wish about reinforcements beyond the point to which you were willing to go – namely the 6 earliest monitors. We are now fully agreed that the Fleet is not to attempt to rush the Narrows but is to support the Army in its gradual advance upon the forts by land. Orders in this sense have been given with which you were in complete accord.

It seems to me that the only course now is to hold on, to go slow, putting as many ships as possible in Malta and the Canal, out of harm's way, and using the destroyers which are out there to hunt the submarines and convoy the army corps which is now starting. If you came into the Admiralty tomorrow for the first time and looked at the problem as it now is, you would advise this as the only practical course. You must feel as I do and as the War Council decided – that whoever may be responsible for the original step, to withdraw now cannot be contemplated.

The announcement of your resignation at this juncture will be accepted everywhere as proof that the military operations as well as the naval at the Dardanelles have failed. The position of the Army which has suffered a loss of 30,000 men in a joint operation will be jeopardized. The admission of failure at the Dardanelles, for so your resignation would be exploited all over the world, might prove the deciding factor in the case of Italy, now trembling on the brink. The knowledge of these facts forces me, not for my own sake (for the fortunes of individuals do not matter now), to appeal to you not to make your resignation operative until at least Italy has declared herself, for which the latest date is the 26th. Meanwhile Sir Arthur Wilson could, if you desire it, do your work.

There ought to be no reproaches between us, and you, my friend, must at this moment in your long career so act that no one can say you were unmindful of the public interests and of the lives of the soldiers and sailors.

In any case, whatever you decide, I claim, in the name of friendship and in the name of duty, a personal interview – if only for the purpose of settling what explanation is to be offered to Parliament.[43]

Fisher was past the point of no return, and his reply was terse:

Dear Winston:

As usual, your letter is most persuasive, but I really have considered everything and I have definitely told the Prime Minister that I leave to-morrow (Monday).

Please don't wish to see me. I could say nothing, as I have determined not to. *I know I am doing right.*

Fisher[44]

Britain's naval destiny now hung in the balance, and nowhere was this more significant than in the Admiral's cabin in HMS *Iron Duke*, riding at anchor in Scapa Flow. Fisher's secretary, Captain T E Crease, had the sad but essential duty of informing the Commander-in-Chief, Grand Fleet, of the flood of events at the Admiralty. He wrote on 17 May to Jellicoe:

I write with a heavy heart, by direction of Lord Fisher, to tell you that he has felt compelled to resign from the position of First Sea Lord; that to-day is his last official day in that capacity and that tomorrow at 11.30 am, he leaves London for the Duke of Hamilton's place near Glasgow. The Government have put all kinds of pressure on him to remain, and the Prime Minister has not accepted his resignation so far, but Lord Fisher is quite determined.

Crease explained that it was an impossibility to continue to serve at the Admiralty under Churchill. The main difficulty, said Crease, was the Dardanelles, and that 'the First Lord is determined in his own mind (though he always professes to the contrary) to ram the fleet again at the Narrows forts and minefields unaided by the Army rather than give up the operations.' The last straws were sending out further naval units from England and making plans to use heavy naval guns ashore, guns for the mounts being constructed for warships then being built. 'Lord Fisher told the Prime Minister that the general effect of the way the Admiralty business was carried on was that he had to spend his whole time watching the First Lord instead of the Germans, and that it could not continue.'[45] In other words, Fisher had been distracted from his professional obligations by political intervention.

That same day, Churchill made one last desperate attempt to keep Fisher at the Admiralty. This was surely designed to maintain his own position, now deteriorating rapidly. Thinking that Fisher wanted more power, he offered the admiral enhanced powers along the line of those enjoyed by Lord Kitchener, a sort of Secretary of State for Naval Affairs. Churchill enjoyed no such authority. He even, without authorisation, went so far as to offer Fisher a seat in the Cabinet, which would place him on a par with Kitchener, a Secretary of State. George Lambert, the Civil Lord, transmitted the offer verbally.[46] Not only did Fisher refuse, but he also promptly wrote to Bonar Law to relay this information and his rejection of the offer: 'I rejected the 30 pieces of silver to betray my country.' His decision to leave the Admiralty was final and absolute, he declared: the real danger was Churchill. He urged Bonar Law not to remain silent, as then Churchill would remain at his post: 'I don't want to stay, but W.C. MUST go at all costs! AT ONCE ... The P.M. will stick at nothing to keep W.C. ... *a very great national disaster is very near us in the Dardanelles*! ... W.C. is a bigger danger than the Germans by a long way.' For the moment, Fisher told Bonar Law, he would have nothing to do with Balfour, who had been a party to Churchill's machinations throughout the Dardanelles enterprise.[47]

To Reginald McKenna, his old boss at the Admiralty, Fisher let loose on Churchill: 'He talks of a mighty enterprise which will certainly be carried to success! Nothing will turn him! At every turn he will be thinking of the military and not the naval side – he never has done otherwise. His heart is ashore, not afloat! The joy of his life is to be 50 yards from a German trench!'[48]

Breaking point

Unknown to Churchill or Fisher, on 17 May the Admiralty crisis was subsumed in a much larger one. The revelation of 14 May regarding the shells shortage was the breaking point for many of the more militant Unionists. To this point the Liberal government existed thanks to the political truce between the Liberals and the Conservatives, or Unionists, in the Commons. On 15 May Professor William Hewins, MP, a leading member of the influential Unionists, warned Asquith that he intended to raise questions in the House of Commons at the earliest possible moment regarding the shells crisis. Hewins had been a proponent of Empire tariff reform and of pressing for a victory over Germany's trade positions at the close of the war. He was a commanding presence with a wide following.[49] He was now to play an important role in national events.

That same day, Bonar Law received in the mail an old newspaper clipping announcing the King's receiving Fisher for an audience. Addressed in Fisher's handwriting, the cryptic message left little doubt that the First Sea Lord had resigned. Bonar Law did not need Fisher's letter of 17 May to realise that Churchill could not remain at the Admiralty. He understood that if Fisher left the Admiralty while Churchill remained, the Unionist backbenches would become uncontrollable and open conflict would ensue in the House of Commons – and, incidentally, his hold on the party might be fatally weakened. Bonar Law resolved to take action.[50]

Early on 17 May, Bonar Law arrived at the Treasury to discuss the situation with Lloyd George – he got along much better with the Chancellor of the Exchequer than he did with the prime minister. Lloyd George confirmed the resignation of Fisher. At this point Bonar Law stated that he could no longer guarantee the survival of the political truce in the House of Commons. Indeed, a parliamentary challenge would ensue if Churchill remained after Fisher had gone. In other words, Churchill must go. Lloyd George grasped the implications immediately. A coalition was now necessary, for the alternative would spell disaster. He walked to 10 Downing Street and put the matter to Asquith. The prime minister at once agreed to the proposition. The Liberal government was dead by noon on 17 May.[51]

Accounts of the swiftly unfolding events differ slightly. One version, related by Lloyd George and Beaverbrook, has Lloyd George returning from his meeting to fetch Bonar Law to 10 Downing Street, where the two leaders agreed to a coalition. The other version, by Austen Chamberlain, has Bonar Law leaving 11 Downing Street while Lloyd George and Asquith met, and consulting Lord Lansdowne and Chamberlain at Lansdowne House. It was only after they discussed the situation, and agreed on a letter that recommended a reconstitution of the government, not necessarily a coalition, that Asquith called Bonar Law to 10 Downing Street. There he offered a coalition. The importance of the difference is a question of who actually proposed the coalition first. However, the more important question is why the leaders agreed to it.[52]

In terms of Asquith's motivations, it has been argued that at this critical hour he was greatly distracted by personal loss. This is undeniable if exaggerated. For several years Asquith had been sustained by his infatuation for the much younger and very beautiful Venetia Stanley, Clementine's first cousin. He poured out his emotions to her in a steady stream of intimate letters. All this suddenly ended on 14 May 1915 when she informed the prime minister that, due to the great disparity in their ages, their relationship was now over and that she intended to marry the gangly and unattractive Edwin Montagu, a member of Asquith's government. Asquith was broken by the revelation: 'This is too terrible; no Hell could be so bad,' he replied in anguish. On the eve of what he regarded as world-shaking events requiring his decisions, he now faced the future 'without your counsel & consent.'[53]

Some have suggested that as a result of this distraction, Asquith was in no condition to fight for his government and meekly conceded to the demands of Bonar Law and Lloyd George.[54] This may be so. Against this argument, however, can be set Asquith's performance in the subsequent construction of the coalition government. He disliked the process of Cabinet formation, reluctant as he was to share the ultimate responsibility for the ministry, but he did not capitulate. He was more than able to manage Bonar Law and ensure that the Unionists were kept out of the key portfolios. The only appointment of any strength given to the Unionists was to replace Churchill at the Admiralty with the former prime minister and chairman of the Committee of Imperial Defence, Arthur Balfour, the perfect choice to cool the hot seat of First Lord. Liberals retained all other key posts – the Exchequer, the Foreign Office, and, of course, the premiership. Asquith was also able to ensure that those of his colleagues he wished to keep, notably Reginald McKenna (First Lord of the Admiralty during Fisher's first term as First Sea Lord; he now became Chancellor of the Exchequer), were retained, even over the vociferous opposition of the Unionists and the press.[55]

Much more plausible is that Asquith, along with Bonar Law and Lloyd George, concluded that a coalition government would be the best option. Bonar Law had played his cards carefully. He wanted to avoid a clash in the House of Commons that would put him in a tight spot, and he had to keep his unruly backbenches in check. A coalition government would accomplish this in due course, he knew. Meanwhile, other scenarios of power-seeking were being played out. Lloyd George wanted the opportunity to take control of munitions away from the War Office – he did this by creating a new Ministry of Munitions, which he headed – and remove Kitchener from his post.[56] For Asquith, a coalition offered a means to secure Unionist support and ensure the continuation of his leadership. Just as important, it meant that blame for failures could be assigned to the Unionists as well as the Liberals. He made sure the Unionists were to have responsibility but no real power. As Asquith commented to Lloyd George on 28 May, of the desirability of the latter accepting a Unionist as Undersecretary of Munitions, 'you ought to have a Tory as a hostage.'[57]

Another consideration was that, according to the Parliament Act of 1911, an election was due by the end of 1915. The prospect of this battle appalled both sides: the Liberals feared defeat as much as the Unionists feared victory. The election could only be postponed by all-party consent, and that would have been impossible if Unionist backbenchers had launched a full assault on the government. A coalition government ensured that all sides would support the indefinite suspension of the pending general election.[58] Thus a backroom deal, in the interests of all concerned, was cemented between Lloyd George, Asquith, and Bonar Law. Bonar Law had bided his time and won.

The decision to form a coalition government sealed the fates of Churchill and Fisher. As has been noted, Churchill was hated, distrusted, and feared by the Unionists. Bonar Law would not serve with him in a reconstructed Cabinet, and he was coolly content to see Churchill, to whom he was always antagonistic, sent into the wilderness. Liberal backbenchers also distrusted Churchill. He was viewed as irresponsible, and his record at the Admiralty from the start of the war was considered chequered. Even if Churchill was not party to a conspiracy about the shells crisis, he was widely believed to have been involved in other such conspiracies against the government, and many Liberals blamed him for the events that led to the coalition government. Several wrote to the prime minister urging that Churchill be excluded from the coalition.[59] Put differently, Churchill was isolated politically; there was practically no group willing to back him in a crisis. Churchill, preoccupied with the demands of his naval administration, did not realise how isolated he had become from his own colleagues.

There was, however, another matter to consider. The clamour of political opposition indicated to Asquith that Churchill was responsible for Fisher's resignation, which was added to the view that he was responsible for all the lack of success at the Dardanelles.[60] Thus Asquith began to put in place his scheme to remove Churchill from the Admiralty and replace him with the steady hand of the cool and dependable Arthur Balfour.

For Fisher the problem was not hostility, as in Churchill's case, but a degree of indifference. The Unionists were far more concerned about removing Churchill than retaining Fisher. They were perfectly willing to have Balfour, their most trusted hand, replace Churchill at the Admiralty, knowing full well that Fisher would not serve under Balfour.[61] (When Fisher heard that Balfour was to become First Lord he cried out, 'Damn it! He won't do: Arthur Balfour is too much of a gentleman.'[62]) No one appeared willing to expend precious political capital to defend a First Sea Lord who had, by some accounts, abandoned his post. They wanted someone more compliant. That seemed like the best solution, and Fisher would have to remain out of the Admiralty.

Later that day, 17 May, largely unaware of the knives drawn against him, Churchill arrived at 10 Downing Street, confident that he could reconstruct the Board of Admiralty. He eagerly awaited the chance to launch a successful defence of the Dardanelles campaign. But events had conspired against him. Asquith told Churchill that he had decided to form a national government with the Unionists, and that a great reconstruction of the Cabinet would be necessary. The prime minister then looked at Churchill and said, 'What are we to do for you?'[63]

Churchill now had his first indication, the first sudden shock, that he might not remain at the Admiralty. For him it was a harrowing thought. While they talked, Lloyd George entered the room and suggested that Churchill could go to the Colonial Office. Churchill responded that he would refuse any office that did not have some responsibility for the conduct of the war. He was, as Fisher had so often said of him, 'a war man'. As he wrote to Asquith that same evening: 'So far as I am concerned if you find it necessary to make a change, I shd be glad – assuming it was thought fitting – to be *offered* a position in the new Government. But I will not *take* any office except a military department, & if that is not convenient I hope I may be found employment in the field.'[64] Asquith, though, had already come to the conclusion that Churchill did not understand the extent of the crisis, and was only concerned with how he would come out of it. When Asquith told Lloyd George that Churchill wanted to speak with the prime minister about the situation, Asquith concluded: 'Which means the situation as it concerns Churchill personally – how far he is likely to be affected. The situation for Churchill has no other meaning but his own prospects.'[65] This is decidedly the case.

Meanwhile, Asquith spelled out to Fisher the intended changes that same day. He wrote: 'I feel bound to tell you for your own information only that a considerable reconstruction of the Government is in contemplation, and in the public interest I trust that you will neither say nor do anything for a day or two.'[66] Fisher agreed to remain in town, and Asquith's words may have led him to believe that he might soon return to power with even greater authority than before. This was Fisher's supreme hope, but it led him to overplay his hand. He sent several detailed operational plans to Captain Crease on 18 May, asking him to draft them into telegrams to be issued the moment he returned to supreme power. He even referred to 'Der Tag', the day the coalition government was to be formed and he would return to the Admiralty.[67]

Of the decisive events of 17 May, Esher provides an excellent summary of Fisher's views:

I saw Fisher later on in the day and he told me that it was impossible for him to stay longer at the Admiralty with Churchill. He had disapproved of the Dardanelles operations from the beginning; he gave all his reasons to the Prime Minister at the time, but was overruled. He says that the Grand Fleet has been dangerously weakened, and that, in fact, the whole margin of preponderance over the Germans has been sent to the Near East. We have a naval force at the Dardanelles stronger than the German High Sea Fleet. Although he has always held that the passage of the Dardanelles was a highly dangerous and almost indeed impossible operation, any chances of success were eliminated by the action of the 17th March. Complete surprise was the only condition under which success might have been achieved. After the first bombardment a few sailors landed unmolested, and destroyed the guns of the outer forts; two days afterwards when the Marines attempted to land they lost 75 per cent of their number. The cause, however, of the quarrel to-day is that Churchill is sending everything upon which he can lay his hands to the Dardanelles, and denuding the Grand Fleet and the Home Defences. Nets – badly wanted for the Irish Channel; the newest type of submarine; a new type of flat-bottomed vessel which can lie up on the sands, carrying a fifteen-inch gun, intended to attack Cuxhaven, are being sent to the Near East. Fisher is convinced that while we might, perhaps, manage with difficulty to hang on in Thrace, it is impossible without grave risks in the other theatres of war to carry the Dardanelles operations through to a successful issue at present.

Besides all this very grave difference of view in matters of high strategy, he complains of Churchill's methods of corresponding with the Admirals in the Mediterranean and his whole plan of concealment. He told me that nothing would induce him to stay any longer at the Admiralty, but that he proposed to give no reason other than that his views and Churchill's upon the naval strategy of the war were wholly incompatible. He showed me a very strong minute written by the Lords of the Admiralty endorsing his views. He told me, however, that none proposed to resign with him, and that Churchill had already asked Wilson to accept the office of First Sea Lord.[68]

By 18 May the press had got wind of the troubles at the Admiralty, as reported in *The Times*: 'It is understood that Lord Fisher has not attended at the Admiralty for the last two days. This fact, coupled with the prolonged interview between the First Sea Lord and the Prime Minister on Saturday, reported in the newspapers on Sunday, has given rise to a variety of rumours.'[69]

There had indeed been wild speculation that Fisher would be selected as some sort of supreme First Lord, much like Kitchener had been made Secretary of State for War. Outsiders thought that Fisher had pulled off a coup. One such, Lewis Harcourt at the Colonial Office, wrote to Esher, 'I think Jacky has triumphed.'[70] Admiral of the Fleet Lord John Hay, a very senior officer, congratulated Fisher on his stand, both over the Dardanelles and over unnecessary civilian interference in the running of the Navy. He even went so far as to say that forcing the reconstruction of the government was 'the greatest service' of his career. Hay also criticised Churchill for interfering in professional issues.[71] Another admiral, Sir Alexander Bethell, told Fisher that the sympathy of the Navy was with him, and 'should the result be that you become the head of the Navy we shall welcome it & back it up through thick & thin.'[72]

Nor was the reality of the situation for Fisher brought home by Esher, who wrote in his journal on 19 May that Fisher objected to Balfour as much as he did to Churchill, and that 'as the Prime Minister has elected to keep Fisher, he must either make Fisher First Lord, or put someone into that position with whom Fisher can act cordially.'[73] In the same vein as his 16 May suggestion that Fisher 'revive the office of Lord High Admiral and take it' himself,[74] Esher wrote to Fisher on 20 May that operations ought to be controlled only and jointly by Kitchener and Fisher: 'To be hanged if they fail. To be crowned with bays if they succeed.'[75]

On 19 May Fisher presented to Asquith six conditions for his remaining at the Admiralty under which 'he could guarantee the successful termination of the war.' If there was any doubt that megalomania was overcoming him, these conditions showed delusions of grandeur now far advanced. The autocrat was exerting himself. Fisher indicated his desire to be untrammelled by politicians getting in his way: 'The 60 per cent of my time and energy which I have exhausted on 9 First Lords *in the past* I wish *in the future* to devote to the successful prosecution of the War. That is my *sole* reason for the six conditions.' First, Fisher demanded that Churchill should not be in the Cabinet 'to be always circumventing me.' Fisher insisted also that he would not serve under Balfour. Second, Fisher desired that his seasoned and reliable professional partner Sir Arthur Wilson leave the Admiralty, the CID, and the War Council, since he would not work with him. (Fisher wrote to Jellicoe on 31 May, '*A.K. Wilson at the Admiralty is a REAL danger!* While I was there it did not signify, as I nullified him.'[76]) Third, a new Board of Admiralty must be appointed. Fourth, Fisher demanded 'complete professional charge of the war at sea, together with the absolute sole disposition of the Fleet and the appointment of all officers of all ranks whatsoever, and absolutely untrammelled sole command of all the sea forces whatsoever.' Fifth, that the First Lord should be free from parliamentary procedure, as Kitchener was; and finally, he demanded complete control over construction policy. Fisher added that these demands should be published so the Fleet might know his position. He also indicated the new men he would appoint, and the abolition of the position of Chief of Staff.[77]

Fisher showed the letter with the conditions to Hankey, who thought Fisher quite mad and advised him at once to withdraw the ultimatum. It was too late, however, since Fisher had already had a copy placed in the hands of Asquith. Asquith was infuriated and thought Fisher had lost his mind: 'Lord Fisher was undoubtedly a man with streaks of genius, but he was afflicted with fits of megalomania, in one of which this extraordinary ultimatum must have been composed ... I always remained on the best of personal terms with him, but the whole of his conduct at this critical time convinced me that it had become impossible that he should remain responsible for the Admiralty.'[78] In communicating Fisher's written demands to the King, Asquith remarked that it 'indicates signs of mental aberration'. Others saw this memorandum as a sign of Fisher's arrogance. Churchill, who didn't know of Fisher's six conditions until 1927, nonetheless told Kitchener on 21 May, speaking generally of the situation at the Admiralty, that 'Fisher went mad.'[79] According to one of Kitchener's biographers, 'that madness took the form of a fit of megalomania ... such was the volcano upon which Churchill had been sitting.'[80] This fit of megalomania was presaged by Fisher's conduct in the months before. Sir Roger Keyes wrote in early December that Fisher had told Captain Philip Dumas that he intended to run the submarine service as he wished, regardless of the wishes of Churchill, and that he was acting similarly in other areas of the Admiralty.[81]

But it was Fisher's disgraceful conduct in deserting the Admiralty and ignoring Asquith's order to return in the King's name that undermined his support, not just in the Cabinet but also among the other Sea Lords. Early on

17 May, Room 40 had observed the usual German signals that tended to precede any sortie in strength by the High Seas Fleet. This turned out to be a false alarm, as the movement was intended to do nothing more than provide cover for minelaying. However, during the alarm, though Churchill hurried back from Cabinet, Fisher was nowhere to be found. As a result, the First Sea Lord's duties had to be assumed by the Second Sea Lord, Admiral Sir Frederick Hamilton. The Sea Lords were appalled that Fisher would abandon his post at what could have been the critical moment of the war. Despite formally expressing their view on 16 May that Fisher ought to remain in office, they now did an about-turn: they contended that Fisher must be removed as First Sea Lord. Inside the Board of Admiralty the winds of change were blowing strongly.

Fearing charges of disloyalty, the Sea Lords did not want to be implicated in Fisher's dismissal, so Hamilton approached Blinker Hall, Director of Naval Intelligence, to 'take steps'. Nothing could be written down, but Hall took on the burden and, using his personal assistant, Commander Dick Herschel, 2nd Baron Herschel, as intermediary, approached Lord Reading, the Lord Chief Justice and a friend of Asquith. In the quiet of Herschel's London flat, Hall put forward the case of the Sea Lords and argued the importance of ensuring that Fisher would not return. It was a sordid but necessary business. Lord Reading did not rush to judgement. For an hour he carefully grilled Hall on his views and the basis for his position. Satisfied with Hall's answers, he finally asked which one should leave the Admiralty, Fisher or Churchill. Hall responded: 'Regretfully, I have to say both.' Reading then stated that he would see Asquith at once and relay the arguments for the necessary steps.[82] Whatever power Fisher had within the Admiralty was now vanished.

Against mounting odds, Churchill continued to believe that he could remain at the Admiralty, and turned to the Tories for support. On the evening of 18 May he met with close political friends F E Smith and Max Aitken at Admiralty House. Aitken told Churchill in no uncertain terms that he could not count on Tory support. Balfour may have been consulted, and word came back that Churchill was not wanted. Next day, and to counter claims that his administration was fraught with difficulties in naval operations, Churchill sent Bonar Law a set of official telegrams regarding earlier naval setbacks in order to show that Tory criticisms of his tenure were unfounded – 'You must not suppose that in sending you these I want to claim all the credit or avoid the blame,' Churchill wrote, 'only hitherto the principle has been that the blame only came to me.' Bonar Law's antipathy to Churchill was long-standing but was not of a hateful sort. Churchill, by contrast, had often been sardonic in treating his opposite. Now at this decisive moment the leader of the Unionists was the last person who would come to Winston's aid, particularly against Fisher, who was the darling of Bonar Law's party.[83] Churchill was cut adrift.

On 20 May Fisher received two letters from Bonar Law regarding the Cabinet shuffle and the likely position of Fisher. In the first letter, Bonar Law told Fisher that he could not meet with him. He advised the First Sea Lord to 'keep yourself free until the new Government is formed or the attempt to form it has failed.' In the second he advised that 'everything is in the melting pot ... you ought not to do anything decisive till you see what kind of metal comes out of the crucible.'[84] Jellicoe wrote the same day to pressure Fisher to stay at the Admiralty and expressed fear that Sir Arthur Wilson would succeed as First Sea Lord. Jellicoe said he and his staff 'distrust his strategic ideas profoundly'. Jellicoe also expressed hope that Fisher would be back on his own terms.[85] Churchill's proposal to recall Wilson to replace Fisher had evoked general horror among the ranking admirals. As Jellicoe stated: '[T]he flag officers afloat are even more distrustful of Sir Arthur Wilson than of Winston Churchill and we should have no confidence whatever in an administration headed by him. I greatly fear that he will eventually be First Sea Lord and I as well as all the rest would view that as a national disaster.'[86]

Churchill learned of Wilson's statement that he would only serve as First Sea Lord under Churchill (and not under Balfour) in the evening of 19 May. Unaware of the admirals' distrust of Wilson, he saw this as a vote of confidence from the Navy and wrote to Asquith in a last-ditch effort the next day, arguing that Wilson's statement was decisive and that it further indicated that Fisher did not have the confidence to allow him to return to his post. Asquith, however, did not circulate Wilson's note.[87]

Clementine Churchill could see the terrible scenario then unfolding. Upset that Asquith was not working harder to keep her husband in office, she wrote to the prime minister pleading for her husband's place:

My dear Mr. Asquith,
For nearly four years Winston has worked to master every detail of naval science. There is no man in this country who possesses equal knowledge capacity & vigour. If he goes, the injury to Admiralty business will not be reparable for many months – if indeed it is ever made good during the war.

Why do you part with Winston? unless indeed you have lost confidence in his work and ability?

But I know that cannot be the reason. Is not the reason expediency – 'to restore public confidence'? I suggest to you that public confidence will be restored in *Germany* by Winston's downfall ...

Winston may in your eyes & in those with whom he has to work have faults but he has the supreme quality which I venture to say very few of your present or future Cabinet possess – the power, the imagination, the deadliness to fight Germany.[88]

Asquith later described this message to Venetia Stanley as 'the letter of a maniac'.[89] He gossiped, in confidence, about Fisher with a degree of self-satisfaction that others found alarming. To treat the man of destiny as an amusing lunatic is a commentary on Asquith and his greatly slipping power at that time. If Fisher and Churchill were to go, Asquith could not be far behind. These were days of great stress at 10 Downing Street. Asquith presented a mellow serenity to the world, but to those who knew him he appeared tired, worried, and preoccupied. Dealing with difficult colleagues and bringing a unity of purpose to the Cabinet posed unimagined difficulties. Haldane was to be removed on account of his attack on Kitchener in the press, the difficult McKenna was to be reassigned, and various Unionists would have to be accommodated in the reconstituted government.

On 20 May Sir George Riddell, proprietor of *News of the World* among other papers, and a confidant of Lloyd George, chanced upon Churchill at the Admiralty. He found Churchill raging at the prospect of his imminent fall from power, as Riddell recorded in his diary:

> [Churchill said] 'I am stung by a viper. I am the victim of a political intrigue. I am finished.'
>
> I [Riddell] said 'Not finished at forty, with your remarkable powers!'
>
> 'Yes,' he said. 'Finished in respect of all I care for – the waging of war; the defeat of the Germans. I have had a high place [Viceroy of India] offered to me – a position which has been occupied by many distinguished men, and which carries with it a high salary. But that all goes for nothing. This is what I live for. LG [Lloyd George] has been partly responsible. Fisher went to him and he told him to resign, or at any rate did not dissuade him ... This is a political intrigue. It centres on LG. He thinks he sees his way to go to the War Office ... The poor devil [Field Marshal Sir John French] is fighting for his life. Had I spent some of my time in lobbying newspapers instead of working twelve hours a day, I should not be in this plight. This is a Northcliffe Cabinet [under the thumb of *The Times*]. He has forced this.'
>
> R[iddell]: 'Do you think the P.M. has been weak in the conduct of the war?'
>
> Winston: 'Terribly weak – supinely weak. His weakness will be the death of him.'
>
> Thus closed ... a most painful and eventful interview and I left this broken man pacing up and down in his room. Early in the conversation he said that his fate was not yet sealed. I think it is. How soon men forget, or appear to forget. I wonder whether Winston remembers McKenna's downfall.[90]

Late that evening, desperately attempting to save his position, Churchill met the stolid Bonar Law, and this led to Winston writing another pleading letter on 21 May. He urged Bonar Law to circulate the letter and the attached specific notes on his naval administration to his Unionist colleagues. Bonar Law stiffly replied that he would show the letters to his colleagues, starting with Austen Chamberlain, but made clear that nothing would change Churchill's fate. That same day Churchill made one final effort with Asquith. He argued that he and Sir Arthur Wilson could bring success to the Dardanelles campaign, while anyone else would not be familiar enough with it. He appealed to Asquith's knowledge of the situation, and argued that he was not clinging to office but 'clinging to my *task* & to my *duty*'. Asquith's reply was devastatingly final: 'I have your letters. You must take it as settled that you are not to remain at the Admiralty.'[91]

Churchill finally realised that his tenure at the Admiralty was at an end. On 21 May *The Times* reported that Balfour was to go to the Admiralty in Churchill's place. Decades later, Churchill's daughter Mary Soames wrote that he 'drew some consolation from the fact that his successor was to be Mr. Balfour, one of his few friends among the Tories, and who, as a member of the War Council, had always supported the plan for the Dardanelles.'[92] *The Times*, which had done so much to discredit Churchill and prop up the Unionists who supported Fisher, hoped that the displacement of Churchill would not also lead to the displacement of Fisher.[93]

Fisher had many admirers in the Service; that was obvious, and the Admirals were likely to close ranks against the Frocks. Beatty, as late as 21 May, believed that Fisher had come through the crisis unscathed: 'It would have been a national calamity if Fisher had gone. He is the only man capable of filling the position adequately, and the Navy breathes freer now it is rid of the *succubus* Winston,' Beatty wrote to his wife, also noting that he had warned Churchill that once Fisher was at the Admiralty, one of them would eventually go and it would not be Fisher.[94]

But the ground was shifting under Fisher, too. With Churchill gone, the Unionists insisted that, in the political sphere, the Admiralty be managed by one of their own who also had credibility with the Liberals. That person was Arthur Balfour, the former Conservative prime minister and a statesman well versed in defence matters and administration. Fisher feared Balfour, with his artful ways and dialectical skills in argument, and had made it unmistakably clear that he was unwilling to serve as First Sea Lord under either Churchill or Balfour. Fisher's message-bearer to Asquith was John Alfred Spender, of the *Westminster Gazette*, a close associate of Asquith. As Fisher noted to Jellicoe, he told Spender that he would only serve under Bonar Law or McKenna.[95] However, the old admiral was running out of time and out of political credit.

These were perilous days for the Navy in London, for who knew what Fisher might say and to whom. The former First Sea Lord posed a clear danger to the government, the Admiralty, Churchill, and even himself. The Secretary of the

War Cabinet, Hankey, foresaw all sorts of difficulties. He knew Fisher was fighting so hard because he feared that if he left the Admiralty now, he would never return. He was fighting for position and reputation. There was a larger issue. He could do incalculable damage to the government and the war effort. Just as he had predicted, on 21 May Hankey heard that Fisher was talking openly with the journalists. Hankey sought some sort of damage control to protect the government and Jacky Fisher. He resolved that the old admiral must be whisked out of London at the first opportunity. The next day he worked with Captain Crease and McKenna to pressure Fisher to get 'away from journalistic influences, as he [Fisher] may do himself and the nation great harm by an indiscretion in his present state.' Hankey told Fisher directly that though he had been injured by events, he must be strong and silent. Fisher took this advice. He packed immediately and caught the last evening train from Euston Station to Glasgow, there to find refuge with the Duke and Duchess of Hamilton. Having not yet secured Asquith's final acceptance of Fisher's resignation, Hankey worked to get this from Asquith, while Fisher told Crease to telegraph it to him at a station along the way.[96] In every way, Hankey succeeded admirably. Asquith accepted Fisher's final resignation that evening with a 'curt' letter: 'I am commanded by the King to accept your tendered resignation of the Office of First Sea Lord of the Admiralty.'[97]

Churchill's last day at the Admiralty, the 'glittering post' that he had so enjoyed, with all its immense challenges, not least of which was dealing with a difficult and independent Fisher, was 27 May. It was a fine, clear day, windy and cold, and young Lady Cynthia Asquith had been asked to join a select luncheon at the Admiralty with the 'setting sun' minister. 'We had all been caught up into a Greek tragedy and are but gradually beginning to realise it,' she confided in her diary in reference to the fact that her father-in-law's administration would now be operating under different rules – answerable to the Conservatives and Unionists:

> Winston came in rather late from the first Coalition Cabinet. He looks unhappy, but is very dignified and un-bitter. I have never liked him so much ... I think his nature – though he may be unscrupulous and inclined to trample on susceptibilities of sailors, or whomever he may have to deal with, from eagerness – is absolutely devoid of vindictiveness, unlike the half-caste Fisher who really runs amok from malevolent spleen and is now saying he will tell the Germans where all our ships are.[98]

She also noted that Winston said that he had been in government for ten years but still was a young man, which was true, and that much might still lie ahead for him. He was, he said of himself, experiencing the 'austerity of changing fortunes', which was equally true. But, with an eye to the future, he complained of the melancholy he would now experience when out of office. A very sad Clementine Churchill was also at the luncheon, among other friends. She told Lady Cynthia that from the day Fisher was appointed she had always known Winston would be forced to leave the Admiralty. Clementine said it would break her husband's heart if the Dardanelles enterprise were now abandoned. One of the reasons that Winston welcomed Arthur Balfour as incoming First Lord of the Admiralty was that he thought Balfour would carry it through.

As for Balfour (her mother's lover), whom Lady Cynthia met later that day, at dinner, he spoke admiringly of Winston, enumerated his marvellous gifts, but said he thought that on account of these he was 'predestined' to failure and vast ambition. Fisher he regarded as mad, though he praised his powers of organisation. Apparently Fisher had threatened to 'break' everyone at the Admiralty. Balfour had met with Jellicoe, learned of the torpedoing of another ship in the Dardanelles, and learned more of the Zeppelin menace (Balfour believed the Admiralty had made a great mistake in not taking up Zeppelins). All in all, Lady Cynthia had had a remarkable day, seeing both First Lords or, as she put it, 'Dash and Sagacity', in obvious reference to Churchill and Balfour. Winston had told Lady Cynthia that Balfour would be much liked by the sailors. 'He is a great luxury,' he added in reference to Balfour, and this she thought a rather nice description.[99]

Before exiting the Admiralty, Churchill, with foresight, took time and care to see that Balfour was well versed on the functioning of Room 40. He explained who worked there and why and, above all, pressed upon his successor the pre-eminence of naval intelligence in waging the war at sea. He also personally spoke to all heads of departments. One of them was the Chief Naval Censor, Rear-Admiral Douglas Brownrigg, who admired Churchill's knowledge, energy, and pluck. He was moved by Churchill's departing message to him. After Churchill had left, Brownrigg returned to his room and wrote down what Churchill had said to him:

> I want to thank you for all you have done for me. I have been surprised, as we did not, I think, like one another at the start; but I have been immensely struck by the way you have done your work, which has been extraordinarily difficult. You have displayed extraordinary tact, shrewdness, and a wide judgement and a broad outlook, and I want to thank you for the wonderfully loyal way you have protected my interests and those of the Service.

To this Brownrigg replied, 'I suppose you will get some other job soon.' Churchill answered, 'Oh yes! I shall turn up again shortly, I expect.'[100]

Asquith gave Churchill the sinecure post of Chancellor of the Duchy of Lancaster, which held minor Cabinet rank but carried no ministerial power. His fall was precipitate and bore a note of finality. He had been sacrificed to national unity and was out of military management. His pay was cut in two and he had to vacate Admiralty House. As their own house was rented out to Sir Edward Grey, Winston and Clementine were offered a house owned by Ivor Guest. Mary Soames wrote of this turn of events: 'These were hard, bleak days for both of them. The sting of public obloquy was added to their feelings of humiliation, and sense of personal betrayal ... As weeks went by, their feelings of bitterness grew towards those who, in their eyes, had betrayed Winston, and above all the "plan" at the moment of greatest trial.'[101]

With no ministerial responsibilities Churchill found plenty of time to brood. He cut a sorry figure. His private secretary, Eddie Marsh, observing Winston close at hand, wrote: 'I am miserably sorry for Winston. You can imagine what a horrible wound and mutilation it is for him to be torn away from his work there – it's like Beethoven deaf ... However he has recovered his serenity since the moment he was convinced it was irrevocable and he has now set his face to the future with his own courage.'[102] People close to Winston said that without Clementine's support he might have gone mad.[103]

For his part, in the days after the establishment of the coalition government, Fisher remained puzzled as to why events had played out as they had. He thought long and hard about what had transpired. The whole seemed strangely unbalanced, even to a man who was himself guilty of instability, alarms, and deviousness. As he told C F G Masterman: 'Kitchener, who can't get a thing right, gets the Order of the Garter, and I get the order of the boot.'[104] To Pamela McKenna, though, Fisher realised that he had fallen by overplaying his hand:

For myself I have been outmanoeuvred! On Monday, May 17, when the Prime Minister wrote me a secret letter that he was going to reconstruct the Government and so inferred that Winston would not be in the Cabinet, I was in the ascendant, and had I left it all there I should presumably have prospered, but in the innocence of my heart I wrote out conditions that in my view made for success in the conduct of the war, and the abolition of the submarine menace ... up to 2 p.m. on Saturday, May 22, the Prime Minister did not give me any idea of his hostility thereto and approved of my coming to Scotland, but the same afternoon he sent a curt dismissal, so I rather suppose something sudden occurred or he would have made some remark as to my leaving for Scotland.[105]

Reginald Tyrwhitt, observing these developments from his command based at Harwich, wrote to Roger Keyes on the change of command:

Towards the end, before the 'debacle', J.F. became impossible ... I am certain that the first 3 months [back at the Admiralty] sapped his brain & it is a d— d good job he has gone.

I am very sorry Winston has gone. I am sure you are of the same opinion. He was always charming to me & I believe in him. He was absolutely fearless & if he had any faults they were his unfortunate journalistic characteristics which kept popping out. Of course he's made mistakes but tell me who hasn't during the war. I saw a good deal of him & I have no hesitation in saying I hope I shall see him again in office & it is quite possible ... I don't know Balfour and have no right to make comparisons but Winston undoubtedly knew all about the Navy & more than many people in high places in the Navy ... No one can take up the strings in five minutes. You can see the difference at the Adty now on the people's faces. There is a look of content & self-satisfaction at having weathered the storm, in place of the hunted round the corner expression. Jackson has taken hold & is I am certain going to be the *find* of the War. You mark my words.[106]

Not everyone was critical of Fisher's second tenure at the Admiralty. Percy Scott, ever loyal, credited Fisher's brief stay for starting the process of reorganising a stagnant and lumbering administration into an efficient war machine, which was finished while Jellicoe was First Sea Lord.[107] James Masterton-Smith, private secretary to successive First Lords of the Admiralty, wrote to Fisher in 1919 of these tumultuous days. He argued that 15 May 1915, the day of Jacky's exit, was Germany's best day of the war. Of Fisher's partnership with Churchill he wrote, 'Together you were invincible and would have gone from triumph to triumph.' But, he wrote, the gods foredoomed the Dardanelles to failure: 'Nothing went right with it, and with it fell the only combination (i.e. yourself and Winston) that could have finished the war with as complete a victory in a third of the time and a fiftieth of the cost, in blood as well as treasure.'[108] Fisher approached the Dardanelles as a naval campaign; Churchill saw it as a political campaign, having confident assurance that Greece would join the Allies and aid in the attack. The Greek government fell, however, and the Dardanelles became a disaster. A G Gardiner, editor of the *Daily News*, wrote at the time of the inevitability of the titans falling out:

Perhaps it ought to have been apparent from the beginning that the Admiralty could not accommodate two such masterful personalities as Mr. Churchill and Lord Fisher. Neither of them has the gift of subordinating himself, and though in time of peace it might be possible for them to observe the true limits of their authority, there was little likelihood of that being the case in time of war, when the political and strategic motives were inevitably complicated.'

Gardiner saw Fisher's exit as a victory scored by Churchill, for Fisher could not obtain Asquith's concurrence that Churchill must go if he, the admiral, were to remain as First Sea Lord. 'It was an unhappy close to the most remarkable naval career since Nelson fell at Trafalgar. But the work Lord Fisher had done remained, and though the instrument on which the security of the country depended had passed out of his hand, it was still the instrument of his creation.'[109] This assessment rings true down through the years.

Amidst all this frenetic activity and turmoil in Whitehall, the war continued to rage out on the seas and margins, guarding seaborne trade against U-boats and torpedo craft, checking for movements of the High Seas Fleet, hunting enemy cruisers, and, not least, continuing with attempts to penetrate the Dardanelles and win the prize of Constantinople with all its benefits, real and imagined. When, by 25 May, news reached British and Australian officers at Mudros that, for certain, Fisher and Churchill had actually gone from the Admiralty, 'it was by no means unpleasing,' as Admiral Rosslyn Wemyss put it in understatement. He added, 'We must now pray that some sympathy and common sense may be brought to bear on our matters out here.'[110] And again, 'Churchill's name will be handed down to posterity as that of a man who undertook an operation of whose requirements he was entirely ignorant. Of Fisher, I will not speak.'[111]

Churchill's fall from power at the Admiralty brought forth much criticism of the man and his methods. Vice-Admiral the Honourable Sir Stanley Colville, a past naval ADC to Edward VII, wrote to George V that Churchill 'was, we all consider, a danger to the Empire', and Jellicoe commented that he had for long 'thoroughly distrusted Mr Churchill because he consistently arrogated to himself technical knowledge which, with all his brilliant qualities, I knew he did not possess.'[112] His old colleague Lloyd George commented to his principal secretary, Albert Sylvester, that Churchill was 'lacking in judgement' and 'is no leader, of course he is not. I know him so well. It is true he is an excellent speaker, but this is not everything. Look at the Dardanelles.'[113] Lloyd George did nothing to save Churchill at the fatal hour; indeed, no Cabinet colleague came to rescue him.

During the days of the May crisis, as it became obvious that Churchill was to lose his post, Kitchener spoke to him reassuringly: 'Well, there is one thing at any rate they cannot take from you. The Fleet was ready.'[114] On the day of his departure from the Admiralty, Kitchener was one of only two persons who came to pay their respects. Churchill never forgot that kindness. Kitchener also was the only man to bring consolation to Haldane, who was excluded from the coalition altogether. Asquith and Grey professed close friendship to Haldane but let him fall from grace without sympathy or regret.[115]

Asquith kept an eye out for Churchill, and when Balfour appeared as the likely successor as First Lord, room was made for Churchill as Chancellor of the Duchy of Lancaster through the intervention of Balfour himself. Thus was

Churchill given some reassurance as to his capabilities, but there too he could not damage the war effort, as the Conservatives feared might be the case had he retained a Cabinet post. The ambitious man in a hurry was now stalled by political events over which he had no influence. This curious state of affairs was anathema to such an active and imaginative leader who liked to keep his hand on the tiller and direct the course of the war. Asquith could have cast him aside, but instead he gave Churchill a new, if partial, lease on life, and the Liberals faced a future without Churchill's vast knowledge of military and strategic affairs. Students of history will continue to discuss the events of May 1915 as a classic fight over civil/military powers of command, arguing the merits of either side in the battle of Churchill versus Fisher. The more fundamental development was the loss of initiative at the Admiralty, for with the titans went the loss of political influence in the War Cabinet. The Dardanelles campaign was now doomed to failure, for Ottoman defences were found to be impenetrable, the disaster of 18 March was not to be repeated on account of attendant risk, and zeal was lacking at the War Office and in command at Gallipoli.

Titans in the wilderness

Like whales washed ashore, Fisher and Churchill found themselves in circumstances not of their own choosing. Fisher had, by his exit, removed himself from the board. And Fisher's actions had made Churchill redundant. Used to being in demand, exhibiting their own autocratic powers, making appointments if and when they chose, they were now in situations where all they could do was read the papers, await any letters and telegrams that came their way, and press on others their points of view, usually to no effect. They were marginal men. Their fall from power had been rapid and complete. The effect on their psyches and senses of well-being must have been traumatic. Under stress they had rocked Whitehall, Parliament, and the press. But their power and magic, in strange combination, had been such that some wondered if they might stage a return or, in fact, be brought back into power by a government reeling under constant difficulties and failures on land and at sea. It is hard to exclude insight and genius from power, especially when so much popularity stood behind them, and this is the reason that for some considerable time the names of Fisher and Churchill remained on many influential lips.

On 22 May Fisher left for Scotland, specifically to Dungavel, near Strathaven, Lanarkshire. There he was happily – 'out of reach of interviews and snapshooters!' – guest of the 13th Duke and Duchess of Hamilton. The Duke, an invalid and the premier peer of Scotland, was a dear old friend and shipmate. The Duchess, Nina, the tall and smiling mother of four sons and three daughters, was a lively conversationalist, an animal rights activist. She possessed an improving instinct backed by evangelical purpose. She adored

Jacky; this was reciprocated. Fisher's strength of purpose and courage attracted her, and as soon as he arrived at the nearby train station she took it upon herself to campaign for his rehabilitation. Nina drew a comparison to Nelson's great love, Emma, Lady Hamilton. Like Emma, the Duchess was a woman of passionate vitality. Emma, remarked Fisher, was 'one mass of sympathy', and Nina had a warm heart and brought abundant sympathy and understanding, and perhaps even a touch of flattery, at a critical hour.

Fisher had gone to Scotland to rest after the strain and excitement of the recent crisis. He got more than fresh air and country views by becoming essentially a partner in the Hamilton estates. The Duke amiably gave him a new assignment, appointing him a trustee of his estates. Nina became his lover. In effect, Jacky was brought within the family. He had full access to the Hamilton residence in St James's Square and a country house, Ferne, near Salisbury. Lady Fisher, so dignified and so sympathetic to her husband, was deeply hurt by Jacky's defection to the Hamiltons, and the matter sorely bothered Jacky. All the same, the new arrangement was permanent. Fisher sent many a letter to the long-suffering Kitty, but only at her death was there reconciliation. Nina, Duchess of Hamilton, became the new woman behind the Fleet, and a powerful one at that. She toiled relentlessly in Fisher's interests and for his return to the Admiralty. Jacky's friends always looked after him.

As an aside, in his *In Search of Churchill*, Martin Gilbert tells how in 1964 Winston's son Randolph Churchill, then writing his father's biography, sent Gilbert to the 14th Duke's castle, Lennoxlove, Scotland, to rummage among the Fisher papers there. Hundreds of letters from Churchill to Fisher awaited him – 'history's gold'. But a notable detail of this story is that while driving up the approach to Lennoxlove, the Duke stopped his Rolls Royce and began to explain how Fisher's papers had ended up in the muniment room of the castellated tower. In Gilbert's words, 'Fisher, it seems, had lived for many years with the Duchess of Hamilton, the duke's mother. She had been his love and his confidante. When Fisher died, all his letters had gone to her. She had guarded them as tenaciously as she had guarded his memory ... What the duke was leading up to, as we sat in his car, was this: some people believed that he, the duke, was not the son of the 13th Duke of Hamilton, but of Fisher.' All the Duke asked was that if the Fisher papers revealed this to be the case, that he be the first to know. Gilbert consented, but found no such evidence.[116] The most moving letters he did find were those written to Fisher 'demanding, urging and pleading' him to return to the Admiralty and see the Dardanelles through. Randolph was furious that it took Gilbert so long to find the essentials, but that was Randolph's intemperate style, and young Gilbert survived the chastisement. He went on to write the third (and monumental) volume of the official biography, all about the Dardanelles. Gilbert concluded that it was

Fisher's energy that most attracted Churchill to him and led him to bring Fisher back to the Admiralty. 'But as the enterprise faltered, Fisher bolted – literally – leaving the Admiralty building for an unknown destination, and alerting the Conservative opposition leaders to the fact that he had gone, that a crisis had arisen which they could exploit.'[117]

As a man of action, Fisher was bound to have second thoughts. Gradually he came to repent his hasty letter to Asquith. Although the Dardanelles campaign, to which he was now opposed, continued on, though not solely 'by ships alone', his resignation had 'stopped the wastage' of the Navy, its ships, and men. His biographer Reginald Bacon says Jacky 'came to see that he might have approached the Prime Minister in a more diplomatic manner and have attained the same end without rupture.'[118] This is a misreading of the events, for the circumstances had led Fisher to his irrevocable decision not to remain at the Admiralty as long as Churchill remained. 'I am absolutely unable to remain with W.C. (HE'S A REAL DANGER!).'[119] At the time Fisher made his ultimate and final resignation, Churchill was firmly in place. However, when Fisher went, so, too, did Churchill, for the Unionists would not allow him to remain, and Fisher's action, as explained, was the Unionists' opportunity. Fisher now found himself in the wilderness, and he hardened in his ways. He fumed from the sidelines and soured in his scepticism. The glowing days of his partnership with Churchill were over, or so he thought. He had brought down the last Liberal government in British history and in doing so had been brought down himself. He yearned to return to power, and he did have strong press backers. Many supporters of Lloyd George believed that Fisher was the man to win the war in a flourish, so they encouraged his restoration. Fisher claimed to be the only man who knew a quick way of winning the war, and some of the shrewdest minds among his contemporaries believed him.[120] These were delusions.

Upon his exit from the Admiralty to the sinecure of Chancellor of the Duchy of Lancaster, Churchill felt acutely the loss of departmental responsibility for the war effort. He was now an outsider, a spectator to events beyond his influence or voice. A war correspondent meeting Churchill at this time remarked how changed he was, looking years older, with a pale face, and much depressed by his loss of the Admiralty.[121] Winston invariably put the best face on his situation. Any explanations given to friends masked the pain,[122] as he recalled in a magazine in the 1920s:

> When I left the Admiralty at the end of May 1915 I still remained a member of the Cabinet and of the War Council. In this position I knew everything and could do nothing. The change from the intense executive activities of each day's work at the Admiralty to the narrowly measured duties of a counsellor left me gasping. Like a sea-beast fished up from the depths, or a

diver too suddenly hoisted, my veins threatened to burst from the fall in pressure. I had great anxiety and no means of relieving it; I had vehement convictions and small power to give effect to them. I had to watch the unhappy casting-away of great opportunities, and the feeble execution of plans which I had launched and in which I heartily believed. I had long hours of utterly unwonted leisure in which to contemplate the frightful unfolding of the War.[123]

For almost half a year, until he realised that political affairs were moving towards disaster for the Liberals, and the coalition government held no promise, Churchill was out of tune and out of favour. His political friends, few in number, could not help. Perhaps never in his active life was there such a period of enforced indolence for this active and creative agent of history.

As best he could, Churchill watched Fisher's progress while both were in the wilderness. On 4 July Fisher – for political and professional reasons, and perhaps even to keep him publicly quiet – was appointed by Balfour to be chairman of the Board of Invention and Research. (Fisher's adventures in this assignment are told in Chapters 11 and 12). Churchill seethed with anger when he read about it in the newspapers. When he protested to Balfour, he was simply told that Asquith had approved the appointment. Churchill, turning his attention to the prime minister, laid bare his views and repeated the basic facts that Fisher was irresponsible and even disloyal:

Fisher resigned his office without warning or parley. He assigned no reason except inability to work with me. The only points of policy under discussion were of minor consequence, & all have been settled by the new Board as I had proposed. You ordered Fisher to return to his post in the name of the King. He paid no attention to yr order. You declared that he had deserted his post in time of war; & the facts are not open to any other construction.[124]

Further, Churchill was outraged that Fisher's apology to Asquith was accepted while no consultation with Churchill was offered, especially 'considering that it was Fisher's unreasonable & extraordinary action that led you to remove me from the Admiralty in time of war, & thus to humiliate me before the whole world.'[125] Behind all this was Churchill's fear that Fisher might become First Lord of the Admiralty; this would block his own return to that coveted post. Churchill 'repeated his slander of Fisher's insanity'.[126] He made a further incautious representation to Balfour, his successor as First Lord of the Admiralty. This brought a riposte from Fisher: 'Winston has remonstrated with A.J.B. at my getting this appointment without Winston having first been consulted!!! A.J.B. replied that he didn't see what concern it was of Winston's!'[127]

Churchill was not alone in watching events. Roger Keyes probably spoke for many naval officers when he wrote: 'I see that J.F. is worming himself back as president of a Committee, he will scheme to get power again. I trust he won't succeed.'[128] Blinker Hall was rather put out and saw larger issues than just Fisher's possible restoration to the Admiralty: 'Behind the scenes at home, I think there is a powerful cabal at work against the Govt. – Northcliffe, Fisher & Co. – and it is strenuous work following up their machinations – some of these old men will not die.'[129]

In fact, Churchill was being shut out of decision-making. He hated inaction. All his life had been at the sharp end of war, participating in it or reporting on it. He had treated the political world as one of combative requirement. He was now without party – the Liberals could not include him; the Unionists would not have him. Like his father he suffered the swings of mood, the emotional ups and downs. Medical matters continue to fascinate in regards to Churchill as they do for many other leaders under stress. Long has it been known that he suffered from a condition he called the Black Dog, referenced by him first in 1911. Churchill was never diagnosed for manic depression (now termed bipolar disorder). But it may account for the mood swings that others observed. I have it on the authority of Dr John Mather, who has studied this matter closely, that Churchill had a mild form of bipolar disorder (bipolar Type II, in which the 'high' moods do not reach the full-blown mania of Type I).[130] Others have different opinions. Mary Soames, Churchill's daughter, wrote that depression had 'been his companion too often in earlier years for him not to know the power of such feelings. But for him the security and loving companionship of marriage had banished "Black Dog" to his kennel.' His writing and painting, she added, were 'sovereign antibodies to the depressive element in his nature.'[131] Sir Martin Gilbert makes the important point that too much emphasis has been put on Churchill's depression: 'Churchill's exceptional resilience was a far more dominant feature of his character than his occasional downheartedness.'[132]

A close observer of Churchill's mood swings at the time of his fall from power was Max Aitken, already mentioned as a confidant and watcher of events as the Admiralty crisis proceeded. We pick up his assessment on the day Churchill was 'suddenly thrown from power into impotence':

What a creature of strange moods he is – always at the top of the wheel of confidence or at the bottom of an intense depression.

Looking back on that long night we spent in the big silent Admiralty room till day broke, I cannot help reflecting on that extreme duality of mind which marks Churchill above all other men – the charm, the imaginative sympathy of his hours of defeat, the self-confidence, the arrogance of his hours of powers and prosperity. That night he was a lost soul, yet full of flashes of wit and humour.

But all those days of our acquaintance were his bad times, and then one could not resist the charm of his companionship or withhold from him the tribute of sympathy.

That Tuesday night he was clinging to the desire of retaining the Admiralty as though the salvation of England depended on it. I believe he would even have made it up with Lord Fisher if that had been the price of remaining there. None the less, so little did he realise the inwardness of the whole situation that he still hoped.[133]

Aitken does not speak of depression or melancholia, only the internal complexities of highs and lows that formed Churchill's emotional character. All the same, it is certain that depression was the direct result of the loss of the Admiralty, that great political prize that he had acquired by his own abilities and Asquith's assistance in 1911. Now that old world had crumbled irrevocably. Churchill was a casualty of war – the war at the top. In larger measure he is a good example of leadership under stress, and after he left the Admiralty, the Black Dog, or some other melancholia, overtook him. Clementine had never seen him so down, and she worried about him continually. His family proved an immense support at this time. At the happy suggestion of his sister-in-law Gwendeline ('Goonie'), he took up painting, a marvellous release from persistent anxieties. He rose quickly to prominence as an oil painter. Some of his first scenes on canvas were of a field of battle, the scarred Belgium landscape near Ploegstreert ('Plugstreet').

'He came, he saw, he capitulated'

Within days of Fisher's final exit from the Admiralty, three U-boats, including *U-21*, made their sinister appearance in the eastern Mediterranean. In mid-May Room 40 determined their appearance and kept Churchill informed of their movements. This was alarming news, for the leading brigades of the new army corps were to arrive toward the end of May, and the safety of the army depended on covering fire from the ships.[134] Indeed, *U-21* sank the battleships *Triumph* (on 26 May) and *Majestic* (27 May), two more British naval fatalities in men and materiel. Other ships were constantly under fire from shore-based guns and were being damaged, which necessitated a passage to Malta for repairs. While eight or ten of the destroyers on station were used as escorts for transports from Gibraltar, the bulk of the Fleet withdrew to safer locations, where they stayed between necessary sorties.

Meanwhile, the Navy was on the hunt for oil tankers and for the German U-boat havens and refuelling bases – the German emperor's villa at Corfu was targeted as one possible site. Secret agents were arranged to operate in neutral territory, and money was immediately made available to retain them. The new worry was that Germany would shift her large submarines to the Mediterranean. If that happened, the consequences would be serious. Destroyers with good sea-keeping abilities would be needed to help minimise the mischief. Nets needed to be rigged at Mudros (the Greek town Moudros on the island of Lemnos, a major Allied base in the Aegean under the command of Admiral Rosslyn Wemyss) and elsewhere to guard against torpedoes. Fleet sweepers and trawlers were placed on steady watch and operations. The French, similarly, deployed cruisers, destroyers, and torpedo boats. The blockade against the Ottoman Empire was tightened, and every effort was made to stop sulphate (used in war materials) entering that country, and oil, horses, warlike stores, and foodstuffs leaving it. British consuls in the islands on the coast of Asia Minor organised a systematic lookout.

In July Asquith considered sending Churchill out to consult with General Sir Ian Hamilton and Admiral de Robeck on behalf of the Cabinet. Kitchener had suggested that Churchill pay the official visit, and Asquith and Balfour had given approval. Churchill was jubilant at the prospect, but once again politics played a fateful hand. Roger Keyes, then in a close working relationship with de Robeck, objected. He sensed that Churchill intended to become 'Generalissimo', and to the complexities already at hand would be added the prospect of Churchill, along the lines of the Antwerp adventure, giving orders to commanders on the spot. Keyes made clear to his superiors that this should not be allowed and, given Churchill's disposition, others saw the same possibility. When they learned of it, the Conservative members of Cabinet vetoed the plan.[135] Churchill was to be kept out of military affairs.

Though on the margins of power, Churchill stood firm on his policy for the Dardanelles. For the moment he acquired powerful reinforcement from the Conservatives, who, strong on imperial influence abroad, held British prestige in the East dear to their hearts. How did this bear on the Gallipoli campaign? 'The idea of British soldiers retiring before Turks was odious to all,' states Beaverbrook. Lord Curzon, Arthur Balfour, Lord Birkenhead, and Lord Lansdowne were all with Churchill in backing the Dardanelles/Gallipoli campaign. They soon came to be regarded as the 'diehards'. Bonar Law, their parliamentary leader, held other views. Perhaps tired of the indifference given to his opinions – Asquith treated him with condescending superiority[136] – Bonar Law, employing powerful logic, began to champion evacuation. He could foresee 'German munitions and officers pouring into Constantinople, and that our men on the shell-swept sea-coast would be in the gravest danger if they were not removed promptly, and a term put to the enterprise which had obviously failed.'[137] His view was that the British should avoid disaster, wind up the campaign, and withdraw. He did not yet command the day but he moved with relentless determination.

There were two more inconclusive battles in June and July, and then General Hamilton planned a new offensive, to begin in early August with a landing at Suvla Bay. Motor lighters, which could hold 500 men or 150 tons of cargo, were used for these landings. Use of these vessels was the idea of Fisher, who had initially intended them to be used as part of his Baltic scheme. Hamilton's request to use them during the April landings had been denied.[138] Fighting continued through much of August, but eventually deteriorated into a stalemate.

Meanwhile, Admiral Weymss and Commodore Keyes made plans for a renewed naval assault to pass through the Dardanelles with old battleships designated for the purpose, a scheme that had a good chance of success. On the Gallipoli peninsula there were Allied gains against strong Ottoman resistance. Had the British pressed on, success might have been attained. But the political circumstances at home and the difficulties in the field combined to suggest that this was a campaign without a satisfactory conclusion in sight. The War Office was indifferent and inclining toward evacuation, and Bonar Law never tired of promoting the idea of winding up the campaign.

In mid-October Sir Ian Hamilton was recalled and Lieutenant General Sir Charles Monro, a 'Westerner', who viewed the Dardanelles campaign as an unnecessary distraction from the key campaign on the Western Front, was sent out to replace him. At dawn on 22 October Churchill was at the train station to see Monro's party off. He threw a bundle of papers into the general's compartment and declared, 'Remember that a withdrawal from Gallipoli would be as great a disaster as Corunna' – a reference to the British army's misfortunes in the Peninsular War in 1809. Once out in the eastern Mediterranean, Monro worked with surgical precision, for he knew in advance what he would recommend: he telegraphed home urging quick evacuation – 'He came, he saw, he capitulated,' wrote Churchill in *The World Crisis*.[139] By this time the Dardanelles had claimed a savage toll: the Allies had lost 46,000 troops, including 8,700 Australians and 2,700 New Zealanders.

Kitchener refused to sign any evacuation orders on grounds that a military disaster might ensue. The government prevaricated, and in the end Kitchener was sent out as an impartial commissioner to report further to Cabinet. The messages passed back and forth between Kitchener and London. Further discussions on the spot could not quell his anxieties. When he got to Cairo, the immensity of defending Egypt was brought home to him, for the officers that he talked to were not interested in a campaign against the Ottomans. 'I thought you were here to protect the Canal,' he chided, 'It seems to me that the Canal is protecting you.'[140] In the circumstances, Kitchener could do nothing but recommend retirement from Gallipoli, leaving the Dardanelles adventure to wind down. The evacuation was completed in December and January and was a brilliant affair.

Upon this last and final act, Fisher was bitter: 'So there you are! ... Those d—d Dardanelles have been evacuated at last! They d—d me! And I remain d—d!!!'[141] Of the evacuation from Gallipoli, Churchill confided to Sir Roger Keyes's wife: 'I cd. not have influenced this tragic event. I was *sure* it was no use my staying [a reference to Churchill's resignation from the Duchy of Lancaster in November 1915]. We have fallen among thieves. But Roger [Keyes] has nothing to regret ... Nothing now remains but to punish the guilty: & for that the time is not yet come.'[142]

The blame game had begun. In the aftermath, Keyes, the key staff officer in the Dardanelles campaign, blamed de Robeck and argued that Churchill would be right to never forgive de Robeck and skewer him after the war.[143] Keyes also exhibited great wisdom when he looked back at Fisher's departure from the Admiralty and the concomitant destruction of Churchill. Keyes carried the arguments even further by blaming Fisher's resignation for the loss of Churchill's drive to see the Dardanelles campaign through.[144] Put differently, the voluntary departure of Fisher left Churchill totally and irreparably isolated, and thereby dragged Churchill into the political wilderness, taking the steam out of the Dardanelles enterprise. Churchill had a broader vision of the failure: 'Not to persevere. That was the crime.'[145]

These were months of great despair, the war going everywhere wrong, with few if any victories for the Allies. Walter Page, the American ambassador in London, believed a turn of the military tide would soon vanquish the English depression. The English, he observed, retained a sense of humour even in these darkest days. Right now John Bull was 'rather pathetic,' he said, 'depressed as he has not been depressed for at least a hundred years. The nobility and the common man are doing their whole duty, dying on the Bosporus or in France without a murmur.' The British leadership, meanwhile, was ageing rapidly on account of the burden of war. Although, the ambassador reported to President Woodrow Wilson of the United States, Lady Jellicoe had gone to Scotland to be with her husband, the admiral. She thought that she would find an old man in charge of the Fleet. Instead, she returned to London jubilant, reporting to Mrs Page, in a rhapsodic way and with evident surprise, that her husband did not seem older. 'The weight of this thing [the war],' Page concluded, 'is so prodigious ...'[146]

The Dardanelles provided lessons for the future and helped lay the groundwork for the establishment of amphibious doctrine: 'Everything is good for something – if only to serve as a horrible example,' writes one historian of naval intelligence.[147] W D Puleston, a captain in the United States Navy and the author of a 1926 examination of the Dardanelles campaign and the things to be learned from its failure, concluded by damning Churchill:

A larger actor in the drama was only temporarily punished, and is once more entrenched in public place. The official Australian history makes the following apt comment on the genesis of the expedition: 'So through Churchill's excess of imagination, a layman's ignorance of artillery, and the fatal power of a young enthusiasm to convince older and slower brains the tragedy of Gallipoli was born.' ... In peacetime the British form of government is delightful; it offers personal liberty and security of property and person, with a minimum of inconvenience to the individual; in wartime with civilian ministers unwilling to be advised, it imperils the existence of the nation and empire. It is doubtful if even Great Britain could survive another World War and another Churchill.[148]

Similarly, even though historian Paul Addison explains that Churchill's responsibilities at the Dardanelles did not extend beyond 18 March and the naval attack of that date (thereafter it was an Army affair, particularly the land campaign that began on 25 April), Addison judges Churchill's responsibility in the affair with this appraisal: 'Churchill's own egotism and impetuosity were factors in his downfall. He was over-confident of success, trumpeting victory in advance and passionately supporting the operation long after most people had written it off. Gallipoli was a cross to which he nailed himself.'[149]

Years after the terrible events of May 1915, Clementine Churchill remembered the pain she had shared with Winston as the Dardanelles drama unfolded. 'I thought he would die of grief,' she told Martin Gilbert, Churchill's biographer, half a century later.[150] Churchill was made the scapegoat of the Dardanelles. Yet it was Kitchener who had pressed for the naval action and Asquith who authorised it. Fisher had blown hot and cold, but at the outset he had concealed his reservations and then expressed great enthusiasm (which he later regretted).

'So closed the Gallipoli episode,' concluded Beaverbrook in his *Politicians and the War*, the book Churchill regarded as the best documentary on the war behind the war. It was, noted Beaverbrook, 'a strange picture of blood and mismanagement, glory and failure.'[151]

The source of the problem lay in London. Admiral Wester Wemyss, who had spent most of the adventure at Mudros, on the island of Lemnos, in observations of the military and naval attempts to force the Dardanelles and control the Gallipoli peninsula, concluded solemnly, 'For ten months were the Allies battering at the outer gate of Constantinople in the well-grounded hope of bringing hostilities to an early conclusion, a hope destined to be shattered, not by the fault of the men on the spot but by the action of those in whose hands lay the conduct of the war.' Deeds of heroism and sacrifice were not in the official documents and chronicles.[152]

Major-General Sir Charles Callwell, who wrote one of the first histories of the Dardanelles, stated in private correspondence that Sir Ian Hamilton and the army were starved logistically and insufficiently supplied to carry the attack to success. The supply arrangements were appalling. As to the affair in the aggregate, he put it this way: 'The whole business was a hideous blunder, for which we have to thank Mr Churchill, although Mr Asquith and Lord Kitchener acquiesced.'[153]

11

Say 'Resurgam'!

Major Churchill, the Queen's Own Oxfordshire Hussars

One man did not wait for the public news of the evacuation from Gallipoli. As the Dardanelles campaign dragged on without success and with high casualties, Churchill continued to defend the project. All the same, it was now clear to him that the game was up. On 18 November he made his resignation speech to the House of Commons, ended his tenure at the Duchy of Lancaster, and retired to the command of a battalion in the trenches of the Western Front.[1]

At this stage of our saga, Churchill was standing on the edge of time, as a literary scribe would say. The higher war direction was categorically closed to him. As mentioned, a consultative role in the Dardanelles was also withdrawn. Then came another, little-known, possibility that derived from the first major conference on Allied strategy, held at Calais in early July 1915. This was a vital step toward an Allied Supreme Command. Among other decisions, it resolved to establish direct maritime and land connections to Russia in order to improve communication and distribution of supplies. The Russian armies were taking the highest casualties of any army in the Great War, and disaffection and despair were spreading in military and civilian life. In London, Hankey proposed to Asquith that Churchill be sent to Russia in order 'to buck up communications of Archangel and Vladivostok for importation of arms and ammunition.' Churchill might have been effective in energising the Russians, but this was not to be. Asquith was reluctant to employ him, and other measures were taken to facilitate support for Russia, including Canadian icebreakers and a new sledge route from near North Cape south to the Gulf of Bothnia.[2]

The House of Commons offered no theatre for Churchill's advancement or defence. 'What about the Dardanelles?' was the taunt constantly thrown at him. The restless thundering of the press was incessant. His political credit had run out. He was the bugbear of the Liberals and the outcast of the Tories. No one wanted to listen to him except his wife and some close friends. Asquith, preoccupied with survival, could offer no prospects. Bonar Law stood adamantly in opposition. Only Lloyd George offered any sort of political hope for the future. Churchill's allies were Kitchener and Balfour, though neither would champion his cause. The war to date had consumed him. Antwerp's fall, loss of capital ships and cruisers, and the rising U-boat menace had happened on Winston's watch at the Admiralty. Zeppelin raids continued. The German High Seas Fleet remained the daily threat. Only soldiering could hold any future, or at least a respite. The Western Front offered the only option.

On the outbreak of war Churchill had hinted at taking a field command. When his brother, Jack, was about to depart for the front, he told him: 'As soon as the decisive battle has been fought at sea – I shall try to come out [to the Front] too, if there is any use for me.'[3] That gesture now was taking on real strength. Churchill's loss of the Admiralty and his exclusion from the Cabinet, putting him on the margins of war direction, had created for him an impossible situation. He could not stay, so he decided it was time to rejoin his old regiment.

Churchill set about preparing his final words to Parliament before his departure for the Front. On 15 November, as the Gallipoli campaign passed through another agonising week, he took this last opportunity in the House of Commons to speak on the Dardanelles campaign. He defended the decision and the campaign, naval and military. He also defended his decision to bring back Jacky. He did not regret having brought Fisher back to the Admiralty a year earlier: Fisher's 'impulse and enthusiasm' had been very welcome in the early phases of the war at sea. As he told the House, he did not wish to discuss the resignation of Fisher six months earlier, in May 1915. Even so, he could not help but make certain pointed remarks about the situation of that previous January when the fateful decision had been made. Certain facts gnawed at him. It was time to bring these into the open. Fisher, he noted, had attended the critically important War Council of 13 January, when the proposed Dardanelles operation was first discussed. Churchill stated that on that occasion 'no expert advisor indicated any dissent', a comment undoubtedly aimed at Fisher. He referred to Fisher's cautionary memorandum of 25 January, but argued that it was not directed against the intended Dardanelles operations, but rather against the depletion of the naval margin of safety in the North Sea. He argued that, though Fisher may have had some doubts, 'on the special technical and professional points involved I received from him at no time any expression of adverse criticism.' In subsequent discussion with the prime minister and Fisher on 28 January, and at War Council of the same day, also attended by Fisher, 'the impression I derived was that Lord Fisher agreed and consented to a purely naval attack on the Dardanelles being made.' Churchill, we read between the lines, had been clearly stung by the actions of his formerly close colleague, Fisher. Their falling out over the Dardanelles operation was, at that point, apparent to all. 'I am not going to embark upon any reproaches this afternoon, but I must say I did not receive from the First Sea Lord either the clear guidance before the event or the firm support after which I was entitled to expect.'[4] This telling comment rings down through the years.

At the time, Fisher thought Churchill's attack in the House of Commons 'malignant'. His initial instinct was to keep silent. It was better, he reasoned, to make no utterance against Churchill's remarks and weighty charges. His loyal secretary Captain T E Crease, and possibly others, thought otherwise. They convinced him to make a brief statement. In the House of Lords next day Fisher gave his measured response:

> I ask leave of your Lordships to make a statement. Certain references were made to me in a speech delivered in the other House yesterday by Mr. Churchill. I have been sixty-one years in the service of my country, and I leave my record in the hands of my countrymen. The Prime Minister said yesterday that Mr. Churchill had said one or two things which he had better not have said, and that he necessarily and naturally left unsaid some things which will have to be said. I am content to wait. It is unfitting to make personal explanations affecting national interests when my country is in the midst of a great war.

According to one journalist present, Fisher 'roared out his speech in a tremendous voice that Winston might have heard while he was receiving his present from the Armoured Car heroes [that is, a farewell gift from the Dunkirk and Antwerp military adventurers]. The peers were thunderstruck ... [and Fisher] with a broad grin on his wrinkled face and a wicked nod of tousled head, turned on his heel, and strode out, as who should say [sic] "Be damned to you all!"' He had no wish to debate or discuss the matter. He had said his piece. The same journalist also wrote that the effect of the speech was tremendous and received favourable reception.[5] Press comment was positive.

On 16 November a farewell lunch was held at the Churchill residence at 41 Cromwell Road, with Winston at his gayest and Clementine admirably calm and brave. However, as Violet Bonham Carter recorded, for most of the guests on that occasion the lunch was a kind of wake.[6] Next day the soldier-statesman supervised the packing of his kit, cigars, liquids, and camping gear. His mother, Jennie, was there, in despair, thinking as many a mother would of the misfortunes her son might face on the Western Front – and regretting his departure on the morrow. She urged Winston to be sensible in the trenches and 'not to play the fool'. 'Remember you are destined for greater things,' she said, 'I am a great believer in your star.'[7] Nothing could keep her from the view that he had been sacrificed to the ineptitude and jealousies of lesser creatures, and that Asquith had, in an act of disloyalty, cast him to the wolves. She knew history would judge Asquith's incompetence.

Thus it was that Major Churchill, the Queen's Own Oxfordshire Hussars, set out to join his yeomanry regiment in France, reporting for full-time military duties as a Territorial Force officer. He wrote later, 'Ministers who resign are always censured; those who cannot explain their reasons are invariably condemned. I crossed the Channel on a leave-boat, studying the varied throng in which were men of every regiment in the Army, going back to the trenches, just as they had come out of them – careless figures, haggard figures – a bustling, good-humoured throng of men.' On arrival at Boulogne, the port landing officer took him aside and told him that he had orders that Churchill was to go, by awaiting car, to see the Commander-in-Chief, Field Marshal Sir John French. A surprised Churchill, expecting lesser attention given his mere officer status, agreed. 'He treated me as if I were still First Lord of the Admiralty, and had come again to confer with him upon the future of the war.'

French's position was weakening daily: 'I am only riding at single anchor,' he told his friend, indicating he was no longer master of events. French gave up his command on 18 December. 'He would much rather have given up his life,' Churchill remarked. French was made 1st Earl of Ypres in 1922; he died three years later. Like Marlborough and Wellington, he had commanded a great British army on the Continent. He had saved the British Army after Mons but was accorded blame for the horrific losses at Neuve-Chapelle, Festubert, and Loos. He did not see eye to eye with Kitchener. 'When you get to the end of your luck,' wrote Churchill of himself when arriving in France on that leave-boat, 'there is a comfortable feeling you have got to the bottom.' Perhaps he was thinking of French's misfortunes, for his study of this 'great contemporary' is one of fascinating appreciation and abundant sympathy.[8] Both were on their way out of high command. French had talked about being at the edge of a precipice; Churchill doubtless felt similarly.

He was attached to the 2nd Grenadier Guards for training, then took command of the 6th Royal Scots Fusiliers. This was a battle-hardened battalion, part of the 9th (Scottish) Division. His brother, Jack, also on the Western Front, imagined Winston being holed up in some exposed dugout. In the regimental mess Churchill brightened proceedings, and his orders for champagne, brandy, and other stimulants never flagged.

From the field, Churchill kept up communications with former colleagues, especially Lloyd George. Westminster and Whitehall were always in his thoughts – and his return to politics was his overriding passion. For political reasons, naturally, much of his correspondence was with Conservatives and Unionists, most of whom were in touch with their old naval apostle Fisher. Churchill expressed hope for a return to power by virtue of the conscription crisis and the plotting to bring down Asquith, whom he regarded as a dead weight on British war fortunes. There was talk of a new Air Ministry, and

Churchill looked for opportunity there. He also hoped to return as First Lord or to succeed Lloyd George as Minister of Munitions. Major-General Edward Spears, the liaison officer to the French military administration, dined with Churchill in late December, after Churchill had made a brief visit to London. Spears wrote in his diary: 'He thinks there is going to be a political crisis on compulsion [that is, conscription, or the draft]. He saw Lloyd George who is going to try & smash the Government when either Bonar Law or LG [Lloyd George] wd be PM & Churchill get Munitions or Admiralty, the remaining one getting the WO [War Office].'[9] The lobbying for office, for power, took on a new guise, and Churchill's campaign for return was waged from battalion headquarters on the French-Belgian border amidst incoming shells from the great Krupp howitzers and others.

'The Board of Intrigue and Revenge'

Meanwhile, as mentioned in Chapter 10, Fisher was ensconced at the Admiralty Board of Invention and Research, soon to be known to his enemies and opponents as the Board of Intrigue and Revenge.

Having exited the Admiralty in mid-May 1915, Fisher spent a couple of weeks in quiet isolation at the Duke and Duchess of Hamilton's estate Dungavel in Lanarkshire, but all too soon he was regretting his hasty departure from Whitehall. He itched for action and eagerly looked for ways to contribute to the war effort – and to clear his name. In mid-June, Fisher wrote to tell the First Lord of the Admiralty, Arthur Balfour, that the powerful J L Garvin of the *Observer* had chided him for now doing nothing with respect to the war. Fisher had decided that he must place himself at Balfour's disposal to serve in any way thought fit. To sweeten the offer he even promised Balfour that he would behave himself and 'give advice *when asked* and ... be silent *when not asked*!'[10] The Dardanelles (and his connection with Churchill) and his intemperate resignation may have haunted him but he was a man of the present and ready for action.

Balfour responded to Fisher's letter with the deft assurance that was his style. Fisher's offer, he said, was just the sort of thing he expected from him. The difficulty presenting itself however, as Balfour put it, was that he was unsure what role Fisher could play: any job at the Admiralty would not be consistent with his stature, given that he had already twice been First Sea Lord.[11] In short, Balfour implied that Jacky was overqualified. But that was only a dodge. Balfour knew instinctively that Fisher wanted supreme power; any sort of secondary disposition was not in his character. He also knew that having Fisher at the Admiralty in any capacity would be difficult. Fisher would be a thorn in the flesh for Balfour – or, for that matter, any other First Lord. How to keep Fisher from meddling while employing him patriotically – or, if we take the view that the First Lord was devious, distracting him into some new line of work – was the trick. Balfour knew Fisher would embarrass the government if unemployed; besides, he was the most popular figure in the land.

At the same time, Balfour had been thinking about the current perplexing situation of the war and of British reverses at sea, particularly those involving submarines. Although among the first to proclaim the diabolical nature of the submarine, Fisher had scant knowledge of anti-submarine warfare measures (ASW). The best way to deal with an enemy submarine was to prevent it exiting its lair. Once at sea a submarine could operate by stealth. Destroyers were used to hunt and seek, and to drop depth charges and to fire mortar bombs, but not until the 'M'-class destroyer did the Navy have a fast (34-knot) sub hunter. Aerial detection of submarines by dirigibles, and particularly Curtiss flying boats, was in its infancy, though this became highly effective in 1918. Direction-finding – taking bearings on enemy ships by electronic means, using intersecting radio signals – aided the finding and tracking of submarines. Room 40 passed this vital information to the Operations Division, which in turn passed specifics to commanders afloat. The U-boat war advanced through various stages, but the Navy's purpose remained the same: to seek and strike. Finding a U-boat on the surface was comparatively easier than detecting an enemy submarine below the sea's surface. Indeed, the latter was a virtual impossibility until invention and implementation of electronic means of detection – first 'passive' detection by hydrophones and later (November 1918) 'active' detection by sound emission and reception (the welcome 'ping,' or echo, of received contacts) became operational. The technological innovation of this war was to find its full flourish in the next.

Given increased depredations by U-boats on Allied shipping, the Admiralty was prepared to consider any measure to locate, track, or evade the enemy's submarines. Suggestions, some bizarre, on how to counter the dreaded submarine poured in, and those believed worthy of investigation were passed to HMS *Vernon*, the torpedo establishment near Portsmouth, or to the National Physical Laboratory at Teddington, near Hampton Court. All sorts of agencies were involved, not least the War Committee of the Royal Society, the War Office Inventions Committee, the Ministry of Munitions, and Sir John French's Committee at the Headquarters of the British Expeditionary Force.[12] Secret research programmes examined the prospects of using seagulls and sea lions as decoys and bait, attracting much interest and merriment. But if dogs and pigeons could be trained for war work, why not seagulls and sea lions? Behaviour science and psychology were being brought in to counter the U-boat scourge.[13]

As the U-boat peril grew, leading scientists became critical of what they saw as a disregard of their expertise.[14] In *The Times* of 11 June 1915, just a week before Fisher's letter to Balfour, acclaimed science fiction writer H G Wells proclaimed the war a 'struggle of invention'; accordingly, in the circumstances, both sides 'must be perpetually producing new devices surprising and outwitting its opponents. Since the war began the German methods of fighting have changed time and time again ... On our side we have not so far produced any novelty at all except in the field of recruiting posters ... We have produced no effective counter stroke at all to the enemy's submarine, and no efficient protection against his improved torpedo.'[15] This call for science to come to the patriotic aid of the state coincided with Fisher's restless desire to return to the Admiralty. For his part, Balfour felt the pressure, as he had many scientific connections at Cambridge, where he had many personal and family contacts. He needed no convincing that the power Britain wielded in science could have advantages for the Navy.

The clever Balfour realised that he could manage these problems by harnessing Fisher's inherent enthusiasm and energy. The day after receiving the admiral's letter, Balfour suggested in a memorandum for the Board of Admiralty that what was needed was a Central Board that could sift through the incoming files of proposals of new or suggested inventions (including U-boat countermeasures) and then refer the worthwhile ones to the appropriate authority or laboratory.[16] Then he sent the following letter to Fisher dated 26 June:

> There *is* a position – though I am by no means sure that you would consent to take it – where your great powers of original thought, combined with your unique experience, would enable you to do great service to the Navy and the Country. Its character is explained in the accompanying Memorandum. If you could see your way to accepting the position of Chairman to the new Inventions Committee you would, I am convinced, be doing a great public service.[17]

Fisher replied with customary vigour and promptness, 'Your kind words leave me no option but to accept the position of Chairman of the Board you mention. I am ready to come any moment you tell me.'[18] Announcement of the appointment appeared in *The Times* of 5 July 1915.

After only forty days in the wilderness, Jacky made his return to Whitehall, with his office in 'Victory House' on Cockspur Street, near Trafalgar Square and just round the corner from the Admiralty. He was back in national service while Churchill was still unsuccessfully looking for meaningful employment at the centre of war administration. There was scant communication between the two at this time. Memories of the turmoil of May remained fresh.

Fisher soon dubbed his headquarters 'the chemist's shop in Cockspur Street'.[19] He warmed quickly to his task and sketched out what needed to be done in the realm of inventions. He argued that the war would be won by inventions and that the first eleven months of the war had shown the British to be 'servile copyists' of the Germans – he named explosive shells, grenades, siege mortars, poison gases, submarines, airships, and mines in particular as examples of weapons introduced by Germany that Britain then studied and produced. Taking a cue from Balfour, who had said, 'Let us collect "brains" and go ahead,' Fisher trumpeted that he needed 'brains' to push the inventors to produce new types of weapons for air and naval attack and defence. Pressing needs were development of airships and bigger and simpler aeroplanes, anti-submarine craft and devices, including mines, and all types of bombs and grenades. He noted how one small bomb dropped on a British factory had killed sixteen men and smashed 50 tons of glass, and he wondered what would happen if a Zeppelin dropped such a bomb on the upper deck of *Iron Duke* and killed Jellicoe. He concluded with '*Man invents. Monkeys imitate!*'[20]

Despite their naval predominance, the British were disadvantaged in the war in the North Sea. Not only were they facing the submarine peril to their surface ships, but they were also contending with Zeppelins in their capacities as spotters, communications specialists, and aerial bombers. Jellicoe, who already had lost ships of the Grand Fleet to submarines, lobbied Balfour and Fisher on 'the absolute necessity for a strong anti-submarine policy, both in regard to new construction and the use of existing vessels. The Zeppelins we cannot tackle, unfortunately. Nothing but sister Zeppelins can do that, and alas! the obstinacy of a few has put us in a position from which we cannot recover.'[21]

The Board of Invention and Research (BIR) consisted of a Central Committee of three members, whom Fisher called the Magi. 'My three Super-Eminent Colleagues,' he commented, ' … were very famous men': Sir J J Thomson, President of the Royal Society, 'a man unparalleled in science'; Sir Charles Parsons, inventor of the turbine (revolutionary in marine engineering), and Sir George Beilby, 'one of the greatest of chemists'. There were also various associates. They faced difficulties, not least ridicule. Fisher again: 'You would have thought that such a Galaxy of Talent would have been revered, welcomed, and obeyed – on the contrary, it was derided, spurned, and ignored.'[22] His target in this was the Admiralty.

The Board's business was done by six sections: airships and general aeronautics; submarines and wireless telegraphy; naval construction; anti-aircraft equipment; ordnance and ammunition; and armament of aircraft, bombs, and bombsights. A subcommittee of three or four scientists, plus a naval officer who acted as secretary, served each section. The second section, developing underwater acoustics for detection of submerged U-boats, became the most important. It covered all aspects of submarine countermeasures, and did research into detection using stray electric fields produced by the subs' own electric motors, induced anomalies in the earth's magnetic field, and thermal variations. Other studies looked at optical detection in clear weather, the emission of sound by submarines under way, and even the use of seagulls and hawks. The Board sifted through more than 37,500 suggestions received from the public, of which 14,000 dealt with submarines, anti-submarine measures, and wireless telegraphy. Many a hare-brained scheme was submitted; few merited study. The BIR tended to stand alone, with no formal co-ordination established between it and other government agencies. Within the BIR, personal contacts were the best means of passing information through the various sections.

Meantime, at the Admiralty, responsibility for combating the U-boat menace at the technical level rested with experimental stations and laboratories under the Director of the Anti-Submarine Committee, the Director of Torpedoes and Mining, and the Director of Naval Ordnance. The main experimental establishment was HMS *Vernon*, the torpedo school near Portsmouth. The Mining School, separate from *Vernon*, concentrated on design and inspection of mines and depth charges. Explosives were developed at the Ordnance Research Department at Woolwich and at HMS *Excellent* (Whale Island). Underwater acoustics were developed at Hawkcraig Admiralty Experimental Station, Aberdour, Scotland, where Commander C P Ryan, a wireless telegraphy genius, was just the man to develop such devices, mainly the directional hydrophone 'Porpoise'. Ryan had been an employee at Marconi and was no stranger to inventions. Of independent mindset, he was suspicious of civilians – like those at the BIR – whom he saw as an encumbrance to naval innovation. Known to Admiral Beatty, he could keep in touch with progress in the Fleet without having to go through the Admiralty.

A US report also recorded the troubles between the naval and BIR scientific establishments.[23] Ryan, who was responsible for the creation of Hawkcraig (his pride and joy), viewed the BIR scientists who had been assigned to that establishment as an imposition and criticised what he saw as their overly academic approach. The BIR scientists, in turn, chafed at the restraints they felt Ryan placed unfairly on their research. These difficulties having reached a crisis, a meeting of all parties was arranged at the Admiralty, where, on 30 March 1916, the main issues were discussed. In the end the Admiralty recommended a separate BIR research station be established (and properly funded), that heads of Admiralty technical departments become associates of the BIR, and that W H Bragg become resident director at Hawkcraig.[24] These were steps in the right direction to bring the Navy and the scientists closer in common cause, but on 12 May Bragg complained to Fisher of conditions at Hawkcraig, in particular the lack of instrument fitters and adequate workshops. He lamented that instrument makers had been allowed to enlist when their specialised trade was so essential to the work at Hawkcraig.

That same month, when BIR representatives travelled to Paris to inspect a captured U-boat, the French learned to their astonishment that the men from BIR had not been told of a report the French had sent to the Admiralty about the U-boat. Balfour later explained this away by saying the report had been 'mislaid' by the Admiralty Intelligence Department. Undoubtedly this was true, but the episode showed the absolute impoverishment in naval administration on this subject. Bragg eventually complained that the Admiralty's responses made him feel 'as if we were playing in a Gilbert and Sullivan opera instead of trying to help to win the war!'[25] By the end of 1916, the relationship between Ryan and the BIR scientists had deteriorated to the point where it was realised that it would be best if the BIR left Hawkcraig and created its own research establishment (the new station, at Harwich, will feature below). Once the BIR left, progress increased at Hawkcraig as Ryan's men had access to the workshops and equipment left behind by the BIR scientists.

Even as relations worsened, tests continued with the object of finding some means of detecting the approach of a submarine in shallow waters. Slow but significant progress was being made on ASDIC (Allied Submarine Detection Investigation Committee) – now commonly known as sonar (Sound Navigation and Ranging). This was of particular interest to Jellicoe, C-in-C of the Grand Fleet, who was haunted by the submarine menace. On 30 April Fisher wrote reassuringly about developments in electronic detection of submarines, especially as regards the research of Professor Bragg, who considered the work almost accomplished. Fisher hinted: 'It is so very simple and ingenious that when the sound is exactly equal on both sides, then you know you are steering direct for the enemy submarine, and, of course, if you have two vessels some distance apart, then you practically fix the position of the enemy submarine by cross bearings!'[26]

On 26 August 1916 the captain of HMS *Dolphin* (home of the Navy's submarine service at Gosport near Portsmouth) reported that he had tested an invention for clearing mined channels in a self-propelled boat. The device was a selenium cell developed by the intriguing inventor Harry Grindell Matthews.[27] The captain reported that he had used a 50ft launch to clear a 100ft-wide channel, cutting mooring lines with paravanes (towed minesweeping devices), which were more useful in pairs.[28] This promised great things. In the 30 April letter to Jellicoe, Fisher had also noted a suggestion to put the selenium cell in a small balloon carrying bombs, so that when the Germans put a searchlight on it, the bombs would go off.

In September 1916 Jellicoe wrote to Fisher about the Fleet's experiments with smokescreens – to provide protection to convoys. They were in full swing, but nothing definite could be said about them. Spotting U-boats from the air had its own problems: 'We don't seem to get on much with rigid airships. I have not heard of one in the air so far. I have an SS [submarine scout airship] with me. She is useful for patrol work and I hope may discover mines. I had a trip in her recently and could see the bottom at five fathoms under favourable conditions.'[29]

Fisher's outspokenness, and the fact that the BIR was independent of the Navy, militated against its acceptance by senior naval officers. He argued that many of the problems were caused by 'a lack of communication between Royal Navy officers, with their pragmatic approach to technical problems, and civilian scientists accustomed to more systematic research.'[30] Balfour kept these issues from becoming public or fodder for gossip among Cabinet colleagues. Fisher, all for publicity, as was his style, wondered how Balfour could be so cordial and supportive to him when, in fact, he was suppressing the letters that Fisher had had printed for circulation to the Cabinet.[31] Balfour was acting as gatekeeper. He did not want to give away scientific and technological secrets, and he knew 'state secrets' made for idle chat in fine dining circles in London. The imprudent Fisher lacked caution.

Balfour naturally looked for early results, but Fisher could not deliver them, and his frustrations grew. A year after his appointment, Fisher had lost interest in the BIR. Even as early as October 1915 he asked again to be 'made some use of' as, according to him, he was 'doing nothing at all'. On 16 October 2015, for instance, he urged Asquith to 'carry out the glorious project of Syria and Mesopotamia'.[32] But what sort of appointment could the old admiral be given, in view of his past history, his enemies, and his age? He disliked being pushed aside, but that was the nature of his position and his power. He would have to live with the circumstances.

In November 1915 a wild rumour circulated that Fisher would be given a seat on the War Council. Jellicoe was secretly appalled. He wrote to the Second Sea Lord, Admiral Hamilton: 'I don't believe J.F. will get on the War Council, but if you really think there is danger I will take steps which may help to stop it. Please let me know about it. I think I can do something very much "entre nous". I think it would be a fatal step.'[33] This is a particularly telling statement since both correspondents were friends of Fisher. Jellicoe owed his position to him, and Fisher spent weekends at Hamilton's place in Scotland.

In January 1916 Fisher began to intrigue to become First Lord of the Admiralty, First Sea Lord, or Controller (Third Sea Lord). Like Churchill he concentrated his attention on those senior British political figures most likely to arrange a shuffle of the Cabinet or even bring down the ministry. He despaired of such a return while Asquith and Balfour held powerful office. He wrote to Hankey: 'For myself I tell them and many others in reply to multitudes of letters that it appears to me that Asquith & Balfour are such astute Parliamentarians that no one will turn them out & they are irremovable! That's my belief – *and so long as they are in I shall be out!*'[34] Early in 1916, he again complained to Hankey of the lack of vigour at the Admiralty and his desire to shake things up once again: 'I know perfectly well I could entirely change the face of the naval situation! YES COMPLETELY ENTHUSE IT!... I have not yet been wrong in any one little detail since June 10 1902 when I became Second Sea Lord.'[35] But Hankey responded: 'The disadvantage of premature action is that you dish your chance of getting in with the present lot and I don't see any serious competitors to them.'[36] (This was most likely a reference to the new First Sea Lord and to the Cabinet composition and opinion at the time.) Fisher, like Churchill, faced the daily agony of being on the sidelines. As Fisher put it to John Leyland, the naval writer, on 2 January 1916: 'It is very hard when one feels at one's zenith to be locked out! Such was the fate of Moses. "His eye was not dim nor his natural force abated," but he was not allowed into the Promised Land, though it was his leadership that had brought the people of Israel to its borders.'[37]

Fisher kept in contact with Lloyd George, writing to compliment the latter on his 20 December 1915 'Too Late!' speech in the House of Commons: 'Your speech will be the history of the War!' Fisher also went out of his way to give Lloyd George credit for helping ensure the '593 vessels' Fisher ordered during his short stint at the Admiralty – the Baltic armada that never was. 'I ... *had a plan* for July 1915, for which those vessels were built,' he wrote. 'That plan was blasted by the Dardanelles, *and so was I*!' He concluded: 'We want another plan,' and expressed his desire to meet with Lloyd George.[38] Was Fisher attempting to get in Lloyd George's good graces, in the hope that he would be restored to power if the 'Welsh wizard' displaced Asquith as prime minister?

He also attempted to bring Bonar Law (the most difficult of all) around to his viewpoint. In a letter of 7 January 1916 Fisher argued that the current Navy was a product of his 'Big Revolution' from 1902 to 1910, and that his stint at the Admiralty in late 1914 and early 1915 had righted mistakes made in the prior four years, especially with respect to submarines and airships (thereby indirectly condemning Churchill's tenure from 1911 to 1914). On politics:

> Balfour ruined his party: I hope he won't ruin his Country! ... [Kitchener] got the Order of the Garter. I got the Order of the Boot! ... For eight months, in the very plenitude of my strength and power, I have been put in charge of a Chemist's Shop, and Balfour says to me in extenuation, when I offered to humiliate myself by joining the Board as Third Sea Lord, so as to get a submarine battleship built in 6 months that would end the War – he said, 'If once you put your foot inside the Admiralty, where should we all be?' and when I told the Prime Minister this story, he said, 'Yes. That's the mischief of it.'[39]

Fisher was helpless, put out to pasture. Like Churchill he believed he had no future.

Churchill calls for Fisher's return

The ghosts of the two men hovered over the Admiralty and haunted the affairs of the Navy. Admiral Sir William James, who knew them both, wrote of the months after their departure: 'The loss of the two men to whom the Navy owed its readiness for war seemed at the time to be a tragedy, and to be suddenly deprived of any control of events at such a critical moment in history must have been Churchill's most bitter experience, but Fisher was ageing and losing grasp and, after the evacuation of the Dardanelles, Churchill would have once again had to endure inaction, enforced by the unalterable pattern of the sea-war.'[40] The Admiralty immediately felt the absence of Churchill's driving power and vision. He would have, says James, 'dispelled the gloomy forebodings during what were called the black months.'[41]

While the duo pursued new concerns and obligations, they retained a sharp if necessarily distant watch on the Fleet. Neither could be muzzled. They were chatterers. Neither could be discountenanced. They worked in strange harness, two oddly shaped thoroughbreds. From their individual vantage points they watched with sadness and horror as the great instrument of British sea power rusted at its moorings in Scapa Flow. The great deterrent served its primary objective as counterweight to the German High Seas Fleet. Given the superiority of British sea power, the restless Churchill and Fisher saw this somnolence as essentially a wasteful tragedy. But their hands were off the levers, and they were on the margins of public affairs.

At the Admiralty, the months of lassitude and inaction continued. One severe problem was the Admiralty's failure to retain skilled craftsmen in the shipyards. There was also a lack of driving power, and a lack of former great sea commanders sitting on the Board of Admiralty. At the same time, no Board members visited the Fleet. They preferred their desk jobs. They were 'out of touch with the sea service'. Hankey said Balfour as First Lord may have been superb and even invaluable on aspects of policy-making but was unsuited in temperament to administer the Admiralty with incessant drive and initiative. Perhaps Jackson was similar to his chief. They were too alike to make a good combination. No changes took place. The Asquith policy was to leave well enough alone. As 1916 began, the Navy, 'which was our main hope and standby for winning the war', occupied little of the attention and energy of the Supreme Command according to Hankey, who was well placed to comment: 'In comparison with the enemy our main fleet was too powerful, and its normal role was so sedentary, that it did not come much into the limelight.'[42]

Then a change came in Berlin. On 15 March 1916, Grand Admiral von Tirpitz was dismissed as Secretary of State of the Imperial Admiralty, an event that aroused anxiety because he had provided unwavering energy and steady direction. Perhaps now the Germans would take the initiative, which would oblige the British Navy to respond.

When Jacky Fisher learned of his opposite's unwanted exit, he wrote a letter to 'Dear Old Tirps':

> We are both in the same boat! What a time we've been colleagues, old boy! However, we did you in the eye over the Battlecruisers and I know you've said you'll never forgive me for it when bang went the 'Blucher' and von Spee and all his host!
>
> Cheer up, old chap! Say 'Resurgam'! You're the one German sailor who understands War! Kill your enemy without being killed yourself. I don't blame you for the submarine business. I'd have done the same myself, only our idiots in England wouldn't believe it when I told 'em!
>
> Well! So long!
>
> Yours till hell freezes,
>
> FISHER
>
> I say! Are you sure if you had tripped out with your whole High Seas Fleet before the Russian ice thawed and brought over those half-a-million soldiers from Hamburg to frighten our old women that you could have got back un-Jellicoed?
>
> R.S.V.P.[43]

Tirpitz was replaced by Eduard von Capelle. Britain now expected a more aggressive turn of events. 'It is inconceivable that a German people would tolerate that the great High Seas Fleet should remain for ever supine without an attempt to break through the steel curtain which shut off Germany from the outer world,'[44] wrote Hankey. The U-boat war against Allied shipping continued in its intensity and, in fact, increased in effectiveness. 'Shoot on sight', something unimaginable heretofore, was now the normal state of affairs.

At Scapa Flow the Commander-in-Chief, Jellicoe, worried incessantly about insufficient numbers of cruisers, destroyers, and minesweepers for the Grand Fleet. In addition to health problems and mental anxieties, he resembled Nelson in an earlier age, never having enough frigates, his sources of information, his first line of defence – what the Americans would call picket ships. Some adjustments were made in the overall deployment of these precious units, which partially helped, but construction was slow and the numbers were never enough. Ottley and Watts, formerly Chief Constructor to the Navy, complained about the slowness of the yards. In particular, Jellicoe complained about delays in finishing the facilities at Rosyth. Such complaints fed Fisher's outrage at the state of affairs at the Admiralty and gave him the ammunition, especially with respect to ship construction, that led to his appearance before the War

Committee in March. Jellicoe, though, urged Fisher to remain out of office, as 'if you are drawn in, you will share the responsibility.'[45]

One of the oddest events in the long interplay of Churchill and Fisher occurred during Churchill's leave in London in March 1916. On his arrival in London, Churchill had learned that the naval estimates would be debated in the House of Commons while he was there. He saw this as an opportunity to demonstrate what he thought was his superior grasp of naval policy. Truth to tell, he had no other cards to play. He had no political credit, so he gathered his political friends around to find the best way to attack the government. He worked diligently on his speech. C P Scott of the *Manchester Guardian,* J L Garvin of the *Observer*, F E Smith, and Sir Francis Hopwood (current Civil Lord at the Admiralty) all met or dined with him at his residence on 3 March. In the rehearsal of Churchill's speech no mention was made of Fisher, but when Hopwood, talked with Churchill as he was leaving: 'C[hurchill] suddenly said that he would teach that d—d old Oriental scoundrel Fisher what it meant to quarrel with him.'[46] At this particular juncture, on the eve of the most astounding about-face, did Churchill really intend to be vindictive and embarrass Fisher? The stage was set for a curious act in the still evolving tragedy punctuated with comic overtones – and an even more curious turnaround.

Scott's role behind the scenes commands particular note, for he consistently attended on Jacky Fisher from 29 February and through the events here described. 'Saw a great deal of Lord Fisher almost always at the Duchess of Hamilton's flat in Cleveland Row where she took part in the conversations – a capable and beautiful woman entirely devoted to his interests. He lives in an atmosphere of intrigue in which he does not appear to play a very skilful part.'[47] Scott encouraged the reconciliation with Churchill. Fisher was enthusiastic about Churchill, believing him to be a future prime minister. Churchill, debating whether to leave the Army and return to the Commons, was faced with the loss of his Army salary. He had no money, said Scott, and had to borrow to provide for his wife and children. Clementine wanted her husband to remain in the Army, and the promise of a battalion was in view.[48] Even so, Churchill was teetering on the edge: he could not resist the challenge, even with its attendant risks, of which he was well aware.

As might be imagined, some of Churchill's political friends were also friends of Fisher, and many of them wished to bring the latter back to the Admiralty. Accordingly, Fisher was invited to lunch, much to the horror of Clementine, who never liked the old admiral. F E Smith, Churchill's dependable friend, who was at the luncheon, reported that Clementine told Fisher point blank: 'Keep your hands off my husband. You have all but ruined him once. Leave him alone.'[49] Despite Clementine's dislike of him, Fisher was invited to Churchill's house on the evening of 5 March. Churchill read his speech to Fisher and revealed that he would end with an appeal for the return of Fisher to the Admiralty. Fisher gleefully wrote Churchill early the next morning full of the old fire: 'I am going to be the humble instrument! ... *We can do it! Come on!*'[50]

That same day, with news flying around Whitehall and the London clubs, Asquith got wind of Churchill's intention to speak in the House of Commons on the 7th. Asquith had Churchill's interests at heart and was always concerned that he might damage himself politically. The Asquiths were dining with the Churchills that night. Asquith's daughter later wrote of that evening: 'My father ... feared that [Churchill] was going to make a most unwise speech ... [and] had done his best to dissuade him from it, but evidently felt that he had failed.' Asquith's wife, Margot, sitting next to Winston, told him how sorry she was to hear that he intended to speak on the Navy, explaining that he had made a good exit from the Admiralty and had taken up an admiring place in the fighting line, risking his life for the country, etc. 'Don't go and spoil it,' she warned. Churchill, she said, seemed to be dreaming of an Opposition that he would lead.[51] Churchill failed to take Margot Asquith's advice or Asquith's either. He did not want to lose an opportunity duly offered.

Morning newspapers on 7 March had no interest in Churchill's pre-occupations. The headlines reported the new terror: Zeppelin raids damaging ports, towns and naval bases. Even in rough weather, on the 5th and 6th, ninety bombs had been dropped over eight counties. In one case, three German airships attacked Rosyth but high winds diverted them to Hull, where they attacked the base, killing eighteen and injuring many more. On the 7th another raid (by five Zeppelins) occurred. One of the craft dropped a 1,000kg bomb on Warrington Crescent, near Paddington, killing, among others, Lena Ford who had written the popular wartime song 'Keep the Home Fires Burning'. That winter heavy snow lay on the ground, and the British Isles had seen some of the coldest weather in years.

In the Commons that day, all the principal characters were seated on the benches or otherwise in the galleries. Asquith was there, and Balfour, the First Lord. From his place in the gallery Hankey, Secretary of the War Cabinet, watched closely. With Churchill due to speak there was tension and anxiety in the air. Hankey, conscious of the unfolding drama, observed Admiral Fisher sitting sphinx-like in his favourite seat behind the clock. He thought the face of the old admiral resembled that of an Indian Buddha.[52]

Then came Churchill's turn: he delivered an impassioned attack on the Admiralty. It was equally an indictment of the government. Churchill, with logical precision, made his arguments. He cited the shipbuilding delays, how Britain was being threatened by Germany at sea. Britain's maritime ascendancy was crumbling. The Admiralty lacked zeal and conviction. Change was required. Then, to the astonishment of all, he strangely and surprisingly appealed for the recall to office of Fisher. The suggestion to reinstate Fisher was met with disbelief. Altogether people were unhappy about the Admiralty, where there was not much drive or punch, said Hankey.[53] He noted in his diary: 'Not very patriotic of Churchill, but he said a lot of true things and his speech was well received by the House except the Fisher suggestion.'[54] Hankey thought Churchill would not do himself or Fisher much good by it.

Clementine considered Churchill's call for Fisher's return a colossal mistake. He had ignored her advice. Margot Asquith, the prime minister's wife, was furious at Churchill's vicious display in the Commons. 'I hope and believe Winston will never be forgiven his yesterday's speech,' she wrote to Balfour the next day from Downing Street. 'Henry & I were thunderstruck at the *meanness* & the gigantic folly of it ... He is a hound of the lowest sense of political honour, a fool of the lowest judgement & contemptible.'[55]

Violet Bonham Carter, too, one of Churchill's closest and most enduring friends had been aghast. 'The debate lives in my memory as one of the most painful I have ever listened to,' she wrote.

> Had I gone mad? Had Winston? He had spoken in calm and measured terms, without excitement and with the utmost deliberation. His speech, as always, had been most carefully prepared. What possessed him? I remembered long talks in which he had poured out his heart to me about Fisher, his vacillations, his constant resignations (my father and I once counted up nine), his desertion. Fisher was responsible for the coerced Coalition, for Winston's exile from the office he loved so dearly, in part at least for the failure of the Dardanelles. He had dealt with him faithfully in his resignation speech. Could he possibly believe in the course which he was advocating? It would be unlike him to swerve from his convictions. Yet if he believed in it he must surely be deranged?
>
> I left the Gallery when he sat down, feeling unable to face what was to follow. I followed Margot to my husband's room. He was speechless. [Churchill's secretary] Eddie Marsh (who never attempted to pass judgment on any speech, even Winston's, saying that he did not know a good speech from a bad one), had tears in his eyes and said to Margot tremulously, 'Do you think he has done for himself?' For once she tempered the wind to the shorn lamb and replied, 'He is young – and if he goes back and fights like a hero it will all be forgotten.'[56]

Violet, with Miss Marple instincts, took an interest in how it had come about. In her book *Winston Churchill as I Knew Him*, she recounted the sequence of events. She knew that Winston had returned on the 2nd and that he had learned the naval estimates were to be debated on the 7th. She knew that

Winston had dined with his mother, and that Garvin of the *Observer*, Fisher's closest press advocate, had been there. She was sure that F E Smith would never have counselled Churchill to do what he had done. C P Scott of the *Manchester Guardian* had been brought into the discussions; he was one of Churchill's most faithful adherents. FE had been at a Cromwell Road lunch at which Fisher had been Winston's guest. It all seemed as if Churchill had been guided to this position, and then taken up the clarion call to bring in the old admiral himself. Violet was sure that a plot had been hatched, that Winston was its chosen tool.[57]

Fisher, unsurprisingly, was ecstatic over Churchill's parliamentary performance. To Jellicoe he wrote: 'Isn't it interesting how personal attacks (IF LEFT ALONE) always rectify themselves? *Vide* Winston's amazing change of front towards me! His speech in the House of Commons was really wonderfully good. HE HELD THE HOUSE ENTHRALLED! Balfour was terribly faltering and halting in his speech. I had an ovation as I left the Peers' Gallery. All the MPs got up and cheered me as I walked out, and the Speaker did not stop them!' Fisher also credited Churchill's attack with breaking up what Fisher thought to be a misguided plan to bring Jellicoe to the Admiralty as First Sea Lord.[58] Fisher never faltered in believing Jellicoe the best commander to fight the German High Seas Fleet if it ever ventured to sea.

Asquith disliked Fisher and was furious at his disloyalty. He would not consider any return of Fisher to the Admiralty. Why Churchill had promoted this idea was beyond his comprehension. All the same he sought to save Churchill from further calamity. He saw Churchill on 9 March at 10 Downing Street and cautioned him against taking rash actions that would damage or even destroy his political career. The way ahead did not involve gathering like-minded dissidents and marshalling strength against the government. Asquith also managed to defuse Churchill's criticism by inviting Fisher to the War Council on 8 March. One further discussion of the issues might clear the air, Asquith thought, and perhaps he was advised in this by Hankey. As requested Fisher attended. But he failed to make a good impression. All the principals were there – Asquith, Balfour, Admiral Sir Arthur Wilson, the Chief of the War Staff, the Chief of the Imperial General Staff, and others. Balfour raised objections to the previous Churchill–Fisher naval administration. In Cabinet Balfour sparkled, and on this occasion gave full vent to his high intelligence and analytical powers. Fisher had no doubts as to the outcome. As he later explained to Hankey, Arthur 'Philosophic Doubt' Balfour 'wiped the floor with me.'[59]

Later that day came Balfour's turn in the House. The First Lord launched a devastating attack on Churchill. He criticised Churchill's claim that the late Board of Admiralty had more 'energy, speed, push and drive' than the present

Board. With customary craftiness he concentrated on the appeal on behalf of Fisher: 'Let me say now one word about the remedy which he proposed at the end. I do not imagine that there was a single person who heard my right hon. Friend's speech who did not listen to this latter part of it with profound stupefaction.' Balfour went on to compare Churchill's earlier words describing Fisher's inability to give advice and his current desire to have him back at the Admiralty. He ridiculed the suggestion of turning out Admiral Sir Henry Jackson in order to bring back Fisher.[60] Balfour's wording bordered on the sardonic, and it played to the view that Churchill had lost his sense of proportion – and was a dangerous man.

In the course of a brief reply, Churchill responded with anger and resentment against the government. He again appealed for the return of Fisher. 'The real fact is that if we could associate in some way or another the driving power and energy of Lord Fisher, with the carrying out of Lord Fisher's programme at the highest possible speed, there is no reason to suppose that great public advantage would not result from that.'[61] But the heat had gone out of the arguments. Churchill had not done himself a favour, and he could not keep out of the arguments, was not prepared to bide his time, and lacked tactical skills in Parliament and in working the press. He had ignored his wife's counsel, and the counsel of more experienced politicians.

Churchill was not without his admirers in Parliament. Chat about the volatile discussions on the naval estimates continued. For instance, on 8 March the industrialist Sir Arthur Markham, a Liberal MP, stated that Balfour's attack on Churchill's statement was 'cheap rhetoric', full of 'cheap sneers'. As to Fisher's possible return, Markham declared that Fisher's return in October 1914 had done wonders at the Admiralty. He quoted Jellicoe: 'no man has ever done more for his country than Lord Fisher did when he was at the Admiralty.'[62] The Earl of Rosebery, a former Liberal prime minister, was also generally supportive of Churchill's speech. He told Fisher: 'Every one has been kicking Winston because he is down. But to me there is something magnanimous and creditable in his coming down and pressing you on the Ministry after his previous speech. But he ought to have given his reasons for his change of view, instead of producing it like a rocket.'[63] Within the Navy, and particularly in higher command, Churchill's call for Fisher's return could not fail to invite concern. All the same, we have this view from one officer who knew Churchill well, feared Fisher, and saw wider horizons against the present uncertainties. Sir Roger Keyes wrote:

Of course everyone will attribute some evil ulterior motives to him. The Admiral [de Robeck] does, but though I think it was ill advised and criminally stupid of him to [call for Fisher's return], I do believe it was in good faith. You remember I said to him he had nursed a viper which had stung – he said quite passionately – 'I'd do it again, even though he did break me – he brought such fire and vim [?] into the construction and production for the Navy and accomplished things which no one else could have done.' Like Lord K[itchener] he [Fisher] had some wonderful qualities. He certainly provided us with some wonderful and invaluable craft, but he ruined the Dardanelles Expedition when he declined to back up W.C. in ordering us to go on on 10th May. And his whole conduct in the Dardanelles business ought to be sufficient to insure his never being allowed to have anything to do with the conduct of the war or the running of the Navy. I may be prejudiced but 99% of officers in the Navy would view his return with the greatest misgiving. I have not met one out here holding any other opinion.[64]

Fisher, as said, attended the War Council on 8 March. He prepared a written statement for the meeting, as he feared that without one his views could be misrepresented as supportive of the current conduct of the war.[65] After the meeting, he wrote: '*I had a splendid time at the War Council* (and lost temper!) and they were quite glad to see me leave the room!'[66] Hankey said Fisher said much of what Churchill did in the Commons. Fisher impressed no one, he admitted, save General Sir William Robertson, who wanted to consult further with Fisher and claimed that the present Admiralty would never accomplish anything. After the meeting, Asquith commented to C P Scott that Fisher was 'a constructor, very fertile and ingenious', but 'not a strategist'. Fisher had 'what the Americans call "hustle"', but so did other officers.[67]

At the same time the War Council deliberated on various matters regarding the conduct of the war, a strange scene was playing itself out in Whitehall. 'Meanwhile,' reported *The Times* on 9 March, '[the street] was lined with sandwich men, who bore appeals for the return of "Jack". About a score of men walked to and fro between Trafalgar Square and the Houses of Parliament. Quotations from both Conservative and Liberal organs calling for the return of Lord Fisher formed the main object of the display, but there was no indication of the source from which the placards emanated. For a few moments the procession halted in front of Admiralty House.' Who paid these men, and who organised this extraordinary demonstration? It might be speculated that Fisher's press friends had engineered the whole thing in vain support of the old sea dog. Professor Marder, who tried to get to the bottom of this, noted that 'a consulting engineer of some repute, Alfred James, was dissuaded by Lambert [George Lambert, a Liberal MP and Civil Lord of the Admiralty] from staging a Fisher-must-return demonstration by sandwichmen in front of Parliament early in March!'[68] While this demonstration did occur, according to the newspaper report, it is unknown from the available evidence whether James was behind it, and whether he operated with the sanction of Lambert.

For his part, Fisher remained hopeful. To C P Scott he wrote: 'McKenna told me ... (THIS IS MOST SECRET!) that if Winston remained he would turn out the Government. Dead. Sure. SO HE WILL!!!'[69] He played to Churchill's vanity. He begged Churchill to resign his Army commission and stay and wage the fight in the Commons in the debate over army estimates. As Fisher wrote on 11 March:

> I've slept over it! I've thought of nothing else! If any specious twaddle about honour or Asquithian jugglery persuades you not to rise from the corner of the Front Opposition Bench next Tuesday to brand the Government with the *massacre* of our *troops* and the utter *ineptitude* of the conduct of the war then I say that *YOU* become the '*Murderer*' because you are the *one and only* man who it is absolutely certain can prevent it and can voice the removal of Kitchener ... *VIA THE ARMY ESTIMATES YOU CAN DO IT!*[70]

Asquith, Balfour, Hankey and others needed Fisher onside, and on 15 March, he attended the CID meeting at the prime minister's request. Fisher commented on Admiralty policy, argued that the Grand Fleet was perilously short of destroyers, and worried that the two light battlecruisers *Glorious* and *Courageous* were taking too long to complete.[71] He had been fed information by Jellicoe, who complained about the slowness of construction and his weakness in small vessels. Fisher sent Asquith and Balfour a number of accusatory letters, charging the administration with naval incompetence.[72] But Fisher was ineffective to change the war machinery. By the end of March he was fed up with the political situation and went into seclusion at the Hamilton country estate, Balcombe Place, Sussex. He compared himself to Elijah 'when he went that day's journey into the wilderness, "and came and sat down under a juniper tree and said, '*It is enough*! Take away my life!'"'[73]

Fisher, however, was not finished. He was restless, and having been sitting down for some time, found it necessary to get up and move. His despair at the conduct of the naval war brought him closer to Churchill, and soon the two were once more on favourable terms, locked in a curious destiny. 'Fisher, the Duchess, and Winston are now bosom friends,' wrote the press proprietor George Riddell on the basis of news received.[74]

Churchill returned to France, but wrote to Asquith about resigning his Army commission. His recent failure to influence the affairs of Parliament only served to strengthen his resolve. He talked with many friends. His wife Clementine again counselled against his return to England. She wrote that he should bide his time for the right moment. She worried he would blemish his reputation further. '"Wait wait have patience, don't pluck the fruit before it is ripe. Everything will come to you if you don't snatch at it." To be great one's actions must be able to be understood by simple people. Your motive for going to the

Front was easy to understand. Your motive for coming back requires explanation.'[75] He ignored her.

Then came a strange turn of events. When his battalion was amalgamated with the 7th Battalion Royal Scots Fusiliers, Churchill found himself made redundant. This was his opportunity, and on 7 May, after six diversionary months on the Western Front, he was back in London. In one of his first speeches in the House of Commons, on 17 May, Churchill defended his conduct of the Admiralty with respect to aerial defence and aeroplane production. He also criticised the newly formed Air Board, under Lord Curzon, as being unable to cope with the problems of the new air service. Instead, he recommended the formation of an Air Ministry with powers equivalent to the other Services. His suggestions, and his defence of his own actions, were undermined by his lack of parliamentary support, as the government could easily afford to contemptuously dismiss him.[76] Only Lloyd George received his criticisms in a friendly manner.[77]

'There seems to be something wrong with our bloody ships today'

We now return to the North Sea, and the dispositions of the German and British fleets. The big event Fisher had forecast, and Churchill had long anticipated, was about to occur. On the brightening morning of 31 May 1916, with a calm sea covered by mist, Vice-Admiral Reinhard Scheer, Commander-in-Chief of the Imperial German High Seas Fleet, set sail with his vast armada of eighteen modern battleships and five battlecruisers in an attempt to set a trap for the enemy. He had persuaded the Kaiser to adopt an aggressive policy at sea and not let his ships and men rot in port as a 'fleet in being'. He did not expect a full action against the larger British Fleet of thirty-one battleships and ten battlecruisers, and only hoped for a partial engagement against the British battlecruisers lured into range. With his battleships he would then put the hammer on the British.

Scheer did not know that the British had cracked the German naval code. By the time he was at sea, Wilhelmshaven disappearing over the horizon to the east, Admiral Sir John Jellicoe and the whole Grand Fleet was making its own independent sweep to the Danish coast of Jutland. In fact, through colossal Admiralty bungling, Jellicoe had no inkling that Scheer had sailed, for the German commander, upon departure from the Jade, had transferred his flagship's radio call sign ashore. In London the Admiralty missed this: the received view was that Scheer had not sailed. By accident, British scouting forces encountered German battlecruisers and other units under Admiral Franz von Hipper. Beatty engaged Hipper's ships, then lured them as well as Scheer's heavy units toward Jellicoe's heavy units. In these circumstances an annihilation of the Germans might have been expected; this had all the appearances of

Jellicoe's day of destiny in which Fisher's prophecy would be fulfilled. After Jellicoe deployed to 'cross the T', the Germans did a 180-degree turn to escape. The German commander artfully deployed his forces after the initial, desultory encounter, and then released his destroyers and their torpedoes, which served to ward off Jellicoe. In the mists and decreased visibility of evening, Scheer made his escape by crossing behind Jellicoe's line and making a safe, night-time run for home. When darkness fell, Scheer had ordered his ships to harbour. The Admiralty made a mess of transmitting to Jellicoe the German radio messages, which were picked up in London. These indicated the route plotted by Scheer for his escape. But by the time Jellicoe knew the precise details it was too late. The Germans were home free.

'There seems to be something wrong with our bloody ships today,' Beatty remarked to Captain Chatfield, the only person who heard this famous comment.[78] *Queen Mary*, whose shooting had been the best of Beatty's ships, had blown up under concentrated fire from *Derfflinger* and *Seydlitz*, with a loss of 1,266 officers and men killed. Jutland revealed a great weakness in Fisher's design theory: his contention that 'speed is armour' proved to be devastatingly foolish, and *Indefatigable* and *Queen Mary* were blown to smithereens. 'The loss of the two battlecruisers,' Beatty wrote in 1934, 'was not the fault of anybody in them, poor souls, but a faulty design... Their [the Germans'] ships were too stoutly built whereas ours went up in a blue flame on the smallest provocation.'[79] Some German vessels suffered heavily in the famous Run to the South but none were lost. With greater armour, stronger construction, superiority in range-finding, and finer armour-piercing shells, the German battlecruisers performed better than the British, even under relatively more inexperienced commanders. Fisher's telling phrases, which he never regretted, that 'speed is the best protection' and that 'hitting is the thing, not armour', cost the British dear at Jutland. Sir Julian Corbett, the official naval historian, said that these dramatic phrases 'haunted the ear, but confused judgement.'[80] While the battlecruiser, as designed under Fisher's committee, was a success at the Falklands, where the longer range British guns could play to advantage on the fleeing German vessels, it proved a disaster in the closer range combat of Jutland. But in consequence of what transpired at Jutland, all eyes were on the Navy, and the glare shone inescapably on Fisher, casting him into deeper shadows.

The first news to reach Britain of a battle in the North Sea came in the form of a German wireless message of 1 June, rerouted through Washington. This announced to the world that 'a portion' of their High Seas Fleet had met the British Grand Fleet in full force and had defeated it. The message described the action and listed the British losses. Similarly suggestive information came unofficially from units of the British Fleet, including some returning to the Firth of Forth. Many people in and near Edinburgh learned that a great sea battle had occurred. Various single 'intercepts' arrived at the Admiralty, specifically messages between Jellicoe and Beatty referring to ships having been sunk. Soon, too, news spread of damaged ships entering east-coast ports with hospital cases on board. Wild rumours flew around the country, since officers and men were wiring to their friends, announcing that they were safe and sound. Some messages were held up for reasons of censorship but the volume of them, six thousand, was so great that before long the Admiralty and the Post Office thought it out of the question to hold them up. The Admiralty was thus faced with an unprecedented situation, for the precise details were not yet to hand at a time when the public and press were clamouring for the hard facts. To maintain further silence was impossible.

In these strange and unbalanced circumstances, and with but one solitary message received on 2 June from the Commander-in-Chief, giving only brief details of what he had received from Beatty, the Admiralty decided to issue an announcement through its Press Bureau. The communiqué (announced to the press at 7pm that same day), with its transparent admissions of British losses being heavier than those inflicted on the enemy, gave the impression that it was a guarded statement of a naval reverse.

This official Admiralty communiqué was received around the world as 'a frightful staggerer, especially to friends of this country in neutral States where German propaganda was going strong, and no doubt our exiled compatriots suffered mentally very acutely.'[81] In the event, those in charge had gone ahead, and Balfour, who was First Lord of the Admiralty; Admiral Sir Henry Jackson, First Sea Lord; and Vice-Admiral Sir Henry Oliver, the Chief of Staff, did their work and told the basic story, detailing how the British ships which bore the brunt of the fighting were those of the Battle Cruiser Fleet ('Among these the losses were heavy') and explaining that the German battle fleet, aided by low visibility, had avoided prolonged action with British main forces and then returned to port, having first received some severe damage from British battleships. The communiqué listed the ships lost, a prodigious number. In all these ways the Admiralty did not presume to keep anything from the press (something unheard of nowadays). What was startlingly clear, in the face of the number of British losses detailed in the German statement, was that, in fact, the British had lost proportionally more ships, more tonnage and more men. A further British communiqué provided additional details.

In the opinion of the chief censor, Rear-Admiral Sir Douglas Brownrigg, who ran the Admiralty's Press Bureau, the Germans suffered irretrievably by the distortions in their original vainglorious communiqué, which they were compelled to alter within days of its issue. But at the time the British press did not see it that way. Balfour was anxious for damage control. Perhaps it was his decision to harness Churchill's literary gifts to present a 'reassuring' view.

Brownrigg gives himself credit for deciding to bring in Churchill with his golden pen to put a new face on the matter. His reasoning was that obtaining the late First Lord's views on the battle could do nothing but good, as Churchill, having become a keen critic of the Admiralty, might be expected to provide an unbiased opinion on it, particularly for consumption in neutral countries (meaning, essentially, the United States). The argument was a bit tortuous, but Brownrigg got on the telephone. He made the proposition. Churchill duly attended on Brownrigg at the Admiralty, who urged and even begged him to undertake the task. At last he consented.

Thus it was that Churchill's statement on Jutland appeared in the papers on Sunday, 4 June. After detailing the losses on both sides he wrote:

> Our margin of superiority is in no way impaired. The despatch of troops to the Continent should continue with the utmost freedom, the battered condition of the German Fleet being an additional security to us. The hazy weather, the fall of night, and the retreat of the enemy alone frustrated the persevering efforts of our brilliant commanders, Sir John Jellicoe and Sir David Beatty, to force a final decision. Although it was not possible to compel the German main fleet to accept battle, the conclusions reached are of extreme importance. All classes of vessels on both sides have now met, and we know that there are no surprises or unforeseen features. An accurate measure can be taken of the strength of the enemy, and his definite inferiority is freed from any element of uncertainty.[82]

The statement was issued in his own name, sparking further accusations of complicity and meddling. Lloyd George was amazed, and alarmed, that Balfour had got Churchill to do the Admiralty's work.[83]

Calling in Churchill to give a reassuring view was fraught with unimagined difficulties, and it turned out to have the opposite result as that intended. 'I never made a greater mistake in my life,' Brownrigg admitted after the war:

> (and that is saying a good deal), for the whole Press let off a scream asking why the Admiralty had given the ex-Minister opportunities of examining all the material denied to everybody else, and they attacked him for having had the temerity to give his views! I apologized to Mr. Churchill very sincerely for having brought down all this abuse on his head, but he took it with characteristic sang-froid, and I believe he thinks, as I do still, that it was a good move. Nevertheless, I was bitterly sorry that I had added to the abuse that was being at that time showered on the Admiralty, for which I was unable, publicly, to shoulder the responsibility.[84]

The press, as stated, expressed outrage that Churchill, no longer a minister of the Crown, had been given access to the secret files, and demanded to know what actually occurred. Churchill was even attacked for having the temerity to express his views. Under pressure, the Admiralty reluctantly allowed journalists access to the essential documentation. Upon hearing of this, Jellicoe, fearing his own command would be compromised by prying newsmen, complained bitterly. The Admiralty then immediately slapped censorship on the reports. Some newspapers got information and others did not; the Admiralty remained silent. The Associated Press of America carried a semi-official account based on an interview with 'a naval officer of high rank'. Three days of confusion and miscommunication helped to create the uncertainty surrounding the battle.[85] The Admiralty Press Bureau and Churchill kept quiet the fact that *Indefatigable* and *Queen Mary* sank because of the bursting of their magazines, but even so, certain items of information got out in published letters that found their way to the Grand Fleet and brought strong protests from Jellicoe.

On Monday, 5 June, the day after Churchill's statement appeared, Fisher told C P Scott, the newspaperman and Liberal politician, that he had seen all the telegrams and documents Balfour had given to Churchill on Friday. Churchill had brought them to Fisher in order to get his assistance in drawing up the report issued to the press. Fisher contended that Jutland amounted to a British defeat because, as Scott wrote in his diary on 5 June, 'even assuming the German losses to be equal to our own that was a wholly unsatisfactory result of an encounter between forces so unequal.'[86]

Fisher made the following criticisms. (1) Timing of British force deployment was atrocious; 'It was all wrong for our battlecruisers to be 2 hours ahead of the fast battleships (*Queen Elizabeths*) and those 2 hours ahead of the battleships.' (2) The Admiralty was to be blamed for this poor co-ordination in concentration of force. (3) 'Beatty blundered. He is not a very clever man, though a very gallant sailor.' He foolishly got caught in an engagement against a superior force. Beatty had no right to sacrifice valuable ships and lives. 'The name he gave to him is "Balaclava Beatty" which sums up the whole thing in 2 words.' He was outmanoeuvred by the Germans: he had allowed his weaker ships (with 7in guns) to lead. 'They were like rabbits against dogs and moreover got in the way of his own fire.' And Beatty compounded his mistakes by being outmanoeuvred so the sun was in his eyes – Cradock's error at Coronel repeated. (4) The Germans rightly retired when Jellicoe and his big guns arrived. (5) Destroyers from Harwich and the Channel, plus submarines and minelayers, should have been sent to cut off the enemy's retreat. (6) The Germans also erred, for when British forces returned to base, German units could have made effective raids on the British coast, and even landed troops or 'behind our lines in France'. Of the Admiralty generally, Fisher thought them in a state of panic, 'having confidence neither in themselves nor in the fleet.'[87]

On the misty margins of these affairs, with the Admiralty casting about widely to maintain control of the 'official story', Churchill was contacted by sources unknown – perhaps Balfour, possibly Brownrigg, or, more likely, the Admiralty Permanent Secretary Sir William Graham Greene – to write an 'appreciation' of the Battle of Jutland. His golden pen would surely bring sense, proportion, and reassurance to an eager if disheartened readership.

Fisher, ever alive to proceedings, attempted to influence Churchill's account, via the naval writer John Leyland, who was to meet with Churchill at 41 Cromwell Road, Churchill's residence, on 9 June. Fisher urged Leyland to put forward his (Leyland's) two views of the battle, which were that 'either we must deplore that the enemy was not allowed to get further north before being attacked, or we must say that Beatty was provided with sufficient force for this business.' In other words, Beatty's actions were to be placed in doubt. Fisher also wanted Leyland to emphasise that mines should have been laid to bar the German fleet's return to port, that submarines should have been sent to intercept their return, and that Tyrwhitt's destroyers and Bacon's monitors should have been sent to make mischief.[88] Nothing seems to have resulted from this, and whatever Churchill wrote appeared in other guises in magazines that same summer.

Fisher was despondent over the news of Jutland. According to Sir Joseph Thomson, a member of the BIR Central Committee, who saw him on the morning after the battle: 'When I got to the office he was pacing up and down the room more dejected than any man I have ever seen. He kept saying time after time, "They've failed me, they've failed me! I have spent thirty years of my life in preparing for this day and they've failed me, they've failed me!" This was the only time I ever knew him to be doubtful about the issue of the war.'[89] The press pestered Fisher. Two days after the battle, he vented to his private secretary Crease:

> I've declined to see *anyone at all* calling here about the [Jutland] disaster ... And Beatty not waiting for his supports. And how slow ships (no matter how heavily armoured) *are no use*! Had the whole of Jellicoe's battleships been speedier, *how different the situation*!! The action began at 2 p.m. He (Jellicoe) only gets up at 6 p.m.! But you see: there'll be an outcry for ships as heavily armoured as a Spithead fort! *That* will be *the* red herring! And why didn't Lord Fisher put on more armour? *Hang Lord Fisher*! The 5 fast battlecruisers might have been in this battle with wonderful results! The 18-inch gun! At a mile beyond von Scheer's range! Von Spee over again at the *Falkland Islands*. I talked to Watts [the naval constructor] this week. These 5 battlecruisers could have been *all* ready last month (May) if pushed as intended.[90]

Describing episodes of the Battle of Jutland in a letter to Lady Jellicoe on 9 June, Fisher referred to Marshal Bosquet's description of the Charge of Light Brigade: '*C'est magnifique, mais ce n'est pas la guerre!*'[91]

The ongoing saga of British official reports about Jutland drew to a close. Two further statements command our attention. The first, Jellicoe's Despatch, as it is called, made public on 6 July, five weeks after the event, stated that the German fleet had been brought to action 'to the westward of the Jutland Bank, off the coast of Denmark'. Thus, 'Jutland', though the Germans called it the Battle of Skagerrak. Jellicoe made clear that it was a British victory. Control of the seas had not been lost, though there were heavy casualties. Visibility had hindered British efforts. The enemy had gone to ground.

The second report, known as the Admiralty's appreciation of the battle, was written by historian Sir Julian Corbett. Brownrigg obtained the necessary official sanction for this, presumably from Balfour, the First Lord. Brownrigg gathered the documentation for Corbett and anxiously awaited the results. Although Brownrigg says it was a true work of art, it had to pass through official channels and did not reach the press for three or four days – altogether too late for damage control. What the press saw as the Admiralty's passive attitude cast further doubts on the naval administration. Admiralty communications gave no indication of any apprehension about future outcomes but only assurances that Britain still dominated at sea. Official statements seemed untrustworthy. Churchill had been further assailed.[92] Had Jellicoe failed at Jutland? The press continued its attacks, and somehow a blind faith developed that Beatty was the true naval leader. And so was born the riddle of Jutland.

As a historian, Churchill came to his own conclusions about British shortcomings and failures at Jutland. Like Fisher, he had been disappointed. Something had gone wrong; indeed, many things had gone wrong. Until Arthur Marder followed up on earlier leads and explained the Admiralty's misreading of German electronic communications and the Admiralty war room's bungling of messages being sent to the Commander-in-Chief during the operations, it seemed as if only Jellicoe could be blamed. Certainly Beatty and others in the Battle Cruiser Squadron thought Jellicoe had arrived too late and really had not faced any enemy gunfire (which is incorrect). Churchill looked at matters from the reports of proceedings, and from Jellicoe's report. He had always appreciated that Jellicoe was the only man on either side who could lose the war in an afternoon, and he wrote just that in *The World Crisis*. He recounts three times during the battle when Jellicoe had the chance to engage the enemy more closely (as Nelson instructed). Churchill understood caution. But he could not comprehend the over-caution that was Jellicoe's style. 'Three times is a lot,' says Churchill.[93] As to the night action, when the Germans passed behind the British Fleet and ran home to safety, Churchill contended that Jellicoe should have been aware of that possibility, and he let the chance of a night engagement pass. Churchill's appraisal of Jellicoe and the Grand Fleet at Jutland is poignant, and it benefited from the fact that he came to write his history of it after Jellicoe's own book *The Grand Fleet*, largely a defence of British naval operations, had been published in 1919. The battle itself now became a battle of words. That is another story for another time and place, and it has become the stuff of legend.

What transpired at Jutland was not the decisive battle as had been expected at sea, not by a long shot. The great, promised day of the Grand Fleet taking on and destroying the German High Seas Fleet did not occur. This was not the Armageddon expected by Fisher and others; this was no Trafalgar. Rather, it was a muddle. Recriminations were bound to follow.

As an historian writing almost immediately after the war, Churchill was in fine position to write his story, select his facts, make his analysis, choose his favourites, and render his judgements. In the second volume of *The World Crisis*, devoted almost entirely to the Dardanelles, Churchill argued that there were two different schools of thought that existed at the Admiralty throughout the war: one was that the war was the business of the Army; the other, that the Navy was an instrument of offensive war.[94] This observation served Churchill well. It was under this general rubric that Churchill, in his third volume, favoured Beatty over Jellicoe. Beatty's spirited actions at Heligoland Bight in August 1914 and Dogger Bank in January 1915, and engagements with the enemy of his battlecruisers and fast division of battleships at Jutland, all won Churchill's heart. The Navy, concluded Churchill, was hobbled by its conservative mindset. Only gradually, he waxed eloquently, did the Navy liberate itself from 'the short-sighted prudent midwifery of the peace-time mind'. 'It stirred beneath the ponderous routine of the line of battle; it sprang into action with the battlecruisers in the North Sea, in the destroyers at Jutland and the Dover Straits, in the submarines of the Heligoland Bight and in the Sea of Marmara, in the motor-launches at Zeebrugge and Cronstadt.'[95] The implication was clear: Jellicoe's command at Jutland was a failure, or at least problematic; his passivity had induced the disaster to which, in private, Fisher referred. This was Churchill's view, but it did not go unanswered.

Years later Admiral Bacon, Fisher's and Jellicoe's faithful biographer, was scathing in his indictment of Churchill's account of the Battle of Jutland that appeared in *The World Crisis*. He complained that many of Churchill's statements were inaccurate, there were conspicuous omissions, and the deductions drawn by Churchill were misleading. Churchill often overstated German strength, therefore insulting the Royal Navy's capabilities, and the book 'unjustly impugns the professional conduct both of the Rear-Admiral commanding the 5th Battle Squadron and also that of the Commander-in-Chief of the Grand Fleet.' Bacon compared Churchill writing his history in his study surrounded by books and charts with the position of Jellicoe on the bridge. He damningly argued that Churchill's judgements were often tinged with an adventurous nature. Devastatingly, he contended that Churchill's prominence and prestige gave unwarranted exercise to his viewpoints, and that 'his account of that battle might well, without exaggeration, be described as a tissue of factual inexactitudes.'[96] These criticisms, however, came long after the event, and by this time many accounts of the smokescreen of Jutland had been written. We return to events, and another episode involving confidentiality of military and political secrets.

Five days after Jutland, early in the morning of 6 June 1916 Churchill went to the office of the War Council to consult records on some historical matters, perhaps the Dardanelles. He sat in Hankey's room, poring over documents to which he had been granted access. Hankey arrived to find Churchill. Not long afterwards his telephone rang. Hankey, answering it, heard the voice of James Masterton-Smith. The Admiralty Secretary told Hankey in cryptic language of the terrible loss of Lord Kitchener and his staff. Masterton-Smith urged total confidentiality, and this brought immediately to Hankey's mind the vain attempt to keep secret the loss of the dreadnought *Audacious* in 1914. Hankey put down the phone. Despite his quiet response, Churchill was on the alert. Hankey recalled:

> Churchill must have recognized some unexpected quality in my voice, for he pricked up his ears and asked if there was any news. I refused to be drawn. I am not sure he ever quite forgave me. But I think I was right. Churchill, it is true, was a Privy Counsellor, an ex-First Lord, the repository of many secrets, and an intimate friend. But he was out of office. The information was given to me by the First Lord's authority in the strictest confidence as likely to affect the proceedings of the War Committee that morning. I was not entitled to reveal it to anyone outside the War Committee. Moreover, the fewer people who know a secret, the less risk there is of its being divulged, whether by chance or design. The news was published officially the same morning.[97]

What had transpired was this: in the previous late evening, Lord Kitchener and his staff, on a mission from the British War Committee, and dispatched to Russia by way of Archangel to give special assurance of Allied support for the beleaguered Eastern Front, had been lost at sea. HMS *Hampshire*, an armoured cruiser, had been sunk off the western approaches to Scapa Flow by a mine, one later proven to have been laid by a U-boat. The loss of Kitchener proved fatal to British efforts to prop up the Russian war machine. While Russian discussions with the British continued into early 1917, from this tragic juncture Russian confidence in the West eroded. British ships continued to pour munitions and other war material into Russia, but there were logistical bottlenecks and soon the British began to doubt the Russian commitment to the Allied cause. The Russians, in turn, had grossly overestimated British promises of assistance. In any event, the great Kitchener had been removed from the scene, the victim of a weapon of underwater warfare.

Coming on top of the Jutland losses, news that Kitchener and *Hampshire* had been lost delivered a heavy shock. There was much anguish among the sailors of the Fleet that this great military figure should have come to his end when in the charge of the Navy. Problems mounted. Rumours that German spies had engineered the tragedy circulated. The Admiralty bungled the press releases; Berlin had news of the sinking before London.

It was also at this time that Imperial Germany announced its dreaded resumption of unrestricted submarine warfare. We return to that presently, but first will examine another form of soft warfare going on at the Dardanelles Commission.

'*What about the Dardanelles?*'

Of all the political figures Churchill was the most anxious for an inquiry. He wanted desperately to defend his administration at the Admiralty and vindicate himself from accusations of recklessness and irresponsibility. To this end, Churchill pressured Asquith to publish the principal Dardanelles documents. Churchill even offered his assistance to work with Hankey on deciding which documents were to be released: 'The series of papers wh I wish to have published cd then be printed provisionally & circulated with those wh others affected may choose. It may be that a few additions will then be thought necessary.'[98]

Asquith was not to be moved, and would not agree to make any documents public for fear of threatening his government and to avoid a heated controversy while the war continued. Hankey, the Cabinet Secretary, also opposed publishing the key documents so soon after the event. The Foreign Office, the War Office, and the Admiralty were all opposed to releasing aspects of the story.[99] Churchill himself had argued in the House of Commons against releasing documents in a response to Lord Charles Beresford's criticism of the conduct of the war at sea on 27 November 1914:

I would say that before it is possible to form a judgement it is necessary that the orders be disclosed, that the telegrams which have been passed should be disclosed, and that the dispositions which prevail, not only at the particular point, but generally throughout the theatre of war, should also in their broad outline and even in considerable detail be made known. That is clearly impossible at the present time. It would be very dangerous for the Minister representing the Admiralty to be drawn into what would necessarily become a controversial, and what might easily become an acrimonious discussion of these matters. And, above all, to disclose partially what has taken place would only lead to demands for fuller and further publication, which would be very prejudicial, not only to actual conduct of the War, but to the general interests of the Naval Service, during the course of the War.

It is not possible, however, desirable it may be, at present for the public or the House to form any judgement on these matters. The only rule which should guide us in regard to information is that nothing must be published which is against the public interest, or hampers naval or military operations.[100]

In regards to the Dardanelles he took a different tack, calling for the release of documents so as to clear his name. This played to the hand of the Unionists: on 1 June Bonar Law, then acting Leader in the House of Commons, announced that papers relating to the Dardanelles would be laid before Parliament. News of the recently fought battle at Jutland soon trickled in and occupied everyone's attention, but only for a while. The gleeful press was soon eager for the documents to be released.

The effect of Bonar Law's action was staggering. The great departments of state received news of the announcement with horror and alarm. Once in public hands the inside story of how the Dardanelles had been launched and carried out was sure to ruin political and service careers, expose the frail workings of the Cabinet to the enemies of the state, and reveal how a war ought not to be fought. The government was exposing itself to attack and ridicule. The principal players quaked in their boots. Hankey, who knew all, discussed the problem with Balfour and, with his backing, decided to ask Asquith to withdraw Bonar Law's foolish promise. Hankey pressed for this withdrawal 'on the ground that we cannot lay papers without exploring our plans in detail, including our intentions after the Dardanelles were past, so that the Turks would then either know that we would never again attempt the passage of the Straits, or would make plans to defeat our action in case we got through. I can imagine nothing more foolish than to do this during the progress of a great war.'[101] Hankey held to the belief that the Turks should be kept guessing; who knew, at some time a fresh attempt might be made, even as a feint, to immobilise a strong garrison in the Gallipoli peninsula and keep it away from other fronts. 'By revealing our earlier plans by publication we should be indicating that we never intended to renew the attack.' Hankey's logic was impeccable. The Foreign Office also objected, worried about diplomatic secrets, and the Admiralty and War Office were also reluctant to disclose ways and means of prosecuting the war, past, present, and future. 'The War Committee, the Service Departments, and the Foreign Office were all in it up to the neck,' says Hankey.[102] As in 1810, when the inquiry into the Walcheren expedition showed that timing was totally incorrect, attention was being drawn to past affairs rather than to prosecuting a gigantic campaign in progress on the Continent.

On 18 July Asquith announced the government would not release the documents because 'the publication at the present time ... could not be made ... without omissions so numerous and so important that the papers actually presented would be incomplete and misleading.' After a long and heated debate, the Asquith government was obliged to set in motion an inquiry into the Dardanelles campaign.[103] Churchill found strange allies with the Conservatives and Unionists who politically despised him and mistrusted his every move. But at this stage the tides of destiny were against him.

The Statutory Commission of Inquiry into the Dardanelles Expedition convened on 23 August 1916 under the chairmanship of Lord Cromer (succeeded on his death by Mr Justice Pickford), then promptly adjourned for twenty-three days to allow Hankey to prepare the papers of the War Council. Announcement of the commission found the dramatis personae scrambling about, getting their hands on documentation and seeking assurance from other principals that they would not wind up without a chair when the music stopped. Under the scrutiny of a protracted inquiry, no government could escape unscathed, no matter how disciplined the purpose and righteous the cause. Cracks developed, disintegration set in. Austen Chamberlain resigned as Secretary of State for India. Lord Kitchener, deceased, began to take on a less than heroic aura. Asquith was under a dark cloud. Balfour, valiant in defence, seemed to be slipping beneath the waves. Grey threatened resignation. Others in the Foreign Office would have preferred a judicial inquiry, but the die was cast, owing to Bonar Law's insistence.

Fisher was similarly concerned: he wanted assurance from Asquith that his opposition at the War Cabinet on 28 January 1915 would be duly noted by the commission – 'and I presume I shall be consulted as to any selection [of documents] that may be made.'[104] Hankey wrote to Fisher in July 1916: 'You and I, I suppose, will have to give evidence on this Dardanelles Committee. Before this we ought to have a talk.'[105] After their chat, where it is likely that Fisher expressed anxiety about his personal reputation and desired assurance that Hankey would back him, the Secretary of the War Council wrote back: 'It is a question of tactics to what extent I should allude to you in my evidence.'[106]

Churchill desired to take the offensive in defending the Admiralty's case against charges. He wrote to Fisher:

My dear Fisher,
Let us meet. You must not be downhearted. I am vy confident that things will right themselves in time. Nothing counts but winning the war... But what a shameful year of cowardice, inertia, futility and insolence has the Arthur

Balfour regime presented. The dead hand lies heavy on our noble fleets: & they even kiss it.[107]

Fisher sought from Churchill specific information of the crucial day of 28 January 1915, seeking to nail down exact details regarding the two War Council meetings of that date. Churchill told him that the minutes were well worth the read.[108] Immediately, Fisher wrote to Hankey to secure those notes. Hankey received permission from the prime minister to show them to Fisher but refused to send them out of the office. He assured Fisher that these records were open to his perusal.[109]

Churchill, always jockeying for position, wrote to Lord Cromer, the Dardanelles Commission chairman, in the second week of August to say what he had prepared for the commission. He said that his evidence would be given in three separate phases: (1) the genesis of the project till early May; (2) events leading up to Suvla Bay in August; and (3) the evacuation. Churchill stated that he was only prepared to deal with the first phase in any detail. He also made clear that he was going to conduct his evidence on his own without counsel, and that he planned to call a number of witnesses and strongly desired to be able to be present during the commission's full run.[110] On 20 September Cromer replied: 'The Commissioners have decided, in respect of all such meetings as are held in secret, not to admit anyone. They are, therefore, unable to comply with your request,' though he did indicate that the evidence of all witnesses would be printed, and witnesses could be recalled to respond to evidence submitted by another person.[111] This was not what Churchill had wanted to hear.

As the commission began its work, Fisher's opinion of Churchill remained high, as it had since March:

Everyone is running down Winston, nevertheless he has the fighting necessities in him:
COURAGE
AUDACITY
CELERITY
IMAGINATION
Those attributes don't exist in any single one of the 23! Not even in Lloyd George! who always stops at the last fence![112]

On 20 August Fisher met with Churchill for a strategy session. Churchill was optimistic about both his prospects and the probability of Asquith's supersession by Lloyd George, who was presumably a more sympathetic judge of these affairs. Churchill made clear that he believed that some hoped the commission would dissolve into a personal battle between the former First Lord and First Sea Lord, which he realised would be a devastating turn of events. He told Fisher he was determined to avoid such a public feud. Churchill wanted all above board: he promised to send Fisher his statement for the commission once he had prepared it.[113]

On 30 August Churchill wrote Fisher to tell him that he had been working on the Admiralty case for the inquiry and again promised him a copy when he had finished. 'I think you will be pleased with it.' He also sent Fisher a copy of Kitchener's statement from the War Office from 13 May 1915 when he was very angry about the withdrawal of *Queen Elizabeth* from the Mediterranean: 'The Admiralty Papers wh they are putting in consist entirely of Oliver's & Jackson's plans with the reports from the Admirals. You and I do not seem to have existed!'[114]

A sidelight on Churchill's insecurity at this time and his fears appears in a note to his friend F E Smith in regard to his statement. Churchill was unsure whether to focus on the naval side specifically or otherwise attempt to demolish myths surrounding the planning of the Dardanelles operation. He was particularly sensitive to the accusations that the operation had been rammed through the War Council secretly, was approved without expert backing, and that the Navy commenced operations that took the Army by surprise.[115] All of these were suppositions of note, and Churchill's fears were well founded.

Jacky Fisher was preoccupied at the same time with another, but related, matter. In a 30 August letter to Hankey he asked the essential question:

> Is your presentment of the Dardanelles case to Lord Cromer's Committee going to be Hamlet with the Prince of Denmark omitted? Bonar Law in his recent public speech to his party said that Lord Fisher's resignation led to the formation of the Coalition Government! What led to the resignation of Lord Fisher? Was it the Dardanelles or was it not? *If it was,* then how funny if you never mention my name! *Especially as being the only dissentient from the very outset!*

Fisher had apparently heard that his name had not appeared in Hankey's statement, though he told him that it was of no consequence since he had sent his own officially acknowledged letter. Also, Lieutenant General Sir Charles Monro, who had succeeded Hamilton in Gallipoli and had carried out the withdrawal, had rendered his testimony in secret. 'Well! "Truth is great and will prevail."'[116] Two days later he wrote to Hankey again, asking him to include Fisher's declaration of 14 May that he was no party to the operation and had stated his opinion to Asquith. This was another reference to the former First Sea Lord's opposition to the Dardanelles. Fisher also asked Hankey if he had in his possession the letter that Fisher had written to the prime minister on 25 January where he threatened resignation.[117]

On receipt of another letter from Hankey on 6 September, Fisher wrote again to express his recollection that both Kitchener and Asquith had known of his disquiet over the Dardanelles from 7 or 8 January and asked the Secretary for access to his materials for the Commission: 'If I ever am allowed hereafter to see what you have prepared for Lord Cromer's Committee of Inquiry I shall be better able to judge of its personal application to myself.'[118]

Fisher was profoundly suspicious of the Dardanelles Commission. A certain MP

had assisted at a séance where the conclusion was reached that ALL would emerge unblemished from the Dardanelles Inquiry with only ONE exception – Lord Fisher!... The contention is that had I not sat down again at the War Council Table on January 28, 1915, and thus resisted Lord Kitchener's entreaty NOT TO RESIGN, THEN the whole affair would have stopped dead!'... But it WILL be funny REALLY that the ONE and ONLY man who objected will be blamed! And the ONLY man who really suffered will be punished! Kitchener got the Order of *the Garter*, Fisher got the Order of *the Boot*![119]

Before Fisher's testimony at the inquiry, he received a telephone call from Lloyd George and met with him for forty-five minutes. 'I was asked what I was going to say about the Dardanelles. I replied, "*The truth*!"' he wrote to George Lambert. He also mentioned to Lambert in the letter 'I'm declining to meet Winston. I think it better not ...'[120] Churchill was careful to warn Fisher about the appearance of collusion – 'But beset as we are by foes it is better to proceed with the utmost caution'[121] – even though Fisher and Churchill had agreed to let Garvin, Fisher's partisan, see Churchill's documents and evidence.

As well, Hankey gave Fisher a 'heads-up' on two areas where in the questioning he was likely to encounter some heavy weather. Lord Nicholson ('Sir William Beelzebub', as Fisher called him on occasion) apparently asked Hankey whether in the circumstances someone remaining silent indicated that person's tacit consent. Hankey replied in the affirmative but told Fisher, 'I had repeatedly pointed out you [Fisher] had implied disagreement when you said the Prime Minister knew your views, even if you had not definitively explained what your disagreement was.' Another member of the inquiry pointed out the inconsistency of Fisher's account on 14 May, where he said that he was not a party to the operation, and the fact that he made no protest at the War Council on 28 January.[122]

Prior to giving evidence in person, Fisher sent in a preliminary draft of his defence to the commission. This was reviewed by Sir W F Nicholson, a long-standing military adviser, and James Masterton-Smith, the Admiralty Secretary. Both warned: 'Remember that the dramatic effect of your statement in the

Lords [on 16 November 1915] was largely due to the simplicity and brevity of what you said, and I cannot help thinking that so successful a precedent should be followed.'[123] Nicholson also warned Fisher against documenting the case too thoroughly, since it would surely make it easier to attract criticism, the last thing wanted. No, keeping it short and simple would suffice.

Fisher's line of reasoning in his submission was that both he and Churchill worked in accord until the Dardanelles operation. The operation, Fisher proclaimed a little artlessly, was something he had been against from the beginning. His long experience had brought him to the early conclusion that an operation to force the Dardanelles would be unsuccessful. He made clear that on that fateful day he was the only member of the War Council to dissent from the decision. Why did Fisher remain in office, then? It was a good question, and remains so to this day. His answer: that he thought it important to stay as First Sea Lord to see through his massive 612-ship construction programme for the Baltic scheme. 'The change in my opinion as to the relative importance of the probable failure in the Dardanelles undertaking began when the ever-increasing drain upon the Fleet ... reached a point at which in my opinion it destroyed the possibility of other naval operations.' And, again: 'In my judgment it is not the business of the chief technical advisers of the Government to resign because their advice is not accepted, unless they are of opinion that the operation proposed must lead to disastrous results.' Fisher explained that at the War Council he held his fire because it would have been unseemly for the First Sea Lord to disagree openly with his political chief. What triggered the resignation was the War Council meeting of 14 May, when it was decided to reinforce further the Dardanelles with ships specifically designed for use in Northern, that is, Baltic waters: 'Gradually the crowning work of war construction was being diverted and perverted from its original aim.'[124]

Fisher finished giving evidence at the Dardanelles inquiry on 11 October, revised the script of it sent him for approval, and returned it to Lord Cromer. To Cromer he also sent a letter in regard to the awkward questioning by Sir F Cawley at the commission, which asked Fisher to reconcile the statement on 14 May 1915 by Kitchener, who claimed the Admiralty proposed the Dardanelles operation, with Fisher's assertion that the idea came from the War Office. In January 1915 Kitchener had asked Churchill about the possibility of a demonstration against the Dardanelles. Fisher gingerly put it this way: 'I repeat that before Kitchener's letter of January 2nd to Mr. Churchill there was no Dardanelles!!' In a postscript he added: 'Mr. Churchill is quite correct. I backed him up till I resigned. *I would do the same again*! He had courage and imagination! *He was a war man*!'

Fisher also reinforced his position that the military and naval advisers were merely counsellors to the War Council, a position that had been openly doubted by Cromer and others: 'If you doubt my dictum that the Cabinet Ministers only were members of the War Council and the rest of us voice-tubes to convey information and advice, ask Hankey to come before you again and state the status! Otherwise the experts would be the Government!' Fisher then quoted from a speech given by Asquith in which he asserted that it was sometimes necessary for a government 'to run risks and to encounter dangers which pure naval or military policy would warn you against.'[125]

Fisher could rightly place blame on Asquith's shoulders. He aimed to make this clear to the commission. He wrote to James Clyde, who had carried out the examination of Fisher at the Dardanelles inquiry, with an addendum to his verbal answers to questions about the 28 January 1915 War Council meeting:

I don't remember how I answered you, but this is what I ought to have said:

'Everyone of them knew' ['of his opinion' – F.].
'I desired no scene.'
'The Prime Minister had decided.'

When I said at the Council table the Prime Minister knew my opinion, *and he did not tell the Council*, THEN I rose from the table intending to leave the Council ...[126]

Churchill also continued to submit memoranda to the Dardanelles Commission, eager as he was that his version of events would prevail. He both justified his support for the Gallipoli campaign in early 1915, and chided the government for not following through after his resignation in May 1915. When Churchill reviewed a draft copy of the interim report in early March 1917, he was upset that it did not include the evidence that would support his positions, even though he came out of the report much better than Asquith or Kitchener. Churchill submitted to the commission a series of notes on what he viewed to be the omissions from the report.[127] Fisher, too, took pains to protect himself. From McKenna he got unreliable news that he was the only one blamed, with Churchill whitewashed and Asquith getting some criticism.[128] And Rosebery also said he believed that the Dardanelles Commission was out to make Fisher the scapegoat.[129] It was Churchill, however, who paid the price for his zeal, initiative, and haste.

The Dardanelles First Report, which covered the origin of the campaign, was released on 12 February and published in *The Times* on 9 March 1917.[130] It stated categorically that the planning at the outset had been disastrous: 'We hold ... that the possibility of making a surprise amphibious attack on the Gallipoli Peninsula offered such great military and political advantages, that it was mistaken and ill-advised to sacrifice this possibility by hastily deciding to undertake a purely naval attack, which from its nature, could not attain completely the objects set out in the decision.'[131] By ships alone was now regarded as an immense blunder in strategy. A hint as to who was to be blamed is revealed in its conclusions: 'But without in any way wishing to impugn his [Churchill's] good faith, it seems clear that he was carried away by his sanguine temperament and his firm belief in the success of the undertaking which he advocated.' On the matter of the Dardanelles, Churchill was forever doomed.

Of course, every prominent person mentioned in the report distanced himself from it immediately, with numerous parties demanding to correct or excise the record, to make additions or emendations, or to add adjectives or qualifiers. The Dardanelles Inquiry Report was therefore designated as interim, and a committee was soon struck to vet the text, with Churchill, Bonar Law, Asquith, Carson, Jellicoe, and Hankey serving as members – hardly an uninvolved assemblage! The future of Ireland, the progress of war involving the Balkans, the future of Egypt and of Mesopotamia – these and other matters, all paramount military concerns – fell into the shadows. The conduct of the war at sea, the needs of merchant shipping, and the requirements for artillery and ammunition for 1918 were held up. All seemed hijacked while the Dardanelles inquiry pressed on its coronary case. 'Surely all this reveals an incredible loss of perspective on the part of Parliament and Press,' noted Hankey sorrowfully on 13 July.[132]

The interim Dardanelles Report made for 'sickening reading', newspaperman Riddell told the First Lord of the Admiralty, Sir Edward Carson, on 10 March. It revealed that no proper organisation existed to carry on the war. The Committee of Imperial Defence had become the Dardanelles Committee, then the War Council, all with ill-defined functions and odd links to Cabinet, the War Office, and the Admiralty. All was muddle: no supreme command existed. That morning, Carson's wife had said to him, 'Now I have read that report I know why you could not sleep when you were in Mr A[squith]'s government.' And I could not, Carson said: 'As I lay awake I could picture those gallant men [waging war and dying], and the mental picture was accompanied by the knowledge of the horrible mismanagement.'[133] And all this was being discussed as the U-boat peril was reaching its most critical state. Carson thought Asquith a great failure as a leader. But would Lloyd George be better?

The interim report came to the House of Commons for debate on 20 March. In anticipation Churchill spent six days carefully preparing his speech. Here was a chance to defend his position and answer his critics. On the day, he expressed general support of the report, but he criticised several specific quotations and the lack of evidence. In particular, he felt that the report had not dealt sufficiently with the shortage of shells in Ottoman forts at the moment when the attack was broken off. Success had escaped the Allies by a hair's breadth. Victory could have been achieved by pressing on. 'Your Commission may condemn the men who tried to force the Dardanelles,' he said, 'but your children will keep their condemnation for all who did not rally to their aid.'[134]

As for Fisher, his claim that he was obliged to yield his professional opinions to those of his superior weakened by the day and was widely discussed. One critic, Admiral Sir Hedworth Lambton Meux, had already commented in *The Times*, with respect to Fisher's claim that he had not been consulted on the Dardanelles operation, that Fisher could have very easily stopped the operation if he had just said he was opposed to it.[135]

It was against this background that Fisher gave his reaction to the release of the Dardanelles Report in the House of Lords on 21 March 1917. 'With your Lordships' permission,' he said, 'I desire to make a personal statement. When our country is in great jeopardy, as she now is, it is not the time to tarnish great reputations, to asperse the dead, and to discover our supposed weaknesses to the enemy; so I shall not discuss the Dardanelles Reports – I shall await the end of the war, when all the truth can be made known.'[136] He did not wish to make this an issue for the press, public, and Parliament to stew about when there were more important matters, and dangers, to consider.

In principle Fisher was right, but already, in practice, the daggers were out, and the daemonic duo faced extinction. Churchill, the last to realise the depth of the criticism levelled against him, wrote cheerily to Fisher: 'There is nothing in the Dardanelles Report which should be permanently injurious to either of us.'[137] Not many shared this view. Admiral Sir David Beatty's reaction to the Dardanelles Report was closer to the mark: 'I should think from it that as far as Winston and Fisher are concerned, they are done ... Enough time has been wasted already, and we had better devote all our time to getting on with the war.'[138]

12

Hazards of War and Last Acts

Churchill's return from the wilderness

In late 1916 and early 1917, as the Dardanelles Commission moved relentlessly toward its final and published conclusions, the political landscape continued to shift. Asquith's first coalition government, formed in consequence of the May 1915 crisis, had brought forward the thrusting Lloyd George as Secretary of State for War in July 1916, in succession to the deceased Kitchener. Bonar Law, underestimated by Asquith as to his character and talents, had acquiesced in Lloyd George's favour. It was a forced appointment certain to bring the new War Secretary into conflict with the generals, and it contained the seeds of the downfall of the Asquith administration and the disruption of the Liberal Party. Lloyd George's reputation was enhanced but Asquith's authority was crumbling. Sooner or later Asquith would have to go. With a reconstructed coalition government imminent, Churchill had high hopes for a return to power and influence. He most feared his old antagonist Bonar Law, who was determined to exclude Churchill from office. In the event, Bonar Law was unable to form a Cabinet, and Churchill calculated that his prospects might be enhanced if Lloyd George became prime minister.[1] In December Lloyd George formed his five-person executive War Cabinet.

In forming his War Cabinet, Lloyd George had to consider Churchill on account of, as the new premier put it, 'his fertile mind, his undoubted courage, his untiring industry, and his thorough study of the art of war.' Lloyd George was not himself averse to offering Churchill a position. However, his government was dependent on Conservative support, and leading Conservatives were dead set against Churchill being given any power or authority. Many Tories blamed Churchill for the early failures of the war and thought him far too prone to taking dangerous risks, as shown by the Antwerp adventure and the Dardanelles disaster. Some had also not forgiven Churchill for crossing the floor to the Liberals in 1904. Lloyd George wrote that some of them were more excited about Churchill's possible appointment than about the war: 'It was interesting to observe in a concentrated form every phase of the distrust and trepidation with which mediocrity views genius at close quarters.' Many believed that in Churchill's powerful mind lay an obscure deficit 'which prevented it from always running true.' They were nervous of a partnership involving Churchill. 'He had in their opinion revealed some tragic flaw in the metal.' Lloyd George thought Churchill had many great qualities, not least imagination, and he cited the tank or, as originally called, the 'land ship' as an example.[2] However, he could not hope to overcome such objections without the Dardanelles Commission at least partially rehabilitating Churchill. Lloyd George relayed this message to Churchill via Sir George Riddell, the *News of the World* proprietor, on 10 December.[3]

After this, Churchill deliberately held himself aloof from opposition groups until the final report of the Dardanelles Commission appeared. But that report, as shown, did not clear him of blame. Churchill remained in the wilderness. In a moment of dismay, he reasoned that had he remained as Chancellor of the Duchy of Lancaster, kept quiet, and drawn his salary, he would by this point have been among the leaders of the nation directing war affairs.[4] That was an error of judgement. The fact of the matter was that he had been unacceptable to the initial coalition – and these same persons who now backed Lloyd George did so on the understanding that Churchill remain out of office. He was unwanted. In the circumstance, Churchill would have to bide his time.

Never idle in advancing his own cause, Churchill meanwhile was active with his pen, his principal means of income. More, though exiled from councils of war, he could use his published articles as his voice, thereby giving him a chance to comment on the war's progress. From October 1916 to March 1917 Churchill wrote for the *London Magazine* and other periodicals.[5] He showed a remarkable inconsistency of argument and a vacillation of purpose, falling into traps of his own making. His first article, published in October 1916, provided much controversy, for he supported the defensive posture of the Grand Fleet and argued that it was being offensive by merely doing nothing. Churchill expressed views that were the exact reverse of what he had advocated when First Lord, 'Without battle we have all that the most victorious of battles could give us ... the action of the British Navy is essentially offensive and aggressive.' He implored the British nation to be satisfied with:

our silent attack upon the vital interests of the enemy ... No obligation of war requires us to go further ... There was no need [at Jutland] for the British to seek battle at all ... What harm does it do us if the German Fleet takes a promenade at sea? Their propellers churn the salt water, their pennants flaunt in the breeze, and the froth soon passes from the waves and the wind blows on – 'whither it listeth'. How does such a performance alter the grim and deadly naval situation from which Germany must find escape or surely perish? If Germany wishes to restore her fortunes, her fleet must not only come out – it must come out to fight, and to fight for a final decision; and it rests with the British Fleet to determine where and under what conditions the battle shall be fought.[6]

By January, Churchill had changed his tune again. He was now urging the Navy to take the offensive and force the Germans into battle. These articles did little to enhance his reputation. They also caused the Admiralty and Jellicoe distress. Vice-Admiral Sturdee, who had been Chief of Staff at the outbreak of the war, came privately to Jellicoe's aid. He wrote a long office memo critical of Churchill's articles for raising doubts in people's minds over the strategic direction of the Navy, and he noted that the views Churchill expressed in the early articles were the exact opposite of what he advocated when he was in office.[7] According to the careful judgement of Vice-Admiral Sir Peter Gretton, 'The most charitable explanation is that he started the series in a spirit of loyalty to the current Admiralty policy, but soon reverted to his own strong convictions on the right way to wage the war.'[8]

Anchored in Scapa Flow, Sir David Beatty, now Commander-in-Chief of the Grand Fleet, was also watching Churchill's actions, and he commented negatively on one of the articles in the *Sunday Periodical* that urged the Navy to become more aggressive. Beatty noted this was the complete opposite of what Churchill had advocated several months earlier. Further:

> It is disgusting that a man who has been a Cabinet Minister and First Lord of the Admiralty should be allowed to write articles in a rag of paper, belittling the officers and the great Service of which he was once the head. It is of course useless to expect a man such as he to do anything but intrigue and he has evidently made use of, or is attempting to make use of, a certain feeling that has been put about by some, that the Navy ought to be doing more, to make capital for himself & assist his intrigues to try and push himself into an office.[9]

Churchill's writings at the time raised larger issues. Was he attempting to be an opposition leader, or an opposition First Lord of the Admiralty? Churchill out of office was a difficult creature for any administration to face, not because of any popularity he might have had with the press or the public, for he did not command that sort of populist appeal, but because of his public pronouncements as a writer and commentator on the progress of the war, ranging far ahead of the politicians and criticising commanders and operations.

In April 1917, after the release of the interim Dardanelles Report – which implicated Churchill but did not draw final conclusions – Lloyd George looked for specific ways to employ the energetic Churchill. Lloyd George discussed with Dr Christopher Addison, the Minister of Munitions, the possibility of Churchill working in that ministry as chairman of a board or committee to examine the development of mechanical aids to warfare. At Lloyd George's suggestion, Addison met twice with Churchill, but nothing came of this.[10] On another occasion, also in April, Churchill met with both Lloyd George and Beatty. According to Beatty, who was seeing his old chief close up once again: 'There is no doubt he is a wonderful man with a mass of energy and will allow nothing to stand in his way when he wants to find out something. Our conversation was interesting and varied and, I hope, will have far reaching results.'[11]

During a secret session of Parliament on the course of the war, Churchill and Lloyd George met by chance behind the Speaker's Chair. According to Churchill, Lloyd George assured him that he desired Churchill to be by his side, and from that moment on, Churchill was a close colleague of the prime minister.[12] As the premier's confidante Frances Stevenson wrote: 'He [Lloyd George] says he wants someone in who will cheer him up and help & encourage him, & who will not be continually coming to him with a long face and telling him that everything is going wrong.'[13]

Lloyd George gave Churchill special assignments. On one of these, in late May, Churchill travelled to France. While there, English newspapers began to report that, on his return, he might join the Cabinet as chairman of the Air Board. This provoked an immediate reaction in Conservative circles. Lord Curzon wrote to Bonar Law on 4 June that 'some of us myself included only joined Ll.G on the distinct understanding that W.Ch was not to be a member of the Govt. It is on record, and to the pledge I and I think all my colleagues adhere.' Lloyd George, with astute judgrment, warned that bringing Churchill into the Cabinet would strain the loyalty of the Conservatives perhaps to the breaking point.[14]

Churchill recognised the constraints under which the new prime minister had to operate. He had held out hope that he could become chairman of the Air Board, which was a post outside Cabinet, but Conservative opposition could not be overcome.[15] Lloyd George considered offering Churchill his old position as Chancellor of the Duchy of Lancaster, which would at least give him a place in the administration, but Churchill had been there before. Why Lloyd George thought he might return to a room with only a view remains a mystery. Churchill responded by stating that he wanted a position in which he could help to defeat the Germans, and would not accept a sinecure.[16]

By mid-1917 a change had come over British political affairs. Lloyd George was in the ascendant and the Conservatives acted in nominal agreement on policy matters. On 16 July Churchill met with Lloyd George at 10 Downing

Street, where the latter, quite independently of other views, invited Churchill to join the government. Churchill was asked what post he preferred and stated his preference for the Minister of Munitions, to which Lloyd George agreed. Lloyd George had no stomach for telling Bonar Law of this development. Max Aitken, now Lord Beaverbrook, was sent for and then dispatched as messenger to ease the process with Bonar Law. The change was announced to the press on 18 July. There was a predictably hostile reaction from both the Tory press and leading Tory politicians. The *Morning Post* chortled that Churchill's appointment 'proves that although we have not yet invented an unsinkable ship, we have discovered the unsinkable politician.' Antwerp and the Dardanelles constituted two Churchillian blunders, said the same newspaper: 'Both expeditions were managed more or less personally by Mr Churchill, whose overwhelming conceit led him to imagine he was a Nelson at sea and a Napoleon on land.' Walter Long, the Conservative Colonial Secretary, wrote to Lloyd George to voice discontent over the move, and the powerful Lord Derby had to be persuaded by Lloyd George not to resign. Derby feared that Churchill would meddle in affairs outside his department. Indeed, as Churchill's aunt Cornelia warned her nephew: 'My advice is to stick to munitions and don't try & run the Govt!' Derby also noted that the move was a shrewd one for Lloyd George personally, as it denied Asquith one of his most powerful lieutenants.[17] To take the heat off Churchill, Lloyd George timed the announcement of the appointment when Lord Northcliffe of *The Times*, a likely opponent of any appointment for Churchill, was in Washington.[18] Lloyd George weathered the storm. Bonar Law was mollified, loyal to Lloyd George out of necessity. As A J P Taylor concludes, correctly, 'Thus did Beaverbrook reopen to Churchill the path to glory.'[19]

In his first months as the Minister of Munitions, Churchill's primary task was to reorganise the department to streamline responsibility and increase efficiency. It was not long, however, before some of his Cabinet colleagues began to question the scope of his activities. Churchill was invited to a War Cabinet meeting of 15 August at which munitions were to be discussed. As Churchill was not a member of the War Cabinet, he was only to offer his opinion when he was asked for it. However, on the question of the allocation of British field guns to Russia, Churchill gave his views unasked. During a second War Cabinet meeting later that afternoon, Churchill gave his opinion on the transfer of naval guns from the Admiralty to the War Office, as there were no representatives from the Admiralty there to challenge him. When the two Service ministers heard what had happened, they were outraged and wrote directly to Lloyd George to protest at Churchill's actions. In the end, both threatened to resign if Churchill was not reined in.[20] The storm passed.

It was not in Churchill's nature to confine his activities to those matters within his assigned administration or jurisdiction. He always expanded beyond borders, filled every space. Here is an example. When Jellicoe had been made First Sea Lord in November 1916, Churchill had congratulated him and had early on pressed upon the admiral that he could 'win for the Navy, without jeopardising its main strength, those opportunities of *minor* offensive action without which neither glory nor in the long run safety can be achieved.'[21] Shortly after returning to the Cabinet as Minister of Munitions, Churchill proposed that the Navy go on the offensive and seize strategic points such as Heligoland, Borkum, or Sylt, as well as use blockships (that is, purposely sunk ships) to seal the submarine exits of German rivers and ports. In effect, Churchill had reverted to his old audacious schemes of offensive action. Jellicoe responded to the more specific proposals (which were surely unwelcome to the First Sea Lord), arguing that they were not feasible and unlikely to achieve success. He did, though, hold out the possibility that if efforts to defeat the submarine menace were unsuccessful on the high seas, operations to inhibit submarine operations and block their exits might be undertaken.[22] By December 1917 Jellicoe had approved planning for an amphibious attack to plug U-boat ports in Belgium. Herein lay the origin of the Navy's remarkable, gallant operation of 23 April 1918 to block Ostend and Zeebrugge and bottle up the U-boats in their lairs and places of refurbishment. In the event the results were mixed and inconclusive but had advantages in morale-building, reminiscent as the operation was of the spirit of Drake and Nelson. Churchill thought the thrilling Zeebrugge episode had returned to the Navy the panache that had been lost at Jutland. Before long U-boats set to sea again on their deadly pursuit of enemy quarry and merchant shipping, but they did so in fewer numbers, and the Dover barrage and North Sea barrage became more effective in lessening the range and activities of the U-boat arm.

BIR *and the submarine menace*

Meanwhile, Fisher, who was still at the Board of Invention and Research, was also working to combat the submarine menace. The site chosen for the new BIR research station (after it moved from Hawkcraig, leaving that station to C P Ryan) was Parkeston Quay at Harwich, the base of Admiral Reginald Tyrwhitt's destroyer and submarine flotillas. Offices were warmly housed in the Great Eastern Railway Hotel, the equipment stashed in a quayside room. Wooden huts housed laboratories, workshops, mess rooms, and kitchen. Most of 1917 was taken up equipping workshops and laboratories as well as acquiring vessels for conducting experiments. *Hiedra* was transferred from Hawkcraig, and *Ivy*, a wooden steam yacht, was purchased. Destroyers from Tyrwhitt's squadron were available as required. Soon the scientific staff at Parkeston Quay had grown to over thirty, and the number of mechanics to over fifty. Work was undertaken on hydrophones, non-contact mines, sound-ranging devices, indicator loops (which could be used both to guide ships and to give warning of hostile craft, by means of cables supplied with alternating current laid on the sea bed), and ASDIC (later known as sonar).

Fisher rejoiced in the progress. To Jellicoe he wrote on 26 January 1917 that if seaplanes could use the direction finder to locate submarines it would be a development of great importance. He also noted that he would soon be travelling to Harwich with his 'Magi', J J Thomson, C Parsons, G T Beilby, and Vice-Admiral Sir Richard Peirse, to see the director, W H Bragg, and to discuss anti-submarine matters.[23] By this time two anti-submarine antidotes were in active preparation. On 17 March Fisher witnessed a demonstration of 'our submarine finder', and proclaimed it privately and secretly as a great success.[24] Here was not only a promising sign but also a talisman of naval warfare for the future.

However, Fisher and the BIR continued to feel ignored and left in the dark by the Navy and other departments of the Admiralty.[25] At a meeting on 27 March complaints were raised by Sir Ernest Rutherford, Bragg, and others about the obstruction they faced from the Navy. They were appalled that they had been denied access to reports of the Navy's successful actions against submarines. In response, Commander S S Hall, representing the Navy at the meeting, stated, 'The only information necessary to be given was that the enemy submarines were in the sea, and that means were required to detect their presence.'[26]

As shipping losses to U-boats rose dramatically, the War Cabinet called Fisher to appear before it in regards to a remark he had made to Sir Edward Carson, the First Lord of the Admiralty, in a letter dated 1 February: 'I've given [Admiral Jellicoe] a plan for dealing effectively with the German submarine menace. If he don't like it, there's an end of it, and if he don't mention it to you, I hope you won't ask him.'[27] The War Cabinet wanted to know its particulars. Fisher duly attended the War Cabinet meeting of 28 March and explained that he had offered to serve under Jellicoe as Controller of the Navy in order to provide more effectually than at present all the apparatus needed to subdue the enemy's submarines.

Two days later, Fisher sent six copies of a BIR memorandum for the War Cabinet's attention. It emphasised how the BIR was being ignored and marginalised by the Navy:

The Board of Invention and Research venture to express their opinion that not withstanding their readiness and desire to bring the combined knowledge of the Board to bear upon such problems, the desire on the part of the Board has not been taken advantage of by the Admiralty to the extent it might have been. On the contrary, the policy of certain Departments has been to adopt such a reticent attitude in dealing with the Board as to create a feeling that the efforts of the latter are viewed with – to say the least – indifference.'[28]

When the businesslike Sir Eric Geddes, former director of North Eastern Railway, became Controller of the Navy in May (and then First Lord of the Admiralty in July), Fisher saw his opening and argued for a reorganisation of the BIR. Fisher claimed that scientists needed to know about all the Navy's anti-submarine actions, successful or not, so that they would be able to learn from operations what countermeasures had already proven effective. The Naval Staff did not want to release details of these actions, which had been kept secret to that point. The Director of Naval Intelligence, Reginald Hall, held that circulation of the reports would 'only lead to irresponsible criticism'. Fisher was livid at what he read as an insult to himself and demanded the removal of Hall. Geddes hauled Hall in for an interrogation and demanded he write a more polite response to Fisher's request as apology, but he refused to fire Hall.[29]

In response to Fisher's agitation, Geddes sent Sir R Sothern Holland, Sir H Ross Skinner, and Captain Alfred C G Egerton with a brief to 'investigate how the work of the Board of Invention and Research can be further aided'. Geddes told Fisher that the goal was to ensure that new inventions were given 'more expeditious and practical effects'.[30] On 21 September, the Holland–Skinner (or Sothern Holland) Report reiterated the well-worn complaints about poor communication and a lack of co-ordination:

> The Navy up to quite a recent date has possessed no research institution and such establishments as now exist have grown up in spite of little encouragement and the absence of any general plan. The Board of Invention and Research ... has not received the full support of the Admiralty ... There has been overlapping of experimental work amongst the various Departments and men of science willing to give their assistance have not been put in the position to get the necessary information to deal effectually with the problems put before them.[31]

The report noted that the BIR's main effort had been directed to 'the provision of means of location and destruction of submarines'. The results were the production of 'a fairly satisfactory hydrophone' and 'a magnetic destructor mine'. On the other hand, the invention of ASDIC was hardly mentioned in the report, which concluded:

> (a) that men of the greatest scientific knowledge are not being used to the fullest extent and are being wasted on committee work; (b) that the B.I.R. does not work in sufficiently close touch with the Admiralty, and *vice versa*; (c) that the scientists are not in and amongst the problems they work on; (d) that the present constitution of the B.I.R. does not admit of the individual driving and co-coordinating power which is so essential to all executive undertakings; and (e) that the multiplication of experimental establishments by the Admiralty must lead to dissipation of forces and to confusion.[32]

Holland and Skinner recommended abolition of the BIR and appointment of a Director of Experiment and Research at the Admiralty. This person would be responsible for the direction of all research, inventions, and experiments under the Third Sea Lord.

Although the Holland–Skinner Report was completed in September, no action was taken for several months, leaving the BIR in a state of acute uncertainty, with some scientists threatening resignation. In December Fisher wrote to ask Geddes his views on the BIR so Fisher would be in a position 'to direct the whirlwind and control the storm'. He made clear he would not resign, because he believed the right attitude was to serve in any way that he was needed – 'we have to say like the Roman Gladiators "Ave Geddes Imperator! Morituri te salutant!"'[33] In response, Geddes told Fisher that he had heard no such complaints, and that while Holland had made his report, he (Geddes) had not acted on the report because he did not know the views of the members of the BIR. He asked Fisher to apprise him of these views. And so the matter went back and forth.[34]

On 26 December Fisher sent Geddes the BIR's views on the report. In general, they agreed with its conclusions, but the delay in implementing recommendations had caused disruptions, uncertainty, and unrest among members and staff. The Admiralty was setting up research organisations that were separate from the BIR, while at the same time the BIR was still attempting to carry out its original terms of reference. Fisher was infuriated that scientific advisers were being 'relegated into answering the bell of Admiralty subordinates'.[35]

Fisher got action. In January 1918 his plan for reorganising the BIR was put in place. Overall supervision of scientific research was transferred to the newly created Department of Experiment and Research at the Admiralty. W H Bragg was attached to the Admiralty's Anti-Submarine Division (ASD), and Professor A S Eve took over Bragg's old post as Resident Director at Parkeston Quay. Parkeston Quay itself was transferred to the ASD, and scientific work there was not affected by changes in the BIR.[36]

But Fisher could not stop complaining, and this led to his final exit from official responsibilities. In January 1918 he wrote a memorandum, 'How the Great War was Carried On', in which he criticised the Admiralty's treatment of the BIR, complaining that 'we were doomed to exasperation and failure by not being able to overcome the pigheadedness of Departmental Idiots. We had to deal with three First Lords, all cordial and appreciative, but they were all equally powerless because none of them would kick anyone out, so at last we had to kick ourselves out ... Never has the Admiralty Executive so wholeheartedly supported the scientific and thoroughly practical proposals of the BIR research.'[37] Geddes could take no more. In a memo 'Organization of

Scientific Research and Experiment' he wrote that the BIR was to be terminated, and Professor J C McLennan, FRS, was to become the head of the Scientific Research and Experiment Department of the Admiralty to deal with scientific questions in the post-war world.[38]

Fisher's last day of association with the BIR was 31 December 1918. He had contributed to the detection of submarines by electronic measures by being the shield protecting the scientists and the naval technicians and experimenters. He had been sidelined from his essential tasks, showed no joy in his work, and was invariably frustrated by the position he held as bystander, critic, energiser, and prodder. The scientists could not work miracles. Turning theory into paradigm into device, and then making the device workable under service conditions, then mass-producing the device and installing it, all in an economically feasible way – this was the challenge.[39] All that lay beyond Fisher.

Even so, the day of ASDIC (later sonar) had arrived. In his concluding 'Report on the Position of Experiment and Research for the Navy', Professor Bragg wrote proudly of 'echo' methods by which 'a beam of sound of a special kind may be emitted under water from the new "Asdic" transmitter in a form as concentrated as that of the searchlight and falling on objects underwater which may give rise to reflected or scattered sound by which the presence and position of the objects can be found. The sound is special in that the wave length is extremely short and the sound cannot be directly detected by the ear.'[40] Of all the methods tried by the French, the British, and the Americans, the most successful so far involved the piezo-electric property of quartz. A submarine lying on the bottom at horizontal distances of 400–700yds, at a depth of 25 to 27 fathoms, could now be detected, and approximate bearings given.[41]

As for Jacky and his leadership at the BIR, Sir Joseph Thomson, Nobel prize-winning physicist of Cambridge, who discovered the electron, wrote this tribute:

I never came across anyone with such pronounced personality, nor with such extraordinary driving power. His method was that of the mailed fist rather than the gloved hand, and in carrying out his schemes he made many enemies and hurt many people's feelings. When different schemes came before him he spent very little time in determining which should be chosen, and in his choice he seemed to be guided by instinct rather than by reason. When he had made his choice, his whole energies were thrown into carrying it into effect. This was a great contrast to the practice I had been accustomed to in University matters. In these, much time and energy is spent in discussing what scheme should be adopted, so much so that one is apt to be tired of the scheme before it is started, and to be languid in carrying it out. There can be no question which is the better method in war-time. Lord Fisher had foresight and imagination as well as energy. He could see the potentiality of inventions which in their early stages had been nothing but failures. He envisaged what service they might render if the purely mechanical difficulties were overcome, as there was a good chance they might be by skill and perseverance, and he did all in his power to expedite this process.[42]

'Won't you handicap your great resolve by associating with me?'

Though the BIR provided a channel for Fisher's seemingly inexhaustible energies, he remained dissatisfied. His letters show his exasperation. He longed for a return to authority and to a prominent role in the war effort. In a letter to Civil Lord of the Admiralty George Lambert, Fisher attached the following kindly and sympathetic newspaper cutting:

TO JACKY FISHER.
To lose a man like you, Sir,
Our land can ill afford,
And in our private view, Sir,
You're with inventions – bored![43]

Admiral Sir Henry Jackson, Fisher's successor as First Sea Lord, had it right when he told Admiral de Robeck in the Mediterranean in early 1916, 'Jacky is tired of being out of the limelight, & been busy intriguing with the press to turn out either Mr. Balfour or myself, with the hope of getting back to the Admiralty. It is not a very patriotic thing to do but that does not count with him.'[44] Fisher continued to insist that he had a plan to end the war in a single decisive stroke. This was typical of the great admiral. He shied away from revealing what this stroke could be, arguing cagily that one should 'never prescribe till you are called in.' As he stated, he feared that his plans would be emasculated if he just handed them in without taking on the responsibility for executing them.[45] That was Jacky's style.

In October 1916 he fulminated against the politicians: 'Balfour is asleep, Asquith is week-ending, Lloyd George is scheming, Bonar Law is Asquithiated.'[46] When rumours of political change reached him the next month, Fisher, ever the opportunist, imagined his moment had arrived. The former First Lord, Reginald McKenna, was plotting to bring back Fisher. Writing to Lambert, his mole, on 16 November: 'I got an urgent telephone to meet McKenna yesterday. He says that Balfour is on his last legs this week! I DON'T BELIEVE IT! McKenna makes out that Asquith very cordial towards me, but he can't force me on Balfour.'[47] Fisher continued trying to pull political strings to arrange high command. All was in vain, for his credit had run out. He had discredited himself in the Dardanelles affair, and many thought his resignation dishonourable. The Board of Invention and Research had yielded no quick fixes to end the submarine peril. If changes were not made in the running of the war at the Admiralty – in particular, if the submarine menace was not 'promptly dealt with' – Fisher believed 'we shall *very shortly* have a COMPULSORY IGNOBLE peace.'[48]

During the changes in the coalition government in December, when Lloyd George became prime minister, Fisher heard various rumours about changes at the Admiralty, including one that said Walter Long was to succeed Balfour as First Lord, conditional on Fisher not being allowed inside the Admiralty.[49] Fisher's return to the Admiralty was blocked. He looked for enemies and wrote to the editor C P Scott on 24 December:

> My enemy, I discover with intense astonishment, is Bonar Law!!! He said three days ago that he was convinced I was 'mad'. (I BEG YOU TO KEEP THIS TO YOURSELF!) So I sent my informant the enclosed letter when I had recovered from the stupefaction of his announcement! But I had but little doubt that Bonar Law had to invent an excuse for his 'volte-face' towards me! He found the Court and Walter Long's party of Tories too much for his friendship for me, and as is the way of politicians 'he ratted'! ... I give my whole mind and thoughts continuously and persistently every second by day and night to thinking out my schemes! *So I am keeping* 'EVER READY'![50]

The move that most impacted Fisher's hopes, though, was not one of the political changes arising from the formation of Lloyd George's coalition government. Rather, it was the appointment of Jellicoe as First Sea Lord a month earlier. Fisher worried about Jellicoe's upcoming summons to the War Cabinet. He must have thought Jellicoe unprepared to deal with what he derisively called the 'frocks', and he put it bluntly in a letter: 'These politicians will get the better of you!' Jellicoe was the essence of the Grand Fleet, Fisher contended. If Jellicoe allowed himself to be promoted out of the Grand Fleet, he would 'betray the country'.[51]

On 8 November Fisher wrote to Jellicoe with respect to rumours of the latter's appointment as First Sea Lord:

> Never in my life have I written a letter with deeper reluctance than this. I have been hoping against hope you would have listened to my entreaty not to give up Command of the Grand Fleet, more especially *just now* when Hindenburg [appointed Supreme Commander] will overcome all German Naval scruples and order out the German Fleet *as he now has the power to do*! He sent those ten German destroyers lately to Boulogne and Folkestone a few days after the German Emperor gave him authority over the German Fleet, when Naval Officers thought it madness, *and he succeeded*! ...
>
> You have agreed with me that the chief danger now threatening us is the German Submarine Menace ... And you now lend yourself to an Effete

Administration which has brought us to the verge of Naval Ruin ...
This is the saddest letter of my life.[52]

The rumours proved true, for on 1 December Jellicoe informed Fisher that he had accepted the post of First Sea Lord. He did so, he said, precisely because he agreed with Fisher on the great threat posed by the German submarine fleet, and he could do nothing to cope with that menace from the command of the Grand Fleet.[53] Beatty, now appointed Commander-in-Chief, Grand Fleet, was generally pleased with Jellicoe's move to the Admiralty, but he shared Fisher's concern. He held the view that 'the trouble with him, i.e. J[ellicoe], is that if [Sir Edward] Carson [First Lord of the Admiralty] doesn't support him, he, Jellicoe, is not strong enough in character to make him [do the Navy's bidding].'[54] Though Fisher continued to support Jellicoe, he came to believe that the latter 'had all Nelsonic attributes except *one* – he is totally wanting in the great gift of Insubordination. Nelson's greatest achievements were all solely due to his disobeying orders! ... He is THE ONE MAN to command the Fleet, BUT he is not the man to stand up against a pack of lawyers clothed with Cabinet garments, and possessed with tongues that have put them where they are!'[55]

Fisher saw himself as Jellicoe's guardian and his adviser. He told Jellicoe that though he would never do anything to subvert him, he would never forgive him for leaving the Grand Fleet and coming to the Admiralty as First Sea Lord. In July 1917 Fisher drafted a bitter letter to Jellicoe which reveals his sense of betrayal, though he apparently did not send it:

It is a strange irony of Fate that you should be the one I selected in 1906 to be Admiralissimo when I predicted at that time that the war with Germany would break out in August 1914 ... and yet you should be the one to twice ruin my hopes of winning the war.

1st by giving up the Command of the Grand Fleet in November 1916 to be First Sea Lord.

2nd by refusing to let me join you as Controller of the Navy on January 31st 1917.

In the first instance you left the appointment for which you were specially fitted on the grounds that you alone could deal with the German Submarine Menace.

In the second instance you refused me as Controller and instead accepted a Railway Engineer [Geddes], concurred in making him into a Vice-Admiral with precisely the powers you refused me.

And now where are you?

Yours,

Fisher[56]

As mentioned earlier in this chapter, Fisher lobbied to return to the Admiralty, offering to serve as Jellicoe's Controller, or Third Sea Lord. He brazenly contended that he could quash the submarine menace. Jellicoe did not want Fisher at the Admiralty. He had been warned of Fisher's conniving. Sir Charles Madden wrote to Jellicoe: 'Beatty told me how dangerous the Fisher cabal has become ... I do hope this catastrophe [Fisher's return to the Admiralty in some capacity] can be averted. Beatty said he was anxious to become Controller. Of course once he got a footing he would intrigue to push you or Sir Edward Carson out or both ... I wish you every success and *no Fisher*.'[57] On 13 February 1917 Jellicoe wrote that there were only two positions Fisher could fill at the Admiralty – First Lord and First Sea Lord. Difficulties would arise with any other post. The next day Fisher wrote that he was 'grieved' by Jellicoe's note, as he was 'confident it would have been a success.'[58]

Widespread suspicion existed in the Admiralty that Fisher would try to use his position at the Board of Invention and Research to return to power and exact vengeance on those who he felt had wronged him. Sir David Beatty, visiting the Admiralty and with a good view of these movements, wrote to his sweetheart, 'What a hot bed of intrigue London is and how old Fisher is enjoying himself. The old rascal, 77 yrs old and he still nobbling weak minded people right and left. I understand I am to get the sack. Not for any Crime but to make room for Bacon!!'[59] (The reference is to Reginald Bacon, unfettered supporter of the great Fisher, and his eventual biographer.)

In a crying letter to Hankey regarding his discarded offer to serve as Controller, Fisher wrote, 'I am not a deserter! I'm an outcast!'[60] This last was correct: he was indeed an outcast, and a troublesome and even pathetic one at that. Marx once wrote that history repeats itself: first as tragedy and then as farce. This was the state with Fisher's attempts to return to the Admiralty. He sounded all the alarm bells. He wrote widely to his friends proclaiming the stupidity of Jellicoe and Carson declining his offer to serve.[61] He tried to exploit the press. He tried to lure in Lloyd George. Jellicoe would have none of it. When Lloyd George went to Carson, the First Lord, 'to beg him to have [Fisher] back at the Admiralty, ... Carson told Lloyd George that Jellicoe objected and he (Carson) would therefore resign sooner than agree ... So *finis* Jellicoe!'[62]

Churchill was also working on Fisher's behalf. On the occasion of the admiral's seventy-sixth birthday, 25 January 1917, Churchill wrote consolingly to Fisher: 'Like you, I have seen no one political. One is quite powerless as far as the war is concerned ... Our common enemies are all powerful today, and friendship counts for less than nothing.'[63] Less than a month later, on 21 February 1917 Churchill came to Fisher's defence in the Commons. Admiral Sir Hedworth Lambton Meux, MP for Portsmouth, had made a speech in which he denounced Fisher for sowing discord in the Navy (reported in *The*

Times, 19 February). Churchill stated that this was not the proper spirit in which to approach 'the appointment of men of the highest ability to the national service', and he argued that Britain needed to use all her talent and all her resources for the war effort. While cautioning that by expressing such an opinion he did not imply any want of confidence in the current Board of Admiralty, he said he hoped the First Lord would be able 'to find some means by which the fertile genius of Lord Fisher can be more effectively associated with the conduct of naval affairs.'[64] On 26 February Meux responded with a litany of complaints about Fisher dating back to the Bacon letters, and contended that when Churchill was First Lord 'he was more or less in the pocket of Fisher.'[65]

Meux also stated that Fisher was at the Admiralty when the three cruisers of the 'live bait squadron' were torpedoed in the North Sea in the autumn of 1914 with heavy loss of life. In a letter to George Lambert, Fisher defended himself: 'I WAS NOT! But directly I returned to Admiralty I took steps to deal with those responsible, and two of them (Admirals H.H. Campbell and Christian) being the King's favourites, I incurred venom!' Fisher claimed that Meux was really after him because of the monies that were saved by Fisher before the war: 'There's a big trade union in the Navy, and I got up against it by getting rid of 19 ½ millions sterling of parasites animate and inanimate! *Hinc illae lachrymae!* (Hence these tears!)'[66] Meux's constituency, Portsmouth, was home to large dockyards, where Fisher's economies would have had an impact.

A week later Churchill wrote to Fisher about Meux's attacks, which were apparently continuing in the Commons and the press: 'His attacks will do you no harm – but rather good.'[67] But Churchill's problem was that he could not leave the matter alone, and when he wrote to Fisher again on 12 March he said, 'I have a strange recurrent feeling that you are going to have another chance. But we must have a talk. Above all don't get downhearted. After all the Falklands and the Big Programme are lasting assets.'[68]

Would that last chance be provided by the catastrophes in the sea war that were regularly being reported, as merchant shipping was sunk by U-boats? For good or ill, Fisher was in no position to influence the conduct of naval policy. The High Seas Fleet remained safely at its moorings. And nothing the Allies did could persuade German high command to send them out. It was preservation of that fleet that mattered, the Kaiser knew. As 1916 had closed on a sour note for Britain, there was no sign of the war's end. Jutland brought no promised victory at sea. The Battle of the Somme had resulted in horrific results to the British armies. And the U-boat peril increased. Jellicoe told Fisher he was pessimistic about the Admiralty's ability to deal with the submarine menace.[69] Jellicoe's pessimism resonated with Fisher. His main concern was that the apathy shown at the Admiralty would soon bring about an ignoble peace.[70]

Churchill, meanwhile, had never abandoned the belief that a Baltic campaign could turn the tide of the war in the Allies favour. He liked war on the margins, away from the Western Front with all its barbed wire chewing away at Allied lifeblood. He returned to this theme, writing to Fisher that a descent on the German coast offered a decisive victory for the Allies, much better than any possible alternatives.[71] He may have been correct. All the same, with preparations underway for the campaign of Passchendaele, the third Battle of Ypres, a strike on the margins by an amphibious force could not be considered. And as long as the German fleet existed as 'a fleet in being' it posed a threat to British security and military operations. The British high command wanted no second front. To Churchill on 11 April Fisher reiterated his usual disgust at the Navy not taking up his Baltic project. 'The Balfourian Apathy at the Admiralty [has] wrecked the war. An un-imaginative Naval Strategy ... Never did a mighty predominant Navy like ours occupy so utterly a humiliating position as it now does!'[72]

Churchill wanted Fisher back at the Admiralty; the cagey old admiral was not so sure. Conscious of the difficulty he might cause Churchill, Fisher put it this way: 'The question is – "Won't you handicap your great resolve by associating me with it?" ... The Public will not reflect that "*A man is only as old as his arteries*"! which reminds me that Sir Bertrand Dawson [Fisher's physician] has invited himself to see mine this very afternoon! being apparently a source of pleasure to him! (I always fear his putting me in the *Lancet* [British Medical Society journal] as a "*freak*"! But truly I am "*exceeding fit*"!)'

In his next breath Fisher listed the vital necessities for the Baltic scheme: 'an immense cloud of aircraft ... prodigious mine-laying facilities ... an *armada* of "submarine-proof" craft...the 500 *self-propelled* barges', or landing craft, that had been intended for an attack on the German coast in July 1915, '*and another mass of them ordered!*' The recapture of Antwerp would follow. This would put heart into Russia, and revive the Russian army.[73]

At the same time, Fisher gave due warning to Lloyd George that the High Seas Fleet might attempt to force a Trafalgar-like battle on the Grand Fleet, and arguing that, to face this threat, Jellicoe should be reappointed to his former post as Commander-in-Chief, Grand Fleet. In making this request, Fisher did not disparage Beatty. Rather, he insisted that Jellicoe was the best man for the job. Fisher also noted his increased fear of invasion, due in particular to the appointment of Hindenburg to lead the German armed forces.[74]

Lloyd George wanted to know more. When Fisher appeared before the War Cabinet on 28 March, he was asked to explain this latter concern. He made it clear that although he had earlier doubted the possibility of invasion, he now believed it to be feasible. The War Cabinet minutes give his seven reasons:

(1.) His diminished confidence, owing to the withdrawal from the command of the Grand Fleet of Admiral Sir John Jellicoe, whom, without disparaging Admiral Sir David Beatty, he had always regarded as the best man and exceptionally qualified for the post, and whom he himself, when in office, had for many years designated as Admiralissimo in time of war;

(2.) The increasing German submarine menace; the numbers of enemy submarines, he pointed out, were now extraordinarily large, and their sea-keeping qualities were increased;

(3.) The demonstration at Gallipoli of the practicability, not only of landing in the face of fire, but of maintaining the expedition on beaches which were under continuous fire;

(4.) The fact that the German Fleet is under the higher command of a military officer, namely, Field-Marshal Hindenburg. He pointed out that a military officer might order the Fleet to take risks that no naval officer would contemplate, and instanced the case of Villeneuve being ordered to sea by Napoleon;

(5.) The risks to the Grand Fleet from mines and submarines in its passage to the vicinity of the landing-places;

(6.) The recent increase in the size of the German Army, which rendered the requisite number of troops available;

(7.) The fact that ample transport is available, 45 per cent. of the German mercantile marine being at Hamburg and Bremen, as well as small craft at Emden, suitable for disembarkation purposes.

For defensive measures, though, without full information of the Admiralty's current dispositions Fisher could recommend nothing more than returning Jellicoe to command of the Grand Fleet.[75] This last had no resonance with the Cabinet, and Fisher's fears of invasion were not confirmed by British naval intelligence. If there had been any doubt, it was clear now that his star was fading fast.

After the War Cabinet meeting of 28 March, Fisher drew up a memorandum to Lloyd George in which he stated that he was appalled that Germany was now able to deal a deadly blow to the Russians by taking St Petersburg, and that the Royal Navy was unable to frustrate this attack: 'All this due to the grievous faulty Naval Strategy of not adopting the Baltic Project put before Mr. Asquith in association with the scheme for the British Army advancing along the Belgian coast by which we should have recaptured Antwerp, and there would have been no German submarine menace such as now is.' He noted that a 612-vessel armada had been constructed for such a plan, but the shipbuilding policy did not cope with the submarine menace, the naval strategy was unimaginative, and secret naval intelligence was good for nothing, as the

Germans were building five submarines a week while the Admiralty believed it was only three, and hence was apathetic. Finally, in a postscript on Jellicoe, 'if any disaster befalls the Grand Fleet owing to Jellicoe not being in Command ... England will be invaded.'[76] He returned to this lost opportunity in a letter to the prime minister on 12 June, arguing that if the Admiralty's plan of November of 1914 had been followed, and the Army had advanced along the Belgian coast, flanked by the gunfire of the Navy, the submarine menace would have been deprived of much of its strength, and German air raids on England would have been much more difficult. He also contended that such an operation could still be attempted, especially as now the US fleet was on station. Fisher pressed Lloyd George on the same matter on 11 July, emphasising the importance of an amphibious operation that would force the High Seas Fleet to fight at a marked disadvantage, thereby allowing the Grand Fleet to triumph and the Allies to win the war. He also recommended greatly increased production of aeroplanes, as 'the Air is going to win the War owing to the sad and grievous other neglects.'[77]

Lloyd George took note of Fisher's importunities and confidently set them aside. He had other urgent matters under consideration. He did not want Jellicoe back at Scapa; he wanted him out of the Admiralty. And, as we shall see, the wheels were being put in motion so that just such an action could be taken by his First Lord of the Admiralty, Geddes, in whom he had complete confidence.

Fisher now began to press for a supreme commander, a person with 'supreme personal direction', as he told Hankey. The Admiralty's influence needed to be expressed. Fisher asked, 'Can the Army win the War before the Navy loses it? That is the vital Question! As the Prime Minister says, "*Blunder after Blunder*"!' Hankey responded: he was in alignment with Fisher that indeed they might win on land but lose at sea.[78]

Throughout 1917 the real crisis of the naval war was the U-boat menace and the dramatic and formidable depredations against merchant shipping, which placed the United Kingdom in the alarming situation of having only three weeks' food supplies remaining. The details have been given in many histories. Fisher was a bystander to events, and so was Churchill. All Fisher could do was send warnings – that Britain would have to sue for an ignoble peace if foodstuffs ran out. On 31 March he wrote to Churchill to comment on an article that appeared in that day's *Daily Mail*. This article reported, via Reuter's offices in Amsterdam, that the Germans were claiming that 781,500 tons of merchant shipping had been sunk in February. Admiral Chapelle, the German Naval Secretary, reported that March's tally would be even larger, with more frequent and efficient U-boats. Of the German boast that they would win, Fisher stated, '*So it will*! unless we have a *Big Change*!'[79] Fisher also sent Churchill several newspaper extracts regarding the extent of claimed German successes in the submarine campaign, and the threat to Britain. From these, Fisher argued that the Admiralty had ample warning of the coming submarine threat.[80]

Observing the trials at the Admiralty from his distant base at Scapa Flow, well informed by letters from Fisher and others, Beatty had a healthy view on the high naval command. He knew Churchill and he knew Fisher, though unlike Jellicoe he owed no allegiance to the old admiral. To Lady Beatty he wrote:

The situation at sea seems to get worser and worser [sic] and it is difficult to see the end, unless it will be the return of the arch devil Jacky Fisher. If he were only 10 or 15 years younger, but he isn't, so there it is ... The heart-breaking point is that the Navy, upon which so much depends, cannot show that they also are the salt of the earth, and we are getting a bad reputation by the muddling of those in authority. And I cannot see the remedy with those in authority remaining where they are and would welcome even Jacky Fisher if I thought it would do any good ...[81]

And a few days later:

... We fly at opposites; first we have Winston with great ideas (generally impossible) and quiet determination, who over-rides a lamentably weak Board of naval officers, including the redoubtable Jacky Fisher; result – disaster. Then we have a philosopher who, learning from his predecessors mistakes & aided by a natural tendency to not interfere, allows an even more lamentably weak Board of sea officers to do worse than nothing; result – literally nothing done and everything allowed to fall into a deplorable condition of unreadiness to meet any menace. And then we have a lawyer, who is still imprisoned by the memory of the disaster caused by the impetuous, interfering Winston, takes over, with a new Sea Board which came into office with all the flair of a sea officer straight from the sea and 2 years experience of war, and the authority of the late Commander-in-Chief, and he also feels with his want of knowledge, he cannot interfere. And the great sea officers are not great enough and fail miserably to appreciate the necessity of the strongest measures, with the result we sink deeper into the mire and are losing ground instead of gaining it. And the lawyer, with his knowledge of human nature and human affairs knows it, and yet feel powerless to put things right, so will take refuge in resigning and let somebody else wrestle with it. Is it possible, do you think, under such circumstances to do anything to pull the fat out of the fire, with an old vulture like J.F. sitting on the rail waiting for the corpse to give its last kick? The man who, if he gets there, has pledged himself to turn me out as I am a danger to the nation because I do not fight the enemy when I meet him. Ye Gods, was there ever such an astoundingly humorous [?] situation? How must they laugh. And in the meantime our magnificent mercantile fleet is rapidly being destroyed. And the task is gradually assuming proportions that the Archangel Gabriel couldn't put right under six months ... There is not a man that I know of who could go to the Admiralty and put it right, not *one*, unless it's Winston!!![82]

Beatty continued to exhibit ambivalence in regards to Churchill and Fisher. He noted disparagingly that Churchill had joined the ranks of those who criticised the inaction of the Grand Fleet. Beatty argued that long before Jutland, in December 1914, he had submitted to Churchill and Fisher bold proposals for offensive action that would have prevented the emergence of the submarine menace, but they had been rejected by the two titans at the Admiralty: 'They have enough material at the Admiralty to stop those two rascals W.C. and J.F. talking for ever.' Two days later, he commented somewhat favourably about Fisher: 'There is a lovely story of old Fisher's that he is coming to stop with me. What a welcome we would give him, but he hasn't been asked yet, and he certainly shall not come unless he is. I have half a mind to ask him anyhow. He is a man, unscrupulous, but still a man. Which is more than anybody at the Admiralty is.'[83] Yes, Jacky was larger than life. Many shared memories of his times in the Admiralty, and his absence, as Beatty said, was noted with regret.

On Christmas Eve 1917 Jellicoe found a blunt letter of dismissal from the First Lord, Geddes, on his desk at the Admiralty. Parliament had risen; no newspapers would be published for the next two days. Geddes's timing was impeccable. Jellicoe had been at the helm of the Grand Fleet for twenty-seven months before coming to the Admiralty as First Sea Lord in November 1916. His worrying temperament, physical difficulties, and his inability to delegate were hidden factors. Upon learning of the dismissal, the Board of Admiralty rose in defence of their chief but then backed down. And so it was that Fisher's favourite was gone from the Admiralty.[84]

In Jellicoe's account of his dismissal as First Sea Lord, he related that, in the aftermath of the 12 December sinking of a Norwegian-bound convoy by German fast destroyers, Geddes informed Jellicoe that he desired an immediate and full inquiry to disclose all the facts. If Jellicoe refused, Geddes said that he would send for Fisher to look into the matter. Jellicoe wrote to Geddes to state that 'it would be very foolish to send Lord Fisher up on such a mission and would cause great ill feeling in the Fleet, and would moreover produce no good result.'[85] This suggests Jellicoe was on the defensive: he would not welcome any outside interference or advice. Jellicoe sensed that Lord Northcliffe, the newspaper baron, was on the warpath against him and the Admiralty. Lloyd George did Northcliffe's bidding. Geddes would give no reasons, but he wrote that Jellicoe 'did not evidence progressive adaptability and effectiveness in decision.'

Churchill was most regretful that Jellicoe had been relieved of his duties. From the Ministry of Munitions he wrote to him: 'It will always be pleasant to me to look back upon our association; upon our hard work together; upon our struggles to secure necessary money for the fleet and for the air, upon the supreme hour which found the Navy ready and its best leader at its head, upon the surmounted difficulties and anxieties of those early months, and upon the pleasant personal relations which always existed between us.' Asquith wrote: 'When history comes to be written, you have no reason to fear the verdict.'[86] And Margot Asquith wrote that she thought the Admiralty insane in its action. With a peerage in the offing, Jellicoe left the Admiralty. Fisher's chosen man and Churchill's selected commander of the Grand Fleet had passed from the apex of power and influence to write his books – and to defend himself against Beatty and others as the long knives were drawn in the extended exhumations and autopsies of British failures at Jutland.

On Christmas Day 1917, before he knew of Jellicoe's departure, Fisher vented his spleen about the conduct of the war in a letter to a friend:

> Our leaders (Political, Military, and Naval) are appalling in their want of '*VISION*'! Stupendous Blunders Afloat and Ashore! The only thing that saves us is that we are the lost tribe of Israel! *A Revolution and a Cromwell both Coming*!!!! The Common People are becoming restive – and Lloyd George knows it – *He is one of them*! ... The astounding miracle is how Balfour has escaped punishment for the Dardanelles, for the Kut disaster, for ignominious truckling at the Foreign Office and for apathy at the Admiralty that has perhaps cost us the war and yet some of the Conservative Party are proposing him as Prime Minister in case Lloyd George is wrecked.[87]

These sad comments show the delusionary position of Jacky Fisher as the crisis of the naval war was reaching its zenith. He imagined somehow that if he dropped in from the clouds all would be well, and with a few vivid strokes from his wonderful pen and some orders barked out he could change the destiny of his nation. He was out of touch with reality, and he was becoming, like Falstaff, a pathetic figure on the stage of history. He kept up his correspondence with Winston Churchill, but it was irregular.

1918

The new year began with no prospect of an end to the War. Fisher lamented the new First Sea Lord, Sir Roslyn Weymss, who, a friend had remarked, 'has never shown any particular talent up to now ... and it is VERY UNUSUAL that a man who HAS any talent does not show any sign of it till he is between 50 and 60 years old.'[88] Russia was in disarray and revolution. Fisher wrote to Churchill on 19 March on the progress of the war: 'It is very sad to think that the

Germans will annex the Russian fleet – a lot of fine new vessels of all types – and worst of all that the Baltic is now fixed up as a German Lake! *And all of it so easily avoidable*! Even now in this eleventh hour it's not too late ... They don't understand the language of War at the Admiralty! No Audacity! No Imagination! No Risks Taken!'[89]

He expanded on the details in a letter to a friend, dated 27 March:

> It has been a most disastrous war for one simple reason – that our Navy, with a sea supremacy quite unexampled in the history of the world (we are five times stronger than the enemy) has been relegated into being a 'Subsidiary Service!' ... What *crashes* we have had: Tirpitz – Sunk. Joffre – Stranded. Kitchener – Drowned. Lord French, Lord Jellicoe, Lord Devonport – Made Viscounts. Fisher – Marooned. Sir W. Robertson – The 'Eastern Command' in Timbuktu. Bethmann-Hollweg, Asquith – Torpedoed ... And a host of minor prophets promoted. (We don't shoot now! we promote!)[90]

Promoted or otherwise honoured. Earlier, in response to a series of KCBs (Knight Commander of the Bath), CBs (Companion of the Bath), and KCMGs (Knight Commander of St Michael and St George), Fisher wrote to Churchill, 'I hear that a new order of Knighthood is on the tapis – O.M.G. (Oh! My God!) – Shower it on the Admiralty!!'[91]

Churchill knew of Fisher's anxieties, and when Jacky told Winston that he intended to make a speech in the House of Lords denouncing timid admirals and generals, Churchill talked him out of it. Again, Fisher became angry with an accusatory article in the *Manchester Guardian* asking why amphibious attacks were not attempted against Zeebrugge and Ostend in late 1914, when Churchill and Fisher were at the Admiralty: the U-boat menace might have ended there and then and other damage done to German war making. Fisher railed against the article. He asked if Churchill was going to allow such a charge to be laid at their feet when the Admiralty had desired just such an operation, only to be foiled by Kitchener's procrastinations and the objections of the French ('WE HAVE TRUCKLED TO THE FRENCH ALL THROUGH!'). He wrote that he desired to make a statement in the House of Lords in ten days, and asked Churchill to get the prime minister's permission, as '*I have not embarrassed him hitherto*.' Fisher unloaded a litany of complaints: he defended his dreadnoughts, arguing that the time of submarine battles (submarines versus submarines) was coming but was not quite yet upon them. Finally, Fisher commented on April raids on the Belgian coast: 'These recent attacks on Zeebrugge and Ostend are heroic and magnificent, "*mais ce n'est pas la guerre*"! We run away. We lose 6 ships more wanted for a vital operation. We lose irreplaceable heroes! It's "tip and run". We want: "*J'y suis, j'y reste.*"'[92]

In response, Churchill urged Fisher to hold his fire: 'A speech from you is a card that you must not play improvidently. It should be a long written statement, *grave, measured, impersonal.*' With respect to the *Manchester Guardian*, Churchill argued that the editor did not need answering. They had done all they could in 1914, and there were insufficient troops for the proposed operations to ensure first-class results. As well, he asserted that the Belgian coast was only an advanced base of submarine warfare, which was true. The Elbe and the Ems were the real bases. Finally, he stated that the successes the Navy was having 'in choking submarines are now becoming very remarkable, and [the operation at] Zeebrugge has given them back the *panache* that was lost at Jutland.'[93]

Fisher replied on 26 May to disagree with Churchill, reasserting his position that 'had the British Army been on the sea flank as it should have been according to common sense, we should have turned the German Flank.' The result would have been entry into the Baltic and the Russians not collapsing, and then a large army would not have been needed for the operations.[94] At this point Fisher seemed to be speaking into a void. His arguments were as wild as they were ineffective. Retrospectives had gone out of style.

Still, Jacky persisted. In a letter to Churchill on 29 August 1918 Fisher again asserted that landing a great army on the Pomeranian Coast was a 'practicable proposition'. With a Navy five times bigger than the enemy's, it would be easy. Fisher went on to urge Churchill to 'entreat the Prime Minister to "*sack the lot*" who now weight him down, and let us go to war in the good old way and turn the German flank, instead of fighting him just where he wishes us always! I feel like Ezekiel among the captives by the River of Chebar, when he saw visions and learnt that in the heavenly places "Whither the spirit was to go they went, and they turned not when they went."'[95]

All Fisher's thoughts turned on the Service and on opportunities missed mainly due to poor administration and faint hearts. Sir Maurice Hankey, the Secretary of the War Council and one of Fisher's closest associates, was well aware of the old admiral's hope of return, and he tactfully told his old chief that no recall to office existed and none would exist in the future. Fisher replied in resignation that he was not disappointed by such news though he still 'yearned for work in the bow' (presumably of the ship of state).[96] Hankey had worked with his old chief for twenty years and knew him as well as any, and he was loyal to him to the last. But he also knew that Fisher's days were numbered and certainly that the bright aurora of earlier days was now flaring out quickly. His job was over. The future of the Navy would turn on the merits of others of younger years who had the political support so necessary to maintain the influence of the Admiralty.

Churchill could never forget the unwillingness of the Admiralty 'in those sad days' to risk its fleets and squadrons in war, and to him this was a matter of strange proportion considering that the generals were confident of breaking the line by massive force, then sending through the cavalry. The Fleet had continued idle at the Dardanelles. Thereafter it maintained that somnolent posture. Ships destined for the scrapyard were not risked 'with the possibility of gaining an inestimable prize.' This was Churchill's view of the great naval mechanism.[97] The men-of-war tugged at their moorings, sortied from time to time in reconnaissance, took up convoy work, hunted U-boats, swept the channels, and kept up Service morale. They were strong in numbers. The Germans dared not interfere. They did not wrest from the British the trident of the seas.

By July 1918, in optimistic circles, it was increasingly clear that the war was coming to an end. Ludendorff's formidable Spring Offensive resulted in an overextended salient that actually weakened the German position. The Allied armies, strengthened by the powerful United States forces, regained the initiative and prepared for what became known, after the event, as 'the last hundred days'. On 21 July Esher, conscious of Fisher's role in readying the Fleet for war and, equally, of the marginalised state of his old friend, wrote comfortingly to Jacky that the impending victory was largely due to him. 'Where should we all be today, were it not for your foresight, your bold determination ... ? My dear, you have had a glorious life, and if there is such a thing as fame you have earned it.'[98] Esher did not exaggerate when he said, 'the prophets were not in it with you.' But the past seemed like a dream and the present something quite elusive.

Bulgaria was the first to surrender, and in the ensuing weeks empires crumbled and kings were toppled. Characteristically, on 14 October Fisher wrote to Churchill that if he were in charge of the High Seas Fleet, he would gallantly sortie into the Channel, cause havoc, sink transports carrying American troops, and intern the fleet in a Spanish port. Fisher was never short of bravado. On the possibility of peace:

The loveliest bit of camouflage in this War is putting up Prince Max of Baden [the new German chancellor and foreign minister] and tame Socialists to lead us to think that Germany is tottering to her fall!!!! We have not struck at a vital spot in Germany. Not a foot of her territory in Germany in our hands. German Armies occupy territories that are not theirs. The German submarine menace shows no sign of lessening. Germany has AT LEAST (yes! AT THE VERY LEAST) twice as many submarines as we have! The German submarine campaign is going to be more intense. (Viscount Jellicoe said it was going to be finished with last August!!!! And heaps of asses have been seeing the end of the War!) NO! WE HAVE NOT YET WON! We may have to go through long weary months yet! (*That is, on the present system*!!)

The shortest way to Berlin is by the sea. The quickest route to end the War is by the sea ...

P.S. Bismarck insisted on marching the German Army through Paris before he dictated peace. Ever since then the French have been a peace-loving nation! So will the Prussians, if we also march through Berlin before we dictate peace.

As I told you, war is *'imagination'* and *'audacity'*, and when these two copulate, the result is 'SURPRISE'! And so we sent von Spee to the bottom! And so we could get to Berlin. For God's sake, don't have a peace with the Germans holding the Rhine, or a single German colony returned to her! SUBMARINES![99]

On 21 October 1918 Fisher outlined to Hankey five points he believed to be vital, from a naval point of view, to any peace with Germany: '(1) The German High Seas Fleet to be delivered up intact. (2) Ditto, every German Submarine. (3) Ditto Heligoland. (4) Ditto, the two flanking islands of Sylt and Borkum. (5) No spot of German Territory in the wide world to be permitted! It would infallibly be a Submarine Base.' He concluded: 'Nelson is turning in his Grave at the passive part played by the British Fleet in this war.'[100] Most of Fisher's points were accepted, but how influential they were in the British pleni-potentiaries' decision-making remains unknown.

Germany was in collapse, her navy in revolt. The Kaiser took refuge in Holland. Then came the Armistice of 11 November, quickly effected. Fisher believed that the Allies were gravely mistaken to accept the Armistice. They should have fought on until the Germans were completely beaten.[101] He was not alone in this view.

After the Armistice, Fisher received a good number of letters praising his role in creating the Grand Fleet as the means by which victory was won. Gerard Fiennes, a naval journalist and friend of Fisher, wrote: 'The Victory is a Victory of Sea Power. *You* made the Fleet; *you* mobilized it; *you* planned the strategy of Falkland Islands, and, whoever else may forget your part as the Organizer of Victory, I do *not*.' He added: 'The war for which you prepared the Empire has been full of disappointments to you, and crowned with sorrow. But Clio [History's muse] sees with clear eyes, and in the future will see you righted. The praise of contemporaries is a small thing compared with the considerable judgment of mankind, and of that verdict you are secure.' Fiennes called Fisher 'the Organizer of Victory', a handsome tribute to the man who had wielded the trident of Neptune.[102] The Armistice terms required German warships, other than caretakers in home ports, to sail within seven days for some neutral port, or ports, but as this was unresolved, they were ordered to be taken in by the Grand Fleet. All U-boats were surrendered. The greatest danger to Britain's sea supremacy had ended.

Twilight of the gods: Fisher's final years

Four days after the Armistice was effected, on 15 November a lone German light cruiser, wearing the flag of a German vice-admiral, arrived in the heavy fog near May Island, Firth of Forth, and dropped anchor. The ship was *Königsberg*. For those who could see it, the German naval ensign flying at the forepeak was brightly lit for the occasion. The war had ended; there would be no further reprisals, no engagement.

The admiral, Hugo Meurer, was representing Admiral Hipper; his mission, to obtain details as to how the German fleet was to be received in accordance with decisions taken at Paris. A boat was lowered and Meurer was conveyed to the stairs of *Queen Elizabeth*, Beatty's flagship. The German admiral's arrival was expected. A cool reception awaited him. The gangway was brilliantly lit. Royal Marines stood at present arms position, bayonets glittering in the light. The German party was ushered down a deck, and when they entered the room where the British admirals and staff sat on the one side, Beatty said to Meurer, 'Pray sit down.' He did so, flanked by assistants.

The German admiral, according to Beatty, looked like death and was terribly crushed and willing to do anything so long as the Germans got peace and food.[103] He told Beatty of the terrible suffering of the German populace. Beatty went over the arrangements, indicating the time and place of the intended rendezvous of the German fleet and its jailers, and forcefully detailing the requirements of the internment. These were accepted. There were no options.

'Of course David's disappointment when he realised that he could never have his great victory at sea was terrible.' So did Lady Beatty confide to her sister-in-law a week after the Armistice came into effect, 'but now he is getting over that and after seeing the Hun Admiral he realises what a great Victory we have had, and *no* lives *lost*.' Lady Beatty speaks of her husband's disappointment, but he was also very angry that the German High Seas Fleet was still in existence. It had not been sunk in battle, and there had been no Trafalgar. These feelings were widespread throughout the British Fleet. There had been victory at sea and victory on land aided and abetted by British sea power. But there had been no great and cataclysmic sea fight – and this fact rankled in the hearts of every officer and bluejacket.[104]

Then came 'der Tag', the day – and not the one hoped for by the Royal Navy. It was a sullen day for the Grand Fleet when, steaming due east, its dreadnoughts, cruisers, and destroyers, flying masthead battle ensigns of supremacy, in dual lines six miles apart, met the late enemy's ships at the appointed position (56° 11' N, 1° 20' W). The British warships, accompanied by Admiral Hugh Rodman's US 6th Battle Squadron, completed majestic 180-degree turns, then brought the remnant pride of the German navy into its grasp. The German ships had come out of the mist as if in some Wagnerian last act. Each British vessel stood at general quarters, 'action stations', with guns loaded and trained fore and aft. British sailors cheered joyously as the gunners at their weapons, dressed in anti-flash smocks, pointed out the grey leviathans of the enemy as they sailed quietly by. Ninety thousand men cheered their Commander-in-Chief. Press and public attention responded to Admiral Sir David Beatty's every word. The preliminary jail for the German dreadnoughts was the Firth of Forth; there an inspection of weapons was to proceed – to make sure they were not armed or ammunition squirrelled away. The German fleet anchored nearly in sight of Edinburgh.

Perhaps forgotten, and certainly uninvited even as observers, on that remarkable day of the internment of the German fleet were persons who had placed the sword of the Grand Fleet in Beatty's hands. The first of them was Lord Jellicoe. His once-bright star had been fading since he was summarily and unkindly removed as First Sea Lord in December 1917. (He had set to writing his books *The Grand Fleet* and *The Crisis of the Naval War*, and then somewhat later found himself in a scrap with Lord Beatty over the official record of Jutland, a story for another time and another place.[105] In the event, Jellicoe would only be made a viscount in comparison to Beatty's earldom, and was sent to distant New Zealand as governor general.)

The other great figure excluded from the internment proceedings was Fisher, the forger of the blade wielded by both Jellicoe and Beatty. He now lived in relative obscurity, increasingly embittered by the ingratitude of a nation he had served for sixty years. The war was over. The German navy was vanquished. New realities needed to be faced. To the current naval administration, Fisher was a potential embarrassment, a problem to be shunted off where he could do little harm. He was still associated with division and controversy and with the incompetence surrounding the Dardanelles operation. There was one further humiliation. Fisher was not invited to the triumphant and moving ceremony of the surrender of the German fleet at sea. Nor was his name included in the King's victory speech to Parliament on 19 November 1918 – 'Yes! King George arranged my omission!' Fisher noted sadly to the newsman C P Scott of the *Manchester Guardian*.[106] One of Fisher's admirers, a senior naval officer on the day when the German ships had come to their jail, wrote consolingly to Fisher on 21 November. He said that Fisher's exclusion was ungracious, but added tellingly, 'history will give you your due. I realise that to-day's victory was yours, and it is iniquitous that you were not here to see it.'[107]

Beatty ordered his famous signal that the German flag was to be hauled down at sunset that day and was not to be hoisted again without permission. At sunset Beatty was cheered throughout his fleet, and double rum rations were issued. The Kaiser's quest for world domination and naval primacy came to an end.

By 27 November all the German ships – eleven battleships, five battlecruisers, seven light cruisers and forty-five destroyers – were at anchor in Scapa Flow, watched over by guard ships of the 1st Battle Cruiser Squadron, which had had more contact with the German navy than any other during the war. Weeks and months passed wearily while various Allied delegates in Paris tried to reach a decision about the future of those ships. The German Admiralty sent direct and indirect instructions to von Reuter to scuttle the ships, and in an act of treachery this was done on 21 June 1919. Fifteen of the capital ships, four of the eight cruisers, and thirty-two destroyers were sunk. Today seven of these ships remain beneath the waves; the remainder have been salvaged. (It has long been a subject of mirth that Wilkinson Sword razor blades were manufactured from Krupp steel salvaged from the guns of the German warships.) By this time, 150 U-boats had been escorted into Harwich, and there the new peril of the seas was extinguished. The end of German naval power had been achieved by Allied uncertainty and differences of opinion as to how the enemy warships should be disposed or apportioned. The German action solved many problems as British naval leadership saw it, but the treacherous move caught the Navy unawares, and Fremantle, the admiral commanding the gaoler squadron, charged the German commander with foul play.

Many ill-feelings remained among the officers and men of both navies, especially the vanquished. The following anecdote survives in the memoirs of the secretary to Captain Hall of British Naval Intelligence. When the U-boats surrendered outside Harwich in 1919, an overwrought German officer said to a British petty officer:

'I will tell you what I think about you and your British flag.'
He then spat viciously into the sea. The Britisher made no retort.
Angrier than before, the German spat again into the sea, saying 'That is what I think of you and your Beatty!'
Our man looked at him for a moment. Then he replied quietly: 'I sympathise with your feelings as a Hun, but don't spit in our sea.'[108]

With war's end, Fisher became even more isolated, ignored, and unappreciated. He thought of himself as having been marooned, cast up on a desert island. His correspondence showed increasingly erratic tendencies, with biblical passages sprinkled through his commentary on policy. To one friend he complained bitterly that 'the Conduct of the War, both by Sea and Land, has been perilously effete and wanting in Imagination and Audacity since May, 1915.' He complained about those who scoffed at his Baltic project and the pandering to allies and the cost of supporting Russia.[109] He was an outcast increasingly consumed by bitterness. He had no use for the current crop of political and military leaders. They had none for him. The world had changed irrevocably since August 1914, empires had fallen, and the Kaiser was in exile in Holland. A new and uncertain form of international order was being talked about at the Paris peace tables and in the drawing rooms.

In the circumstances, Fisher grew more and more outspoken on his concept of democracy, questioning the honours system. He even began to question the idea of the monarchy itself, toying with republican ideals and socialist schemes.[110] He was not alone in these pursuits, but for an Admiral of the Fleet, his proclivities in this regard strike one as bizarre. His restlessness and sense of dissatisfaction knew no bounds. It was in tune with his character.

The Dardanelles haunted Fisher as they did Churchill. In Parliament and in the press that dismal campaign was fought and refought. Fisher had always supported Nelson's arguments that a man-of-war ought never take on a fort in an artillery duel. In regards to the Dardanelles in *Memories*, Fisher disputed the conclusions of G A Schreiner (*From Berlin to Baghdad*) and Henry Morgenthau (*The Secrets of the Bosporus*), who argued that the 18 March 1915 attack on the Dardanelles forts nearly succeeded, as the Turks were down to a few rounds per gun. Fisher supported General Sir Charles Callwell's account, which showed that even if the fixed batteries were put out of commission, the mobile batteries had still to be contended with, as well as mines and torpedoes. As Liman von Sanders, the German commander, wrote: 'The attack on the Straits by the Navy alone I don't think could ever have succeeded. I proposed to flood the Straits broadcast with mines, and it was my view that these were the main defences of the Dardanelles, and that the function of the guns of the forts was simply to protect the minefields from interference.' Fisher placed the blame on the 'political desire of getting possession of the Straits'. The operational commanders were convinced that the operation could be halted at any time. The politicians, however, decided to push ahead.[111]

Then there was the perceived failure at Jutland. Fisher felt betrayed by Jellicoe's book *The Grand Fleet*, published 1919. It showed the alleged unpreparedness of the Navy to fight a war. It was critical of all manner of things relating to mines and torpedoes, docks and dockyards, defences and garrisons, ships and crews. It was also a low-key indictment of naval administration. Jacky thought this book should never have been published. Jellicoe's indictment of naval policy as it was prosecuted immediately before the war had the effect, years later, of getting Beresford excited in the House of Lords. Beresford, always an opportunist, wanted to open old wounds. He wildly proposed a broad resolution condemning the policy of the Admiralty for the unnecessary loss of life and the lack of preparations. In his own defence, Fisher pointed to the fact that there was retrogression from the time of his leaving the Admiralty in 1910 to his return in 1914: this was the interval when McKenna and Churchill were on their own. It would be better, Fisher contended, that naval historical accounts not be written by former commanders-in-chief. As for his hated rival, the man who had been a thorn in his flesh, he now began to blend all the issues together as is shown by the following: 'Beresford should be treated with silent contempt ... But what a sad thing for our naval prestige in this war is all this *"fouling of our own nest"*! Really, Jellicoe ought to be shot!'[112]

After war's end and the demobilisation of the Fleet, Parliament drastically cut naval expenditures. Fisher wrote to Lloyd George's private secretary expressing his interest in helping the Admiralty save money. His own experience as an economiser would be an asset, or so he thought.[113] Fisher fired off a letter to *The Times* expressing outrage at the level of government expenditure. The Fleet was costing £140 million, while in 1904 it stood at £34 million when there was an opponent to build against. 'I have to say from severe experience and great obloquy that Departmental Committees or Cabinet Committees or even Prime Ministers are no use in such an extremity. You must turn out the whole spendthrift crew "neck and crop" who are responsible for this ruinous waste of money. You must be ruthless, relentless, and remorseless! Sack the Lot! If the nation doesn't sack the spendthrifts, "Then is the day of crumbling not far off."'[114] The editor of *The Times* echoed Fisher's sentiments and, in particular, pressed the issue of economy of estimates. Specifically, the editor focused on 'constructive economy' rather than negative economy. 'Let us not rest upon our oars, but determine to lead the world once again in naval construction; to think out the problem of the new engine and the submarine; to be first with the new gun. That is the way of true economy, we take him to say, and very heartily we agree.'[115]

Fisher could not contain himself and let himself be carried away on less important matters, thereby exposing himself to ridicule. On the same day, he wrote disgustedly about the new uniform policies: 'Then, Sir, there follow 12 specific injunctions about cocked hats and gold-laced trousers and midshipmen's jackets! "Give peace in our time, O Lord!" if this indicates the minds of those whose hearts should be filled with the internal combustion engine.' In particular he decried one type of uniform that was only to be worn at His Majesty's Levee, which would presumably not be needed when 'we make the 16th new Republic!'[116] In response, Vice-Admiral Penrose Fitzgerald was, as was his wont, particularly unimpressed. 'When your readers saw a letter from Lord Fisher they probably expected to find something that would be a practical and useful guide to Parliament and the Board of Admiralty in forming sound policy ... Profound, then, must have been their disappointment when they found nothing but a vague and disjointed tirade, which probably reminded them more of the passionate screams of an angry child deprived of his favourite toy.'[117]

In those days there was no more working the backstairs of newspapermen and editors for Fisher, and he took to writing directly to *The Times*. A series known as the 'Scrap-the-lot' letters appeared in September 1919 and, true to form, stoutly defended his policies and his efforts.

> Personally, life would lose its charm for me the day I can't waltz ... What adjectives I got in those stormy years – domineering, demoniacal, sardonic, sinister, saturnine, ruthless, relentless, and remorseless! ... So it came about that when on Trafalgar Day, 1904, I was appointed First Sea Lord of the Admiralty, and breakfasted alone with King Edward at Buckingham Palace, though I had entered the navy penniless, friendless, and forlorn. I was equipped with knowledge and power sufficient to say to anyone who obstructed me '*You be damned*,' and he was damned.
>
> First I felt certain sure that democracy was required in the Navy. The motive power had been sails aloft, it was now machinery; those who controlled the sails had not stooped to oil their fingers, and the real masters of the Navy were the despised engineers, whose mammas were not asked to teas by those other mammas.

In another letter, Fisher defended *Dreadnought* on indisputable grounds that it froze the shipbuilding of other powers for sixteen months. '*The damned thing was so different.*' Fisher also defended his precious battlecruisers and emphasised the importance of superior speed.[118] In one of the later articles, Fisher wrote of his critics (especially Beresford) and the abolition of overseas squadrons: 'Each Admiral thought he was being humiliated by his ships being taken away a few at a time and brought home. Some of them mutinied and ought to have been shot, but we only shoot a poor devil like Byng who had no friends ... What I think is one of the fearful things of the late war is that we had no Admirals or Generals shot – we only promoted them.'[119]

On 16 September 1919 we find Fisher writing on the conservation of coal in warships. Such a letter left him open to critique on other matters, such as the Dardanelles.[120] Admiral of the Fleet Sir Arthur Fanshawe was unimpressed by Fisher's tirade. He contended that Fisher's 'extraordinary ebullition ... should remain unanswered', and he attacked Fisher for not being critical of himself, arguing that some of his reforms and decisions had proved problematic at best.

> It has been to some of us a great surprise that Lord Fisher's great talents were not more conspicuously displayed (whether or no he may have approved of the undertaking) in the preliminaries of the Dardanelles expedition, which so nearly succeeded in spite of all mistakes and miscalculations ... I cannot believe that the tone of Lord Fisher's various letters, &c., containing so unnecessary a number of forceful adjectives (not usually employed among gentlemen, and certainly hitherto employed between naval officers ...) can promote either respect for himself or add force to the opinions he expresses.

The description of those who differ from him (amongst whom I claim a place) as 'fools' and 'idiots' is, beyond measure, discourteous and uncalled for.[121]

Fisher could not stay out of the fray. He wrote again, complaining bitterly: 'We are not free yet. Nearly a year after the most humiliating and crushing armistice ever known, this slave-driven country is spending two millions sterling a day more than income ... And all the People cry "Sack the Lot," But the Lot are our Masters and we are the Slaves ... to avoid waste we must scrap all that is obsolete ruthlessly, relentlessly, and remorselessly ... Sir, we must Sack the Lot!'[122]

Fisher continued to fulminate in letters to the editor of *The Times*. He was still furious about the 'bloated' estimates and the focus on surface vessels: 'It's as clear as daylight that future war at sea absolutely precludes the use of any vessel of war that can't go under water, because aircraft will compel it! So why keep any of the present lot? Not only that but you've got also to scrap all the admirals and superior officers because they won't do for the new job! Put them all in some museum like Greenwich Hospital.'[123] Then it was time to turn on the politicians. His last public blast, a letter to *The Times* on 12 June 1920, took on 'Our plutocratic, effete, despicable House of Commons ... The so-called Labour leaders have not a touch of Parnell or Bradlaugh in them!'

A growing sense of mortality came over Fisher in these late days. There were consolations, not least the friendship of Nina, Duchess of Hamilton. The poet Dryden's bust in Westminster Abbey always offered inspiration and much-needed solace. Whenever he passed it he read the great words, which he saw as being appropriate to the close of a busied life:

Not Heaven itself upon the past has Power;

What has been has been, and I have had my hour.

But what sort of literary remembrance could Jacky leave for posterity? He thought long and hard about this. He knew of how the historian William Lecky, a fellow holder of the Order of Merit, had toiled over his final book, *The Map of Life*, devoting more than three years to it and giving more attention to the revision of the last of its chapters than to all of his other works.[124] All the principal figures in the war, political, diplomatic, military, and naval, were penning memoirs for a burgeoning public readership. The Cabinet Office commissioned official histories of naval and military operation and other subjects. Fisher was inspired to write his own story. But what form should this take? A friend, Sir George Reid, warned him of the perils of autobiography: 'You only know one view of yourself – others see you all around.' However, Fisher replied that he saw no problem in publishing his 'memories', and that 'there's one side no one else can see, and that's "the inside"!' Lord Rosebery, a noted biographer as well as a statesman, had been 'emphatic' in advising that Fisher and not someone else must write the book. Fisher decided to begin, at least.

At this stage Fisher had no capacity for sustained thought, and no abilities that would allow him to write an extended work, even a concise survey, giving the main features of his life. He thought in paragraphs, staccato – like bullets that burst forth in regular succession. He had always prided himself on his persuasive powers. As early as 1911, as he told Hankey, he had begun 'collecting incidents of my life which I am writing down with absolute frankness and fullness without a thought as to the proprieties of publication. Someone else can prune. I don't want a flatulent panegyrist to make a plaster saint of me when I am gone, or my enemies to picture me with horns and a forked tail!'[125]

In April 1918 Jacky had privately printed, in 100 copies, his 'life'. *Some Notes by Lord Fisher to His Friends* was 310 pages and carried the alluring subtitle *To be in Three Portions: One now – one later – one after death*. The Westminster Press prepared this work. Copies appear at auction and in antiquarian bookstores from time to time.

The secret story of this mysterious 'life' can be reconstructed through the story told by the remarkable writer Esther Meynell, who wrote under the pen name E Hallam Moorhouse. A noted book reviewer and novelist, her career as a supposed masculine naval author always amused Jacky. She was an expert on Nelson and Emma, Lady Hamilton. Fisher, when First Sea Lord before the war, had got wind of Esther, made her acquaintance, showed her his collection of Nelson letters and antiquities, and befriended her family. What odd jobs in the literary line she did for him is not known. In early spring 1918 he induced her to come at once to Wiltshire, where he was with the Duke and Duchess of Hamilton, to put into order his ideas and texts. The Duchess offered her a nearby manor house complete with cook and housekeeper. Esther accepted and with her two daughters was happy to escape hateful London. 'I doubt if Cinderella was more enchanted when the fairy godmother stepped into her kitchen,' she wrote in her memoir. Once arrived she was greeted next day by the tinkling of sleigh bells, and a carriage drawn by four Shetland ponies brought the admiral accompanied by the smiling Duchess to her doorstep. They had come from nearby Ferne House. 'Now, don't make any mistake about it, you are here to work!' Fisher told Esther. He opened a bursting dispatch box, explained different snippets of enticing autobiography to her, told her to burn what she didn't like, and then drove off with the Duchess. He would not leave Esther alone and brought additional items. He could not decide if the whole thing was drivel, announcing, 'Burn the whole d—d lot!' Then when she suggested what should be left out, he would complain, with grieved expression, 'But that's the best thing of the lot! That's real Bovril.' And so the work went on, bit by bit. Despite rapidly advancing years, he was in good spirits, and of a photo taken of Jacky with Esther on one side and Nina on the other, he cheerily described himself as 'a rose between two thorns'.[126] The work went on for six weeks, and then the text was finished, and ready for private printing.[127]

Somehow the managing partner of the London house Hodder & Stoughton, Sir Ernest Hodder-Williams, got word of this strange collation called *Some Notes*. Another literary project was in view. An arrangement was entered into for a different sort of book – one of 'memoirs'. It is likely that Esther Meynell did the heavy lifting in the literary line. Jacky was not good at this sort of paperwork. He told Lord Esher of his newly found literary joy, and on 20 August 1919 his ever-loyal correspondent and adviser replied that nothing could touch him more than the inclusion of some of his own words in Fisher's work. 'I shall love to read your notes on a life that has been and is so splendid. What "they" have lost and robbed the county of I know well. However, as you say in Dryden's wonderful phrase, they cannot rob the nation of all that you did in those great years. And the span of life is narrow – even for bureaucrats and politicians!'[128] At the time, Esher was unsuccessfully wrangling to be official historian to write the British military history of the war, but the Cabinet Office, influenced by the opinion of Hankey and Corbett, would not have it, and the task fell to others.

Fisher's published book, a sensation, was entitled *Memories*. In the introduction, Fisher justified the book by stating, 'I believe that the vindication of a man's lifework is almost an impossible task for even the most intimate of friends or the most assiduous and talented of Biographers, simply because they cannot possibly appreciate how great deeds have been belittled and ravaged by small contemporary men.'[129] At Hodder & Stoughton, Hodder-Williams noted that in the few weeks that *Memories* was being prepared, Fisher sent over one thousand words of instructions, exhortations, protestations, and congratulations. In addition, the editor noted that the staff were compelled to ask Fisher's permission to edit some of the more turbulent passages in the work. Fisher took care so as not to wound the personal feelings of any living person. He was equally concerned not to wound the feelings of survivors or to damage the reputation of those departed. Fisher dealt with a particular passage dealing with Beresford in the original manuscript: 'a long passage dealing, and dealing faithfully with Lord Beresford [was] crossed out with the splutter of the quill pen, and these words added as a note: "Within a few hours of penning the above remarks I had news of his death. *De mortuis nil nisi bonum*. I have scratched out what I had been going to say."'

Memories, on the bookstands on Trafalgar Day 1919, was sharp, to the point, entertaining, and biblical. There was no shortage of lively yarns and breezy comments. The frankness of the book was everywhere leavened by a sense of humour. It was egotistical, dogmatic, fearlessly outspoken, and sometimes bitingly outrageous. More than all these things, it was Fisher's salute to history. It was his story, one so uncharacteristic of naval autobiography or memoir. You will not find its likeness anywhere. From the pages we hear him saying, 'I told you so, I forecast this, I was present at the creation.' Fisher was a man of war, and the book showed it. He was, too, the literary man of the month. Royalties from *Memories* put Fisher's bank account into the black for the first time in years, or so he said, and also allowed him to take a holiday in the south of France with friends.

Truth to tell, *Memories* is not much of a memoir – indeed, it never could be – and it tells all too little about the Navy. But it was vintage Fisher. That was what counted. Some thought Fisher had not done himself justice by it. The publisher noted that the book did not do justice to the full range of Fisher's power, as the printed word could not convey the power of his personality. Hodder-Williams stated that if Fisher had had his way, there would have been no such book. He undertook the task of composing *Memories*, though, as a matter of duty to the nation and to the Navy.[130]

The Times praised Fisher's book and the man himself. In particular, the editor focused on Fisher's foresight and his grasp of economy. 'The way to be economical is not to ignore the necessity for change, but to take it as an axiom to predict its effects and to provide against them in good time. This is the moral of Lord Fisher's book, as it is the gospel which he is continually preaching to the country.'[131] The work, too, was a social commentary on the times. 'These new pronouncements on Naval history and policy, on the conduct of the war, on men, women, dancing, religion, and many other topics, are supplemented with extracts from the miscellaneous writings which Lord Fisher has, since his retirement from the Admiralty in 1915, been collecting and printing for ultimate circulation among his personal friends.' Excerpts of Fisher's book appeared in advance of publication and then in six instalments in *The Times*.[132]

As for the reviews and the reviewers, *Memories* did not pass unscathed, though few were the critics in the press of the book by 'Breezy Jack'. Of the dozens of press reviews, only three highly critical ones are to be found.[133] One of them, Arthur H Pollen in the *Sunday Times* of 2 November 1919, wrote that the book had pathos and that Fisher never knew what a fleet was for: 'He did not trouble about the principles of fighting, or about the strategy that would compel the enemy to fight, or about the means by which weapons should be used so as to fight with the best effect, or about the tactics which the changes in weapons produce, simply because he never looked on fighting as the one and only thing which a fleet has to do.' Pollen, most visceral of critics, was later to expound on British disasters at Jutland. But his review of Fisher's *Memories* was riddled with the old shibboleths and the old incantations. 'There never were any plans, any tactical doctrines, any technique at all.' In the *Daily*

Express (21 October 1919) and in *Empire News* (26 October 1919), Fisher's severest naval critic, H C Ferraby, thought *Memories* a cruel self-portrait of a hasty, hectoring, untamed spirit that time had soured and not mellowed. The man who had dictated its pages to his secretary was not the same who had, between 1904 and 1910, prepared the British Navy for the 1914 war. The Rt Hon J M Robertson in the *Nottingham Journal*, the *Yorkshire Observer*, and the *Star* (24 October 1919) thought Fisher had contrived at one stroke to put his country to shame: 'Copenhagening' the German fleet at Kiel was a deplorable adventure never, happily, brought about. The disclosure of it discredited Britain in the eyes of the world. Others thought differently.

In early November 1919 his publisher announced that the companion to *Memories*, known as *Records*, would soon be published. The date had been fixed at 8 December, the fifth anniversary of the defeat of von Spee's squadron at the Falkland Islands by Fisher's 'greyhounds of the sea'. Extracts were published in *The Times* on 24, 25, and 26 November. Fisher, now a celebrated author, planned to publish an autobiography entitled *Visions*, which he was working on at the time of his death. However, *Memories* and *Records* ended up standing as a compromise between the no-book of Fisher's wish and the orderly, complete autobiography that the public desired.[134] Already critics had noted that Fisher could no more write a regular book than Vesuvius could write one, and in one instance a reviewer opined that only a biographer like Sir Julian Corbett could do him the justice that he could not do himself.[135]

The clouds had already begun to close on Fisher by this time, his private life then one of some darkness and complexity. His growing closeness to the Duchess of Hamilton came at a cost to his wife, Frances Katharine Josepha Delves Broughton, Baroness Fisher, who died 18 July 1918 at Malmesbury, Wiltshire. Of his wife's death, Fisher himself remarked that it was 'a most perfect, peaceful, blissful end'.

> And such was Katharine Delves Broughton, for fifty-two years the wife of Admiral of the Fleet Lord Fisher of Kilverstone, having married him as a young lieutenant without friends or money or prospects, and denied herself all her life long for the sake of her husband and her children – to them she was ever loyal, faithful and steadfast, and to such as condemned them she was a Dragon.[136]

She was buried at Kilverstone. Lord Esher sent condolences. 'Memories of old days crowd upon me, and I have thought much of you these last few hours ... Where should we all be to-day were it not for your foresight, your bold determination, and the atmosphere of Reform in which SHE had so large a share.' What a great story could be written of the Navy's revitalisation and of Balfour's role, and dear old Stead's press accounts. 'Really the prophets were not in it for you.' That was Esher's judgement. He understood the battle and the breeze as well as any, and he lamented Fisher's decline and imminent departure from this Earth. He sensed its coming. 'My dear, you have had a glorious life, and if there is such as thing as fame you have earned it.'[137]

Fisher's movements were more restricted now, though his imagination was as always unimpaired. All attention was now drawn to the post-Armistice settlements and to a supposed new world order. Every figure of any importance was going to Paris, and so the admiral had to make his appearance there. Fisher went to Paris twice. In June he made a whirlwind trip to Paris during the Peace Conference. In a Rolls-Royce car lent to him by Churchill he was rocketed through town and country in Fisher style, 'mostly at 70 miles an hour.' He ate several meals with Lloyd George and enjoyed a good dance at the famed Majestic Hotel.[138] In all, it was a whirl of happiness. He told his daughter, 'Perhaps I shall bring a French maid for myself back with me from Paris! ...'[139]

During the visit a wild rumour circulated that Fisher might be named Britain's ambassador to the United States. It might have started with Jacky himself. He had been on good terms with the US Navy going back to the days of Admiral William Sampson, when Fisher had been C-in-C, North America and the West Indies. Having a senior naval officer as ambassador may have been good in view of the focus on naval affairs in Anglo-American diplomacy. Churchill liked the idea and apparently paid a visit to Fisher to tell him that he had written to Lloyd George to press the appointment. On the American side, the admiring Colonel Edward House told Fisher how wonderful it would be if he were named ambassador to Washington. In view of Fisher's opinionated positions and erratic behaviour it is impossible to believe such an idea would be given much consideration at the Foreign Office and elsewhere where such a decision would be made. Fisher might have liked the idea but privately he realised the unlikelihood of such an appointment.[140] The task went to Sir Edward Grey.

On 18 July 1919 Fisher turned up in Paris again, this time with the fabulous Nina, 'his duchess'. He 'was in the most uproarious form,' observed Maurice Hankey, keeping 'all Paris roaring at the funny stories he tells.' Fisher and the Dowager Duchess attended service at a Presbyterian church in the company of President and Mrs Woodrow Wilson, Lloyd George and his daughter Megan, and Hankey.[141] Gaiety, feasting, and good fun were the order of the day. It all suited Fisher famously, for he hated being on the margins of great events and now filled every room in which he appeared with warmth and good humour. Even to the last he gathered attention to himself, always pressing on with his customary solecisms and odd explanations of history and his role in the past – and wild predictions of the future. There was a darker side, too. Fisher believed that the British government delegation was making a hash of the negotiations on the German question at Versailles. In his reading of events, this was due primarily to the incompetence of Balfour and Lord Robert Cecil. He thought they were giving the country away to the League of Nations, and in so doing would let Germany off easy. He also concluded that a revolution in Britain was likely.[142]

Beginning on 17 March 1920, Fisher underwent four separate surgical procedures to remove cancer of the prostate, all of which failed to save his life. In June his physical condition quickly deteriorated. He lost weight, slipping to about 130lbs (59kg). One of the last letters written by Fisher was to his old friend Admiral John Moresby. The letter was uncharacteristically sober; no doubt the old sailor was in pain: 'I am dictating these few lines to you to show you I have you in remembrance. I have had a serious setback. They tried the X-ray treatment on me before leaving London, and the shock was too great. But I have a very eminent physician looking after me, and he takes a cheerful view.'[143] The country life at Ferne provided some consolation, among the roses and the company he so loved of Nina, Duchess of Hamilton, his faithful friend. He travelled to London to deal with medical matters as required.

On 10 July 1920 the end came for Admiral of the Fleet Lord Fisher of Kilverstone, GCB, OM, GCVO, LLD. He died at the London residence of the Duchess of Hamilton, 19 St James's Square. He was seventy-nine. His will had been written down in Fisher's own hand on notepaper a few days after the death of Lady Fisher. His estate was valued at £23,767, not a large sum considering his station, and was divided among his four children.[144] The ever-faithful George Lambert and Nina, Duchess of Hamilton, were named literary executors. The vast trove of Fisher's papers, chiefly correspondence, was sent in steamer trunks to be stored in the tower at the Hamilton estate, Lennoxlove, Scotland (these documents were catalogued by Ruddock Mackay of the University of St Andrews and acquired by the Churchill Archives Centre, Churchill College, Cambridge).

Then came the great funeral procession and service of 13 July, said to rival that for Fisher's particular friend Edward VII. An honour guard of 100 Royal Marines and 100 bluejackets pulling the gun carriage bearing the coffin, draped with a Union Jack, departed St James's Square for Westminster Abbey. The route, lined by spectators, lay along Pall Mall, past the palace of three monarchs that Fisher had served, then on through the Admiralty Arch to Trafalgar Square and the Nelson monument, also close to his old offices in Spring Gardens and the Admiralty Building. Then it passed down Whitehall to the Abbey, burial site of heroes, where Fisher had spent so many hours in prayer and reflection. Eight admirals served as pall-bearers: Jellicoe, Henry Jackson, H King-Hall, Cecil Thursby, R F H Henderson, Francis Bridgeman, Reginald Bacon, and Arthur Moore. (Four of them had been among Fisher's 'seven brains' who had aided his naval revolution – Jellicoe, Jackson, Henderson, and Bacon). Admiral

Hedworth Meux, one of Fisher's old sparring partners, represented George V. Another admiral, Percy Scott, was unable to be a pall-bearer because of a leg infection. United States naval officers were stationed with British officers in the west door of the Abbey when the procession arrived.

The Board of Admiralty was represented by Beatty, Chatfield, and Walter Long. Churchill came but left no record of observations. Also attending were Prince Louis of Battenberg, Lord Northcliffe, Admiral Sir Charles Ottley, Lady Bridge (widow of Admiral of the Fleet Sir Cyprian Bridge), Herbert and Margot Asquith, Maurice Hankey, Viscount Knollys, Reginald McKenna, Admiral William Fisher, Arnold White, the journalist, Sir Alfred Yarrow, the ship constructor and designer, and Sir Philip Watts, the naval architect. Esher, regretfully, could not be in attendance 'at dear old Jackie's last attendance in the Abbey.'[145] Corbett, the historian who was now writing the official history, was there to say goodbye to his old friend.

Fisher's publisher, Hodder-Williams, took his place in the parade among the civilians. Of the procession he wrote with unrestrained emotion that it seemed as if Nelson was giving Fisher his salute as the cortege passed by:

I know that that little smoke-grimed figure with armless sleeve and cocked hat stood at the salute at the top of his high column as we swung behind the Bluejackets round Trafalgar Square, our eyes fixed on the Union Jack at half-mast. By the Cenotaph in Whitehall the sailors changed into that perfect slow march which only the Navy can march to perfection, the tramping of which is like a tattoo of death. I know that Lord Fisher would have wished that all the fine conventions of Admiralty could be observed, but I for one would have liked that at some point in the memorial march and service convention had been crashed through, and that some wild, stirring, heartening song of battle and of victory had been played as a welcome to the hero – coming home.

Around the coffin in the Abbey, with its covering of the Union Jack – oh the pathos of that lonely cocked hat and sheathed sword, and the beautiful memories of the single sprig of myrtle – were grouped 'Jacky' Fisher's men, and behind them one who looked like an Admiral in mufti – Reginald McKenna [who of all the First Lords of the Admiralty had most brought about the Fisher naval revolution in materiel and who had defended him against Beresford].

The 'Last Post' lifted the service from the mournful depths of sorrow, and made it worthy of a most gallant and victorious warrior. It was played superbly, but not in the usual long-drawn wail of sadness, but triumphantly blaring, quickly, joyously – as the glad call to rest for one whose day's work was well and gladly done.[146]

The funeral cortège was impressive. Of the service, *The Times* thundered: 'Here, at least, all criticism is stilled, all calumny silent. Now we know him for what he was and would fain tell him that the Empire knows its debt to him.' And by the same: 'The people, in its silent, stolid, reverent British way, wrote its affection and admiration for "Jacky Fisher" upon the social history of our time.'[147]

Fisher's body was sent to Golders Green for cremation. The ashes were taken via train from Liverpool Street Station to Thetford, Norfolk, on 14 July. A Royal Navy officer and eight ratings acted as escort to the private burial service at Kilverstone. On a simple farm wagon covered with the same Union Jack used at the funeral of Lady Fisher the remains were conveyed across the lawn to the churchyard. Canon Edgar Sheppard, Sub-Dean of the Chapels Royal, acting on a promise made to Fisher, officiated. Admiral of the Fleet Sir Arthur Wilson, Fisher's fellow keeper of secret naval war plans, attended. Fisher's ashes were buried beside those of his wife. He had chosen Proverbs 22:29 for the text of his stone:

> Seest thou a man diligent in his business?
> he shall stand before kings,
> He shall not stand before mean men

And on the footstone was carved the resounding motto he had selected ten years earlier: FEAR GOD AND DREAD NOUGHT.

Today the lichen-encrusted headstone shows relentless effects of sun, wind, and storm off the North Sea. Still, the baron's coronet can be made out, an adornment of faithful service to the Crown as it is a testament to a quixotic life. The place, down a long, narrow lane from the war memorial to the Great War's local fallen, is in out-of-the-way St Andrew's churchyard, little visited these days. A century ago, Jacky had been placed there to rest at last, and across the gently flowing pasture to the creek and dark trees beyond lies a spaciousness such as Jacky never enjoyed save at sea, his ship caught in the irons of the doldrums (and then not for long).

Nowadays the historian-biographer finds puzzling the balancing of the turmoil of Jacky's life with the quietude of his resting place, but as my comforting companion reminded me, *Sic transit gloria mundi*. No one could wish for a more pleasant place of repose, free from the anguish and agonies of this life and world.

Below the coronet, too, you can just make out:

In Proud Memory of
John Arbuthnot Fisher
1st Baron of Kilverstone

And below again:

G.C.B. O.M. G.C.V.O.
Admiral of the Fleet
Organizer of the Navy
that won the Great War
Departed this life July 20th 1920
in the 80th year of his age.

To the south stands the stone of Frances Katharine Josepha, wife of John, Baron Fisher. To the north, in succession, stand those of Beatrix Alice, eldest daughter of Lord and Lady Fisher and wife of Admiral Neeld; then Jane, wife of 2nd Baron Fisher (1885–1955); then Cecil, 2nd Baron of Kilverstone (1868–1955); and last of all, John Vavasseur, 3rd Baron Fisher of Kilverstone, DSC (1921–2013).

Jacky's son Cecil became 2nd Baron Fisher of Kilverstone. The Lords Commissioners of the Admiralty directed Sir Oswyn Murray, Permanent Secretary of the Admiralty, to write to him:

The extraordinary services which your father rendered during his long and distinguished career in the Royal Navy, both in the Navy itself and in administration offices on shore, are too well known to be recounted here. There is no part in the multitudinous activities of modern naval service in which his influence has not been felt. The nation has been fortunate in having at its disposal, during the greatest period of naval development and progress the world has seen, Lord Fisher's unrivalled qualities of untiring zeal, brilliant genius, and whole-hearted devotion. His remarkable abilities were displayed alike in the technical development of the Fleet and all its appurtenances, in the training and education of the personnel of the Royal Navy, and in the strategical disposition of the Sea Forces of the country, both in preparation for and in actual operations of war, and three successive Sovereigns and their Ministers have enjoyed the benefit of his counsels during one of the most critical and eventful periods of the history of this realm. His loss is irreparable, but their lordships are glad that he lived to see the triumphant conclusion of his labours in the surrender of the German Fleet, and the successful issue of the late war. My lords desire me to express to you their profound sympathy with you and with the rest of his family in their bereavement, which is, indeed, shared not only by the Royal Navy, but by the Empire.[148]

So passed from the scene one of the most remarkable men of the age or, for that matter, of any age. Certainly he ranks among the most unlikely of admirals in the lengthy and illustrious annals of the Royal Navy. His endless reforming zeal stood him apart from any other Sea Lord. He had passed from the age of sail through to electronic means of detecting submarines. He was forward-thinking even if he did not understand the full intricacies of rapidly changing technology. He was just as assuredly the guardian of the nation and the Empire, and no one could question his unbridled patriotism. He was the last to realise his own shortcomings – hasty actions, breaches of confidence, and vindictive-ness toward those who stood in his way. He believed he was on a mission to keep the sea security of the British Isles and its essential trade, and this he did with unremitting zeal in the years of greatest challenge.

As for Admiral Sir David Beatty, he became First Sea Lord in 1919. 'When Admiral Beatty's flag is hauled down today,' said the *Daily Express*, with wisdom, 7 April 1919, 'there passes from the great stage that new Armada which, under Providence, has saved humanity ... To all ranks of that great Fleet every citizen of all free States owes homage, for the very battles that won the war rested ultimately for their issue on this Fleet's power to keep the seas.'

Postscript: 'History will give you your due'

Readers of history and biography will have noticed that for many a great saga there often appears a denouement – the tying up of loose ends, the reckoning of final results, the parsing out of the careers and characteristics of the main actors, and more. And so it is here where, in the afterlife, stories take on enlarged meaning and resound down the years.

Churchill and Fisher had been locked in strange destiny almost from the time Asquith named Churchill to the Cabinet in 1908. They remained linked in the telling and retelling of the history of the First World War. Even in death the interlocking lives of these titans form a legendary pairing. Re-evaluations of the Dardanelles adventure continue to prod many inquiries, as do the building of the great capital ships, the emergence of the submarine, the quest for oil and oil empires in eastern lands, and the personalities of the key players involved ashore and afloat. Given the personalities of Churchill and Fisher, these sea lords were invariably in the public eye – and together they formed an explosive and controversial relationship continuously calling back to their time students of history, political affairs, and naval relations at the level of higher command.

'Ruthless, relentless, remorseless'

Fisher's death prompted the earliest public reappraisals, focused specifically on the career of the most famous admiral since Nelson. Three days after his passing, *The Times* brilliantly assessed Fisher's career:

> Conventions and customs, which, in his opinion, had served their time, he over-rode with a fearless disregard for anything that might be said in criticism of his actions. The personnel of the Navy, he treated in the same way. For inefficiency, whether in ships or men, he had to adapt a phrase ... 'ruthless, relentless, and remorseless' ... The reforms themselves were invaluable. But the steps taken to carry them out were sometimes too brusque, too defiant of

494

tradition – in a word, too ruthless to commend them ... They often gave rise to bitter controversy and opposition ... there was always a party in the Navy which criticized more than it respected his policy.[1]

This was true. No observer of Fisher's fortunes had watched him more closely than Lord Esher, who had counselled the intemperate admiral on many an occasion. Esher, ever the friend and the critic, after hearing of Fisher's death wrote:

> I heard late last night that poor dear Jackie had gone aloft. Well, he had many crowded hours of glorious life and few men have ever enjoyed the press and lull of battle more than he. He elbowed his way through love and war with a directness and self-confidence that never blenched at any obstacle. He and Stead were fighters, but clean fighters, whatever their beaten enemies may have said. They were both men of strong intellectual passions, a bit ruthless, but ever seeking truth and finding it oftener than most men. Jackie was a Maccabean – a true believer in the God of Battles, in the Jahveh of the ancient Hebrews. His Bible was the Old Testament, which he knew by heart, without a dash of the New in his disposition.

He added, with a note of compassion, 'Jackie, I am sure, never hurt a human being, in spite of his being a Son of Thunder, but he was according to the lights of the hypocrite both a publican and a sinner. Anyhow, he could both love and hate strongly; but both his love and hatred stopped short of action. It was a pure intellectual exercise! In the web of which his character was woven the threads were of many colours and they ran crossways in many directions.'[2]

Not all persons saw Fisher in the same clear light that Esher cast upon his friend. By war's end the Navy had passed into another era, and a change had come over the admirals who still wrote letters and articles to the prominent periodicals and papers. They distanced themselves from Fisher; they had new concerns quite clear of his ancient obsessions. In the circumstances, they hardly spoke of Fisher in regards to the progress of the war. Time had swept away the compulsion of his actions, the resonance of his voice, and the power of his influence. His friend and fellow admiral, the ever-devoted John Moresby, noticed this when an 'article-writing' admiral sent him a letter in which Fisher's name had not been mentioned, nor his services alluded to. 'I returned it, saying it was the play without Hamlet,' Moresby told Fisher. 'You might be wrong, or despised, but you could not be *ignored*.' Moresby went on to chronicle the changes effected under Fisher: the Navy revolutionised, Osborne Naval College created, obsolete cruisers scrapped, a naval base shifted from Portland to Rosyth, dreadnought battleships and battlecruisers invented, the victory at the Falklands, and so on. 'He might as well talk of Rome without Caesar ... He

replied and said you were an Enigma, and that covered it all! There is some
truth to this, for such are all born leaders of men.'³ A great personage had
passed from the scene but inhabited the ghostly margins of the times.

On 27 March 1923 Lord Esher wrote tellingly of the Churchill–Fisher
relationship and the enduring struggle between the two, the echoes of which
come down to us to this day. His comments were made in consequence of
Churchill's soon-to-be released (and defensive) first volume of *The World Crisis*:

> I think the book shows the folly of going on building these great armoured
> castles that you have to keep in harbour and protect as though they were
> Dresden china. No battleships did a single thing during the whole war. They
> just 'menaced' each other at a safe distance. Jellicoe was terrified the whole
> time, unless every sort of device and in harbour protected him.
>
> Of course, Jackie is the hero of the whole story. The one presiding genius
> over preparation for war! – and, had he been loose [given a free hand], the
> winner of the war in two years instead of four.
>
> Winston backed up well from 1912. He had this merit that he listened to
> Jackie and chose his fighting sailors well.
>
> Jellicoe was a 'safe' man. You can detect the writhing of Beatty, Keyes,
> Pakenham – the dashers – all the time. They wanted to be up and doing.
>
> So the navy held the gate. The other school – Nelson's – were saying: 'Let
> us have a go and we will plump the army down within fifty miles of Berlin.'
>
> This controversy will never be settled.⁴

Esher was right: discussions as to why the Navy failed to bring the Germans to
account at sea will never end. Among the post-mortems was that of hard-hitting
British naval commentator Hector Bywater. Writing in the 1930s, he
condemned the Fisher regime at the Admiralty because it crushed opposition
and pushed aside those who dissented from his doctrines. Bywater argued that
it was impossible to know how many great officers had been swept aside: 'Their
subsequent treatment at the hands of the high priest, Lord Fisher, is an abiding
scandal.' And in the same writer's view, Fisher was also largely to blame for the
fall of the Navy in the public eye.⁵ These views prevailed, and they took up
commanding positions.

Not long before his death, Fisher received a tender letter from James
Masterton-Smith, formerly private secretary to successive First Lords, including
Churchill. He pointed to Fisher's exit from the Admiralty, 'what happened in
that fateful month of May', as the deciding event of the war:

> The 15th of May, 1915, was the best day the Germans had in the War. The
> breach between yourself and Winston was the tragedy – in my judgment the
> outstanding tragedy – of the War. Together you were invincible and would

have gone from triumph to triumph. But the high gods willed otherwise, and from the first foredoomed the Dardanelles to failure. Nothing went right with it, and with it fell the only combination (i.e. yourself and Winston) that could have finished the War with as complete a victory in a third of the time and a fiftieth of the cost, in blood as well as treasure.[6]

That too, was an exaggeration and is one of the accumulating 'ifs' of this story of the titans.

From the time of his departure from the Admiralty until his death, Fisher kept quiet on the matter of Churchill's interventions. He made no public issue of the business; he kept his complaints to his private correspondence and his discussions with intimates. It was Jellicoe who was the most significant naval professional to complain about Churchill. He was critical of Churchill's *The World Crisis*, arguing that there were 'countless mis-statements', such as the question of basing the Fleet at Rosyth.[7]

Harold Begbie, one of Fisher's friends among the many political journalists, commented shortly after the admiral's death that Jacky would never be numbered among the saints but, happily, was not destined to be found among the martyrs. 'No man I have met ever gave me so authentic a feeling of originality as this dare-devil of genius, this pirate of public life, who more than any other Englishman saved British democracy from Prussian domination.'[8] Fair comment – and the reason is easier to see in retrospect than it was in those terrible times. Fisher brought one tremendous purpose to life, a purpose exalted into a greatness and singularity unknown to most of his age, save Churchill. This singleness of purpose tended to reduce him to something quite childlike, as others saw it. But Begbie claimed Fisher was one of the greatest Englishmen of all time; he was possessed with genius.

Fisher called England 'God's Breakwater against Germany'. His consuming passion was to make the Navy fit and ready for the war that he saw was coming long before 'the Day'. 'All his genius and strength, and all his imagination, and the immense drive of his nature was in it, and his tremendous courage. That never failed, but there were bad times.'[9] So wrote Esther Meynell. He was a patriot of a most unusual kind, placing his devotion to England above all else. He was daemonic, too, in seeking the safety, honour, and glory of Britain and the Empire. Conscious of his own powers, he exhibited an inspiration not possessed by fellow mortals in the Service or at the Admiralty. His patriotism was his saving grace and made him unquestionable in the eyes of history. Only his methods made him suspect. He had no political party to back, only that which favoured the Navy. Had his contemporaries been travelling wholeheartedly in the same direction, and at the same speed, he might have figured in the annals of the Admiralty as something of a saint.

But his naval contemporaries were not similarly driven. They found his urgings inconvenient, vexatious. Accordingly, they resisted him to the point of exasperation. When conflict arose, they departed – to fight in the back rooms or to lay snares at his feet. Vilification became a natural order of the day, and with it came a dark and dreary cloud of sadness bordering on pathos. As a revolutionary, Fisher moved too quickly ahead of those who might have been able to help him.

In later years, far from being at centre stage for the rejuvenation and reorganisation of the Service under Selborne and McKenna, those First Lords of the Admiralty who stand above the rest or, again, in the cut and thrust of battle planning with Churchill, Fisher found himself in a state of loneliness and assumed a watchful position uncharacteristic of his disposition. Exhausted by labours and wearied by the endless battles that are the wont of the reformer, Fisher climbed his own Olympus. All too soon he was a man of yesteryear. The Board of Invention and Research held no charm. No one paid him homage there, or came to give respect or ask advice. These were the deepest cuts of all. He had been swept aside by events, made sadly redundant. Fisher, save for the odd sortie from various country haunts to London, was out of sight and out of mind. His attendance in the House of Lords was irregular and sparse. His letters to *The Times* were bolts from the blue, erratic and unpredictable, guaranteeing a further gratuitous appreciation of lunatic forces at work.

He grew apart from politicians. More, his contempt for them increased daily. He damned them with all the vigour of the Old Testament vernacular. He had always got on best with the Conservatives, or Unionists. How different they were to work with than the problematic, uncertain Liberals. But like all of them in post-war times he was jockeying for position, reacting to the buffeting political winds of fate. He was not cut out for survival in this line of work, no matter how great a shipbuilder he was or an economiser in the use and deployment of naval assets. To him, politicians, the 'frocks', lacked character. This was his conclusion. They were spineless. They lacked vision, had no appreciation of anything long-range. Except for one or two who had leadership qualities of a minor degree, the bulk of his contemporaries fell below his expectations, failed to meet the mark. 'To find men at the heart of so great a nation with no courage in the heart, with no exaltation of captaincy in the soul, without even the decency to make sacrifices for principle made him bitterly contemptuous,' wrote a contemporary, with wisdom, of Fisher. 'At first he could scarcely bridle his rage, but as years went on he used to say that the politicians had deepened his faith in Providence.' Put differently, Fisher believed that England would have perished long ago had not God been looking after her. And in later years he unceasingly quoted the poet William Watson:

Time and the Ocean, and some fostering star
In high cabal have made us what we are.[10]

When it came, Fisher's exit from this world left in its wake a divided Navy and an embittered officer elite. Many years would pass before old wounds were healed. A subsequent dispute between Admirals Jellicoe and Beatty (and their respective followers), fought out largely behind the scenes, tended to dampen the dust that had arisen during Fisher's momentous days.

For almost six years as First Sea Lord, Jacky Fisher had shaken up the Navy, leading a revolution in naval affairs. Obstruction, reaction, and prejudice prevented easy passage of his reforms. As late as 1900 the Navy retained its late-Victorian character. Boarding pikes were still to be seen. Such bugle calls as 'Away boarders' and 'Prepare to ram' could still be heard. At general quarters, officers put on frock coats and swords. A midshipman passing for lieutenant in seamanship was asked by the president of his board to describe the procedure for hanging a man at the yardarm. Spit and polish was at its zenith. Gunnery practice was conducted at short range, but this was expensive. As the charming saying went, 'Attitude and action are the art of gunnery and whiskers make the man.' Fleet manoeuvres were practised, but with the costs of steam coal ever a worry.

In his time, Fisher saw many of these older customs swept aside. With a flourish of his pen he discarded those old 'useless vessels of war whose officers were shooting pheasants up Chinese Rivers.' Opponents squirmed when those vessels were swept away, for they knew that in a future war they might well be used for convoy work or observation duties. They squirmed again when he brought in the revolutionary *Dreadnought*, and yet again when he promoted the submarine as the future weapons platform of naval war. The water-tube boiler was revolutionary, and the turbine, too. He attempted to reform naval education, creating a system of common entry for all officers. Work was pressed on at Scapa Flow for the new base of operations. Naval forces were brought home from distant margins and concentrated in home waters to work and drill over their future battleground. He overhauled dockyards, speeded up ship construction, established a Royal Naval Volunteer Reserve. Nucleus crews had been introduced. He improved provisions and seamen's working conditions, and revised punishments. He developed logistical support in the form of Royal Fleet auxiliaries. He foresaw aviation and the prodigious 15in gun.

Not least, he had talent-spotted, sometimes against the views of the First Lord, the great sea commanders of the future, including Jellicoe and, to a lesser extent, Beatty. Jellicoe had been one of 'the seven brains' employed privately by Fisher to advance his reforming agenda under Lord Selborne. Popular among other officers and the lower deck, Jellicoe was a born leader, if a centraliser.

Unimpressive in appearance, his personality was such that he gained the confidence of the Fleet. He had high professional competence and an 'eye for battle'. He was capable of making quick decisions. He probably gave those under him too little critique for their failings. More seriously, he was incapable of delegating authority. This stemmed from his immense capacity to do administrative work.

Sir David Beatty, vice-admiral commanding the Battle Cruiser Squadron, was a well-known figure in social circles and had married handsomely. He was a handsome fellow with broad vision in naval affairs. He possessed spirit and could distinguish between issues and unimportant matters. He was independent in character, with abundant self-confidence. His jaunty disposition attracted much interest, and those who knew him well swore by his professional expertise. Beatty, whom Churchill had raised over the heads of so many others when he was given command of the Battle Cruiser Squadron, went on to perhaps the most famous career in naval administration. He became First Sea Lord in 1920. With him to the Admiralty he brought Admiral Osmond de B Brock, the Vice Chief of the Naval Staff, and Captain Ernle Chatfield, his flag officer at Jutland. Many others were brought along at the same time. Beatty arrived just in time to examine the text of the report by Captain J E T Harper, prepared for the Board of Admiralty, on the Battle of Jutland. Like Jellicoe he was conscious of how history would view him, and like Churchill, too, was keen to correct the record. Beatty disagreed with many of the details as presented by Harper, and a long battle ensued, backed by Brock and others, that led to the Harper Record being placed on hold, as it turned out, forever. Meanwhile, the press were clamouring for Harper's details, and in Parliament probing questions were asked. Montagues and Capulets abounded. Positions favouring Jellicoe or Beatty were taken. A general rancour ensued, prejudicial to the Navy. History-writing admirals had a field day, and even the 'official history' written by Corbett, *Naval History of the World War*, volume 3 (1923), failed to meet with the Board of Admiralty's approval. In fact, this disclaimer was entered into the flyleaf of the book: 'The Lords Commissioners of the Admiralty have given the author access to official documents in the preparation of this work, but they are in no way responsible for its production or for the accuracy of its statements. Their Lordships find that some of the principles advocated in the book, especially the tendency to minimise the importance of seeking battle and of forcing it to a conclusion, are directly in conflict with their views.' History was in the dock, and the Admiralty and the Navy were on trial.

Beatty campaigned hard for the Navy in the post-war years, an extraordinarily difficult job given the general state of the economy and the rising influence and demands of the Royal Air Force, the biggest empire-builder in history since the Romans according to some British admirals. Beatty devoted his last years to country pursuits, especially the hunt. He was ill when news of Jellicoe's death on 20 November 1935 reached him. 'So Jellicoe has gone! Well, I feel I shall be the next to be summoned. I do not think the call will be long. I am tired. I am tired.' Despite cold weather and the advice of his medical adviser, Beatty was determined to take part in the ceremony in which his old commander-in-chief was borne to St Paul's. 'What will the Navy say if I fail to attend Jellicoe's funeral?'[11] He carried out his duties as pall-bearer, and he looked so deathlike passing through Fleet Street that a welcome glass of brandy was brought out to him from a nearby newspaper office.

George V died on 20 January 1936, another sign of the disappearing old order. Beatty, who regarded the King as his best friend, was determined to honour him by attendance. He accompanied the gun carriage pulled by sailors from the Fleet, with spectators once again noticing how ghastly he looked. He died on 11 March 1936. The Archbishop of Canterbury took the service. *The Times* recounted the details: 'Sailors marched beside his pall through the cold misty morning to St Paul's. His body was brought upon a gun carriage and lifted by blue jackets down the Cathedral aisle. Over the coffin was flung the Union he had flown as Admiral of the Fleet.' The dead admiral was laid beside the tomb of Jellicoe. 'Deep in the Crypt not far from the sarcophagus of Nelson they were left in peace. In death they were not divided and the strange skein which had so often entangled their careers was smoothed out by the Fates.'

The women behind the Fleet played their devoted part. That Beatty was placed beside Jellicoe in the Crypt upset the Dowager Countess Jellicoe. She sought to have Beatty buried in a corner other than the naval one. 'I do appreciate the fact you and the Admiralty are not to blame about St. Paul's,' she wrote in anger to the First Sea Lord, Admiral of the Fleet Sir Ernle Chatfield (Beatty's flag captain at Jutland). 'Strange that the Church instead of giving you Peace of Mind should destroy it.'[12] The controversy of Jutland, which simmered until the end of the War, had a new lease of life that stretched well into the beginning of the Second World War, and is now legendary.

The deaths of Jellicoe and Beatty marked the end of the Fisher era at a time when the Navy was alarmed by the naval preparations of future enemies: Imperial Japan, Mussolini's Italy, and Nazi Germany. The old blame game receded in importance. New and urgent calculations presented themselves.

In his time, Jacky Fisher was one of the most remarkable of men – adored by some, dreaded by others, despised by not a few. He was one of the great figures of any age. In his passage he left a great sea wash. He was a human dynamo. He moved at the speed of one of his torpedo-boat destroyers. An expert in torpedoes and in gunnery, he was a materialist of naval power. He prided himself on being a seaman. He loved the Royal Navy with all his heart. He deplored the old methods of promotion on the grounds of seniority alone, for he held firmly to the belief that the best way of promoting efficiency was to see that persons he liked and trusted should be given preferment in appointment and advancement in the Service. That got him into trouble. He equally hated the old system of training officers, thinking it class-ridden and technologically backward, and he called for a wholesale revision to naval training and education that included the introduction of new courses of study and the building of the Britannia Royal Navy College in Devon. In everything he was an iconoclast and was widely seen as a revolutionary and troublemaker. But he rose to the top, partly on the basis of his own manifold abilities and equally on the basis of the support that various politicians gave him. When he came to the Admiralty as First Sea Lord on the eve of Trafalgar Day 1904, he did so with the (nervous) backing of the government of the day. And when the Liberals came to power in 1906, Fisher was firmly entrenched in position. Before long his famed innovation, the battleship *Dreadnought*, was in commission sporting its great armour, guns, and speed. Soon to appear were the fast battlecruisers, giving wide-ranging mobility to British naval power. He advocated the idea of flotillas, though he seldom saw them in action. He became the greatest administrator of the Royal Navy since Lord Barham and, as the great historian Arthur Marder proclaimed, his name will always be connected with the Navy at the apex of its power.

When Fisher left the Admiralty for what he thought was the last time, officially on New Year's Day 1910, having been elevated to the House of Lords and made Admiral of the Fleet, there was even then a cloud over his head. The intrigue with Beresford was the cause, and Asquith's suspicions against the old admiral never faded. Churchill nourished a different view. When Churchill needed a First Sea Lord to replace Prince Louis Battenberg in October 1914, he hauled in Fisher despite objections that Fisher was past his prime. These were immensely challenging times, for the war was not over by Christmas as had been predicted, the Kaiser's navy was not easily brought to account, and well into the early months of 1915 the Royal Navy missed many opportunities for victory against the enemy. During these lamentable months, Churchill and Fisher operated in loose and disjointed harness. But incompatibility of temperament and outlook prevented them from working in harmony for long. They kept different hours at the Admiralty and often communicated by memo or note. Grave difficulties lay ahead.

Fisher always believed that the Navy – and the British war effort – needed 'one man' to win the war. Fisher had no doubt that he himself was the one who could win the war – by allowing Britain's advantage in sea power to exercise its function, and by lightning strikes of amphibious forces against the enemy. But from time to time he let it be known to Churchill that he believed Winston was 'the man'. In any event, Fisher's Baltic project got nowhere, though he did build a fleet of shallow-draught monitors and other vessels.

The War Cabinet had its mind fixed on the Dardanelles as a means of knocking the Ottoman Empire out of the war, securing Constantinople (Istanbul) for the Russians, and keeping up the Eastern Front so as to preoccupy the Germans in that theatre. By January 1915 the Dardanelles campaign was no longer an *idée fixe*: it was an accepted feature of British government policy. Churchill believed that in the absence of any military force, which was not forthcoming from Lord Kitchener, the Secretary for War, the Dardanelles could be taken 'by ships alone'. Thus was launched the ill-fated Dardanelles campaign. Churchill forced the pace, made the scheme his own. Fisher may have swallowed his misgivings, but what about Kitchener? Churchill's account of attempts to persuade a tardy Kitchener to release the 29th Division for the operation runs counter to the War Council minutes, later released to the public, that Churchill intended to use the troops not for an attack at the Dardanelles, but to give weight to British diplomacy, and to garrison Constantinople. Unsurprisingly, Kitchener did not agree to send the division until 10 March. Fisher, who knew the risks, nonetheless contended that it could be accomplished if done right away, but weeks passed before ships were in place, the necessary supplies sent, and the attack begun to force the Ottoman forts to submit to British and French naval gunnery. The 29th Division was eventually committed to the campaign, and ANZAC forces were thrown in, beginning 25 April. But the campaign never succeeded despite repeated attempts and changes of command, and by December it was over – with attacking forces withdrawn to other obligations and challenges.

The association of these two titans continued until mid-May 1915, when a struggle based on irreconcilable principles about who was in charge led to Fisher's resignation – and Churchill's exit from the Admiralty. The powerful and impossible combination came to a crashing close, sending the contestants into the wilderness. There were many other combinations at the Admiralty, but most of them were quiet and ineffective and undoubtedly slow and ponderable. Selborne and McKenna were the best First Lords of the Admiralty under whom Fisher served. The Churchill–Fisher combination has been harshly judged as among the failures, or worse.[13]

'Winston is back'

Churchill, as we have seen, was devastated by his loss of the Admiralty and his exit from the centre of direction of the war effort. Fisher continued his behind-the-scenes conniving, weakened now because of his disgraceful abandonment of his post. For a time he headed the Bureau of Invention and Research, looking for technical means of hunting the dreaded new threat, the U-boat, which was mauling Allied merchant shipping and threatening the survival of the nation. He never found a countermeasure to the U-boat, though promising advances were made in underwater electronic detection. Meanwhile, Fisher and Churchill co-operated on the evidence they presented to the searing inquiries of the Dardanelles Commission. Churchill, throughout, was loyal to his friend and never deserted him. Fisher was more suspicious. Because he could not out-argue Winston, as he told his political head just before his exit, he was obliged to leave the Admiralty.

For a time Churchill was prepared to let bygones be bygones. He had said all he wanted to about his administration at the Admiralty in *The World Crisis*. It was a stout defence. Fisher had not given him the support he contended he deserved. He had no further desire to open old wounds; indeed, he would have been happy to leave Fisher as a piece of memory. That was not to be, for in 1929 Admiral Reginald Bacon, a trusted Fisherite, biographer of Jellicoe, and a man devoted to the memory of Jacky, produced a *Life of Lord Fisher*, which was entirely laudatory of his old chief. Fisher's literary executors had entrusted the work to him; he did not disappoint. In Churchill's opinion, Bacon discharged his duties as biographer in a partisan manner – and in a fashion designed to revive old animosities and quarrels. Once Bacon had laid out the charges against Churchill, the latter could not leave them uncontested. Thus, in an article in *News of the World* entitled 'Lord Fisher and his Biographer', he moved to get his own back and to exert what nowadays is called damage control. 'To impart a mood of hatred and spiteful controversy into the discussion of the memorable transactions with which Lord Fisher was concerned, was to render no true service to his memory,' wrote Churchill. That critique received an extended lease of life when Churchill's hot-selling *Great Contemporaries*, first published by Thornton Butterworth in 1937, was issued in a revised, extended edition in 1938. This last contained four new articles on Charles Stewart Parnell, Lord Baden-Powell, President Franklin Delano Roosevelt, and, of particular interest to us here, Churchill's assault on Fisher and Bacon.

Churchill's retrospective views on Fisher had been long awaited. He warmed to his topic. A flash of light always came from Fisher, said Churchill, yet there was always something foreign to the Navy about Fisher. He was never of the 'band of brothers' that marked the Nelsonic touch. He was the 'dark angel' of the naval service, and he gloried in it. 'Ruthless, relentless, remorseless' was his favourite epithet about himself. Fisher was partisan; he was the author of his own misfortune, inviting vendettas and manoeuvres. 'But behind him and his professional progeny, the bloodhounds followed sniffing and padding along, and now and then giving deep tongue.'

Churchill made no attempt to sidestep the fact that it was he who had brought Fisher back to the Admiralty, no matter how disastrous the decision. As he told Admiral Keyes, he would do so again with the knowledge he had at that time and in that circumstance. Fisher brought energy to the Admiralty. He was a builder of warships. His genius was that of a constructor, organiser, and energiser. 'He cared little for the Army and its fortunes.' And he delighted in trampling on the Treasury. Build ships – that was his message and his mission – and that he did. But he was old, and increasingly in a position of declining health. In fact, Churchill stated – for the first time – that it was always his belief that Fisher had suffered a nervous breakdown at the critical juncture. This last may be true, though unlikely. If it is correct, it emphasises yet again the importance of the study of health in regards to statecraft and the running of great departments of state or the naval service. Perhaps Churchill's retrospective was running a bit wild, for there is no confirming evidence Fisher suffered a nervous breakdown. Churchill disliked the partisan nature of Fisher's biographer, Bacon, of that there can be no doubt. Thus, when the abridged, one-volume edition of *The World Crisis* appeared in 1931, the reinforced view Churchill held of Fisher's mental instability gave the reading public the general account of this state of affairs that has become what we might call the received version. Then again, Churchill always had the last word: referring to Fisher's ultimatum of May 1915 in which he set forth to Asquith his demands so that he could head up the Admiralty, Churchill wrote, 'Nothing could more clearly, more cruelly, expose the mental distress and wild excitement into which the strain of war had plunged the old Admiral. Nothing could portray more vividly the volcano upon which I had been living and upon which grave decisions of war and policy had been pursued.'[14]

Then there was Churchill's treatment of Jellicoe in *The World Crisis*. Understandably, material consideration had brought ill-success: Jellicoe's tactics reflected his abiding worries about enemy torpedoes, submarines, attacking light surface craft, and the deadly mine. The battlecruisers possessed intrinsic design defects, and Churchill distanced himself from admiration of a vessel of the greatest power and speed incapable of facing a strong battleship. Deficiencies in design proved fatal. The fast division of *Queen Elizabeth*-class ships were kept from battle, not deliberately but by neglect. Moreover, prudent rearming induced tactical schemes unworthy of the Navy's tradition. Churchill then directed salvos against his principal sea commander:

> The ponderous, poignant responsibilities borne successfully, if not triumphantly, by Sir John Jellicoe during two years of faithful command, constitute unanswerable claims to the lasting repect of the nation. *But the Royal Navy must find in other personalities and other episodes the golden links which carried forward through the Great War the audacious and conquering traditions of the past*; and it is to Beatty and the battle-cruisers, to Keyes at Zeebrugge, to Tyrwhitt and his Harwich striking force, to the

destroyer and submarine flotillas out in all weathers and against all foes, to the wild adventures of the Q-ships, to the steadfast resolution of the British Merchant Service, that the eyes of rising generations will turn.[15]

In his retelling of the Jutland episode, Churchill seized upon the partisan and inaccurate *Naval Staff Appreciation of Jutland*, commissioned by Beatty and compiled by Alfred and Kenneth Dewar, and used it extensively. Although release of that publication was suspended, Churchill possessed one of the few copies that had not been recalled. A flawed work, its messages and information found wide readership in Churchill's volume.[16]

In the years since the disappointing and inconclusive Battle of Jutland, Churchill had shown a strong preference for Beatty over Jellicoe. This was not so much because the former had once been his naval assistant but because the latter had so disappointed Churchill in his actions, or his want of actions due to what Winston regarded as his cautiousness. Jellicoe missed opportunities.

Beatty was at the Admiralty as First Sea Lord when Churchill was named Chancellor of the Exchequer for Stanley Baldwin's Conservative government. He wrote on 11 November 1924 to the fifty-three-year-old Beatty:

> My Dear Beatty:
> I am so grateful for your kind letter of congratulations ... I am one of your great admirers, and I never cease to proclaim you as the inheritor of the grand tradition of Nelson.
> How I wish I could have guided events a little better and a little longer. Jutland would have had a different ring if the plans already formed in my mind after Dogger Bank for securing you the chief command had grown to their natural fruition.
> I live a good deal in those tremendous days.
> Once more my sincere thanks,
> Yours ever,
> Winston S.C.[17]

A tinge of sadness coupled with touches of resignation and regret is here disclosed. Then again, Churchill had many regrets. The Dardanelles campaign will long be studied as one of those might-have-beens of history. What might have happened if the Allies had pressed their military means just a little longer? Even more puzzling: what would have happened if Churchill's advice to Parliament in March 1916 had been followed? He had made a speech rationalising and justifying that campaign and his involvement in it. The speech was well-prepared, and all sides of the House listened to it with respect and interest. Then, at its close, to the astonishment of all, he proposed as a solution the recall of Fisher to the Admiralty. At that time Fisher was politically unacceptable, and Churchill equally so.

Many lessons were learned from the experiences of the Great War. Not least among them was that Churchill discovered his Service chiefs could be egotistical and domineering men. That Churchill outlasted most of them owes much to his challenging tug-of-war with Fisher. In the final analysis it was Fisher who prepared the great naval instrument of the Allied victory, and it was Churchill who placed the Grand Fleet at its battle station, with its watchtower at Scapa Flow. These were notable and noble achievements, not to be forgotten. The torpedo may have ended the possibility of a close blockade of the enemy's ports and coasts, the mine caused many a casualty, and the armed merchant cruisers did their jobs, but the grinding influence of Britain's naval power, which was ubiquitous if not always crushing in its encounters with the enemy, played a great role in the final outcome. Britannia still held the trident of Neptune. But the Britannic tragedy had already occurred on Churchill's and Fisher's watch at the Admiralty.

When Churchill's own account of the First World War was published, he exposed himself to much criticism, including renewed criticism for the Dardanelles disaster. In the opening volume of *The World Crisis* (1923) he wrote of his supervising role at the Admiralty. These are his anodyne words: 'It was no part of my duty to deal with the routine movements of the Fleet and its squadrons, but only to exercise a general supervision.' One can almost believe that Churchill, for all his interventions and energy, all his desires for action this day (which he learned from Fisher), and all his inventiveness and countless new ideas, exercised only general management of the war at sea. This was unconvincing to many, not least to Lord Selborne, Fisher's old and sagacious acquaintance, who had effected the Selborne Scheme when Jacky first became First Sea Lord. In regards to Churchill's statement that he only exercised a general supervision, Selborne wrote:

> These are Churchill's own words, and yet his book is one long record of constant interference in routine and consequent failure of supervision. The fundamental fault of his system is its restlessness. Great as his services were, they would have been greater if he could have refrained from trying to do his colleagues' and his subordinates' work as well as his own. The result was a diminution of his otherwise splendid driving power and a grievous injury to the value of his supervision. For what is the value of a man's criticism, when the order has been drafted by himself, or his supervision, when he himself is the author, approver, and executor of the policy?

Lord Selborne gave further advice, and it may have been intended for Churchill. Perhaps he had in mind a second world war: 'If any future First Lord finds himself in that great position in another Armageddon, I hope that the courage of Mr Churchill will wrap him as a cloak, but I hope also that he will shun as poison the temptation to do the work of his naval and technical advisers, of his administrative officers and of the Secretariat, as well as his own.'[18]

When the bells proclaimed the Armistice throughout Britain, Churchill was within easy walking distance of so many places that had been part of his restless political life to this date – and would be so in the future. He was in the Hotel Metropole, Northumberland Avenue, at the time, just around the corner from the National Liberal Club. Not far away was the august Admiralty, with its naval intelligence unit and its operations room to which Churchill had been irresistibly drawn, the nerve centre of the British Empire's naval web of influence, the most powerful and independent office of the State. Near it stood the War Office, and beyond that 10 Downing Street and the new Air Ministry. Beyond that, again, stood the House of Commons, that great theatre of politics, where he had stoutly and ably defended the great naval estimates of 1913, and also where, in a flight of fancy lacking sober judgement after the Dardanelles and Gallipoli reverses, he had called in March 1916 for Fisher's return to the Admiralty.

On 3 September 1939, the day Britain declared war on Hitler's Germany, Churchill returned to the Admiralty as First Lord. He looked back on his earlier time there as the 'Golden Age', and recounted in *The Gathering Storm* how he 'came again to the room I had quitted in pain and sorrow almost exactly a quarter of a century before, when Lord Fisher's resignation had led to my removal from my post as First Lord and ruined irretrievably, as it proved, the important concept of forcing the Dardanelles.' He called for the return of his old table: it was retrieved. The old maps and charts of naval dispositions were similarly uncovered. At the first Board meeting of the Admiralty he was filled with emotion, and he told his colleagues what a privilege and honour it was to be again in that chair. 'Gentlemen,' he said, 'to your tasks and duties.' And from that moment on, exerting energy and showing stamina, he, as he put it, 'laid my hands upon the naval affairs.'[19] The machinery of administration began to move more vigorously, and in naval circles his 'First Lord's prayers' – 'Pray inform me' – showed his constant concern and quest for 'action this day'. Officers recalled his earlier days at the Admiralty, and his interference in professional matters beginning in 1911 and ending in 1915. They had reason to wonder what might transpire in this new, second, world war.

And what, we might ask, did Winston Churchill learn about the direction of war and, in particular, how the supreme command can function in times of stress? What difference did he see between political power as a statesman and professional power as conducted and implemented by naval officers? Given the extensive historical discussion about whether Churchill meddled in naval operational matters in the Second World War – Arthur Marder proved that he never did when First Lord of the Admiralty, but other views are that Churchill never stopped meddling – it is safe to say this will be a discussion without end.[20]

Captain Stephen Roskill, in *Churchill and the Admirals*, argued that Churchill's intense and complex relationship with Fisher coloured subsequent relationships with admirals in the Second World War. In particular, Churchill was always on the lookout for those who showed too much independence or obstinacy, clearly wishing to avoid having another 'Fisher' who would be obstructive and attempt to run things his own way.[21] Churchill, like Fisher, appointed officers, naval, land, and air, to places of prominence and influence in order to advance his own views or strengthen his own positions. Few historians, if any, have said otherwise. What Marder did, in opposition to Roskill, was show that during the Second World War Churchill did not interfere with the naval professionals at the Admiralty in the conduct of operations *when he was First Lord of the Admiralty*. Roskill resoundingly responded to him in the negative, and echoes of this come down to us.[22] We know of cases where admirals, generals, and air marshals outlasted Churchill in argument or in listening. But many commanders lost their posts. In Admiral Sir Dudley Pound, First Sea Lord, Churchill had a professional colleague who could not be easily moved, but whether he managed to control Winston's enthusiasms and endless operational plans is a story for another time and place.[23]

His tremendous powers of concentration amounting to obsession led him into difficulties that he could not foresee. Frustrated by Kitchener's unwillingness to commit an early division to the Dardanelles led him foolishly to 'by ships alone'. Churchill then failed to get Fisher's complete concurrence on the naval operation. Churchill moved too far ahead of his chief counsellors of war. No wonder he was distrusted. His genius often outranged lesser mortals, to his cost. This was his fatal flaw.

If strong positions are taken in favour of or against Churchill in his manipulating and energising role in the conduct of war at the top, there can be no doubt that he learned greatly from the experience of the First World War, and took greater care in the exercise of his responsibilities in 'the supreme command' in the Second. However, ample evidence exists that he would still run a whole campaign on his own authority, against professional opinion. There is no better example of this than Operation Menace, the debacle at Dakar, West Africa, in September 1940. He overpowered his armed service advisers and staff. No foothold for General de Gaulle and the Free French could be obtained there in the face of the resistance of Vichy French and German forces.

The division that developed between Churchill and Fisher had begun months before the May 1915 crisis in Whitehall over the Dardanelles. The previous December, Churchill, in his search for a naval offensive, had pressed hard upon Fisher his own special plan for the occupation of Borkum, holding it with a garrison, and using that island as a base for submarines and light craft that would cause the High Seas Fleet to come out of its lairs and do battle with the Grand Fleet. As much as Churchill pleaded the case, which he always did in ardent form, he could not get his First Sea Lord to move the project forward to the detail stage. In his retelling of events, Churchill blamed Fisher for not taking action on an operation he thought bound to be successful, and even accused him of lassitude – perhaps the only time Jacky was ever charged with that fault. In the preliminary chapters of *The World Crisis 1915*, the second volume of his expansive history, Churchill describes how Fisher seemed to stand in his way. He gives no credit to the view that his professional colleague had justifiable reasons for opposing the capture of Borkum and all its attendant consequences, including perhaps the loss of the Royal Navy's command of the North Sea. Borkum in British hands would have been a hostage to fortune. We see here the risks Churchill was prepared to take. He knew about the fortunes of war, and once the opportunity for taking Borkum passed, 1915 became the ill-fated year for the Allied powers, one that led to further disasters which Churchill thought might have been avoided had decisive action been taken against the German High Seas Fleet. What would have happened if the British had captured Borkum? Here is one of the might-have-beens of history, and it was Churchill's good luck to outlive Fisher and his supporters and, not least, to have the final word.

Above all, and in summary, a delectable quote A J P Taylor unearthed from the documents rings down to us through the years. 'All I asked was compliance with my wishes after reasonable discussion.'[24] Churchill was inexhaustible: he wore people down, and as old Jacky Fisher complained, he could not out-argue Churchill. Very few people could, save perhaps Clementine.

List of Abbreviations

Adm	Admiralty Papers, TNA
Beatty Papers	*The Beatty Papers*, ed Bryan Ranft, 2 vols
Cab	Cabinet Papers, TNA
CAC	Churchill Archives Centre, Churchill College, Cambridge
CHAR	Chartwell Papers, CAC
CHUR	Churchill Papers, CAC
Cmd	Command papers (papers that originate outside Parliament and are presented to Parliament by command of His [Her] Majesty or by command of the House of Commons)
DRBK	de Robeck's Papers, CAC
Esher, Letters and Journals	*Journals and Letters of Reginald Viscount Esher*, ed Maurice V Brett, 3 vols; Oliver, Viscount Esher, 1 vol
ESHR	Esher Papers, CAC
FDSF	*From the Dreadnought to Scapa Flow*, Arthur J Marder, 5 vols
FGDN	*Fear God and Dread Nought* [Fisher letters], ed Arthur J Marder, 3 vols
FISR	Fisher Papers, CAC
FO	Foreign Office Papers, TNA
HMSO	His/Her Majesty's Stationery Office
HNKY	Hankey Papers
Jellicoe Papers	*The Jellicoe Papers*, A Temple Patterson, 2 vols
Keyes Papers	*The Keyes Papers*, ed Paul G Halpern, 3 vols
RNM	Royal Naval Museum, Portsmouth
SLGF	Shane Leslie Papers, CAC
TNA	The National Archives, Kew, Surrey

References

Introduction

1 Barry M Gough, *Pax Britannica: Ruling the Waves and Keeping the Peace before Armageddon* (Basingstoke: Palgrave Macmillan, 2014).

2 Winston S Churchill, *The World Crisis* (London: Thornton Butterworth, 1923–31), 1:23, 24. Throughout I have used the London edition, which has different pagination from the New York edition.

3 It bears repeating that the Royal Navy was also essential to the economic well-being of the British Isles. By 1913 a sixth of the entire British workforce was reliant on naval contracts. See Hew Strachan, *The First World War*, vol 1 (Oxford: Oxford University Press, 2001), 375.

4 Blanche Dugdale, *Arthur James Balfour: First Earl of Balfour, 1906–1930* (London: Hutchinson, 1936), 2:143.

5 Quoted in Dugdale, *Balfour*, 2:184. See also John Ehrman, *Cabinet Government and War, 1890–1940* (Cambridge: Cambridge University Press, 1958), 59.

6 Taprell Dorling, *Men o' War* (London: Philip Allan, 1929), viii and 221.

7 Norman Dixon, *On the Psychology of Military Incompetence* (London: Pimlico, 1994), 336–7.

8 Richard Ollard cited in Robert Blake and William Roger Louis, *Churchill* (New York and London: W W Norton, 1993), 381.

9 A Ewing, *The Man of Room 40: The Life of Sir Alfred Ewing* (London: Hutchinson, 1939), 187.

10 Lord Beaverbrook, *Politicians and the War,*

1914–1916 (London: Thornton Butterworth, 1928), 107.

11 Ewing, *Man of Room 40*, 142.

12 See Oliver Johnson, 'Class Warfare and the Selborne Scheme: The Royal Navy's Battle over Technology and Social Hierarchy', *Mariner's Mirror*, 100:4 (November 2014), 422–33. Custance to Bridge, 3 June 1902, Bridge Papers, BRI 15, National Maritime Museum. Quoted in ibid, 422. The learned journals of the day covered these matters, many speaking about technical issues. As Johnson observes, the naval professional commentary addressed mainly social issues. See also below, where the Selborne Scheme, opposition to it, and its implementation are discussed.

13 Reginald Bacon, *A Naval Scrap-Book First Part 1877–1900* (London: Hutchinson, 1925), vii.

14 Arthur J Marder, 'Reflections on an Era', in *Victory and Aftermath (January 1918– June 1919)*, vol 5 of *From the Dreadnought to Scapa Flow: The Royal Navy in the Fisher Era, 1904–1919* (hereafter *FDSF*) (London: Oxford University Press, 1970).

15 Louis Le Bailly, *From Fisher to the Falklands* (London: Marine Management (Holdings) for the Institute of Marine Engineers, 1991), 19.

16 Sigmund Munz, *King Edward VII at Marienbad: Political and Social Life at the Bohemian Spas* (London: Hutchinson, 1934), 13.

17 Baron von Eckardstein, *Ten Years at the*

Court of St James' (London: Thornton Butterworth, 1921); Sidney Lee, *King Edward VII: A Biography* (London: Macmillan, 1927), 2:11.

18 I once asked my historian friend Correlli Barnett the best way to start a chapter. His remark has stuck with me, though I have seldom been able to implement the suggestion: 'I always think that a man coming into a room armed with a loaded revolver gets the most attention.' Norfolk conversation of June 2014.

19 S Lee, *King Edward VII*, 2:10.

20 Ibid, 2:12.

21 W S Churchill, *World Crisis*, 1:26.

22 Ibid, 1:5.

Chapter 1

1 Jan Morris kept a photo of Jacky to hand for years before embarking on a brilliant portrait of the man: *Fisher's Face* (London: Viking, 1995).

2 Esther Meynell, *A Woman Talking* (London: Chapman & Hall, 1940), 65.

3 Unknown naval writer or editor in 1905, quoted in Reginald Bacon, *The Life of Lord Fisher of Kilverstone: Admiral of the Fleet* (London: Hodder, 1929), 2:2.

4 Meynell, *A Woman Talking*, 79.

5 Gentleman with a Duster [Harold Begbie], *The Mirrors of Downing Street: Some Political Reflections* (London: Mills and Boon, 1920), 37–8.

6 Quoted in Meynell, *A Woman Talking*, 73.

7 See, for example, Fisher from his father, 15 May 1854, in Arthur J Marder, *Fear God and Dread Nought: The Correspondence of Admiral of the Fleet Lord Fisher of Kilverstone* (hereafter *FGDN*) (London: Jonathan Cape, 1952), 1:24–5: 'You must recollect I am very poor and that you have a great many brothers and sisters, and I cannot give you much pocket money.'

8 See David Cannadine, *The Decline and Fall of the British Aristocracy* (New York: Vintage Books, 1999), 264–80.

9 Sir N Barnaby to Fisher, 15 January 1910, in John Arbuthnot Fisher, *Memories* (London: Hodder and Stoughton, 1919), 256.

10 Richard Hough, *Admiral of the Fleet: The Life of John Fisher* (New York: Macmillan, 1969), 21.

11 Arthur J Marder, *The Anatomy of British Sea Power: A History of British Naval Policy in the Pre-Dreadnought Era, 1880–1905* (New York: Knopf, 1940), 21.

12 Fisher, *Memories*, 93.

13 Quoted in William Goodenough, A *Rough Record: The Life of Admiral Sir William Goodenough* (London: Hutchinson, 1943), 59.

14 Quoted in Virginia Cowles, *Edward VII and His Circle* (London: Hamish Hamilton, 1956), 318.

15 Aubrey Mansergh, 'Another Look at Lord Fisher', *Naval Review*, 62, no. 3 (July 1974), 270.

16 Alan Cowpe, 'The Royal Navy and the Whitehead Torpedo', in *Technical Change and British Naval Policy, 1860–1939*, ed Bryan Ranft (London: Hodder and Stoughton, 1977), 24.

17 William Jameson, *The Fleet That Jack Built: Nine Men Who Made a Modern Navy* (New York: Harcourt, Brace & World, 1962), 97.

18 Quoted in ibid.

19 Fisher to Lord Esher, 21 December 1903, ESHR 10/41.

20 'The Bombardment of Alexandria "Jubilee"', *Illustrated London News*, 16 July 1932.

21 On Fisher and especially Beresford in these Egyptian events, see Geoffrey Bennett, *Charlie B: A Biography of Admiral Lord Charles Beresford of Metemmeh and Curraghmore* (London: Peter Dawnay, 1968), 88–93.

22 Earlier in 1882 Fisher became known to Queen Victoria when she visited Mentone, on the Riviera, and his ship *Inflexible* was guard ship. After Alexandria, she sent her congratulations, and her regret at the casualties sustained by *Inflexible*. See Jameson, *Fleet That Jack Built*, 99–100.

23 Reginald Viscount Esher, *The Tragedy of Lord Kitchener* (London: John Murray, 1921), 6.

24 Quoted in ibid.

25 Marder, *Anatomy of British Sea Power*, 119–43. Also Stanley Bonnett, *The Price of Admiralty: An Indictment of the Royal Navy, 1805–1966* (London: Robert Hale, 1968), 157–63, which testifies to Stead's words ringing with Fisher's phrases. The admiral quoted by Marder (119) is

Reginald Bacon, *A Naval Scrap-Book First Part 1877–1900* (London: Hutchinson, 1925).

26 Successive crises down to 1905 are analysed in Marder, *Anatomy of British Sea Power*, 144ff.

27 *FGDN*, 1:335.

28 Quoted in *The Times History and Encyclopedia of the War*, part 149 (26 June 1917), 228.

29 Letter to his daughter Beatrix, Mrs R R Neeld, 23 March 1899, in *FGDN*, 1:139–40.

30 Captain W H Pigott to Fisher, 9 January 1898; also Fisher to Admiralty, 17 January 1898, Adm 1/7339B.

31 Andrew Gordon, *The Rules of the Game: Jutland and British Naval Command* (London: John Murray, 1996), 196.

32 I have elaborated on these themes in my *Pax Britannica*, 233–45.

33 Nicholas Lambert, *Sir John Fisher's Naval Revolution* (Columbia: University of South Carolina Press, 1999), 74.

34 Cited in *Review of Reviews*, February 1910. See also Diana Preston, *Wilful Murder: The Sinking of the Lusitania* (London: Doubleday, 2002), 15.

35 Quoted in Ruddock F Mackay, *Fisher of Kilverstone* (Oxford: Clarendon Press, 1973), 221.

36 Rolf Hobson, *Imperialism at Sea: Naval Strategic Thought, the Ideology of Sea Power and the Tirpitz Plan, 1875–1914* (Boston and Leiden: Brill Academic, 2002). On Tirpitz, see Peter Padfield, *The Great Naval Race: Anglo-German Naval Rivalry 1900–1914* (London: Hart-Davis, MacGibbon, 1974), 35–47 and passim; also Robert K Massie, *Dreadnought: Britain, Germany, and the Coming of the Great War* (New York: Random House, 1991).

37 Winston S Churchill, *The World Crisis* (London: Thornton Butterworth, 1923–31), 1:88.

38 Cowles, *Edward VII and his Circle*, 321.

39 Ibid, 220.

40 Quoted in Holger H Herwig, *'Luxury' Fleet: The Imperial German Navy 1888–1918*, rev edn (London and Atlantic Highlands, NJ: Ashfield Press, 1987), i.

41 William James, *Admiral Sir William Fisher* (London: Macmillan, 1943), 36.

42 Quoted in ibid, 26.

43 The author of this undated letter is Admiral Sir Heathcote Grant, quoted in Bacon, *Life of Lord Fisher of Kilverstone*, 1:115.

44 Geoffrey Penn, *Infighting Admirals: Fisher's Feud with Beresford and the Reactionaries* (Barnsley: Leo Cooper, 2000), 70–1.

45 Fisher to his wife, 29 September 1900, in *FGDN*, 1:161.

46 Marder, *Anatomy of British Sea Power*, 111–12.

47 T D Manning, *The British Destroyers* (London: Putnam, 1961), lists all the classes and specifications.

48 Quoted in Marder, *Anatomy of British Sea Power*, 398.

49 Marder, *Anatomy of British Sea Power*, 396–7.

50 Quoted in ibid, 400.

51 Selborne to Curzon, 19 April 1901, quoted in George D Boyce, ed, *The Crisis of British Power: The Imperial and Naval Papers of the Second Earl of Selborne, 1895–1910* (London: The Historians' Press, 1990), 113.

52 Marder, *Anatomy of British Sea Power*, 403.

53 Rhodri Williams, *Defending the Empire: The Conservative Party and British Defence Policy, 1899–1915* (London and New Haven, CT: Yale University Press, 1991), 30–3.

54 Selborne's memorandum to the Cabinet, 16 November 1901, and another of 26 February 1904, quoted in Boyce, *Crisis of British Power*, 6–7.

55 Bacon, *Naval Scrap-Book*, 254–5.

56 Philip Watts, 'Ships of the British Navy on August 4, 1914, and Some Matters of Interest in Connection with Their Production', *Transactions of the Institution of Naval Architects*, 61 (1919), 63.

57 Fisher to Selborne, 22 May 1901, in *FGDN*, 1:193–206.

58 Fisher to James R Thursfield, 6 November 1900, in *FGDN*, 1:163–4.

59 Fisher to Arnold White, [March 1901], in *FGDN*, 1:187.

60 Epitome of Mediterranean Fleet Exercises, 1899 to 1902, in FISR 8/13, 4728, to which is attached detailed 'Précis of Exercises'.

61 Fisher to Selborne, 5 January 1901, in

FGDN, 1:174–9. See also Boyce, *Crisis of British Power*, 108–12.

62 And when not observed had fatal consequences. Vide loss of HMCS *Athabaskan*, 29 April 1944.

63 Fisher to Selborne, 9 August 1901, in *FGDN*, 1:204–6.

64 Fisher to Selborne, 16 January 1901, in *FGDN*, 1:182–4.

65 Charles Beresford, *Memoirs of Admiral Lord Charles Beresford* (London: Methuen, 1914), quoted, interestingly enough, in John Arbuthnot Fisher, *Records* (London: Hodder and Stoughton, 1919), 265.

66 Quoted in Williams, *Defending the Empire*, 36.

67 Geoffrey Penn, *'Up Funnel, Down Screw!' The Story of the Naval Engineer* (London: Hollis & Carter, 1955), 138–9.

68 Peter Kemp, 'The Royal Navy', in *Edwardian England, 1901–1914*, ed Simon Nowell-Smith (London: Oxford University Press, 1964), 494–5.

69 *FDSF*, 1:29.

70 Admiral W H Henderson, 'Life of Lord Fisher: Reminiscences', *Naval Review*, 18 (1930), 194.

71 *FDSF*, 1:29.

72 Donald M Schurman, *Julian S Corbett, 1854–1922: Historian of British Maritime Policy from Drake to Jellicoe* (London: Royal Historical Society, 1981), 29.

73 Cited in Mackay, *Fisher*, 274.

74 Schurman, *Corbett*, 26–8.

75 Lord Selborne to Walter Kerr, 2 May 1901, in Boyce, *Crisis of British Power*, 119–20.

76 Boyce, *Crisis of British Power*, 119.

77 Selborne to Kerr, 16 December 1901, in Boyce, *Crisis of British Power*, 136.

78 Kerr to Selborne, 21 May 1901, in Boyce, *Crisis of British Power*, 121–2.

79 Kerr to Selborne, 17 December 1901, in Boyce, *Crisis of British Power*, 138.

80 Ibid, 137–8.

81 Selborne to Kerr, 16 December 1901, in Boyce, *Crisis of British Power*, 136–7.

82 Cited in Mackay, *Fisher*, 255.

83 Admiral Sir Barry Domvile, *From Admiral to Cabin Boy* (London: Boswell, 1947), 14–15.

84 Cited in Mackay, *Fisher*, 276.

85 Quoted in Louis Le Bailly, *From Fisher to the Falklands* (London: Marine Management (Holdings) for the Institute of Marine Engineers, 1991), 5.

86 John Arbuthnot Fisher, 'The Engineer Question, 1902', in John B Hattendorf et al, eds, *British Naval Documents, 1204–1960* (London: Navy Records Society, 1993), 972–4. Italics in original.

87 Mackay, *Fisher*, 266.

88 Memorandum by Selborne, 25 February 1902, in Boyce, *Crisis of British Power*, 139–41.

89 Kerr to Selborne, 11 March 1902, in Boyce, *Crisis of British Power*, 141.

90 Mackay, *Fisher*, 275–6.

91 Fisher to Cecil Fisher, 14 November 1902, in *FGDN*, 1:266.

92 Quoted in Mackay, *Fisher*, 278.

93 *Admiralty Memorandum*, dated 16 December 1902, Parliamentary Papers, Cmd 1385.

94 Cited in Mackay, *Fisher*, 278–80, and Penn, *Up Funnel, Down Screw!*, 140.

95 Notations in Memorandum of 1906 (printed February 1906), FISR 4752. See also Mackay, *Fisher*, 280.

96 *FDSF*, 1:30.

97 *FDSF*, 1:49.

98 Penn, *Up Funnel, Down Screw!*, 142.

99 Mackay, *Fisher*, 296; *FDSF*, 1:46.

100 Fisher to Corbett, 3 May 1903, in FISR 1/3, 106.

101 *FDSF*, 1:47.

102 *FDSF*, 1:48–9.

103 Penn, *Up Funnel, Down Screw!*, 142–3.

104 Fisher, *Records*, 167–9.

105 Mackay, *Fisher*, 283.

106 For extended treatment and sources, see Donald M Schurman, *The Education of a Navy: The Development of British Naval Strategic Thought, 1867–1914* (Chicago: University of Chicago Press, 1965), 118–21.

107 See Esher to MVB, 22 February 1902 and 8 March 1902, in Maurice V Brett, *Journals and Letters of Reginald Viscount Esher* (hereafter *Esher Journals and Letters*) (London: Nicholson and Watson, 1934), 1:325–6.

108 Mackay, *Fisher*, 282.

109 Esher to MVB, 11 February 1906, in *Esher Journals and Letters*, 2:141–3.

110 Cited in Penn, *Up Funnel, Down Screw!*, 145.

111 *FDSF*, 1:47.

112 *FDSF*, 1:49.
113 See *FDSF*, 1:30; and Admiral Sir John Hopkins to Fisher, 16 April 1906, and Sir Henry Benbow to Fisher, 20 April 1906, both in Fisher, *Records*, 170–1.
114 Fisher to John Leyland, 17 October 1911, in *FGDN*, 2:393.
115 DRLN, 'A Review of "Thirty-Six Years at the Admiralty", by Sir Charles Walker', *Naval Review*, 22, no. 4 (1934), 823.
116 *FDSF*, 1:50.
117 Penn, *Up Funnel, Down Screw!*, 149.
118 Viscount Hythe, ed, *The Naval Annual: 1913* (original, Portsmouth: J Griffin and Co, 1913; reprint Plymouth: David and Charles Reprints, 1970), 29.
119 Cited in Mary Arnold-Forster, *The Right Honourable Hugh Oakeley Arnold-Forster, A Memoir, by His Wife* (London: Edward Arnold, 1910), 191–2.
120 Rudyard Kipling to L C Cornfold, nd but July 1904, in Thomas Pinney, ed, *Letters of Rudyard Kipling*, vol 3, *1900–1910* (Houndmills: Macmillan, 1996), 146–57.
121 Speech to Royal Academy Banquet, 2 May 1903, in Fisher, *Records*, 79–83, and FISR 8/14, 4734. See also Taprell Dorling, *Men o' War* (London: Philip Allan, 1929), 231.
122 James Lees-Milne, *The Enigmatic Edwardian: The Life of Reginald 2nd Viscount Esher* (London: Hodder and Stoughton, 1986), 145. On other suggested persons to serve on this committee, see Esher to MVB, 21 September 1902 and 24 September 1902, in *Esher Journals and Letters*, 2:14–16. See also Peter Fraser, *Lord Esher: A Political Biography* (London: Hart-Davis, MacGibbon, 1973), 92–6.
123 Frederick Ponsonby, *Recollections of Three Reigns* (London: Eyre and Spottiswoode, 1951), 129.
124 Esher to MVB, 19 October 1902, in *Esher Journals and Letters*, 2:28–9.
125 Esher to MVB, 4 November 1902, in ibid, 2:30.
126 See Fisher to Esher, 7 and 20 December 1903, in Fisher, *Memories*, 169–70. For Clarke on Fisher, see *FDSF*, 1:342–3.
127 Fisher to Esher, 19 November 1903, in Fisher, *Memories*, 166–7.
128 Mackay, *Fisher*, 293.
129 Fisher to Esher, [?] March 1904, cited in Fisher, *Memories*, 176.
130 Haig to Esher, 23 March 1904, in *Esher Journals and Letters*, 2:50–1.
131 Fisher to Esher, 17 January 1904, and a subsequent letter perhaps of the same date, ESHR 10/41.
132 Fisher to Esher, 22 January 1904, ESHR 10/41.
133 W J McDermott, 'British Strategic Planning and the Committee of Imperial Defence, 1871–1907' (PhD dissertation, University of Toronto, 1970), 102–5. See also 'Report of the Esher War Office (Reconstruction) Committee, 1904', in Joel H Weiner, ed, *Great Britain: The Lion at Home; A Documentary History of Domestic Policy, 1689–1973*, vol 3 (New York: Chelsea House Publishers, 1974), 2257–73.
134 Charles à Court Repington, *Vestigia* (London: Constable, 1919), 258–60.
135 Reginald Bacon, *From 1900 Onward* (London: Hutchinson, 1940), 114–15.
136 Lord Knollys to Fisher, 22 February 1904, cited in Fisher, *Records*, 24.
137 Dorling, *Men o' War*, 233.
138 Fisher to Esher, 5 August 1904, in *FGDN*, 1:323.
139 Sigmund Munz, *King Edward VII at Marienbad: Political and Social Life at the Bohemian Spas* (London: Hutchinson, 1934), 168–9.
140 Ibid, 169. See page **96** in Chapter 2 below.

Chapter 2

1 Esher to Fisher, 6 August 1904, FISR 1/4, 132. See also *FGDN*, 1:324.
2 Fisher to Esher, 28 July 1904, ESHR 10/41.
3 Fisher to Esher, 17 and 21 August 1904, ESHR 10/41.
4 Esher to MVB, 6 August 1904, in *Esher Journals and Letters*, 2:59–60.
5 Fisher to Esher, 21 August 1904, and Esher to Fisher, 24 August 1904, in ibid, 2:60–1.
6 Prince of Wales to Fisher, 23 August 1904, FISR 1/4. See also *FGDN*, 1:326.
7 Esher to Fisher, 31 August 1904, FISR 1/4, 130.
8 Esher to MVB, 26 September 1904, in *Esher Journals and Letters*, 2:64–5.
9 Fisher to Knollys, [late August 1904], in *FGDN*, 1:327.
10 Fisher to Richard Haldane, 3 May 1904, in *FGDN*, 1:314. See also FISR 1/4, 123.
11 Fisher to [?], 22 February 1905, in *FGDN*, 2:51.

12 Peter Kemp, ed, *Papers of Admiral Sir John Fisher* (London: Navy Records Society, 1960), 1:xv.

13 For this I am indebted to Paul Haggie, 'The Royal Navy and War Planning in the Fisher Era', *Journal of Contemporary History*, 8, no. 3 (1973), 113.

14 Translation of 'A Seaman' found in *Le Phare,* 15 January 1905, in FISR 8/14, 4739.

15 Fisher to Esher, 25 September 1904, in ESHR 10/41.

16 Sidney Lee, *King Edward VII: A Biography* (London: Macmillan, 1927), 2:329, 330–3.

17 See also, Richard Hough, *Former Naval Person: Churchill and the Wars at Sea* (London: Weidenfeld and Nicolson, 1985), 24–6.

18 These observations from *FGDN*, 1:279.

19 Fisher to Tweedmouth, 5 October 1906, in *FGDN*, 2:95–6.

20 For discussion of this matter, see Rhodri Williams, *Defending the Empire: The Conservative Party and British Defence Policy, 1899–1915* (London and New Haven, CT: Yale University Press, 1991), 61–6, where this segment of the memo is published.

21 Recall that this was the issue on which long-standing Liberal leader and prime minster W E Gladstone tendered his final resignation in 1894.

22 Fisher, 'Naval Questions', 12 July 1907, in CHAR 2/32.

23 'Report of the Estimates Committee', 26 November 1904, in FISR 8/14, 4736, 1.

24 'Coast Guard', June 1906, in John Arbuthnot Fisher, *Records* (London: Hodder and Stoughton, 1919), 120–4.

25 'Observatories', 11 August 1906, in Fisher, *Records*, 124–6.

26 Fisher to Esher, 17 June 1904, cited in John Arbuthnot Fisher, *Memories* (London: Hodder and Stoughton, 1919), 179–80, and ESHR 10/41.

27 Fisher to Sir George Clarke, 12 September 1907, in *FGDN*, 2:133.

28 Barry M Gough, 'Admiral Sir (later Baron) John Arbuthnot Fisher', in *The First Sea Lords*, ed Malcolm H Murfett (Westport, CT: Praeger, 1995), 20–1; and Hew Strachan, *The First World War*, vol 1

(Oxford: Oxford University Press, 2001), 378, 381–2.

29 Fisher to Selborne, 29 July 1901, in *FGDN*, 1:202–4.

30 Fisher to Selborne, 25 February 1902, FISR 1/3, 90.

31 Mark Kerr, *Prince Louis of Battenberg, Admiral of the Fleet* (London: Longman, 1934), 144–9.

32 Cited in William James, 'Churchill and the Navy', in *Churchill, By His Contemporaries*, ed Charles Eade (London: Hutchinson, 1953), 91.

33 I first found this in Canadian Forces College, Toronto, and have it mounted in my Archives Room to this day as a reminder of his thoughts on this matter.

34 Fisher to Corbett, and enclosed minute by Corbett, 22 May 1905, in FISR 1/4, 166, and Corbett to Fisher, 13 May 1906, in FISR 1/5, 202.

35 Esher to Hankey, 15 March 1915, in *Esher Journals and Letters*, 3:221; *FDSF*, 1:404.

36 For further citations and discussions of these strategic issues, see Barry M Gough, 'Maritime Strategy: The Legacies of Mahan and Corbett as Philosophers of Sea Power', *Journal of the Royal United Services Institute for Defence Studies*, 133, no. 4 (Winter 1988), 55–62.

37 I owe this astute observation to Nicholas Black, whose book on the subject is heavily rooted in the primary sources: Nicholas Black, *The British Naval Staff in the First World War* (Woodbridge: Boydell Press, 2009), 54–5.

38 'Statement of the First Lord of the Admiralty Explanatory of the Naval Estimates, 1912–1913, Appendix: Naval War Staff', 1 January 1912, Cmd 6106 (1912); see Marder's comments in *FDSF*, 1:404n.

39 Admiral Walter Kerr to Selborne, 2 September 1901, in D George Boyce, ed, *The Crisis of British Power: The Imperial and Naval Papers of the Second Earl of Selborne, 1895–1910* (London: The Historians' Press, 1990), 123.

40 Cited in Barry M Gough, 'The Royal Navy's Legacy to the Royal Canadian Navy in the Pacific, 1880–1914', in *The RCN in Retrospect, 1910–1968*, ed James A Boutilier (Vancouver: UBC Press, 1982), 7.

41 Battenberg to Fisher, 20 January 1902, FISR 1/2, 186.

42 See Fisher, 'Strategical Distribution of our Fleets', [1902], FISR 1/3, 90.

43 Louis Battenberg, [Untitled Memorandum on Cables and Cable-Laying], 15 March 1903, FISR 1/3, 96.

44 See various naval minutes by Battenberg, Fisher, and Selborne, 7–9 November 1904, in FISR 1/4, 139.

45 Fisher to Beresford, 27 February 1902, FGDN, 1:233.

46 Fisher to Selborne, 19 October 1904, FGDN, 1:330–2.

47 Prince of Wales to Fisher, 23 August 1904, in FGDN, 1:326.

48 'Report of the Estimates Committee', 26 November 1904, in FISR 8/14, 4736, 3–4.

49 Annual Register for 1905, 62–4.

50 'Distribution and Mobilisation of the Fleet', Cabinet Memorandum by Lord Selborne, 6 December 1904, in Boyce, Crisis of British Power, 184–90.

51 Barry M Gough, Britannia's Navy on the West Coast of North America, 1812–1914 (Surrey, BC: Heritage House, 2016), 300–2; and Gough, 'The Royal Navy's Legacy', 5–8.

52 Fisher to Edward VII [nd], in Lee, Edward VII, 2:332–3. The King sided with Fisher.

53 Fisher to Tweedmouth, 4 October 1906, in FGDN, 2:93–5.

54 Fisher, 'The Use of the Gunboat [1906]', in Records, 118–20.

55 Rear-Admiral Hedworth Lambton to the Prince of Wales, [?] November 1904, FISR 1/4, 137.

56 The Prince of Wales to Fisher, 10 November 1904, FISR 1/4, 138. Also see FGDN, 2:48–9.

57 Lambton to Selborne, 3 December 1904, in Boyce, Crisis of British Power, 184.

58 FDSF, 1:71–3.

59 Fisher to Tweedmouth, 11 October 1906, in FGDN, 2:98–9.

60 Fisher to King Edward VII, 22 October 1906, and enclosed for the Prince of Wales, 23 October 1906, in FGDN, 2:102–5.

61 FGDN, 2:105n; and the Prince of Wales to Fisher, 21 December 1906, FISR 1/5.

62 Richard Hough, Admiral of the Fleet: The Life of John Fisher (New York: Macmillan, 1969), 198.

63 For a start, see Charles H Fairbanks, Jr,

'The Origins of the Dreadnought Revolution: A Historiographical Essay', International History Review, 13 (May 1991), 246–72; Jon Sumida, 'Sir John Fisher and the Dreadnought: The Sources of Naval Mythology', Journal of Military History, 59, no. 4 (October 1995), 619–37; Nicholas Lambert, 'Admiral Sir John Fisher and the Concept of Flotilla Defence, 1904–1909', Journal of Military History, 59, no. 4 (October 1995), 639–60.

64 Philip Watts, 'Ships of the British Navy on August 4, 1914, and Some Matters of Interest in Connection with Their Production', Transactions of the Institution of Naval Architects, 61 (1919), 1–65.

65 Andrew Roberts, Salisbury: Victorian Titan (London: Weidenfeld and Nicolson, 1999), 281.

66 Fisher to Selborne, 2 August 1904, in FGDN, 1:321–2.

67 Annual Register for 1905, 63.

68 Selborne to Fisher, 3 July 1905, FISR 1/4, 177.

69 On torpedo advances, see Oscar Parkes, British Battleships, 'Warrior' to 'Vanguard': A History of Design, Construction and Armament, 2nd ed (Annapolis, MD: Naval Institute Press, 1990), 506; on effects, see Robert Gardiner and Andrew Lambert, eds, Steam, Steel and Shellfire: The Steam Warship (London: Conway, 1992), 167. Fisher's claim that the 6in gun had been made redundant by the torpedo proved a false argument, though it was dogmatically articulated and credulously accepted.

70 Fisher to Arnold White, 28 January 1901, in FGDN, 1:185.

71 Fisher to Selborne, 5 January 1902, in FGDN, 1:174–9.

72 Fisher to Selborne, 19 December 1900, in FGDN, 1:170–4.

73 Fisher to Tweedmouth, 26 September 1906, in FGDN, 2:90–3.

74 Quoted in A J A Morris, The Scaremongers: The Advocacy of War and Rearmament 1896–1914 (London: Routledge and Kegan Paul, 1984), 167.

75 A J A Morris, The Scaremongers, 370.

76 Frederic C Dreyer, The Sea Heritage: A Study of Maritime Warfare (London: Museum Press, 1955), 57.

77 Rear-Admiral F S Inglefield to Fisher, 20

December 1907, CHAR 2/32, 13.

78 Fisher to Tweedmouth, 16 October 1906, in *FGDN*, 2:101.

79 Parkes, *British Battleships*, 478, 483. Also Watts, 'Ships of the British Navy', 7–8.

80 Details in 'Proposals Respecting Designs of the New Vessels to be Laid Down in 1906–7 and Employment of Armed Merchant Cruisers', January 1906, FISR 8/15, 4750.

81 Fisher to Andrew Noble, 14 April 1906, in *FGDN*, 2:74–5.

82 Fisher to Corbett, 2 January 1906, FISR 1/5, 212.

83 See Lieutenant-Commander William S Sims, USN, to Fisher, 3 November 1906, and enclosed, 'The Inherent Tactical Qualities of All-Big-Gun, One-Calibre Battleships, Large Displacement, and Gun Power', September 1906, in Kemp, *Papers of Admiral Fisher*, 1:343–77.

84 Fisher to Tweedmouth, 5 October 1906, in *FGDN*, 2:95–7.

85 Mark Kerr, *The Navy in My Time* (London: Rich and Cowan, 1932), 47; Parkes, *British Battleships*, 495.

86 Fisher to Tweedmouth, 10 and 14 September 1906, in *FGDN*, 2:87–9.

87 Fisher to a friend, 20 April 1904, quoted in Taprell Dorling, *Men o' War* (London: Philip Allan, 1929), 232.

88 Fisher, *Records*, 176.

89 William Jameson, *The Most Formidable Thing: The Story of the Submarine from Its Earliest Days to the End of World War I* (London: R H Davis, 1965), 253.

90 The above follows Arthur J Marder, *The Anatomy of British Sea Power: A History of British Naval Policy in the Pre-Dreadnought Era, 1880–1905* (New York: Knopf, 1940), 360–7.

91 Roger Keyes, *Naval Memoirs of Admiral of the Fleet Sir Roger Keyes, vol 1, The Narrow Seas to the Dardanelles, 1910–1915* (London: Thornton Butterworth, 1934), 24.

92 Fisher to Battenberg, [?] January 1904, in FISR 1/3, 112.

93 Fisher, 'Submarines' and 'Submarines: Second Postscript', both to the Controller of the Navy, 20 April 1904, in ESHR 10/41. See also Fisher, *Records*, 174–6, and *FGDN*, 2:308–9.

94 Fisher to Lord Cromer, 22 April 1905, in *FGDN*, 2:54.

95 Fisher to Esher, [ca 23 April 1904], in *FGDN*, 1:310–11.

96 C F Aspinall-Oglander, *Roger Keyes, Being the Biography of Admiral of the Fleet Lord Keyes of Zeebrugge and Dover* (London: Hogarth Press, 1951), 82–4; quotes here are from 84.

97 Ibid, 86.

98 Strachan, *First World War*, 390–2; Andrew Gordon, *The Rules of the Game: Jutland and British Naval Command* (London: John Murray, 1996), 584.

99 'Distribution and Mobilisation of the Fleet', Cabinet Memorandum by Lord Selborne, 6 December 1904, in Boyce, *Crisis of British Power*, 184–90.

100 Anthony Carew, *The Lower Deck of the Royal Navy, 1900–1939: The Invergordon Mutiny in Perspective* (Manchester: Manchester University Press, 1981), 47.

101 Ruddock F Mackay, *Fisher of Kilverstone* (Oxford: Clarendon Press, 1973), 379.

102 Ibid, 284.

103 Carew, *Lower Deck*, 47.

104 Jon Sumida, 'British Naval Administration and Policy in the Age of Fisher', *Journal of Military History*, 54, no. 1 (January 1990), 10.

105 Mackay, *Fisher*, 379–80.

106 Sumida, 'British Naval Administration', 10.

107 Mackay, *Fisher*, 380.

108 Ibid; and Dan van der Vat, *Standard of Power: The Royal Navy in the Twentieth Century* (London: Hutchinson, 2000), 6–7.

109 Carew, *Lower Deck*, 25–7.

110 Ibid, 47.

111 Fisher to Yexley, 13 January 1910, in *FGDN*, 2:290.

112 Carew, *Lower Deck*, 49.

113 Fisher to Yexley, 3 August 1910, FISR, 2075.

114 Fisher to Esher, 5 August 1910, in Fisher, *Memories*, 200–1.

115 Carew, *Lower Deck*, 53–4.

116 Mackay, *Fisher*, 379.

117 Carew, *Lower Deck*, 54.

118 Fisher to Yexley, 5 October 1911, in FISR, 2151.

119 Fisher to Yexley, 11 October 1911, in FISR, 2153.

120 Carew, *Lower Deck*, 43.

121 Mackay, *Fisher*, 427 and 435–6.

122 Cited in Mackay, *Fisher*, 427.
123 Fisher to J A Spender, 8 August 1910, in *FGDN*, 2:335.
124 Fisher to McKenna, 22 August 1910, in *FGDN*, 2:337.
125 Fisher to Esher, December 1911, in Fisher, *Memories*, 207.
126 From Remarks by the British Naval Attaché at Paris, in *Memoranda by Sir John Fisher, 1903–04*, ESHR 7/3.
127 Fisher to James Thursfield, 29 November 1901, in *FGDN*, 1:217–18.
128 Fisher to Arnold White, 6 August 1902, in *FGDN*, 1:259–62.
129 Balfour to Selborne, 5 April 1902, in Boyce, *The Crisis of British Power*, 142.
130 For discussion of Chamberlain's attempts to ally with Germany, see Robert K Massie, *Dreadnought: Britain, Germany, and the Coming of the Great War* (New York: Random House, 1991), 242–6, 291–309.
131 Bryan Ranft, 'Parliamentary Debate, Economic Vulnerability, and British Naval Expansion, 1860–1905', in *War, Strategy, and International Politics: Essays in Honour of Sir Michael Howard*, ed Lawrence Freedman et al (Oxford: Clarendon Press, 1992), 77–93. See also Bryan Ranft, 'The Royal Navy and the Mercantile Marine, 1860–1914: Partners in Ignorance', in *Charted and Uncharted Waters*, ed S Palmer and G Williams (London: National Maritime Museum, 1982), 197–217; and Adm 116/866B, NID Memo: 'The Protection of Trade: Remarks on Various Methods of Stationing Cruisers', 30 March 1905, adopted by Admiralty 30 April 1905 (minutes of Admiralty meeting on 'Protection of Ocean Trade in War Time', Adm 116/866B), and Orders to Commander-in-Chief, Channel, 6 May 1905, Adm 116/900B.
132 Admiral Sir Cyprian Bridge to Selborne, 14 February 1904, in Boyce, *Crisis of British Power*, 168–9.
133 Admiral Bridge held the view that Britain's alliance with Japan was as much to keep Japan out of any other great power's alliance as it was due to any desire to join with Japan. See Bridge to Selborne, 22 April 1902, in Boyce, *Crisis of British Power*, 142–3.
134 See, for example, Intelligence Officer, Singapore to Admiralty, 26 April 1905, FISR 1/4, 155.
135 Fisher to Lansdowne, 25 April 1905, in *FGDN*, 2:55–7.
136 Balfour to Fisher, 26 April 1905, and Fisher to Balfour [ca 26 April 1905], in *FGDN*, 2:57–8.
137 Lansdowne to Sir Francs Leveson Bertie, 27 April 1905, in FISR 1/4, 157; Bertie to Lansdowne, 27 April 1905, in *FGDN*, 2:58–9n; and Lansdowne to Fisher, 27 April 1905, FISR 1/4, 156.
138 C L Ottley to Fisher, 1 May 1905, in FISR 1/4, 164, and *FDSF*, 1:111.
139 I have not attempted in this book to explore the evolution of the fight between the War Office and the Admiralty, 1901–1914, and the complications of the CID. It is clear that Fisher and Churchill were obstacles to inter-Service planning, with disastrous results to the development of what might be called 'a supreme command'. On this see Nicholas J d'Ombrain, *War Machinery and High Policy: Defence Administration in Peacetime Britain 1902–1914* (Oxford: Oxford University Press, 1973).
140 Louis Mallet to C I Thomas, 23 April 1905, FISR 1/4, 151, and *FGDN*, 2:57n.
141 E N Anderson, *The First Moroccan Crisis* (Hamden: Archon Books, 1966), 228. See also Edward E Bradford, *Life of Admiral of the Fleet Sir Arthur Knyvet Wilson* (London: John Murray, 1923), 199.
142 Sir Frederick Maurice, *Haldane*, vol 1 (London: Faber and Faber, 1937), 173–6.
143 Fisher to Lansdowne, 22 April 1905, in *FGDN*, 2:55.
144 Mallet to Bertie, 25 April 1905, Bertie MSS, quoted in Zara S Steiner, *The Foreign Office and Foreign Policy, 1898–1914* (Cambridge: Cambridge University Press, 1965), 66.
145 Steiner, *Foreign Office and Foreign Policy*, 66.
146 See ibid, 98–9. See also Michael Howard, *The Continental Commitment: The Dilemma of British Defence Policy in the Era of Two World Wars* (1972; London: Ashfield, 1989), on the Foreign Office's views on Germany; also Steiner, *Foreign Office and Foreign Policy*, passim.
147 Fisher told this to J A Spender in late 1904. See *FGDN*, 2:20n.
148 Philip Magnus, *King Edward the Seventh*

149 Esher to the King, 18 January 1906, in *Esher Journals and Letters*, 2:136–9.

150 Fisher to Esher, 7 October 1907, FISR 1/5, 264a. See also *FGDN*, 2:144–6.

151 W J McDermott, 'British Strategic Planning and the Committee of Imperial Defence, 1871–1907' (PhD dissertation, University of Toronto, 1970), 273–4. See also Maurice Hankey, *The Supreme Command* (London: George Allen and Unwin, 1961), 1:52.

152 Fisher to Tweedmouth, 9 July 1906, in *FGDN*, 2:83, and McDermott, 'British Strategic Planning', 289.

153 Maurice, *Haldane*, 174.

154 Fisher to Tweedmouth, 26 September 1906, in *FGDN*, 2:90–3.

155 Esher to MVB, 14 January 1905, in *Esher Journals and Letters*, 2:134–5.

156 Esher to Fisher, 18 February 1906, in *Esher Journals and Letters*, 2:145.

157 Wilson to Fisher, 9 March 1906, FISR 1/5, 195.

158 Battenberg's success in tactical exercises led Fisher in late 1902 to call him to the Admiralty as Director of Naval Intelligence; Fisher also appointed him to the *Dreadnought* design committee. See Marder, *Anatomy of British Sea Power*, 368–70.

159 'Renewal of the Anglo-Japanese Alliance: Naval Aspect of the Question', Confidential No. 2 [June, 1906], in FISR 8/15, 4745. Also in FISR 8/15 are details on Gibraltar being handed over to the War Office, as well as how it was to be defended.

160 Esher to MVB, 28 July 1905, in *Esher Journals and Letters*, 2:96.

161 Fisher to Corbett, 28 July 1905, in *FGDN*, 2:63.

162 Esher to MVB, 21 December 1906, in *Esher Journals and Letters*, 2:209.

163 Stephen W Roskill, *Hankey: Man of Secrets* (London: Collins, 1970–1974), 1:76–9.

164 Mackay, *Fisher*, 366–77.

165 Esher Journal, 21 August 1908, in *Esher Journals and Letters*, 2:332.

166 Anon, 'German Feelings about War with England in December 1906', in FISR 1/5, 264a.

167 See Jonathan Steinberg, 'The Copenhagen Complex', *Contemporary History*, 1 (1966), 23–46.

168 *FDSF*, 2:xi.

169 Giles MacDonagh, *The Last Kaiser: William the Impetuous* (London: Weidenfeld and Nicolson, 2000), 291 and 306–7.

170 Ibid, 291.

171 E F Benson, *The Kaiser and English Relations* (London: Longmans, Green, 1936), 251.

172 Fisher to Esher, March 1909, ESHR 10/42.

Chapter 3

1 Fisher to Lord Knollys, 17 December 1906, in *FGDN*, 2:107.

2 Fisher to Tweedmouth, 5 October 1906, in *FGDN*, 2:97.

3 Andrew Roberts, *Salisbury: Victorian Titan* (London: Weidenfeld and Nicolson, 1999), 281–2. See also Salisbury to Selborne, 27 February 1901, in D George Boyce, ed, *The Crisis of British Power: The Imperial and Naval Papers of the Second Earl of Selborne, 1895–1910* (London: The Historians' Press, 1990), 112.

4 C Holland to Fisher, 22 March 1905, in FISR 1/4, 147.

5 King Edward to Fisher, 8 January 1905, in FISR 1/4, 143.

6 V Wemyss, *The Life and Letters of Lord Wester Wemyss* (London: Eyre and Spottiswoode, 1935), cited in *Naval Review*, 23 (1935), 595.

7 Fisher to Lord Knollys, 24 December 1905, in *FGDN*, 2:66.

8 Esher to Fisher, 15 October 1907, in ESHR 10/42.

9 Esher to Fisher, 21 October 1906, in FISR 1/5, 205a.

10 Fisher to Esher, 21 December 1903, in ESHR, 10/41.

11 Fisher to Corbett, 11 February 1907, in FISR 1/5, 227. See also Fisher to Corbett, 15 January 1907, in *FGDN*, 2:113.

12 John Winton, 'Life and Education in a Technically Evolving Navy, 1815–1925', in *Oxford Illustrated History of the Royal Navy*, ed J R Hill (Oxford: Oxford University Press, 1996), 274.

13 Fisher to Major-General Sir John Moody, RMLI, 28 December 1904, in FISR 1/4, 140.

14 Kenneth Rose, *King George V* (1983;

London: Phoenix, 2000), 17.

15 Fisher to Prince of Wales, 28 April 1905, in *FGDN*, 2:60. King's Lynn is in the same county (Norfolk) as Sandringham.

16 Battenberg to Fisher, 3 June 1905, in FISR 1/4, 169.

17 Esher to MVB, 3 September 1906, in *Esher Journals and Letters*, 2:179.

18 Esher to Fisher, 5 September 1906, in ibid, 2:181–8.

19 Esher to Fisher, 21 October 1906, in ibid, 2:198–9.

20 Haldane, Secretary of State for War, had referred his whole scheme for War Office reforms, while Morley, Secretary of State for India, had referred the Afghanistan frontier question, with Kitchener's associated scheme.

21 Esher to Fisher, 4 February 1907, in *Esher Journals and Letters*, 2:219–20.

22 Fisher to [?], 3 January 1907, in *FGDN*, 2:111.

23 Esher to MVB, 3 January 1907, in *Esher Journals and Letters*, 2:215.

24 Cited in Gerald French, ed, *Some War Diaries, Addresses and Correspondence of Field Marshal the Earl of Ypres* (London: Herbert Jenkins, 1937), 113.

25 Fisher once commented that John Morley, a leading Liberal and Little Englander, told him he would rather face a contested election against anyone other than Beresford. See Fisher to Earl Spencer, 28 March 1902, in *FGDN*, 1:237–8.

26 Churchill, Parliamentary Debates, quoted in Reginald Bacon, *The Life of Lord Fisher of Kilverstone: Admiral of the Fleet* (London: Hodder, 1929), 2:29.

27 A Roberts, *Salisbury*, 559.

28 Bacon, *Life of Lord Fisher*, 1:30–1.

29 The Unionists were technically a coalition of Conservatives and Liberal Unionists, the latter being former Liberals who had split from the party over Irish Home Rule, and who were led by Joseph Chamberlain and the 8th Duke of Devonshire (formerly the Marquess of Hartington).

30 Barry M Gough, *Pax Britannica: Ruling the Waves and Keeping the Peace before Armageddon* (Basingstoke: Palgrave Macmillan, 2014), 19–23.

31 See especially Nicholas Lambert, *Sir John Fisher's Naval Revolution* (Columbia: University of South Carolina Press, 1999).

32 Hew Strachan, *The First World War*, vol 1 (Oxford: Oxford University Press, 2001), 381 and 389–90. Nicholas Lambert, in *Sir John Fisher's Naval Revolution*, has analysed this issue more deeply and rightly connects the Fisher–Beresford dispute to questions of strategy and force structure.

33 Fisher to Rear-Admiral Wilmot Fawkes, 27 June 1901, in *FGDN*, 1:197.

34 Fisher to Beresford, 27 February 1902, in *FGDN*, 1:232.

35 Fisher to Earl Spencer, 28 March 1902, in *FGDN*, 1:237.

36 Cyprian Bridge, Reginald Custance, Charles Penrose Fitzgerald, Carlyon Bellairs.

37 Bacon to Fisher, 12 and 15 April 1906, in *FGDN*, 2:72–4 and 76–7.

38 Fisher to Tweedmouth, 24 April 1906, in *FGDN*, 2:79–80. The short service men signed up for five years' active service in the Navy and another seven years in the Reserve instead of the usual twelve years on the active service list.

39 Rear-Admiral F S Inglefield, Commander, 4th Cruiser Squadron, Bermuda, to Fisher, 9 March 1908, in FISR 1/6, 295.

40 Esher to MVB, 7 March 1907, in *Esher Journals and Letters*, 2:223–5.

41 Battenberg to the naval correspondent of *The Times*, J Thursfield, 23 January 1907, cited in Mark Kerr, *Prince Louis of Battenberg, Admiral of the Fleet* (London: Longman, 1934), 221.

42 Ibid.

43 Fisher to Beresford, 22 April 1907, in *FGDN*, 2:121.

44 Beresford to Fisher, 22 April 1907, in *FGDN*, 2:121. A copy of the letter was sent to Esher. See ESHR 10/42.

45 Fisher to George Lambert, 21 January 1907, in *FGDN*, 2:115.

46 Fisher to Beresford, 30 April 1907, in *FGDN*, 2:122.

47 Beresford to Fisher, 2 May 1907, in *FGDN*, 2:123.

48 Tweedmouth to Fisher, 8 June 1907, in *FGDN*, 2:125.

49 *FDSF*, 1:93–5. Admiralty Memorandum, 'Remarks on Interview with Commander-in-Chief, Channel Fleet, Friday, July 5, 1907'.

50 Admiralty Board Minute, 15 August 1907, in FISR 1/5, 252.

51 Admiralty Board Minute, 15 August 1907, in FISR 1/5, 252.

52 Fisher to Tweedmouth, 1 October 1907, in *FGDN*, 2:139.

53 Fisher to King Edward, 4 October 1907, in *FGDN*, 2:142.

54 Fisher to Hurd, 7 October 1907, in RNM 1998/35 (13).

55 Fisher to King Edward, 4 Oct 1907, in *FGDN*, 2:142.

56 Ponsonby to Fisher, 8 October 1907, FISR 1/5, 259.

57 Percy Scott, *Fifty Years in the Royal Navy* (London: John Murray, 1919), 202–3.

58 FDSF, 1:97–99; and Geoffrey Penn, *Infighting Admirals: Fisher's Feud with Beresford and the Reactionaries* (Barnsley: Leo Cooper, 2000), 186–9.

59 Charles à Court Repington, *Vestigia* (London: Constable, 1919), 278–80.

60 Balfour had stated in the House of Commons in 1905, while still prime minister, that there was not a serious risk of an invasion of the British Isles. See *FDSF*, 1:348.

61 Niall Ferguson, *The Pity of War* (New York: Basic Books, 1998), 11 and 13–14.

62 Fisher to the Prince of Wales, 16 Oct 1907, in *FGDN*, 2:147.

63 Fisher to Corbett, 28 September 1907, in *FGDN*, 2:138. See also FISR 1/5, 257.

64 Fisher to John Leyland, 22 September 1907, in *FGDN*, 2:136–7.

65 *FDSF*, 1:349, and Penn, *Infighting Admirals*, 160.

66 Fisher to Sir George Clarke, 12 September 1907, in *FGDN*, 2:132–3.

67 Esher to Fisher, 29 August 1907, in *Esher Journals and Letters*, 2:247–8.

68 Fisher to Esher, 8 September 1907, in ibid, 2:248.

69 Esher to Fisher, 1 October 1907, in ibid, 2:249.

70 Fisher to Esher, 7 October 1907, in ibid, 2:250.

71 Esher to Fisher, 15 October 1907, in ibid, 2:251–2.

72 Esher Journal, 27 and 28 November 1908, in ibid, 2:263.

73 Corbett to Fisher, 31 January 1908, in FISR 1/6, 286. Fisher did ask for Corbett's help in refuting Repington's initial testimony to the inquiry. See Fisher to Corbett, 4 December 1907, and Corbett's

affirmative reply of the same day, in *FGDN*, 2:152–3.

74 *FDSF*, 1:349–50.

75 8 November 1907, ESHR 10/42.

76 Fisher to Corbett, 4 December 1907, in *FGDN*, 2:152.

77 Esher Journal, 24 November 1907, in *Esher Journals and Letters*, 2:262.

78 Esher to Fisher, 7 November 1907, in FISR1/5, 264a.

79 Fisher to Esher, 8 November 1907, in ESHR 10/42.

80 Esher Journal, 24 November 1907 and 4 February 1908, in *Esher Journals and Letters*, 2:262 and 280; and Sir Frederick Maurice, *Haldane*, vol 1 (London: Faber and Faber, 1937), 184.

81 *FDSF*, 1:349, and Penn, *Infighting Admirals*, 163. See also Haldane to Esher, 23 August 1907, and Esher to MVB, 24 August 1907, in *Esher Journals and Letters*, 2:246–7.

82 This may be followed in *FDSF*, 1:350, and Penn, *Infighting Admirals*, 164–5.

83 Tweedmouth to First Sea Lord, Controller, Financial Secretary, and Fourth Sea Lord, 23 November 1907, in FISR 1/5, 267.

84 Ruddock F Mackay, *Fisher of Kilverstone* (Oxford: Clarendon Press, 1973), 388–91. Fisher initially recommended, among other means of ensuring the reductions desired by Cabinet, that the battleship be dropped from the estimates.

85 The standard source for this Cabinet crisis is Esher's Journal, 7 February 1908, in *Esher Journals and Letters*, 2:280–4. See also Mackay, *Fisher*, 391, and *FDSF*, 1:137–8.

86 Fisher to Cawdor, 25 November 1907, in *FGDN*, 2:151.

87 Bridgeman to Fisher, 4 January 1908, in FISR 1/6, 273.

88 Fisher to Bridgeman, 5 January 1908, in *FGDN*, 2:154.

89 Fisher to Esher 18 January 1908, in ESHR 10/42.

90 Fisher to Sir Edward Grey, 23 January 1908, in *FGDN*, 2:156. The response to Beresford's request that the Director of Naval Intelligence pay him a visit was a cold one. 'As his request seemed to indicate a misapprehension as to the functions of the Intelligence Department, a reply was sent to the effect that it would be preferable

if he obtained this assistance from his own Chief of Staff.' See Fisher to McKenna, 26 May 1908, in *FGDN* 2:179.

91 Fisher to Esher, 31 January 1908, in *FGDN*, 2:160.

92 Memorandum drafted by Esher, 25 January 1908, in FISR 1/6.

93 Esher to Fisher, 24 January 1908, in FISR 1/6, 281.

94 Esher to Fisher, 9 February 1908, in FISR 1/6, 290.

95 F E Smith to Fisher, 31 January 1908, in FISR 1/6, 285.

96 Esher to the Secretaries of the Maritime League (Wyatt & Smith), 22 January 1908, FISR 1/6, 278.

97 Esher Journal, 7 February 1908, in *Esher Journals and Letters*, 2:284.

98 Cited in ibid, 2:285n.

99 J A Spender, *Fifty Years of Europe: A Study in Pre-War Documents* (London: Cassell, 1933), 274–5.

100 Cited in Robert K Massie, *Dreadnought: Britain, Germany, and the Coming of the Great War* (New York: Random House, 1991), 529.

101 Spender, *Fifty Years of Europe*, 274.

102 Esher Journal, Esher to the King, and the King to Esher, 19 February 1908, in *Esher Journals and Letters*, 2:285–8.

103 Esher Journal, 19 February 1908, in ibid, 2:286.

104 Marder makes clear in his examination of the Tweedmouth–Kaiser exchange that the First Lord did indeed make details available to the Kaiser that he should not have revealed, and this necessitated his retirement from the Admiralty. See *FDSF*, 1:140–2.

105 Repington, *Vestigia*, 285–6.

106 Esher Journal, 7 March 1908, in *Esher Journals and Letters*, 2:293.

107 Fisher to King Edward, 8 March 1908, in *FGDN*, 2:167.

108 Esher to MVB, 9 March 1908, and Esher Journal, 14 March 1908, in *Esher Journals and Letters*, 2:293–5.

109 Asquith to Venetia Stanley, 31 October 1914, in Michael and Eleanor Brock, eds, *H H Asquith: Letters to Venetia Stanley* (Oxford: Oxford University Press, 1982), 299–300.

110 Cited in Mackay, *Fisher*, 373. Mackay suggested that Fisher based his 'knowledge'

on Tweedmouth's reluctance to take decisive action against Beresford in the midst of the Fisher–Beresford crisis.

111 King Edward to Fisher, 14 April 1908, in FISR 1/6, 305. See also *FGDN*, 2:172n.

112 Fisher to McKenna, 16 April 1908, in *FGDN*, 2:173. See also Fisher to King Edward, 11 April 1908, in *FGDN*, 2:172, and FISR 1/6, 306.

113 Fisher to McKenna, 26 May 1908, in *FGDN*, 2:177–9.

114 Fisher to Esher, 8 October 1908, in ESHR 10/42.

115 McKenna to Beresford, 1 July 1908, in FISR 1/6, 317.

116 C I Thomas to Beresford, 1 July 1908, in FISR 1/6, 318.

117 Esher to MVB, 2 May 1908, in *Esher Journals and Letters*, 2:307–8.

118 Esher to MVB, 14 May 1908, in ibid, 2:312.

119 From *FGDN*, 2:43.

120 Cited in *FDSF*, 1:102.

121 F Bullen, Editor of *Daily Mail*, to Fisher, 12 July 1908, in ESHR 10/42.

122 Esher to Lord Knollys, 12 July 1908, in *Esher Journals and Letters*, 2:328.

123 Fisher to McKenna, 11 August 1908, in *FGDN*, 2:186–7.

124 Esher to MVB, 13 September 1909, in *Esher Journals and Letters*, 2:409.

125 Esher Journal, 3 and 9 November 1908, in ibid, 2:354–5 and 357–8.

Chapter 4

1 David Lloyd George to Churchill, 3 January 1903, in Randolph S Churchill, *Winston S Churchill 1: Youth, 1974–1900* (London: William Heinemann, 1966), 516.

2 Lloyd George's dislike of Jellicoe dates from this time. Lloyd George charged that the Admiralty exhibited 'shameful neglect' in not bringing the particulars of the German menace to light earlier, but McKenna, to Lloyd George's embarrassment, stated that in 1907 Lloyd George had dismissed the issue thusly: 'It's all contractors' gossip' – or words to that effect. Jellicoe prepared the 'memo' of this for McKenna, which had proof positive that as of 3 December 1907 the First Lord and the four Sea Lords were 'very anxious about the possibility of accelerated German shipbuilding, and that anxiety is now fully justified.' Memoranda and Jellicoe

correspondence, printed in Frederic C Dreyer, *The Sea Heritage: A Study of Maritime Warfare* (London: Museum Press, 1955), 68–71.

3 Esher Journal, 12 February 1909, in *Esher Journals and Letters*, 2:369–70.

4 Quoted in Peter W Gretton, *Former Naval Person: Winston Churchill and the Royal Navy* (London: Cassell, 1968), 30.

5 Quotes from Reginald Bacon, *The Life of Lord Fisher of Kilverstone: Admiral of the Fleet* (London: Hodder, 1929), 2:88 and 89, respectively.

6 *FGDN*, 2:207.

7 Winston S Churchill, *The World Crisis* (London: Thornton Butterworth, 1923–31), 1:36–7.

8 Chamberlain's comments about the naval scare and Fisher are in Charles Petrie, *The Life and Letters of the Right Hon Sir Austen Chamberlain*, vol 1 (London: Cassell, 1939), 224.

9 W S Churchill, *World Crisis*, 1:37.

10 Oscar Parkes, *British Battleships, 'Warrior' to 'Vanguard': A History of Design, Construction and Armament*, 2nd ed (Annapolis, MD: Naval Institute Press, 1990), 519.

11 For the 1909 naval scare, see *FDSF*, 1:151–85. See also Peter Padfield, *The Great Naval Race: Anglo-German Naval Rivalry 1900–1914* (London: Hart-Davis, MacGibbon, 1974), which brilliantly counterpoises the German to the British positions in politics and shipbuilding. In the end, the four additional dreadnoughts were ordered, not because of any German threat, but due to the knowledge that both the Austrians and the Italians were going to embark on a dreadnought-construction programme.

12 *FDSF*, 1:188.

13 Esher to Lord Knollys, 5 April 1909, in *Esher Journals and Letters*, 2:380.

14 Beatty to Lady Beatty, 20 February 1909, in Bryan Ranft, ed, *The Beatty Papers*, 2 vols (hereafter *Beatty Papers*) (London: Navy Records Society, 1989, 1993), 1:20.

15 Battenberg to Admiral Sir George King-Hall, 24 February 1909, in Mark Kerr, *Prince Louis of Battenberg, Admiral of the Fleet* (London: Longman, 1934), 225–6. See also Ruddock F Mackay, *Fisher of Kilverstone* (Oxford: Clarendon Press,

1973), 363.

16 Esher, no ally of Beresford, conceded that the letter was 'very temperate and well written'. See Esher to J S Sandars, 20 April 1909, in *Esher Journals and Letters*, 2:384.

17 *FDSF*, 2:189–90. Esher believed that the inquiry was agreed to in order to divert attention from the controversy over the 1909/10 naval construction programme. See Esher to Balfour, 15 April 1909, in *Esher Journals and Letters*, 2:383.

18 Fisher to Esher, 13 April 1909, in *FGDN*, 2:211.

19 Esher to Balfour, 15 April 1909, in *Esher Journals and Letters*, 2:383.

20 *FDSF*, 1:190. Esher told Fisher 'nothing but a "file of marines" should get him out of the Admiralty.' See Esher Journal, 14 April 1909, in *Esher Journals and Letters*, 2:382–3.

21 Fisher to Ponsonby, 24 April 1909, in *FGDN*, 2:247.

22 See Fisher to Esher, 12 June 1909, in *FGDN*, 2:251, and Fisher to Esher, 16 June 1909, in ESHR 10/43.

23 Important to the historiography of this subject, the damning evidence against Beresford revealed by this inquiry has been disclosed in Richard Freeman, *The Great Edwardian Naval Feud: Beresford's Vendetta against 'Jackie' Fisher* (Barnsley: Pen and Sword, 2009), 186–220.

24 Fisher to Ponsonby, 4 May 1909, in *FGDN*, 2:248.

25 Fisher to W T Stead, 6 May 1909, in *FGDN*, 2:249.

26 Fisher to Mrs Neeld [Fisher's daughter], May 1909, in *FGDN*, 2:249.

27 Fisher to Esher, 15 June 1909, in ESHR 10/43.

28 Fisher to Esher, 3 July 1909, in *FGDN*, 2:255–6.

29 *FDSF*, 1:190–1.

30 Fisher to Esher, 3 July 1909, in *FGDN*, 2:255–6. See also ESHR 10/43.

31 *FDSF*, 1:199–200.

32 Esher to Balfour, 15 August 1909, in *Esher Journals and Letters*, 2:399–400.

33 Fisher to McKenna, 19 August 1909, in *FGDN*, 2:260.

34 Fisher to Crease, 22 August 1909, in *FGDN*, 2:214.

35 Fisher to Esher, 28 August 1909, ESHR 10/43.

36 Fisher to Esher, 27 October 1909, ESHR 10/43.
37 Esher to J S Sandars, 9 September 1909, in *Esher Journals and Letters*, 2:406–7.
38 Esher to MVB, 7 October 1909, in ibid, 2:412–13.
39 Esher Journal, 17 November 1909, in ibid, 2:421.
40 Taprell Dorling, *Men o' War* (London: Philip Allan, 1929), 233.
41 Quoted in Mackay, *Fisher of Kilverstone*, 347–8.
42 Fisher to Esher, 2 February 1910, ESHR 10/43.
43 Edward E Bradford, *Life of Admiral of the Fleet Sir Arthur Knyvet Wilson* (London: John Murray, 1923), 223–4.
44 Beatty to Lady Beatty, nd (but mid-December 1909), SLGF 12/4.
45 Shane Leslie, 'Memories of Beatty' (unpublished MS, SLGF 12/4), Ch 7.
46 John Arbuthnot Fisher, *Some Notes by Lord Fisher to His Friends* (privately printed, 1918); James Lees-Milne, *The Enigmatic Edwardian: The Life of Reginald 2nd Viscount Esher* (London: Hodder and Stoughton, 1986), 208.
47 Lees-Milne, *Enigmatic Edwardian*, 208.
48 Esher to Fisher, 24 May 1910, in *Esher Journals and Letters* (1930), 3:4.
49 Barbara W Tuchman, *The Guns of August* (New York: Ballantine Books, 1994), 14.
50 Esher to J A Spender, 8 August 1910, and Esher to Balfour, 16 August 1910, in *Esher Journals and Letters*, 3:12–14.
51 Esher to Balfour, 30 September 1910, in ibid, 3:24–5.
52 Esher to J S Sandars, 7 February 1911, in ibid, 3:46–7.
53 Esher to Fisher, 27 April 1911, in ibid, 3:51–2.
54 Esher to Fisher, 31 December 1911, in ibid, 3:76–7.

Chapter 5
1 David Jablonsky, *Churchill, the Great Game and Total War* (London: Cass, 1991).
2 See Douglas S Russell, *The Orders, Decorations and Medals of Sir Winston Churchill*, 2nd edn (Washington, DC: Churchill Centre, 2004).
3 Anthony Storr, *Churchill's Black Dog, Kafka's Mice, and Other Phenomena of the Human Mind* (New York: Grove, 1988), 3–50, quotation at 46. Also Wilfred Attenborough, *Churchill and the 'Black Dog' of Depression* (Basingstoke: Palgrave Macmillan, 2014).
4 A J P Taylor, *English History, 1914–1945* (Oxford: Clarendon, 1965), 4n1.
5 Beatty to Lady Beatty, [20 September 1902], *Beatty Papers*, 1:11–12.
6 John H Mather, 'Sir Winston Churchill: His Hardiness and Resilience', in *Churchill Proceedings 1996–1997* (Washington, DC: Churchill Centre, 2000), 83–97.
7 Esher to MVB, 9 January 1907, in *Esher Journals and Letters*, 2:215–16.
8 Esher to MVB, 30 April 1908, in ibid, 2:306–7.
9 Esher Journal, 22 June 1908, in ibid, 2:323–4.
10 Esher Journal, 26 June 1908, in ibid, 2:325–6.
11 Esher Journal, 8 July 1908, in ibid, 2:326–7.
12 Esher Journal, 15 April 1909, in ibid, 2:369–70 and 384.
13 Esher to Lord Morley, 13 October 1909, in ibid, 2:417–18.
14 Esher Journal, 27 September 1908, in ibid, 2:344–5.
15 George Allardice Riddell, *More Pages from My Diary, 1908–1914* (London: Country Life, 1934), 1, 18.
16 Quoted in Mary Soames, ed, *Speaking for Themselves: The Personal Letters of Winston and Clementine Churchill* (London: Doubleday, 1998), 17.
17 Sonia Purnell, *First Lady: The Life and Wars of Clementine Churchill* (London: Aurum, 2015).
18 Ronald Hyam, *Elgin and Churchill at the Colonial Office, 1905–1908: The Watershed of the Empire-Commonwealth* (London: Macmillan, 1968), 489–506; Hopwood quotation at 502.
19 Beatty to his wife, 6 December 1909, in *Beatty Papers*, 1:28.
20 Esher to MVB, 30 January 1910, in *Esher Journals and Letters*, 2:444–5.
21 Esher to MVB, 16 February 1910, in ibid, 2:451–2.
22 David Stafford, *Churchill and Secret Service* (New York: Overlook Press, 1998), 24–8.
23 Ibid, 26–31.

24 Ibid, 33–42.
25 Quote from Churchill's *World Crisis* in Randolph S Churchill, ed, *Churchill Documents 3: Early Years in Politics, 1901–1907* (Hillsdale, MI: Hillsdale College, 2007), 528.
26 Fisher to Arnold White, 19 January 1907, in *FGDN*, 2:114.
27 Fisher to Tweedmouth, 10 April 1907, in *FGDN*, 2:114n.
28 King Edward VII to Lady Londonderry, 4 April 1907, in Sidney Lee, *King Edward VII: A Biography* (London: Macmillan, 1927), 2:534.
29 Fisher to Churchill, 27 April 1907, CHAR 2/32, 12–13.
30 Fisher to Churchill, 9 January 1908, CHAR 2/32, 16.
31 Fisher to Esher, 19 January 1908, in *FGDN*, 2:155.
32 Fisher to Esher, 1 August 1911, *FDSF*, 1:211.
33 A J P Taylor, *The Struggle for Mastery in Europe 1848–1918* (Oxford: Oxford University Press, 1971), 467–73.
34 Margot Asquith (Countess of Oxford and Asquith), *Off the Record* (London: Frederick Muller, 1943), 30.
35 Peter W Gretton, *Former Naval Person: Winston Churchill and the Royal Navy* (London: Cassell, 1968), 36.
36 Richard Burdon, Viscount Haldane, *Richard Burdon Haldane: An Autobiography* (London: Hodder and Stoughton, 1929), 223–5.
37 Quoted in Roy Jenkins, *Churchill: A Biography* (New York: Farrar, Straus and Giroux, 2001), 212.
38 Churchill to Clementine, 2 and 6 August 1911, in Randolph S Churchill, *Winston S Churchill 2: The Young Statesman, 1901–1914* (London: William Heinemann, 1967*)*, 510–11.
39 Burdon, *Richard Burdon Haldane*, 226–7.
40 Maurice Hankey, *The Supreme Command* (London: George Allen and Unwin, 1961), 1:81–2. Fisher, however, backed Admiral Wilson. See Fisher to Hankey, [undated], in ibid, 1:83. The Admiralty's meritorious plan at this stage imagined all sorts of peripheral actions necessary for victory, but the case suffered in its presentation.
41 Winston S Churchill, *The World Crisis* (London: Thornton Butterworth, 1923–

31), 1:56.
42 Quoted in Michael McMenamin, 'Action This Day', *Finest Hour*, 151 (Summer 2011), 30.
43 Zara S Steiner, *Britain and the Origins of the First World War* (New York: St Martin's Press, 1977), 70–8; and, by the same, *The Foreign Office and Foreign Policy, 1898–1914* (Cambridge: Cambridge University Press, 1969), 140–2; also, Robert K Massie, *Dreadnought: Britain, Germany, and the Coming of the Great War* (New York: Random House, 1991), ch 39.
44 Churchill to McKenna and Churchill to Asquith, both 13 September 1911, quoted in McMenamin, 'Action This Day', 30. Also, for reception and consequences, see Gretton, *Former Naval Person*, 36–9.
45 Violet Bonham Carter, *Winston Churchill as I Knew Him* (London: Eyre and Spottiswoode and Collins, 1965), 236.
46 The exchange of offices took place 23 October 1911.
47 Esher Journal, 24 November 1911, in *Esher Journals and Letters*, 3:74.
48 Ruddock F Mackay, *Fisher of Kilverstone* (Oxford: Clarendon Press, 1973), 432.
49 Quoted in ibid, 433.
50 Fisher letters of various dates, 10 October 1911 to 7 March 1912, in John Arbuthnot Fisher, *Memories* (London: Hodder and Stoughton, 1919), 206–8; some are duplicated, and supplemented by others, notably to John Leyland, 7 November 1911, in Reginald Bacon, *The Life of Lord Fisher of Kilverstone: Admiral of the Fleet* (London: Hodder, 1929), 2:134–6, 140–2.
51 Hew Strachan, *The First World War*, vol 1 (Oxford: Oxford University Press, 2001), 382.
52 Quoted in Leslie Gardiner, *The British Admiralty* (Edinburgh: William Blackwood, 1968), 318.
53 Gretton, *Former Naval Person*, 2. When asked if he had made that famous comment, Churchill replied that no, he had not, but wished he had.
54 S S Hall to Fisher, 17 February 1914, in FISR 1/14, 783.
55 Nicholas Lambert, 'Admiral Sir Arthur Knyvet-Wilson, VC', in *The First Sea Lords*, ed Malcolm H Murfett (Westport, CT: Praeger, 1995), 35–53.

56 W S Churchill, *World Crisis*, 1:62.

57 See *FDSF*, 1:252n.

58 William James, 'Churchill and the Navy', in *Churchill, By His Contemporaries*, ed Charles Eade (London: Reprint Society, 1953), 88.

59 Gretton, *Former Naval Person*, 1.

60 Riddell, *More Pages from My Diary*, 78.

61 William James, *The Eyes of the Navy: A Biographical Study of Admiral Sir Reginald Hall* (London: Methuen, 1955), 81–2; and Patrick Beesly, *Room 40: British Naval Intelligence, 1914–1918* (London: Hamish Hamilton, 1982), 134–5.

62 Fisher to Churchill, 22 April 1912, Fisher to Esher, 29 April 1912, and Fisher to Cecil V Fisher, 4 April 1912, in *FGDN*, 2:450–2, 457–9, and 445. See also Mackay, *Fisher of Kilverstone*, 436–7.

63 Esher to Fisher, 29 March 1912, in *Esher Journals and Letters*, 3:85–6.

Chapter 6

1 For discussion of Churchill's memo of 28 October 1911 and Wilson's response, see Peter W Gretton, *Former Naval Person: Winston Churchill and the Royal Navy* (London: Cassell, 1968), 79–82. Also Edward E Bradford, *Life of Admiral of the Fleet Sir Arthur Knyvet-Wilson* (London: John Murray, 1923), 229.

2 Nicholas Lambert, 'Admiral Sir Francis Bridgeman-Bridgeman', in *The First Sea Lords*, ed Malcolm H Murfett (Westport, CT: Praeger, 1995), 57.

3 Oliver Warner, *Command at Sea: Great Fighting Admirals from Hawke to Nimitz* (New York: St Martin's Press, 1976), 166.

4 Nicholas Lambert, 'Admiral Sir Arthur Knyvet-Wilson, VC', in Murfett, *The First Sea Lords*, 48.

5 Winston S Churchill, *The World Crisis* (London: Thornton Butterworth, 1923–31), 1:93.

6 Esher to Churchill, 8 January 1912, and Esher to Fisher, 9 January 1912, in *Esher Journals and Letters*, 3:77–8.

7 Hew Strachan, *The First World War*, vol 1 (Oxford: Oxford University Press, 2001), 381 and 400–1; and Maurice Hankey, *The Supreme Command* (London: George Allen and Unwin, 1961), 1:85–101.

8 Beatty to Lady Beatty, 24 March 1912, and 'Beatty's Paper for Winston Churchill on Naval Dispositions in a War Against Germany', in *Beatty Papers*, 1:35–45.

9 Esher to Fisher, 4 August 1912, in *Esher Journals and Letters*, 3:104–5.

10 Esher to Knollys, 29 September 1912, in ibid, 3:109–10.

11 Esher to Stamfordham, 26 October 1913, in ibid, 3:142.

12 David Lloyd George, *War Memoirs*, new edn (London: Odhams, 1938), 1:5.

13 Admiral Sir Barry Domvile, *From Admiral to Cabin Boy* (London: Boswell, 1947), 14.

14 George Allardice Riddell, *More Pages from My Diary, 1908–1914* (London: Country Life, 1934), 51.

15 Randolph S Churchill, *Winston S Churchill 2: The Young Statesman, 1901–1914* (London: William Heinemann, 1967), 529; also Daniel Yergin, *The Prize: The Epic Quest for Oil, Money and Power* (New York: Free Press, 1992), xiv.

16 John Arbuthnot Fisher, *Memories* (London: Hodder and Stoughton, 1919), 116.

17 Fisher to Arnold White, 28 January 1901, in *FGDN*, 1:185.

18 Fisher to Selborne, 26 March 1902, in *FGDN*, 1:235.

19 Cited in Peter Kemp, 'The Royal Navy', in *Edwardian England, 1901–1914*, ed Simon Nowell-Smith (London: Oxford University Press, 1964), 505–6.

20 Ibid, 506.

21 Ruddock F Mackay, *Fisher of Kilverstone* (Oxford: Clarendon Press, 1973), 387.

22 Fisher to Esher, 5 August 1910, in Fisher, *Memories*, 200–1.

23 Fisher to J A Spender, 8 August 1910, in *FGDN*, 2:335.

24 Fisher to Arnold White, 31 January 1911, in *FGDN*, 2:355.

25 Fisher to Jellicoe, 13 December 1911, in *FGDN*, 2:420–1.

26 Quoted in Yergin, *The Prize*, 140.

27 Mackay, *Fisher of Kilverstone*, 437.

28 Cited in 'Liquid Fuel for the Navy', in *The Times*, 30 July 1912, 6.

29 Beatty to Lady Beatty, 24 May 1912, Admiralty Yacht, SLGF 12/4.

30 Beatty to Lady Beatty, 27 May 1912, SLGF.

31 Violet Asquith, diary 24 May 1912, in R Churchill, *Churchill 2: Young Statesman*, 586.

32 Violet Asquith, diary 24 May 1912, in ibid.

33 Mackay, *Fisher of Kilverstone*, 437–8; Beatty to Lady Beatty, 24 May 1912, in *Beatty Papers*, 1:45–6.

34 John Arbuthnot Fisher, *Records* (London: Hodder and Stoughton, 1919), 194.

35 Churchill to Fisher, 11 June 1912, cited in Mackay, *Fisher of Kilverstone*, 438.

36 Mackay, *Fisher of Kilverstone*, 438.

37 Cited in 'Liquid Fuel for the Navy'.

38 'Liquid Fuel for the Navy'.

39 Michelle Cosentino and Ruggero Stanglini, *British and German Battlecruisers: Their Development and Operations* (Barnsley: Seaforth, 2016), 134.

40 Fisher to Esher, 20 September 1912, in *FGDN*, 2:478–9.

41 Mackay, *Fisher of Kilverstone*, 440.

42 Ibid, 441.

43 From J W Reed, engine manager, Jarrow on Tyne, Palmers Shipbuilding and Iron Company, 24 December 1912, copy, CHAR 2/92.

44 Jon Sumida, 'British Naval Administration and Policy in the Age of Fisher', *Journal of Military History*, 54, no. 1 (January 1990), 16–17.

45 Fisher's own account of Deterding and his testimony is given in 'Notes on Oil and Oil Engines', in Fisher, *Records*, 201–2.

46 Memorandum in regard to Outline Scheme for Supply of Oil Fuel (Secret), 7 March 1913, Adm 116/1219.

47 Mackay, *Fisher of Kilverstone*, 444.

48 Dr George T Beilby's correspondence with Fisher, 7 September 1913, in FISR 1/14, 728.

49 Mackay, *Fisher of Kilverstone*, 441.

50 Cited in ibid, 454.

51 Yergin, *The Prize*, 144–7.

52 Martin Gilbert, ed, *Churchill Documents 6: At the Admiralty, July 1914–April 1915* (Hillsdale, MI: Hillsdale College Press, 2008), 16–17.

53 Yergin, *The Prize*, 147.

54 Fisher to Churchill, mid-1917, in CHAR 2/92.

55 Slade's report, 'The Petroleum Situation in the British Empire' (29 July 1918), which examined the problems and sources of British oil fuel supplies, urged strong British control of the oil fields. His suspicion of the Royal Dutch Company was not supported by the Cabinet, with Balfour worried about imperial ambitions as a war policy, one with serious consequences to national obligations and international respect. The Admiralty position and sources may be followed in Marion Kent, *Oil and Empire: British Policy and Mesopotamian Oil, 1900–1920* (London: Macmillan, 1976), 125.

56 Strachan, *First World War*, 377.

57 Esher to Balfour, 1 July 1912, in *Esher Journals and Letters*, 3:95–8.

58 Esher to MVB, 2 July 1912, and Esher Journal, 5 July 1912, in ibid, 3:99–100.

59 Gretton, *Former Naval Person*, 136–7.

60 Fisher to Jellicoe, 13 December 1911, in *FGDN*, 2:420.

61 Cited in *FDSF*, 1:269.

62 Four ships had been planned (*Queen Elizabeth*, *Warspite*, *Valiant*, and *Barham*). A fifth, *Malaya*, was ordered soon thereafter when the Federated States of Malaya offered not less than £2.25 million for the construction of a first-class armoured ship. See Viscount Hythe, ed, *The Naval Annual: 1913* (Portsmouth: J Griffin and Co, 1913; reprint, Plymouth: David and Charles Reprints, 1970), 25–6.

63 Andrew Gordon, *Rules of the Game: Jutland and British Naval Command* (London: John Murray, 1996), 8; Mackay, *Fisher of Kilverstone*, 435; and *FDSF*, 1:268.

64 Gordon, *Rules of the Game*, 34–5; Mackay, *Fisher of Kilverstone*, 437; and *FDSF*, 1:268–9.

65 See for instance, contemporary discussion on the subject of 'differentiation of naval force' by the naval correspondent of *The Times*, J R Thursfield, *Naval Warfare* (Cambridge: Cambridge University Press, 1913), 111–28. This makes clear that battleships were still regarded as ships that could 'stand in line' but that battlecruisers, now outgrowing themselves as to size and speed, had been assigned duties that were uncharacteristic of earlier classes and were either a danger or a misfit. Perhaps they might be described as waifs and strays. *Hood* was a battlecruiser, last of a breed.

66 Gordon, *Rules of the Game*, 13–15.

67 *FDSF*, 1:420.

68 *FDSF*, 1:329.

69 *FDSF*, 1:329.

70 *FDSF*, 1:328–9.

71 Mackay, *Fisher of Kilverstone*, 377.

72 Reproduced in *FDSF*, 2:75–6, and elsewhere.

73 *FDSF*, 2:70–81, reviews the matter and cites the relevant memoranda and correspondence.

74 Mackay, *Fisher of Kilverstone*, 441–2.

75 Fisher to Arnold White, 13 March 1913, in *FGDN*, 2:484.

76 Stephen W Roskill, *Hankey, Man of Secrets* (London: Collins, 1970–1974), 1:129–30.

77 Fisher to Stamfordham, 25 June 1912, in *FGDN*, 2:468–9; FISR 5/17, 4281; and Mackay, *Fisher of Kilverstone*, 442.

78 Mackay, *Fisher of Kilverstone*, 442–3. See also Cab 2/2/3.

79 Richard Hough, *Admiral of the Fleet: The Life of John Fisher* (New York: Macmillan, 1969), 168.

80 Mackay, *Fisher of Kilverstone*, 444.

81 Ibid, 445.

82 Balfour to Fisher, 6 May 1913, in *FGDN*, 2:485.

83 Mackay, *Fisher of Kilverstone*, 445–6. See also Hankey Papers, typescript, 4 pp, covered by Fisher to Hankey, 16 May 1913.

84 FISR 5/18, 4284.

85 Mackay, *Fisher of Kilverstone*, 447. See also Balfour to Fisher, 6 May and 20 May 1913, in *FGDN*, 2:485–6.

86 Various prints of the memo appear in FISR 5/18, 4290, Nos 1–4. No. 3 has Jellicoe's marginalia.

87 Sydenham to Fisher, 24 and 28 June 1913, in FISR 704 and 705.

88 Mackay, *Fisher of Kilverstone*, 450.

89 Balfour to Fisher, 12 September 1913, in FISR 1/14, 731.

90 Fisher to Corbett, 29 November 1913, in *FGDN*, 2:494–5.

91 Corbett to Fisher, 30 November 1913, in FISR 1/14, 752.

92 Mackay, *Fisher of Kilverstone*, 450–1; Corbett to Fisher, 30 November 1913, in FISR 1/14, 752, and Corbett to Fisher, 4 December 1913, ibid, 756.

93 Mackay, *Fisher of Kilverstone*, 451.

94 Churchill to Fisher, 12 December 1913, in FISR 1/14, 759.

95 Mackay, *Fisher of Kilverstone*, 452, and FISR 1/14, 763.

96 Mackay, *Fisher of Kilverstone*, 453.

97 Ibid, 453.

98 Ibid, 453–54. See also *FGDN*, 2:507.

99 *FDSF*, 1:339.

100 Fisher to Churchill, 10 November 1911, in Randolph S Churchill, *Churchill Documents 4: Minister of the Crown, 1907–1911* (Hillsdale, MI: Hillsdale College Press, 2008), 672.

101 *FDSF*, 1:336–7.

102 Hythe, *The Naval Annual: 1913*, 168–9; and *FDSF*, 1:336.

103 *FDSF*, 1:339–40.

104 *FDSF*, 1:340–1.

105 *FDSF*, 1:338.

106 *FDSF*, 1:337–8.

107 *FDSF*, 1:333, 338.

108 Allan Westcott, ed, *Mahan on Naval Warfare* (Boston: Little, Brown, 1942), 322–4.

109 Richard Burdon, Viscount Haldane, *Richard Burdon Haldane: An Autobiography* (London: Hodder and Stoughton, 1929), 239–45. By no means was there Cabinet unanimity regarding Haldane's missions and messages. Haldane remarked that he found himself more popular in Germany than in England. See Stephen E Koss, *Lord Haldane: Scapegoat for Liberalism* (New York: Columbia University Press, 1969), ch 3.

110 Holger H Herwig, 'The Failure of German Sea Power, 1914–1945: Mahan, Tirpitz, and Raeder Reconsidered', *International History Review*, 10, no. 1 (March 1988), 80; and Niall Ferguson, *The Pity of War* (New York: Basic Books, 1998), 84–5. On the financial limitations to German armaments, see Niall Ferguson, 'Germany and the Origins of the First World War: New Perspectives', *Historical Journal*, 35, no. 3 (1992), 725–52.

111 *FDSF*, 1:429–30.

112 R Churchill, *Churchill 2: Young Statesman*, 584.

113 Correlli Barnett, *The Swordbearers: Studies in Supreme Command in the First World War* (London: Eyre and Spottiswoode, 1963), 109–110.

114 Shane Leslie, 'Memories of Beatty', unpublished manuscript, SLGF 12/4, unpaginated.

115 Quoted in ibid, 8th page.

116 Ibid, SLGF 12/2.

117 John D Grainger, *The British Navy in the Baltic* (Woodbridge: Boydell, 2014), 236, citing Adm 1/8384/186.

118 Roskill, *Hankey, Man of Secrets*, 1:104.
119 John Gooch, 'The Myth of Imperial Defence' (University of London, Institute of Commonwealth Studies, paper RHC/73/4, 15 November 1974).
120 A E M Chatfield, *The Navy and Defence: The Autobiography of Admiral of the Fleet Lord Chatfield* (London: William Heinemann, 1942), 116–20 (quotation at 120).
121 Ibid, 120.

Chapter 7
1 Winston S Churchill, *The World Crisis* (London: Thornton Butterworth, 1923–31), 1:190.
2 Lewis Bayly, *Pull Together! The Memoirs of Admiral Sir Lewis Bayly* (London: George G. Harrap, 1939), 158–9.
3 Richard Hough, *Admiral of the Fleet: The Life of John Fisher* (New York: Macmillan, 1969), 259.
4 Churchill to Clementine Churchill, 24 July 1914, quoted in Martin Gilbert, *Winston S Churchill 3: The Challenge of War, 1914–1916* (London: William Heinemann, 1971), 4–5.
5 W S Churchill, *World Crisis*, 1:193
6 Mark Kerr, *Prince Louis of Battenberg, Admiral of the Fleet* (London: Longman, 1934), 243.
7 M Gilbert, *Churchill 3: Challenge of War*, 6.
8 Kerr, *Battenberg*, 243.
9 M Gilbert, *Churchill 3: Challenge of War*, 6–7.
10 George Cassar, *Asquith as War Leader* (London: Hambledon, 1994), 15.
11 Churchill to Clementine, 28 July 1914, in Randolph S Churchill, *Winston S Churchill 2: The Young Statesman, 1901–1914* (London: William Heinemann, 1967), 710.
12 Max E Hertwig, 'The "Kingly Conference", 1914: Churchill's Last Try for Peace', *Finest Hour*, 163 (Summer 2014), 20–1. Foreign Office opinion held correctly that such a conference would not work unless called by Russia and Austria.
13 Cassar, *Asquith as War Leader*, 15.
14 The authoritative biography of Jellicoe is A Temple Patterson, *Jellicoe* (London: Macmillan, 1969).
15 These telegrams were published for all to see in 1936, in Jellicoe's official biography:

Reginald Bacon, *Life of John Rushworth Earl Jellicoe* (London: Cassell, 1936), 199–201. See also John Winton, *Jellicoe* (London: Michael Joseph, 1981), 140–3; and Correlli Barnett, *The Swordbearers: Studies in Supreme Command in the First World War* (London: Eyre and Spottiswoode, 1963).
16 Cited in A Temple Patterson, ed, *The Jellicoe Papers: Selections from the Private and Official Correspondence of Admiral of the Fleet Earl Jellicoe of Scapa*, 2 vols (hereafter Jellicoe Papers) (London: Navy Records Society, 1966, 1968), 1:41–2.
17 Churchill to Lady Jellicoe, 1 August 1914, in *Jellicoe Papers*, 1:41. It has been argued in German sources that the replacement of Callaghan by Jellicoe constituted a conscious decision by the Admiralty in favour of a defensive mindset over an offensive one. See Hew Strachan, *The First World War*, vol 1 (Oxford: Oxford University Press, 2001), 414.
18 Jellicoe to Hamilton, 7 August 1914, in *Jellicoe Papers*, 1:48.
19 Preface reprinted without additional comment in 2nd and enlarged edtion (1978); *FDSF*, 3:vii.
20 Winton, *Jellicoe*, 144.
21 Barnett, *The Swordbearers*, 109.
22 W S Churchill, *World Crisis*, 1:212.
23 Ibid, 1:213n.
24 Lord Beaverbrook, *Politicians and the War, 1914–1916* (London: Thornton Butterworth, 1928), 35–6.
25 For discussion of the relevant documents, see M Gilbert, *Churchill 3: Challenge of War*, 8–9, 13, 23, and 25.
26 Beaverbrook, *Politicians and the War*, 35–6.
27 B H Liddell Hart, *History of the First World War* (London: Pan, 1972), 460.
28 Christopher Clark, *The Sleepwalkers: How Europe Went to War in 1914* (New York: Harper Collins, 2013), 538–47.
29 Hankey to Esher, 31 July 1914, cited in Strachan, *First World War*, 374.
30 M Gilbert, *Churchill 3: Challenge of War*, 23–4.
31 Cassar, *Asquith as War Leader*, 18.
32 Beaverbrook, *Politicians and the War*, 176–86.
33 W S Churchill, *World Crisis*, 1:228; also Peter Padfield, *The Great Naval Race:*

Anglo-German Naval Rivalry 1900–1914 (London: Hart-Davis, MacGibbon, 1974), 332.

34 Quoted in A J A Morris, *The Scaremongers: The Advocacy of War and Rearmament 1896–1914* (London: Routledge and Kegan Paul, 1984), 344.

35 M Gilbert, *Churchill 3: Challenge of War*, 31.

36 Richard Toye, *Lloyd George and Churchill: Rivals for Greatness* (London: Pan, 2008), 127.

37 John Buchan, *The King's Grace, 1910–1935* (London: Hodder and Stoughton, 1935), 115.

38 Quoted in Peter Ackroyd, *London: The Biography* (London: Vintage, 2002), 721–2.

39 Fisher to Churchill, 9 September 1914, cited in M Gilbert, *Churchill 3: Challenge of War*, 3:64. The friend was Hankey.

40 M Gilbert, *Churchill 3: Challenge of War*, 191–2.

41 Unknown to the British, *Goeben*'s boiler had serious defects that limited top speed during the first days of the war to 18 knots.

42 Paul G Halpern, *A Naval History of World War I* (Annapolis, MD: Naval Institute Press, 1994), 54–5.

43 Admiralty to C-in-C, 30 July 1914, Cab 37/119/59. Also Admiralty correspondence with admirals and captains afloat, in Adm 137/879. The majority of these are printed for convenience in E W R Lumby, ed, *Policy and Operations in the Mediterranean, 1912–1914* (London: Navy Records Society, 1970), 146–237. Also M Gilbert, *Churchill 3: Challenge of War*, 17–18.

44 Churchill and Battenberg to Milne, 2 August 1914, cited in M Gilbert, *Churchill 3: Challenge of War*, 26.

45 Churchill to Milne, 3 August 1914, in Lumby, *Policy and Operations in the Mediterranean*, 150.

46 Cited in Geoffrey Bennett, *Naval Battles of the First World War*, rev edn. (London: Pan, 1983), 17.

47 H H Asquith, *The Earl of Oxford and Asquith: Memories and Reflections, 1852–1927* (Boston: Little, Brown, 1928), 2:21.

48 M Gilbert, *Churchill 3: Challenge of War*, 28–30; and K G B Dewar, 'Escape of the *Goeben* and *Breslau*', *Naval Review*, 44,

no. 1 (February 1956), 38.

49 William James, *The Eyes of the Navy: A Biographical Study of Admiral Sir Reginald Hall* (London: Methuen, 1955), 60–1.

50 Eric Bush, *Gallipoli* (London: George Allen and Unwin, 1975), 29.

51 W S Churchill, *World Crisis*, 1:250.

52 H H Asquith, *Memories and Reflections*, 2:21.

53 Winston S Churchill, *My Early Life* (London: Eland, 2000), 176.

54 For Troubridge's decision not to engage, see *FDSF*, 2:26–9. Troubridge had initially wavered but was influenced by his Flag Captain, Fawcet Wray, to not engage. Troubridge had also been an observer at the Battle of Tsushima, and had seen the effect of modern naval ordnance. Strachan, *First World War*, 646.

55 Halpern, *Naval History of World War I*, 54–6; and Ulrich Trumpener, 'Turkey's Entry into World War I: An Assessment of Responsibilities', *Journal of Modern History*, 34, no. 4 (December 1962), 181.

56 Beaumont to Grey, 6 August 1914 [received 7 August 1914], and two messages from Beaumont to Grey, 7 August 1914 [received 8 August 1914], cited in David H Stevenson, ed, *British Documents on Foreign Affairs: Reports and Papers from the Foreign Office Confidential Print*, part 2, *From the First to the Second World War*. Series H, *The First World War, 1914–1918*, vol 1, *The Allied and Neutral Powers: Diplomacy and War Aims, I: August 1914–July 1915* (Frederick, MD: University Publications of America, 1989), 5–6 and 7–8.

57 See Geoffrey Miller, *Superior Force: The Conspiracy Behind the Escape of Goeben and Breslau* (Hull: University of Hull Press, 1996).

58 Trumpener, 'Turkey's Entry into World War I', 178–9; and Mr Erskine to Grey, 5 August 1914 [received 6 August 1914], in Stevenson, *British Documents on Foreign Affairs*, Series H. *The First World War*, 3–4.

59 Trumpener, 'Turkey's Entry into World War I', 180–1 and 183.

60 Beaumont to Grey, 9 August 1914 [received same day], in Stevenson, *British Documents on Foreign Affairs*. Series H, *The First World War*, 9.

61 Strachan, *First World War*, 648–9.
62 Milne to Churchill, 12 August 1914, and Churchill to Grey, 12 August 1914, in Lumby, *Policy and Operations in the Mediterranean*, 434; Asquith to Venetia Stanley, 12 August 1914, in Michael and Eleanor Brock, eds, *H H Asquith: Letters to Venetia Stanley* (Oxford: Oxford University Press, 1982), 167–9.
63 Trumpener, 'Turkey's Entry into World War I', 172.
64 Beaumont to Grey, 16 August 1914, in Lumby, *Policy and Operations in the Mediterranean*, 441.
65 H H Asquith, *Memories and Reflections*, 2:26.
66 Asquith to King George V, 17 August 1914, cited in C Jay Smith, Jr, 'Great Britain and the 1914–1915 Straits Agreement with Russia: The British Promise of November 1914', *American Historical Review*, 70, no. 4 (July 1965), 1018.
67 Churchill to Grey, 17 August 1914, in Lumby, *Policy and Operations in the Mediterranean*, 441–2.
68 Sir L Mallet to Grey, 17 or 18 August 1914, in ibid, 445–6; and M Gilbert, *Churchill 3: Challenge of War*, 194–8.
69 Lumby, *Policy and Operations in the Mediterranean*, 230–2.
70 *FDSF*, 2:31–2.
71 Minute by Battenberg, 7 September 1914, Adm 137/879.
72 *FDSF*, 2:34–5.
73 Barry M Gough, *Historical Dreadnoughts: Arthur Marder, Stephen Roskill, and Battles for Naval History* (Barnsley: Seaforth, 2010), 116–20.
74 Lumby, *Policy and Operations in the Mediterranean*, 396–7.
75 Admiralty to Rear-Admiral, 2nd Light Cruiser Squadron, 11 January 1915, in ibid, 235–6.
76 Admiralty to Marine, Bordeaux (via French naval attaché), 20 September 1914, in ibid, 454.
77 Lumby, *Policy and Operations in the Mediterranean*, 411–22.
78 Cited in M Gilbert, *Churchill 3: Challenge of War*, 42. Italicisation of the ship's name by the author.
79 Corbett, quoted in *FDSF*, 2:20; Rear-Admiral Eardley-Wilmot, 'How Did the 'Goeben' Escape?', *Stead's Magazine*, 8 January 1921.
80 K G B Dewar, 'Escape of the *Goeben* and *Breslau*'.
81 Fisher to Yarrow, 10 February 1918, cited in *FGDN*, 3:335n.
82 Cited in Bennett, *Naval Battles of the First World War*, 14.
83 Quoted in Halpern, *Naval History of World War I*, 64; also Miller, *Superior Force*, 251.
84 W S Churchill, *World Crisis*, 1:255. For a review of the circumstances, see Miller, *Superior Force*, ch 15.
85 W James, *Eyes of the Navy*, 63.
86 Hall's account is in Patrick Beesly, *Room 40: British Naval Intelligence, 1914–1918* (London: Hamish Hamilton, 1982), 80–2. See also David Stafford, *Churchill and Secret Service* (New York: Overlook Press, 1998), 76–7; and W James, *Eyes of the Navy*, 60–4.
87 Frederic C Dreyer, *The Sea Heritage: A Study of Maritime Warfare* (London: Museum Press, 1955), 80.
88 Jellicoe to his mother, 7 August 1914; full letter printed in Bacon, *Jellicoe*, 220–1.
89 John Rushworth Jellicoe, *The Grand Fleet, 1914–1916: Its Creation, Development, and Work* (London: Cassell, 1919), 37–9.
90 Andrew Gordon, *The Rules of the Game: Jutland and British Naval Command* (London: John Murray, 1996), 34.
91 Ibid.
92 *The Times*, 9 September 1919.
93 Jellicoe, *Grand Fleet*, 26–7.
94 Julian Corbett, *History of the Great War: Naval Operations*, vol 1 (London: Longmans Green, 1920), 38–9. For particulars on minelaying and minesweeping see Norman Friedman, *Fighting the Great War at Sea: Strategy, Tactics, and Technology* (Annapolis, MD: Naval Institute Press, 2014), 335–50.
95 Robert Rhodes James, ed, *Winston S Churchill: His Complete Speeches, 1897–1963* (New York: Chelsea House, 1974), 3:2324–5.
96 Fisher to Lady Jellicoe, 16 August 1914, in *FGDN*, 3:51.
97 Jellicoe to Battenberg, 18 August 1914, in *Jellicoe Papers*, 1:50.
98 W S Churchill, *World Crisis*, 3:106.
99 *FDSF*, 2:42–9.

100 Richmond diary, 24 October 1914, in Arthur J Marder, ed, *Portrait of an Admiral: The Life and Papers of Sir Herbert Richmond* (London: Jonathan Cape, 1952), 121.

101 Eric W Osborne, *The Battle of Heligoland Bight* (Bloomington: Indiana University Press, 2006).

102 For discussion, see Robin Prior, *Churchill's 'World Crisis' as History* (London: Croom Helm, 1983), 16–18. Prior cites original sources for comparison to Winston's prose.

103 Quoted in his biography in *Oxford Dictionary of National Biography*.

104 O Murray to Beatty, 22 October 1914, with Jellicoe's covering letter of 29 October 1914, copy, in SLGF 3/3.

105 Cited in M Gilbert, *Churchill 3: Challenge of War*, 58.

106 In Robert K Massie, *Castles of Steel: Britain, Germany, and the Winning of the Great War at Sea* (New York: Random House, 2004), 106–7.

107 Ibid. Keyes to de Robeck, 29 September 1914, in Paul Halpern, ed, *The Keyes Papers*, 3 vols (hereafter *Keyes Papers*) (London: Navy Records Society, 1972–1981), 1:31–5.

108 Winston S Churchill, 'The U-Boat War', in *Thoughts and Adventures: Churchill Reflects on Spies, Cartoons, Flying, and the Future*, ed James W Muller with Paul Courtenay and Alana Barton (Wilmington, DE: ICI Books, 2009), 131.

109 Tobias R Philbin, *Admiral Von Hipper: The Inconvenient Hero* (Amsterdam: B R Grüner, 1982), 40.

110 Fisher to John Leyland, 15 October 1914, in *FGDN*, 3:63.

111 Jellicoe to the Secretary of the Admiralty, in *Jellicoe Papers*, 1:69.

112 Philbin, *Admiral Von Hipper*, 41–2.

113 Stafford, *Churchill and Secret Service*, 60–2; and Strachan, *First World War*, 422–3.

114 Max Hastings, *Catastrophe: Europe Goes to War 1914* (London: William Collins, 2013), 162–4, 181, 187–93, 213, 444, 543.

115 Churchill's dynamic leadership in the air defence of Britain in the 1914–1918 war has never been appreciated and awaits further study. For an introduction to this topic, see Stephen W Roskill, ed, *Documents Relating to the Naval Air Service*, vol 1, *1908–1918* (London: Navy Records Society, 1969). The air offensive is described in Walter Raleigh, *The War in the Air, Being the Story of the Part Played in the Great War by the Royal Air Force*, vol 1 (Oxford: Clarendon, 1922), 374–88.

116 Churchill to Battenberg and Sir Frederick Hamilton, 16 August 1914, cited in M Gilbert, *Churchill 3: Challenge of War*, 47–8.

117 M Gilbert, *Churchill 3: Challenge of War*, 54–6.

118 Donald M Schurman, *Julian S Corbett, 1854–1922: Historian of British Maritime Policy from Drake to Jellicoe* (London: Royal Historical Society, 1981), 158.

119 Admiral Fisher to Cecil Fisher, 6 September 1914, in *FGDN*, 3:57.

120 Citation for the letter unknown (perhaps *The Times*, 9 September 1914). Announcement of the Naval Brigade was made 7 September. A K Wilson was named honorary colonel of the 2nd Royal Naval Brigade, and Beresford honorary colonel of the Royal Marine Brigade.

121 'Some of the Meditations of Lord Fisher', in his own hand, nd but late 1917, Beaverbrook Papers, BC-MS, Harriet Irving Library, University of New Brunswick.

122 From Max Hastings, comp, *Oxford Book of Military Anecdotes* (Oxford: Oxford University Press, 1985), 328–9.

123 Violet Bonham Carter, *Winston Churchill as I Knew Him* (London: Eyre and Spottiswoode and Collins, 1965), 329.

124 James E Edmonds, *Military Operations: France and Belgium, 1914*, 3rd edn (London: Macmillan, 1933), 18–19. I have also relied on Julian Thompson, *The Royal Marines: From Sea Soldiers to a Special Force* (London: Pan, 2000); and Leonard Sellers, *The Hood Battalion: Royal Naval Division – Antwerp, Gallipoli, France 1914–1918* (London: Leo Cooper, 1995).

125 M Gilbert, *Churchill 3: Challenge of War*, 97–100.

126 Viscount Grey of Fallodon, *Twenty-Five Years: 1892–1916* (London: Hodder and Stoughton, 1925), 2:81.

127 Quoted in M Gilbert, *Churchill 3: Challenge of War*, 103–7.

128 Asquith to Venetia Stanley, 3 October

1914, quoted in M Gilbert, *Churchill 3: Challenge of War*, 107.

129 It survived however. See J M N Jeffries, 'Doom Over Antwerp', in *The Great War – I Was There*, ed John Hammerton (London: Amalgamated Press, 1938), ch 39, 179. See also Sellers, *The Hood Battalion*, 16–17. Further particulars of Churchill and Antwerp will be found in William Manchester, *The Last Lion: Visions of Glory, 1874–1932* (Boston: Little, Brown, 1983), 497–505.

130 Quoted in Lewis Broad, *Winston Churchill 1874–1945* (London: Hutchinson, 1945), 180.

131 Cited in M Gilbert, *Churchill 3: Challenge of War*, 107.

132 Ibid, 108–11.

133 Churchill to Asquith, 5 October 1914, cited in ibid, 111–22.

134 A J P Taylor, *Beaverbrook* (New York: Simon and Schuster, 1972), 104.

135 Asquith to Venetia Stanley, 5 October 1914, cited in M Gilbert, *Churchill 3: Challenge of War*, 113.

136 M Gilbert, *Churchill 3: Challenge of War*, 114.

137 Celia and John Lee, *Winston and Jack: The Churchill Brothers* (London: Authors, 2007), 266.

138 Reginald Viscount Esher, *The Tragedy of Lord Kitchener* (London: John Murray, 1921), 68.

139 Asquith to Venetia Stanley, 6 October 1914, cited in M Gilbert, *Churchill 3: Challenge of War*, 117.

140 M Gilbert, *Churchill 3: Challenge of War*, 121.

141 Ibid, 137.

142 Hastings, *Catastrophe*, 72.

143 Douglas Jerrold, *The Royal Naval Division*, 2nd edn (London: Hutchinson, 1927), 24. Also C and J Lee, *Winston and Jack*, 266–7.

144 M Gilbert, *Churchill 3: Challenge of War*, 125–7.

145 Ibid, 129–30.

146 Cited in ibid, 130.

147 Brock, *Asquith: Letters to Venetia Stanley*, 276.

148 Beatty to Lady Beatty, 18 and 20 October 1914, cited in M Gilbert, *Churchill 3: Challenge of War*, 133–4.

149 Fisher to Mrs McKenna, early October 1914, in *FGDN*, 3:61.

150 A J P Taylor, *English History, 1914–1945* (Oxford: Clarendon, 1965), 11.

151 M Gilbert, *Churchill 3: Challenge of War*, 137.

152 Churchill, Speech to the House of Commons, 15 November 1915, in R R James, *Churchill: His Complete Speeches*, 3:2392–4.

153 Quoted in Thompson, *Royal Marines*, 72.

154 Viscount Grey of Fallodon, *Twenty-Five Years: 1892–1916* (London: Hodder and Stouton, 1925), 2:83.

155 It may be seen at the National Museum of the Royal Navy, Portsmouth Dockyard. See Matthew Sheldon, *HMS M.33* (Stroud: Pitkin, 2015).

156 R R James, *Churchill: His Complete Speeches*, 3:2336–7.

157 *FDSF*, 2:48.

158 *FDSF*, 2:48 and 48n11.

159 Lord Stamfordham to Maurice Bonham Carter, 22 September 1914, Asquith papers, cited in *FDSF*, 2:48n10.

160 C F Aspinall-Oglander, *Roger Keyes, Being the Biography of Admiral of the Fleet Lord Keyes of Zeebrugge and Dover* (London: Hogarth Press, 1951), 98–9; M Gilbert, *Churchill 3: Challenge of War*, 85.

161 Fisher to Jellicoe, 28 October 1914, BL Add MSS 49009; Churchill's order of 25 September 1914, Adm 137/47; for discussion see Nicholas Black, *The British Naval Staff in the First World War* (Woodbridge: Boydell Press, 2009), 110–11.

162 Fisher to Mrs McKenna, early October 1914, in *FGDN*, 3:61.

163 Beatty to Churchill, 17 October 1914, SLGF/3/3.

164 Filson Young, *With the Battlecruisers* (1921; Annapolis, MD: Naval Institute Press, 1986), 56.

165 Philip Watts, 'Ships of the British Navy on August 4, 1914, and Some Matters of Interest in Connection with Their Production', *Transactions of the Institution of Naval Architects*, 61 (1919), 11.

166 M Gilbert, *Churchill 3: Challenge of War*, 141–2.

167 Asquith to Venetia Stanley, 28 October 1914, in Brock, *Asquith: Letters to Venetia Stanley*, 290–2 and note.

168 Douglas Brownrigg, *Indiscretions of the*

Naval Censor (London: Cassell, 1920), 32–4. See also Jellicoe, *Grand Fleet*, 152–3.

Chapter 8

1 From a letter by L Mountbatten 1914, quoted in Philip Ziegler, *Mountbatten* (New York: Knopf, 1985), 35.

2 Battenberg had been born in Graz, Austria, in 1854. On the press agitation, as well as the high regard for Battenberg in the Service, see Robert K Massie, *Castles of Steel: Britain, Germany, and the Winning of the Great War at Sea* (New York: Random House, 2004), 165–78.

3 Asquith to Venetia Stanley, 24 October 1914, in Michael and Eleanor Brock, eds, *H H Asquith: Letters to Venetia Stanley* (Oxford: Oxford University Press, 1982), 284–6.

4 M Gilbert, *Winston S Churchill 3: The Challenge of War, 1914–1916* (London: William Heinemann, 1971), 147.

5 Cited in ibid, 144.

6 Asquith to Venetia Stanley, 27 October 1914, in Brock, *Asquith: Letters to Venetia Stanley*, 287–8.

7 His letter is printed by Churchill in *The World Crisis* (London: Thornton Butterworth, 1923–31), 1:400–1.

8 Battenberg to Churchill, 29 October 1914, CHAR 13/27A; also John B Hattendorf, 'Admiral Prince Louis of Battenberg', in *The First Sea Lords*, ed Malcolm H Murfett (Westport, CT: Praeger, 1995), 87.

9 Quoted in Harold Nicolson, *King George the Fifth: His Life and Reign* (London: Constable, 1952), 251.

10 Quoted in Martin Gilbert, *Churchill, A Photographic Portrait* (New York: Wings Books, 1993), caption for photo 88. Could it be that the mortification Churchill felt at having to surrender to popular clamour was in later years mitigated by the fact that he was able to provide Prince Louis's son, Lord Louis Mountbatten, with opportunities for high achievement? For a partial answer, I give the following: 'That Lord Louis was dashing, fearless, and always encouraging new technical ideas and gifted with the mystique of leadership Mr. Churchill knew. As a blood relative of royalty, he stood for certain intangible traditional values at a time when our life was being chipped away. He had known

Lord Louis all the years of his life and owed his father a great debt for shouldering the full responsibility for the initial disasters of the First World War. Mr. Churchill has an elephantine memory for old friends and past services.' Brian Connell, *Manifest Destiny: A Study in Five Profiles of the Rise and Influence of the Mountbatten Family* (London: Cassell, 1953), 149.

11 Asquith to Venetia Stanley, 28 October 1914, in Brock, *Asquith: Letters to Venetia Stanley*, 290–2.

12 Asquith to Venetia Stanley, 29 October 1914, in Brock, *Asquith: Letters to Venetia Stanley*, 295–7.

13 Quoted in Nicolson, *King George the Fifth*, 252.

14 Asquith to Venetia Stanley, 30 October 1914, in Brock, *Asquith: Letters to Venetia Stanley*, 297–8.

15 Quoted in Nicolson, *King George the Fifth*, 251.

16 *The Times*, 29 October 1914, 8.

17 Battenberg to Churchill, 28 October 1914, cited in M Gilbert, *Churchill 3: Challenge of War*, 149–50.

18 Fisher to Esher, 1 November 1914, in ESHR, also in Martin Gilbert, ed, *Churchill Documents 6: At the Admiralty, July 1914–April 1915* (Hillsdale, MI: Hillsdale College Press, 2008), 243.

19 W S Churchill, *World Crisis*, 1:403–4.

20 Ibid, 1:405.

21 Willian James, *The Eyes of the Navy: A Biographical Study of Admiral Sir Reginald Hall* (London: Methuen, 1955), 82.

22 Douglas Brownrigg, *Indiscretions of the Naval Censor* (London: Cassell, 1920), 17–18.

23 Percy Scott, *Fifty Years in the Royal Navy* (London: John Murray, 1919), 294–5.

24 Esher Journal, 4 November 1914, in *Esher Journals and Letters*, 3:193–4.

25 Beatty to Lady Beatty, 30 October, 2 and 3–4 November 1914, in *Beatty Papers*, 1:148–54.

26 W S Churchill, *World Crisis*, 1:433.

27 Violet Asquith in her diary, 19 May 1915, cited in Brock, *Asquith: Letters to Venetia Stanley*, 294.

28 Lord Beaverbrook, *Politicians and the War, 1914–1916* (London: Thornton Butterworth, 1928), 104.

29 M Gilbert, *Churchill 3: Challenge of War*, 155.

30 Arthur J Marder, ed, *Portrait of an Admiral: The Life and Papers of Sir Herbert Richmond* (London: Jonathan Cape, 1952), 133.

31 Keyes to his wife, Eva Keyes, 11 November 1914, in *Keyes Papers*, 1:51–2. See also Keyes to Captain S S Hall, 20 January 1915, in *Keyes Papers*, 1:74–7, where Keyes praised Fisher's personnel reforms of 1902, which 'swept away all the hidebound restrictions of generations, as only he could.'

32 Keyes to Eva Keyes, 31 October and 1 November 1914, in *Keyes Papers*, 1:41–2.

33 Keyes to Eva Keyes, 4 and 7 December 1914, in ibid, 1:53–6.

34 Keyes to Eva Keyes, 15 January and 2 February 1915, and Keyes to de Robeck, 18 January 1915, in ibid, 1:71, 73–4, and 79.

35 Taprell Dorling, *Men o' War* (London: Philip Allan, 1929), 220. See also W S Churchill, *World Crisis*, 1:78–9.

36 The following owes much to *FDSF*, vol 2, ch 5; Barrie Pitt, *Coronel and Falklands* (1960; London: Cassell, 2002); and Geoffrey Bennett, *Coronel and the Falklands*, rev edn (London: Pan, 1968).

37 For a translation of instructions, and discussions of options presented to him, see Keith Yates, *Graf Spee's Raiders: Challenge to the Royal Navy 1914–1915* (Annapolis, MD: Naval Institute Press, 1995), 24–5. See also Hew Strachan, *The First World War*, vol 1 (Oxford: Oxford University Press, 2001), 466–80.

38 W S Churchill, *World Crisis*, 1:418.

39 Peter W Gretton, *Former Naval Person: Winston Churchill and the Royal Navy* (London: Cassell, 1968), 185.

40 Julian Corbett, *History of the Great War: Naval Operations*, vol 1 (London: Longmans Green, 1920), 346–7.

41 *FDSF*, 2:111.

42 Harold Hickling, quoted in *FDSF*, 2:114.

43 Frederic C Dreyer, *The Sea Heritage: A Study of Maritime Warfare* (London: Museum Press, 1955), 90.

44 Mark Kerr, *Prince Louis of Battenberg, Admiral of the Fleet* (London: Longman, 1934), 244.

45 Ibid, 244–5.

46 Churchill to Kitchener, 5 November 1914, cited in M Gilbert, *Churchill 3: Challenge of War*, 158–9.

47 Asquith to Venetia Stanley, 4 November 1914, in Brock, *Asquith: Letters to Venetia Stanley*, 309.

48 Ibid; and M Gilbert, *Churchill 3: Challenge of War*, 158.

49 Frances Stevenson, diary, 5 November 1914, cited in M Gilbert, *Churchill 3: Challenge of War*, 159.

50 W S Churchill, *World Crisis*, 1:415 and 422. The whole sequence, backed by telegrams and correspondence, can be found at 407–38. For discussion of this, see Pitt, *Coronel and Falklands*, 24–5.

51 Fisher to Tweedmouth, 16 October 1906, in *FGDN*, 2:101.

52 Brownrigg, *Indiscretions of the Naval Censor*, 20–1.

53 Gretton, *Former Naval Person*, 185–6.

54 See Herbert W Richmond's foreword to Lloyd Hurst, *Coronel and After* (London: Peter Davies, 1934), xiv–xvi.

55 See, for example, Jellicoe to Fisher, 11 November 1914, and Jellicoe to Beatty, 12 November 1914, in *Jellicoe Papers*, 1:81–2.

56 Jellicoe to Admiralty, 12 November 1914, and Fisher to Jellicoe, 16 November 1914, in *Jellicoe Papers*, 1:82–4.

57 Gretton, *Former Naval Person*, 186.

58 W S Churchill, *World Crisis*, 1:452.

59 M Hankey, diary, 4 and 5 March 1915, HNKY 1/1.

60 W S Churchill, *World Crisis*, 1:436.

61 Churchill to Fisher, 10 December 1914, cited in M Gilbert, *Churchill 3: Challenge of War*, 183–4.

62 Bennett, *Coronel and the Falklands*, 166.

63 Fisher to Churchill, 25 December 1914, in M Gilbert, *Churchill 3: Challenge of War*, 184.

64 For this press release, see Brownrigg, *Indiscretions of the Naval Censor*, 23–31.

65 Richmond in his diary, 13 December 1914, Marder, *Portrait of an Admiral*, 130–1.

66 The exchange of telegrams may be traced in Bennett, *Coronel and the Falklands*, 171–3.

67 Gretton, *Former Naval Person*, 187. See, however, Fisher's comment to Jellicoe: 'It is kind of you to prune down Sturdee's reports. MUCH WANTED!' Fisher to

Jellicoe, 20 February 1915, in *FGDN*, 3:158–9.

68 Richard Hough provides extensive treatment of Sturdee's reception in *The Pursuit of Admiral von Spee: A Study in Loneliness and Bravery* (London: George Allen and Unwin, 1969), 165–9.

69 Fisher to a friend, 22 August 1917, in John Arbuthnot Fisher, *Records* (London: Hodder and Stoughton, 1919), 231–2. A similar appraisal of the consequences of the annihilation of Admiral von Spee's fleet is in Fisher's manuscript, 'Some of the Meditations of Lord Fisher', nd but late 1917, Beaverbrook Papers, BC-MS, Harriet Irving Library, University of New Brunswick.

70 Dreyer, *Sea Heritage*, 101–4.

71 Fisher to Jellicoe, 20 December 1914, and Fisher to Mrs R W Lovett, 20 December 1914, *FGDN*, 3:100–1 and 98–9 respectively.

72 Quoted in Nicolson, *King George V*, 257.

73 Churchill to Fisher, 23 December 1914, in *FGDN*, 3:109.

74 Jellicoe to Fisher, 18 December 1914, and Beatty to Jellicoe, 20 December 1914, in *Jellicoe Papers*, 1:107–12.

75 David Stafford, *Churchill and Secret Service* (New York: Overlook Press, 1998), 66–8; Gretton, *Former Naval Person*, 190.

76 Fisher to Jellicoe, 17 December 1914, in *Jellicoe Papers*, 1:106.

77 Fisher to Jellicoe, [ca 21 December 1914], in ibid, 1:113.

78 Ibid, 1:113–14.

79 Fisher to Jellicoe, 20 December 1914, *FGDN*, 3:99.

80 Brayton Harris, *The Navy Times Book of Submarines: A Political, Social, and Military History* (New York: Berkley, 1997), 173–6. Also Gaddis Smith, *Britain's Clandestine Submarines 1914–1915* (New Haven, CT: Yale University Press, 1964).

81 John Arbuthnot Fisher, *Memories* (London: Hodder and Stoughton, 1919), 86–90, and *Records*, 230.

82 Fisher to Jellicoe, 23 December 1914, in *Jellicoe Papers*, 1:115.

83 W S Churchill, *World Crisis*, 1:428–32.

84 Martin Gilbert, ed, *The Churchill War Papers*, vol 1, *Churchill at the Admiralty September 1939–May 1940* (New York and London: W W Norton, 1993), 63.

85 *FDSF*, 2:96.

86 Paul Hayes, 'British Plans for Attacking Germany, 1906–1915', in *War Strategy and International Politics*, ed Lawrence Freedman et al (Oxford: Clarendon Press, 1992), 99.

87 John D Grainger, *The British Navy in the Baltic* (Woodbridge: Boydell, 2014), 234. See also Shawn T Grimes, *Strategy and War Planning in the British Navy, 1887–1918* (Woodbridge: Boydell, 2012), 58–60.

88 Peter K Kemp, ed, *Papers of Admiral Sir John Fisher* (London: Navy Records Society, 1964), 2:316–17.

89 Hayes, 'British Plans for Attacking Germany', 97–9.

90 Churchill to Asquith, 31 July 1914, cited in M Gilbert, *Churchill 3: Challenge of War*, 20–1.

91 M Gilbert, *Churchill 3: Challenge of War*, 37–8.

92 Ibid, 180–1.

93 See Michael Wilson, *Baltic Assignment: British Submarines in Russia, 1914–1919* (London: Leo Cooper in association with Secker and Warburg, 1985); Paul G Halpern, *A Naval History of World War I* (Annapolis, MD: Naval Institute Press, 1994), 187–190 (for 1914), 199–205 (for 1915).

94 M Gilbert, *Churchill Documents 6: July 1914–April 1915*, 46 and 53.

95 Strachan, *First World War*, 402.

96 Printed in Fisher, *Records*, 217–22 (quotation at 222).

97 Churchill to Fisher, 22 December 1914, in M Gilbert, *Churchill Documents 6: July 1914–April 1915*, 326; and Hayes, 'British Plans for Attacking Germany', 100.

98 Churchill to Jellicoe, 9 March 1915, in *Jellicoe Papers*, 1:150–1.

99 Hayes, 'British Plans for Attacking Germany', 102–5.

100 Thomas G Frothingham, *The Naval History of the World War: Offensive Operations, 1914–15* (Cambridge, MA: Harvard University Press, 1924), 1:156.

101 Fisher to Churchill, 4 January 1915, in M Gilbert, *Churchill 3: Challenge of War*, 239.

102 Churchill to Fisher, 4 January 1915, in ibid, 239; and W S Churchill, *World Crisis*, 2:63–4.

103 Churchill's memo of 1 January 1915, and

extracts of the Secretary's Minutes of 7 January 1915 War Cabinet, in Stephen W Roskill, ed, *Documents Relating to the Naval Air Service*, vol 1, *1908–1918* (London: Navy Records Society, 1969), 188–92.

104 Captain Murray F Sueter to Fisher, 6 February 1915, FISR 1/18.

105 George Holt Thomas to Fisher, 25 February 1915, FISR 1/18, 946 (from Airships Ltd).

106 Rear-Admiral Sir Charles Ottley to Captain T E Crease, 24 February 1915, FISR 1/18, 945.

107 W S Churchill, *World Crisis*, 2:77–8

108 Keyes to the Chief of the War Staff, 1 November 1914, in *Keyes Papers*, 1:42–9.

109 Rear-Admiral George A Ballard to Keyes, 20 December 1914, in ibid., 1:62–3.

110 Fisher to Jellicoe, 28 November 1914, in *Jellicoe Papers*, 1:100.

111 Jellicoe to Fisher, 2 December 1914, in ibid, 1:101–2.

112 Lionel Dawson, *Flotillas: A Hard-Lying Story* (London: Rich and Cowan, 1933), 198–9.

113 Fisher to Jellicoe, 21 November 1914, in *Jellicoe Papers*, 1:98.

114 Fisher to Jellicoe, 30 November 1914, in ibid, 1:100–1.

115 See Jellicoe to the Secretary of the Admiralty, 4 December 1914, and Jellicoe to Fisher, 5 December 1914, in ibid, 1:102–4.

116 Admiralty to Jellicoe, 16 November 1914, and Jellicoe to Fisher, 18 November 1914, in ibid, 1:93–4 and 96.

117 Jellicoe to Fisher, 2 December 1914, in ibid, 1:101–2.

118 Fisher to Jellicoe, 20 and [ca 21] December 1914, in ibid, 1:112–14.

119 Admiralty to Jellicoe, 20 December 1914, in ibid, 1:112.

120 Jellicoe to Fisher, 23 December 1914, in ibid, 1:114.

121 Roy Jenkins, *Churchill: A Biography* (New York: Farrar, Straus and Giroux, 2001), 263.

122 Fisher to Jellicoe, 26 and 28 December 1914, in *Jellicoe Papers*, 1:115–17.

123 Fisher to Jellicoe, 11 January 1915, in ibid, 1:122.

124 Asquith to Venetia Stanley, 23 October 1914, in Brock, *Asquith: Letters to Venetia*

Stanley, 282–3.

125 John Rushworth Jellicoe, *The Grand Fleet, 1914–1916: Its Creation, Development, and Work* (London: Cassell, 1919), 48–9.

126 Jellicoe to Fisher, 17 January 1915, in *FGDN*, 3:129–32.

127 Fisher to Churchill, 20 January 1915, in FISR 1/18; see also *FGDN*, 3:134–6.

128 Memo by Fisher, 20 January 1915, in FISR 1/18, 914; see also *FGDN*, 3:136–8.

129 Fisher to Jellicoe, 21 January 1915, in *Jellicoe Papers*, 1:127.

130 Churchill to Fisher, 20 January 1915, in *FGDN*, 3:138–40. See also Speech by Churchill, 27 November 1914, in Robert Rhodes James, ed, *Winston S Churchill: His Complete Speeches, 1897–1963* (New York: Chelsea House, 1974), 3:2342–8.

131 Churchill to Fisher, 19 January 1915, cited in *FGDN*, 3:134n.

132 I owe this appraisal to John Winton, *Jellicoe* (London: Michael Joseph, 1981), 154–5.

133 W S Churchill, *World Crisis*, 1:418–19.

134 Churchill, 'Business as Usual', in R R James, ed, *Churchill: His Complete Speeches*, 3:2340ff.

135 W S Churchill, *World Crisis*, 2:57; Lewis Bayly, *Pull Together! The Memoirs of Admiral Sir Lewis Bayly* (London: George G Harrap, 1939).

136 Churchill to Jellicoe, 11 January 1915, cited in M Gilbert, *Churchill 3: Challenge of War*, 185.

137 W S Churchill, *World Crisis*, 2:126.

138 Ibid, 2:127. Instructions are printed at ibid, 2:126; see also Stafford, *Churchill and Secret Service*, 68–70; Filson Young, *With the Battlecruisers* (1921; Annapolis, MD: Naval Institute Press, 1986), 174.

139 Gretton, *Former Naval Person*, 194.

140 Beatty to the Admiralty, 24 January 1915, in FISR 1/18, 922.

141 Churchill to French, 24 January 1915, cited in M Gilbert, *Churchill 3: Challenge of War*, 262.

142 Fisher to Beatty, 25 January 1915, in *FGDN*, 3:146. See also FISR 1/18.

143 Fisher to Beatty, 27 January 1915, in FISR 1/18. See also *FGDN*, 3:146–7.

144 Fisher to Asquith, 28 January 1915, in *FGDN*, 3:148.

145 Fisher to Jellicoe, 6 February 1915, in *Jellicoe Papers*, 1:141.

146 Fisher to Beatty, 31 January 1915, in FISR 1/18. Also *FGDN*, 3:150–1.

147 Beatty to Jellicoe, 8 February 1915, in *Jellicoe Papers*, 1:143–5.

148 Jellicoe to the Admiralty, 10 February 1915, in ibid, 1:145.

149 See Secretary of the Admiralty to Jellicoe, 7 March 1915, in ibid, 1:150 and note; and Gretton, *Former Naval Person*, 195.

150 Strachan, *First World War*, 438.

151 Fisher to Beatty, 6 February 1915, in W S Chalmers, *The Life and Letters of David, Earl Beatty* (London: Hodder and Stoughton, 1951), 198.

152 Fisher to Beatty, 8 and 12 February 1915, FISR 1/18, 939 and 942. See also *FGDN*, 3:155–6.

153 Jellicoe to Beatty, 7 February 1915, in *Jellicoe Papers*, 1:142–3.

154 Jellicoe to Churchill, 7 February 1915, in FISR 1/18, 936.

155 Beatty to Jellicoe, 8 February 1915, in *Jellicoe Papers*, 1:143–5.

156 Fisher to Jellicoe, [nd, but evidently early February 1915], in ibid, 1:141.

157 Gretton, *Former Naval Person*, 195.

158 Fisher to Jellicoe, 2 February 1914 and [nd, but early February 1915], in *Jellicoe Papers*, 1:132 and 141.

159 Memorandum, 'A Plea for Strengthening the Grand Fleet by the Battleships now at Portland', late March 1915, in FISR 1/18, 962.

160 Minute by Churchill, 27 March 1915, in FISR 1/18, 962.

161 Tyrwhitt to Keyes, nd [early March 1915], in *Keyes Papers*, 1:98–100.

162 Fisher to Jellicoe, 25 March 1915, in *Jellicoe Papers*, 1:153.

163 Fisher to Jellicoe, 9 April 1915, in ibid, 1:156.

164 Fisher to Jellicoe, 13 April 1915, in ibid, 1:156.

165 Jellicoe to Hamilton, 14 April 1915, in ibid, 1:157.

166 Stafford, *Churchill and Secret Service*, 71.

167 Naval Staff Monograph, *Home Waters, From February to July 1915*, 29; also *FDSF*, 2:344.

168 Quoted in Edward E Bradford, *Life of Admiral of the Fleet Sir Arthur Knyvet Wilson* (London: John Murray, 1923), 242.

169 For example, without the sinking of *Lusitania*, the US would never have entered the war; Imperial Germany would not have been defeated; and the Nazis therefore would never have come to power.

170 This is the proven argument of Robert Ballard. See his *Lusitania: Probing the Mysteries of the Sinking That Changed History* (Edson, NJ: Chartwell, 2007).

171 Diana Preston, *Wilful Murder: The Sinking of the Lusitania* (London: Doubleday, 2002), 436–44. For the cruise of *U-20* and consequences, see Thomas Bailey and Paul Ryan, *The Lusitania Disaster* (New York: Free Press, 1975). Bailey asked Marder if any evidence existed as to a conspiracy theory, and the answer was a clear no. Marder paid no attention to the disaster in his own great work. In doing so he negligently failed to point a finger at Churchill or Fisher, or both.

172 Esher Journal, 9 May 1915, in *Esher Journals and Letters*, 3:231–2; and Preston, *Wilful Murder*, 404.

173 David Ramsay, *Lusitania: Saga and Myth* (New York: Norton, 2002), 75, for the Gilbert and Sullivan reference.

174 Colin Simpson, *Lusitania* (London: Longman, 1972), 169. Simpson states that Fisher was responsible, but that is another conspiracy theory.

175 Information from David Ramsay, 17 August 2016.

176 Preston, *Wilful Murder*, 399–406; and Stafford, *Churchill and Secret Service*, 72–5.

177 Webb's memo is in Adm 137/1058; printed, in part, in Simpson, *Lusitania*, 177–8. On Webb's prejudicial report see Daniel Allen Butler, *The Lusitania: The Life, Loss, and Legacy of an Ocean Legend* (Mechanicsburg, PA: Stackpole, 2000), 206–11.

178 Preston, *Wilful Murder*, 314–16; and Stafford, *Churchill and Secret Service*, 72–5. See also respective documents in Adm 137/1058.

179 Mersey Papers, quoted in Simpson, *Lusitania*, 232.

180 David Ramsay, whose reliable book on the *Lusitania* disaster is the best to date, places the business within the context of the stream of events of the whole war.

181 Esher to [?], 26 April 1912, in *Esher Journals and Letters*, 3:89–92.

182 Marder, *Portrait of an Admiral*, 92.

183 W S Churchill, *World Crisis*, 1:93.
184 A J P Taylor, *Politics in Wartime* (New York: Atheneum, 1965), 21.
185 Roy Jenkins, *Asquith: Portrait of a Man and an Era* (New York: Dutton, 1964), 387. Also Gordon Craig, 'Political Leader as Strategist', in *Makers of Modern Strategy from Machiavelli to the Nuclear Age*, ed Peter Paret (Princeton, NJ: Princeton University Press, 1986), 485–7.
186 Cited in Stephen E Koss, *Asquith* (London: Allen Lane, 1976), 160.
187 M Gilbert, *Churchill 3: Challenge of War*, 226.
188 Hankey to Fisher, 21 January 1915, FISR 1/18.
189 Corbett, in *FDSF*, 2:420.
190 Bentley Brinkerhoff Gilbert, *David Lloyd George: A Political Life*, vol 2 (Columbus: Ohio State University Press, 1992), 200–2.
191 Asquith's comment as early as 12 August 1914 bears witness: 'Lord K[itchener] has rather demoralised the War Office with his bull in the china shop manners and methods, and particularly his ignorance of & indifference to the Territorials.' Asquith to Venetia Stanley, 12 August 1914, in Brock, *Asquith: Letters to Venetia Stanley*, 167–9.
192 Paul Guinn, *British Strategy and Politics: 1914 to 1918* (Oxford: Clarendon Press, 1965), 34.
193 Margot Asquith diary, 21 March 1915, and Asquith to Venetia Stanley, 24 March 1915, in M Gilbert, *Churchill 3: Challenge of War*, 361–2; and Jenkins, *Asquith*, 339–40.
194 Asquith to Venetia Stanley, 9 and 26 February 1915, in Brock, *Asquith: Letters to Venetia Stanley*, 421–3 and 449.
195 See Asquith to Venetia Stanley, 6 November 1914, in ibid, 311–12 and 312n5.
196 Kitchener to Churchill, 18 December 1914, not sent, cited in M Gilbert, *Churchill 3: Challenge of War*, 166.
197 Fisher to Jellicoe, 4 January 1915, in *FGDN*, 3:120.
198 Maurice Hankey, *The Supreme Command* (London: George Allen and Unwin, 1961), 1:255.
199 M Hankey, diary, 29 March 1915, HNKY 1/1, 18–19.

Chapter 9
1 Fisher to Churchill, 5 April 1915, in Winston S Churchill, *The World Crisis* (London: Thornton Butterworth, 1923–31), 2:303.
2 C F Aspinall-Oglander, *History of the Great War, Based on Official Documents. Military Operations: Gallipoli*, 2 vols (London: William Heinemann, 1929, 1932). Throughout I have relied on Tim Travers, *Gallipoli 1915* (Stroud: Tempus, 2002).
3 Trumbull Higgins, *Winston Churchill and the Dardanelles: A Dialogue in Ends and Means* (New York: Macmillan, 1963), 10.
4 Fisher to F Ponsonby, 16 August 1906, in *FGDN*, 2:85–6.
5 Higgins, *Winston Churchill and the Dardanelles*, 10.
6 Charles E Callwell, *The Dardanelles* (London: Constable, 1919), 2.
7 CHAR 13/27; also Martin Gilbert, ed, *Churchill Documents 6: At the Admiralty, July 1914–April 1915* (Hillsdale, MI: Hillsdale College Press, 2008), 81–2; Callwell, *Dardanelles*, ch 1.
8 Martin Gilbert, *Winston S Churchill 3: The Challenge of War, 1914–1916* (London: William Heinemann, 1971), 3:203.
9 Higgins, *Winston Churchill and the Dardanelles*, 14.
10 Christopher Bell, *Churchill and the Dardanelles* (Oxford: Clarendon, 2017), 7.
11 John Arbuthnot Fisher, *Memories* (London: Hodder and Stoughton, 1919), 50 and 52.
12 W S Churchill, *World Crisis*, 2:539
13 M Gilbert, *Churchill 3: Challenge of War*, 220–1.
14 Robert B Asprey, *The German High Command at War* (New York: Quill, 1991), 130–1.
15 Memorandum by Hankey, 28 December 1914, cited in Paul Guinn, *British Strategy and Politics: 1914 to 1918* (Oxford: Clarendon Press, 1965), 53–4. See also Maurice Hankey, *The Supreme Command* (London: George Allen and Unwin, 1961), 1:248–9.
16 Hankey, *Supreme Command*, 1:252; and W S Churchill, *World Crisis*, 2:44.
17 Asquith to Venetia Stanley, 30 December 1914, in Michael and Eleanor Brock, eds, *H H Asquith: Letters to Venetia Stanley*

(Oxford: Oxford University Press, 1982), 345–7. See also M Gilbert, *Churchill 3: Challenge of War*, 225–8.

18 M Gilbert, *Churchill 3: Challenge of War*, 228–9.

19 C R M F Cruttwell, *A History of the Great War, 1914–1918*, 2nd edn (Oxford: Oxford University Press, 1936), 206.

20 Kitchener to Lieutenant-General Sir John Maxwell, 24 February 1915, cited in Guinn, *British Strategy and Politics*, 48.

21 M Gilbert, *Churchill 3: Challenge of War*, 232–3.

22 Ibid, 234.

23 Roger Keyes, *Naval Memoirs of Admiral of the Fleet Sir Roger Keyes, vol 1, The Narrow Seas to the Dardanelles, 1910–1915* (London: Thornton Butterworth, 1934), 219–21.

24 Fisher to Churchill, 3 January 1915, *FGDN*, 3:117–18.

25 Fisher to Balfour, 4 January 1915, *FGDN*, 3:118–119.

26 Fisher to Churchill, 3 January 1915, in W S Churchill, *World Crisis*, 2:95–6, and *FGDN*, 3:117.

27 Lawrence's arguments for Alexandretta, and his post-war comments to Basil Liddell Hart, are in David Garnett, ed, *The Essential T E Lawrence* (Harmondsworth: Penguin, 1956), 73–5.

28 Churchill to Fisher, 4 January 1915, *FGDN*, 3:121.

29 M Gilbert, *Churchill 3: Challenge of War*, 236.

30 Fisher to Churchill, 4 January 1915, *FGDN*, 3:122.

31 Fisher to Churchill, 4 January 1915, in M Gilbert, *Churchill Documents 6: July 1914–April 1915*, 239; also *FGDN*, 3:124.

32 W S Churchill, *World Crisis*, 2:63.

33 Reginald Bacon, *The Life of Lord Fisher of Kilverstone: Admiral of the Fleet* (London: Hodder, 1929), 2:206.

34 M Gilbert, *Churchill 3: Challenge of War*, 237.

35 Ibid, 240–5.

36 George Allardice Riddell, *Lord Riddell's War Diary 1914–1918* (London: Ivor Nicholson and Watson, 1933), 53.

37 Bacon, *Life of Lord Fisher*, 2:207.

38 M Gilbert, *Churchill 3: Challenge of War*, 248–51; and W S Churchill, *World Crisis*, 2:109.

39 Esher Journal, 13 January 1915, in *Esher Journals and Letters*, 3:203–4.

40 Hankey to Balfour, 10 February 1915, Balfour MSS, Add MS 49703, British Library. See also Arthur J Marder, *From the Dardanelles to Oran: Studies of the Royal Navy in War and Peace 1915–1940* (1974; reprint Barnsley: Seaforth, 2015), 2.

41 Cited in M Gilbert, *Churchill 3: Challenge of War*, 252.

42 Churchill's minute, 14 January 1915, in W S Churchill, *World Crisis*, 2:112.

43 Churchill to Carden, 15 January 1915, in ibid, 2:111.

44 Riddell, *Lord Riddell's War Diary*, 47.

45 Jellicoe to Fisher, 17 and 18 January 1915, in *FGDN*, 3:129–32; see also W S Churchill, *World Crisis*, 2:150.

46 Fisher to Churchill, 18 January 1915, in *FGDN*, 3:132–3.

47 Cited in Cruttwell, *History of the Great War*, 209.

48 Fisher to Jellicoe, 19 January 1915, in M Gilbert, *Churchill Documents 6: July 1914–April 1915*, 259; see also *FGDN*, 3:133.

49 Minute by Churchill, 20 January 1915, in M Gilbert, *Churchill Documents 6: July 1914–April 1915*, 120.

50 H H Asquith, *Memories and Reflections, 1852–1927* (Boston, MA: Little, Brown, 1928), 2:67; and Hankey, *Supreme Command*, 1:269.

51 Fisher to Beatty, 20 January 1915, in FISR 1/18.

52 Fisher to Churchill, 20 January 1915, in *FGDN*, 3:140.

53 W S Churchill, *World Crisis*, 2:153–54.

54 Fisher to Jellicoe, 21 January 1915, in *FGDN*, 3:141–2.

55 Fisher to Jellicoe, 23 January 1915, in *FGDN*, 3:144–5.

56 'Lord Fisher Indisposed', *The Times*, 23 January 1915, 8; and 'The King and Lord Fisher', *The Times*, 26 January 1915, 8.

57 Fisher to Churchill, 25 January 1915, FISR 1/18.

58 Memo by Fisher, 26 January 1915, FISR 1/18. According to Hankey, who played a role in drafting this memorandum, little of it was actually written by Fisher himself. See Hankey, *Supreme Command*, 1:269.

59 Churchill to Fisher, 26 January 1915, FISR 1/18, 920.

60 Guinn, *British Strategy and Politics*, 57.
61 Churchill to Fisher, 26 January 1915, cited in M Gilbert, *Churchill 3: Challenge of War*, 265.
62 Hankey to Churchill, 26 January 1915, FISR 1/18.
63 Fisher to H H Asquith, 28 January 1915, FISR 1/18; see also *FGDN*, 3:147–8; and M Gilbert, *Churchill 3: Challenge of War*, 268–9.
64 Fisher to Churchill, 28 January 1915, in M Gilbert, *Churchill 3: Challenge of War*, 269.
65 Churchill to Fisher, 28 January 1915, in ibid, 270; see also *FGDN*, 3:149.
66 *FDSF*, 2:210.
67 See also Hankey's notes of the meeting, in which Kitchener, Balfour, and Grey, in addition to Churchill, expanded on the perceived advantages of an attack against the Dardanelles. Hankey, *Supreme Command*, 1:271.
68 Fisher, *Memories*, 80. Jeffrey Wallin, *By Ships Alone: Churchill and the Dardanelles* (Durham, NC: Carolina Academic Press, 1981), 93–4. Asquith held that in the decade of his experience on the Committee of Imperial Defence he had never known the technical (military and naval) experts to show any reluctance to make comments, whether invited or uninvited; this was the same view taken by his ministerial colleagues on the War Council.
69 Newspaper clipping, nd, FISR 1/18, 149. For the published version, see Fisher, *Memories*, 59n.
70 Asquith to Venetia Stanley, 28 January 1915, *Asquith: Letters to Venetia Stanley*, 405; also, H H Asquith, *Memories and Reflections*, 2:70.
71 H H Asquith, *Memories and Reflections*, 2:106–7.
72 Hankey, *Supreme Command*, 1:267.
73 Minutes of the 9th Meeting of the War Council, 28 January 1915, FISR 1/25, 1413.
74 Quoted in M Gilbert, *Churchill 3: Challenge of War*, 273.
75 Guinn, *British Strategy and Politics,* 57.
76 War Council Minutes, 28 January 1915, in ESHR 17/5; Guinn, *British Strategy and Politics*, 57.
77 Lloyd George to Fisher, 30 January 1915, FISR 1/18.
78 Esher Journal, 29 January 1915, in *Esher Journals and Letters*, 3:212.
79 H H Asquith, *Memories and Reflections*, 2:71.
80 Fisher to Jellicoe, 29 January 1915, in *FGDN*, 3:149–50.
81 Arthur J Marder, ed, *Portrait of an Admiral: The Life and Papers of Sir Herbert Richmond* (London: Jonathan Cape, 1952), 135–6.
82 Ibid, 140.
83 Ibid, 137–8.
84 W S Churchill, *World Crisis*, 1:439–40.
85 Mary Soames, *Clementine Churchill* (London: Cassell, 1979), 120. Also M Gilbert, *Churchill 3: Challenge of War*, 419; and Martin Gilbert, *In Search of Churchill: A Historian's Journey* (New York: HarperCollins, 1994), 264.
86 The first time I met Mary Soames, I gained in conversation the distinct impression of that suspicion of Fisher that is dominant in the Churchill strain and is pronounced in Churchill's own writings that deal with the Dardanelles debacle. My various addresses to the International Churchill Society on the Fisher–Churchill relationship, though central to modern history, tended always to be treated as curiosities, for Fisher was one of many 'great contemporaries' but a very dark and troublesome figure. To keep the record accurate and the memory green was Lady Mary Soames's abiding charge to ICS, and indeed beneficial to all who want to see Winston Churchill in all his guises and all his greatness and even his faults. About this same time I read in A J P Taylor's *English History* that he regarded Churchill as 'the saviour of his country', the highest and unassailable compliment (Taylor, *English History, 1914–1945* [Oxford: Clarendon, 1965], 4n1). That was in regards to the Second World War. The same could be said of Fisher in the First World War, for the Navy Jack built saved the British Empire.
87 William James, *The Eyes of the Navy: A Biographical Study of Admiral Sir Reginald Hall* (London: Methuen, 1955), 82.
88 Information from Len Barnett, 21 April 2015.
89 M Gilbert, *Churchill 3: Challenge of War*, 279.
90 War Council Minutes, 9 February 1915, in ESHR 17/5.
91 W S Churchill, *World Crisis*, 2:109.

92 Hankey to Balfour, 10 February 1915, cited in Paul G Halpern, *A Naval History of World War I* (Annapolis, MD: Naval Institute Press, 1994), 111.

93 Marder, *Portrait of an Admiral*, 142–5.

94 Fisher to Beatty, 26 February 1915, FISR 1/18, 947.

95 Esher Journal, 28 February 1915, in *Esher Journals and Letters*, 3:218.

96 Vice-Admiral A H Limpus to Rear-Admiral Sir Richard Fortescue Pillmore, 14 March 1915, FISR 1/18, 950.

97 M Gilbert, *Churchill 3: Challenge of War*, 314–16.

98 Ibid, 316.

99 Churchill to Kitchener, 4 March 1915, cited in ibid, 325.

100 Esher Journal, 12 August 1914, *Esher Journals and Letters*, 3:176.

101 Fisher to Churchill, 4 March 1915, cited in M Gilbert, *Churchill 3: Challenge of War*, 326, and W S Churchill, *World Crisis*, 2:301.

102 Fisher to Churchill, 15 March 1915, in M Gilbert, *Churchill 3: Challenge of War*, 346.

103 Churchill to Fisher, 15 March 1915, in ibid, 346

104 Halpern, *Naval History of World War I*, 112–13.

105 Churchill to Carden, 11 March 1915, cited in M Gilbert, *Churchill 3: Challenge of War*, 337; and Patrick Beesly, *Room 40: British Naval Intelligence, 1914–1918* (London: Hamish Hamilton, 1982), 82.

106 For details surrounding the change in command, see Keyes to Eva Keyes, 17 March 1915, in *Keyes Papers*, 1:108–10; and Halpern, *Naval History of World War I*, 114. By this point, Fisher did not much approve of Carden anyway: 'Who expected Carden to be in command of a big fleet? He was made Admiral Superintendent of Malta to shelve him!' Fisher to Jellicoe, 16 March 1915, *FGDN*, 3:165–6.

107 Guinn, *British Strategy and Politics*, 69.

108 From 'Lord Fisher's Notes of His Own Special Interventions at War Council Meetings', in Fisher, *Memories*, 83.

109 Fisher to Vice-Admiral de Robeck, 20 March 1915, in M Gilbert, *Churchill 3: Challenge of War*, 358.

110 Major-General Charles Callwell to Fisher, 20 March 1915, FISR 1/18, 953.

111 Churchill to First Sea Lord and Others, 22 March 1915, FISR 1/18, 955.

112 A K Wilson to Fisher, 22 March 1915, FISR 1/18, 954.

113 Limpus to Secretary of the Admiralty, Secret, 23 March 1915, FISR 1/18, 957.

114 A S Malta to Admiralty, 23 March 1915, FISR 1/18, 963.

115 Vice-Admiral de Robeck to Limpus, 26 March 1915, in Paul G Halpern, ed, 'De Robeck and the Dardanelles Campaign', in *The Naval Miscellany*, vol 5, ed N A M Rodger (London: Navy Records Society, 1974), 445.

116 De Robeck to Admiralty, 23 March 1915, FISR 1/18, 963, in M Gilbert, *Churchill 3: Challenge of War*, 364.

117 Fisher to Churchill, 24 March 1915, quoted in M Gilbert, *Churchill 3: Challenge of War*, 367; see also *FGDN*, 3:169.

118 Fisher to Churchill, 24 March 1915, quoted in M Gilbert, *Churchill 3: Challenge of War*, 367.

119 Churchill quote is in A J P Taylor, *The War Lords* (New York: Athenaeum, 1978), 76–7. Further references and discussion in Barry M Gough, *Historical Dreadnoughts: Arthur Marder, Stephen Roskill and Battles for Naval History* (Barnsley: Seaforth, 2010), 228–9.

120 Churchill at Dardanelles Commission, 28 September 1916, FISR 1/23, 1284. See also Halpern, *Naval History of World War I*, 115.

121 Fisher to Churchill, 26 March 1915, in M Gilbert, *Churchill 3: Challenge of War*, 375.

122 Fisher to Churchill, 29 March 1915, in ibid, 378.

123 W S Churchill, *World Crisis*, 2:298.

124 Fisher to Churchill, 5 April 1915, in ibid, 2:303.

125 Board of Admiralty to Fisher, 8 April 1915, FISR 1/19, 971; also *FGDN*, 3:188–90.

126 Fisher to Board of Admiralty, 8 April 1915, in FISR 1/19, 971; also *FGDN*, 3:190–1.

127 Churchill to Fisher, 8 April 1915, CHAR 13/57/3. This (from Churchill's own papers) does not survive in the Fisher Papers, perhaps indicating that Churchill never sent it. Information from Allen Packwood.

128 Fisher to Churchill, 2 April 1915, FISR 1/19, also *FGDN*, 3:183. This may also be followed in W S Churchill, *World Crisis*, 3:302–3.

129 Churchill to Fisher, 11 April 1915, cited in M Gilbert, *Churchill 3: Challenge of War*, 394.

130 Originals in FISR 1/19, 981–2.

131 In M Gilbert, *Churchill 3: Challenge of War*, 398–9.

132 Gwynne to Wilson, 12 April 1915, in Keith Wilson, ed, *The Rasp of War: The Letters of H A Gwynne to the Countess Bathurst, 1914–1918* (London: Sidgwick and Jackson, 1988), 78.

133 M Gilbert, *Churchill 3: Challenge of War*, 410.

134 Churchill to Fisher, 3 May 1915, cited in ibid, 411–12.

135 Vice-Admiral, Eastern Mediterranean, to Admiralty, 10 May 1915, FISR 1/19, 989.

136 Memorandum by Fisher to Churchill, 11 May 1915, secret, FISR 1/19, 990; also *FGDN*, 3:215–18; W S Churchill, *World Crisis*, 2:343. This memorandum was also forwarded to Asquith on 12 May 1915. See H H Asquith, *Memories and Reflections*, 2:108.

137 Churchill to Fisher, 11 May 1915, FISR 1/19, 991; also *FGDN*, 3:218–19; M Gilbert, *Churchill 3: Challenge of War*, 421.

138 M Gilbert, *Churchill 3: Challenge of War*, 420.

139 Hankey diary, quoted in ibid, 421.

140 Fisher to Churchill, 12 May 1915, in ibid, 421–2.

141 Fisher had been long concerned about the arrival of enemy submarines at the Dardanelles: 'I have only one anxiety; the German and Austrian submarines – *when they appear the game will be up!*' Fisher to Churchill, 20 March 1915, in *FGDN*, 3:163; and W S Churchill, *World Crisis*, 2:302.

142 For the sinking of the *Goliath*, see Halpern, *Naval History of World War I*, 117.

143 Guinn, *British Strategy and Politics*, 75; and M Gilbert, *Churchill 3: Challenge of War*, 422–3.

144 Churchill in the House of Commons, 13 May 1915, in Robert Rhodes James, ed, *Winston S Churchill: His Complete Speeches, 1897–1963* (New York: Chelsea

House, 1974), 3:2377.

145 Cited in M Gilbert, *Churchill 3: Challenge of War*, 426.

146 Fisher to Asquith, 13 May 1915, in *FGDN*, 3:220–1.

147 M Gilbert, *Churchill 3: Challenge of War*, 423.

Chapter 10

1 R J Q Adams, *Bonar Law* (London: John Murray, 1999), 176–9; and Martin D Pugh, 'Asquith, Bonar Law, and the First Coalition', *Historical Journal*, 17, no. 4 (1974), 821–4.

2 Stephen E Koss, *Asquith* (London: Allen Lane, 1976), 183; and Asquith to Venetia Stanley, 6 February 1915, in Michael and Eleanor Brock, eds, *H H Asquith: Letters to Venetia Stanley* (Oxford: Oxford University Press, 1982), 421–3.

3 Britain was not the only major combatant to suffer from a munitions shortage. All of the major powers had a shortage of shells in 1914 and 1915, as the war proved to be much longer than had been expected. See Hew Strachan, *The First World War*, vol 1 (Oxford: Oxford University Press, 2001), 993–1005.

4 Koss, *Asquith*, 181.

5 For a discussion of relations between Kitchener and Sir John French, see Reginald Viscount Esher, *The Tragedy of Lord Kitchener* (London: John Murray, 1921), 110–31.

6 This visit was admitted by Asquith in the House of Commons on 12 May.

7 Roy Jenkins, *Churchill: A Biography* (New York: Farrar, Straus and Giroux, 2001), 269.

8 Stephen E Koss, 'The Destruction of Britain's Last Liberal Government', *Journal of Modern History*, 40, no. 2 (June 1968), 257–77, and, also by Koss, *Lord Haldane: Scapegoat for Liberalism* (New York: Columbia University Press, 1969), 184–218; and *Asquith*, 180–97. The latter, more recent, work contains a new version of his theory revised in light of criticisms of the original.

9 See, for example, Northcliffe's comment to an associate in December 1915: 'I wish you would not start "booming" Churchill again. Why do you do it? We got rid of the man with difficulty and he is trying to come

back. "Puffing" will bring him back.' See Reginald Pound and Geoffrey Harmsworth, *Northcliffe* (London: Cassell, 1959), 491.

10 See Bentley Brinkerhoff Gilbert, *David Lloyd George: A Political Life*, vol 2 (Columbus: Ohio State University Press, 1992), 194 and 199.

11 Alan Moorehead, *Gallipoli* (London: Hamish Hamilton, 1956), 141.

12 Martin Gilbert, *Winston S Churchill 3: The Challenge of War, 1914–1916* (London: William Heinemann, 1971), 431–3; John Arbuthnot Fisher, *Memories* (London: Hodder and Stoughton, 1919), 83; Geoffrey Penn, *Fisher, Churchill, and the Dardanelles* (Barnsley: Leo Cooper, 1999), 175–7.

13 M Hankey, diary, 14 May 1915, HNKY 1/1.

14 Edward E Bradford, *Life of Admiral of the Fleet Sir Arthur Knyvet Wilson* (London: John Murray, 1923), 243.

15 *Précis of Lord Fisher's Case*, September 1916, printed, copy, FISR 1/19, 968. The original Fisher sent to Churchill, 2 April 1915. See Catalogue of the Fisher Papers, Churchill Archives Centre, 324.

16 Churchill to Asquith, 14 May 1915, in Winston S Churchill, *The World Crisis* (London: Thornton Butterworth, 1923–31), 2:353–4. The crisis may also be followed in various documents in Martin Gilbert, ed, *Churchill Documents 6: At the Admiralty, July 1914–April 1915* (Hillsdale, MI: Hillsdale College Press, 2008), 884–903.

17 Fisher, *Memories*, 83; William Manchester, *The Last Lion: Visions of Glory, 1874–1932* (Boston: Little, Brown, 1983), 1:554. For the pertinent memorandum, see Churchill to Fisher, 14 May 1915, and encl, in *FGDN*, 3:222–6. Note that the key recommendation regarding the two additional submarines was not included by Churchill in his reprint of the memoranda in his war history. See W S Churchill, *World Crisis*, 2:354–6.

18 For resignation letter, see Fisher to Churchill [copy to Asquith], 15 May 1915, in *FGDN*, 3:228. Also Fisher to Captain Crease, 19 February 1917, in *FGDN*. 3:433.

19 Memo by Fisher, 15 May 1915, FISR 1/19,

1003.

20 Fisher to Churchill, 15 May 1915, Churchill papers, 13/57; also FISR 1/19, 1004, and printed FGDN, 3:228.

21 M Hankey, diary, 15 May 1915, HNKY 1/1.

22 Manchester, *The Last Lion*, 1:554.

23 Fisher to Churchill, [May 16, 1915], in *FGDN*, 3:230–1. See also Fisher to Churchill, 15 May 1915, FISR 1/19, 1004.

24 Fisher to Asquith, 15 May 1915, FISR 1/19, 1005; see also, H H Asquith, *The Earl of Oxford and Asquith: Memories and Reflections, 1852–1927* (Boston: Little, Brown, 1928), 2:109.

25 Asquith to Fisher, 15 May 1915, Cab 1/33. The letter was entrusted to Churchill's private secretary, James Masterton-Smith. See H H Asquith, *Memories and Reflections*, 2:109.

26 Jenkins, *Churchill*, 271.

27 Esher Journal, 15 May 1915, in *Esher Journals and Letters*, 3:235.

28 Leslie Gardiner, *The British Admiralty* (Edinburgh: William Blackwood, 1968), 332.

29 M Gilbert to author, 7 February 1999. As Fisher's letters indicate, Balcombe Place was a frequent location for him in later years, as were 36 Berkeley Square and 19 St James's Square, Ferne, near Salisbury, Hamilton Palace in Lanarkshire, and other properties of the Hamilton Trust, of which Fisher became a trustee after his departure from the Admiralty. Balcombe Place was also connected to Lady Denman and later to the Women's Institute and the Women's Army. It is now a wedding venue and care home.

30 Asquith was attending the wedding of Geoffrey Howard, a Liberal Whip.

31 Cited in M Gilbert, *Churchill 3: Challenge of War*, 438–9.

32 David Lloyd George, *War Memoirs*, new edn (London: Odhams, 1938), 134–5.

33 Ibid, 135.

34 Reginald McKenna to Fisher, 16 May 1915, in *FGDN*, 3:232. It seems from this letter that McKenna knew where Fisher was holed up.

35 Bradford, *Life of Admiral of the Fleet*, 243–4.

36 A K Wilson to Fisher, 16 May 1915, FISR 1/19, 1009.

37 Letter from Sea Lords to Asquith, 19 May

1915, in H H Asquith, *Memories and Reflections*, 2:110. See also Sea Lords' letter, 16 May 1915, FISR 1/19, 1007 and in *FGDN*, 3:234–5.

38 Fisher to the Sea Lords, 16 May 1915, in FISR 1/19, 1007 and *FGDN*, 3:234–5.

39 Fisher to Captain Crease, 17 May 1915, in *FGDN*, 3:239.

40 Esher Journal, 16 May 1915, in *Esher Journals and Letters*, 3:236.

41 Esher to Fisher, 16 May 1915, FISR 1/19, 1008

42 W S Churchill, *World Crisis*, 2:364.

43 Churchill to Fisher, 16 May 1917, FISR 1/19, 1011; *FGDN*, 3:233–4.

44 Fisher to Churchill, 16 May 1915, FISR 1/19, 1012.

45 Crease to Jellicoe, 17 May 1915, in *Jellicoe Papers*, 2:161.

46 According to Marder, Churchill received no sanction from Asquith or anyone else to make such a proposal. See *FGDN*, 3:238n.

47 Fisher to Bonar Law, 17 May 1915, in *FGDN*, 3:237–8. Gilbert dates this exchange and the offer that caused it as occurring on 19 May. See M Gilbert, *Churchill 3: Challenge of War*, 456.

48 Fisher to McKenna, 16 May 1915, *FGDN*, 3:232.

49 See the *Oxford Dictionary of National Biography* entry on him by A C Howe.

50 Adams, *Bonar Law*, 181–4. Koss has also argued that Balfour was making an attempt to reassert himself as leader, and that Bonar Law pushed for a coalition to keep the leadership for himself. See Koss, 'The Destruction of Britain's Last Liberal Government', 268–70.

51 Adams, *Bonar Law*, 184–5; B B Gilbert, *David Lloyd George*, 194–5; and Pugh, 'Asquith, Bonar Law, and the First Coalition', 826–7.

52 Pugh, 'Asquith, Bonar Law, and the First Coalition', 827–8.

53 From Asquith's letter to Venetia, quoted in Martin Gilbert, *In Search of Churchill: A Historian's Journey* (New York: HarperCollins, 1994), 63.

54 Manchester, *The Last Lion*, 1:557; Jenkins, *Asquith*, 359–66.

55 Pugh, 'Asquith, Bonar Law, and the First Coalition', 830.

56 Asquith may have shared this desire, but it

was thwarted by a massive public showing of support for Kitchener after Northcliffe's *Daily Mail* denounced him on 21 May. See Koss, 'The Destruction of Britain's Last Liberal Government', 270–1.

57 Asquith to Lloyd George, 28 May 1915, cited in Pugh, 'Asquith, Bonar Law, and the First Coalition', 832.

58 Pugh, 'Asquith, Bonar Law, and the First Coalition'.

59 See, for example, W M R Pringle to Asquith, 20 May 1915, cited in M Gilbert, *Churchill 3: Challenge of War*, 460.

60 C F Aspinall-Oglander, *Roger Keyes, Being the Biography of Admiral of the Fleet Lord Keyes of Zeebrugge and Dover* (London: Hogarth Press, 1951), 165.

61 B B Gilbert, *David Lloyd George*, 194.

62 Burton Kendrick, *Life and Letters of Walter H Page* (New York: Doubleday, Page, 1926), 2:101–2.

63 W S Churchill, *World Crisis*, 2:366.

64 Churchill to Asquith, 17 May 1915, in ibid, 2:369.

65 Cited in M Gilbert, *Churchill 3: Challenge of War*, 451.

66 Asquith to Fisher, 17 May 1915, FISR 1/19, 1017, and *FGDN*, 3:239.

67 Fisher to Captain Crease, 18 May 1915, in *FGDN*, 3:240. See also Fisher to Mrs Reginald McKenna, 29 May 1915, in *FGDN*, 3:250.

68 Esher Journal, 17 May 1915, in *Esher Journals and Letters*, 3:236–8.

69 'Lord Fisher and the Admiralty', *The Times*, 18 May 1915, 9.

70 M Gilbert, *Churchill 3: Challenge of War*, 452.

71 Admiral of the Fleet Lord John Hay to Fisher, 19 May 1915, FISR 1/19 [?].

72 Admiral Sir Alexander Bethell to Fisher, 18 May 1915, FISR 1/19, 1020.

73 Esher Journal, 19 May 1915, in *Esher Journals and Letters*, 3:240.

74 Esher to Fisher, 16 May 1915, FISR 1/19, 1008.

75 Esher to Fisher, 20 May 1915, FISR 1/19, 1025. See also Ruddock F Mackay, *Fisher of Kilverstone* (Oxford: Clarendon Press, 1973), 501n.

76 Fisher to Jellicoe, 31 May 1916, in *Jellicoe Papers*, 2:165.

77 For this memorandum, see FISR 1/19, 1021; *FGDN*, 3:241–3; and H H Asquith,

Memories and Reflections, 111–13.

78 H H Asquith, Memories and Reflections, 113.

79 M Gilbert, Churchill 3: Challenge of War, 466–7.

80 Philip Magnus, Kitchener: Portrait of an Imperialist (London: John Murray, 1958), 340.

81 Keyes to Eva Keyes, 7 December 1914, in Keyes Papers, 1:55–6.

82 William James, The Eyes of the Navy: A Biographical Study of Admiral Sir Reginald Hall (London: Methuen, 1955), 83–5; David Stafford, Churchill and Secret Service (New York: Overlook Press, 1998), 82; and Patrick Beesly, Room 40: British Naval Intelligence, 1914–1918 (London: Hamish Hamilton, 1982), 136–7.

83 M Gilbert, Churchill 3: Challenge of War, 455–6.

84 Bonar Law to Fisher, two letters dated 20 May 1915, FISR 1/19, 1026 and 1027.

85 Jellicoe to Fisher, 20 May 1915, FISR 1/19, 1028; in FGDN, 3:243–4.

86 Nicholas Lambert, 'Admiral Sir Arthur Knyvet-Wilson, VC', in The First Sea Lords, ed Malcolm H Murfett (Westport, CT: Praeger, 1995), 49.

87 Churchill to Asquith, 20 May 1915, cited in M Gilbert, Churchill 3: Challenge of War, 458.

88 Clementine Churchill to Asquith, 20 May 1915, in Mary Soames, Clementine Churchill (London: Cassell, 1979), 123. See also M Gilbert, Churchill 3: Challenge of War, 459.

89 Cited in M Gilbert, In Search of Churchill, 64. Also [Harold Begbie], The Mirrors of Downing Street: Some Political Reflections by a Gentleman with a Duster (New York: G P Putnam, 1921), 37.

90 Sir George Riddell, diary, 20 May 1915, cited in B B Gilbert, David Lloyd George, 197. For a somewhat shorter but no less weakened version see George Allardice Riddell, Lord Riddell's War Diary 1914–1918 (London: Ivor Nicholson and Watson, 1933), 89–90.

91 M Gilbert, Churchill 3: Challenge of War, 461–5.

92 Soames, Clementine Churchill, 122.

93 'A Significant Meeting', The Times, 21 May 1915, 9–10.

94 Beatty to his wife, 21 May 1915, Beatty Papers, 1:273–4.

95 Fisher to Jellicoe, 22 May 1915, in FGDN, 3:245.

96 Maurice Hankey, The Supreme Command (London: George Allen and Unwin, 1961), 1:317–18; and Hankey to Fisher, 23 May 1915, in FGDN, 3:248.

97 Asquith to Fisher, 22 May 1915 [Postmark: 7.45pm], in FGDN, 3:247. This was the first communication Fisher had received from Asquith since 17 May.

98 L P Hartley, ed, Lady Cynthia Asquith Diaries, 1915–18 (London: Century, 1968), 31.

99 Ibid, 31–2.

100 Douglas Brownrigg, Indiscretions of the Naval Censor (London: Cassell, 1920), 35–6.

101 Soames, Clementine Churchill, 124–5.

102 Christopher Hassall, Edward Marsh, Patron of the Arts: A Biography (London: Longmans, 1959), 340.

103 Richard Hough, Former Naval Person: Churchill and the Wars at Sea (London: Weidenfeld and Nicolson, 1985), 119. One of these people was William Blunt.

104 Cited in Lucy Masterman, C F G Masterman (London: Nicholson and Watson, 1939), 289.

105 Fisher to Mrs McKenna, 29 May 1915, in FGDN, 3:250.

106 Tyrwhitt to Keyes, nd [early June 1915], in Keyes Papers, 1:14447. Tyrwhitt's views had changed somewhat from the month before, when he claimed that both Fisher and Churchill were 'dangerous people'. See ibid, 145n.

107 Peter Padfield, Aim Straight: A Biography of Sir Percy Scott, the Father of Modern Naval Gunnery (London: Hodder and Stoughton, 1966), ix.

108 James Masterton-Smith to Fisher, 30 October 1919, in FGDN, 3:597–8.

109 A G Gardiner, The War Lords (London: J M Dent, 1915), 318–19.

110 Lord Wester Wemyss, The Navy in the Dardanelles Campaign (London: Hodder and Stoughton, 1924), 124.

111 Ibid, 136.

112 Hough, Former Naval Person, 117.

113 Cited in Lord Moran, Churchill: Taken from the Diaries of Lord Moran; The Struggle for Survival, 1940–1965 (Boston: Houghton Mifflin, 1966), 349.

114 Cited in M Gilbert, *In Search of Churchill*, 292.

115 A J P Taylor, *Beaverbrook* (New York: Simon and Schuster, 1972), 95.

116 The papers eventually went to St Andrew's University where another historian, Ruddock Mackay, catalogued them prior to writing his biography of Fisher. Then they went to the Churchill Archives Centre, Churchill College, Cambridge, where they are part of the great treasures of that repository. Intriguingly, most of Churchill's papers are there too, in almost adjacent shelves. That the great literary fragments of these two intertwining lives should be in such proximity long after the deaths of these titans of the Admiralty is a subject for wonder and congratulations to naval historian Stephen Roskill (and others) and to the successive Keepers and Archivists and the Master and Fellows of Churchill College, the National Memorial to Churchill.

117 M Gilbert, *In Search of Churchill*, 19–22.

118 Reginald Bacon, *The Life of Lord Fisher of Kilverstone: Admiral of the Fleet* (London: Hodder, 1929), 2:285.

119 Fisher to Bonar Law, 17 May 1915, in *FGDN*, 3:237.

120 A J P Taylor, 'Big-Gun Man', *Observer*, 26 April 1959.

121 Soames, *Clementine Churchill*, 126.

122 Cited in Manchester, *The Last Lion*, 1:564–5.

123 Winston S Churchill, *Thoughts and Adventures: Churchill Reflects on Spies, Cartoons, Flying, and the Future*, ed James W Muller with Paul Courtenay and Alana Barton (Wilmington, DE: ICI Books, 2009), 307.

124 Churchill to Asquith, 6 July 1915, in M Gilbert, *Churchill 3: Challenge of War*, 506.

125 M Gilbert, *Churchill 3: Challenge of War*, 507.

126 M Gilbert, ed, *Churchill Documents 7: 'The Escaped Scapegoat', May 1915–December 1916* (Hillsdale, MI: Hillsdale College Press, 2008), 1072. See also Penn, *Fisher, Churchill and the Dardanelles*, 205.

127 Fisher to Mrs Reginald McKenna, 12 July 1915, in *FGDN*, 3:278.

128 Keyes to his wife, 17 July 1915, in *Keyes Papers*, 1:161–3.

129 W R Hall to Keyes, 18 July 1915, in ibid, 1:163–4.

130 Communication from Dr John Mather, 9 November 2016.

131 Quoted in David Owen, *In Sickness and in Power: Illness in Heads of Government during the Last 100 Years* (London: Methuen, 2008), 40–1, who notes that Churchill still got depressed in later years, and quotes authorities on this (ibid, 41–2).

132 M Gilbert, *In Search of Churchill*, 209.

133 Lord Beaverbrook, *Politicians and the War, 1914–1916* (London: Thornton Butterworth, 1928), 124.

134 Stafford, *Churchill and Secret Service*, 78–9.

135 On this, see *Keyes Papers*, 1:163; also, M Gilbert, *Churchill 3: Challenge of War*, 510–14.

136 Taylor, *Beaverbrook*, 97.

137 Beaverbrook, *Politicians and the War*, 160.

138 C F Aspinall-Oglander, *History of the Great War, Based on Official Documents. Military Operations: Gallipoli* (London: William Heinemann, 1929–32), 2:131–2.

139 W S Churchill, *World Crisis*, 2:489.

140 Beaverbrook, *Politicians and the War*, 168.

141 Fisher to Sir Hedley Francis Le Bas, 10 January 1916, in Le Bas Papers, scrapbook in 'Articles Donated by Archives Centre Readers' at the Churchill Archives Centre, Cambridge.

142 Churchill to Eva Keyes, 14 December 1915, in *Keyes Papers*, 1:283.

143 Keyes to his wife, 31 December 1915, in ibid, 1:300–3.

144 Speech by Admiral of the Fleet Sir Roger Keyes speech 7 May 1940, cited in Martin Gilbert, ed, *The Churchill War Papers*, vol 1, *Churchill at the Admiralty September 1939–May 1940* (New York and London: W W Norton, 1993), 1214.

145 W S Churchill, *World Crisis*, 2:169.

146 Kendrick, *Life and Letters of Walter H Page*, 2:101–2, 141.

147 Jonathan Haynes, 'Gallipoli and the Role of Intelligence', *Naval Institute Proceedings* 121 (June 1995), 76.

148 Captain W D Puleston, *The Dardanelles Expedition: A Condensed Study*, 2nd edn (1926; Annapolis, MD: Naval Institute Press, 1927), 168.

149 Paul Addison, *Winston Churchill* (Oxford: Oxford University Press, 2007), 36.

150 Soames, *Clementine Churchill*, 122.
151 Beaverbrook, *Politicians and the War*, 174.
152 Wester Wemyss, *Navy in the Dardanelles Campaign*, 9.
153 Charles Callwell to D A Buxton, 25 July 1920, author's collection.

Chapter 11

1 Lord Beaverbrook, *Politicians and the War, 1914–1916* (London: Thornton Butterworth, 1928), 174.
2 At the same time, the Russian attaché in London was urging the Chief of the Naval Staff, Rear-Admiral Henry Oliver, to take action in the Baltic. In his unsatisfactory answer, Oliver 'pointed out the difficulties of operations in the Baltic, mentioned as an example the failure of the Dardanelles enterprise, and declared that if the British Fleet attempted to enter the Baltic, the immediate consequence would be the occupation of the Danish Islands by Germany, which would soon cut off the Fleet from its bases.' Just as Fisher's and Churchill's schemes for a war in the Baltic had come to naught so did the Russians appeal in vain. None of Fisher's shallow-draught *Courageous*-class battlecruisers, which would be used for such an attempt, could be ready until 1917. The Grand Fleet continued in a virtually inactive state, commanded by an increasingly pessimistic commander. I owe this to the highly original findings of Philip K Lundeberg, 'Undersea Warfare and Allied Strategy in World War I, Part 2, 1916–1918', *Smithsonian Journal of History*, 1, no. 4 (Winter 1966), 52–4. See also Maurice Hankey, *The Supreme Command* (London: George Allen and Unwin, 1961), 1:433.
3 Churchill to Jack Churchill, 26 August 1914, cited in Martin Gilbert, *Winston S Churchill 3: The Challenge of War, 1914–1916* (London: William Heinemann, 1971), 58.
4 Speech in House of Commons, 15 November 1915, in Robert Rhodes James, ed, *Winston S Churchill: His Complete Speeches, 1897–1963* (New York: Chelsea House, 1974), 3:2390–2403. On 4 November 1915, when Churchill dined with Sir Roger Keyes, they talked of Jacky and his return to the Admiralty in 1914 at Churchill's insistence. Keyes told Churchill

categorically, 'Well, you nursed a viper when you took him back.' Churchill's response to Keyes's doubts was that he would do so again. From Keyes's diary entry for 4 November 1915, in *Keyes Papers*, 1:228–9.
5 Speech, House of Lords, 16 November 1915, in John Arbuthnot Fisher, *Records* (London: Hodder and Stoughton, 1919), 86. The journalist's reaction is in *FGDN*, 3:272–3. Three months later Churchill retracted these charges. See *FGDN*, 3:332.
6 William Manchester, *The Last Lion: Visions of Glory, 1874–1932* (Boston: Little, Brown, 1983), 573.
7 Quoted in Anne Sebba, *Jennie Churchill: Winston's American Mother* (London: John Murray, 2007), 303. See also Celia and John Lee, *Winston and Jack: The Churchill Brothers* (London: Authors, 2007), 286.
8 Churchill's 'Sir John French', probably written at the subject's death, appeared in print later; it was reprinted in Winston S Churchill, *Great Contemporaries: Churchill Reflects on FDR, Hitler, Kipling, Chaplin, Balfour, and Other Giants of His Age*, ed James W Muller with Paul H Courtenay and Erica L Chenoweth (Wilmington, DE: ISI Books, 2012), 79–92 (and see notes, 437–44); Churchill quote at 91.
9 Major-General Edward Spears in his diary, 27 December 1915, cited in M Gilbert, *Churchill 3: Challenge of War*, 622.
10 Fisher to Balfour, 18 June 1915, in *FGDN*, 3:262. On Balfour, see Robert K Massie, *Dreadnought: Britain, Germany, and the Coming of the Great War* (New York: Random House, 1991), ch 18.
11 Balfour to Fisher, 21 June 1915, in *FGDN*, 3:262–3.
12 Willem Hackmann, *Seek and Strike: Sonar, Anti-Submarine Warfare, and the Royal Navy, 1914–1954* (London: HMSO Books, 1984), 15. See also John Rushworth Jellicoe, *The Crisis of the Naval War* (London: Cassell, 1920), 10–11, which describes material attempts to deal with the U-boat menace. This is now out of date. See also John Terraine, *Business in Great Waters: The U-Boat Wars, 1916–1945* (London: Leo Cooper, 1989). On naval intelligence and unrestricted submarine

warfare and countermeasures, see Patrick Beesly, *Room 40: British Naval Intelligence, 1914–1918* (London: Hamish Hamilton, 1982), ch 15.

13 Among other studies, see David A H Wilson, 'Avian Anti-Submarine Warfare Proposals in Britain, 1915–1918: The Admiralty and Thomas Mills', *International Journal of Naval History*, 5, no. 1 (April 2006), 1–25.

14 These themes are thoroughly explored in Jack K Gusewelle, 'Science and the Admiralty during World War I: The Case of the BIR', in *Naval Warfare in the Twentieth Century*, ed Gerald Jordan (London: Croom Helm, 1977), 105–17.

15 Hackmann, *Seek and Strike*, 13–14.

16 Ibid, 16.

17 Balfour to Fisher, 26 June 1915, in *FGDN*, 264.

18 Fisher to Balfour, 28 June 1915, in *FGDN*, 264.

19 Hackmann, *Seek and Strike*, 18.

20 Fisher to Balfour [?], 5 July 1915, in *FGDN*, 276–7.

21 Fisher to Balfour, 7 July 1915, in *FGDN*, 277–8.

22 Fisher, *Records*, 65–6. Balfour's description of BIR goals, 10 July 1915, is in Adm 116/1430.

23 Beatty to Wemyss, 10 August 1918, in *Beatty Papers*, 1:535–6, discloses Beatty's support for Ryan and his experimental directional hydrophone Porpoise.

24 Bragg took up this appointment in April 1916.

25 Cited in Hackmann, *Seek and Strike*, 25–6.

26 Fisher to Jellicoe, 30 April 1916, in *FGDN*, 3:345–6.

27 Grindell Matthews has been acclaimed as the inventor of the mobile phone, the world's first talking picture (an interview with Ernest Shackleton in 1921, before he left for Antarctica), a 'death ray' for shooting down aircraft, and others. The Admiralty paid him £25,000 for the patent for this selenium cell, demonstrated in Richmond Park's Penn Pond in 1911.

28 Report of the Captain, HMS *Dolphin*, 26 August 1916, FISR 1/23, 1265.

29 Jellicoe to Fisher, 18 September 1916, in *FGDN*, 3:372.

30 Hackmann, *Seek and Strike*, 17.

31 Fisher to C P Scott, 31 March 1916, in *FGDN*, 336.

32 Fisher to Asquith, 16 and 28 October 1915, in *FGDN*, 3:281.

33 Jellicoe to Vice-Admiral Sir Frederick Hamilton, 9 November 1915, in *Jellicoe Papers*, 2:186–7.

34 Fisher to Hankey, 7 January 1916, in Martin Gilbert, ed, *Churchill Documents 7: 'The Escaped Scapegoat', May 1915–December 1916* (Hillsdale, MI: Hillsdale College Press, 2008), 700.

35 Fisher to Hankey, 26 January 1916, in ibid.

36 Hankey to Fisher, 27 January 1916, in FISR 1/18.

37 Fisher to John Leyland, 2 January 1916, cited in *FGDN*, 3:273.

38 Fisher to Lloyd George, early January 1916, in *FGDN*, 3:286–7.

39 Fisher to Bonar Law, 7 January 1916, in *FGDN*, 3:288–90.

40 William James, 'Churchill and the Navy,' in *Churchill, By His Contemporaries*, ed Charles Eade (London: Hutchinson, 1953), 147.

41 Ibid.

42 Hankey, *Supreme Command*, 2:488.

43 Fisher to Tirpitz, 29 March 1916. Unknown newspaper printing of this letter; reprinted first in John Arbuthnot Fisher, *Memories* (London: Hodder and Stoughton, 1919), 31. For a comparison of these two, see Paul Kennedy, 'Fisher and Tirpitz: Political Admirals in the Age of Imperialism', in Jordan, *Naval Warfare in the Twentieth Century*, 45–59. See also *FGDN*, 3:334.

44 Hankey, *Supreme Command*, 2:488–9.

45 Jellicoe to Fisher, 18 and 20 January 1916, in *FGDN*, 3:290–1.

46 M Gilbert, *Churchill 3: Challenge of War*, 708.

47 C P Scott, diary, undated (between 29 February and 3 March 1916), in Trevor Wilson, ed, *The Political Diaries of C P Scott, 1911–1928* (London: Collins, 1970), 186.

48 C P Scott, diary, 6–8 March 1916, in ibid, 186–7.

49 M Gilbert, *Churchill 3: Challenge of War*, 709.

50 Fisher to Churchill, 6 March 1916, in ibid, 710–11.

51 Quoted in ibid, 713.

52 Stephen W Roskill, *Hankey, Man of Secrets* (London: Collins, 1970–74), 1:254. See

Parliamentary Debates, Commons, 5th series, 7 March 1916, vol 80, cols 1401–20 for Balfour's speech and col 1420 for Churchill's.

53 Hankey, *Supreme Command*, 2:490.

54 M Hankey, diary, 7 March 1916, in Martin Gilbert, ed, *Churchill Documents 8: War and Aftermath, December 1916–June 1919* (Hillsdale, MI: Hillsdale College, 2008), 1442.

55 M Gilbert, *Churchill 3: Challenge of War*, 729.

56 Violet Bonham Carter, *Winston Churchill as I Knew Him* (London: Eyre and Spottiswoode and Collins, 1965), 448.

57 Ibid, 449.

58 Fisher to Jellicoe, 9 March 1916, in *FGDN*, 3:321.

59 Fisher to Hankey, 11 May 1916, in Roskill, *Hankey*, 1:255.

60 Speech by Balfour, 8 March 1916, in M Gilbert, *Churchill 3: Challenge of War*, 726–8. Report on naval debates, March 1916, *Annual Register*, 1916, 81.

61 Speech by Churchill, 8 March 1916, in M Gilbert, *Churchill 3: Challenge of War*, 728.

62 *Parliamentary Debates*, Commons, 5th series, vol 80, cols 1586–91.

63 Rosebery to Fisher, 30 March 1916, in *FGDN*, 3:335–6.

64 Keyes to his wife, 14 March 1916, in *Keyes Papers*, 1:343–4.

65 Fisher to T E Crease, 7 March 1916, in *FGDN*, 3:320.

66 In M Gilbert, *Churchill Documents 7: May 1915–December 1916*, 1445.

67 Cited in Ruddock F Mackay, *Fisher of Kilverstone* (Oxford: Clarendon Press, 1973), 511. See also J L Hammond, *C P Scott of the Manchester Guardian*, rev edn (London: Bell, 1934), 195–6.

68 *FGDN*, 3:273.

69 Fisher to Scott, 9 March 1916, in M Gilbert, *Churchill 3: Challenge of War*, 732–3.

70 Fisher to Churchill, 11 March 1916, in M Gilbert, *Churchill 3: Challenge of War*, 734.

71 Fisher to Lloyd George, 15 March 1916, in CHAR 2/92, 62.

72 The letters are mentioned in Fisher to Archibald S Hurd, 29 March 1916; Rosebery to Fisher, 30 March 1916; and

Fisher to C P Scott, 31 March 1916, in *FGDN*, 3:334–6.

73 Fisher to C P Scott, 27 March 1916, cited in *FGDN*, 3:274.

74 G Riddell, diary, 13 April 1916, in George Allardice Riddell, *Lord Riddell's War Diary 1914–1918* (London: Ivor Nicholson and Watson, 1933), 173.

75 Quoted in M Gilbert, *Churchill 3: Challenge of War*, 748.

76 Stephen W Roskill, *Churchill and the Admirals* (London: Collins, 1977), 58–9.

77 Ibid, 63.

78 Captain A B Sainsbury confirmed this comment from a statement induced by D Bonner Smith, Admiralty Librarian, who in 1937 was seeking verification for inclusion in the *Oxford Dictionary of Quotations*. Chatfield stated that Beatty said no more than the words quoted here. Stephen W Roskill, *Admiral of the Fleet, Earl Beatty: The Last Naval Hero; An Intimate Biography* (London: Collins, 1981), 160.

79 Quoted in V E Tarrant, *Jutland, the German Perspective: A New View of the Great Battle, 31 May 1916* (Annapolis, MD: Naval Institute Press, 1995), 98.

80 Quoted in ibid, 13.

81 My account draws heavily on the memoir of the Rear-Admiral Sir Douglas Brownrigg, chief censor at the Admiralty, *Indiscretions of the Naval Censor* (London: Cassell, 1920), 48–59, with the quotation from 51.

82 Printed in *Times History of the War* (London, 1916), 9:131. The other statements, German and British, are printed in this work.

83 T Wilson, *Political Diaries of C P Scott*, 212–13.

84 Brownrigg, *Indiscretions of the Naval Censor*, 54.

85 Langhorn Gibson and J E T Harper, *The Riddle of Jutland* (New York: Coward-McCann, 1934), 268–75. The 'naval officer of high rank' was never identified.

86 T Wilson, *Political Diaries of C P Scott*, 210.

87 Ibid, 210–11, 213.

88 Leyland to Fisher, 7 June 1916, and Fisher to Leyland, 9 June 1916, in *FGDN*, 3:354 and note.

89 Cited in *FGDN*, 3:274.

90 Fisher to T E Crease, 3 June 1916, in *FGDN*, 3:353.

91 Fisher to Lady Jellicoe, 9 June 1916, in *FGDN*, 3:355. Fisher misidentified Bosquet as Marshal MacMahon.

92 A useful summary of statements, interpretations, propaganda, and unjustifiable abuse placed on Churchill may be found in Henry Newbolt, *Naval Operations*, vol 4 (London: Longmans, Green, 1928), 1–18.

93 W S Churchill, *World Crisis*, 3:161.

94 Ibid, 2:541–2.

95 Ibid, 2:542.

96 Reginald Bacon, 'Mr Churchill and Jutland', in *The World Crisis by Winston Churchill: A Criticism*, ed Lord Sydenham et al, 2nd edn (London: Hutchinson and Co, [1927?]), 120–87.

97 Hankey, *Supreme Command*, 2:505.

98 Churchill to Asquith, 2 June 1916, in M Gilbert, *Churchill 3: Challenge of War*, 778.

99 Roskill, *Churchill and the Admirals*, 62–3.

100 Speech by Churchill, 27 November 1914, in R Rhodes James, *Churchill: Complete Speeches*, 3:2342–8.

101 Hankey, diary, 3 June 1916, in Hankey, *Supreme Command*, 2:318.

102 Hankey, *Supreme Command*, 2:522.

103 M Gilbert, *Churchill 3: Challenge of War*, 789.

104 Fisher to Asquith, 2 June 1916, in M Gilbert, *Churchill 3: Challenge of War*, 779.

105 Hankey to Fisher, 22 July 1916, in FISR 1/23, 1248.

106 Hankey to Fisher, 25 July 1916, in FISR 1/23, 1249.

107 Churchill to Fisher, [?] June 1916, in M Gilbert, *Churchill 3: Challenge of War*, 776.

108 Churchill to Fisher, 28 July 1916, in FISR 1/23, 1251.

109 Fisher to Hankey, 28 July 1916, in FISR 1/23, 1252; for Hankey's reply, see Hankey to Fisher, 29 July 1916, in FISR 1/23, 1253.

110 Churchill to Cromer, 12 August 1916, in M Gilbert, *Churchill 3: Challenge of War*, 804.

111 Cromer to Churchill, 20 September 1916, in ibid, 808.

112 Fisher to George Lambert, 18 August 1916, in *FGDN*, 3:364.

113 Fisher to George Lambert, 21 August 1916, in *FGDN*, 3:365–6.

114 Churchill to Fisher, 30 August 1916, in M Gilbert, *Churchill 3: Challenge of War*, 806.

115 Churchill to F E Smith, 8 September 1916, in ibid, 806.

116 Fisher to Hankey, 30 August 1916, in *FGDN*, 3:368.

117 Fisher to Hankey, 1 September 1916, in *FGDN*, 3:370–1; see also Fisher, *Memories*, 74.

118 Fisher to Hankey, 6 September 1916, in Fisher, *Memories*, 76.

119 Fisher to George Lambert, 6 September 1916, in *FGDN*, 3:372.

120 Fisher to Lambert, 21 September 1916, in *FGDN*, 3:373.

121 Churchill to Fisher, 20 September 1916, in FISR 1/23, 1272.

122 Hankey to Fisher, 28 September 1916, in FISR 1/23, 1275.

123 W F Nicholson to Fisher, 30 Sept 1916, and encl Fisher's document to Dardanelles Commission, in FISR 1/23, 1278.

124 'Summary for the Chairman of Lord Fisher's Evidence', 7 Oct 1916, FISR 1/18.

125 Fisher to Cromer, 11 October 1916, *FGDN*, 2:374–5. See also FISR 1/24, 1288. FISR 1/24, 1332, is a different version of this letter.

126 Fisher to James Clyde, 12 October 1916, in *FGDN*, 3:376.

127 Martin Gilbert, *Winston S Churchill 4: World in Torment, 1916–1922* (London: William Heinemann, 1975), 6–11.

128 Fisher to George Lambert, 4 March 1917, in *FGDN*, 3:436–7.

129 Fisher to George Lambert, 19 March 1917, in *FGDN*, 3:440–1

130 'The Dardanelles Report', *The Times*, 9 March 1917, 9–12.

131 *Dardanelles Commission: First Report and Supplement, 1917*, 12 February 1917, HMSO, Cmd 8490, 42.

132 M Hankey, diary, 13 July 1917, in Hankey, *Supreme Command*, 2:529.

133 Riddell, *Lord Riddell's War Diary*, 243–5.

134 M Gilbert, *Churchill 4: World in Torment*, 11–13.

135 'Navy and Lord Fisher: Criticism by Sir Hedworth Meux', *The Times*, 19 February 1917, 10.

136 Speech, House of Lords, 21 March 1917,

in Fisher, *Records*, 87.

137 Churchill to Fisher, 3 March 1917, FISR 1/24,1320. *Dardanelles Commission: Final Report and Appendices, 1919.* HMSO, Cmd 371, was made public in 1919.

138 Beatty to Lady Beatty, 12 March 1917, *Beatty Papers*, 1:409.

Chapter 12

1 Stephen W Roskill, *Churchill and the Admirals* (London: Collins, 1977), 64.

2 David Lloyd George, *War Memoirs*, new edn (London: Odhams, 1938), 1:635–8.

3 Further details can be found in Richard Toye, *Lloyd George and Churchill: Rivals for Greatness* (London: Pan, 2008), 180–5.

4 Churchill to Archibald Sinclair, 20 December 1916, cited in Martin Gilbert, *Winston S Churchill 4: World in Torment, 1916–1922* (London: William Heinemann, 1975), 4–5.

5 These articles may be found, along with all his others, in Michael Wolff, ed, *Winston S Churchill: The Collected Essays*, 4 vols (London: Library of Imperial History, 1976).

6 Churchill, 'The War by Land and Sea', *London Magazine*, October 1916. Years later he changed his mind again and put it this way: 'I am shaken in my view as to the small consequences which would have resulted from a complete victory at Jutland. I think there is no doubt we could have entered the Baltic, with consequences on Russia which no man can measure, at the end of 1916 and in 1917 ... One feels ... that a shrinking hand and anxious doubting spirit guided the British Fleet that melancholy day and night. (Churchill to Keyes, 25 August 1924). It was in this tone, Marder observes with clarity, that the Jutland chapters of *The World Crisis* were written in 1927. See *FDSF*, 3:263.

7 Sir Doveton Sturdee, 'Remarks on the Main Naval Strategy of the War', 24 November 1916, in *Jellicoe Papers*, 2:98–101. Also to be found in Jellicoe's *The Submarine Peril: The Admiralty Policy in 1917* (London: Cassell, 1934), 25–34, where it had wide currency.

8 Peter W Gretton, *Former Naval Person: Winston Churchill and the Royal Navy* (London: Cassell, 1968), 229–30.

9 Beatty to Lady Beatty, 3 July 1917, *Beatty Papers*, 1:444.

10 M Gilbert, *Churchill 4: World in Torment*, 15–16.

11 Beatty to Lady Beatty, [15 April 1917], *Beatty Papers*, 1:415.

12 M Gilbert, *Churchill 4: World in Torment*, 17.

13 Frances Stevenson in her diary, 19 May 1917, cited in ibid, 18. Like Lloyd George, Asquith appreciated Churchill's vitality and originality, and liked how he constantly worked on new schemes to defeat the Germans. See Asquith to Venetia Stanley, 24 October 1914, in Michael and Eleanor Brock, eds, *H H Asquith: Letters to Venetia Stanley* (Oxford: Oxford University Press, 1982), 284–6.

14 M Gilbert, *Churchill 4: World in Torment*, 23–6.

15 Ibid, 3–4.

16 Ibid, 26–7.

17 Ibid, 28–31.

18 Gretton, *Former Naval Person*, 230.

19 A J P Taylor, *Beaverbrook* (New York: Simon and Schuster, 1972), 131.

20 M Gilbert, *Churchill 4: World in Torment*, 32–44.

21 Churchill to Jellicoe, 2 December 1916, in *Jellicoe Papers*, 2:108.

22 'Jellicoe's Comments ... on a Project of Attacking Heligoland, Borkum, and Sylt put forward by Churchill', July 1917, in *Jellicoe Papers*, 2:174–9.

23 Fisher to Jellicoe, 26 January 1917, in FISR 1/18.

24 Fisher to George Lambert, 18 March 1917, in *FGDN*, 3:440.

25 In Willem Hackmann, *Seek and Strike: Sonar, Anti-Submarine Warfare, and the Royal Navy, 1914–1954* (London: HMSO Books, 1984), 29.

26 Ibid, 30.

27 Fisher to Carson, 1 February 1917, in *FGDN*, 3:426.

28 Cited in Hackmann, *Seek and Strike*, 30. See also Fisher to Hankey, 29 March 1917, FISR 1/25, 1335, and Fisher to Hankey, 30 March 1917, FISR, 1/25, 1340.

29 William James, *The Eyes of the Navy: A Biographical Study of Admiral Sir Reginald Hall* (London: Methuen, 1955), 86–7.

30 Geddes to Fisher, 24 August 1917, FISR 1/26, 1371.

31 Cited in Hackmann, *Seek and Strike*, 32–3.
32 Cited in Ruddock F Mackay, *Fisher of Kilverstone* (Oxford: Clarendon Press, 1973), 506.
33 Fisher to Geddes, 20 December 1917, cited in Hackmann, *Seek and Strike*, 35.
34 Geddes to Fisher, 20 December 1917, FISR 1/26, 1380.
35 Fisher to Pierse, 22 December 1917, FISR 1/26, 1382.
36 Hackmann, *Seek and Strike*, 37.
37 Cited in ibid, 37.
38 Geddes to Fisher, 18 December 1918, FISR 1/25, 1426.
39 Jack K Gusewelle, 'Science and the Admiralty during World War I: The Case of the BIR', in *Naval Warfare in the Twentieth Century*, ed Gerald Jordan (London: Croom Helm, 1977), 114.
40 Adm 116/1430, report, 10, cited in Mackay, *Fisher of Kilverstone*, 508.
41 Adm 116/1430, report, 17–18, cited in ibid, 509.
42 Cited in *FGDN*, 3:270.
43 Fisher to George Lambert, 21 August 1916, in *FGDN*, 3:367.
44 Admiral Sir Henry Jackson to Vice-Admiral John de Robeck, 9 February 1916, in de Robeck MSS, DRBK 4/31; cited in Paul G Halpern, ed, *The Royal Navy in the Mediterranean 1915–1918* (London: Navy Records Society, 1987), 100.
45 Fisher to a friend, nd [1916?], and Fisher to a Privy Councillor, 27 December 1916, in John Arbuthnot Fisher, *Memories* (London: Hodder and Stoughton, 1919), 36–9.
46 Fisher to George Lambert, 24 October 1916, in *FGDN*, 3:377–8.
47 Fisher to George Lambert, 16 November 1916, in *FGDN*, 3:388–9.
48 Fisher to Jellicoe, 20 November 1916, and Note by McKenna, in *FGDN*, 3:390 and note 2. Fisher threatened to make this statement about the 'compulsory ignoble peace' in the House of Lords but was dissuaded by McKenna.
49 Fisher to George Lambert, 24 November 1916, in *FGDN*, 3:394.
50 Fisher to C P Scott, 24 December 1916, in *FGDN*, 3:407.
51 Fisher to Jellicoe, 4 November 1916, in *Jellicoe Papers*, 2:93.
52 Fisher to Jellicoe, 8 November 1916, in FISR 1/25, 1310. The copy in *Jellicoe Papers*, 2:104–5 dates the letter as 28 November.
53 Jellicoe to Fisher, and Fisher to Jellicoe, 1 December 1916, in *Jellicoe Papers*, 2:107–8.
54 Beatty to his wife, 15 December 1916, *Beatty Papers*, 1:386–7.
55 Fisher to Ernest G Pretyman, 27 December 1916, in Fisher, *Memories*, 37–9. See also *FGDN*, 3:407–9.
56 Fisher to Jellicoe, 16 July 1917, cited in Mackay, *Fisher of Kilverstone*, 511–12.
57 Madden to Jellicoe, 12 February 1917, in *Jellicoe Papers*, 2:144.
58 Jellicoe to Fisher, 13 February 1917, and Fisher to Jellicoe, 14 February 1917, in *FGDN*, 3:428–9.
59 Beatty to Eugenie, 4 March 1917, SLGF 1/4A
60 Fisher to Hankey, 30 March 1917, in FISR 1/24, 1340.
61 Fisher to C P Scott, 23 February 1917, in *FGDN*, 3:434–5.
62 Fisher to the Duchess of Hamilton, nd [mid-February 1917?], in *FGDN*, 3:429.
63 Churchill to Fisher, 25 January 1917, in *FGDN*, 3:423.
64 'House of Commons Debate', *The Times*, 22 February 1917, 10; and Hansard for 21 February 1917.
65 'The Navy Estimates: Admiral Meux and Lord Fisher', *The Times*, 27 February 1917, 8.
66 Fisher to George Lambert, 18 February 1917, in *FGDN*, 3:432.
67 Churchill to Fisher, 3 March 1917, in FISR 1/24. 1320.
68 Churchill to Fisher, 12 March 1917, in FISR 1/24.
69 See Fisher to George Lambert, 21 November 1916, in *FGDN*, 3:389n.
70 Fisher to Jellicoe, 16 January 1917, FISR 1/24.
71 Churchill to Fisher, 25 January 1917, in *FGDN*, 3:423.
72 Fisher to Churchill, 11 April 1917, CHAR 2/92.
73 Fisher to Churchill, 15 April 1917, in *FGDN*, 3:450–1. See also FISR 1/24, 1345.
74 Fisher to Lloyd George, 14 and 20 March 1917, in *FGDN*, 3:438–9 and 441–2; and Hankey to Fisher, 26 March 1917, in FISR 1/24, 1327.

75 War Cabinet Minutes, 28 March 1917, in FISR 1/24, 1340.

76 Fisher to Lloyd George, 28 March 1917, FISR 1/24, 1331. See also *FGDN*, 3:443–4, and John Arbuthnot Fisher, *Records* (London: Hodder and Stoughton, 1919), 222–3. Another letter to Lloyd George of the same date exists in the Fisher Papers that is similar but not exactly the same. It is unclear which was sent (FISR 1/24, 1332).

77 Fisher to Lloyd George 12 June and 11 July 1917, in Fisher, *Records*, 234–6. See also FISR 1/25, 1361.

78 Fisher to Hankey, 23 April 1917, in FISR 1/24, 1347, and Hankey to Fisher, sd, in FISR 1/24, 1346. See also *FGDN*, 3:453–5.

79 Fisher to Churchill, 31 March 1917, CHAR 2/92.

80 Fisher to Churchill, 1917, CHAR 2/92 and FISR 1/25, 1288.

81 Beatty to Lady Beatty, 27 April 1917, *Beatty Papers*, 1:419.

82 Beatty to Lady Beatty, 3 May 1917, in *Beatty Papers*, 1:421–2.

83 Beatty to Lady Beatty, 8 and 10 May 1917, in *Beatty Papers*, 1:423–5.

84 S W Roskill, 'The Dismissal of Admiral Jellicoe', *Journal of Contemporary History*, 1, no. 4 (October 1966), 69–93.

85 'Jellicoe's Account of the Circumstances Leading Up to his Dismissal from the Post of First Sea Lord', in *Jellicoe Papers*, 2:240–5.

86 See, among others, letters from Geddes, Asquith and Churchill in *Jellicoe Papers*, 2:240–63.

87 Fisher to the Duke of Buccleuch, 25 December 1917, in FISR 1/26, 1383.

88 Fisher to Churchill, 13 March 1918, in *FGDN*, 3:521–2.

89 Fisher to Churchill, 19 March 1918, in CHAR 2/92.

90 Fisher to a friend, 27 March 1918, in Fisher, *Records*, 246–7.

91 Fisher to Churchill, 9 September 1917, in Fisher, *Memories*, 78.

92 Fisher to Churchill, 17 May 1918, in *FGDN*, 3:533–55.

93 Churchill to Fisher 19 May 1918, in FISR 1/25, 1414. See also *FGDN*, 3:535–6.

94 Fisher to Churchill, 26 May 1918, FISR 1/25, 1415. See also *FGDN*, 3:536–7.

95 Fisher to Churchill, 29 August 1918, FISR 1/25, 1420. See also *FGDN*, 3:549–50.

96 Fisher to Hankey, 22 July 1918, in Stephen W Roskill, *Hankey, Man of Secrets* (London: Collins, 1970–1974), 1:580.

97 W S Churchill, *World Crisis*, 6:321–2.

98 Esher to Fisher, 21 July 1918, in James Lees-Milne, *The Enigmatic Edwardian: The Life of Reginald 2nd Viscount Esher* (London: Hodder and Stoughton, 1986), 316.

99 Fisher to Churchill, 14 October 1918, FISR 1/25, 1421. See also *FGDN*, 3:552–3.

100 Fisher to Hankey, 21 October 1918, FISR 1/25, 1422. See also Fisher, *Records*, 244; and Fisher, *Some Notes by Lord Fisher to his Friends* (privately printed, 1918), iii. A copy of *Some Notes* is in ESHR 17/5.

101 Fisher to George Lambert, 31 October 1918, in *FGDN*, 3:556–7.

102 Gerard Fiennes to Fisher, 11 November 1918, in *FGDN*, 3:557.

103 Ethel Beatty to her sister-in-law, 18 November 1918, SLGF 3/13.

104 Particulars of this episode and surrender are in W S Chalmers, *The Life and Letters of David, Earl Beatty* (London: Hodder and Stoughton, 1951), 341–9.

105 See Andrew Gordon, *The Rules of the Game: Jutland and British Naval Command* (London: John Murray, 1996), passim; also Barry M Gough, *Historical Dreadnoughts: Arthur Marder, Stephen Roskill and Battles for Naval History* (Barnsley: Seaforth, 2010), 256–68.

106 Richard Hough, *Admiral of the Fleet: The Life of John Fisher* (New York: Macmillan, 1969), 356.

107 An admirer to Fisher, 21 November 1918, in Fisher, *Records*, 247–8. See also Lord Winster's 'Six Years That Shook the Navy', *Evening Standard*, 5 May 1942 (copy in FISR 15/5).

108 Hugh Cleland Hoy, *40 OB or How the War Was Won* (London: Hutchinson, 1935), 247.

109 Fisher to a friend, 25 January 1918, in Fisher, *Memories*, 240–2.

110 Fisher to a friend, 9 June 1918, in ibid, 76.

111 Fisher, *Memories*, 84–5.

112 Fisher to Lambert, 4 April 1919, in *FGDN*, 3:577.

113 Fisher to Frances Stevenson, 20 August 1919, in FISR 1/25, 1431. See also *FGDN*, 3:586–7.

114 'Lord Fisher on Waste', *The Times*, 2 September 1919, 11.

115 'Lord Fisher Again', *The Times*, 5 September 1919, 11.

116 'Lord Fisher on the Fleet', *The Times*, 5 September 1919, 11.

117 Vice-Admiral C C Penrose Fitzgerald, 'To the Editor of *The Times*', *The Times*, 8 September 1919, 12.

118 'The Navy – Changes in Men and Ships', *The Times*, 8 September 1919, 11–12.

119 'The Navy – A Prescription for Building', *The Times*, 11 September 1919, 11.

120 'Still Wasting Money', *The Times*, 16 September 1919, 11.

121 'The Debit Side', *The Times*, 20 September 1919, 11–12.

122 'Where the Last War Left Off', *The Times*, 27 September 1919, 8.

123 'Blinded', *The Times*, 31 October 1919, 8.

124 Fisher, *Memories*, 281.

125 Fisher to Hankey, 3 April 1911, in Maurice Hankey, *The Supreme Command* (London: George Allen and Unwin, 1961), 1:147.

126 Esther Meynell, *A Woman Talking* (London: Chapman and Hall, 1940), 63–84. Of all the sources on Fisher, this is the most elusive, but Marder and Jan Morris learned about it, and I combed bookstores until I located a copy of this delightful reminiscence.

127 The drafts were placed in the hands of Fisher's literary executors.

128 Esher to Fisher, 20 August 1919, in Esher, *Letters and Journals*, 4:242.

129 Fisher, *Memories*, x.

130 Barry M Gough, 'Rulers of the Waves: British Naval Memoirs', in *Political Memoir: Essays on the Politics of Memory*, ed George Egerton (London: Frank Cass, 1994), 145–7.

131 'Lord Fisher's Gospel', *The Times*, 21 October 1919, 13.

132 'Lord Fisher's "Memories"', *The Times*, 8 October 1919, 9. Excerpts published 11, 13, 14, 15, 16 and 17 October.

133 From the dozens of reviews that survive in FISR 15/5.

134 Gough, 'Rulers of the Waves', 145–7.

135 *The Observer*, unsigned, 2 November 1919, copy in FISR 15/5.

136 Quoted in *FGDN*, 3:413.

137 Esher to Fisher, 21 July 1918, in Fisher, *Some Notes by Lord Fisher*, v–vi. However, see copy of letter in Esher, *Letters and Journals*, 4:207–8, which omits 'she': 'Where should we all be to-day, were it not for your foresight, your bold determination?'

138 Fisher to Cecil Fisher, 11 June 1919, in *FGDN*, 3:583.

139 Fisher to Lady Dorothy Fullerton, 9 May 1919, in *FGDN*, 3:581–2.

140 Fisher to Earl of Rosebery, 9 May 1919, in *FGDN*, 3:582.

141 Roskill, *Hankey*, 2:91.

142 Fisher to Admiral John Moresby, 7 February 1919, in *FGDN*, 3:574–6.

143 Fisher to John Moresby, 6 July 1920, in *FGDN*, 3:634.

144 'Lord Fisher's Will', *The Times*, 5 October 1920, 10.

145 Esher to LB, 14 July 1920, in Esher, *Letters and Journals*, 4:263.

146 In *The British Weekly of Social and Christian Progress*, 15 July 1920, 306. Fisher's publisher, Sir Ernest Hodder-Williams, proprietor of Hodder and Stoughton, doubtless wrote this.

147 'Lord Fisher, Funeral Service at the Abbey', *The Times*, 14 July 1920, 12.

148 O Murray to Cecil Fisher, 14 July 1920, *FGDN*, 3:635.

Postscript

1 'Lord Fisher,' *The Times*, 12 July 1920, 15. Likely by James Thursfield, naval correspondent.

2 Esher to LB, 11 July 1920, in Esher, *Letters and Journals*, 4:262–3.

3 Moresby to Fisher, 9 July 1918, in John Arbuthnot Fisher, *Records* (London: Hodder and Stoughton, 1919), 248.

4 Esher to LB, 27 March 1923, in Esher, *Letters and Journals*, 4:287–8.

5 Hector Bywater, *Searchlight on the Navy* (London: Constable, 1935), 49.

6 J Masterton-Smith to Fisher, 30 October 1919, War Office, in *FGDN*, 3:597–8.

7 Endorsement by Jellicoe, in Jellicoe to the Secretary of the Admiralty, 14 September 1916, in *Jellicoe Papers*, 2:71–5.

8 Gentleman with a Duster [Harold Begbie], *The Mirrors of Downing Street: Some Political Reflections* (London: Mills and Boon, 1920), 32, 36, which I have used

extensively here.

9 Esther Meynell, *A Woman Talking* (London: Chapman and Hall, 1940), 86.

10 In John Arbuthnot Fisher, *Memories* (London: Hodder and Stoughton, 1919), x.

11 Quoted in Shane Leslie, 'Memories of Beatty' (unpublished MS, SLGF 12/4), 11.

12 Information from Marder files; Barry Gough, 'Introduction', in Arthur J Marder, *From Dreadnought to Scapa Flow*, vol 3 (Barnsley: Seaforth, 2014). Also, Barry M Gough, *Historical Dreadnoughts: Arthur Marder, Stephen Roskill and Battles for Naval History* (Barnsley: Seaforth, 2010), 127.

13 Reginald Bacon in Eugene L Rasor, *Winston S Churchill, 1874–1965: A Comprehensive Historiography and Annotated Bibliography* (Westport, CT: Greenwood, 2000), 162.

14 Winston S Churchill, *The World Crisis*, abridged edn (New York: Scribners, 1931), 471.

15 Winston S Churchill, *The World Crisis* (London: Thornton Butterworth, 1923–31), 3:169–70. Italics added.

16 On this, in reference to Churchill, see introduction to William Schleihauf, ed, *Jutland: The Naval Staff Appreciation* (Barnsley: Seaforth, 2016). This work contains additional editorial comment by Stephen McLaughlin.

17 In Charles Beatty, *Our Admiral: A Biography of Admiral of the Fleet Earl Beatty* (London: W H Allen, 1980), 136.

18 Lord Selborne, *National Review*, August 1923, 838; also Peter W Gretton, *Former Naval Person: Winston Churchill and the Royal Navy* (London: Cassell, 1968), 197–8. When Churchill's *The World Crisis* was published in all its volumes, Selborne was one of several who immediately commented on it in print.

19 Winston S Churchill, *The Second World War*, vol 1 (London: Cassell, 1948), 320–1.

20 Marder's '"Winston Is Back": Churchill at the Admiralty, 1939–40', first published in *English Historical Review* (1972) as a supplement, was an extensive, ground-breaking investigation with compelling evidence gleaned from participants. It was reprinted in Arthur J Marder, *From the Dardanelles to Oran: Studies of the Royal Navy in War and Peace 1915–1940* (1974; reprint Barnsley: Seaforth, 2015), 105–78; see also Gough, *Historical Dreadnoughts*, 226–42.

21 Stephen W Roskill, *Churchill and the Admirals* (London: Collins, 1977), 280.

22 Gough, *Historical Dreadnoughts*, 216–51.

23 See Robin Brodhurst, *Churchill's Anchor: The Biography of Admiral of the Fleet Sir Dudley Pound* (Barnsley: Leo Cooper, 2000).

24 A J P Taylor, *The War Lords* (New York: Athenaeum, 1978), 76–7.

Acknowledgements

I must first extend my gratitude to the Master, Fellows and Scholars of Churchill College, Cambridge, for twice electing me Archives By-Fellow. To successive Keepers of the Churchill Archives Centre – Correlli Barnett, Piers Brendon, and Allen Packwood – and the Archives Committee, I extend appreciation for their sponsorship and hospitality. And to the diligent staff of the Churchill Archives Centre, I express gratitude for many kindnesses, notably much sound advice, that spurred this project and speeded its conclusion. Holdings of that Centre lie at the heart of modern historical scholarship in military, naval, and political affairs, particularly that dealing with Churchill and Fisher; to have unfettered access to these papers for extended months and even terms over the past score of years has been a boon to this project. To have at my disposal the holdings of the library there, notably works collected or written by Captain Stephen Roskill, accelerated my progress and stimulated my inquiries.

Next to thank are the staff and keepers of The National Archives (the former Public Record Office) in Kew, Surrey. Finding aids and digitalised listings made many visits a delight (though invariably a withering chase against time); the newer documents retrieval systems and electronic inventories made the researcher there feel a little like a rider on a point-to-point course, and always with a flourishing finish.

As Caird Fellow at the National Maritime Museum, Greenwich, I had for three months the run of the extensive library and archival holdings. These were of particular value to me as I studied how naval historians had evaluated the naval war at sea, 1914–1918. A preliminary look at the Beatty papers fuelled my interest in the sailor Churchill said was Nelson's true successor (Fisher had Jellicoe in mind). The Montagues and Capulets continue their quarrel in the documents, articles, and books.

To librarians and staff of the following, I extend grateful thanks for allowing me to carry on research, often from remote locations: the Athenaeum, the

British Library, the London Library, Beineke Library Yale University, the University of New Brunswick, McGill University Library and Archives, and the US Naval Academy. Postcard photos come from my own collection. For photographic advice I acknowledge the assistance of Brian L Winter.

I am grateful to Wilfrid Laurier University, Waterloo, Ontario, for grants in aid of research during various phases of this project and for electing me University Research Professor. Dr Wesley Ferris and Robert Davison provided research help. Students in naval history and war studies courses at the University, as also at Canadian Forces College, Toronto, for the Royal Military College of Canada, provided unsuspecting sounding boards and sparked many a discussion and debate. A travel grant from the Churchill Center and Churchill Museum assisted research in later stages of the work.

Over the course of two decades I have had occasion to speak to many audiences on the subjects featured in this book. To hosts in such diverse locations as Bermuda, Singapore, London, Anchorage, Washington, DC, and Phoenix, I express thanks. I will concede that the questions (always stimulating) at these events on the might-have-beens of a Dardanelles/Gallipoli campaign carried to a successful conclusion always ended with some evasion on my part. But what I will not dodge is the effect that ill-starred Dardanelles affair had on Winston Churchill. If the learning curve was steep for him in 1915, and his heart broken by what transpired, there is no doubt that the whole episode steeled him for the events of the Second World War. He possessed undaunted courage. When, in 1939, he returned as First Lord of the Admiralty – 'Winston is back!' was telegraphed throughout the Fleet – these lessons well learned were not lost on him. But that is another story, one well worth the telling in a companion book.

Vice-Admiral Sir Peter Gretton and Captain Stephen Roskill wrote books on Churchill and the Navy, with particular attention to the Admiralty and commanders at sea; these encompass both world wars. Gretton had the advantage of the Royal Archives; Roskill, his extensive network among naval officers and archivists. These two historians lit my path here. As will be seen in my endnotes, I am beholden to the late Arthur J Marder for his editing of the Fisher papers and, more, for his examination of the politics of British naval supremacy in the era beginning in the late 1880s and continuing through to the end of the First World War and after. His publications 'Winston is Back' and *Operation Menace*, details of which are to be found in the Bibliography, deserve closest attention, for they were based not so much on Admiralty papers as on contemporary evidence gleaned from participants in the formation of policy and in the operations themselves. A strong theme in these works is the degree to which, and in what ways, Churchill overly interfered in the planning and implementation of naval operations. I express thanks to the late Sir Martin

Gilbert, who assisted me in my investigation into where Jacky Fisher escaped to – was it the Charing Cross Hotel? – on the day of his final resignation from the Admiralty. His volumes of the Churchill biography and his documentary collection of Churchill companion volumes provided much guidance and a beginning point for attendant searches in the archives. This book owes much to Marder and to Gilbert, and it could not have been completed without their conscientious and detailed work. As my work rests heavily in the political story of naval supremacy (and not in the history of technology or of finance), the literary paths illuminated by these prodigious scholars are of fundamental value.

To the following individuals I express thanks for information, advice, and encouragement: David Boler, Ronald Cohen, Paul Courtenay, Robert Courts, Carlo D'Este, Peter Dixon, James Goldrick, John Mather, Kenneth McKenzie, James Muller, Malcolm Murfett, Lawrence Phillips, David Ramsay, the late John Ramsden, Eugene Rasor, Nicholas Roskill, Douglas Russell, the late Captain A Sainsbury, and William Schaub. For assistance and providing comments on the text, when in gestation or draft, I thank Christopher Bell, Paul Courtenay, Jan Drent, Kenneth Hagan, Brian Jameson, Richard Langworth, John Maurer, the late William Schielhauf, Neville Thompson, Tim Travers, and Bernie Webber. I am grateful for new perspectives brought to naval history by recent scholarship on the Fisher era (1904–1910), notably by Jon Sumida, Nicholas Lambert, Christopher Bell, and Matthew Seligmann. The late Richard Ollard, biographer and editor, provided guidance on formulating the core themes that inspired this book, most notably on the remarkable personalities of the daemonic duo. I regret that he did not live to see the results of labours expended toward the aim of describing the remarkable, often disputatious, interaction of two unusual persons thrown together in the clutches of history. This book is an exploration of how difficult it is in wartime for a premier maritime power to exert compelling influence on a dominant continental power, an observation made so clearly by Sir Julian Corbett, Stephen Roskill, and Sir Herbert Richmond, and I acknowledge their insights here. Then again, the theories of Alfred Thayer Mahan and Halford Mackinder provide yet another theoretical backdrop, and I am grateful to Kenneth Hagan and Paul Kennedy for elucidation of arguments about sea power's influences in littoral and continental struggles.

I wish also to thank my publishers and their associates, and particularly Julian Mannering and Robert Gardiner, who have brought this work into print. My esteemed personal editor Audrey McClellan made many rough places plain, and has provided a continuity over the years and decades that are essential to ease the passage of the historian's ideas and writings. And finally, my thanks to family and friends, as well as to my late parents, for their abiding support, essential contributions to divine guidance, and never-failing companionship.

A Note on Sources

The conscientious historian is faced with many difficulties in determining the reliability and disinterestedness of the sources available. For a book such as this, unique challenges present themselves. Chief among them is the fact that Fisher and Churchill were quite capable of using history to their own ends. Both were masters of the English language and the alluring turn of phrase that carried a sense of conviction. Their artful language reflects their personalities and character.

Fisher's letters are a delight to read and are full of insight. To some extent they represent the man himself, but in other ways they mask a deeper and more complex individual. For all his woes and difficulties, Fisher put a bright face on his personal relationships, as shown in his correspondence. His letters therefore require deeper evaluation of the official correspondence and memoranda of the day. Commentaries by third-person observers, notably Lord Esher, help explain Fisher's actions. Other observers of this complex scene are Maurice Hankey and Herbert Richmond, casting light similarly on Churchill. Although Fisher wrote two published works that might classify as memoirs – they are really rough fragments of autobiography, a stringing together of literary snippets – he had no capacity to sit down and work out an extended evaluation of British naval power and statecraft. This he could have done in later years, in the five years between his resignation and his death. He chose otherwise. And so whereas just about any other statesman, soldier, or sailor of any significance wrote up their memoirs, Jacky Fisher left us fragments of memory and experience.

Churchill was keen to protect himself from future criticism by historians, and his attempt at 'gatekeeping' against the official Cabinet Office historian, Sir Julian Corbett, constitutes the earliest demonstration of this. Robin Prior, Donald M Schurman, and David Reynolds are our guides here. The powerful and influential style of Churchill's *The World Crisis* has the air of authenticity. However, a probing examination behind the scenes, so to speak, shows

Churchill's careful massaging of the particulars to his own advantage in his own defence. He fought a running battle against official historians – and others. And in writing his own account of Jutland he used a partisan, now discredited, account, *Naval Staff Appreciation of Jutland*, written by A C and K G B Dewar (available in a volume edited by William Schleihauf, published by Seaforth in 2016). The original printing was destroyed by order of the First Sea Lord, Admiral Sir Charles Madden. Churchill had one of the five surviving copies and used it to his undoubted advantage. Admiral Sir Reginald Bacon's 1933 assault on Churchill's version appeared in Lord Sydenham et al, *The World Crisis by Winston Churchill: A Criticism*, 2nd edn (London: Hutchinson, 1927), and is also to be found in John Harper and Reginald Bacon, *The Jutland Scandal: The Truth about the First World War's Greatest Sea Battle* (Barnsley: Frontline, 2015), ch 12. Though Jutland may be a battle without end, it is clear that Churchill got much of it wrong in the selection of evidence and the telling of the story.

Churchill differs from Fisher in one special way: he was an historian of considerable merit. He also had time on his side. He was well favoured by outliving Fisher – and having the last word on the controversy that led to his wilderness years after the Cabinet and Admiralty crisis of May 1915. Specifically, he had the benefit of that last word in a review of Bacon's 1929 biography of Fisher, and in a revised version of his essay on the famed and controversial admiral that first appeared in the second edition of Churchill's *Great Contemporaries*, 1937 (I have written more fully about this in *Finest Hour*, 150 (Spring 2011)).

Following in Admiral Bacon's wake, many historians have directed attention to Churchill and his writing of history – and to his self-justification. Attention is particularly drawn to Robin Prior's work, *Churchill's 'World Crisis' as History*, and David Reynolds's book on a similar theme in regards to the next war, *In Command of History: Churchill Fighting and Writing the Second World War*. I have also dealt with these matters in *Historical Dreadnoughts*, all about Arthur Marder and his sparring partner Stephen Roskill. *The World Crisis*, that remarkable five-volumes-in-six chronicle Churchill produced between 1923 and 1931, is an alluring source for the general reader but full of minefields and pitfalls for the working historian. The often-overlooked final volume, *The Aftermath*, yields perspectives on Turkey and the Ottoman Empire. The distinguished authority Richard Langworth has written in *A Connoisseur's Guide to the Books of Sir Winston Churchill*: 'Like all of his war books where he is involved, it is highly biased and personal, tending to magnify and defend his own role in affairs.' Among Churchill's endearing characteristics was his unabashed honesty. Of *The World Crisis* he declared that it was 'not history, but a contribution to history'; later, of his six-volume *The Second World War*, he would say similarly, 'This is not history; this is my case.' For this entirely correct reason, I have distanced myself from it except to exploit Churchill's commentary or judgements on certain points or issues. Wherever possible I have used the first English edition of each volume, for the reason that the one-volume compendium (published in 1931) that is now so well circulated by no means tells the full story, and is generally devoid of maps. Noteworthy and often overlooked is the fact that the 1931 printing contains new material added by Churchill, and considerable revisions. Therein he states: 'I have had to record a somewhat different account of Lord Fisher's resignation from that which appeared in the original edition. Mr. Asquith's disclosures in his "Memoirs" and Lord Fisher's own biographers have cast a less charitable light upon the conduct of the old Admiral than that in which I had viewed it.' On this, Langworth comments: 'Asquith's memoirs disclosed that Fisher had written an incredible letter offering to remain at the Admiralty if vested virtually with dictatorial powers, refusing to serve either under Churchill or his successor Arthur Balfour' (114).

Although in the main I have used primary sources in original manuscript form, no student of the history of this era can do work without ready access to various printed sources and the editorial apparatus that accompanies these. I have been blessed inasmuch as the key documents used in this study are available in print, where the inquisitive can consult them (and find innumerable diversions). Most are also available on the web.

I draw attention particularly to that mine of information, the published correspondence of Fisher edited by Arthur Marder, *Fear God and Dread Nought*. Many letters not included by Marder have appeared in other publications, including Richard Hough's life of Fisher, *Admiral of the Fleet*, and Ruddock F Mackay's *Fisher of Kilverstone*. There is, however, no substitute for consulting the full run of the Fisher correspondence at the Churchill Archives Centre. The same is true for the diaries and letters of Lord Esher, in the same repository.

We should be mindful of what the distinguished bibliographer of naval history Eugene Rasor (*British Naval History Since 1815*) said about the official Churchill biographies: that although they were much anticipated because they would throw light on contentious matters, they had, unfortunately, consistently avoided final resolution of so much that was controversial about Churchill. Put differently, critique of Churchill would have to lie with naval history and naval historians. Among naval papers, the *Jellicoe Papers* and *Beatty Papers* published by the Navy Records Society (NRS), as selected by their respective editors, A Temple Patterson and Bryan Ranft, are of inestimable value, containing as they do Churchill and Fisher materials or comments on the protagonists. Among the other publications of the NRS are to be found real gems, such as Paul G Halpern's cluster of papers on Admiral John de Robeck and the Dardanelles campaign, published in N A M Rodger, ed, *Naval Miscellany*, volume 5. Other volumes published by the NRS of value include *Policy and Operations in the Mediterranean 1912–14*, edited by E W R Lumby, and *The Royal Navy in the Mediterranean 1915–1918*, and the *Keyes Papers*, both edited by Paul G Halpern. Note, too, that Nicholas Tracy's *Sea Power and the Control of Trade*, also published by NRS, contains a comprehensive discussion of the paper world that British naval commanders inhabited in regards to belligerent rights (many rules changed with the Hague Conferences and the Declaration of London); these subjects are not included in my book. Full details of these works are given in the Bibliography. Of superb value, also, are the Selborne papers, edited by D George Boyce for The Historians' Press, and numerous memoirs or autobiographies as noted in the Bibliography. This work probes the face of naval battle on the home front, in the offices, newspaper columns, drawing rooms, and elsewhere, of the nation. Memoirs and private letters are naturally self-serving, as are authorised biographies, though to a lesser extent; nonetheless, when used with caution, they provide behind-the-scenes viewpoints on character and circumstance. Violet Bonham Carter's *Winston Churchill as I Knew Him*, for example, is a work of unique observation marred by personal devotion to the subject, yet provides material not found elsewhere. The memoir of Fisher's private secretary, Mrs Esther Meynell, *A Woman Talking*, opened many new vistas on the private life and literary visions of Jacky.

To various historians and biographers who have written on aspects of my subject, I express thanks for the guidance supplied. In particular I thank Trumbull Higgins, Peter Gretton, and Stephen Roskill. Arthur Marder explored the relationship of Fisher and Churchill in *From the Dreadnought to Scapa Flow*, volumes 1 and 2, and these are unsurpassed as a narrative of the naval war, though they are by no means perfect. *The Official History of Naval Operations*, by Julian Corbett and Henry Newbolt, gives an altogether unfortunate story of the war at sea, and has now been supplanted by many other works. Just as Marder sought to analyse 'the war behind the war', so too did Stephen Koss provide the same sort of critical and visceral discussion of Asquith's administration and its difficulties in two commendable biographies: *Asquith* and *Haldane*. As a guide to the naval literature I have depended on Eugene Rasor, *British Naval History Since 1815: A Guide to the Literature* (first published New York: Garland, 1990; now updated and online at the University of Essex). *The Naval Who's Who 1917* (reprinted 1981) lists ranks, promotion dates, and honours of naval officers, plus other items of use to the historian, including a list of officers' services from 1914 to 1916 and Jellicoe's Jutland Despatch.

A note on *The Official Churchill Biographies* and *The Churchill Documents* (the latterly formerly known as *Churchill Companion Volumes*)

I list here only the works used in my study of Churchill and Fisher.

1. *The Official Churchill Biographies*

By Randolph S Churchill

> *Winston S Churchill 1: Youth, 1974–1900.* London: William Heinemann, 1966. Reprinted with new introduction (2005) by Martin Gilbert. Hillsdale, MI: Hillsdale College Press, 2006.

> *Winston S Churchill 2: Young Statesman, 1901–1914.* London: William Heinemann, 1967. Reprinted with new introduction (2007) by Martin Gilbert. Hillsdale, MI: Hillsdale College Press, 2007.

By Martin Gilbert

> *Winston S Churchill 3: The Challenge of War, 1914–1916.* London: William Heinemann, 1971. Reprinted Hillsdale, MI: Hillsdale College Press, 2008.

> *Winston S Churchill 4: World in Torment, 1916–1922.* London: William Heinemann, 1975. Reprinted Hillsdale, MI: Hillsdale College Press, 2008.

2. *The Churchill Documents*

Correspondence files of Winston Churchill, gathered together as essentials for the official biography, were printed in a series known as *The Churchill Companion Volumes*. All serious students of history are indebted to them.

But take note: these are now correctly titled *The Churchill Documents*, nineteen volumes to date, edited initially by Randolph Churchill and continued by Martin Gilbert and, since 2015, by Larry P Arnn. These volumes also contain 'refugia' from other locations – elusive diary entries of others, odd Admiralty files, remote political commentary, etc. These companion volumes are much more than the Churchill story as revealed through selected correspondence to and from Winston Churchill. They offer a window on the ever-changing world with which Churchill found himself engaged.

The Churchill Documents, nineteen volumes to date, covering Churchill's life to the eve of D-Day, are published by Hillsdale College Press (www.hillsdale.edu), where further particulars may be found. The volumes I referred to in the course of my research are listed below. Dates of first publication also included.

Randolph S Churchill, compiler
    Vol 1: *Youth, 1874–1896.* 2006, 1967.

Vol 2: *Young Soldier, 1896–1900*. 2006, 1967.
Vol 3: *Early Years in Politics, 1901–1907*. 2007, 1969
Vol 4: *Minister of the Crown, 1907–1911*. 2008, 1977.
Vol 5: *At the Admiralty, 1911–1914*. 2007, 1969.

Martin Gilbert, compiler
Vol 6: *At the Admiralty, July 1914–April 1915*. 2008. 1972.
Vol 7: *'The Escaped Scapegoat', May 1915–December 1916*. 2008. 1972.
Vol 8: *War and Aftermath, December 1916–June 1919*. 2008. 1977.
Vol 9: *Disruption and Chaos, July 1919–1921*. 2008. 1977.
Vol 14: *At the Admiralty, September 1939–May 1940*. 2011. 1993.

Bibliography

Ackroyd, Peter. *London: The Biography*. London: Vintage, 2002.

Adams, R J Q. *Bonar Law*. London: John Murray, 1999.

Addison, Paul. *Winston Churchill*. Oxford: Oxford University Press, 2007. This is based on Addison's entry for Churchill in *Oxford Dictionary of National Biography*. Online. Oxford: Oxford University Press, 2004–.

Anderson, E N. *The First Moroccan Crisis*. Hamden: Archon Books, 1966.

Annual Register for 1905.

Arnold-Forster, Mary. *The Right Honourable Hugh Oakeley Arnold-Forster, A Memoir, by His Wife*. London: Edward Arnold, 1910.

Aspinall-Oglander, C F. *History of the Great War, Based on Official Documents. Military Operations: Gallipoli*. 2 vols. London: William Heinemann, 1929–32.

———. *Roger Keyes, Being the Biography of Admiral of the Fleet Lord Keyes of Zeebrugge and Dover*. London: Hogarth Press, 1951.

Asprey, Robert B. *The German High Command at War*. New York: Quill, 1991.

Asquith, H H. *The Earl of Oxford and Asquith: Memories and Reflections, 1852–1927*. 2 vols. Boston: Little, Brown, 1928.

Asquith, Margot (Countess of Oxford and Asquith). *Off the Record*. London: Frederick Muller, 1943.

Attenborough, Wilfred. *Churchill and the 'Black Dog' of Depression*. Basingstoke: Palgrave Macmillan, 2014.

Bacon, Reginald. *From 1900 Onward*. London: Hutchinson, 1940.

———. *Life of John Rushworth Earl Jellicoe*. London: Cassell, 1936.

———. *The Life of Lord Fisher of Kilverstone: Admiral of the Fleet*. 2 vols. London: Hodder, 1929.

———. 'Mr Churchill and Jutland', in *The World Crisis by Winston Churchill: A Criticism*, ed Lord Sydenham of Combe, et al, 2nd edn, 120–87. London: Hutchinson, [1927?].

———. *A Naval Scrap-Book First Part 1877–1900*. London: Hutchinson, 1925.

Bailey, Thomas, and Paul Ryan. *The Lusitania Disaster*. New York: Free Press, 1975.

Ballard, Robert. *Lusitania: Probing the Mysteries of the Sinking That Changed History*. Edson, NJ: Chartwell, 2007.

Barnett, Correlli. *The Swordbearers: Studies in Supreme Command in the First World War*. London: Eyre and Spottiswoode, 1963.

Bayly, Lewis. *Pull Together! The Memoirs of Admiral Sir Lewis Bayly*. London: George G Harrap, 1939.

Beatty, Charles. *Our Admiral: A Biography of Admiral of the Fleet Earl Beatty*. London: W H Allen, 1980.

Beaverbrook, Lord. *Men and Power, 1917–1918*. London: Hutchinson, 1956.

——. *Politicians and the War, 1914–1916*. London: Thornton Butterworth, 1928.

Beesly, Patrick. *Room 40: British Naval Intelligence, 1914–1918*. London: Hamish Hamilton, 1982.

[Begbie, Harold]. *The Mirrors of Downing Street: Some Political Reflections by a Gentleman with a Duster*. New York: G P Putnam, 1921.

Bell, Christopher M. *Churchill and the Dardanelles*. Oxford: Oxford University Press, 2017.

——. *Churchill and Sea Power*. Oxford: Oxford University Press, 2015.

Bennett, Geoffrey. *Charlie B: A Biography of Admiral Lord Charles Beresford of Metemmeh and Curraghmore*. London: Peter Dawnay, 1968.

——. *Coronel and the Falklands*. Rev edn, London: Pan, 1968.

——. *Naval Battles of the First World War*. Rev edn, London: Pan, 1983.

Benson, E F. *The Kaiser and English Relations*. London: Longmans, Green, 1936.

Beresford, Charles. *Memoirs of Admiral Lord Charles Beresford*. London: Methuen, 1914.

Black, Nicholas. *The British Naval Staff in the First World War*. Woodbridge: Boydell Press, 2009.

Blake, Robert, and William Roger Louis, eds. *Churchill*. New York and London: W W Norton, 1993.

Bonham Carter, Violet. *Winston Churchill as I Knew Him*. London: Eyre and Spottiswoode and Collins, 1965.

Bonnett, Stanley. *The Price of Admiralty: An Indictment of the Royal Navy, 1805–1966*. London: Robert Hale, 1968.

Boyce, D George, ed. *The Crisis of British Power: The Imperial and Naval Papers of the Second Earl of Selborne, 1895–1910*. London: The Historians' Press, 1990.

Bradford, Edward E. *Life of Admiral of the Fleet Sir Arthur Knyvet Wilson*. London: John Murray, 1923.

Brett, Maurice V, ed. *Journals and Letters of Reginald Viscount Esher*. 3 vols. London: Ivor Nicholson and Watson, 1934. Volume 4 of the same title, ed Oliver, Viscount Esher. London: Ivor Nicholson and Watson, 1938.

Broad, Lewis. *Winston Churchill 1874–1945*. London: Hutchinson, 1945.

Brock, Michael, and Eleanor, eds. *H H Asquith: Letters to Venetia Stanley*. Oxford: Oxford University Press, 1982.

Brodhurst, Robin. *Churchill's Anchor: The Biography of Admiral of the Fleet Sir Dudley Pound*. Barnsley: Leo Cooper, 2000.

Brownrigg, Douglas. *Indiscretions of the Naval Censor*. London: Cassell, 1920.

Buchan, John. *The King's Grace, 1910–1935*. London: Hodder and Stoughton, 1935.

Burdon, Richard, Viscount Haldane. *Richard Burdon Haldane: An Autobiography*. London: Hodder and Stoughton, 1929.

Busch, Briton C. *Britain, India, and the Arabs, 1914–1921*. Berkeley: University of California Press, 1971.

Bush, Eric. *Gallipoli*. London: George Allen and Unwin, 1975.

Butler, Daniel Allen. *The Lusitania: The Life, Loss, and Legacy of an Ocean Legend*. Mechanicsburg, PA: Stackpole, 2000.

Bywater, Hector. *Searchlight on the Navy*. London: Constable, 1935.

Callwell, Charles E. *The Dardanelles*. London: Constable, 1919.

Cannadine, David. *The Decline and Fall of the British Aristocracy*. New York: Vintage Books, 1999.

Carew, Anthony. *The Lower Deck of the Royal Navy, 1900–1939: The Invergordon Mutiny in Perspective*. Manchester: Manchester University Press, 1981.

Cassar, George. *Asquith as War Leader*. London: Hambledon, 1994.

Chalmers, W S. *The Life and Letters of David, Earl Beatty*. London: Hodder and Stoughton, 1951.

Chatfield, A E M. *The Navy and Defence: The Autobiography of Admiral of the Fleet Lord Chatfield*. London: William Heinemann, 1942.

Churchill, Randolph S. See notes on the official Churchill biographies and the Churchill Documents above.

Churchill, Winston S. *My Early Life*. Published 1930 and in print ever since. London: Eland, 2000.

———. *Great Contemporaries: Churchill Reflects on FDR, Hitler, Kipling, Chaplin, Balfour, and Other Giants of His Age*. Ed James W Muller with Paul H Courtenay and Erica L Chenoweth. Wilmington, DE: ISI Books, 2012.

———. *The Second World War*. Vol 1. London: Cassell, 1948.

———. *Thoughts and Adventures: Churchill Reflects on Spies, Cartoons, Flying, and the Future*. Ed James W Muller with Paul Courtenay and Alana Barton, 129–45. Wilmington, DE: ISI Books, 2009.

———. *The World Crisis*. 5 vols in 6 parts [sometimes incorrectly described as in 6 vols]. London: Thornton Butterworth, 1923–31. Individual volumes, with titles and dates of first publication are: vol 1: *The World Crisis 1911–1914* (April 1923); vol 2: *The World Crisis 1915* (October 1923); vol 3: *The World Crisis 1916–1918 Parts I and II* (January 1927); vol 4: *The World Crisis: The Aftermath* (March 1929); and vol 5: *The World Crisis, The Eastern Front* (November 1931).

———. *The World Crisis*. Abridged edition. New York: Scribners, 1931.

Clark, Christopher. *The Sleepwalkers: How Europe Went to War in 1914*. New York: Harper Collins, 2013.

Connell, Brian. *Manifest Destiny: A Study in Five Profiles of the Rise and Influence of the Mountbatten Family*. London: Cassell, 1953.

Corbett, Julian. *History of the Great War: Naval Operations*. Vol 1. London: Longmans Green, 1920. See also Henry Newbolt.

Cosentino, Michele, and Ruggero Stanglini. *British and German Battlecruisers: Their Development and Operations*. Barnsley: Seaforth, 2016.

Cowles, Virginia. *Edward VII and His Circle*. London: Hamish Hamilton, 1956.

Cowpe, Alan. 'The Royal Navy and the Whitehead Torpedo', in *Technical Change and British Naval Policy, 1860–1939*, ed Bryan Ranft, 23–36. London: Hodder and Stoughton, 1977.

Craig, Gordon. 'Political Leader as Strategist', in *Makers of Modern Strategy from Machiavelli to the Nuclear Age*, ed Peter Paret, 481–509. Princeton, NJ: Princeton University Press, 1986.

Cruttwell, C R M F. *A History of the Great War, 1914–1918*. 2nd edn, Oxford: Oxford University Press, 1936.

Dardanelles Commission: First Report and Supplement, 1917, and *Final Report and Appendices, 1919*. HMSO, Cmd 8490, Cmd 371.

DRLN. 'A Review of "Thirty-Six Years at the Admiralty", by Sir Charles Walker', *Naval Review*, 22, no. 4 (1934), 821–6.

David, Edward, ed. *Inside Asquith's Cabinet: From the Diaries of Charles Hobhouse*. London: John Murray, 1977.

Davison, Robert L. *The Challenges of Command: The Royal Navy's Executive Branch Officers, 1880–1919*. London: Routledge, 2016.

Dawson, Lionel. *Flotillas: A Hard-Lying Story*. London: Rich and Cowan, 1933.

Dewar, A C. 'Admiral Bacon's Life of Lord Fisher: A Review', *Naval Review*, 18 (1930), 181–9.

Dewar, K G B. 'Escape of the *Goeben* and *Breslau*', *Naval Review*, 44, no. 1 (February 1956), 33–44.

———. *The Navy from Within*. London: Gollancz, 1939.

Dixon, Norman. *On the Psychology of Military Incompetence*. London: Pimlico, 1994.

d'Ombrain, Nicholas J. 'Churchill at the Admiralty and the Committee of Imperial Defence, 1911–1914', *Journal of the Royal United Services Institution*, 115, no. 657 (March 1970), 38–41.

———. *War Machinery and High Policy: Defence Administration in Peacetime Britain, 1902–1914*. Oxford: Oxford University Press, 1973.

Domvile, Barry. *From Admiral to Cabin Boy*. London: Boswell, 1947.

Dorling, Taprell. *Men o' War*. London: Philip Allan, 1929.

Dreyer, Frederic C. *The Sea Heritage: A Study of Maritime Warfare*. London: Museum Press, 1955.

Dugdale, Blanche. *Arthur James Balfour: First Earl of Balfour, 1906–1930*. 2 vols. London: Hutchinson, 1936.

Eade, Charles, ed. *Churchill, By His Contemporaries*. London: Hutchinson, 1953.

Eardley-Wilmot, Rear-Admiral. 'How Did the "Goeben" Escape?', *Stead's Magazine*, 8 January 1921.

Eckardstein, Baron von. *Ten Years at the Court of St James'*. London: Thornton Butterworth, 1921.

Edmonds, James E. *Military Operations: France and Belgium, 1914*. 3rd edn, London: Macmillan, 1933.

Ehrman, John. *Cabinet Government and War, 1890–1940*. Cambridge: Cambridge University Press, 1958.

Epkenhans, Michael. 'Imperial Germany and the Importance of Sea Power', in *Naval Power in the Twentieth Century*, ed N A M Rodger, 27–40. Basingstoke: Macmillan, 1996.

Esher, Reginald Viscount. *The Tragedy of Lord Kitchener*. London: John Murray, 1921.

———. *Esher Journals and Letters*. See Brett, Maurice V, and Oliver, Viscount Esher.

Evans, David C, and Mark R Peattie, *Kaigun: Strategy, Tactics, and Technology in the Imperial Japanese Navy, 1887–1941*. Annapolis, MD: Naval Institute Press, 1997.

Ewing, A. *The Man of Room 40: The Life of Sir Alfred Ewing*. London: Hutchinson, 1939.

Fairbanks, Charles H, Jr. 'The Origins of the *Dreadnought* Revolution: A Historiographical Essay', *International History Review*, 13 (May 1991), 246–72.

Ferguson, Niall. 'Germany and the Origins of the First World War: New Perspectives', *Historical Journal*, 35, no. 3 (1992), 725–52.

———. *The Pity of War*. New York: Basic Books, 1998.

Fisher, John Arbuthnot. 'The Engineer Question, 1902', in *British Naval Documents, 1204–1960*, ed John B Hattendorf et al, 972–7. London: Navy Records Society, 1993.

———. *Memories*. London: Hodder and Stoughton, 1919.

———. *Records*. London: Hodder and Stoughton, 1919.

———. *Some Notes by Lord Fisher to His Friends*. Privately printed, 1918.

Fraser, Peter. *Lord Esher: A Political Biography*. London: Hart-Davis, MacGibbon, 1973.

Freeman, Richard. *The Great Edwardian Naval Feud: Beresford's Vendetta against 'Jackie' Fisher*. Barnsley: Pen and Sword, 2009.

French, Gerald, ed. *Some War Diaries, Addresses and Correspondence of Field Marshall the Earl of Ypres*. London: Herbert Jenkins, 1937.

Friedman, Norman. *The British Battleship 1906–1946*. Barnsley: Seaforth, 2015.

———. *Fighting the Great War at Sea: Strategy, Tactics, and Technology*. Annapolis, MD: Naval Institute Press, 2014.

Frothingham, Thomas G. *The Naval History of the World War: Offensive Operations, 1914–15*. Cambridge, MA: Harvard University Press, 1924.

Gardiner, A G. *The War Lords*. London: J M Dent, 1915.

Gardiner, Leslie. *The British Admiralty*. Edinburgh: William Blackwood, 1968.

Gardiner, Robert, and Andrew Lambert, eds. *Steam, Steel and Shellfire: The Steam Warship*. London: Conway, 1992.

Garnett, David, ed. *The Essential T E Lawrence*. Harmondsworth: Penguin, 1956.

Gentleman with a Duster [Harold Begbie]. *The Mirrors of Downing Street: Some Political Reflections*. London: Mills and Boon, 1920.

German, A B. 'Fighting the Submarine: A Chronology', *Canadian Defence Quarterly*, Special Issue (December 1985/January 1986), 40.

Gibson, Langhorn, and J E T Harper. *The Riddle of Jutland*. New York: Coward-McCann, 1934.

Gilbert, Bentley Brinkerhoff. *David Lloyd George: A Political Life*. Vol 2. Columbus: Ohio State University Press, 1992.

Gilbert, Martin. See notes on the official Churchill biographies and the Churchill Documents above.

———. *Churchill, A Photographic Portrait*. New York: Wings Books, 1993.

———, ed. *The Churchill War Papers*. Vol 1, *Churchill at the Admiralty September 1939–May 1940*. New York and London: W W Norton, 1993.

———. *In Search of Churchill: A Historian's Journey*. New York: Harper Collins, 1994.

Goldrick, James. *Before Jutland: The Naval War in Northern European Waters, August 1914–February 1915*. Annapolis, MD: Naval Institute Press, 2015.

———. *The King's Ships Were at Sea: The War in the North Sea, August 1914–February 1915*. Annapolis, MD: Naval Institute Press, 1984.

Gooch, John. 'The Myth of Imperial Defence', University of London, Institute of Commonwealth Studies, paper RHC/73/4, 15 November 1974.

Goodenough, William E. *A Rough Record: The Life of Admiral Sir William Goodenough*. London: Hutchinson, 1943.

Gordon, Andrew. *The Rules of the Game: Jutland and British Naval Command*. London: John Murray, 1996.

Gough, Barry M. 'Admiral Sir (later Baron) John Arbuthnot Fisher', in Murfett, *The First Sea Lords*, 17–33.

———. *Britannia's Navy on the West Coast of North America, 1812–1914*. Surrey, BC: Heritage House, 2016.

———. *Historical Dreadnoughts: Arthur Marder, Stephen Roskill and Battles for Naval History*. Barnsley: Seaforth, 2010.

———. 'Maritime Strategy: The Legacies of Mahan and Corbett as Philosophers of Sea Power', *Journal of the Royal United Services Institute for Defence Studies*, 133, no. 4 (Winter 1988), 55–62.

———. *Pax Britannica: Ruling the Waves and Keeping the Peace before Armageddon*. Basingstoke: Palgrave Macmillan, 2014.

———. *The Royal Navy and the Northwest Coast of North America, 1810–1914: A Study of British Maritime Ascendancy*. Vancouver: UBC Press, 1971.

———. 'The Royal Navy's Legacy to the Royal Canadian Navy in the Pacific, 1880–1914', in *The RCN in Retrospect, 1910–1968*, ed James A Boutilier, 1–12. Vancouver; UBC Press, 1982.

———. 'Rulers of the Waves: British Naval Memoirs', in *Political Memoir: Essays on the Politics of Memory*, ed George Egerton, 131–50. London: Frank Cass, 1994.

Grainger, John D. *The British Navy in the Baltic*. Woodbridge: Boydell, 2014.

Gretton, Peter W. *Former Naval Person: Winston Churchill and the Royal Navy*. London: Cassell, 1968. Also published as *Winston Churchill and the Royal Navy*. New York: Coward and McCann, 1969.

Grey, Viscount of Fallodon. *Twenty-Five Years: 1892–1916*. 2 vols. London: Hodder and Stoughton, 1925.

Grimes, Shawn T. *Strategy and War Planning in the British Navy, 1887–1918*. Woodbridge: Boydell, 2012.

Guinn, Paul. *British Strategy and Politics: 1914 to 1918*. Oxford: Clarendon Press, 1965.

Gusewelle, Jack K. 'Science and the Admiralty during World War I: The Case of the BIR', in Jordan, *Naval Warfare in the Twentieth Century*, 105–17.

Hackmann, Willem. *Seek and Strike: Sonar, Anti-Submarine Warfare, and the Royal Navy, 1914–1954*. London: HMSO Books, 1984.

Haggie, Paul. 'The Royal Navy and War Planning in the Fisher Era', *Journal of Contemporary History*, 8, no. 3 (1973), 113–31.

Halpern, Paul G. 'De Robeck and the Dardanelles Campaign', in *The Naval Miscellany*, ed N A M Rodger, vol 5, 439–98. London: Navy Records Society, 1984.

———. 'Fisher, John Arbuthnot', in *Oxford Dictionary of National Biography*. Online. Oxford: Oxford University Press, 2004–.

———, ed. *The Keyes Papers*. 3 vols. London: Navy Records Society, 1972–1981.

———. *A Naval History of World War I*. Annapolis, MD: Naval Institute Press, 1994.

———, ed. *The Royal Navy in the Mediterranean 1915–1918*. London: Navy Records Society, 1987.

Hamilton, C I *The Making of the Modern Admiralty: British Naval Policy-Making, 1805–1927*. New York: Cambridge University Press. 2011.

Hammond, J L. *C P Scott of the Manchester Guardian*. Rev edn, London: Bell, 1934.

Hankey, Maurice. *The Supreme Command*. 2 vols. London: George Allen and Unwin, 1961.

Harley, Simon. '"It's a Case of All or None": "Jacky" Fisher's Advice to Winston Churchill, 1911', *Mariner's Mirror*, 102, 2 (May 2016), 174–90.

Harris, Brayton. *The Navy Times Book of Submarines: A Political, Social, and Military History*. New York: Berkley, 1997.

Hartley, L P, ed. *Lady Cynthia Asquith Diaries, 1915–18*. London: Century, 1968.

Hassall, Christopher. *Edward Marsh, Patron of the Arts: A Biography*. London: Longmans, 1959.

Hastings, Max. *Catastrophe: Europe Goes to War 1914*. London: William Collins, 2013.

———, comp. *Oxford Book of Military Anecdotes*. Oxford: Oxford University Press, 1985.

Hattendorf, John B. 'Admiral Prince Louis of Battenberg', in Murfett, *The First Sea Lords*, 75–90.

Hayes, Paul. 'British Plans for Attacking Germany, 1906–1915', in *War Strategy and International Politics: Essays in Honour of Sir Michael Howard*, ed Lawrence Freedman et al, 95–116. Oxford: Clarendon Press, 1992.

Haynes, Jonathan. 'Gallipoli and the Role of Intelligence', *Naval Institute Proceedings* 121 (June 1995), 75–6.

Hazelhurst, Cameron. *Politicians at War, July 1914–May 1915*. London: Jonathan Cape, 1971.

Henderson, Admiral W H. 'Life of Lord Fisher: Reminiscences', *Naval Review*, 18 (1930), 189–202. Note: This item, and other contributions to the *Naval Review* by A C Dewar and A H Pollen in the same issue (given as separate entries in this Bibliography), prompted further discursive comment in a successive issue of the same periodical (not listed here). To be observed is that among the more insightful of these was that by Lord Sydenham of Combe (Sir George Clarke), who was the moving force in the publication of the collection of critical essays *The World Crisis by Winston Churchill: A Criticism*.

Hertwig, Max E. 'The "Kingly Conference", 1914: Churchill's Last Try for Peace', *Finest Hour*, 163 (Summer 2014), 20–1.

Herwig, Holger H. 'The Failure of German Sea Power, 1914–1945: Mahan, Tirpitz, and Raeder Reconsidered', *International History Review*, 10, no. 1 (March 1988), 68–105.

———. *'Luxury' Fleet: The Imperial German Navy, 1888–1918*. Rev edn, London and Atlantic Highlands, NJ: Ashfield Press, 1987.

Higgins, Trumbull. *Winston Churchill and the Dardanelles: A Dialogue in Ends and Means*. New York: Macmillan, 1963.

Hobson, Rolf. *Imperialism at Sea: Naval Strategic Thought, the Ideology of Sea Power and the Tirpitz Plan, 1875–1914*. Boston and Leiden: Brill Academic, 2002.

Holmes, Richard. *In the Footsteps of Churchill*. New York: Basic Books, 2005.

Hore, Peter. *Dreadnought to Daring: 100 Years of Comment, Controversy and Debate in the Naval Review*. Barnsley: Seaforth, 2012.

Hough, Richard. *Admiral of the Fleet: The Life of John Fisher*. New York: Macmillan, 1969. Also published as *First Sea Lord: An Authorised*

Biography of Admiral Lord Fisher. London: Allen and Unwin, 1969.

———. *Former Naval Person: Churchill and the Wars at Sea*. London: Weidenfeld and Nicolson, 1985.

———. *The Pursuit of Admiral von Spee: A Study in Loneliness and Bravery*. London: George Allen and Unwin, 1969.

Howard, Michael. *The Continental Commitment: The Dilemma of British Defence Policy in the Era of Two World Wars*. 1972; London: Ashfield, 1989.

Hoy, Hugh Cleland. *40 OB or How the War Was Won*. London: Hutchinson, 1935.

Hurst, Lloyd. *Coronel and After*. London: Peter Davies, 1934.

Hyam, Ronald. *Elgin and Churchill at the Colonial Office, 1905–1908: The Watershed of the Empire-Commonwealth*. London: Macmillan, 1968.

Hythe, Viscount, ed. *The Naval Annual: 1913*. Portsmouth: J Griffin and Co, 1913. Reprint, Plymouth: David and Charles Reprints, 1970.

Jablonsky, David. *Churchill, the Great Game and Total War*. London: Cass, 1991.

James, William. *Admiral Sir William Fisher*. London: Macmillan, 1943.

———. 'Churchill and the Navy', in *Churchill, By His Contemporaries*, ed Charles Eade, 139–56. London: Hutchinson, 1953.

———. *The Eyes of the Navy: A Biographical Study of Admiral Sir Reginald Hall*. London: Methuen, 1955.

Jameson, William. *The Fleet That Jack Built: Nine Men Who Made a Modern Navy*. New York: Harcourt, Brace and World, 1962.

———. *The Most Formidable Thing: The Story of the Submarine from Its Earliest Days to the End of World War I*. London: R H Davis, 1965.

Jeffries, J M N. 'Doom Over Antwerp', in *The Great War – I Was There*, ed John Hammerton, ch 39. New printing of *Daily Mail* report of Naval Division and fall of Antwerp. 3 vols. London: Amalgamated Press, 1938.

Jellicoe, John Rushworth. *The Crisis of the Naval War*. London: Cassell, 1920.

———. *The Grand Fleet, 1914–1916: Its Creation, Development, and Work*. London: Cassell, 1919.

———. *The Submarine Peril: The Admiralty Policy in 1917*. London: Cassell, 1934.

Jenkins, Roy. *Asquith: Portrait of a Man and an Era*. New York: Dutton, 1964.

———. *Churchill: A Biography*. New York: Farrar, Straus and Giroux, 2001.

Jerrold, Douglas. *The Royal Naval Division*. 2nd edn, London: Hutchinson, 1927.

Johnson, Oliver. 'Class Warfare and the Selborne Scheme: The Royal Navy's Battle over Technology and Social Hierarchy', *Mariner's Mirror*, 100, 4 (November 2014), 422–33.

Jordan, Gerald, ed. *Naval Warfare in the Twentieth Century, 1900–1945: Essays in Honour of Arthur Marder*. London: Croom Helm, 1977.

Kemp, Peter, ed. *Papers of Admiral Sir John Fisher*. 2 vols. London: Navy Records Society, 1960, 1964.

———. 'The Royal Navy', in *Edwardian England, 1901–1914*, ed Simon Nowell-Smith, 489–516. London: Oxford University Press, 1964.

Kendrick, Burton, ed. *Life and Letters of Walter H Page*. 2 vols. New York: Doubleday, Page, 1926.

Kennedy, Paul. 'Fisher and Tirpitz: Political Admirals in the Age of Imperialism', in Jordan, *Naval Warfare in the Twentieth Century*, 45–59.

Kent, Marion. *Oil and Empire: British Policy and Mesopotamian Oil, 1900–1920*. London: Macmillan, 1976.

Kerr, Mark. *The Navy in My Time*. London: Rich and Cowan, 1932.

———. *Prince Louis of Battenberg, Admiral of the Fleet*. London: Longman, 1934.

Keyes, Roger. *Adventures Ashore and Afloat*. London: Harrap, 1939.

———. *Naval Memoirs of Admiral of the Fleet Sir Roger Keyes*. 2 vols. London: Thornton Butterworth, 1934.

Koss, Stephen E. *Asquith*. London: Allen Lane, 1976.

———. 'The Destruction of Britain's Last Liberal Government', *Journal of Modern History*, 40, no. 2 (June 1968), 257–77.

———. *Lord Haldane: Scapegoat for Liberalism*. New York: Columbia University Press, 1969.

Laffin, John. *Damn the Dardanelles: The Agony of Gallipoli*. Gloucester: Alan Sutton, 1989.

Lambert, Andrew. *Admirals: The Naval Commanders Who Made Britain Great*. London: Faber and Faber, 2008.

Lambert, Nicholas. 'Admiral Sir Arthur Knyvet-Wilson, VC', in Murfett, *The First Sea Lords*, 35–53.

———. 'Admiral Sir Francis Bridgeman-Bridgeman', in Murfett, *The First Sea Lords*, 55–74.

———. 'Admiral Sir John Fisher and the Concept of Flotilla Defence, 1904–1909', *Journal of Military History*, 59 (October 1995), 639–60.

———. *Sir John Fisher's Naval Revolution*. Columbia: University of South Carolina Press, 1999.

Langworth, Richard M. *A Connoisseur's Guide to the Books of Sir Winston Churchill*. London: Brassey's, 1998.

Le Bailly, Louis. *From Fisher to the Falklands*. London: Marine Management (Holdings) for the Institute of Marine Engineers, 1991.

Lee, Celia and John. *Winston and Jack: The Churchill Brothers*. London: Authors, 2007.

Lee, John. *A Soldier's Life: General Sir Ian Hamilton 1853–1947*. Basingstoke: Pan, 2001.

Lee, Sidney. *King Edward VII: A Biography*. 2 vols. London: Macmillan, 1925–27.

Lees-Milne, James. *The Enigmatic Edwardian: The Life of Reginald 2nd Viscount Esher*. London: Hodder and Stoughton, 1986.

Leslie, Anita. *The Marlborough House Set*. New York: Doubleday, 1973.

Leslie, Shane. 'Memories of Beatty'. Unpublished manuscript, SLGF 12/4.

L'Etang, Hugh. *The Pathology of Leadership: A History of the Effects of Diseases on 20th Century Leaders*. New York: Hawthorne, 1970.

Leylan, John, ed. *Brassey's Naval Annual, 1916*. London: William Clowes and Sons, 1916.

Liddell Hart, B H. *History of the First World War*. London: Pan, 1972.

Lloyd George, David. *War Memoirs*. New edn, London: Odhams, 1938.

Lumby, E W R, ed. *Policy and Operations in the Mediterranean, 1912–1914*. London: Navy Records Society, 1970.

Lundeberg, Philip K. 'Undersea Warfare and Allied Strategy in World War I, Part 2, 1916–1918', *Smithsonian Journal of History*, 1, no. 4 (Winter 1966), 52–4.

MacDonagh, Giles. *The Last Kaiser: William the Impetuous*. London: Weidenfeld and Nicolson, 2000.

Mackay, Ruddock F. *Fisher of Kilverstone*. Oxford: Clarendon Press, 1973.

Magnus, Philip. *King Edward the Seventh*. London: John Murray, 1964.

———. *Kitchener: Portrait of an Imperialist*. London: John Murray, 1958.

Mahan, A T. *The Influence of Sea Power upon History, 1660–1783*. Boston: Little, Brown, 1890.

Manchester, William. *The Last Lion: Visions of Glory, 1874–1932*. Boston: Little, Brown, 1983.

Manning, T D. *The British Destroyers*. London: Putnam, 1961.

Mansergh, Aubrey. 'Another Look at Lord Fisher', *Naval Review*, 62, no. 3 (July 1974), 267–72.

Marder, Arthur J. *The Anatomy of British Sea Power: A History of British Naval Policy in the Pre-Dreadnought Era, 1880–1905*. New York: Knopf, 1940.

———, ed. *Fear God and Dread Nought: The Correspondence of Admiral of the Fleet Lord Fisher of Kilverstone*. 3 vols. London: Jonathan Cape, 1952–59.

———. *From the Dardanelles to Oran: Studies of the Royal Navy in War and Peace 1915–1940*. 1974. Reprint. Barnsley: Seaforth, 2015.

———. *From the Dreadnought to Scapa Flow: The Royal Navy in the Fisher Era, 1904–1919*, 5 vols. London: Oxford University Press, 1961–1970. The complete work was reprinted, with introductions by Barry Gough, by Seaforth, 2013–14.

———. *Operation Menace: The Dakar Expedition and the Dudley North Affair*. 1976. Reprint, Barnsley: Seaforth, 2016.

———, ed. *Portrait of an Admiral: The Life and Papers of Sir Herbert Richmond*. London: Jonathan Cape, 1952.

———. '"Winston is Back": Churchill at the Admiralty, 1939–40', revised version of that first issued in *English Historical Review*, Supp 5, Longman, 1972. Reprinted in Marder, *From the Dardanelles to Oran*, 105–78, and containing critique of S W Roskill's views on Churchill's naval administration: 'Musing on a Bolt from Olympus', 173–8.

Mason, David. *Churchill, 1914–1918.* New York: Ballantine, 1973.

Massie, Robert K. *Castles of Steel: Britain, Germany, and the Winning of the Great War at Sea.* New York: Random House, 2004.

———. *Dreadnought: Britain, Germany, and the Coming of the Great War.* New York: Random House, 1991.

Masterman, Lucy. *C F G Masterman.* London: Nicholson and Watson, 1939.

Mather, John H. 'Sir Winston Churchill: His Hardiness and Resilience', in *Churchill Proceedings 1996–1997*, 83–97. Washington, DC: Churchill Centre, 2000.

Maurer, John. '"The Ever-present Danger": Winston Churchill's Assessment of the German Naval Challenge before the First World War', in *Churchill and Strategic Dilemmas before the World Wars*, ed John Maurer, 7–50. London: Frank Cass Publishers, 2003.

Maurice, Sir Frederick. *Haldane.* Vol 1. London: Faber and Faber, 1937.

McDermott, W J. 'British Strategic Planning and the Committee of Imperial Defence, 1871–1907'. PhD dissertation, University of Toronto, 1970.

McMenamin, Michael. 'Action This Day', *Finest Hour*, 151 (Summer 2011), 30–1.

Meynell, Esther. *A Woman Talking.* London: Chapman and Hall, 1940.

Miller, Geoffrey. *Superior Force: The Conspiracy Behind the Escape of Goeben and Breslau.* Hull: University of Hull Press, 1996.

Moorehead, Alan. *Gallipoli.* London: Hamish Hamilton, 1956.

Moran, Lord. *Churchill: Taken from the Diaries of Lord Moran; The Struggle for Survival, 1940–1965.* Boston: Houghton Mifflin, 1966.

Morris, A J A. *The Scaremongers: The Advocacy of War and Rearmament 1896–1914.* London: Routledge and Kegan Paul, 1984.

Morris, Jan. *Fisher's Face.* London: Viking, 1995.

Munz, Sigmund. *King Edward VII at Marienbad: Political and Social Life at the Bohemian Spas.* London: Hutchinson, 1934.

Murfett, Malcolm H, ed. *The First Sea Lords: From Fisher to Mountbatten.* Westport, CT: Praeger, 1995.

Naval Who's Who 1917. New edn, Polstead, Suffolk: J B Hayward, 1981. Contains Jellicoe's Despatch, including warship losses and human casualties.

Newbolt, Henry. *Naval Operations.* Vol 4. London: Longmans, Green, 1928. This is the continuation of the three volumes written by Corbett and, similarly, for the Committee of Imperial Defence (and not the Admiralty).

Nicolson, Harold. *King George the Fifth: His Life and Reign.* London: Constable, 1952.

Noppen, Ryan K. *Ottoman Navy Warships 1914–18.* Oxford: Osprey, 2015.

Oliver, Viscount Esher. *Journals and Letters of Reginald Viscount Esher.* 2 vols (1910–1930). London: Ivor Nicholson and Watson, 1938. First three vols of the same title, ed Maurice V Brett. London: Ivor Nicholson and Watson, 1934.

Ollard, Richard. *Fisher and Cunningham: A Study of the Personalities of the Churchill Era.* London: Constable, 1991.

Osborne, Eric W. *The Battle of Heligoland Bight.* Bloomington: Indiana University Press, 2006.

Owen, David. *In Sickness and in Power: Illness in Heads of Government during the Last 100 Years.* London: Methuen, 2008.

Padfield, Peter. *Aim Straight: A Biography of Sir Percy Scott, the Father of Modern Naval Gunnery.* London: Hodder and Stoughton, 1966.

———. *The Great Naval Race: Anglo-German Naval Rivalry 1900–1914.* London: Hart-Davis, MacGibbon, 1974.

Parkes, Oscar. *British Battleships, 'Warrior' to 'Vanguard': A History of Design, Construction and Armament.* 2nd edn, Annapolis, MD: Naval Institute Press, 1990.

Penn, Geoffrey. *Fisher, Churchill, and the Dardanelles.* Barnsley: Leo Cooper, 1999.

———. *Infighting Admirals: Fisher's Feud with Beresford and the Reactionaries.* Barnsley: Leo Cooper, 2000.

———. *'Up Funnel, Down Screw!' The Story of the Naval Engineer.* London: Hollis and Carter, 1955.

Petrie, Charles. *The Life and Letters of the Right Hon Sir Austen Chamberlain.* Vol 1. London: Cassell, 1939.

Philbin, Tobias R. *Admiral Von Hipper: The Inconvenient Hero.* Amsterdam: B R Grüner, 1982.

Pinney, Thomas, ed. *Letters of Rudyard Kipling.* Vol 3, *1900–1910.* Houndmills: Macmillan, 1996.

Pitt, Barrie. *Coronel and Falklands.* 1960; London: Cassell, 2002.

Pollen, A H. 'The Tragedy of Lord Fisher of Kilverstone: How He Failed and Why', *Naval Review*, 18 (1930), 151–80.

Ponsonby, Frederick. *Recollections of Three Reigns.* London: Eyre and Spottiswoode, 1951.

Ponting, Clive. *Churchill.* London: Sinclair-Stevenson, 1994.

Pound, Reginald, and Geoffrey Harmsworth. *Northcliffe.* London: Cassell, 1959.

Preston, Diana. *Wilful Murder: The Sinking of the Lusitania.* London: Doubleday, 2002.

Prior, Robin. *Churchill's 'World Crisis' as History.* London: Croom Helm, 1983.

Pugh, Martin D. 'Asquith, Bonar Law, and the First Coalition', *Historical Journal*, 17, no. 4 (1974), 813–36.

Puleston, Captain W D. *The Dardanelles Expedition: A Condensed Study.* 2nd edn, 1926. Annapolis, MD: Naval Institute Press, 1927.

Purnell, Sonia. *First Lady: The Life and Wars of Clementine Churchill.* London: Aurum, 2015.

Ramsay, David. *Lusitania: Saga and Myth.* New York: Norton, 2002.

Raleigh, Walter. *The War in the Air, Being the Story of the Part Played in the*

Great War by the Royal Air Force. Vol. 1. Oxford: Clarendon, 1922.

Ranft, Bryan, ed. *The Beatty Papers*. 2 vols. London: Navy Records Society, 1989, 1993.

———. 'Parliamentary Debate, Economic Vulnerability, and British Naval Expansion, 1860–1905', in *War, Strategy, and International Politics: Essays in Honour of Sir Michael Howard*, ed Lawrence Freedman et al, 77–93. Oxford: Clarendon Press, 1992.

———. 'The Royal Navy and the Mercantile Marine, 1860–1914: Partners in Ignorance', in *Charted and Uncharted Waters*, ed S Palmer and G Williams, 197–217. London: National Maritime Museum, 1982.

———, ed. *Technical Change and British Naval Policy, 1860–1939*. London: Hodder and Stoughton, 1977.

Rasor, Eugene L. *Winston S Churchill, 1874–1965: A Comprehensive Historiography and Annotated Bibliography*. Westport: Greenwood, 2000.

Reynolds, David. *In Command of History: Churchill Fighting and Writing the Second World War*. London: Allen Lane, 2004.

Repington, Charles à Court. *Vestigia*. London: Constable, 1919.

Rhodes James, Robert. *Churchill: A Study in Failure, 1900–1939*. London: Weidenfeld and Nicolson, 1970.

———, ed. *Winston S Churchill: His Complete Speeches, 1897–1963*. 8 vols. New York: Chelsea House, 1974.

———. *Gallipoli*. London: Batsford, 1965.

Richmond, Herbert. 'Foreword', in Lloyd Hurst, *Coronel and After*. London: Peter Davies, 1934.

———. *Sea Power in the Modern World*. New York: Reynal and Hitchcock, 1934.

Riddell, George Allardice. *Lord Riddell's War Diary 1914–1918*. London: Ivor Nicholson and Watson, 1933.

———. *More Pages from My Diary, 1908–1914*. London: Country Life, 1934.

Ridley, Jane, and Clayre Percy, eds. *The Letters of Arthur Balfour and Lady Elcho 1885–1917*. London: Hamish Hamilton, 1992.

Roberts, Andrew. *Salisbury: Victorian Titan*. London: Weidenfeld and Nicolson, 1999.

Roberts, John. *The British Battlecruisers 1905–1920*. Barnsley: Seaforth, 2016.

Rodger, N A M. *The Admiralty*. Lavenham: Terence Dalton, 1979.

———, ed. *The Naval Miscellany*. Vol 5. London: Navy Records Society, 1984.

———, ed. *Naval Power in the Twentieth Century*. Basingstoke: Macmillan, 1996.

Rose, Kenneth. *King George V*. 1983; London: Phoenix, 2000.

Roskill, Stephen W. *Admiral of the Fleet, Earl Beatty: The Last Naval Hero; An Intimate Biography*. London: Collins, 1981.

———. *Churchill and the Admirals*. London: Collins, 1977.

———. 'The Dismissal of Admiral Jellicoe', *Journal of Contemporary History*, 1, no. 4 (October 1966), 69–93.

———, ed. *Documents Relating to the Naval Air Service*. Vol 1, *1908–1918*. London: Navy Records Society, 1969.

———. *Hankey, Man of Secrets*. 3 vols. London: Collins, 1970–1974.

———. *HMS Warspite*. London: Collins, 1957.

Ruge, Friedrich. *Scapa Flow 1919: The End of the German Fleet*. London: Ian Allen, 1973.

Russell, Douglas S. *The Orders, Decorations and Medals of Sir Winston Churchill*. 2nd edn. Washington, DC: Churchill Centre, 2004.

Scheer, Admiral. *Germany's High Sea Fleet in the World War*. New York: Peter Smith, 1934.

Schleihauf, William, ed. *Jutland: The Naval Staff Appreciation*. Barnsley: Seaforth, 2016.

Schurman, Donald M. *The Education of a Navy: The Development of British Naval Strategic Thought, 1867–1914*. Chicago: University of Chicago Press, 1965.

———. *Julian S Corbett, 1854–1922: Historian of British Maritime Policy from Drake to Jellicoe*. London: Royal Historical Society, 1981.

Scott, Percy. *Fifty Years in the Royal Navy*. London: John Murray, 1919.

Sebba, Anne. *Jennie Churchill: Winston's American Mother*. London: John Murray, 2007.

Seligmann, Matthew. 'Naval History by Conspiracy Theory: The British Admiralty before the First World War and the Methodology of Revisionism', *Journal of Strategic Studies*, 38, no. 7 (2015), 966–84. Published online 19 April 2015.

———. 'New Weapons for New Targets: Sir John Fisher, the Threat from Germany, and the Building of HMS *Dreadnought* and HMS *Invincible*, 1902–1907', *International History Review*, 30, no. 2 (June 2008), 239–58.

———. *The Royal Navy and the German Threat 1901–1914*. Oxford: Oxford University Press, 2012.

———. 'Switching Horses: The Admiralty's Recognition of the Threat from Germany, 1900–1905', *International History Review*, 30, no. 2 (June 2008), 239–58.

Seligmann, Matthew S, Frank Nagler, and Michael Epkenhans, eds. *The Naval Route to the Abyss: The Anglo-German Naval Race, 1895–1914*. London: Navy Records Society, 2015.

Sellers, Leonard. *The Hood Battalion: Royal Naval Division – Antwerp, Gallipoli, France 1914–1918*. London: Leo Cooper, 1995.

Sheldon, Matthew. HMS *M.33*. Stroud: Pitkin, 2015.

Simpson, Colin. *Lusitania*. London: Longman, 1972.

Smith, C Jay, Jr. 'Great Britain and the 1914–1915 Straits Agreement with

Russia: The British Promise of November 1914', *American Historical Review*, 70, no. 4 (July 1965), 1015–54.

Smith, Gaddis. *Britain's Clandestine Submarines 1914–1915*. New Haven, CT: Yale University Press, 1964.

Soames, Mary. *Clementine Churchill*. London: Cassell, 1979.

———, ed. *Speaking for Themselves: The Personal Letters of Winston and Clementine Churchill*. London: Doubleday, 1998.

Spender, J A. *Fifty Years of Europe: A Study in Pre-War Documents*. London: Cassell, 1933.

Stafford, David. *Churchill and Secret Service*. New York: Overlook Press, 1998.

Steinberg, Jonathan. 'The Copenhagen Complex', *Contemporary History*, 1 (1966), 23–46.

Steiner, Zara S. *Britain and the Origins of the First World War*. New York: St Martin's Press, 1977.

———. *The Foreign Office and Foreign Policy, 1898–1914*. Cambridge: Cambridge University Press, 1965.

Stevenson, David H, ed. *British Documents on Foreign Affairs: Reports and Papers from the Foreign Office Confidential Print*. Part 2, *From the First to the Second World War*. Series H, *The First World War, 1914–1918*. Vol 1, *The Allied and Neutral Powers: Diplomacy and War Aims, I: August 1914–July 1915*. Frederick, MD: University Publications of America, 1989.

Storr, Anthony. *Churchill's Black Dog, Kafka's Mice, and Other Phenomena of the Human Mind*. New York: Grove, 1988.

Strachan, Hew. *The First World War*. Vol 1. Oxford: Oxford University Press, 2001.

Sumida, Jon. 'British Naval Administration and Policy in the Age of Fisher', *Journal of Military History*, 54, no. 1 (January 1990), 1–26.

———. 'The Historian as Contemporary Analyst: Sir Julian Corbett and Admiral Sir John Fisher', *Mahan Is Not Enough: The Proceedings of a Conference on the Works of Sir Julian Corbett and Admiral Sir Herbert Richmond*, ed James Goldrick and John B Hattendorf, 125–40. Newport: Naval War College Press, 1993.

———. 'Sir John Fisher and the *Dreadnought*: The Sources of Naval Mythology', *Journal of Military History*, 59, no. 4 (October 1995), 619–37.

Sydenham of Combe, Lord [Clarke, Sir George]. *My Working Life*. London: John Murray, 1927.

———, et al. *The World Crisis by Winston Churchill: A Criticism*. 2nd edn, London: Hutchinson, [1927?].

Tarrant, V E. *Jutland, the German Perspective: A New View of the Great Battle, 31 May 1916*. Annapolis, MD: Naval Institute Press, 1995.

Taylor, A J P. *Beaverbrook*. New York: Simon and Schuster, 1972.

———. *English History, 1914–1945*. Oxford: Clarendon, 1965.

———. *Politics in Wartime*. New York: Atheneum, 1965.

————. *The Struggle for Mastery in Europe*. Oxford: Oxford University Press, 1971.

————. *The War Lords*. New York: Athenaeum, 1978.

Temple Patterson, A. *Jellicoe*. London: Macmillan, 1969.

————, ed. *The Jellicoe Papers: Selections from the Private and Official Correspondence of Admiral of the Fleet Earl Jellicoe of Scapa*. 2 vols. London: Navy Records Society, 1966, 1968.

Terraine, John. *Business in Great Waters: The U-Boat Wars, 1916–1945*. London: Leo Cooper, 1989.

Thompson, Julian. *The Royal Marines: From Sea Soldiers to a Special Force*. London: Pan, 2000.

Thursfield, J R. *Naval Warfare*. Cambridge: Cambridge University Press, 1913.

Toye, Richard. *Lloyd George and Churchill: Rivals for Greatness*. London: Pan, 2008.

Tracy, Nicholas, ed. *Sea Power and the Control of Trade: Belligerent Rights from the Russian War to the Beira Patrol, 1854–1970*. Aldershot: Ashgate for The Navy Records Society, 2005.

Travers, Tim. *Gallipoli 1915*. Stroud: Tempus, 2002.

Trumpener, Ulrich. 'Turkey's Entry into World War I: An Assessment of Responsibilities', *Journal of Modern History*, 34, no. 4 (December 1962), 169–80.

Tuchman, Barbara W. *The Guns of August*. New York: Ballantine Books, 1994.

van der Vat, Dan. *The Grand Scuttle: The Sinking of the German Fleet at Scapa Flow in 1919*. Annapolis, MD: Naval Institute Press, 1986.

————. *The Ship that Changed the World*. London: Hodder and Stoughton, 1985.

————. *Standard of Power: The Royal Navy in the Twentieth Century*. London: Hutchinson, 2000.

Wallin, Jeffrey. *By Ships Alone: Churchill and the Dardanelles*. Durham, NC: Carolina Academic Press, 1981.

Warner, Oliver. *Command at Sea: Great Fighting Admirals from Hawke to Nimitz*. New York: St Martin's Press, 1976.

Watt, D C. *How War Came – The Immediate Origins of the Second World War 1938–1939*. New York: Pantheon, 1989.

Watts, Philip. 'Ships of the British Navy on August 4, 1914, and Some Matters of Interest in Connection with Their Production', *Transactions of the Institution of Naval Architects*, 61 (1919), 1–65.

Weiner, Joel H, ed. *Great Britain: The Lion at Home; A Documentary History of Domestic Policy, 1689–1973*. Vol 3. New York: Chelsea House Publishers, 1974.

Wemyss, V. *The Life and Letters of Lord Wester Wemyss*. London: Eyre and Spottiswoode, 1935.

Westcott, Allan, ed. *Mahan on Naval Warfare*. Boston: Little, Brown, 1942.

Wester Wemyss, Lord. *Naval War in the Dardanelles Campaign*. Churchill College Archives.

———. *The Navy in the Dardanelles Campaign*. London: Hodder and Stoughton, 1924.

Williams, Rhodri. *Defending the Empire: The Conservative Party and British Defence Policy, 1899–1915*. London and New Haven, CT: Yale University Press, 1991.

Wilson, David A H. 'Avian Anti-Submarine Warfare Proposals in Britain, 1915–1918: The Admiralty and Thomas Mills', *International Journal of Naval History*, 5, no. 1 (April 2006), 1–25.

Wilson, Keith, ed. *The Rasp of War: The Letters of H A Gwynne to the Countess Bathurst, 1914–1918*. London: Sidgwick and Jackson, 1988.

Wilson, Michael. *Baltic Assignment: British Submariners in Russia, 1914–1919*. London: Leo Cooper in association with Secker and Warburg, 1985.

Wilson, Trevor, ed. *The Political Diaries of C P Scott, 1911–1928*. London: Collins, 1970.

Winton, John. *Jellicoe*. London: Michael Joseph, 1981.

———. 'Life and Education in a Technically Evolving Navy, 1815–1925', *Oxford Illustrated History of the Royal Navy*, ed J R Hill, 230–79. Oxford: Oxford University Press, 1996.

Wolff, Michael, ed. *Winston S Churchill: The Collected Essays*. 4 vols. London: Library of Imperial History, 1976.

Woodward, E L. *Great Britain and the German Navy*. London: Oxford University Press, 1935.

Yates, Keith. *Graf Spee's Raiders: Challenge to the Royal Navy 1914–1915*. Annapolis, MD: Naval Institute Press, 1995.

Yergin, Daniel. *The Prize: The Epic Quest for Oil, Money and Power*. New York: Free Press, 1992.

Young, Filson. *With the Battlecruisers*. 1921. New edition with introduction by James Goldrick. Annapolis, MD: Naval Institute Press, 1986.

Ziegler, Philip. *Mountbatten*. New York: Knopf, 1985.

Index

586

size 306, 312–14, 342–3, 361, 362–3, 366–7, 381, 425, 432; diminished for Battle of Falklands 287; Dogger Bank action 308; fear of mines, torpedoes, subs 248–9; Jutland 439–40; loss of capital ships 305; minimum strength 362; plan to take more active role 299–300; plays waiting game 249, 267, 303, 313, 324, 424; surrender of German Fleet 477–9, *pl 33*; weakened by Dardanelles campaign 389. *See also* Admiralty; Beatty, Admiral Sir David; Churchill, Winston Spencer; Fisher, Admiral Sir John Arbuthnot; High Seas Fleet; Home Fleet; Jellicoe, Admiral Sir John; Royal Navy

Great Britain: close to civil war 210–11; closer relationship with US 16; conscription 373, 415; Continental Commitment xxxvi, 87–8, 93–4; declares war on Germany 221–3, 228–9; decolonisation 87–8 (*see also* Royal Navy: fleet redistribution); election (1885) 13; election (1906) xxxvii, 100; election (1915), suspended 387; expects naval battle xxxiv, 425; failure of intelligence system 231–3, 239, 251–2; fear of invasion xxv, xxxiv, 46, 96, 99, 115–19, 152–3, 192, 193, 303, 313, 467–9; fights war on credit 321; First Moroccan Crisis 93, 94–5; German raids on Yorkshire coast 292–3; humour in darkest days 409; importance of control of seas xxiv–xxv, 12, 13, 17, 29, 44, 87, 184, 218, 345; intelligence system 152–4, 229 (*see also* Naval Intelligence; Room 40); invasion of Belgium 221–2; Mediterranean policy 21–4; Middle East and Near East foreign policy 185, 336; 'Milestones to Armageddon' xxxvii; naval challenge from Germany 25; naval superiority 71–2, 73, 134; need for alliances 87–8; no proper war organisation 450; not great military power 87; oil concessions in Persia 175, 183; Ottoman navy 225, 233–4; plans to energise Russians 412; protection of merchant marine 61, 89–90; Russo-Japanese War 91–3, 94–5; threats of surprise attack 48–9, 96, 98, 100; war with Ottoman Empire 328, 331. *See also* Entente Cordiale; Ireland

Great War: alternatives to Western Front 328, 332–3 (*see also* Baltic Sea; Dardanelles campaign); Armistice 476, 508; assassination of Archduke Franz Ferdinand 205; attempts to shorten 362 (*see also* Dardanelles campaign); darkest days for Allies 409; decisive day 217–18; events preceding declaration xxvi–xxvii, 203–4, 209–23; 'last hundred days' 475; official British military history 485; 'one man' to win the war xxxv, 323, 335–6, 469, 502; 'struggle of invention' 418; Western Front 264, 299; 'Westerners' and 'Easterners' 328, 332. *See also* Schlieffen Plan; *specific countries, battles and, commanders*

Greece 22, 23, 232, 355, 399
Gretton, Vice-Admiral Sir Peter 167, 454
Grey, Sir Edward: Agadir crisis 156–8, 159–61; assessment of WSC 150, 152; British ambassador to US 488; consents to secret French talks 94, 218–19; Dardanelles campaign 348; Dardanelles Commission 444; defence of Antwerp 260; inquiry into naval policy 121–2; Kaiser Wilhelm II 19, 101; 'lamps are going out' 223; reluctant to adjust

to realities of war 321; residence 53; speech on GB's guarantee to Belgium 222; supports naval estimates (1909) 132, 133–4; WSC's 'naval holiday' idea 102; WSC's Antwerp adventure 267

Guest, Captain Freddie 323, 374
guns, naval: after *Dreadnought* 76; challenged by new technology 189–90; crack easily 105; development of 11–12, 69; effect of torpedoes 70–1; effect on naval tactics 81; fire control systems 78, 110, 310; inefficiency 10–11; long-range guns key to naval warfare 27, 28, 68, 71; on super-dreadnoughts 165–6, 188. *See also* Board of Invention and Research
Gwynne, H A 114, 265, 364

Haig, General Sir Douglas 46, 230
Haldane, R B: Agadir crisis 158, 159–61; attacked by WSC on army estimates 149–50, 155; attacks Kitchener in press 394; coalition government 400; desire to reform Admiralty 155, 160, 162–3; Germanophile 164; halts army manoeuvres (1911) 142; JF–Beresford quarrel 122, 125, 139; lack of Army–Navy co-operation 97; laments JF's departure (1910) 142; 'Little Navy' faction 131; preparations for war 202, 230; reforms War Office xxviii, 162, 171; residence 53; supports return of JF and Wilson to Admiralty 274; supports RN at CID inquiry 119; threat of foreign espionage 153; trims army estimates 120; Scapa Flow defences 173; works with CID 106. *See also* British Army; War Office
Hall, Captain Reginald 'Blinker': BIR's anti-sub research 459; blocks JF's return to Admiralty 392; danger of subs 194; JF's health 353; *Lusitania* 317–18; naval intelligence 204, 253, 278; Ottoman ammunition shortage 356–7; out-argued by WSC 167–8; 'powerful cabal at work' 405; RN transit of Dardanelles 241–2
Hall, Rear-Admiral S S 167, 182, 458
Hamilton, Admiral Sir Frederick 392, 422
Hamilton, Duchess of (Nina Douglas-Hamilton): JF's lover and confidante 7, 402, 488, 488–9; JF's memoirs: 484–5; in London 53, 426; refuge after JF resigns 379, 396, 401–2
Hamilton, Duke of (Alfred Douglas-Hamilton) 396, 401–2
Hamilton, Emma 5, 402, 484
Hamilton, General Sir Ian 180, 230 323, 355, 360, 408
Hamilton, Vice-Admiral Sir Frederick 362, 381
Hankey, Colonel Maurice: concern about war-readiness of RN 160, 162; Dardanelles campaign 341, 345, 353, 355, 366–8, 375–6; Dardanelles Commission 444–7, 450; economic war 172; GB's obligation to enter war 219; JF in Paris in 1919 488; JF's appearance at War Council 429, 431; JF's funeral 490; JF's grievances 324, 343, 348, 422–3; JF's resignation 377, 379, 391, 395–6; Kitchener's death 441; lack of naval action 320–1, 424, 425; loyal to JF 474; naval war plans (1906/7) 99, 297; official history of war 485; Official Secrets Act 154; opposes releasing Dardanelles documents 442–3; proposal to force Dardanelles 333, 336–8; suggests WSC go to Russia 412; WSC's speech on naval estimates (1912/13) 205; WSC's

Index of Ships

Ships are HMS (His/Her Majesty's Ship) unless otherwise indicated.
HMY = His/Her Majesty's Yacht; RMS = Royal Mail Ship; SM = *Seiner Majestät* (His Majesty's, used for submarines); SMS = *Seiner Majestät Schiff* (His Majesty's Ship); USS = United States Ship
Br = British; Fr = French; Ge = German
pl # = plate number (in one of the two photo sections); italicised when photo includes the ship